ELECTRONIC OFFICE PROCEDURES

ELECTRONIC OFFICE PROCEDURES

Rosemary T. Fruehling
Director, Office of Software and Courseware Technology
Minnesota Department of Economic Development

Constance K. Weaver
Director, Planning Systems
McGraw-Hill, Inc.

Gregg Division
McGRAW-HILL BOOK COMPANY

New York   Atlanta   Dallas   St. Louis   San Francisco
Auckland   Bogotá   Guatemala   Hamburg
Lisbon   London   Madrid   Mexico   Milan   Montreal
New Delhi   Panama   Paris   San Juan   São Paulo
Singapore   Sydney   Tokyo   Toronto

Sponsoring Editor □ Roberta Moore
Editing Supervisor □ Alfred Bernardi
Design and Art Supervisor/Text Designer □ Caryl Valerie Spinka
Production Supervisor □ S. Steven Canaris
Photo Editor □ Rosemarie Rossi

Cover Designer □ Sulpizio Associates
Technical Art □ Burmar Technical Corp., Interactive Graphics, Inc., Sulpizio Associates

Library of Congress Cataloging-in-Publication Data

Fruehling, Rosemary T.
    Electronic office procedures.

    Includes index.
    1. Office practice—Automation.   2. Electronic
office machines.   I. Weaver, Constance K.   II. Title.
HF5547.5.F78   1986   651   86-10326
ISBN   0-07-022534-6

The manuscript and line art for this book were prepared electronically.

Electronic Office Procedures

2 3 4 5 6 7 8 9 0   VNHVNH   8 9 3 2 1 0 9 8 7

ISBN 0-07-022534-6

Dr. Rosemary T. Fruehling is currently Director of the Office of Software Technology Development for the State of Minnesota.

An internationally known educator and lecturer in the field of business education, Dr. Fruehling has taught office education at both the high school and the postsecondary levels. She has also conducted business education teacher-training seminars for the McGraw-Hill International Division and for the U.S. Department of Defense.

Dr. Fruehling has served as a consultant to such business firms as International Milling, General Mills, Honeywell, and Warner-Lambert Pharmaceutical Company. Just prior to her current appointment, Dr. Fruehling served as Postsecondary Vocational Education Section Manager, in the Division of Vocational-Technical Education of the Minnesota State Department of Education.

Dr. Fruehling is coauthor of other publications with McGraw-Hill, among them, *Business Correspondence: Essentials of Communication,* Sixth Edition, *Business Communication: A Problem-Solving Approach,* Third Edition, and *Psychology: Human Relations and Work Adjustment,* Sixth Edition.

Dr. Fruehling received her B.S., M.A., and Ph.D. degrees from the University of Minnesota in Minneapolis.

Constance K. Weaver currently serves as Director, Planning Systems, for McGraw-Hill, Inc.

In addition to her extensive experience in business, Ms. Weaver has spent several years developing and marketing educational materials in the field of business education. She has conducted business education teacher-training seminars for McGraw-Hill in the areas of office automation and microcomputer applications. She has also taught at the postsecondary level.

Ms. Weaver has a wide-ranging background and practical experience in microcomputer applications and office systems and has recently completed coordinating the implementation of an integrated office system within the Corporate Planning Department of McGraw-Hill.

Ms. Weaver received her B.S. degree from the University of Maryland, College Park, Maryland.

Photo Credits

Original text photographs by Jules Allen, John Cavanagh, Will Faller, Richard Hackett, and Bob Rogers as indicated below. Other photographs reproduced with permission of the following:

Jules Allen: pages 27 (left), 79,85, 89 (bottom), 103, 108, 116, 171, 172 (bottom right), 210 (top and bottom), 213, 243, 273 (top), 275, 295, 325, 330, 342, 345, 364, 450, 461, 466, 483, 488, 512, 518, 522; **Apple Computer, Inc.:** pages 34, 81; **Peter Arnold/Gerhard:** page 360; **Art Resource:** page 119; **Ashton-Tate:** page 196; **AT&T, Bell Laboratories:** pages 111, 197, 322 (left, middle, and right), 323, 336, 385, 411, 501; **BASF Systems Corporation:** page 247 (top); **Bettmann Archive:** page 468; **Burroughs Corporation:** page 169; **Candee and Associates/Click Chicago:** page 372; **John Cavanagh:** pages 61, 90, 313, 314, 315 (top and bottom), 316, 375, 425; **Control Data Corporation:** pages 172 (top left and top right), 299; **Culver Pictures, Inc.:** page 24 (top left and top right); **Datapoint Corporation:** page 271; **Devoke Data Products:** page 248 (top and third from top); **Digital Equipment:** page 248 (fourth from top); **Essete— Pendaflex Corporation:** page 241; **Will Faller:** pages 12, 61, 75, 90, 96, 162, 165, 167, 201, 218, 219 (top and bottom), 220, 270, 346, 347 (top and bottom), 349 (top and bottom), 350 (top and bottom), 352 (top and bottom), 354, 357, 381, 400 (left); **Fugitsu Imaging Systems of America:** page 170; **Paul Fusco/Magnum Photos:** page 472; **Richard Hackett:** pages 72, 87, 101, 104, 107, 109, 157, 186, 228, 277, 305, 329, 371, 374, 400 (right); **Erich Hartmann/Magnum Photos:** pages 89 (top), 148, 151, 179, 266 (right), 403; **Hayes Microcomputer Products:** page 298 (left); **Michael Heron:** page 182; **Honeywell Information Systems, Inc.:** page 18; **Houston Instruments:** pages 172 (bottom left), 269; **IBM Corporation:** pages 11, 27 (bottom right), 32 (top); **Mike Kagan/Monkmeyer Press:** page 258; **Lotus Development Corporation:** page 202; **Dick Luria/Photo Researchers:** page 456; **Cathlyn Melloan/Click Chicago:** page 383; **Moog, Inc.:** page 174; **National Computer Systems:** page 37; **NEC Information Systems:** page 266 (left); **NYNEX Information Resource Company:** page 331; **Panel Concepts, Inc.:** page 84; **Robert Phillips/Image Bank:** page 496; **Pitney-Bowes:** page 292; **Ricoh Corporation:** page 303; **Bob Rogers:** pages 9, 152 (left and right), 168 (top and bottom), 190 (bottom), 240, 249, 283, 298 (top), 327, 338, 379, 394, 397, 404, 424, 504, 519; **Sepp Seitz/Woodfin Camp and Associates:** page 33; **Silver Reed America, Inc.:** page 209; **Sperry Corporation:** pages 30, 32 (bottom), 137, 516; **Storage Systems, Inc.:** page 255; **Texas Instruments:** page 194; **3M Corporation:** pages 248 (bottom), 251, 252 (left and right); **U.S. Postal Service:** page 288; **Alex Webb/Magnum Photos:** page 474; **Wang Laboratories, Inc.:** page 362; **Western Union:** page 307.

Contents

PART 2
INFORMATION PROCESSING
TECHNOLOGY
AND PROCEDURES   97

PART 3
ADMINISTRATIVE
SUPPORT FUNCTIONS 343

Chapter 16
Arranging Business Trips   392

Chapter 17
Financial and Legal Functions   418

Preface

"Information flow will be more important than the hierarchy."[1]

Peter Drucker, Clarke Professor of Social Sciences and Management at the Claremont Graduate School, California, and well-known author of business management books, made this statement in reference to the changing structure of the electronic office.

In the same article Drucker wrote that he disliked the word *automation* because it emphasized machines, "whereas what we are really talking about is *organizing work around the flow of information*" (emphasis added).

Electronic Office Procedures gives you a detailed view of how the information processing cycle is being changed by today's technology. It shows you how and why this change is taking place. It recognizes that today "knowledge workers"—among whom are the office employees—make up more than half of the work force. The text clearly describes the processing of information—inputting, processing, outputting, storing, and distributing—contrasting procedures in traditional and electronic offices.

To help you put into perspective and comprehend the changes that are occurring and to help you see how they have evolved, the text discusses the three stages of the business office: the traditional office, the word processing office, and the electronic office. This approach serves two purposes:

☐ First, all three types of offices exist today, so this text prepares you for work in any one of them.

☐ Second, by detailing how the electronic office evolved out of the traditional office and the ways it changed procedures, the text makes it easier for you to understand the new procedures and your role.

The electronic office makes it possible to process great amounts of information quickly and accurately. In the course of this text, you will learn about the kinds of equipment available for processing information and how you will use such procedures as electronic mail, electronic records management, and teleconferencing in the electronic office. The text makes it clear, however, that doing tasks faster is not the sole difference in the electronic office. Functions themselves are changed. Office workers are doing things differently.

---

[1]Peter Drucker, in *On Human Factors*—a source booklet of comments and observations by experts in the field of human factors and office automation, Wang Laboratories, Inc., 1983.

The traditional division of office work between managers on the one hand and administrative support workers on the other is blurring. The text shows how office functions are being rethought and redefined in the face of the new technology. New job descriptions reflect new responsibilities and assignments. All of this, as the book shows, adds up to new opportunities and challenges for the office worker.

The increasing use of sophisticated technology has tremendous implications for those entering the business office, especially those who see themselves moving into supervisory and even managerial roles in the years ahead. As you will read, the new technology can open up avenues of advancement that previously did not exist.

The successful office employee of the future will need to be familiar with more than one function. Specialists will still be needed, of course, in areas such as word processing and data processing. But increasingly, all office workers will be expected to perform many different *information processing* functions. The sophisticated computer systems described in *Electronic Office Procedures* make this not only desirable but also possible.

Secretaries, administrative assistants, and future office managers being trained today must acquire certain skills to be data processors, systems analysts, information system managers, and utility managers, as well as word processors or data processors. Those wishing to advance will need to have knowledge of how systems work. One section of this book deals with the issues and decisions a company faces when establishing an electronic system. Having the ability to train others, both new personnel and managers, in the use of a new system will be necessary.

To an increasing extent, data processing, systems analysis, and the management of information systems will be an integral part of the future office worker's job rather than separate functions. New job titles reflect this broadening scope of responsibilities: *information processing specialist* and *information processing supervisor* are two examples, as you will read.

Machines by themselves are powerless. Information that is unused is worthless. People continue to be the main element in the electronic office, as this text makes clear. Human relations skills, important as ever, are interwoven with technical information in this text, which stresses those that are important to your career. Ultimately, it is the integration of people and machines that makes a system work.

You will learn about the traditional leadership skills still required and look at how the decision to automate an office is made and then implemented. You will read about job opportunities in the electronic office and the ways to launch your successful career.

This text will prepare you for entering a business world in which you will find traditional systems alongside electronic systems. It points out the significant trends. By keeping informed of the new technology, making sense of it, and, most important, grasping its implications—none of which is an easy task—you can have an exciting and interesting career in the business office of the eighties and nineties.

Acknowledgments

We would like to acknowledge Neild Oldham for his assistance in preparing and revising the manuscript for publication. For their reviews of the manuscript thanks go to Brenda Breton, Director of Electronic Office Management, Westbrook College, Portland, Maine; Ralene Kroenke, Instructor, Integrated Information Systems Specialist Program, Alexandria Technical Institute, Alexandria, Minnesota; Joan Lacombe, Chairman, Secretarial Studies Department, Bay Path Junior College, Somers, Connecticut; and Marilyn Sarch, formerly Dean, Taylor Business Institute, Paramus, New Jersey.

For their input in the early stages of the project's development, we wish to recognize Patricia Garner, Instructor, Golden Gate University, Los Angeles, California; Dr. Mary Margaret Hosler, Associate Professor, University of Wisconsin, Madison; and Dr. Carmela Kingston, Professor of Business, Trenton State College, Trenton, New Jersey.

Many other people contributed their time and technical expertise to the development of this project. To all of them we extend our grateful acknowledgment.

Rosemary T. Fruehling
Constance K. Weaver

part 1
An Overview of the Electronic Office

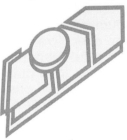

The business office is rapidly changing from a manual-based system to an electronic computer-based system. Automation of manual tasks is a concept that sums up this change. But the change is more than working faster with computers. The change is altering the relationship between office workers and managers.

Using sophisticated equipment in the electronic office, office workers will make decisions, analyze data, organize information, create graphics, and set up conferences.

Individuals who have well-rounded traditional office skills and who also can use the new technology will be in great demand. Office automation will not diminish the secretary's role but enhance it.

In the transition period, businesses will continue to use traditional equipment, such as the electric typewriter, the U.S. Postal Service, and telephones, along with computer systems. Obviously, there will always be a need for some traditional equipment, but electronic systems will increasingly dominate.

The chapters in Part 1 tell you how automation is affecting the basic office function of information processing and describe the electronic office of today. You will see why these are exciting times to start a business office career and why additional skills are important for advancement.

Automation notwithstanding, we will certainly never reach a "peopleless" office. In your work you will always deal with people. That being the case, Part 1 includes a discussion of human relations skills as well.

chapter 1
The Changing Office

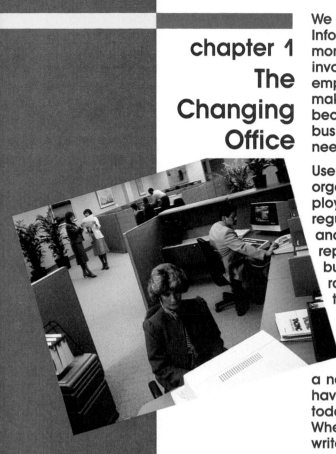

We live in what is presently known as the Information Age. For the first time in history, more Americans are employed in jobs that involve processing information than are employed in jobs that produce goods. This makes it an exciting time to be in business because information is the lifeblood of the business world. Business organizations need information in order to function.

Users of business information include an organization's customers, clients, or employees; outside suppliers; government regulatory agencies; and other people and organizations. A corporation's annual report to its shareholders is an example of business information, and so is a memorandum from an administrative assistant to an executive regarding a vacation schedule. Every time a company makes a sale, purchases supplies, acquires new customers, expands its staff, introduces a product, or explores a new market, it generates information. We have more information at our disposal today than at any other time in history. Whenever scientists uncover facts, authors write books, creative thinkers come up with new theories, or inventors develop new devices, more information is generated.

In the 1970s computerization hit the American business office. Along with computers came an "information explosion" that has vastly increased the amount of information office workers have to deal with. Today more than 60 percent of all workers have occupations that are involved in the exchange of information. Compare this with the situation in 1950, when most people worked in manufacturing jobs and only 17 percent worked in offices, and you will see the impact of the "information explosion."

To cope with this explosion, businesses have to find more efficient ways to process information. Office workers find that they have to learn to operate new, complex machines, and they have to learn a whole new vocabulary of technological terms. New information processing technology is also changing the way office workers perform their jobs. Computers now handle many of the repetitive, tedious tasks that used to take up so much time. This leaves more time for office workers and their managers to devote to responsibilities that require creativity, judgment, and the ability to make decisions.

In this chapter you will learn how Information Age technology is changing the very nature of office work. You will also learn some of the new computer-related terminology that you will need to know to progress through this course and to work in a modern business office. And you will learn about the changing role of office workers in the new Information Age.

What Is Information?

To define information, we must also define data. The terms *data* and *information* both mean *facts*. The difference is that **data** usually refers to a group of facts, usually in the form of words or figures— for example, a list of names and addresses or a sheet of sales figures. Often these facts are unorganized. **Information** refers to facts that have been processed or organized in some fashion. When you type a list of names and addresses in alphabetic order, or when you prepare a chart showing average monthly sales receipts, you are creating information. You are taking the data and organizing it into useful information, which can then be communicated to others.

An example that illustrates the difference between data and information is the U.S. census. Conducted every ten years, the census involves the collection of data: the number of people in each household and their ages, incomes, occupations, and so on. The data is then converted into information, such as the average household income in a particular city or a list of the fastest-growing cities. People can use such information to figure out future housing needs or to plan sales or marketing campaigns. Other examples of organized or processed facts are letters, inventories, reports, memos, expense accounts, schedules, and purchase orders.

High Tech in the Office

The need to find more efficient ways of handling the rapidly growing mountain of business information has been the driving force behind the development of office technology. When people talk about office technology or office automation, what they are really talking about is creating a workplace where sophisticated computers and other electronic equipment carry out as many of the office's routine jobs as possible. The basic reason for bringing electronic technology, or **high tech** as it is often called, into the office is to increase productivity. In a narrow sense, **increased productivity** means that more work can be done by employees in the same period of time or that employees can do the same amount of work in a shorter period of time. It can also mean that fewer employees can perform the same amount of work. In a broader sense, increased productivity can mean that workers have greater flexibility in accomplishing their tasks. Thus, the quality of their work can be improved, as well as the efficiency.

Until the 1980s the major application of technology to improve productivity was in the shop or factory, not the office. One reason for this is that the need for efficiency in the factory is greater than in the office. But another important factor is that in the shop and factory it is easier to find and identify those jobs which are repetitive and can be broken down into **algorithms**, that is, repetitive, step-by-step procedures that can more easily be computerized. Assembly-line jobs such as filling bottles with catsup and welding auto bodies are examples of factory jobs that lend themselves easily to automation. It is not surprising, therefore, that the first computers to enter the office world were used to automate labor-intensive, routine business functions in accounting and financial operations. (**Labor-intensive** refers to tasks that require many work hours to complete.) There is no question that electronic equipment can greatly speed up the performance of many specific office tasks, but real increases in productivity will not be realized unless technology is applied to the functions of the office as a whole.

Office Functions, Tasks, and Procedures

An office **function** can be defined as a series of acts or operations expected from a person or thing; it is a set of responsibilities imposed by one's occupation. A **task** is an assigned piece of work, often to be completed within a given time frame. A function is composed of a series of tasks. For example, dictation, transcription, keyboarding, editing, proofreading, copying, mailing, and filing are the series of office tasks that make up the function of processing written documents. To perform each task in this series, the office worker must follow a **procedure**, which is a set of defined steps that outline the elements of a task and provide a framework for getting the job done. Office procedures define not only how a particular task is to be done but also the time frame in which it is to be accomplished, the materials and equipment to be used, and the individuals or departments with whom or with which the worker must interact to complete the task. Through the use of office procedures, a business can carry out its functions in a predictable and orderly way.

DEFINITION	EXAMPLE
FUNCTION The acts or operations expected from a person or thing; a series of tasks or responsibilities imposed by one's occupation.	**FUNCTION** ■ Scheduling meetings.
TASK An assigned piece of work, often to be completed within a given time frame.	**TASK** ■ Set up staff meeting.
PROCEDURE A series of steps followed in a regular, definite order.	**PROCEDURES** ■ Check boss's calendar. ■ Call staff members to announce time and date. ■ Reserve meeting room. ■ Distribute memo confirming date, time, place. ■ Prepare materials needed for the meeting.

Categorizing a job duty as a function or as a set of tasks sometimes depends on the level of the job. For a manager such job duties as budgeting, scheduling, negotiating, and monitoring are functions. Tasks associated with the budgeting function might be forecasting expenses, analyzing expenditures, identifying line items to cut or add, identifying areas of increasing costs, balancing the final budget figures, and preparing a draft of the budget for keyboarding.

The administrative assistant to the manager might be responsible for several of the tasks that make up the budgeting function, such as gathering information, calculating the figures, and processing the final document. Some of the procedures might be to prepare the budget in a specified format, to submit it to upper management on a specific date, and to get a specified number of approvals before money can be spent. The administrative assistant would probably have some role in carrying out all the budgeting procedures.

The goal of applying automation to the budgeting function would involve using technology to improve the quality of information that goes into the budget and the efficiency of the entire budgeting process. This goal would be more likely to result in an increase in productivity than would the goal of using technology to speed up isolated tasks, such as calculating the final figures or keyboarding final copy.

The ultimate goal in applying technology to the business office, then, is not merely to automate various tasks such as typing, filing, and calculating but to help the company perform major functions such as producing goods and services, negotiating contracts, receiving and filling orders, and making and receiving payments. It follows that the most efficient office is one where office automation encompasses virtually all the routine information processing tasks and functions performed by the employees in that office. When the computer performs a function, or a whole series of tasks, it is being used in a much more productive and efficient manner.

How can this broader goal of automating office functions be accomplished? To find out, it is necessary to look at how office technology evolved and to discover where the true power of the technology lies.

Information Processing Technology

What do we mean when we talk about information processing? Essentially, we are talking about the transformation of data into useful information. This process can be broken down into five functional areas: input, process, storage, output, and distribution/communication.

These functions can be thought of as the categories of tasks and procedures that deal with the processing of data into information. They can also be looked at from the standpoint of how information processing technology works.

Input is the entering of prepared data into the computer.

Processing is the organization and calculation of words and numbers carried out by the computer.

Storage is the recording of information so that it can be recalled and used again.

Output is the processed data, or information, which can be displayed on the computer screen or printed out as a paper document.

Distribution/communication is the movement of information from one location to another.

The evolution of the computer in the areas of processing, storage, and distribution/communication is where we find the greatest impact of electronic technology (Fig.1-1). While the input and output functions have also changed, the significant advancements in these areas are really a part of the processing function. For example, more complex input procedures such as the keyboarding of commands are really giving the computer processing instructions. Similarly, it is the enhancement of the processing capabilities of the computer that has expanded the options available in the forms of computer output.

Processing, storage, and distribution/communication technology developed separately but simultaneously. When we examine the developments in the area of distribution/communication, we will look at the *communication* aspect as it relates to the ability to transfer information through the use of communications technology. If we look at the impact of technology on the series of tasks that make up these functions, we will see how the merging of technology in these areas made office automation possible.

Processing, Storage, and Communication

Human beings have been processing, storing, and communicating information for thousands of years. Goatherds who tied knots in lengths of rope to keep count of their flocks in ancient Greece were processing and storing information. Scholars who collected and stored papyrus scrolls in the great libraries of ancient Egypt and Greece were storing information for future generations. African tribes who used drums to send messages and Indians who used

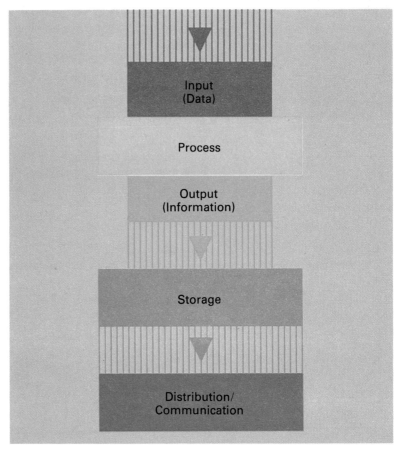

Fig. 1-1 The computer has had the greatest impact on processing, storage, and distribution/communication. Although input and output are affected, changes here are part of the processing function.

smoke signals to talk to people from other tribes were communicating information.

As civilizations developed, the technology for processing, storing, and communicating information became progressively more efficient. In the earliest business offices, clerks used clay tablets and abacuses to note and calculate daily transactions. Later they progressed to pens and paper. But since all information is made up of words and numbers, more modern devices such as the adding machine, the calculator, and the typewriter had a great impact on the processing of information in business offices. The storing of information progressed from clay tablets and papyrus to books and paper. In today's modern office, information is stored not only on paper in file folders but on microfilm and on computer disks that can hold enormous amounts of data in a very small space. The telephone was the first big technological breakthrough to permit people to communicate information quickly and easily over long distances.

Then came radio, television, and communications satellites that link places all over the world.

Processing   Automation was first applied to the processing function in the office. The reason for this has already been mentioned; that is, the processing tasks could be more easily broken down into step-by-step procedures for computerization. In fact, it was the application of the computer to business data processing tasks that led to the information explosion. Because computers can perform at astounding speeds, businesses could process more data and therefore generate much more information than they could produce before. Traditionally, processing in the business world has been divided into two broad areas: data processing and word processing.

The term **data processing** originally was used to describe what computers do. Its meaning has become so general that many people use it to describe any computer activity. Sometimes it is modified as *electronic data processing* (EDP) or *automatic data processing* (ADP). Both terms were coined to stress the automatic as opposed to manual manipulation of data. EDP often means computing that focuses on business applications. Another term used for business applications is *business data processing* (BDP). Payroll, inventory control, accounting, and sales are typical activities for business data processing applications.

The next major area of use for processing technology was **word processing**, which is the manipulation of text. The term *word processing* was first applied to an electronic typewriter. Today, though, the term has come to mean using a computer to create, edit, revise, format, or print out text.

EARNINGS	HOURS	CURRENT	YEAR TO DATE	DEDUCTIONS	CURRENT	YEAR TO DATE
REGULAR PAY	1	27692	638460	FICA	9130	45650
TOTAL PAY	1	27692	638460	FEDERAL	23543	117715
				NEW JERSEY	2642	13210
				NJ UNEM/DISA	638	3192
				PENSION CONTR	957	2538
				TAX DEF SAVING	12769	63845
				COMP MED-FAM	554	2770
				L T D SUPP I	322	1604
				UNITED WAY	500	2500
				CREDIT UNION	10000	50000
				NET PAY	66637	335436

STATEMENT OF EARNINGS NOT NEGOTIABLE

SOCIAL SECURITY NUMBER	DEPT.	CO.
123-45-6789	0000	00

PERIOD ENDING	PER WK YR
03/09/86	00 00

10130628

One of the first uses of computers by business was to prepare payrolls and issue checks. As shown, a payroll check stub has a lot more information than amount of pay.

One of today's leading computer manufacturers, International Business Machines (IBM), coined the term in 1964 as part of a marketing strategy for a new kind of typewriter. This was the Magnetic Tape Selectric Typewriter, known as the MT/ST. You will read more about this in Chapter 2, which traces the evolution of word processing. The big difference between the MT/ST and other electric typewriters was that it could record words on a magnetic tape. In a sense, IBM combined a tape recorder and a typewriter. The MT/ST speeded the preparation of typed documents considerably by allowing the typist to make a limited number of corrections and revisions without retyping the whole document. It also made it possible for typists to produce endless numbers of original or personalized letters, since different names and other information could be easily inserted and the new versions typed out by the MT/ST very quickly.

This was just the beginning. For an idea of how quickly word processing took hold, consider that IBM planned to sell about 5000 MT/STs altogether. By 1980 a single vendor was selling 20,000 word processing systems a year.

Modern word processors go way beyond the MT/ST. They allow secretaries to make unlimited corrections and alterations before the final document is stored and produced. A secretary can even lift paragraphs and pages from one document and transfer them to another. If a secretary is preparing a final report from a draft, for example, he or she needs only to retrieve the draft from the computer disk and make the required changes without having to go through the task of retyping the entire report.

Word processing is the cornerstone of the electronic office. For a time many people developed the impression that word processing was all there was to office automation. Now systems have been developed that allow word processing and data processing functions to be accomplished on one piece of equipment. This breakthrough in processing technology has allowed people to think in broader terms, and thus the concept of **information processing**, or the transformation of data into useful information, as the major activity of the automated office is fast becoming a reality. But processing is only one part of the information processing activity.

Storage When a document is processed on a word processor or computer, an electronic image is produced. When viewed on the screen, this image is called **soft copy**. This image can be stored temporarily in the machine's memory. Temporary files can be retrieved and used while information is being processed, or information can be stored permanently on a magnetic medium such as tape or on a floppy diskette. The electronically stored documents are called **electronic files.** When the copy is printed out on paper, it is called **hard copy.**

This diskette can hold the approximate equivalent of 180 pages of text.

Some people have referred to the electronic office as the "paperless" office. This is one myth that needs to be dispelled. A paperless office at some time in the future is conceivable, but so far the electronic office has generated more paper, not less. This is not too surprising when you think about it. Computers have the ability to gather and process facts with amazing speed. Consequently, more usable information is available for office workers and managers. Trying to read it all or work with it on a computer screen is not feasible. People still need to see hard copy.

However, storage in the electronic office has broader implications than choosing between the use of hard copy and the use of soft copy in retrieving information. Electronic storage technology makes it possible to store vast amounts of information in very small spaces. It makes it possible to very easily and quickly retrieve and use the information that was stored. And it makes it possible to reuse processed documents without having to rekeyboard them.

The ability of computers to store more and more information in smaller and smaller spaces is changing the way offices carry out their operations. Today's personal computer can perform the same functions as a computer that used to take up a whole room. Why? Because the instructions the computer needs to perform complex functions can now be stored in a space the size of a fingernail. It is this capacity that allowed manufacturers to produce the computers that can sit on a desk top, bringing technology to the office worker's fingertips.

This means that anyone in the office who has the equipment can easily obtain information stored electronically. Managers and professionals with computer terminals on their desks can retrieve information with the push of a button. Secretaries can store forms and documents that have to be used over and over again, cutting back on hours spent rekeyboarding. And more important, information that has been collected and stored can be quickly retrieved for use in making better business decisions and in enhancing business operations.

For example, consider a company that wants to improve health benefits for its employees but cannot afford to increase them across the board. One way to identify the areas where an increase would most benefit the workers is to analyze the types of health-care services that employees have used most frequently in the past. If this information is stored only on paper documents, it could take weeks or even months to collect the information and organize it so that it can be analyzed. However, if employee insurance claims are stored electronically, this information can be retrieved and printed out in a matter of minutes. Think what this would mean to the manager responsible for this business decision in terms of expediency and assurance of the accuracy of the information. Think also what it would mean to the company's employees who would be able to benefit from the manager's ability to retrieve and analyze the information and make the decision to increase benefits within a much shorter time frame.

Communication   The ability to utilize vast amount of electronically stored information and retrieve it quickly would be limited if organizations had access only to information stored in their own electronic files. The ability is unlimited, however, when information can be transferred from computer to computer and retrieved from remote locations.

The impact of technology on the distribution and communication functions of information processing may be the most dramatic advantage of office automation and the one with the greatest capacity to increase productivity. Communications technology allows the linkage of information processing equipment both internally (within the organization) and externally (outside the organization). Documents can be electronically transferred from one location to another in soft-copy form. The receiver of a document can print out a hard copy, if desired. Information that is sent electronically, then held in storage until it is either read in soft copy form or printed as hard copy, is called **electronic mail**.

Since electronic messages can be sent from one computer to another, it is possible to cut back on the use of the telephone. Of course, we will always use the telephone when we need to reach someone right away to pass on information, but the telephone has drawbacks:

■ Often there is a busy signal, which wastes time.

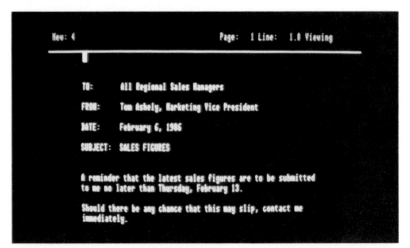

Electronic messages, like the one above, can be received and read in soft-copy form. This method is more efficient than using the telephone or distributing hard copies of interoffice memos.

- Even more often the person being called is not in, and a message has to be left. If the original caller is not in when the call is returned, the result is a round of "telephone tag."

- Receiving telephone calls can be disruptive, particularly if the message from the caller is not urgent. Use of a computer message system allows workers to deal with nonurgent messages at their own convenience, not at the convenience of the caller.

Communication in the automated office is also made easier by the fact that people can hold meetings using electronic technology. A **teleconference** is a meeting in which several people can participate by using telephones, and computers can be linked to the telephones so that documents can be exchanged during the meeting. An enhancement of the teleconference is the **video teleconference**, in which participants who may be in several different cities can see each other on a screen and show charts or products.

Technological Evolution

The technological advancements in the areas of processing, storage, and communication are exciting when viewed separately. But it is the merging of these functions through the use of electronic equipment that has resulted in a major impact on the office environment. This merging, or integration, of computer technology forces us to change the way we view the overall work flow in the office.

This flow of work is often referred to as the **information processing cycle.** If you consider the functions of information processing technology that were outlined earlier—input, processing, storage, output, and distribution/communication—you will see how technological developments have changed the information processing cycle from a step-by-step linear flow to a dynamic, integrated process (Fig. 1-2). For example, take the job function of processing documents. The tasks involved in processing a letter are to take down the dictation; transcribe, edit, and proofread the letter; and make carbons or photocopies of it. You then place the letter in an envelope and send it through the U.S. Postal Service. You file copies of the letter in the appropriate file folders, which are kept in a file cabinet. These are distinct steps that you take, one after the other, until the job is done. In the traditional office, you would think of these steps in this order:

1. Input (take dictation)

2. Process (transcribe, edit, proofread)

3. Output (make copies)

4. Distribute (send through U.S. Postal Service)

5. Store (file)

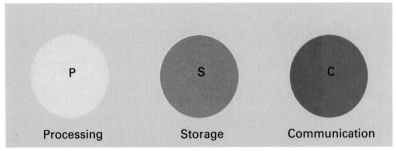

Fig. 1-2a Technology in these three areas developed separately.

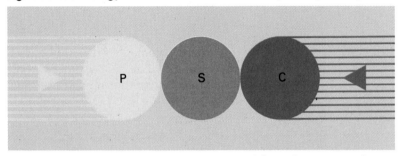

Fig. 1-2b The evolution of technology caused them to merge or become integrated.

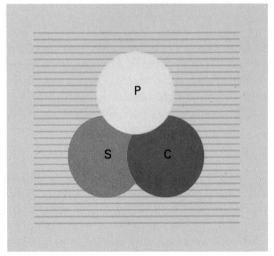

Fig. 1-2c Through this integration electronic equipment became more powerful.

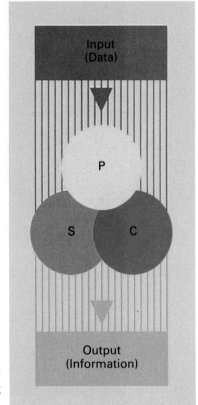

Fig. 1-2d Use of integrated equipment has changed the work flow in the office.

If you worked in an electronic office, you would still take dictation. You would keyboard the letter on a computer. You would edit and proofread the letter on the screen and store it as an electronic file, and when you were finished, you might even use the computer to distribute the letter. That is, you would send the letter from your computer to the computer of the person or persons to whom it is addressed. In this example you would have processed the document, stored it, and communicated the information almost at the same time. This merging of tasks parallels the merging of the technology and has resulted in many major changes in the way office functions and tasks can be carried out. Now information processing is no longer a series of steps that take place one after the other. Instead, processing, storage, and communication can take place almost simultaneously during the processing stage.

From the previous example, it is easy to see why office automation was first applied to the secretarial/clerical function of document preparation. The tasks that constitute the processing phase of this function—formatting, editing, and manipulating text—are tasks that can be broken down into a set of repetitive, logical steps for computer programming.

Increases in productivity could be measured by faster, higher-quality production of documents. With the evolution and merging of processing, storage, and communication technology, however, many new options for increasing productivity were opened. It became apparent that technology could be applied to higher-level functions in the office to achieve the higher level of productivity goals mentioned earlier. This means that office automation must be applied to the administrative support and management functions.

Administrative Support Functions

When widespread use of processing technology came to the office, many people thought that automation of the processing function was office automation itself. The first reaction to the influx of word processing equipment in the office was an increase in productivity in the area of document production. In the late 1970s and even into the early 1980s, this was considered to be a very progressive use of automated office equipment.

As a result, organizations began separating the word processing/document production function from the traditional secretarial/administrative assistant functions. Large companies began setting up special departments, usually called word processing centers. These centers processed the majority of paper documents that were needed for both external and internal distribution. New positions were created for word processing operators and word processing specialists. Many administrative secretaries and office managers moved into the position of word processing supervisor.

As a result of this new organization, the secretarial role became separated into two functions: word processing and administrative

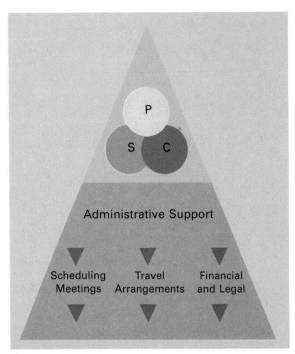

Fig. 1-3 Administrative support functions incorporate some tasks that can be automated; however, a high level of human interaction and decision making is involved in them.

support. The administrative support function incorporates all those duties which cannot be fully automated (Fig. 1-3). Duties such as organizing and controlling the work flow, making travel arrangements, gathering information, planning and setting up meetings, keeping financial and legal records, and handling telephone calls and visitors are all a part of the administrative support role. These duties are composed of tasks that have individual requirements. They also incorporate tasks that require a highly developed skill in decision making.

While this organization is still used in many businesses today, the proliferation of microcomputers in the office in the early 1980s caused a shift back to combining the document production and administrative support functions in one job. The merging of processing, storage, and communication technology and the ability to install these capabilities in a computer small enough to sit on the top of a secretary's desk made this possible.

Now the power of the technology can be used to do more than process large numbers of documents faster and faster. Such tasks as scheduling and keeping calendars, sending and receiving messages, gathering information, keeping records, filing, and handling expense accounts and other financial items can all be done more productively through the use of technology at the administrative support workstation.

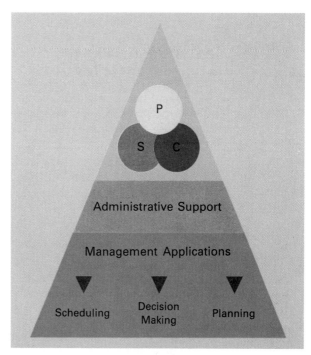

Fig. 1-4 The automation of the managerial workstation can improve the way this function is carried out.

Managerial Functions

In today's electronic office, the management function is, of course, also being automated. This means that information can be sent electronically from the manager's desk to the secretary's. Notes, calendars, messages, expenses, and schedules can all be kept on the computer. With the decentralization of document production in many automated offices, managers will be able to have direct access to processed documents and electronic files.

The automation of the administrative support and managerial functions in the office will bring about increased productivity in the broad office functions described earlier: budgeting, negotiating contracts, filling orders, and so on (Fig. 1-4). The automation of the administrative support and managerial functions is also leading to a shifting of responsibilities in the office.

Changing Roles

We've been using the terms *secretary* and *office worker* to talk about the people who process information in America's business offices. But what do these job titles mean?

Office worker is, of course, a very broad term covering every kind of office job classification: file clerk, mail clerk, stenographer, receptionist, word processor, data processor, secretary, executive assistant, administrative assistant, and correspondence secretary, to name a few.

Secretary is more restrictive in meaning, but it can include word processor, executive assistant, administrative assistant, personal secretary, corporate secretary, and correspondence secretary.

Secretary originally implied *private* or *confidential,* but changing practices made it necessary to specify *personal* or *corporate.* The word has a long and honorable history. Its present meaning of one who processes correspondence, keeps records, and transacts business for others dates back to before 1500. And secretaries of all kinds will continue to be needed in the automated, electronic office.

Secretaries and office workers are members of a vital and growing occupation. In his book *Megatrends*, John Naisbett notes, "We now mass produce knowledge, and knowledge is the driving force of our economy." In fact, one term that is coming into common use to describe people who work with information is **knowledge workers**. The term can be applied to lawyers, managers, insurance adjusters, clerical workers, and secretaries, among others. In this book we will use the terms *secretary* and *office worker* wherever it is appropriate, unless we are discussing a specific job such as file clerk.

As business offices increase their use of electronic technology to improve productivity, the role of the secretary in the electronic office will increase in significance and responsibility. The secretary of the future will be more an information processing specialist, with primary skills in administrative support and secondary skills in typing. It is even likely that as more sophisticated computer systems are established, secretaries will be able to use them to perform functions now carried out by special departments, such as accounting, inventory control, order entry, sales, and financial analysis.

The use of electronic technology is causing a change in the roles of office workers. Secretarial responsibilities will change to reflect the new skills required in today's office.

Not only will office automation increase the responsibilities of secretaries; it will also upgrade their stature as employees. In the electronic office, they will be skilled operators of highly technical equipment. In addition, they will be trusted to perform a wide range of duties—such as researching, editing, and supervising and hiring other employees—that were once done by middle-level managers. Secretaries will be free to carry out more creative duties and use their own judgment and initiative. This will make their work more challenging and interesting than it has ever been before.

■ Summary

- We live in what is known as the Information Age. The use of computers in the business office has created an "information explosion," which has led to the development of new information processing technology.

- Office jobs are organized into functions, tasks, and procedures. The major reason for office automation is to increase productivity. This requires that technology be applied not only to office tasks but to the broad functions of the office.

- Information processing can be broken down into five functional areas: input, processing, storage, output, and distribution/communication. Human beings have always processed, stored, and communicated information. The impact of technology on these three functions has changed the way offices process information.

- Processing has traditionally been broken down into two areas: data processing and word processing. New technology allows these functions to be performed on one type of equipment.

- Electronic files are documents stored on electronic media. They can be viewed on the screen as soft copy or printed out as hard copy. Electronic files can also be retrieved and re-used to create new documents without rekeyboarding.

- Electronic storage technology makes it possible to store vast amounts of information in very small spaces and to retrieve it instantaneously. This improves the ability to gather information needed to make business decisions.

- Communications technology allows the linkage of information processing equipment so that information can be transferred from computer to computer.

- Advances in information processing technology have resulted in the automation of many administrative support and managerial functions. This will mean greater improvements in productivity. Such advances are causing a shifting of responsibilities and roles in the office.

Review Questions

1. What is the difference between data and information? Give examples of each.

2. Explain the difference between a task and a function. What are office procedures, and how do they help office workers perform their jobs?

3. What does increased productivity mean? How does high technology help businesses increase their productivity?

4. Name the three major areas of technology that have changed the way office workers perform information processing functions.

5. Give examples of how technological developments in processing, storage, and communication improve the ability to perform office tasks.

6. What is the difference between data processing and word processing? How has this changed?

7. What are four administrative support tasks that have been affected by office automation?

8. Explain how office automation is changing the roles of secretaries and office workers.

Technical Vocabulary*

data
information
high tech
increased productivity
algorithm
labor-intensive
function
task
procedure
input
processing
storage
output

distribution/communication
data processing
word processing
information processing
soft copy
electronic file
hard copy
electronic mail
teleconference
video teleconference
information processing cycle
knowledge workers

Discussion and Skills Development

1. Reporters discuss data and information daily in magazines and newspapers. Select three articles that use either data or information. Be prepared to explain to the class why your examples are data or information.

2. Contact an admissions office, a bank, a newspaper, a library, a doctor's office, or an insurance company, and ask the of-

*The terms listed in the Technical Vocabulary section at the end of every chapter in this book are presented in the order in which they are discussed within the text in order to facilitate easy reference.

fice workers there what kind of office automation they use regularly and what tasks it is used for. Ask them how well they like it, what its limitations seem to be, and how recently the equipment was installed. Summarize your findings in a report to the class.

3. It is useful to be able to think through a project and figure out what the individual steps are that must be taken to complete the project. Think through a project you might have coming up, such as planning a party or a trip to the theater. Write down all the tasks you can think of that you will need to accomplish to complete this project. Organize them into the logical order in which they must be done—first, second, and so on. Which tasks require judgment and decision making? Which tasks could be automated? Which tasks depend on something else being done first? Which tasks can be done simultaneously? Keep your notes on this project; file them away for future reference. As you progress through this text, you will be referred back to this exercise.

chapter 2
Modern Office Technology

Computers are everywhere. We can't buy a loaf of bread, take money out of the bank, or check into a hospital without encountering a computer. Our homes have been inundated not only with computers but with many other technological marvels such as cordless telephones and videocassette recorders. The new technology is in our lives to stay, and it has moved into the business office as well.

Your first office job may not require you to operate anything more complicated than an electric typewriter, but sooner or later you may be required to use an electronic typewriter, a word processor, or a microcomputer. The technology for processing, storing, and communicating information is still changing rapidly. If you are to keep up with these changes, you need a basic understanding of how the most up-to-date equipment works and what it does in the modern business office.

This chapter will trace the development of modern office technology from the typewriter to the computer. And you will see how advancements in the processing, storing, and communication of information are revolutionizing the way modern offices function.

Word Processing— An Overview

To trace the history of processing technology, it is necessary to first look at the typewriter. Nothing, not even the telephone, which had a great impact on communications, changed the business office quite so much as the typewriter—or, as it was first called, the type writer. The first really usable typewriter was made in the nineteenth century by Christopher Sholes, a printer and inventor in Milwaukee, Wisconsin. By 1909 no fewer than 89 separate manufacturers were turning out these popular new machines.

The typewriter business in the early part of this century was much like the computer boom in recent years. Many people wanted to produce typewriters, and manufacturers kept introducing improvements. Buyers were often bewildered and a little afraid because there were many different kinds of models to choose from, and they couldn't be sure which type of writing machine was best. Within a few years, however, many manufacturers had gone out of business, and a standard model typewriter produced by a few companies remained.

Three stages in the evolution of the typewriter were (*top left*) manual, (*top right*) electric, and (*bottom*) electronic.

Before the invention of a practical typewriter, office workers were all men. After typewriters came into the business office, women graduates of clerical schools founded by typewriter manufacturers took over the all-male clerical jobs.

Those Typing Machines

The purpose of the typewriter was to speed up the process of putting words on paper, and it was a revolutionary improvement over writing documents out by hand or having them set in type. The typewriter proved to be revolutionary in another sense as well. To generate a mass market for their machines, early manufacturers started hundreds of schools to train office workers to use the typewriters. When it became apparent that most of their pupils were women, the companies capitalized on that fact by advertising their machines as a means for women to win economic freedom. Within a decade or two, the male clerks in most business offices were replaced by women, and secretarial and clerical work became a traditional woman's occupation. That tradition is beginning to change as office automation continues to elevate the status of office workers and more men enter the clerical field.

Only a few years after the first practical typewriters appeared, electric typewriters were introduced, further automating and speeding up the process of putting words on paper. The first electric typewriter was produced in 1925 by E. Remington & Sons, manufacturers of sewing machines and guns and of the first commercial typewriter. In 1934 IBM also brought out an electric typewriter.

Electric typewriters made typing easier and faster, since typists needed to apply only a little pressure to depress the keys. Another major change was the introduction of the "RETURN" key. Instead of having to reach up and push a bar at the end of every line, typists merely had to hit an extra key without taking their fingers off the keyboard to make the carriage return.

Computerized word processors refined this capability further by introducing **word wrap**. With word wrap you do not even need to hit a "RETURN" key at the end of every line because the computer automatically starts a new line. You only need to hit the "RETURN" key when you want to start a new paragraph.

By the 1950s the electric typewriter had replaced most manual typewriters in the business office, but even today you can still find manual typewriters in some offices. After the 1950s the pace of change accelerated as each succeeding development in the typewriter took it a step closer to full-scale word processing.

A significant step in that evolutionary process was a change in the way in which the letters were put onto the paper. The standard manual and electric typewriters were all typebar machines. That is, each character was on an individual bar that struck against the ribbon and paper when the typist pressed the key.

Most portable typewriters still are typebar machines, but the standard typewriter in the business office is now a single-element machine. On single-element machines, a ball, called an **element**, replaces the typebar. On such typewriters the carriage does not move back and forth. Instead, the ball moves and rotates so that it strikes the ribbon with the right character at the right spot on the paper. The single-element machine is faster than a typebar machine. Even more important, different elements can be used on one machine, giving different sizes or styles of type.

As with other changes in the typewriter, this innovation also anticipated further improvements that computer technology would bring to word processing: modern word processors can print out type in a wide variety of formats quickly and easily.

TYPE TERMINOLOGY

Typists using sophisticated machines need to understand terminology that was once used only by printers. Many commonly used terms refer to either the size or the style of type. Terms that describe size include:

- **Elite**—the smaller of the two common sizes on typewriters. It is also known as *12-pitch,* since 12 elite characters fit in an inch.
- **Pica**—the larger of the two common sizes on typewriters. It is also known as *10-pitch,* since 10 characters of pica size fit in an inch. In printing, a pica is a unit of measure equivalent to ⅙ inch.
- **Point**—a unit of measure in printing. Twelve points make up one pica; a point is ¹/₇₂ inch. Typists should become familiar with the point system, since many word processing computers and printers produce typed copy in point sizes. Standard sizes for text are 8, 10, and 12 points—the smaller the number, the smaller the type.

Terms that describe style include:

- **Boldface/Bold**—terms for type that is heavier and darker than normal.
- **Face/Typeface**—a general term for style of type.
- **Font**—refers to the size of the typeface; a style of type has more than one font.
- **Ital/Italic**—a slanted typeface, somewhat in between script and standard.
- **Script**—a style of typewriter type that looks somewhat like flowing handwriting.
- **Standard**—term for common typewriter type as opposed to script.
- **Typescript**—typewritten copy.
- **Typeset**—printed copy.

Self-correcting typewriters were another major advance for typists. Although the term *self-correcting* is something of an exaggeration, machines with this capability do simplify making corrections, at least on the original. If you use one of these machines, you can use a special key and tape to correct a mistake without having to erase the error or retype the entire page. You would still have to erase the error on the carbon manually, however.

Electric adding machines and calculators joined the electric typewriter in the office. A general term for all these electric devices is **electromechanical,** to distinguish them from electronic devices.

Electronic Typewriters

Electronic typewriters were yet another step in the evolution of the typewriter. Essentially, electronic typewriters are electric typewriters with some computerized functions. They bridge the gap between electromechanical machines and computers.

The more sophisticated electronic typewriters are sometimes called text-editing machines because they allow the user to alter the copy. The term *word processing* was coined to describe what these electronic typewriters do. In 1964, when International Business Machines (IBM) developed the Magnetic Tape Selectric Typewriter (MT/ST), an electronic typewriter, the company used the term to market it.

As the name implies, this first word processor was an electric typewriter attached to a device that stored keystrokes by recording them on magnetic tape. When you typed corrections, the MT/ST automatically made a new recording of the text. This allowed you to make a tape that was free of errors and then replay it to produce a perfect copy of the text. The tape—or a section of it—could be replayed any number of times, causing the MT/ST to type copies automatically at 150 words a minute. With this machine you could produce multiple original copies much faster than with a standard typewriter.

Some MT/STs featured storage consoles with dual recording tapes, one for the text of a form letter and another for a mailing list. This model could automatically merge information from the two tapes to produce an individually typed copy addressed to each recipient.

Unlike more modern word processors, the MT/ST did not feature **random access,** which is the ability to retrieve a document electronically without looking at any of the other documents recorded on the storage medium. If you wanted to produce a third document on the tape, you had to play through the first two.

In 1969 IBM introduced the Magnetic Card Selectric Typewriter, usually referred to as the *Mag Card.* The first Mag Cards worked like the MT/STs, except that they recorded keystrokes on magnetically coated cards instead of tapes. Each card could hold one page of text. Separating the stored text into pages this way made it possible to print any single document or page without replaying others.

A later version, the Mag Card II, was the first word processor with an internal electronic memory as well as an attached storage unit. The memory could retain up to 8000 characters as long as the typewriter was turned on. Thus you could make your revisions before transferring the text from the internal memory to the storage card.

The Mag Card II also included a correcting ribbon that lifted errors from the page as you struck over them. Thus you could produce a usable copy of the corrected text as you keyboarded it, as opposed to having to print out a corrected version.

Today manufacturers make electronic typewriters that offer larger internal memories as well as other features not found on earlier models. They may have small, usually one-line, display screens and a limited capability to communicate with each other over telephone lines or cables.

Word Processors

The concept of word processing came to full bloom in the 1970s. In 1972 the first video display screen was introduced, and at the same time Comptek Research became the first company to introduce the use of disks, storage devices external to the machine, with a word processor. As major manufacturers such as Olivetti, Royal, Xerox, Lanier, and Digital Equipment Corporation began to manufacture word processing equipment, technological advances became more and more rapid. With the introduction of the IBM Displaywriter in 1980 and the entry of major computer manufacturers such as Burroughs and Honeywell onto the word processing scene, the merging of computer technology and word processing technology was complete.

Two widely used word processors are the IBM Displaywriter (*left*) and the Wang Alliance (*right*).

Now, when we think of word processing, we think of computers. Traditionally, a word processor was a piece of electronic equipment that processed only words, while a computer was a device for processing numerical data. However, this distinction is becoming obsolete. Nowadays most general-purpose computers can be set up to handle word processing, and most modern word processors are, in fact, computers.

When using a word processor, you see the words appear on a full-sized screen as you type. You can go to any word or place on the screen by using keys that move a **cursor**, which is a blip of light or some other symbol that you can move around on the screen. By positioning the cursor in the appropriate place, you can change, correct, and edit the document you are typing at any point without having to retype the entire page. You can easily move words, sentences, and paragraphs around, delete them, underline them, put them in boldface, or use any of a number of other features because at this point the document exists only as blips of light on the screen.

As you work along, you can store the document in the computer. When you finish keyboarding, you can press a few more keys and produce a paper copy of the document. If you have made an error, you can recall the document from the computer's memory back onto the screen, correct the error, and print out another, corrected, paper copy. When the document is displayed on the screen, it is called soft copy, to distinguish it from hard copy. The word processor can be set up to communicate with other computers so that a letter can be sent from one terminal to another in the next office or in another city.

The word processor has enormous advantages over the typewriter, even the electronic typewriter, because it permits typists to make unlimited corrections and changes. Word processors also perform a great many formatting tasks almost effortlessly, such as numbering pages, setting margins, centering titles, highlighting passages, and dividing copy into multiple columns.

The word processor saves thousands of hours of retyping a year. It enables office workers to store immense amounts of information in very small spaces, and it allows them to retrieve the information quickly and easily. All of these improvements mean that businesses become more productive because their employees can perform more work in much less time. Office workers also enjoy their jobs more because they don't have to perform so many tedious, mechanical jobs such as formatting, retyping, and retrieving papers from files.

Most word processors are computers, but not all computers are word processors. It's true that you can do some word processing on just about any computer, but many small computers—such as the ones you take home and connect to your television set—allow for only limited amounts of storage and processing. Their display screens usually can show you only 22 lines of type 40 characters wide, while word processors can display 54 lines of type 80 characters wide. Some large office computers are set up to perform both data processing and word processing, and some perform only word processing functions. Computers that are "dedicated" solely to word processing can generally perform a wide range of processing, formatting, and calculating. However, because they cannot perform the broad range of functions that other computers can, more and more microcomputers are being purchased for use in the office. Consequently, use of dedicated word processing equipment is on the decline.

Impact on the Office Since the arrival of the new technology in the business office, desks have become workstations and typewriters have become word processors. The term **workstation** incorporates the idea of all the equipment, furnishings, and accessories needed to perform work in an electronic environment. Word processing brought many significant changes to the office, which include:

- Increased efficiency through greater typing speed coupled with higher quality.
- Reduced retyping and proofreading time.
- Reduced time spent on routing repetitive chores.
- More time for administrative support services.
- Greater and more efficient use of office equipment.
- More and better career opportunities for office workers, with higher pay scales.

Computers have brought even more significant changes in the way offices function. In the following pages we will take a look at the definition, history, and operation of computers in general.

Computers— An Overview

There are many different types of computers that do many different things, from controlling the heat in a microwave oven to flying an airplane. In the business office the computer is an extraordinarily efficient machine for processing, storing, and distributing information.

A computer can add, subtract, multiply, divide, and make logical decisions, such as whether one thing is equal to, greater than, or less than another. A computer used to schedule students' classes, for example, could make the following decision: "The number of students signed up for a course equals the number of seats available in the lecture hall; therefore, the course is filled." It is the capacity to perform these logical functions that makes computers so much more than just super calculating machines.

Computers "read" bits of information that are recorded as electrical or magnetic fields on magnetic tapes and disks. A computer looks at the electrical field and senses whether it is on or off, or it looks at the magnetic field and senses whether it is positive or negative. In effect, then, computers can make decisions only on the basis of the answers to "yes" and "no" questions. To use the earlier example, the computer would decide "Yes, there is a seat left" and issue a course assignment, or it would decide "No, there are no seats left" and announce that the course is filled. It is because computers can make thousands of these yes/no decisions a minute that they can be instructed to perform functions as complicated as word processing.

Most information processing computers are **digital** computers. That means they can count numbers (digits) that represent letters, numerals, or other symbols. They use the binary code (zeros and ones) to do this. In a computer's language, the zeros are negative magnetic fields and the ones are positive magnetic fields. The letter C, for example, would look like this to a computer: 11000011. The binary code is simply a means for the machine for answering a yes/no question by reading the magnetic medium.

Computer Processing

Computers were originally designed to carry out complicated math processes quickly and accurately, in short, to compute. The first electronic automatic computer was known as ENIAC, which stands for Electronic Numerical Integrator and Computer. Developed at the University of Pennsylvania in 1945, ENIAC filled a room 50 by 30 feet and cost more than $400,000. Today a computer with similar capabilities would fit on your desk.

The First Generation As computers evolved, it became customary to refer to the successive improved machines in terms of generations. The very first computers were thus first-generation computers.

First-generation computers such as ENIAC, shown above, used vacuum tubes. They were large and generated a lot of heat.

First-generation computers used vacuum tubes, and ENIAC had 18,000 of them. It was programmed by connecting wires in various configurations and operated through a series of more than 6000 switches. ENIAC was designed to compute the trajectory of shells for the U.S. Army. It did this faster than people could, but it was a cumbersome, awkward machine requiring trained technicians to operate it.

The first computer designed to process business data was called UNIVAC I (*UNIV*ersal *A*utomatic *C*omputer). It was developed in 1951 by the Remington-Rand Corporation (the same company that manufactured the first commercial typewriter). In 1952 the CBS broadcasting network used UNIVAC I to predict the results of the U.S. presidential election. After analyzing only 5 percent of the vote, UNIVAC I correctly predicted that Dwight Eisenhower would defeat Adlai Stevenson. This feat made the general public conscious of computers and their power. Some feared these machines that could "outthink" people.

In 1953 IBM, the maker of the MT/ST which had joined the growing ranks of computer manufacturers, announced the IBM 650 Electronic Computer. The IBM 650 was the first medium-sized machine specifically built for business applications. With this computer, IBM, already a leader with its punched-card accounting devices and typewriters, moved to the front of the new industry.

The Second Generation   Until the late 1950s, all computers used vacuum tubes. Then the vacuum tube gave way to the transistor, and the next generation of computers was born.

The second generation began about 1959 with what is called *solid-state* circuits on transistors. **Transistors** are electronic devices consisting of substances that conduct electricity. Invented at Bell Laboratories in the late 1940s, transistors were already used in radios and televisions.

Transistors in computers did the same work as vacuum tubes, but they were better for three very important reasons:

1. They were smaller, so they took up less space.

2. They generated less heat (special cooling was required for the large vacuum tube computers to prevent them from melting).

3. They were more reliable.

Because computers using transistors were smaller, faster, less expensive, and more reliable than first-generation computers, more businesses could afford them. The second-generation transistorized computers had a tremendous impact on business. In 1955 fewer than 250 computer systems existed in the United States. Within five years 2500 transistorized computer systems were humming and buzzing. By 1964 the number of such systems had soared to more than 18,000. The Information Age was well on its way when the next improvement arrived.

The IBM System/360 was one of the first computers to use the microchip. This launched a new generation of computer technology.

The Third Generation Third-generation computers made their debut on April 7, 1964, when IBM launched its new System/360 computer using the latest technological development: microchips. **Microchips**, known formally as *microprocessors* or informally as *chips*, are slivers of silicon about the size of a baby's fingernail. Unlike other computer circuits, chips can be mass-produced, so they are cheaper. Also, they are even more reliable than transistors. With the advent of microchips, computers became practical and affordable for small businesses as well as for government and large corporations. By 1980 tiny semiconductor chips capable of containing as many circuits as 70,000 transistors were available. And the amount of information or memory these tiny chips can contain is increasing constantly.

Modern computers use the microchip, which is very small but which can store tremendous amounts of data.

Microcomputers, the smallest, least expensive computers, are found in offices of all sizes, even small ones.

Today computers are classified in three broad categories depending, essentially, on how powerful they are, which is to say how many tasks they can perform and how quickly.

Mainframes **Mainframe** computers have larger storage capacities and can process information faster than any other category of computers. They are so fast that they can process about 5 million instructions a minute. They are usually used by the government, by universities, by institutions such as hospitals, and by companies that sell computer time to other smaller companies.

A mainframe computer which is among those with the highest speed, largest functional size, biggest physical dimensions, or greatest monetary cost is called a supercomputer. An example of this is the Cray 2 supercomputer at the University of Minnesota Supercomputer Institute. The Cray 2 uses the most advanced technology available. It allows many types of users to solve problems that cannot be solved with other computers.

Minicomputers Smaller and usually less powerful than mainframes, all **minicomputers** are third-generation computers. Because of the microchip, some are actually more powerful than first-generation mainframes. These computers are also used by the government and by large businesses. Because they are less expensive and easier to operate than mainframes, they are also used by moderate-sized companies. They perform the same kinds of tasks that mainframes do in processing alphanumeric data. Some minicomputers are designed to do specific tasks, such as word processing.

Mainframe computer systems are used by large companies that have massive amounts of data to be processed.

Microcomputers   The smallest computers, taking their name from the microchip that made them possible, **microcomputers** can perform a wide variety of functions, including word processing. These are the computers that individuals can keep on their desks and use in their homes.

Microcomputers are found in all kinds of offices. A physician's office, for example, may use a single microcomputer for word processing, billing, and keeping patients' medical records. A small real estate sales company might use a microcomputer to keep track of houses for sale, sales commissions, and other data. The real estate office might have its microcomputer connected via telephone lines with a minicomputer or mainframe computer to receive information about houses for sale all over the region, state, or country.

Computer Storage

Computers can read and store millions of these bits or pieces of information. Their capacity to store information is called **memory**. The more memory a computer has, the more information it can store and the faster it can process it.

People have been seeking ways to store information for 30,000 years. Books eventually became our greatest single means for storing information. Computers are now assuming an increasing importance because the growth of information has become so great that libraries of conventional books can no longer keep up. With their vast storage capacity, computers help us to contain and use the increasing flood of information that our society generates. A single disk, for example, is able to hold the entire catalog of books contained in the Library of Congress.

Because of this ability to store and process immense amounts of information, computers have had an astonishing impact on business and government. It used to take the U.S. Census Bureau almost the entire decade between one census and the next to tabulate the results. Now the same work can be done in months. Businesses that used to lose days of productive work annually to count their inventories can now do the job in seconds. Records that would take up floors of file cabinets can be placed on a few reels of computer tape or in a single disk pack. Computers have made it possible for small companies to expand their business activities and services far beyond their former limits, and they have made it possible for very large businesses, such as department store chains and utility companies, to serve their customers much more quickly and effectively.

Computer Communication

The computer's ability to communicate has been enhanced by developments paralleling those of increasing its storage capacity and processing capabilities. There would be little point in having so much information stored in a computer if we could not easily retrieve it in order to distribute it throughout the world—in short, communicate it.

As you read earlier, the big technological breakthrough in communication was the telephone, followed by radio, television, and communications satellites. Transferring messages and information from computer to computer is playing an increasingly important role in the office environment today. Linking computers or word processors for the purpose of enabling people to share equipment and information is neither a novel nor new development. Terminals

Fig. 2-1 Linkage of equipment brings computer resources to multiple users of a system.

tied to larger computer or word processing systems have done the job for years.

An example of one of the early systems designed to communicate is IBM's 360 computer system, discussed earlier in this chapter. Intracompany linkage is a common practice today in companies that have mainframe and minicomputer systems. Now, through the use of microcomputers, systems can be set up so that many different departments located throughout the organization can utilize the resources provided by the larger system. This type of linkage is called an **electronic network**. In an electronic network, computers and other devices located in various places are connected electronically so that data and other computer resources can be shared and exchanged (Fig. 2-1). Workers can access **internal files**, that is, data held on the computer system within the organization, or **external files**, data held on computer systems outside the organization.

Computer Hardware

Regardless of what functions they perform, all computers have the same basic units or physical components, which are called **hardware**. Because they are made up of different units, computers are often referred to as **computer systems,** even the small microcomputers.

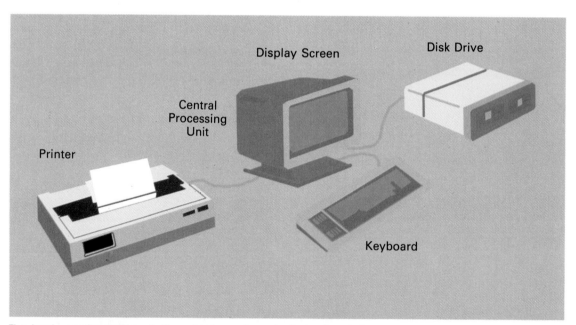

The basic configuration of all computer systems includes input devices (keyboard), storage/processing devices (central processing unit), external storage devices (disk drive), output devices (printer and display screen), and as an option, communications devices.

The basic units of all computer systems are:

- Input devices.
- Central processing unit.
- Storage devices.
- Output devices.

In addition, systems designed to communicate with one another will have communication devices. Note that the units of the computer system reflect the flow of information through an office that you read about in Chapter 1: input, processing, storage, output, and distribution/communication (IPSOD).

Let's take a closer look at each of the basic units.

Input Devices
These devices are used to enter data into the computer. You are familiar with the most common device: the typewriterlike keyboard. The keyboard is usually linked directly to the computer. It has more keys than a regular typewriter keyboard; the additional keys are used to carry out special functions.

Another primary input device that is being used increasingly is the optical character reader (OCR). This is a device that can "read" ink (text) on paper—written, typed, or printed—and put it into the computer system. OCR devices are quite common today, and you may have seen them being used. They scan and read the bar codes on goods you buy in the supermarket. The checkout clerk just passes an item over the OCR, which reads the price contained in the bar code, rings it up, and adds it to the total. OCRs are also used to process checks and read price tags in department stores.

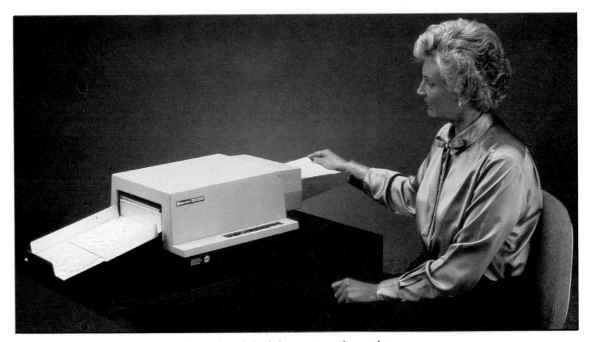

The OCR scanner can be used to enter data into a computer system.

Central Processing Unit

The heart of the computer system is the central processing unit (CPU). It receives data from the input devices, carries out the various operations, and sends out the results to output devices. The CPU consists of three principal parts:

- **Control Unit**. This is the part of the CPU that causes the system to carry out instructions. It is a kind of internal "traffic cop" that routes information here and there within the computer for processing, storage, and communication.

- **Arithmetic-Logic Unit**. This unit does the arithmetic functions of adding, subtracting, multiplying, and dividing. It can determine if a number is larger or smaller and if it is negative or positive. In that way it is able to make logical decisions (the yes/no routine mentioned earlier).

- **Memory**. This is sometimes called *main memory* or *temporary memory* or *internal memory*, as opposed to *file storage* or *auxiliary memory*. The memory in the CPU holds data that is input and sends it out as necessary to the arithmetic-logic unit or to output devices. It also holds the instructions or program to carry out the functions.

Storage Devices

The ability to store large amounts of data is essential to a computer. As noted above, the computer stores data in its temporary memory. When the computer has finished processing the data, it must be given instructions to store or "file" it permanently.

The most commonly used storage media for computer files are magnetic disks, which look like small records in their jackets, and magnetic tapes, which are similar to music tapes. In business offices disks are used most often. The computer can transfer data electronically to these disks and tapes. Just as you can go to the file drawer and get the copy you filed, you can have the computer retrieve data stored on a disk or tape.

CPUs are often equipped with **disk drives**, which are devices into which the disks are placed so that they may be "read" or "written on" by the system. Some computers have similar devices to do the same thing with tapes.

Storage and retrieval are very important parts of any business office procedure. There would be no sense in filing anything if you didn't expect to look at it again. Computers are invaluable in the business office because they satisfy so well the three most important demands of a good filing system:

1. They have a large capacity and can store a lot of information in a small space.

2. They allow speedy access to needed data.

3. They store information relatively cheaply.

Output Devices

The most commonly known electronic output device is the **printer**, a machine that allows the computer system to present a paper copy of its results to you. The paper copy is called a **printout**, or hard copy.

Another common output device is the **video display terminal (VDT)**. This is also known as the display screen or a **cathode-ray tube (CRT)**. It looks very much like a television screen, and on it the computer operator can see the data that is being input and processed. If you were using a word processing system, you would see the letters you are typing—the soft copy—appear on the VDT as you type them.

Communication Devices

Computer systems can be connected to each other by special wires and cables so that they can communicate. When computer systems are connected by wires for communication, they are said to form a local area network. A **local area network (LAN)** can allow computer systems to communicate locally, within the same office or between offices in the same building. Through telecommunications, communication can take place between computers in different buildings. A computer system in New York, for example, can be hooked up to one in San Francisco. This is very important for companies whose business spans the continent or the world. The home office can quickly exchange information with any of its branch offices.

Even if they are not hooked up with special wires and cables, computer systems can communicate with each other over regular telephone lines. To do this, they need a device called a modem. **Modem** stands for *mo*dulator-*dem*odulator. A modem can convert digital communication signals, used for computer communication, into analog signals that can be sent over telephone wires. At the receiving end, the modem converts the analog signals back into digital signals, which can be read by the receiving computer. This process is called *data communication.*

Data communication allows computers in remote locations to send data to and receive data from each other. It is possible, for example, for you to sit at a computer in your school and retrieve information from a library in Washington, D.C., or in New York City. You will read more about communicating with computers in later chapters.

Computer Software

To make all the hardware you have been reading about work, the computer must be given programs or instructions. These programs and instructions are called **software**. Computers are relatively useless pieces of machinery without software. Without software, the computer is like a camera without film or a stereo without records.

Software exists in three broad categories: programming software, operating or systems software, and applications software.

Programming Software

The programming software consists of the instructions or programs implanted in the circuits of the CPU. These instructions make the computer operate, but the ordinary user does not interact directly with them.

Operating or Systems Software

Additional instructions or programs are required to allow the system to operate with and interact with the applications software. An example of systems software might be a program to schedule which of several waiting jobs the computer should carry out next. Users usually don't need to worry about systems programs.

Applications Software

The specific programs that individuals run are known as the applications software. There are thousands of specialized applications programs packages. For example, word processing programs and accounting programs are applications programs. So are games or medical diagnostic programs. You can expect to use some applications programs in the electronic office.

Computer System Configurations

The processing, storage, and communicating equipment that forms a computer system can be configured, or set up, in many different ways. Minicomputers and mainframe computers often have their components spread over many different offices or buildings. The CPU may be in one building, the keyboard and display screen in another, and the printer in the same building as the keyboard and display screen, but in another room. One CPU is usually connected to several keyboards, display screens, and printers.

A typical business office workstation could consist of a microcomputer CPU, a keyboard, a display screen, and a printer all at one location. Generally, microcomputers are self-contained, with all their components able to fit on one desk. Because they are self-contained, they are called **standalones**. Now that personal computers and word processors have become common tools within the office environment, many companies are looking ahead to the next step—gaining greater productivity by linking different systems and components together. The advantages to such an electronically linked office are becoming obvious. Such factors as cost savings on shared equipment, shared information, and improved electronic communications are only a few of the possibilities.

Shared Resource Systems

A common configuration in a business office is to have two or more systems share the same peripherals. Such a configuration is called a **shared resource system** (Fig. 2-2). In a shared resource system each workstation functions independently and does not share a common central processing unit. They may, however, share peripherals. **Peripherals** are devices such as printers, modems, and storage units, that are housed separately from the computer itself, yet are dependent on the CPU to operate. There are many benefits that

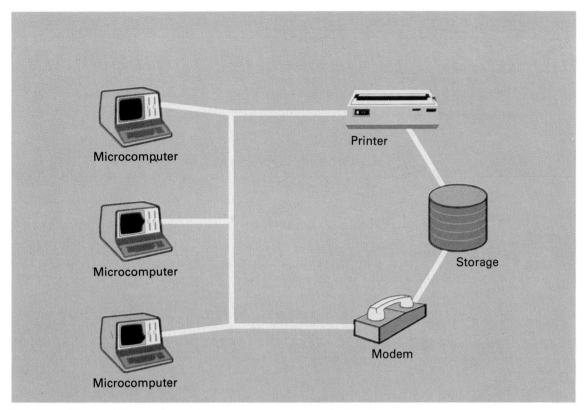

Fig. 2-2 In this shared resource system, each microcomputer has its own CPU and shares the printer, storage, and modems.

are gained from such a configuration. Although the computer or word processing terminal may be in use a major portion of the day, often peripherals such as printers, central storage units, and modems are used only periodically. The cost of providing peripherals for each workstation can be quite high. In the case of printers, for instance, there are several different types of printers that produce different outputs and may be used to complete different jobs. By tying several computers or word processors to one or more printers, a high level of productivity and variety can be achieved for a more economical cost. An additional benefit of this type of configuration is that systemwide breakdowns are reduced. If you are working on a project at your station and the central processing unit at another station is down, it will not affect your workstation.

Shared Logic Systems

A **shared logic system** is a configuration in which several workstations share or access a central processing unit (CPU) (Fig. 2-3). The workstations connected to the CPU are called **terminals**. A terminal consists of a keyboard and a display screen; these always form the basic workstation of a system when the CPU and printer are located elsewhere.

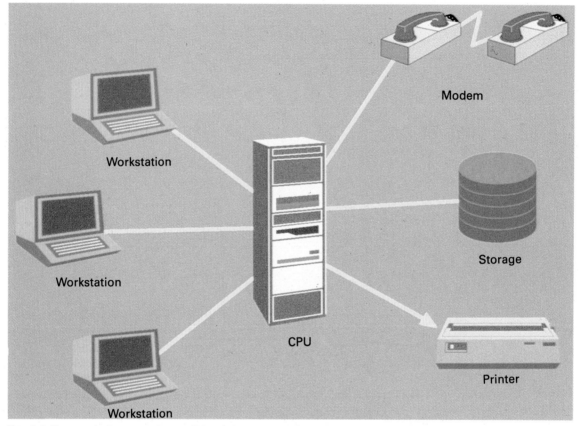

Fig. 2-3 The central processing unit in a shared logic system is bigger and far more powerful than CPUs for standalone equipment.

The central computer's CPU is generally larger and more powerful than the CPU of a standalone. Shared logic systems often provide greater editing, memory, and storage capacities. In this type of system, the fact that the CPU is shared allows word processor or microcomputer operators to exchange documents electronically with each other and with their supervisors. This feature can increase productivity, especially when several people are working on the same document in order to finish it quickly. Many of today's large office word processing systems are shared logic systems. Although several workers may have a CRT at their desks, the central processing and storage systems are often housed and maintained in a separate location.

The biggest drawback of a shared logic system is that when the CPU breaks down, all the workstations connected to it are also shut down. With some systems, this happens frequently. In addition to leaving operators unable to work, these failures can erase or scramble the documents being worked on.

Some organizations solve these problems by equipping their shared logic systems with workstations that have their own small processing units. This setup is called a **distributed logic system**, and the workstations with their own processing units are called **intelligent workstations**. In a setup where the workstation consists of only a keyboard and a display screen, the workstation is called a **dumb terminal** because the processing capability is located not in the workstation but in a separate location.

The ability to link microcomputers and mainframes into these kinds of networks has had such an impact on the modern electronic office that it has changed the way work flows through the office. In Chapter 3 we will examine how these changes have occurred and how they benefit office workers and managers.

■ Summary

- The typewriter changed the business office more than any other invention, beginning with the manual typewriters that were developed by the late 1800s. They were replaced by electric typewriters in the mid-1900s. The newer, more sophisticated electronic typewriters can store words for editing and correcting, and some with even more computerized functions can display text and can communicate with each other over telephone lines.

- The term *word processing* was coined by IBM in 1964, when its MT/ST electronic typewriter was introduced. As more and more manufacturers came on the scene, technological advances in the areas of electronic storage, video display, and communications led to an expansion of the application of computer technology to word processing.

- Word processors permit typists to make unlimited corrections and changes without retyping. Word processors also perform automatically many formatting tasks, such as numbering pages, centering, setting margins, and setting up columns. Word processors can also perform numerical calculations and other complex functions that overlap with the capabilities of computers.

- Word processing has had a major impact on the office. It has led to increased efficiency, better quality in document processing, and efficient use of equipment. Less time spent on routine, repetitive chores has meant more time for administrative support services. This has led to an expansion of career opportunities for office workers.

- Computers are machines that can perform arithmetic functions and can make logical decisions such as less than/greater than so quickly that thousands of these choices can be made in a minute. In addition, more information can be stored in a smaller space than ever before.

- The first computers were large and cumbersome. Computer technology has changed from vacuum tubes to transistors to, more recently, microchips. The newest computers are small and affordable, and they can perform more tasks than ever before.

- All computers have physical components, called hardware, which are units for input, central processing, storage, and output, and sometimes for communication as well. With the use of telecommunications, it is possible for computer systems to be connected to each other either in the same building or across the country via telephone lines.

- Microcomputers, the smallest computers, contain all the components in a space the size of a desk top, and so they are called standalones. But it is common in an office to find minicomputers and mainframes, the largest computers, with components spread over several workstations.

- When one CPU does all the processing for several workstations, this is called a shared logic system. When the workstations in a system can do some processing on their own, this is called a distributed logic system. These groupings of components are called networks. In the business office, networks have changed the way work flows from one person or place to another.

- Computers have had an impact on speed and quality in typing and on efficiency in the use of office space and office workers' time. They have also made it possible for secretaries and administrative assistants to provide more administrative support and so improve their career opportunities and pay.

■ Review Questions

1. Discuss the ways that the evolution of electromechanical typewriters anticipated the changes in computerized word processing.

2. What computerized functions do electronic typewriters have?

3. Discuss some of the advantages of a word processor over a typewriter.

4. What are some ways in which word processors have increased office efficiency?

5. Describe briefly the development of the three generations of computers.

6. Trace the flow of information (input, processing, storage, output, and distribution/communication) you learned about in Chapter 1 through the units of a typical computer system.

7. Magnetic tapes or magnetic disks can have more than one use in a computer system. Describe their uses.

8. What are the main advantages of electronically linked computer systems?

9. Describe briefly the three kinds of software that most computers require in order to operate. What purpose does each kind serve?

10. Discuss the similarities and differences between shared logic systems and distributed logic systems. What is the advantage of one over the other?

■ Technical Vocabulary

word wrap	computer system
element	disk drive
electromechanical	printer
random access	printout
cursor	video display terminal (VDT)
workstation	cathode-ray tube (CRT)
digital	local area network (LAN)
transistor	modem
microchip	software
mainframe	standalone
minicomputer	shared resource system
microcomputer	peripheral
memory	shared logic system
electronic network	terminal
internal files	distributed logic system
external files	intelligent workstation
hardware	dumb terminal

■ Discussion and Skills Development

1. Find an electric or electronic typewriter that has elements in a variety of styles and sizes. Choose any paragraph out of a newspaper or magazine, and type it out in all the sizes and styles you can, including selecting the incorrect pitch specified for the style. Now take a look at all the samples. What happened when you selected the wrong pitch? What kind of style do you think you would select for what purpose (letter, memo, report, envelope, and so on)? What advantage do you gain in space by selecting a certain type size?

2. At the end of Chapter 1, in your last activity, you were asked to develop a list of tasks that you have to accomplish to complete a project. Find your list, and using a manual typewriter, an electric typewriter, and an electronic typewriter

each in turn, make typed copies of that list. Be sure to warm up on each machine. What are the differences in typing time? What did you like or dislike about using each machine? Which do you feel is best suited to this use? (Save these typed lists and file them with your task list.)

3. Go to your school or local library, and using the *Reader's Guide to Periodical Literature*, look up articles written from 1950 to 1955 in national magazines about computers, even UNIVAC I, by name. Read about business and public reactions to the new technology. Look especially for predictions of what computers would do in the future. Then write a one-page essay on the reactions and predictions. Notice and comment on the reactions that may have been justified, and discuss the predictions that have come true or even been exceeded.

chapter 3
Office Systems and the Flow of Information

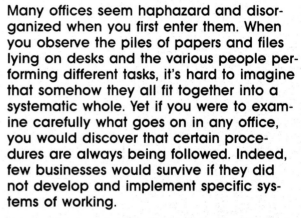

Many offices seem haphazard and disorganized when you first enter them. When you observe the piles of papers and files lying on desks and the various people performing different tasks, it's hard to imagine that somehow they all fit together into a systematic whole. Yet if you were to examine carefully what goes on in any office, you would discover that certain procedures are always being followed. Indeed, few businesses would survive if they did not develop and implement specific systems of working.

As you have already learned, all offices process information, and there are more similarities than differences in the ways businesses do this. Office workers in the sales office of a major automobile dealership perform functions that are similar to those performed by office workers in a small-town insurance brokerage. So do the individuals who process credit transactions in a store or who handle correspondence and filing in a law office. They are all engaged in processing information.

This chapter takes you on a guided tour of information processing: from the initial gathering of data to the final stage of sending it out. You'll see how various office functions fit together into a systematic flow, and you'll see why it is possible to compare the work of people employed by companies as dissimilar as computer manufacturing firms and real estate agencies.

The main difference between office jobs lies not in what people do but in how they do it. Depending on whether people work in a traditional, word processing, or electronic office, they will have different ways of performing the basic office functions. In this chapter you'll learn how computers affect the traditional flow of information and about the savings in time and effort that can be achieved in an electronic office.

The Flow of Information

The automation of an office means using technology to change the way in which information is processed or restructuring the flow of information to take full advantage of the uses of the technology. In Chapter 1 we talked about converting raw data into useful information in five steps and in the general terms of input, processing, storage, output, and distribution/communication. This chapter is going to go into some detail about information processing *systems*. A system is simply an organized or established set of procedures.

First, however, it should be noted that every office is unique, with its own methods, procedures, personnel, and problems. Offices are also in widely varying stages in terms of how far they have gone toward adapting the use of technology to meet their individual needs. Some offices are using almost exclusively traditional methods of carrying out office functions, others have widespread use of word processing, and still others are functioning as fully electronic offices. It is for this reason that each of us will need to have a thorough understanding of information processing systems. Another reason is that office workers today will be expected to bring to their jobs new ways of using the information processing system so as to increase office productivity.

Figure 3-1 shows how the information process has worked traditionally. The flow of information is **linear**, meaning that the information flows in a straight line, beginning with input and ending with storage. Each step—input, process, output, distribution, and storage—takes place one at a time and in the same order. If you wanted to reuse information—such as a list of sales figures or a description of your company's services—that had already gone through the whole process, you would have to repeat all five phases.

In the past this five-phase sequence never varied. But, as you have already learned, modern technology has made some important

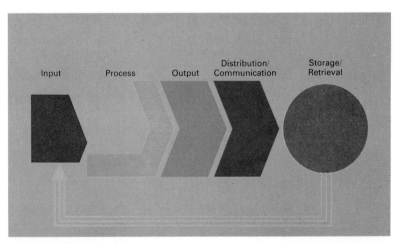

Fig. 3-1 In the past, information always flowed through an office in this linear fashion.

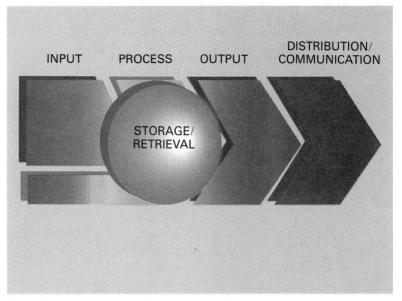

INPUT   **PROCESS**   **OUTPUT**   **DISTRIBUTION/ COMMUNICATION**

STORAGE/ RETRIEVAL

Fig. 3-2 In an integrated information processing system the phases of information processing overlap. This gives the worker far more flexibility and a greater range of options for performing individual tasks.

changes in the way information is processed. Figure 3-2 represents an integrated information processing system in which the phases of information processing overlap. This system, or what we call the electronic office, is more flexible and more efficient. It offers many new options and challenges to today's office workers.

To fully appreciate these changes, you need to learn more about the developments that have been taking place. In order to do this, it is necessary to look at the evolution of information processing systems in three stages: the traditional office, the word processing office, and the electronic office.

Keep in mind that these distinctions are being used to facilitate the explanation of how the use of office technology has evolved. Today there is really no such thing as a "typical" office. Some still use the traditional methods of working, while others have brought in all the latest electronic equipment. In between are those offices which have started to modernize but which are not fully electronic. Usually the first piece of electronic equipment that a business acquires is a word processor. For this reason we refer to the nontraditional but not yet fully automated office as the word processing office. You might get a job in any one of these three types of offices, so you need to know how each type operates.

The Traditional Office

A traditional office uses no computers. Information flows in a linear path, from input to storage. Workers in a traditional office use typewriters for processing information, and they store the information in file drawers. When some of that filed information is needed, someone locates it, retypes it for its new use, distributes it, and stores it again for future use.

Thousands of American companies have traditional office systems. If you go to work in a traditional office, you will be able to make use of many of the basic secretarial skills, such as taking shorthand, typing, filing, and handling mail.

The Word Processing Office

As computers have become smaller, less expensive, and more sophisticated, more and more offices have begun to use them in some capacity. Most often these computers are used strictly for word processing tasks, usually taking the place of the typewriter. These computers do not interact with mainframes or other systems and do little communicating with other computers.

In a word processing office, the information flow becomes cyclical to the extent that the use of the computer moves the storage/retrieval phase from the end to the middle of the process. In effect, storage occurs automatically at the input stage, and retrieval can be carried out automatically at any time. Also, it is possible to input data without keyboarding through the use of electronic scanners that can read text and enter it into the computer. Distribution is mostly manual, just as in the traditional office. However, some word processing offices do use electronic communications.

Most offices today fall into this word processing category. But most offices do not take full advantage of their computers' capability to store and retrieve information. In many word processing offices, hard copy is still generated and filed in the traditional manner.

The Electronic Office

Many offices are moving toward maximum usage of computers so that the processing of information becomes almost totally electronic. In these offices there is complete interaction among computer systems and much communicating ability with other computers.

In the electronic office, information storage occurs as information is input into the computer. This is similar to storage in the word processing office. The key difference, however, is that almost all information is stored electronically, not as hard copy in file drawers. All information is therefore also retrieved electronically; that is, to get at information, an office worker commands the computer to find the data, which is then displayed on a screen or printed out as hard copy.

In an electronic office, workers have access to more information than that which exists in their own computer files. The computers have the ability to communicate with computers in other offices, giving the workers access to information in those offices' files as well. In networked systems data retrieval from remote locations is possible. It is this kind of networking that most distinguishes the electronic office from the word processing office.

All data stored in computer files can be manipulated electronically and reused in new documents with little or no rekeyboarding. Secretaries and administrative assistants are then freed to carry out many more administrative support activities and become more involved in data analysis and decision making.

Input, storage, and retrieval are not the only phases of the process that are changed in the electronic office. Documents and data can also be distributed electronically. A document prepared in one office can be sent from that office's computer to another computer in the same building or to another location altogether. Electronic distribution/communication is speedier than traditional distribution and involves less paper.

If the office follows the traditional model, information is always processed in the following way: input > process > output > distribution/communication > storage. All information processing is done manually, and always in this order. If, however, the office is modernized or is in the process of modernizing, information processing will follow the following pattern: input > process > storage > output > distribution/communication. You will recall this sequence more easily if you memorize the acronym **IPSOD**. Moving the storage stage to a central point means that information can be accessed at any step within the cycle once it has been input. This change also means that information can be communicated or transmitted from computer to computer before it is output as hard copy.

But, you may be asking, how will this really affect the flow of information and my day-to-day work? The rest of this chapter will explore the answer to this question.

Stages of Information Processing

Because offices are in various stages of transition, it is not possible to choose a representative office to use as the model for following information processing from start to finish. It is more useful to examine information processing in all three of the types of offices we have described: traditional, word processing, and electronic. This will help you prepare to cope with information processing in whatever business environment you find yourself.

It should be emphasized that while word processing offices and electronic offices have certain advantages over traditional offices, work can be and is being done efficiently in traditional offices throughout the world. After all, the methods employed in these offices have been used successfully for centuries. And many of the methods and procedures used in these offices will continue to be used, even in the most modern offices. Also, while the order of stages in the flow of information changes, the basic steps remain the same regardless of the type of office.

Input

If you go to work in a traditional office, you will gather data for input from sources such as previously processed documents stored in tra-

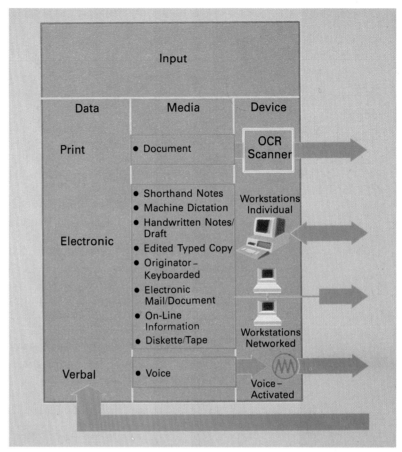

Fig. 3-3 In the electronic office options for handling input are greatly expanded. Data is created electronically, in print, and orally. Types of input media include those used in the traditional and word processing offices, plus more. Different types of equipment and equipment configurations are available.

ditional files (Fig. 3-3). These may be in the form of letters, memos, reports, or other kinds of written documents. You will usually find data concerning customers or clients, such as addresses and contact names, in organized filing systems, such as card files, or lists that are periodically updated within the department. To obtain mailing lists or lists containing large amounts of numerical information, such as sales figures or inventory numbers, you may have to go to another department, such as the data processing department. Regardless of where you go to get the information, you will be getting it by hand out of files, by telephone, or by filling out requests for other people to get it for you.

With a traditional filing system, it is the rare office that manages to keep its files absolutely correct, up to date, and intact. More than likely, some files will be lying around outside of the file drawers, others will be misfiled within the file drawers, and still others will be missing altogether. Tracking down missing files is a time-consuming process that greatly interrupts the flow of information through an office.

Once you have gathered the data you need, you must convert it into a medium that can be understood. This means that your handwritten notes, shorthand notes, machine dictation, statistics, and so on, must be assembled into a format from which they can be input for processing. In a traditional, word processing, or electronic office, machine dictation, shorthand, and longhand are still the most common formats used for preparing data for input.

In a traditional office, the input device is the typewriter, which will usually be electric or electronic. It is also important to remember, however, that the typewriter is also the processor and output device. Thus, each time a keystroke is entered, simultaneously output is generated. In a word processing office, much information will still be gathered by hand, but you will input it on a word processor rather than a typewriter. It is also possible that some of the data you need to prepare your input will have already been prepared on the word processor. In that case, you will be able to retrieve it electronically, which will save you some legwork. Once the data has been input on the word processor, it remains in temporary memory until it is either stored, edited, or output.

In the electronic office, data is stored in the computer system. This data may be stored locally on a disk or it may be stored on a computer a great distance away and retrieved through the use of telecommunications. You will be able to access it by giving appropriate commands to the computer. You will then be able to manipulate the data electronically to suit your purposes. Data may also be prepared for entry into the system using the same media that were described for the traditional and word processing environments.

As you learned in Chapter 2, in a word processing or electronic office, there are devices other than the keyboard that may be used for inputting. The optical character reader (OCR) can scan a printed or typed document electronically and transfer the characters to the word processor.

In the electronic office, since all levels of office workers, including principals, have computer workstations, it is becoming more and more common for executives to keyboard drafts of their input and then send the drafts to their secretary's computer for final formatting, editing, and printing. If more executives had keyboarding skills, this practice would probably be more widespread. A more sophisticated technology that more executives may have access to in the future is voice-activated input. Systems that are able to convert human speech into a digital format are available today but are quite expensive. As this technology undergoes further development, causing its price to decline, you can expect to see more widespread use of it. Another form of input can be found on systems that have display screens that are sensitive to touch. You can input and manipulate data by touching different parts of the screen.

Processing   In the traditional office, the processing phase involves both nontyping and typing tasks. Nontyping tasks include setting format specifications such as margins, tab stops, line spacing, and positioning of the first line of text. Once you finish these preliminary steps, you type the document at your best speed without making errors. Your next step is to proofread and, if necessary, edit the document. If there are minor mistakes, you can correct them easily if you have a self-correcting typewriter. If not, each mistake must be corrected by covering over it with correction tape or correction fluid and then typing the correction only. If the errors are more substantial, you may need to totally retype one or more pages. You must also correct any carbon copies you have made.

If you are either very lucky or very good at your job, the person for whom you prepared the document will not request any further changes. When further changes are necessary, however, you will have to retype part or all of the document. You must then proofread again and resubmit the document for approval. Occasionally, more changes will be requested, and the process begins again. Thus processing in a traditional office may involve retyping a document several times, even though most of the text remains unchanged.

In a word processing or electronic office, you will be spared much of the above work. Margins, indents, and line spacing can be set or changed at will and the text adjusted to fit the new specifications automatically. You can also program the computer to number pages automatically. Then, if the document length changes, the computer will provide the new, correct page numbers. You can perform editing tasks such as adding or deleting one or more words without retyping whole pages. And you can instruct the computer to insert headings for each page. The computer will even proofread your work for spelling errors if it has a built-in dictionary or a software program with a dictionary. You will still need to read the work, however, because the computer cannot discriminate between homonyms such as *there* and *their*, nor can it know if you left out a word or misused punctuation.

After you have printed out a hard copy of your finished document and submitted it for approval, you can easily correct errors or make changes by editing the soft copy and then print out a revised document. No matter how many changes you make, the new copy will be clean, with no evidence of the many revisions it has been through. Figure 3-4 compares processing in the three types of offices, illustrating the differences in equipment and procedures used.

Traditional Office-Processing

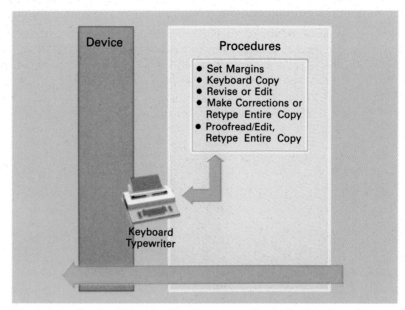

Fig. 3-4*a* In the traditional office the typewriter is the input device and the processor. Formatting and editing procedures are done manually.

Word Processing Office-Processing

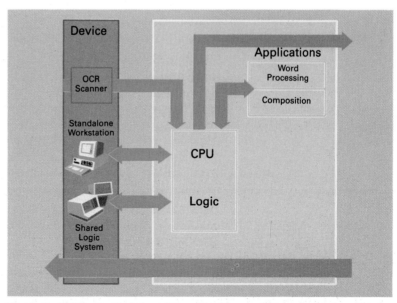

Fig. 3-4*b* In the word processing office the equipment may be stand-alone or part of a shared logic system. Word processing and composition applications are processed by the CPU, based on commands input by the operator.

Electronic Office-Processing

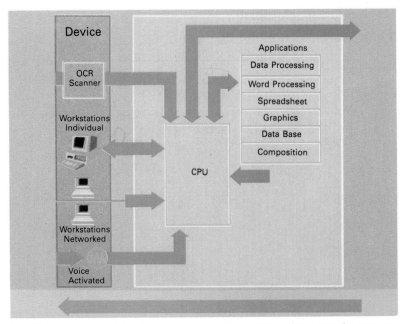

Fig. 3-4c Processing in the electronic office differs from word processing in that systems are networked and there are many more processing applications.

Merging Information With a computer you can **merge**, or combine, information from different computer files. For example, say you have to send the same letter to ten different people. Once you have typed the letter, you can merge it with a file that contains a list of names, addresses, and salutations. The computer will then print the same letter ten times with the different headings.

Data Analysis In an electronic office, where all data is stored electronically, the computer can make comparisons of all stored data. It can also be commanded to convert the data into different formats, such as bar graphs or variable two-line charts. In a traditional and word processing office, such tasks would be done by the general manager or by an accountant. But in the electronic office, any office worker who has been trained to use the computer would be able to prepare the required information.

Data Bases In an electronic office, you can use the computer to gain access to data bases. A **data base** is a stored collection of data on a particular subject. One company might, for example, create a data base consisting of the selling prices of various competing products. Another might list the names, sizes, and locations of all its retail outlets in a data base. You can use a data base to assemble reports or other documents. The data can be manipulated in many ways to show different aspects of the same information. Tasks such as this take many hours of concentrated work in a traditional or word processing office.

Decision-Support Applications Whereas the major application of the word processor is the processing and production of documents, in the electronic office a wide variety of other applications can be performed. These are often referred to as **productivity tools** or **decision-support tools** because they allow complex, time-consuming tasks to be done in a fraction of the time it takes to do them manually. In addition to word processing, these applications include:

- *Data processing*, the manipulation of alphanumeric data.

- *Spreadsheeting*, the use of a grid or matrix, in the form of columns and rows on the screen, to perform mathematical calculations.

- *Graphics*, the creation of charts, graphs, and other types of pictorial images.

- *Data base management*, the entering, organizing, storing, and retrieving of data in a format and order specified by the user.

- *Composition*, electronic typesetting of words and images.

 Storage
In a traditional office, the storage phase of the information flow does not come until the very end, after the data has been input, processed, output, and distributed. In an electronic office and, to a lesser extent, in a word processing office, storage is an automatic part of the input and processing phases. Whenever you keyboard a document, it is stored by the computer, first temporarily in the electronic circuits of the system and then permanently when you command the computer to save it. It can then easily be retrieved and reused for input.

Today most data is stored on disks, which may be referred to as floppy diskettes or disks, depending on their size and type. Some systems also store data on tape.

One major difference between storing information on disks and storing it as hard copy is in the amount of physical space required. A single 5¼-inch disk can hold hundreds of letters. You could easily file 100 disks, holding many hundreds of letters, memos, and reports, in two small boxes that could sit on your desk. It would take several full-sized file drawers to hold the same amount of hard-copy information.

Retrieval involves locating the appropriate disk and then having the computer find the information you want on that disk. This step is similar to the retrieval phase in a traditional office, where the hard-copy document must be located in a file drawer. The main difference is that with disks you do not have to get up from your desk to retrieve information.

Electronic filing solves many of the problems associated with traditional files. For example, files stored on a computer's hard disk can be protected so that only certain people have access to them.

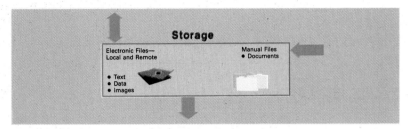

Fig. 3-5 In the electronic office hard copies of documents are greatly reduced. Text, voice, and images can be stored on a variety of storage media.

Instead of having to lock file cabinets and sign documents in and out of files, users of a word processing system can secure their files by using a password system. Under this system, all individuals who are allowed to use the files are assigned a password. They must enter the password into the computer before they can gain access to any of the information stored there. To achieve additional security, some companies change the password regularly.

Word processing and electronic offices do keep paper records of many of their documents just as traditional offices do. (Figure 3-5 shows the various types of storage media used in the electronic office.) Many people feel that this is necessary in case of accidental erasure of data or in case of a power failure. In a power failure, whatever is stored in the temporary memory of the computer is lost unless it has been stored on a disk. Also, data already stored on a disk can become garbled if a power surge precedes the power failure. Many larger companies that rely heavily on their computers have backup power generators for precisely this reason. One way to reduce the problem of accidental loss of electronically stored data is to make backup copies of all disks and to update these regularly.

But even barring these problems, many companies store hard-copy records because they are not yet completely comfortable with the concept of electronic storage of data. In a word processing office, where not everyone necessarily knows how to operate the computers, it may not make sense to limit access to data stored on computers to the few people who know how to use the computers. Therefore, hard copy may be filed for use by the noncomputer users. A word processing office also needs traditional files for storing documents that were not prepared on its word processing system.

Output In a traditional office, the output is the finished document and the main output device is the typewriter. If you need duplicates of the finished product, you use carbon paper or make photocopies.

Most word processing offices still have typewriters, so these are included among the output devices used by this kind of office. The output devices of the word processors, however, are the printers to which they are connected. These can be either draft quality or letter quality. Typically, the draft-quality printers, or **dot matrix printers**, make neat copies, but they do not have the polished appearance of typewritten or typeset copy. The letters are formed from series of dots with regular spaces between them. **Letter-quality printers**, on the other hand, produce copy that looks like typeset material, usually with variable spacing for different letters and dark, clean letters. Each letter is individually printed, much the same as with a typewriter. The difference is that the typing is controlled by a computer rather than a person. The main drawback of letter-quality printers is that they tend to be slower than dot matrix printers.

If you need to have a document typeset, you may be able to use your word processor to prepare the manuscript for setting. As was discussed earlier, information can be transferred directly from a word processor or computer to a composition system for the production of typeset material. As you input the words, you can also input instructions in the form of special codes that will tell the compositor how the document is to look. You would either send your disk to the compositor or transmit the information electronically through the use of telecommunications. This system saves an operator from having to rekeyboard the document into the typesetting machine.

Some electronic offices use laser printers. A **laser printer** uses a combination of electronics and photography to produce beautifully printed originals with incredible speed. Because the laser printer is so fast, it can be used instead of a photocopier to make duplicates (that are actually originals). Most of the other printers that are used with word processors are too slow to be considered useful for making duplicates, so photocopiers are usually used, as in traditional offices.

In a word processing office hard copy is produced locally. The printing device is usually tied directly to the word processing system through a cable. In the electronic office, much of your output is originally generated in the form of soft copy before it is printed. The hard copy may be output locally or transmitted to a remote location. That is, it is sent from your computer to the screen of another computer, where it is received as soft copy. The recipient may view the soft copy and may print out a hard copy or save the document on a disk. This may be done with lengthy documents, but electronic messages are usually just deleted from the system, although they can be saved or printed, if necessary.

All offices, no matter what their level of sophistication, need to collate, fold, bind, or otherwise prepare for distribution hard copies of documents. A laser printer can automatically collate material, but the papers must still be folded or bound by hand. Some photocopiers also have a collating capability. Figure 3-6 shows output in the electronic office.

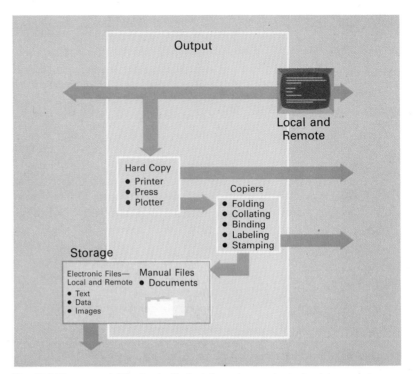

Output

Local and Remote

Hard Copy
- Printer
- Press
- Plotter

Copiers
- Folding
- Collating
- Binding
- Labeling
- Stamping

Storage

Electronic Files—
Local and Remote
- Text
- Data
- Images

Manual Files
- Documents

Fig. 3-6 The capability for both local and remote output is a major change from the word processing to the electronic office.

Distribution/ Communication

The distribution/communication phase of information processing involves getting the information you have prepared out to the people who need to receive it (see Fig. 3-7). As with other stages in the IPSOD process, the way you do this depends on the type of office you work in. In a traditional office, output is distributed within the office via interdepartmental mail. For distribution outside of the office, either the U.S. Postal Service or a private courier service such as Federal Express or Purolator is used.

In the word processing office, some distribution is handled in the same way. In other cases word processors are linked to each other and the output is sent as soft copy to other machines tied to the network within the building. The receiving workstations then store it in their systems and print it out as hard copy if needed. The advantage of this method is that distribution can be completed in minutes instead of the days it would take if output were distributed by mail.

Even the electronic office, however, needs to use some of the manual distribution methods (mail and courier service) to reach offices that do not have electronic equipment. But in a fully electronic office, virtually all employees have computer terminals at their workstations. These terminals are linked to each other and to a central computer, and they may be linked to computers at remote locations. In addition, they are linked to other equipment, such as microfilm files and printer/copiers. These links allow the people and equipment in the system to communicate with each other—and perhaps with outsiders—instantaneously through the use of electronic mail.

An electronic network provides instant communication of three kinds: between one person and another, between a person and a computer or other equipment, and between two pieces of equipment.

Instant communication of this sort can save at least several days and sometimes even weeks in the distribution/communication phase of the information processing cycle. Furthermore, it allows people to receive immediate feedback to help them make decisions. This timesaving dimension of the electronic office has the potential of revolutionizing the ways in which business people make decisions that affect basic business functions.

Electronic mail can be most useful when complex information is needed immediately. Imagine that you needed the most recent sales figures from ten branch offices. In a traditional office, you would have to make ten phone calls or write ten memos requesting the information. Even if you used an express mail service, you would

```
Msgs: New: 3              Mar 21,86 12:22 PM Document:
                             MESSAGE DISPLAY
  TO   Janet Kimball

  From:  Pam Brown
Postmark:  Mar 21,86    10:45 AM
Status:   Certified  Urgent
Subject: Budget
----------------------------------------------------------------
Message:
      Mr. Johnston asked me to obtain a copy of last year's budget for a
      meeting he's attending in 45 minutes.  Can you please get a copy to
      me as soon as possible?

      Thank you.



----------------------------------------------------------------
Pick one: (1. View content, 2. File, 3. Reply, 4. Forward,
          5. Delete, 6. Next message, 7. Print, 8. Remail)
```

The sender of this message was able to save a lot of time by using electronic mail rather than standard mail services. The receivers of the message can act immediately to fulfill the request.

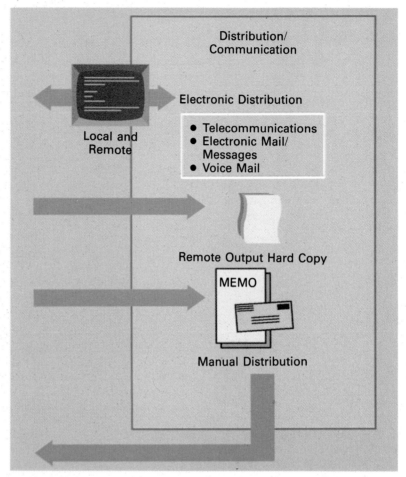

Fig. 3-7 The immediacy of distribution in the electronic office will have a major impact on the way businesses function. As communications technology advances there is a potential for networking on a global scale.

have to wait at least one day to get the information. But with electronic mail, you can send the requests for information to each office simultaneously. In seconds all ten branch offices would have your request. If no one is attending one of the machines to which the mail is being sent, the computer will store the information until the person returns and turns on the system. The information you require will be sent back to you as quickly as the people on the other end can command their computers to supply it (probably in a matter of minutes).

Voice Mail **Voice mail** links telephones and computers. With voice mail you do not even need to type in your message or request for information. Suppose that you work in the head office in New York, and it is 9 a.m. You need the latest projected sales figures from the branch office manager in San Francisco, where it is only 6 a.m. You are going to an all-day meeting, so you won't be able to make the call later. You can telephone the San Francisco branch now, where the computer will answer the phone, take your message, and alert the San Francisco manager that there is a message waiting. When the manager opens up the office, he or she will see the light and can respond immediately to your message.

Teleconference   As mentioned in Chapter 1, a teleconference enables several people in different locations to hold a conference just as if they were all in the same room. There are two types of teleconferences: audio and video.

An **audio teleconference** is a telephone call that links several people in different locations at once. This type of teleconference can take place in traditional and word processing offices as well as in electronic offices. During an audio teleconference, the people involved may use a facsimile machine or some other device to exchange documents visually during their conversation.

A **video teleconference** uses closed-circuit television and computers, telephones, and electronic devices to enable people to see each other as well as hear each other. A video teleconference is possible only in an electronic office. It is perhaps the most sophisticated form of communication today, affording many benefits. It allows people in widely separated locations to hold discussions, see each other's facial expressions and gestures, look at charts and graphs together, exchange documents and data, and give demonstrations. It makes possible face-to-face meetings without the expense and time required to have all the people involved travel to the same location for their meeting.

Although the start-up costs for video teleconference capabilities are substantial, higher productivity and lower costs over the long run are the ultimate benefits. The video teleconference demonstrates how people and electronic equipment can work together to process information more quickly and more efficiently than ever before.

■ Three Office Models

Figures 3-8, 3-9, and 3-10 depict the flow of work in the three office models presented in this chapter. Compare the five phases of information processing and the overall flow of work to gain a clear understanding of the impact of technology on office systems.

Changing Responsibilities

Office workers at all levels are affected by changes in information processing technology. If you become a secretary or administrative assistant, you will find that you can provide a much higher level of administrative support if you work in an electronic office. You will even be able to participate in decision making to a degree impossible in the traditional or word processing office.

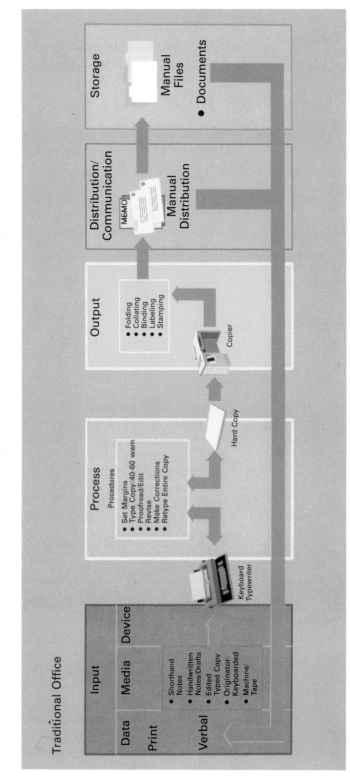

Fig. 3-8 In a traditional office, printed and verbal data is gathered and input through the use of various input media. The typewriter is both the input device and the processor. After the information is typed and corrected, it is copied and made ready for distribution by hand or by mail. A copy is then filed by hand for office records.

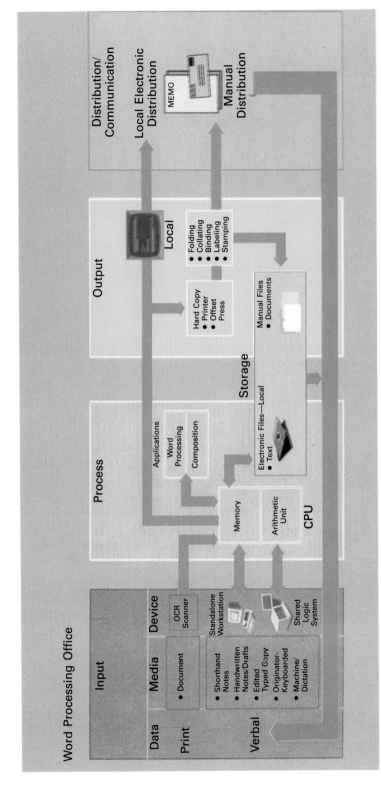

Fig. 3-9 In the word processing office the input data and media are the same as in the traditional office. The keyboard is the input device but the processing is done by the CPU, allowing for the manipulation of text in soft-copy form. Storage and retrieval can occur in the middle rather than at the end of the process. The output and distribution stages of information processing are similar to that of the traditional office, except that local soft copy output is available.

The Electronic Office

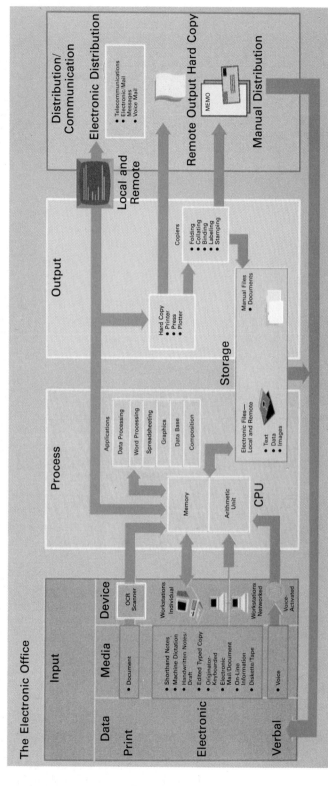

Fig. 3-10 In the electronic office there are more options available for the input data, media, and devices. In the processing phase applications that go way beyond text manipulation can be accessed through the CPU. As in the word processing office, the storage/retrieval phases are moved to the middle of the process, where they occur simultaneously or automatically. In the electronic office, however, all data can be accessed electronically and paper and traditional files are greatly reduced. Output can be in soft-copy or hard-copy form and distribution can be instantaneous through the use of local and remote networks.

TRADITIONAL OFFICE	WORD PROCESSING OFFICE	ELECTRONIC OFFICE
• Accounting	• Accounting	• Accounting
• Shorthand	• Shorthand	• Shorthand
• Filing/Records Management	• Filing/Records Management	• Electronic Filing/Records Management
• Business English and Communication	• Business English and Communication	• Business English and Communication
• Typing	• Keyboarding	• Keyboarding/Input Devices (voice, mouse, digitizer)
• Secretarial Office Procedures:	• Word Processing Operations	• Word Processing Operations
Human Relations	• Secretarial Office Procedures:	• Secretarial Office Procedures:
Letter, Memo, and Report writing	Human Relations	Human Relations
Filing	Letter, Memo, and Report writing	Letter, Memo, and Report writing
Travel Arrangements	Electronic Filing	Electronic Filing
Telephone Techniques	Travel Arrangements	Travel Arrangements
Resource and Reference Materials	Telephone Techniques	Telephone Techniques
Adding, Calculating, and Transcribing	Resource and Reference Materials	Resource and Reference Materials
Conferences and Meetings	Adding, Calculating, and Transcribing	Adding, Calculating, and Transcribing
Appointment Scheduling	Conferences and Meetings	Conferences and Meetings (audio/video teleconferences)
	Appointment Scheduling	Electronic Calendaring
	Word Processing and Writing Tool Software	• Computer Literacy Skills (file management, data base management, communications, operating systems)
		• Applications Software (writing tools, spelling checkers, spreadsheets, data bases, graphics)
		• Interactive Capabilities (local and remote networks)

Fig. 3-11 This chart shows the changing nature of the basic and support functions performed by secretaries and administrative assistants in the three types of offices: traditional, word processing, and electronic.

In performing tasks such as preparing an annual report, you will take on the responsibility of developing the necessary charts and graphs—with the aid of a computer and either your company's or an external data base. You will have to exercise judgment regarding which statistics are relevant to your report and which are not.

In a traditional office and, to a lesser extent, in a word processing office, your duties may be more mechanical and repetitious in preparing such a report. You might have to do a lot of typing and retyping of pages until the report is finished. In the electronic office, your typing and mechanical chores are reduced significantly, freeing you to do more creative work. Figure 3-11 shows a comparison of responsibilities in the three types of offices.

The revolution in computer technology touches all of our lives every day. Regardless of what type of office you work in, the way you work will be increasingly affected by the new technology. Using it effectively will help you process more information more efficiently. Its greatest value, however, lies not in its ability to speed up individual tasks but in its ability to help us uproot old operations and perform them in a more efficient way.

■ Summary

■ All offices process information. Modern electronic technology has changed the way information is processed and the sequence in which it is processed.

- There is no such thing as a "typical" office today. Offices may be traditional, word processing, or electronic.

- A traditional office relies on nonelectronic equipment to process its information. Typical equipment includes typewriters and photocopying machines.

- A word processing office uses some electronic technology in the form of word processors.

- An electronic office uses sophisticated electronic equipment in the form of mainframe or minicomputers, computer terminals at each workstation, and integrated systems that enable people to use computers to communicate with other computers.

- Information processing consists of five phases, regardless of the type of office: input, process, output, distribution/communication, and storage.

- In a traditional office, information processing occurs in a linear fashion, with storage at the end.

- In an electronic office, and to a lesser degree in a word processing office, storage occurs simultaneously with input and processing. Information then flows in the following way: input, process, storage, output, and distribution/communication. This sequence may be remembered by memorizing the acronym *IPSOD*.

- Input consists of gathering information from traditional or electronic files.

- During the processing phase, the data is converted into a medium that can be used by other people. The typewriter is the main piece of processing equipment in the traditional office. In a word processing or electronic office, many of the repetitive tasks that are associated with typing are automated.

- In a traditional office, documents are stored on paper. Word processing and electronic offices can store data on disks or tapes, as well as in traditional paper files.

- Output from a traditional office consists of typed documents that may be duplicated on a copying machine. The output device of a word processor is its printer. Printers vary in speed and quality of print.

- The main channels of distribution in a traditional office are interdepartmental mail, the U.S. Postal Service, and private courier services. In a word processing and electronic office, however, computers can communicate with each other.

- Audio and video teleconferences enable people in different locations to hold meetings without traveling.
- Changes in information processing technology are changing the nature of office work. Office workers can expect to take more responsibility as the more repetitious aspects of their jobs are automated.

■ Review Questions

1. Describe the information flow in the traditional office, giving the steps and telling how they occur.

2. What happens to the information flow in an electronic office? How is it different from the information flow in a traditional office?

3. What does the acronym *IPSOD* stand for?

4. Write a brief description of each IPSOD phase in the electronic office.

5. Even though a word processing office may have word processing computers, why is it still not considered an electronic office?

6. Define a data base and how it is used for input in the electronic office.

7. What options are available for output in the electronic office that do not exist in the traditional or word processing office?

8. How are storage and retrieval made easier in the word processing and electronic office?

9. Describe how the preparation of letters for ten branch offices is speeded up in the word processing or electronic office as compared with the preparation of the letters in the traditional office.

10. What are some of the communication methods available to the worker in the electronic office?

■ Technical Vocabulary

linear
IPSOD
merge
data base
productivity tools
decision-support tools

dot matrix printer
letter-quality printer
laser printer
voice mail
audio teleconference
video teleconference

■ Discussion and Skills Development

1. Visit a local business office, or talk to a friend or relative who works in a business office. From what you see or hear, determine what category—traditional, word processing, or electronic—the office falls into. Describe how it fits that category.

2. Check with your school office to determine how it handles a major report, such as an attendance report. Try to identify the various stages of the information flow in relation to the preparation of the report. How is input accomplished? What processing is done and how is it done? What form does the output take? At what point does storage/retrieval take place? How is communication/distribution carried out? Into which of the three categories of offices does your school office fall?

3. Find some magazines about the business office in your library. Magazines to look for include *Office Administration and Automation, The Office, Today's Office, Words,* and *Management Technology.* Look for articles describing office automation (OA) or the office of the future. Read one or two, and make notes to discuss in class.

4. Visit an office-supply store. Identify the different types of supplies and equipment carried. Determine what is available for the different types of offices—traditional, word processing, and electronic. Check the Yellow Pages of a local telephone book or visit a local dealer in computers and software to see what equipment is available which an electronic office could use and which the office-supply store does not carry (a modem, for example). Prepare a report for class discussion.

chapter 4
Working in Today's Office

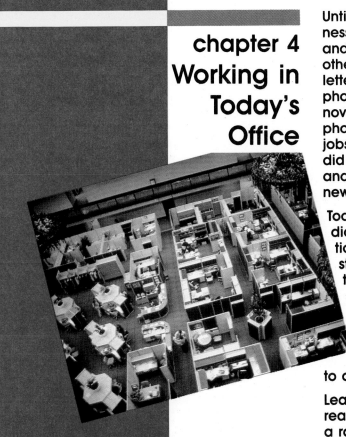

Until computers began to transform businesses, office work was fairly predictable and unchanging. For years secretaries and other office personnel took dictation, typed letters and reports, answered the telephone, and maintained filing systems. Innovations such as electric typewriters and photocopying machines had made their jobs easier. But on the whole, their work did not change much from year to year, and there was little opportunity to learn new skills or advance to higher positions.

Today the basic office skills—keyboarding, dictation and transcription, communications and language arts, and filing—are still very much in demand. But added to these important skills is a need for adaptability. Never before have office workers been expected to master change as rapidly as they have in the past few years. And it is likely that the rate of change will continue to accelerate.

Learning new skills or transferring skills already learned is the key to adaptability in a rapidly changing office environment. In addition, people need to be well informed about individual job requirements and about equipment and procedures in order to make wise decisions and avoid costly errors.

This chapter explores how the technological revolution in the office is leading to a greater need for decision-making skills—in managers and in their support staffs. It also explains the ways in which the office has been changing and suggests ways that you can learn to adapt to changes in the work environment.

Finally, it looks into some new ideas about worker comfort and morale. You'll find out why there's a new emphasis on furniture design and office layout, and you'll discover how planners go about trying to achieve the ideal office environment.

Automation and People

When typewriters were first introduced in the 1870s, office workers, who took pride in the quality of their handwriting, reacted with outrage. They were insulted. They feared that a clickety-clacking machine would replace their skilled art. In time, however, the typewriter came to be valued. The increased speed and legibility with which this machine produced documents ensured its place at the center of office procedures.

People had a similar reaction in recent years when businesses first began to automate. Many workers feared that computers would soon do away with the need for human labor in the office. So far, however, these fears have been unfounded. The demand for office workers has continued to increase despite automation. The Bureau of Labor Statistics estimates that the number of office workers in the United States, which was about 38 million in the 1970s, will rise to more than 55 million in the 1990s. While some jobs are indeed being eliminated, many more are being created. No matter how much sophisticated electronic equipment employers install, people are still needed to operate the equipment and make the decisions required to process information.

There's no denying, however, that automation will eliminate some jobs and require the redefinition of others. For example, when employees can send their coworkers messages that they can read on their computer terminals, their employer is unlikely to need as many mail-room workers as he or she did when messages had to be sent as hard copies through the interoffice mail. Some organizations

Adaptability to change is a key skill required of all workers in the electronic office.

that tie their automated business systems together into networks find that operations become so much more productive that they need fewer workers. On the whole, though, automation is not likely to eliminate many jobs, but it is very likely to change the nature of office work. If you want to be a successful office worker, you will have to develop the ability to view changes as opportunities to help your employer meet business goals and increase your own value as an employee.

Mastering Change

People tend to cling to the familiar and to resist the unfamiliar. Because of this human tendency, one of the hottest topics of discussion in today's business world is that of mastering change.

The first step in mastering change is to recognize and accept that some changes are inevitable. Then you need to develop an ability to evaluate the old and welcome the new and the unexpected. Few people do this easily. Consider your gut reactions when your plans are changed or when you have to start doing things in a different way. Most people resist change on some level. The saying that we are creatures of habit contains more than just a grain of truth.

Another step in mastering change is to gain the ability to accept the truth, even when it is unpleasant. Most of us want to believe that certain aspects of our lives are permanent and will continue in a familiar way. This notion gives us security and makes us feel comfortable. It allows us to see what we want to see. But today, in both our business lives and our personal lives, the ability to cope successfully depends upon looking at things with more objectivity. We need to have untrapped minds—minds that can recognize the reasons for changes.

Mastering change also requires us to be tolerant of errors and to accept them as a natural part of risk taking. Being willing to take risks encourages future risk-taking behavior. The reason for this is simple: as we take risks, we learn that the results of risk taking are not as devastating as we may have feared. The consequences, even of a bad error, are generally not grave. A lack of tolerance for errors may cause some people to resist change, however. We all need to remind ourselves from time to time that failure, while always a disappointment, need not be a defeat. Many people, when facing a risky decision, ask themselves, "What's the worst thing that could happen?" If they are honest with themselves, they will usually find that the worst thing is not really very bad.

You will also be able to master change more easily if you learn to recognize your own ignorance. It's easy to see ignorance in others, but it's not always so easy to acknowledge your own. Unless you can freely admit that you don't know some things, you can hardly begin to learn new tasks and procedures.

People who learn to master change successfully are able to understand and explain what is happening around them. It is for this reason that this book is encouraging you to understand the changes

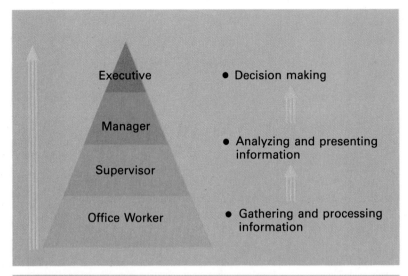

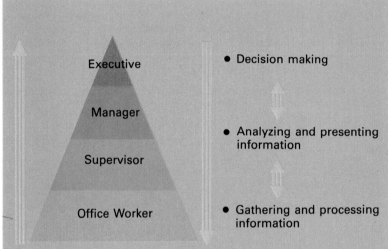

Fig. 4-1 Office automation will result in the elimination of some jobs, but secretaries will gain new skills and new opportunities will open up for them. In the electronic office, they will be more involved in decision making and analyzing and presenting information, as well as gathering and processing it.

that are taking place in the business world. Knowing what to expect in your future office job will help you adapt to its requirements and make progress in achieving your future career goals. Figure 4-1 illustrates the changing role of the office worker from one of gathering and processing information to greater participation in analyzing and presenting the information as well as making decisions.

Basic and Traditional Office Skills

You will find that the basic English and math skills which you began acquiring in your earliest school days will still be useful in today's electronic office. A working knowledge of arithmetic, grammar, spelling, and punctuation is always essential in the workplace. The abilities to follow instructions, to think abstractly, and to organize material are also a necessity. Even though computers process numbers and verbal data automatically, you need these basic skills to check the results you get and to evaluate material.

Because business functions are integrated in the electronic office, a single, seemingly minor mistake can affect not only your own business function but also others throughout the organization. Suppose, for example, that you are using your computer terminal to process a budget, and because of a simple keyboarding error, you enter a number with the decimal point in the wrong place. If you do not check your work, the incorrect figure will be permanently stored. The computer will then use this incorrect number in calculating budget figures automatically, and these figures also will be incorrect.

When people talk about "computer errors," they are usually referring to mistakes such as the one just described. Computers do, in fact, give incorrect information from time to time, but when this happens, it is almost always because people have given the computers incorrect data to begin with. Computer technicians sometimes use the term *GIGO* in referring to this all-too-common occurrence. **GIGO** stands for "garbage in, garbage out." If what we send

```
Msgs: New:  0              Feb 07,86  2:00 AM Document: MARKETING PLANS
                                   DRAWERS

    Dr        Personal        Owner
              Drawers         Count
    1    ANNUAL REPORT 1985      1
    2    ANNUAL REPORT 1986      1
    3    PERSONNEL A-H           1
    4    PERSONNEL I-P           1
    5    PERSONNEL Q-Z           1
    6    SALES 1985              1
    7    SALES 1986              1




    Pick one: (1. Folders, 2. Other cabinet, 3. View or Change, 4. Create,
              5. Delete, 6. Reformat or Print menu) █
    Drawer number(s):
```

Electronic filing requires the same organizational skill as traditional filing. Files must be broken up into logical units for easy storage and retrieval.

into a computer is wrong, what we get out will also be wrong. Office workers can prevent or correct many so-called computer errors by proofreading numbers and estimating arithmetic answers to see that the data they input is correct and that the output information makes sense.

Many of the new procedures found in electronic offices require traditional skills, or new skills based on them. If you're producing a letter, for example, you need the skills of establishing a format and proofreading, whether you are typing it on a typewriter in a traditional office or on a computer in an electronic office.

In fact, word processing in the electronic office provides a good illustration of why you need basic office skills as well as additional new skills. To be good at word processing, you must have good typing skills in addition to knowing how to operate the machine. Furthermore, when storing a letter electronically on a computer disk, you will be using the same organizing skills that you would use in storing a hard copy in your file drawer. No matter how much processing you do automatically with computers, you still have to remember the basic and traditional office skills that you have been learning ever since you started school.

Decision-Making Skills

Because computers perform so many tasks automatically, you might think that there are fewer decisions to be made in the electronic office than in the traditional office. Actually, the reverse is true. Electronic technology can help managers and other office workers make faster and better decisions by making information available quickly. At the same time, technology presents us with more options than we have in traditional offices, which means that there are more decisions to be made. In the electronic office, decision-making skills are more important than they have ever been.

Decision making is a major part of a manager's job. Managers must decide how to achieve the organization's goals, while at the same time serving as the link between management and staff. Managers hire employees and assign them to tasks that best utilize their abilities. They evaluate work performance and decide whom to promote and whom to let go, while all the time trying to increase productivity and maintain steady performance.

To make decisions wisely, managers need information. Electronic technology has given them access to vast amounts of information that might have taken them weeks or months to gather by traditional methods—and to some information that they might not have obtained at all.

To illustrate this, let's say that the merchandise manager for a chain of shoe stores is about to place orders with manufacturers for a three-month supply of shoes for the stores. She reviews the quarterly sales report, and then, using the computer terminal on her desk, she retrieves information from the company's data base to find out which styles and sizes have been increasing in sales and which have been decreasing. These figures can help her to decide which styles to restock and which to discontinue. They can also help her see trends in fashion. If patent leather shoes are selling briskly, for example, she might decide to add several new styles of patent leather shoes to the stores' stocks. Moreover, the computer can process the sales figures to help her estimate how many pairs of shoes she should order in each style and size for each of the chain's stores.

To obtain this information by traditional means, the merchandise manager might have spent days or even weeks reading reports from stores, extracting figures from these reports, and making estimates with a calculator. Electronic technology has helped her to make her ordering decisions much more quickly.

The same technology might also give the merchandise manager more decisions to make, however. Before she places her order, she can write a summary of her plans and send this summary electronically to all the store managers, along with a request for their comments. Depending on their responses, which could be received in a matter of hours, she may refine her plans to match the wishes of customers more closely.

She might learn that customers in several stores have been asking for high-quality running shoes, which the stores do not stock. Now she has a new decision to make: should she add these running shoes to her order list? This new information presents her with an opportunity to plan her business operations more effectively. In a traditional office, the merchandise manager might not have been able to solicit the store managers' responses to purchasing plans in time to meet the order deadlines. She would have needed more time to make her decision, and the decision would not have been based on the most up-to-date facts. You can follow the store manager's decision-making process and how technology was utilized by comparing the top and bottom portions of Fig. 4-2.

The choices presented by electronic technology have increased the importance of decision-making skills for secretaries, clerks, and other members of managers' support staffs, as well as for the managers themselves. Imagine, for example, that you are the merchandise manager's administrative assistant. You made several decisions in processing the memo to the shoe store managers. First, you decided to keyboard the manager's memo rather than use the typewriter because this would enable you to correct errors and format during the input phase, which would be faster than making corrections separately. Next, to save time, you decided to transmit the document directly to the store managers' computers rather than print and mail hard copies. Finally, you decided that printing a hard copy of the memo for your own files was unnecessary because you had a soft copy stored on the computer disk.

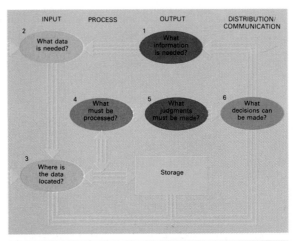

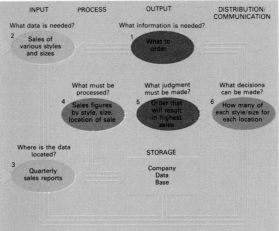

Fig. 4-2 This schematic represents a decision-making process built around the technology available in the electronic office. It is called the "backward approach" because it starts with determining the needed output—What information is needed? Step 2 is to determine what data is needed, and Step 3 is to locate the data. In Step 4 the data is processed into a new form that will be useful in Step 5, making a judgment based on the output. In Step 6 this judgment can be communicated in the form of a final decision. The bottom portion of the figure shows how this decision-making scheme can be applied to the example used here.

In the traditional office, you would have had fewer decisions to make in processing the memo. You would have had no practical alternative to typing it, no way of sending it to the store managers except through a manual delivery system, and no way to store it other than by filing a carbon or photocopy. In the electronic office, the availability of equipment provided choices that required several decisions.

Choosing the Technology for the Function

How do people go about choosing the best way to do a particular job? Electronic technology has presented office workers with alternative ways for doing their work. Often they have to make a decision about the best equipment to use for a particular task or function. In order to make correct decisions, they need to consider some important factors relating to the functions for which the equipment is required. Let's examine the four factors of cost, speed, quality, and confidentiality to see how they interact with each other to determine the best way to get a job done.

Cost　As a responsible office worker, you should usually choose the method of work that allows you to accomplish your goal with the lowest possible cost to your employer. Suppose, for example, that your company subscribes to an outside data bank. A **data bank** is a data base or a collection of data bases maintained by an organization and made available electronically to other companies for a fee. Your company pays by the minute or by the hour for the time it spends obtaining information from the data bank. If it costs $75 an hour with a one-hour minimum to obtain information from the data bank, you probably will not use it if you can obtain the information from a

The mix of equipment in offices today makes it necessary for the worker to decide which piece of equipment is the best to use for a particular task. In this office, the worker has the choice of sending a memo or letter electronically over the computer or conventionally through the U.S. Postal Service. Before making a decision, the worker will have to answer such questions as: How quickly does the information need to reach the recipient? Which is the least expensive way to send this information? Is an immediate reply necessary?

free library just down the street. On the other hand, it might be worth the cost if your boss needs the information in a hurry, or if it would take too much of your time to obtain it by some other means.

Speed   In some instances speed is more important than economy. For example, if you had to get a document to a branch office in another city by the close of the business day, you would not use the U.S. Postal Service, even though it is the least expensive means of external distribution in most cases. Electronic technology, while sometimes more expensive, usually offers the fastest means of communication and can provide time savings in all phases of information processing.

Quality Standards   Many information processing tasks require that your output meet certain quality standards of appearance, and knowing what standards to meet will help you determine which technology to use. For example, a computer system may include several printers, some of which are faster than others. However, the output from the fast printers may not be as presentable as the documents produced by the slower machines. You should probably choose the higher-quality printer for documents intended for customers and others outside your organization and the lower-quality printer for internal memos.

Confidentiality   Sometimes information needs special protection because it is confidential or because your employer's business would suffer if the information were altered or lost. The need for security might affect your decisions about how to process certain kinds of information. If you were sending a confidential document to a remote electronic office, for example, you might want to send it electronically so that the recipient could read a soft copy on a computer screen. The document could not be lost in the mail that way, and you would retain a copy of it on the electronic storage medium in your office. Since people in a large network must generally identify themselves to the computer before they can gain access to electronic files, electronic communication could also reduce the chances of unauthorized personnel seeing the information.

Human Relations Skills

While electronic office technology can save time and help you process information, it may also reduce your opportunity for human contact. For example, sending interoffice messages through electronic mail will cut back on telephone calls and "drop-in" visits, and teleconferencing will cut back on meetings in person. Similarly, if customers can order merchandise from your company by electronic mail, your employer's sales representatives will spend less time in face-to-face contact with them.

In each of these examples, electronic technology enables the employer to carry out business more efficiently. However, when the amount of human contact in business is reduced, it is possible that

Because people are the foundation of any business, it is important that they participate in the implementation of office automation and understand its effect on their contribution to the organization. Interviewing employees about methods and procedures used prior to automation is one way to get their support for a new system.

human relations will suffer unless specific steps are taken to curb the erosion that can occur.

High Tech/High Touch Technological advances have been accompanied by an awareness of a need to examine their effects on people. John Naisbitt studied the phenomenon in his book *Megatrends*, in which he pointed out that every era of "high tech," or advanced technology, has brought a move toward "high touch," or sensitivity to human needs. This means that as a society becomes more technologically oriented, the need for personal contact doesn't diminish but instead finds new ways to express itself.

According to Naisbitt, "whenever new technology is introduced into society, there must be a counterbalancing human response—that is, *high touch*—or the technology is rejected." He cites examples such as advances in medical technology that created increased concern for issues such as patients' rights, the quality of medical care, and the "quality of death." Other examples are jet air travel, which created the opportunity for more face-to-face meetings, and communications technology, which makes it easier and less costly to communicate with people in distant places.

Naisbitt predicted that technological developments which lead to less frequent contact between people and possible isolation will catch on very slowly or be rejected entirely. Among these he noted the electronic cottage (people doing secretarial/clerical work from home), electronic banking, and teleconferencing.

The move toward a balance between high tech and high touch takes place almost automatically as people bring new technology into their lives. In the office, awareness of the human factors has led to new approaches to office automation. One of the most successful techniques used today is the **participative approach**. Using this approach, management involves the workers in making decisions and implementing new procedures. The most prevalent factors behind people's resistance to change are fear of the unknown, insecurity, and the fear of being replaced by machinery. Here are some of the ways in which the participative approach can circumvent these problems:

■ Employees are told in advance that the office will be automated. Individual job functions are reviewed, and employees are consulted on the tasks they perform before final decisions are made.

■ The reasons for redefining jobs or reorganizing the staff are explained, and employees are given a clear idea of what their new duties will be.

■ In some cases redefining job functions may result in more responsibility, a higher rate of pay, or greater opportunity for advancement.

■ To avoid having people feel insecure and threatened by their lack of knowledge, equipment installation and training can take place simultaneously.

■ Those who catch on quickly may be asked to help others so that there is a sharing of experiences, which reduces the level of tension.

■ The office environment can be changed to ensure the physical comfort of employees.

Of course, each employee must take responsibility for making the work environment a pleasant one by making a special effort to have good human relations on the job. Here are some things to keep in mind that will help you:

■ Remember that the key to effective human relations is your attitude toward yourself. If you feel good about yourself, it is easier to get along with others.

■ Try to understand others and to care about what they are thinking or feeling.

■ Practice reciprocal behavior; that is, behave toward others as you would wish others to behave toward you. If you follow this rule in positive ways, you will find that people will react in kind.

■ Have goals, and be able to identify them specifically. If you find yourself in a situation that is causing you stress because you are dissatisfied, examine your feelings and determine whether you need to redefine your goals or look for another way to satisfy them.

- Be flexible, and learn to deal with your frustrations in a positive way by making an effort to relax at work, setting priorities rather than trying to do everything at once, solving problems as they arise, and putting enthusiasm into your job.

The Office Environment

As you learned in Chapter 3, businesses are in various stages of automating their office functions. Some businesses do not use any electronic technology; others have automated some functions but have not coordinated their computerized operations into a unified system. Still other businesses use integrated electronic technology in all their functions. For the purpose of understanding the evolution of technology and the information processing cycle, we have categorized these stages of automation as traditional, word processing, and electronic. However, when you enter the business world, you may encounter many different stages of automation. It is likely that you will encounter one of four common situations:

- The experimenting office.
- The electronic office with a traditional backup.
- The electronic office that must communicate with traditional offices.
- The office with several incompatible systems.

Experimentation Before making an expensive purchase, many businesses try out several kinds of electronic equipment. During these experimental periods, manual methods and systems remain in use. Your employer may encourage you to use the new equipment for tasks that are not urgent but to stick to traditional methods when there is little time for learning new procedures.

Backup Systems Sometimes computers and other electronic devices do not work the way they are supposed to. New computer systems sometimes malfunction. Many employers back up their new systems by keeping old systems in place in case such an emergency should occur. If the word processor breaks down when you are trying to get a letter into the afternoon mail, you can probably find a typewriter in the office and finish the task using this traditional office machine.

Communicating with Other Offices Even if you go to work for an employer whose entire business is electronically integrated, you will undoubtedly be doing business with other companies that use traditional methods for sending and receiving information. You will

Many business offices today are a mix of traditional and electronic equipment, so that workers must be familiar with procedures used in both.

be able to store the documents you generate on disks rather than on paper, but you will still need a traditional filing system for papers you receive from outsiders. And no matter how much electronic communications equipment is available, large automated offices will still need a mail room to handle the regular postal mail.

Equipment Incompatibility In electronics, **compatibility** refers to the ability of one kind of computer to accept and process disks or tapes that have been prepared on another type of computer. In word processing, for example, two different systems would be compatible if the disks prepared by a secretary using one kind of equipment could be passed on for further input to another secretary with another kind of equipment. By automating business functions one at a time, many large companies have ended up with several computers made by different manufacturers. A business might, for example, use three different computer systems for inventory control, accounting, and word processing. These systems may not be compatible. When this situation occurs, the company has to use traditional procedures and equipment, such as photocopiers and interoffice mail, to communicate between departments.

Determining the Benefits of Change

To overcome the factors that slow down the process of automation in the office, managers must be able to identify the benefits automation will bring. Like the father in *Cheaper by the Dozen*, who set out to increase the productivity of his 12 children by doing a time study of them as they performed their household chores, an office manager has to identify the possible gains his or her office would achieve through the purchase of new equipment. One way this can be done is by performing a feasibility study.

Before most companies invest heavily in automation, they conduct feasibility studies, part of which requires finding out how long it takes to perform a particular task.

A **feasibility study** takes into consideration all the office tasks and includes an analysis of procedures, equipment, and productivity in regard to time, costs, and benefits. Through such a study—which can be used to examine any number of possible changes, not just those related to automation—a business can determine if specific changes in office methods and equipment are desirable.

Basically, a feasibility study is concerned with people, procedures, and equipment—the three elements that make up an office system. For example, in a feasibility study devoted to studying automation, the human issues would involve the perceptions and reactions of the office staff and the necessary training of personnel. The procedural issues would involve productivity, security, and the new procedures that would be needed with the new equipment. And the technological issues would involve decisions about which functions and tasks to automate, how to effect a transition to automation, and how to ensure compatibility of equipment.

More and more businesses are conducting feasibility studies on automation and deciding to implement the transition to automation, but each business does this at its own pace and in its own way. In the business world today, you will find offices in all stages of automation, using many different information processing systems.

Changing Office Equipment

The problems involved in choosing and purchasing new equipment can be staggering, especially to smaller businesses that do not have electronics experts on their staffs. Consider that in 1909 no fewer than 89 separate manufacturers were turning out new typewriters. In the 1980s a similar situation exists with computers. The vast array of computers, software (IBM alone offers hundreds of programs), and accessories is indeed bewildering.

The pocket calculator is another good example of how fast technology in office equipment changes. Twenty years ago calculators were bulky and expensive, and they had limited capabilities. Today they are small, inexpensive, and capable of performing many functions very quickly.

Given the pace with which technology has been changing, today's highly touted electronic wonder can easily become tomorrow's dinosaur. Consequently, fear of buying the wrong equipment is one reason why businesses have been hesitant to invest in electronic systems. Although costs are declining, they are still high. Many organizations, large and small, are reluctant to commit much money to installing new equipment and retraining people, especially when they can get the work done some other way. They would rather wait until the situation stabilizes, but that may not come about for a long time. And meanwhile, other companies are greeting the rapid developments enthusiastically, automating their offices, and changing their systems when more sophisticated equipment becomes available. In the future these companies are likely to have a decided edge over their nonautomated competitors.

When a company is planning a sizable capital investment in computers, many questions must be answered:

■ What office functions are to be automated?

■ What software is needed?

■ What is the best equipment for the job?

■ What kind of environment is best for the equipment?

■ How many employees will need equipment?

■ Who will provide service for the system, and how reliable and quick is it?

These are just a few of the many questions that must be answered. They may give an idea of the decisions involved in automating an office.

Despite the fact that computers have only recently become widely used, the number of companies making equipment and the amount of software available is truly remarkable.

You may understand the transition to automation better if you think of yourself as the "manager" of your stereo collection and imagine that your stereo system has broken and you need to buy new equipment. You're aware that the technology has been changing and that there are now several different systems to choose from. You could buy a new record player, or a cassette player, or a compact disk player. There are advantages and disadvantages to each choice. You have to consider the size and condition of your record collection. If you change to compact disks, you'll have to start a whole new collection, but the quality of the sound will be improved. If you choose a cassette player, you can record some of your favorite music, and you will be able to use the cassettes in your car as well as at home. If you stick with standard records, you won't have to spend money on new records or tapes. Like an office manager trying to decide on the best electronic system for a particular office, you have to take all the options into account and then make the choice that best suits your needs and budget.

Ergonomics The introduction of electronic equipment into the workplace has had some far-reaching effects. One of the most noticeable is in the way people have been adapting the work environment to the new ways of working. Standard desks are being replaced by workstations designed to accommodate a computer and software instead of a typewriter and files. Meanwhile, psychologists, architects, and other specialists are exploring other ways to improve the work environment.

Today there is a whole field of study called **ergonomics** that is devoted to examining how the physical work environment affects the worker and his or her job performance. The focus of ergonomics is on the ways an existing work situation can be modified, or a new work situation planned, to meet the needs of each worker. Ergonomists and most employers today know that people are most productive when they are physically and psychologically comfortable. Detailed attention is now being paid to designing work spaces, furnishings, and equipment with the workers' well-being in mind.

Floor Plans As technology changes, the movement of people through office space often changes as well. Fewer trips to the copying machine may be needed because printers at individual workstations can make copies of material that is stored electronically. Visits to the central records room become unnecessary because people can use their terminals to access the company's data bases electronically. To accommodate the changing flow of people, office planners try to place walls, furnishings, and equipment so that both people and information can reach their most frequent destinations as efficiently as possible. At the same time, they consider the working conditions that people need in order to do their jobs.

Since office automation often evolves gradually, an office's floor plan may change as the process develops. To cope with such changes, many employers are turning to **office landscaping**, an approach to layout in which a large, open room is sectioned off by movable partitions into a number of workstations. Acoustic panels, shelving units that can be rearranged, easy-to-place storage units, and modular furniture form a workstation that is convenient, comfortable, and economical for a company that is expanding or changing its current system. Office landscaping provides great flexibility and can cut business costs dramatically. A 15-year study by Office Landscape Users Group, an organization of employers, shows that remodeling under an office landscaping plan costs one-tenth as much as remodeling in a space with fixed walls.

Besides saving money, office landscaping offers individual workers some control over their own environment. They can reorganize their work space to meet changing needs, and they can create a comfortable and pleasant atmosphere in which to work.

Furniture and Equipment Design Landscaped offices usually include **modular furniture**, which consists of desk tops, shelves, cabinets, and other furnishings of uniform design that attach to partitions. You can arrange these furnishings in whatever way allows you to do your job with the greatest efficiency. In addition to allowing flexibility for individual office workers' needs and tastes, modular furniture unifies the decor and keeps an open office from looking cluttered and unprofessional.

Ergonomics plays an important role in the design of modular office furniture. Specially designed tables for people who use com-

Like the equipment itself, offices are continually being redesigned to afford the most comfortable working conditions. This office has an ultramodern, modular design which allows easy movement from one area to another. The furniture is specially designed to hold the equipment and ensure the physical comfort of the worker. Acoustics, lighting, and other environmental factors have all been given special consideration in this design.

puters have several surfaces for storing components at different levels. You may be able to adjust the heights of these surfaces so that the keyboard and VDT are both placed for maximum comfort.

Specially designed chairs can also be adjusted in several ways so that workers can change the height or the angle of the back to reduce strain and fatigue.

Computer equipment is continually being redesigned to make it easier to use. In the first word processors, the keyboard and VDT were one unit. Later, the keyboard was separated from the VDT so that users could move both pieces individually to the position that was best suited for them.

Computer equipment itself is continually being redesigned to make it easier and more comfortable to use. In early word processors, the VDT and keyboard were one solid unit. Now most keyboards are separate from their VDTs, allowing you to move either one to any position you wish. Also, the VDTs are made so that you can tilt and turn the screen easily to set it in the position that is most suitable for your height and situation. Special screens have been designed to reduce glare, a problem with any kind of TV screen.

Ergonomists have spent a lot of time studying color combinations to determine which colors are best for the characters and background on the screen. This is of special concern for workers who have to spend long hours at the screen, such as is the case for word

Common color combinations used on a monochrome screen are amber, green, or white characters on a black background. Blue is another common background color used on color monitors.

processing or data processing operators. As yet there is no general agreement on the best combination, although many users claim that green or amber characters on black backgrounds are best for preventing eyestrain, headaches, and fatigue.

Lighting Office lighting is another concern of ergonomists. Most offices use fluorescent light, which produces less glare and heat than incandescent bulbs and costs less to operate. The sun is, of course, the least expensive source of light, and natural daylight is generally preferred by most people. Many new office buildings have glass exterior walls to admit as much light as possible. An unfortunate property of sunlight, however, is that it causes the worst possible glare on display screens. Workstations need to be carefully placed to avoid this problem.

Acoustics Offices can be noisy: telephones ring, people talk, printers and typewriters rattle and hum. While noise is inevitable in an office, excessive noise distracts and irritates people and lowers their productivity. It can be especially troublesome in landscaped, open offices because partitions do not block sound as effectively as walls.

Ergonomists use various methods for reducing noise levels. In large, open offices they may recommend draperies, carpeting, and textured ceilings to help absorb noise. Acoustic partitions that are specially designed to absorb sound may also be suggested. Particularly noisy pieces of equipment, such as printers and photocopiers, may be located in a room separated from the workstations. Printers that cannot be isolated in this way may be made quieter by the use of specially designed covers.

Climate Temperature, humidity, and air quality can affect the performance of electronic equipment. The electric circuits inside computers generate heat. Since the equipment will fail if it overheats, temperature control is very important.

Temperature control is very important for people too. Studies have shown that people are most comfortable—and most productive—when the temperature is about 68°F. Your own experience probably tells you that you are less effective when the temperature is significantly higher or lower than this. Some historians even believe that climate has played a large role in the location of major civilizations throughout the history of humanity. From ancient Greece and Rome to the modern-day United States and Europe, the major civilizations have been located in places where the temperature averages are in the optimum range for productivity. If you look on a world map, you will see that almost without exception, the major world civilizations throughout history have been located between 30 and 50 degrees north of the equator, where temperature averages are around 68°F.

Air quality in an office is also important, and one of the most common problems is cigarette smoke. Many nonsmokers object to the smell of cigarette smoke, and today it is widely believed that breathing in cigarette smoke from the air is almost as harmful to health as smoking itself. Aside from the human problem, smoke can also cause problems for computers. If smoke particles enter a computer or get on disks, malfunctions can occur. For all these reasons, smoking is usually banned in word processing and electronic offices.

Humidity is an important factor in climate too. Air that is too dry or too humid not only makes people uncomfortable and therefore less productive but can also cause equipment malfunctions. In an effort to control the inside climate, architects have designed sealed windows for many new office buildings, and these have necessitated the constant use of air conditioning, heating, and air-exchange systems, regardless of the weather. Some buildings have computers that monitor climate-control equipment so that the temperature, humidity, and air quality in the offices are maintained at the desired levels. The energy crisis, however, has recently raised questions as to the wisdom of this approach to climate control.

Creating Standards

The transition from the traditional office to the electronic office has had some consequences that few people anticipated. Workers have experienced unexpected health problems. Complaints about eyestrain, fatigue, muscular pains, and stress have multiplied in recent years. As a result, union and government officials have become active in trying to introduce standards for the design of office furniture and electronic equipment.

Why should the electronic office cause health problems? Consider that the workers in a traditional office generally have an opportunity to move about in their daily routines. When they type a letter, they might get up to check a file, find a report, or borrow a calculator. In contrast, workers in an electronic office may have little reason to move from their seats during the workday, since the computer contains most of the information they need.

Sitting in one place and looking at a VDT for long periods of time can cause fatigue and stress. It is for this reason that union and government officials are becoming involved in setting standards. One recommendation that experts have made for reducing fatigue and maintaining productivity is that workers never spend more than two hours at a computer without a break or without changing to an activity requiring different movements and a different posture.

■ Summary

■ Many workers fear that automation will eliminate the need for human beings in the workplace. While it is true that some jobs will no longer be necessary, many others will be created, and there will be an increased demand for office workers with a solid foundation in the basic skills and a thorough understanding of fundamental information processing procedures.

- Most people resist change. Learning to recognize that change is inevitable is one step toward mastering it. Mastering change also requires people to recognize the truth and to be tolerant of errors.

- Decision-making skills and human relations skills are important in the electronic office. Successful office workers must be able to adapt to change and learn new skills that can help both them and their employers achieve business goals.

- Because they usually have more options open to them, people who work in electronic offices will often have to exercise more judgment than people who work in traditional offices. They will have to decide which technology is best to use for a particular task in terms of economy, speed, quality, and security.

- People adapt to "high tech" with "high touch." One way managers can avoid problems when the office automates is to let the workers participate in making decisions and implementing new procedures.

- People who work in electronic offices will still use some traditional office equipment and procedures, often because employers keep old systems in place as they experiment with new ones. Traditional equipment and procedures are also maintained to enable electronic offices to communicate with their traditional counterparts.

- Incompatibility of equipment can be a major problem in companies that automate gradually. Many managers have to compromise in order to achieve compatibility.

- Some companies conduct feasibility studies to determine what electronic equipment they should acquire.

- Some companies have been slow to automate because of rapid changes in technology, the high cost of electronic equipment, the complexity of the computer market, the incompatibility of different types of equipment, and the natural tendency of people to resist change.

- Companies planning to invest in computers need to decide what functions can be automated, what software is needed, what equipment would be best for the job, and how many employees would be affected.

- Technology is changing the physical environment of office workers as well as the equipment and procedures they use. In planning offices today, businesses must consider the sensitive electronic equipment as well as the needs and comfort of the workers.

■ Ergonomists try to arrange walls, furnishings, and equipment so that both people and information can circulate through the office efficiently. Many employers purchase furnishings and equipment that are designed for maximum employee comfort and productivity.

■ Review Questions

1. List reasons why companies may choose to automate gradually rather than all at once.

2. What effects has office automation had on the number and types of jobs available to office workers?

3. Why are basic math skills still important in electronic offices in which computers perform calculations automatically?

4. Why do decision-making skills have increased importance in electronic offices?

5. Why do fully electronic offices still need to use some traditional office procedures?

6. What factors should office workers consider when selecting the most appropriate technology for a particular task?

7. Give an example of how electronic technology can change movement patterns of people in an office.

8. What advantages does office landscaping offer employers?

9. Explain how concern for user comfort has influenced the design of computer terminals.

10. What are some of the factors in the environment that can affect the productivity of both people and equipment?

■ Technical Vocabulary

GIGO	feasibility study
data bank	ergonomics
participative approach	office landscaping
compatibility	modular furniture

■ Discussion and Skills Development

1. Assume that you work in the admissions department of a large hospital. The department manager, Anna Rabinowitz, has been a prime mover behind automating the admissions procedures. Each worker in the department has a microcomputer, and they are all linked electronically. When a person is admitted, you must obtain information, including name, date of birth, address, phone number, place of employment, and the extent of the person's insurance coverage, including the name of the insurance company and numbers of insurance policies.

Much of this information is also collected independently by the billing department. Ms. Rabinowitz wants to establish an electronic connection with the billing department so that the two departments can exchange information and save the trouble of collecting it separately. The hospital administrator is concerned about the cost of doing this and is also concerned about the possibility of "computer error."

If you were Ms. Rabinowitz, how would you explain to the administrator how most "computer errors" occur? Bear in mind that when Ms. Rabinowitz hires office workers, she always selects people with good training in basic and traditional office skills. How would this play a part in her discussions with the hospital administrator?

2. In your job you communicate with various insurance companies. Some of these are small firms that do not use much electronic equipment. You often speak on the phone with their representatives. But most of the insurance companies you deal with are large and technologically sophisticated. Most of your communication with them is done electronically. Ms. Rabinowitz encourages you to get to know the people at the large firms by name and to conduct some business with them by telephone even when you could use the computer.

Do you think that this is good business practice? Discuss the effect of electronic technology on human relations.

3. In your office you have old and new equipment: typewriters, microcomputers, copying machines, and filing cabinets. In each of the following situations, describe how old and new equipment would come into play.

- You must exchange information with a large insurance company that has automated equipment.
- The hospital administrator decides to link your department and the billing department electronically. Your department (admissions) will gather the information and pass it along. For the next few months, you must keep a backup system.

4. Consider the following facts about your job and the hospital admitting office:

- You must interview incoming patients and relatives.
- There are only four workers.
- Sometimes people must wait to be interviewed.
- You use traditional and electronic equipment.
- Only two of the five rooms in your department have windows.
- You must spend considerable time at your station.

Assuming that you were asked to help redesign the office, what ergonomic factors should you consider?

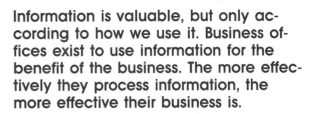

part 2
Information Processing Technology and Procedures

Information is valuable, but only according to how we use it. Business offices exist to use information for the benefit of the business. The more effectively they process information, the more effective their business is.

Part 2 shows how a modern office gathers, processes, and distributes information. In the electronic office sophisticated machines facilitate the information cycle. You will learn about how that cycle operates in both the traditional and the electronic office.

Regardless of how extensively we use computers, the starting point of the information cycle is always a person. And the ending point is also a person. A person's actions result in the creation of data. A person's use of the data justifies gathering and distributing it. So the human factor remains important. For that reason Part 2 covers such basic human interactions as speaking, listening, and writing.

Part 2 also shows how the computerized information processing cycle operates. The chapters review hardware (computers themselves) and software (the programs that run the computers) found in business offices today. Electronic retrieval of data and electronic storage, both significant changes, are covered.

Information distribution represents another difference between traditional and electronic offices. Part 2 covers ways of distributing information, including electronic mail, telecommunications, and teleconferencing.

chapter 5
Business Communication Skills

Business communication is the exchange of information in the business office. It is divided into two main branches: oral communication and written communication. Oral communication—speaking and listening—is a basic human skill that we use throughout our lives. In the business office, oral communication is an important skill. We use it every time we make an appointment, answer the telephone, or ask a question.

Communication is an important step in the information processing cycle—input, processing, storage, output, distribution/ communication (IPSOD)—because without communication there would be no point in processing information in the first place. It would be like making cars with no way to get them to their dealerships, or putting out a newspaper with no carriers to deliver it to the readers.

Companies process information because they need to move it from one office to another or from one company to another so that it can be used to accomplish their goals. Take, for example, an office manager who writes and mails a letter to an office equipment firm to arrange to purchase various items of equipment. He or she has processed information (compiled the list of items) and communicated it (sent the letter) in order to accomplish a goal (purchasing the equipment). If the office manager had omitted the step of sending the letter, nothing would have been accomplished.

In this chapter you will learn a little about communication theory—how people send and receive information. You will learn the meaning of misinformation and how to avoid it, and you will learn some basic techniques for oral business communication. These techniques will help you handle office visitors, address groups of people, and interact with office coworkers.

The Communication Process

Communication is the process by which information is exchanged. You communicate—read, write, listen, and speak—a large part of each day, both at home and at work. When it happens in the workplace, it becomes **business communication**. Everything you do on the job involves communication.

Most businesses have their own specific ways of communicating certain things (the format for a memo, for example, or a certain phrase to use when answering the phone), but most of the time you will need to know and use some of the generally accepted methods of business communication described in this chapter.

Elements in Business Communication

Keep in mind that people communicate with each other. In the electronic office, with computers sending information to and receiving information from other computers across the building or across the country, it sometimes seems that the machines are doing the communicating. It is important to remember that there is always a person who prepared and sent the message and another who received it and responded.

All communication requires a sender, a receiver, and a message. The **sender** is the person who creates and sends the message, and the **receiver** is the person who detects and interprets it. In addition, for information to be exchanged, it is necessary for the receiver to respond. The terms given to this familiar dynamic of speaking, listening, and answering are **encoding** and **decoding**. (See Fig. 5-1.)

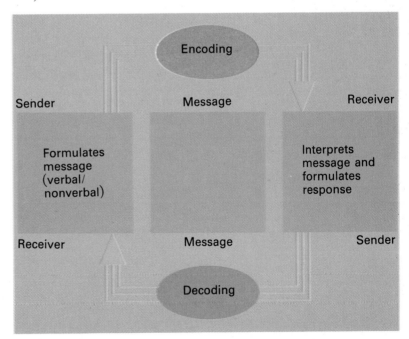

Encoding

Sender | Message | Receiver

Formulates message (verbal/nonverbal)

Interprets message and formulates response

Receiver | Message | Sender

Decoding

Fig. 5-1 People communicate by encoding and decoding messages. The sender encodes the message; the receiver decodes it.

Encoding takes place when a sender formulates the message to be sent. This form may be verbal, which is communication through the use of written or spoken words, or it may be nonverbal, which is communication through the use of symbols, pictures, or hand and body gestures. Nonverbal communication that depends on behavior—gestures, facial expressions, and posture—is called **body language**.

After the message is encoded, it is sent from the sender to the receiver, where it is decoded, or interpreted. Messages are decoded when they pass through the receiver's **mental filters**. These are all the ideas, facts, attitudes, emotions, experiences, and memories in the receiver's mind that distinguish the ways in which he or she detects and interprets a message. Each person's mental filters are different, so each person interprets a message in his or her own way. The decoding process triggers a response that starts the sender-message-receiver cycle all over again.

Miscommunication

Miscommunication occurs when something goes wrong between the sender and the receiver. The sender may send an inaccurate or confusing message, or the receiver may mishear or misunderstand the message he or she receives. With so many messages coming and going and so many ways for our unique mental filters to interpret them, miscommunication is bound to happen once in a while. In a business situation, miscommunication can cause serious errors. A company might receive a wrong shipment or a busy executive might miss an important appointment because incorrect information was sent.

Good communication depends on messages being encoded and decoded accurately, but sometimes there are situations in the business office that can interfere with the routine encoding and decoding process and result in bad communication. Let's take a close look at how this happens.

The normal, everyday routines of speaking, listening, reading, gesturing, and making facial expressions are all dependent on interactions between signals and sensory receivers. A **signal** is something in our environment that stimulates us—something we see, hear, taste, smell, or feel. A **sensory receiver** is a body organ that can detect and interpret signals—our eyes, ears, tongue, nose, or fingertips. Without our being aware of it, our bodies are receiving and interpreting many signals simultaneously, often all in combination. For example, it is possible for you to read a report, eat a sandwich, smell a visitor's cigar or perfume, and hear the phone ringing—all at the same time.

Normally, we can handle the bombardment our senses receive each moment because our mental filters tune out the effects of some of the signals on our sensory receivers. An example is the way we tune out some sounds so that they become background noises of which we are barely conscious. Miscommunication occurs when

Trying to interpret too many signals at once leads to miscommunication.

our mental filters tune out the wrong signal or when we try to handle two competing signals at once. If you were talking to one person on the telephone while another person was talking to you across your desk, for example, you could easily become too distracted to understand what either was saying to you.

Because miscommunication is quite common, especially in large organizations, the process of communication is being studied by psychologists and sociologists to see what goes wrong and what can be done to prevent it. New theories and techniques are being developed all the time. Some are well known and are being used in the workplace. A company you work for may sponsor a seminar or workshop on communication in an effort to improve the exchange of information in the office.

It is easy to tell when successful communication has taken place. The message has been detected and interpreted the way the sender intended it to be, and so things run smoothly and happen as expected. When miscommunication occurs, its effects may show up almost immediately, or they may not be apparent for quite a while. Sooner or later, something does not happen as expected, someone spots a mistake, or someone misunderstands a message and does the wrong thing. Ideally, the best time to detect and correct a miscommunicated message is as soon as it occurs.

There are some techniques that you can use to improve message reception and to minimize the possibilities of miscommunication:

■ **Concentrate.** When there is a lot of activity in a business office— telephones ringing, intercoms buzzing, and people coming and going near your workstation—it can be difficult to read, listen, or respond accurately. Concentrating consciously on one thing can help you tune out distractions.

■ **Be aware of your own mental filters**. Mental filters vary in kind. An example might be a word with a special meaning in the region where you grew up or a long-standing fear, such as a fear of being criticized or of handling numbers. Sometimes we ascribe our mental filters to a "mental block"; we might claim, for example, "I never could spell very well." Being aware of your mental filters can help you overcome them.

■ **Be aware of other people's mental filters**. You may discover, for example, that your supervisor does not remember messages unless they are written down. Using a combination of written and spoken messages with such people will help you work around their mental filters and communicate successfully with them.

■ **Request and provide feedback**. Giving **feedback** means responding in some way to confirm that you have received and understood a message, or it may mean giving people an opinion about something they are doing. It might mean simply repeating what you have just heard in order to confirm that you understand a request, or it might mean letting people know how well they are performing a task you have asked them to do.

Preparing Messages

Communication requires preparation. Whether you plan to speak or write to one person or to a dozen, you need to perform a few basic steps in order to communicate effectively:

1. Create an idea.
2. Identify the audience.
3. Gather data.
4. Process the information.
5. Choose the method of communicating.

In routine conversation all these steps occur so quickly that you are not even aware of them. In the business office, however, oral communication requires thought and organization.

Creating Ideas To communicate effectively, you need to have a clear idea of what you want to say. Do you need to explain a procedure to a new employee? Do you want to send out a memo explaining your company's new travel policy? Before you start, decide what you want to say: What points will you cover? In what sequence? In how much detail?

Identifying the Audience Before you gather information in support of your idea or decide how you will send your message, you need to determine who your audience is likely to be. In a business setting, you might be communicating with your supervisor, your colleagues, or your subordinates. It might be helpful to ask yourself these questions:

1. Who needs to know this information?

2. What will they already know about this topic?

3. What will be the best way to send this message?

4. Will I need a response from the receivers?

Gathering Data Data gathering is collecting information to add substance to and provide explanations for the idea you want to communicate. Typical data-gathering methods are reading files, records, and reference materials; using computer data banks; and consulting with experts.

How involved the data-gathering process will be depends on the scope of the idea. It can be as simple as finding a telephone number in the Yellow Pages or as extensive as collecting all the figures that are necessary for preparing an annual budget for your department. It is a good idea for you, as an office worker, to learn about all the sources of information at your disposal. Many companies have in-house libraries. With electronic technology you may also have access to computer files and data banks. Learn whom in your workplace you can refer to for information. Once you have gathered your data, you can begin to create your message.

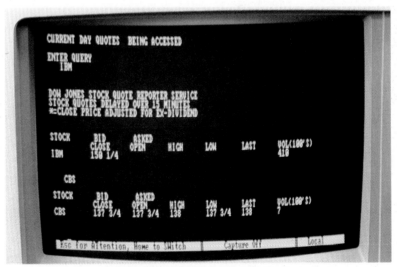

Before you can communicate a message, you have to gather the data you need by researching files and reference books, and by consulting the appropriate experts. In the electronic office it is possible to have access to research and information through the use of on-line retrieval services.

Processing Information   Since elementary school you have heard about the need to prepare an outline before you begin to write. Outlines are necessary whether you plan to speak or write your message. Processing the information means organizing it in a way that allows your reader or listener to understand it. When writing stories, journalists always make sure they have answered the five Ws: Who? What? When? Where? and Why? These are good guidelines for anyone to use in preparing an outline. Ask yourself those questions as you begin to organize your information.

Choosing a Method of Communication   Certain kinds of information require certain methods of communication. You would not choose to write a memo and send it through interoffice mail if a quick phone call would serve the same purpose. On the other hand, it would be hard to communicate highly detailed statistics by telephone, so you would choose a written form of communication.

In the traditional office, you will most commonly communicate verbally—face to face, over the telephone, or through written messages such as letters and memos. In the electronic office, you may also have computers and other electronic devices to help you send messages. There may be other methods at your disposal as well. A hands-on demonstration or the use of illustrations can be very helpful. Because individuals absorb information in different ways, it is a good idea for message senders to use as many methods of communication as they may need to get the job done.

Suppose, for example, that you, as an administrative assistant, have been assigned the task of training a new employee in the use

Hands-on practice can be the best way to show a coworker how to operate a new piece of equipment. Choosing the right method for communicating information is an important office skill.

of the company's copier. You will have to decide what method of communication will be best. You may decide that the new employee should read the operating manual. Or you may decide to explain the equipment aloud while you demonstrate its use. Or you may have the new person try it out for himself or herself. Probably, you will choose to use some combination of all these methods. After the employee has had time to read the manual and practice operating the copier, you can check to see that the information you provided has been received accurately. You might ask the new person to describe the process and then demonstrate the proper use of the copier for you. As an experienced user, you will know right away if a miscommunication has occurred.

Oral Communication Skills

The exchange of information through speaking, listening, and using body language happens so frequently and so effortlessly that we do not often think of it as a skill that needs to be mastered. Yet it can become one of our most powerful skills on the job because of its immediacy. When we speak or listen, we are usually face-to-face with our receivers or senders. In our personal lives, we soon learn that once we have spoken aloud to someone, we can't take back our words, no matter how hurtful or thoughtless they may be. It is the same way in the business office. Oral communication is our most important human relations skill because what we say to visitors and coworkers creates impressions and attitudes that are difficult to change.

One major factor influencing the impression you create in the business environment is your use of the language. It is important to take note of the way you speak at home and among your friends. Would this same manner of speaking be understood and accepted by people who don't know you and whose expectations are that you communicate with them in a way that is generally considered to be the norm? For example, at home or at school when you greet your friends or are introduced to someone, it is acceptable to say "Hi" or "Hi'ya." However, in a business environment, this type of greeting would be considered inappropriate, particularly if you were speaking to someone outside the company, or to someone at a higher level in the company. The appropriate greeting in this situation is "How do you do." This is a common phrase that you have heard all of your life, but it may sound and feel strange to hear yourself say it if you are not accustomed to speaking this way. However, you should practice using this phrase and other more formal speech patterns until you feel comfortable with them. Remember that the goal of communication is to be understood. Speaking standard business English will make your message clearer to others because the message will not get caught in the receiver's preconceived notions (mental filters) about people who do not speak the language of the business world.

FORMAL AND INFORMAL SITUATIONS

Here are some typical formal communications situations encountered most often by office workers:

- Presenting information or a report to a supervisor or colleagues.
- Having a job interview.
- Conducting a training program.
- Making a sale to a customer.
- Participating in staff meetings, seminars, or workshops.

Some typical informal communications settings are:

- Answering the phone.
- Greeting visitors or customers.
- Receiving instructions from your supervisor.
- Handling inquiries from colleagues or subordinates in your own department or in other departments.
- Training a new staff member.

Oral communication can occur in both formal and informal settings. In the business office, however, even informal communication has to be given more thought and care than casual, everyday conversation at home and among friends. Here are some standard guidelines, in addition to those discussed earlier, for preparing and sending messages that you, as the speaker, can use in both formal and informal situations:

- **Have something worthwhile to say**. In the business office, time is money, and time that someone spends listening to you is valuable. Be sure that what you say is to the point, is timely, and has substance and value to the listener.

- **Be sensitive to your audience**. From the moment you begin to speak, be aware of your listeners. Make sure they can hear you; notice their expressions; be conscious of their body language. Adjust your speaking to meet their needs, and if it seems necessary, stop to get feedback by saying something like "Can you all hear me?" or "Are there any questions so far?"

- **Develop voice control and quality**. Your voice should be appropriately loud for your audience. The tone of your voice should be well modulated within your physical limitations. We don't all have to sound like radio or television announcers, but we do want our listeners to concentrate on what we say, not on how we sound. Your voice should be expressive, with emphasis in the appropriate places and with enough variety to maintain interest. Speak from your diaphragm and drop your voice an octave; that will give your voice more carrying power.

- **Avoid a tentative tone**. Many pauses or filling in with "ums," "ahs," and "you knows" will erode your credibility. Also, you should avoid ending your sentences with a questioning tone.

- **Use correct English**. Good grammar and a solid vocabulary will help you create an impression of authority and professionalism. You should always be aware of correct subject-verb agreement, parts of speech, mood, tense, and sentence structure. Misuse of grammar can change the whole meaning of a sentence and result in a serious miscommunication. Incorrect pronunciation of words can confuse your listener and erode your credibility. You should take particular care with names. The correct pronunciation of people's names sends the message that you are sufficiently interested in those people to learn their names.

- **Be sensitive to timing**. In informal communication, choose a time to speak that is not hectic or stressful for the listener. In formal settings, be aware of the time allotted for the topic you are addressing. Save questions for a question-and-answer period, or save ones that might not be of general interest for a later time when you can approach the questioner. In any communication situation, avoid interrupting.

- **Maintain a good appearance**. Dressing appropriately will make you more comfortable and confident when you speak and help establish your professionalism. There are many advice books on this topic, but remember that "image building" is only part of your effort to succeed in communication. You can look like an office superstar in your best suit or dress and spoil the image by speaking like someone with a third-grade education.

Presenting the appropriate image is a key to success in any communication situation.

Listening Skills

Receiving oral communication—listening—is also a skill that can be put to good use in the office. Listening is a combination of hearing and understanding. Every day we hear things that do not make a distinct impact on our consciousness because we don't listen carefully. Here are some techniques that will help you build your listening skills:

- **Be prepared**. Familiarize yourself with the speaker's topic. This will give you a framework into which to fit new information and prepare you to ask intelligent questions.

- **Concentrate and listen actively**. Consciously consider what the speaker is saying, and mentally sum up each major thought that is presented.

- **Interact with the speaker**. Look the speaker in the eye except when you are taking notes. Use appropriate body language, nodding or shaking your head. Make pertinent comments at appropriate times to give the speaker feedback.

- **Take notes**. Taking notes will help you remember what was said afterward. But be careful not to overdo it. Do not try to write down everything; just put down the important points briefly. Otherwise, you might become so involved in writing that you lose track of what is being said.

- **Try to be comfortable**. Sit where you can hear and see the speaker. (His or her body language is information for you.) Try to avoid distractions such as glaring lights or humming air conditioners.

- **Avoid anticipating what you will hear**. Do you recall what you learned about mental filters? If you think you know what you are going to hear, you may not hear accurately what the speaker really says.

- **Make time to recycle the message**. If an opportunity to provide feedback and double-check for understanding does not present itself in the course of a conversation, consciously make time. It may save time in the long run if you can avoid a time-consuming and embarrassing follow-up phone call or, worse, an error.

- **Complete follow-up work right away**. Except for your notes, your only record of the message is in your head. Do any follow-up work before you forget what you heard.

Taking notes is a good way to listen effectively when others are communicating information to you.

Nonverbal Skills

During our discussion of speaking and listening, we have referred several times to body language. Body language is a powerful communicator and miscommunicator. Animated facial expressions, head movements, hand gestures, and posture can add meaning to your words, but you should be sure that they are coordinated with your speaking. For example, if you say "I am so glad to see you here this morning" but do not smile or look at your audience while you say it, your listeners will doubt your sincerity.

You should always be conscious of your facial expression, and you should establish eye contact with your listeners whenever possible. Looking someone in the eye conveys authority, honesty, recognition, and self-confidence. Avoiding a person's eyes means just the opposite.

Typical Business Communication Roles

Any of the speaking, listening, and body language skills you have learned will make you a better communicator in any situation in or out of the workplace. Let's take a closer look at some of the typical business situations you may find yourself in, and let's see what communication techniques you can add to those you have already acquired.

Person to Person

Most person-to-person communication in the business office is informal. The kinds of person-to-person situations you are likely to deal with include greeting visitors, answering the phone, responding to questions and requests for information, and giving and taking instructions.

If it is likely that you will be greeting visitors, you should familiarize yourself with the names, titles, organizations, and agendas of frequent callers and visitors. Be sure to share this information with coworkers and supervisors so that they are prepared to greet and help visitors as well. Unless you are asked to do otherwise, you should always use a visitor's last name and his or her title—Mr., Mrs., Dr., Senator, and so on.

As an office worker you can expect to greet many visitors and clients. Often these situations will require that you make introductions.

Even if you are busy, take time to acknowledge visitors or callers and assure them that you will get to them as soon as you can. For example, if you are on the phone, you can smile and nod to your visitor to put him or her at ease.

You may be required to introduce visitors to your supervisor, and so you should develop your interpersonal skills. Know how to shake hands and formally introduce people. Offer a visitor refreshments if they are available, and be aware of the special needs of disabled visitors. These are all courtesies that convey your sense of professionalism.

Sometimes you may have to deal with an angry or upset visitor. For example, a visitor might show up without an appointment, demand to speak to the boss, and refuse to state his or her name or business. When you have to communicate with such visitors, you should try first to identify them and find out the purpose of their visit. Second, you should try to protect yourself and your coworkers from unnecessary interruptions. The best way to achieve these objectives is to be as tactful as possible. **Tact** is the ability to avoid offending or embarrassing people. Remain objective, and do not take the visitors' tone or manner personally; courteously try to assist them. Avoid being abrupt or defensive. Once you have identified a visitor's problem, do your best to solve it yourself or refer the visitor to the most appropriate office. As a last resort, you may have to telephone the supervisor or coworker your visitor is demanding to see. Don't say anything to commit your supervisor to a meeting. Instead, you might suggest that your supervisor and the visitor arrange a future meeting.

Some person-to-person exchanges are formal and have a specific purpose. For example, if you were employed as a legal secretary, part of your duties might be to interview your employer's clients to collect information needed to prepare a will or take out a mortgage. All the general rules about oral communication and interpersonal skills apply here. Be courteous, be on time, and be prepared. That is, know the client's name and the purpose of the interview or meeting. When the meeting is coming to a close, take time to summarize the main points, and after the meeting is over, think back over the conversation and make any additional notes you may require. If you are the one being interviewed, for a job or a promotion, for example, watch and listen to your interviewer carefully and respond to questions directly and honestly.

Many of your person-to-person exchanges will be by telephone. Perhaps it will be your job to screen your boss's telephone calls or to set up meetings by telephone. When using the phone, remember that you need to find ways to compensate for the fact that you can't see the person to whom you are speaking (and can't, therefore, read his or her body language) and for the fact that you can't be seen either. Techniques for using the telephone effectively are described fully in Chapter 13.

Person to Group

Person-to-group communication can take place at a board meeting, at a seminar, at a staff meeting, or in any other kind of situation where you are asked to speak to a group or participate in a group discussion. It is in these kinds of meetings that big decisions are made and important information is communicated. Here are some strategies for succeeding in person-to-group exchanges:

- **Be prepared**. In all communication situations, preparation is important, but in person-to-group exchanges, it is especially so. If you are presenting information, know your topic cold; have your data gathered and carefully processed; and have a typed agenda to help your audience receive your message accurately. Sometimes you can make good use of nonverbal materials or graphics, such as charts and diagrams, to make your point. If you are a listener, you should read up on the topic to be discussed, review the agenda, and develop questions you may want answered to help you understand the message.

- **Make sure your audience is comfortable**. Minimize distractions. Do you have enough chairs? Is there enough light? Can everyone hear?

- **Summarize and ask for questions**. After you have stated your message, briefly restate your main points; then answer any questions your audience may have. This is the time to get the feedback you need to make sure you've delivered your message accurately.

Teleconferences

When you have to participate in an audio or video teleconference, all the techniques we have covered so far will help you communicate effectively in this situation. In addition, you will have to be espe-

As the cost of using electronic technology decreases, more and more businesses will use video teleconferences to conduct meetings.

cially aware of the limitations of the equipment you are using. For example, if the video is focusing on the graphics you have prepared, then the audience may not be able to see your body language at the same time.

If you are part of a teleconference without video, it may be necessary to identify yourself when you speak until everyone can recognize your voice.

Communication and IPSOD

As we have said all along, communication (or distribution) is one step in the IPSOD process. It is interesting to note that communication itself can be broken down into IPSOD steps.

When someone sends a message, input consists of listening—hearing and understanding the message. You add it to the information you already have, and if you discover that more information is needed, you ask questions or research the subject until you are satisfied. This is the same thing as retrieving information from storage, which is another means of input.

Processing is thinking about the message and formulating a reply. Output is the response, the written or spoken message you send back to the person you are communicating with. You can also distribute/communicate the response to new receivers, say by circulating a memorandum. The receivers, in turn, start the cycle all over again. And, of course, the message can be stored—in your mind or on paper, computer disk, or microfilm.

This communication and information processing cycle is repeated constantly and without conscious thought as you communicate with friends and family throughout the day. In the business office, the same process applies to virtually everything you do, from talking to a coworker to using the most sophisticated word processing computers.

To communicate well, you have to think clearly, speak and write well, and demonstrate good interpersonal skills. Your main job in the business office is to be understood, and good communication skills make that possible. In this chapter you have seen how oral communication works. In the next chapter you will learn how to apply many of these same principles to written communication.

■ Summary

■ Business communication is the exchange of information, or messages, in the business office. Messages can be verbal or nonverbal. All communication requires a sender, a receiver, and a message.

■ Sometimes in the business office, messages are miscommunicated because our sensory receivers fail to detect them clearly or because our mental filters misinterpret them.

■ To ensure successful communication, we should prepare messages carefully. To prepare a message, the sender creates an idea, identifies the audience, gathers data, processes it into information, and chooses the best method of communication.

- Oral communication—speaking and listening—is our most powerful communication method because of its immediacy. In the workplace oral communication can take place in both formal and informal settings.

- To communicate orally, you should make sure you have something worthwhile to say. You should watch and respond to your audience and speak clearly. Also, make sure you use good English and present a well-groomed appearance.

- Listening is an important oral communication skill. Good listeners familiarize themselves with the speaker's topic, listen actively, and take notes.

- Body language, a form of nonverbal communication, refers to how speakers and listeners use facial expressions, gestures, and posture to communicate.

- The basic rules for use of the telephone in business include answering promptly, speaking clearly, listening carefully, and being polite.

- In most person-to-person exchanges, being prepared, helpful, and polite are basic courtesies expected of the professional office worker.

- Talking to a group is usually a formal communication situation. When you talk to a group, you need to know your material, gather the information you need, and provide an agenda.

- Talking to another person over the telephone and participating in a group meeting by means of a teleconference are examples of oral communication by machine.

- Communication itself can be broken down into IPSOD steps.

■ Review Questions

1. Define communication, and describe what is meant by the elements of communication.

2. Explain the difference between verbal and nonverbal communication.

3. How does miscommunication occur, and what steps can be taken to avoid it?

4. What are the basic steps that have to be followed before you can communicate either orally or in writing?

5. In any oral communication, there are some general guidelines that a speaker can follow to ensure successful communication. What are they, and why are they important?

6. What techniques can you use to build your listening skills?

7. List the typical business situations in which oral communication can occur, and give one example of each.

8. Explain how communication can be broken down into IPSOD steps.

■ Technical Vocabulary

communication
business communication
sender
receiver
encoding
decoding
body language

mental filter
miscommunication
signal
sensory receiver
feedback
tact

■ Discussion and Skills Development

1. It is hard to imagine how you appear when you speak. An audiotape or videotape of yourself can be very instructive. Prepare a short oral presentation describing, for example, one of the courses you are taking. Make notes, but do not write out verbatim what you wish to say. Then locate a tape recorder or, better still, a videotape camera, and ask a friend to tape you while you make a presentation. Review the tape and note how you sound and/or look. Listen and watch especially for your tone of voice, verbal skills and habits, and body language. Then present your talk again, being conscious this time of anything you need to improve. Review the tape again. How did you do this time?

2. "Rumor" or "Whisper down the lane" is a game that many people played when they were younger. It is based on the premise that if a message is repeated often enough, it is bound to be misinterpreted. Try to organize a half dozen to a dozen of your classmates to play a variation of this game. Put together a message that describes a meeting—where, what day, what hour, what will be discussed, who should attend—and have it passed orally from person to person throughout the course of a day. Have the last person to receive the message write it down, and compare his or her version with the original message. How do they differ? What other methods of communication would have ensured that the message would come back accurately?

3. Attend a public lecture or talk at your school or in the community. Listen, using all the listening skills you have learned in this text. Take notes. When it is over, review your notes and memory. What was the speaker's main point? Did the speaker answer the questions Who? What? When? Where? Why? and How? Did the speaker interact with the audience? What kinds of body language did he or she use? Did you interact with the speaker? If you attend this lecture with a friend, compare notes. Did you both come to the same conclusions about what was said?

chapter 6
Writing
Business
Communications

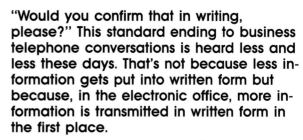

"Would you confirm that in writing, please?" This standard ending to business telephone conversations is heard less and less these days. That's not because less information gets put into written form but because, in the electronic office, more information is transmitted in written form in the first place.

Business people need to see things in writing—either on paper or on a VDT—for several reasons. Often it is necessary to have documentation as proof that certain agreements have been made or to confirm information given over the telephone. Also, it is easier to analyze, verify, and store written information.

The written word, then, remains a basic means of communication in the business office. The advent of the electronic office has brought about new forms of written communication, thereby increasing the amount of written material.

Electronic messages and electronic mail do not require paper, of course, but they do require writing skills. In fact, they call for more advanced writing skills than those needed for traditional forms of written communication.

Like the oral communication skills that you learned about in Chapter 5, written communication skills can be improved with knowledge and practice. This chapter reviews standard types of business communications and explains why tone and presentation are important. You'll see samples of the different formats used for business communications, and you'll learn what forms of communication should be used for specific situations.

Remember that every memo, letter, or report that you send out says something about you as a communicator and, more important, about the company that you represent.

Writing Skills in Today's Office

No matter what kind of office you work in, you will find that written communication is an important part of the information flow. It always has been, and it will continue to be in the future. In the electronic office, good writing skills are just as important as they are in the traditional office, and perhaps even more so.

In an electronic office, you must often "communicate" with a computer: give it commands, ask it questions. Usually, you communicate with the computer by writing words, which you input by using the keyboard. Correct spelling and punctuation are particularly important. Computers are not "smart"; they are programmed to understand certain specific commands. Any variation from these commands will not be understood. If you make an error, the computer will give an error message, but it cannot proceed until you give it the correct input.

You also use written words to communicate with people via computer. Using the computer allows you to send messages to people very quickly. In some cases your message arrives as soon as you type it. With this kind of system, you will not have time to erase or correct any errors before the recipients see them. Another kind of system allows you to type your message, read and edit it, and then send it. This way, you can correct errors before other people see them. But in either case, you need to have good writing skills to communicate effectively.

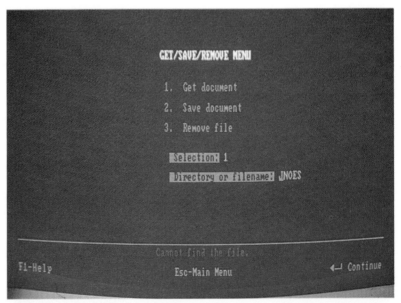

Correct spelling and punctuation are essential when using the computer. If file names are not input correctly, you will get an error message.

Another reason why good writing and editing skills are more important in an electronic office stems from the change in the way information flows through the office. You will remember that storage/retrieval moves from the end of the information processing flow to the middle. Your words go into storage when you input them, so it is important either to be correct the first time around or edit and correct the material that is being input. If you are writing a letter or report on a word processor, it's easy to make changes and corrections, but you still need editing skills in order to know what corrections are needed.

Proofreading, a central component of good writing skills, is a very important part of the writing process in the electronic office. Once an error or misinformation has been input and stored in a computer, it can be used unwittingly by many people and remain there undetected, only to continue causing problems further down the line.

You probably know people who edit themselves as they speak. It can be difficult to listen to people who do this because they are forever backtracking, pausing, repeating, correcting, and qualifying their statements. In the end, the receiver (listener) of such a conversation may be more confused than if the sender (speaker) had simply talked without editing himself or herself. Written communication differs from oral communication in an important respect. The sender (writer) can usually edit the message before the receiver (reader) gets it. The "drawback" is that the reader will therefore expect the message to be clear, grammatical, and correctly spelled. Let's look at some ways of sharpening your written communication skills.

The Written Word

The written word is one of civilization's most distinguishing characteristics. Without the written word, civilization as we know it could not exist. Written communication does, however, lack the immediacy of oral communication. When you speak to someone, the information is sent and received instantaneously, and you also get immediate feedback in the form of a reply.

While written communication does not have this spontaneity, it does have its own advantages: time to prepare and a permanent record to store or file. In oral communication, unless the listener takes notes, storage takes place only in the form of memory, which can be faulty. Consider how many times you've incorrectly remembered the price of something you saw or the details of what someone said. It happens to all of us, proving that the human memory is not a reliable record of information.

Time to Prepare

In ordinary, day-to-day oral communication, you have little or no time to prepare exactly what you are going to say or plan how you will say it. But if you are going to make a formal speech or address a large group, you usually do have some time to prepare. A major part of your preparation for such a presentation is writing down your thoughts.

When you communicate in writing, you almost always have time to think about what you will say and how you will say it. The amount of time you will have, however, is largely determined by the kind of office you work in. In any office one factor that influences how much time you have to prepare is the accepted **turnaround time** (time from when a task is given to when it is expected to be completed) for typical business correspondence. The longer the accepted turnaround time, the more time you will have to prepare your written communication. Another factor that influences how much time you have to prepare is the deadline of any particular project. Again, a deadline that is far off in the future will give you more time to prepare than one that is only a few hours or days ahead.

If you work in an electronic office, you have an advantage over your counterpart who works in a traditional office. The technology available to you in an electronic office will enable you to edit and make changes in your written communication much more quickly and easily. Since it will take you less time to input, process, store, and retrieve information, you will have more time available to you for the actual preparation of your document.

There are exceptions to this, however. You may sometimes communicate with another person via machine in an interactive situation. An **interactive** situation is one in which you at your terminal exchange information with someone at another terminal. You "talk" back and forth, exchanging information, giving and receiving feedback by writing words that appear simultaneously on both your screen and the other person's screen. You then read what the other person replies. In such a situation, where you will not have the opportunity to edit yourself, good writing skills are clearly important.

Permanent Records

When you communicate in writing, you always have a permanent, verifiable record of the information that was exchanged. If anyone challenges the record, forgets it, or remembers it incorrectly, the written communication is available to correct and refresh memories.

Because they are permanent, written communications should be carefully and thoughtfully prepared. They should reflect your best efforts, for they are a permanent record by which not only you but also your company will be judged. A sloppy, poorly constructed letter with misspellings and incorrect grammar is evidence of a poorly run company. Many people avoid doing business with such companies. They reason that the quality of a company's correspondence reflects the quality of the company's work, and to a very large extent, this is a valid assumption. You should always keep this in mind when preparing written correspondence.

The Rosetta stone, discovered in 1799, has provided a permanent record of writing that was done almost two thousand years ago. Although you cannot expect your business communications to be preserved for two thousand years, writing does provide a permanent record. The author of this communication, Ptolemy V of Greece, also had time to prepare his document, another advantage of written communication.

The Act of Writing

Like anything else, writing is a skill that can be acquired and, with practice, improved. The importance of this skill is attested to by the amount of time schools spend teaching spelling, grammar, and punctuation.

Many of the techniques that improve oral communication can also be used to improve written communication. Preparation is one important technique. Being comfortable, having the right tools or instruments, and suiting your message to the situation are others. There are also general techniques and usage skills that can be applied specifically to improving writing skills. Let's review a few of them.

General Techniques There is no cut-and-dried formula that will make a competent writer, but there are several techniques you can employ to increase the effectiveness of your written communication.

■ **Be yourself**. This is true in writing as well as in any interpersonal activity. When you speak, you do not suddenly try to use big words and long sentences to impress the receiver of your message. If you did, you would probably miscommunicate and sound silly, or at least stiff and pretentious. The same is true with writing. Writing is a more structured and formal exchange of information than is oral communication, which means that you have a little more leeway to use a higher level of vocabulary and more eloquent sentences, but nonetheless, you should be yourself and sound natural (Fig. 6-1).

RAZ-MA-TAZ NOVELTIES

1543 Ventura Avenue

Freeport, CA 90028

January 4, 1987

Mr. William Baker
2124 Sunset Road
Wingham, MA 02745

Dear Mr. Baker:

Regrettably, the item to which you made reference in your recent missive can no longer be purchased. Our supplier has terminated production and is not replacing the item with merchandise of similar function. Your full reimbursement and our most sincere apologies are enclosed.

Sincerely,

RAZ-MA-TAZ NOVELTIES

Diane DiBendetto
Assistant Manager

cnj

Fig. 6-1 The writer of this letter sounds like a stuffy, pompous person. In reality, she is a very pleasant young woman. The letter would have sounded better if it had been written in a more natural tone.

- **Know your reader**. When writing, you should have in mind who the receiver or reader of the message will be. This is necessary whether there will be one or a hundred people reading your message. If you have an image of the reader(s) in mind, you will more likely aim your message accurately.

- **Exercise empathy**. Empathy is the ability to understand and feel what others feel. This is related to the previous technique. Identify your reader(s), and then put yourself in their shoes as you read over the message you have prepared.

- **Be courteous**. Even though writing is not a direct person-to-person activity, human relations are important. Being business-like does not mean being brusque or short. A written business message should quickly reach the point, but not so fast that it strikes the receiver(s) as rude. Studies have indicated that when people communicate via computer, either interactively or by leaving messages, they tend to be brusque and less polite. This is something to watch for in yourself if you are in a position to communicate via computer.

- **Keep to the point**. Without sacrificing courteousness, do keep to the point. Being too short can seem rude, but, a wordy, rambling message wastes the receiver's time, which is the ultimate rudeness. A well-written message exhibits a skillful balance.

- **Be results-oriented**. Know what you want your message to achieve so that you can write it accordingly. Although courteous in both instances, you might adopt one tone when writing a valued client about a missed payment and another tone when writing to a problem client who often misses payments.

- **Organize your message**. Present points logically. For a long message, preparing an outline will help.

- **Be clear and specific**. Give the reader as much information as you can—anything that would be helpful. For example, if you have the responsibility for arranging a conference and you must write to the convention site about your needs, it is better to write "We will need a room that will hold at least 50 people" rather than "We will need a large room."

- **Be complete**. Make sure that you include all pertinent information. Journalism's Who? Where? When? What? and Why? are good guidelines for you to follow. Not all your messages will require answers to each of these questions, but making it a routine always to check your message against them will ensure that you've left nothing out.

- **Be accurate**. Always cross-check and verify your data. Use a dictionary to make sure your spelling is correct.

- **Avoid jargon. Jargon** is specialized technical language not normally used in everyday communication. In this book we have talked about *hard copy* and *soft copy*, for example. These terms represent the jargon of the electronic office. You should avoid such terms in written messages to people outside your office unless you are certain they will understand them.

- **Proofread**. This is the most important habit to develop. If you do not proofread your written messages carefully before you send them, you waste the effort you put into improving your writing, and you waste the advantage of having time to prepare that writing gives you over speaking (Fig. 6-2).

```
                    MODERN OFFICE SUPPLIES

                   12345 Southern Boulevard

                   Paxton Corners, IL 60708



         February 22, 1987



         Ms. Marcia Longchamps
         98 Carlson Road
         Marlboro, NJ 07746

         Dear Ms. Longchomps:

         Thankyou for your resent request for sampels of our product.
         A box of our unique folders bindrs, and other oficce materials
         are being shiped under seperate cover.  In it their are also
         our latest catalog and a clean order from.

         Thank you,

         MODERN OFFICE SUPPLIES

         Richard Mellon
         Richard mellon
         Sales Representative

         cnj
```

Fig. 6-2 The writer of this letter did not proofread before sending the communication. The letter represents the company badly as a result.

Usage Skills   The most important usage skills are knowing grammar, punctuation, and spelling, as well as having a good vocabulary. In addition to a dictionary and a **thesaurus** (a book that lists synonyms, or words that can be used for other words), you should have a good reference book on grammar and punctuation at your desk, and you should refer to it whenever in doubt. *The Gregg Reference Manual*, sixth edition, is an example of such a book. Major newspapers such as *The New York Times*, universities such as the University of Chicago, and the U.S. government all publish manuals of style that answer many questions about usage and are available to the general public. Another excellent resource that any person preparing a written message should have at hand is *The Elements of Style*, by William Strunk, Jr., and E. B. White. This slim volume is packed with a wealth of good advice for all writers.

Here are a few generally accepted principles of good usage that you should be aware of when preparing a written message. Some will parallel or reinforce techniques already discussed.

- **Be consistent**. Once you decide on the format for your message, stick with it throughout. In writing, **format** means the general appearance of your message. If you decide to indent the first line of paragraphs, do so throughout. Will you capitalize abbreviations, such as *A.M.* and *P.M.,* or write them in lowercase? Either way is correct, as long as you use only one way throughout.

- **Use the active voice**. You can write in either an active voice or a passive voice. Experts recommend using the active voice as much as possible in writing. The active voice is direct and to the point: "We appreciate your order" is better than "Your order is appreciated." The former is the active voice; the latter the passive.

- **Be concise**. Some people believe that their writing appears more formal when they use long sentences and many words. Not so. In oral communication, the phrase *you know* is an example of useless words that people often insert in their speech. People often insert such useless words in their written messages as well. Consider these examples: *due to the fact that* should be simply *because*; *the general consensus of opinion* is not only wordy but redundant. *Consensus* means *collective opinion* and gains nothing from the modifier *general*. Keep an eye out for the useless *you know*s when you write, and edit them out before you send your message.

- **Do not overexplain**. Some writers believe that putting in a lot of details will help make the subject matter clearer to the reader. This is not necessarily so. Too much detail or explanation can confuse rather than clarify, especially in a business communication.

- **Remember the second comma**. Parenthetic phrases (those not essential to the meaning of the sentence) should be set off with commas. Always be sure to put in the second one. Many writers put in the first comma and forget to use the second one. This rule also applies to the second comma after the year in a date or the state in an address when it is contained in a sentence: "On April 24, 1985, we received your order." "We shipped the order to your Akron, Ohio, office."

- **Use positive expressions**. Be definite and firm in your written messages. Instead of writing "We do not believe that we can accept your offer at this time," write "We cannot accept your offer at this time."

- **Use the first or third person**. This refers again to the active or passive voice. Many writers of business messages begin sentences with the word *it*, as in "It is found that . . . ." This is a weak way to state something, and you should avoid it when possible. Instead, try to be more direct and say "We have found that . . . ."

Reading the Written Communication

Just as there are techniques you can acquire to become a good listener when taking part in oral communication, there are techniques you can practice to improve your reading skills. Many are similar to those used for listening. As with writing, practice will improve your reading skills.

Here are some techniques to practice or keep in mind when you are reading:

- **Be comfortable**. This is true for all activities. The more comfortable you are, the better you can concentrate. If your back hurts or your legs are falling asleep, your mind will be on your physical discomfort rather than on what you are reading. Be sure that your chair and desk are adjusted so that you are physically at ease.

- **Have adequate lighting**. The company you work for is required by law to provide adequate and safe working conditions, which include adequate lighting. One problem with reading in the electronic office is glare on VDT screens. They should be placed in such a way as to avoid glare. If the glare is still objectionable, you can put an antiglare shade on the screen.

- **Have a noise-free environment**. Again, your company is responsible for providing an environment that is relatively noise-free. Some noise cannot be avoided in large offices. Do what you can to minimize it.

- **Keep eyeglasses clean**. If you must wear glasses to read, make sure they are clean.

- **Highlight important points**. In letters and memos, highlight with a colored marker or by underlining the important points so that you can see them at a glance. For long reports or books, make notes of the important points.

If your job requires you to read many long reports or books, there are speed-reading courses you can take. For ordinary work, such as reading letters, memos, and reports, this is probably not necessary. If your job is in a highly technical field, you will have to learn the jargon of the field and train yourself through practice to read technical material.

A good reading technique in any situation is scanning. Go through the material quickly at first, reading the table of contents and subheads, getting a picture in your mind of what the material is about and how the information flows. Then look for summary paragraphs at the ends of the chapters. After you have the general idea, go back and read more closely.

Forms of Written Business Communication

In the business office, most written messages take one of three forms:

- **Interoffice memorandums**—brief, direct, sometimes informal communication between or among people inside the organization.

- **Letters**—more formal communication with people outside the organization.

- **Reports**—often lengthy, researched, written messages communicating information in depth to people both inside and outside the organization.

You will encounter these typical forms of written communication on the job, both in hard copy and in soft copy. Because you will be involved in writing them as well as reading them, you should be familiar with each one.

Interoffice Memos

Like all other written communications, memos serve two basic functions: they transmit information, and they provide a record of the information and the fact that it was transmitted. Memos are most useful in the quick exchange of information among coworkers. Unfortunately, though, people do sometimes overuse them. In some organizations, people get into the habit of sending memos on everything they do. They do this for a good reason—to avoid being misunderstood—and for a questionable reason—to protect themselves by having a record. This way they can always prove exactly what their actions were in any situation. In most cases this is not necessary.

One good reason for using a memo is to avoid interrupting coworkers with telephone calls for business that is not really urgent. For messages that are complicated or where a record is really needed, memos are usually the best medium to use.

To speed up the preparation of memos, some companies provide forms with preprinted headings. The headings and the rest of the memo usually follow a set format:

- **Preprinted heading**—this usually includes the company's name or **logo** (identifying symbol), the title *Interoffice Memorandum*, and the words *To, From, Dept., Subject,* and *Date.*

- **Body**—the main part or message.

- **Closing**—the sender's signature or initials. Since the full sender's name is typed at the top after the word *From*, it is rarely typed again at the bottom. That would be a waste of time. It is customary for the person typing the memo to type his or her initials at the lower left margin.

Figure 6-3 shows a typical format for an interoffice memo.

In electronic and word processing offices memo formats can be stored on the system. Also, much information that is repeated can be automatically inserted.

Hard copies of memos are distributed by hand. You might deliver a memo personally if you needed an immediate response because of time pressures. Otherwise, you would use interoffice mail. Most larger companies have messengers who deliver interoffice mail, which is put in special envelopes for this purpose. In an electronic office, you would send memos via the electronic mail system.

Letters

When you or your supervisor must communicate in writing with someone outside your organization, the most common method would be by letter. Letters are usually more formal than memos because they mostly go to people outside doing business with your company. For this reason, it is essential that they create a good impression.

Like memos, letters have standard parts or sections. Since everyone is familiar with and expects to see these parts of a letter, using them helps the process of communication. Not using them or using them incorrectly can hinder communication. Let's take a look at the accepted parts of a letter:

- **Heading**—includes the company name or logo, which is usually preprinted and is called the **letterhead**, and the date line (giving the date the letter is written, which should be the same as the date when it is sent).

- **Opening**—includes the **inside address** (name, title, and address of the receiver) and **salutation** (greeting to the receiver: "Dear Ms. Jones" or "Dear Sally," depending on the degree of familiarity).

- **Body**—includes the subject line, if used (a brief statement of the main topic), and the text of the message.

- **Closing**—includes a complimentary phrase; the company signature (optional); the sender's signature and title; the typist's initials; notice of enclosure(s), if any; and notice of those receiving

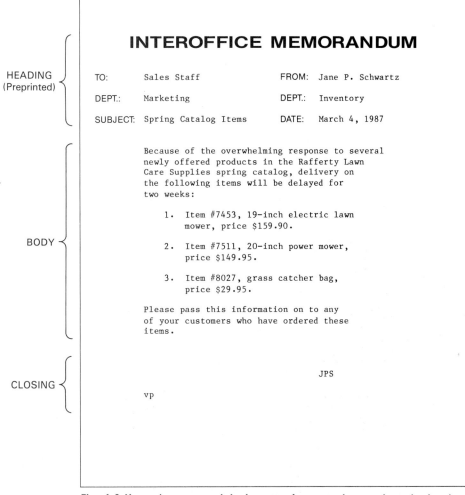

HEADING (Preprinted)

INTEROFFICE MEMORANDUM

TO: Sales Staff   FROM: Jane P. Schwartz

DEPT.:   Marketing   DEPT.: Inventory

SUBJECT: Spring Catalog Items DATE: March 4, 1987

BODY

Because of the overwhelming response to several newly offered products in the Rafferty Lawn Care Supplies spring catalog, delivery on the following items will be delayed for two weeks:

1. Item #7453, 19-inch electric lawn mower, price $159.90.

2. Item #7511, 20-inch power mower, price $149.95.

3. Item #8027, grass catcher bag, price $29.95.

Please pass this information on to any of your customers who have ordered these items.

JPS

CLOSING

vp

Fig. 6-3 If you have preprinted memo forms and are using electronic equipment, you must calculate where the words in the heading will fall so that they are positioned correctly after the guide words.

copies, if any. Sometimes a notice of those receiving "blind" copies is included. This appears on the sender's copy and selected others, but not on the receiver's copy, since the receiver is not to be informed of those receiving "blind" copies. A letter might also have a **postscript**, which is an addition to the body of the letter placed in the closing because the writer either forgot to include it earlier or intentionally wanted to emphasize this point. Figure 6-4 shows the parts of a typical business letter.

Business letters are written in one of four generally accepted formats. As you read earlier, formatting has to do with line indentation,

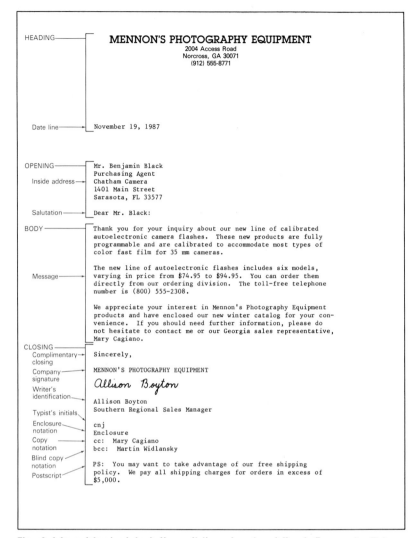

Fig. 6-4 In a block style letter, all lines begin at the left margin. This format is the easiest and fastest to type.

margins, and to some extent, punctuation. Let's look at the accepted letter formats:

■ **Block format.** In the block format, all letter parts begin at the left margin. This is the format of the letter shown in Fig. 6-4.

■ **Modified-block, standard format.** In this format all parts begin at the left margin except the date line, the complimentary closing, and the writer's identification, which start at the horizontal center of the page. Look at Fig. 6-5 for an example of a modified-block, standard format letter.

■ **Modified-block, indented paragraphs.** In this format the first line of each paragraph is usually indented five spaces. The date

ILLINOIS OFFICE TECHNOLOGIES, INC.
3200 South Michigan Avenue
Chicago, IL 60611
(312) 555-8700

August 22, 1987

Ms. Diane Nelson
Advertising Manager
Business Network Supplies Center
220 Delaware Avenue
Buffalo, NY 14202

Dear Ms. Nelson:

Would you please send me your current office supplies catalog
and price list? I am in charge of our company's reference
center and receive requests from my coworkers for office
supplies and equipment catalogs.

May I be put on your mailing list so that I will receive new
catalogs as they are available?

Sincerely,

ILLINOIS OFFICE TECHNOLOGIES, INC.

David P. Weinstein

David P. Weinstein
Reference Center Associate

pd

Fig. 6-5 The modified-block, standard format is the most frequently used format in business correspondence.

line, the complimentary closing, and the writer's identification start at the horizontal center of the page. Figure 6-6 shows a modified-block, indented paragraph format letter.

■ **Simplified format**. In this format all letter parts begin at the left margin. There is no salutation or complimentary closing, and the subject line and writer's identification are capitalized. See Fig. 6-7.

In the electronic and word processing office, the formats for these letter styles can be set up and stored on the system.

Although the general rule is to keep letters short—no more than one page—sometimes that isn't possible. When you have letters

```
                                        113 Oak Street
                                        Ridgewood, NJ 07451
                                        April 3, 1987


        Mr. William Chang
        Personnel Director
        The New Jersey Sentinel
        315 Terrace Avenue
        Hackensack, NJ 07604

        Dear Mr. Chang:

            Your advertisement for a well-rounded student with organi-
        zational skills for a summer word processing job was posted in
        the guidance center of Carlton Business School, where I am a
        student. I believe I am the student for whom you are looking.
        Let me explain why.

            As the enclosed resume illustrates, I am about to receive
        an associate's degree from Carlton, where I have been an honor
        student. My course of study has included not only shorthand
        and transcription, which, I'm sure you'll agree, are important
        skills, but also experience on most word processing equipment.
        In addition, for the last summer, I worked as a word processing
        operator at Hines & Crawford, a law firm in my home town of
        Ridgewood. I believe both my educational background and my
        work experience will help me satisfy the requirements for the
        job you need to fill this summer.

            I can begin work any time after June 15.

            You can reach me at 555-5165 any day after 4 p.m. May I
        have a personal interview at your convenience?

                                        Sincerely,

                                        Brenda Coleman

                                        Brenda Coleman

        Enclosure
```

**Fig. 6-6 A letter in modified-block style with indented paragraphs; the
paragraphs are usually but not always indented five spaces.**

consisting of two or more pages, you need a format for the pages
after page 1. The following rules can apply to all letters:

- Use plain paper without a letterhead but of the same size and
  quality as page 1.

- Have the same side margins as on page 1.

- Start the first line at least 1 inch, but no more than 2 inches, from
  the top.

- Have a heading on each page after page 1 that includes the addressee's name, the page number, and the date. These can all be
  on one line, which saves space; or each element can be on a
  separate line.

STETSON'S EDUCATIONAL AMUSEMENTS
718 Stadium Drive
San Antonio, TX 78412
(512) 555-7355

February 17, 1987

Tots & Teddy Bears
Nursery Schools, Inc.
116 West 3rd Street
Tulsa, OK 74103

NURSERY SCHOOL EDUCATIONAL PRODUCTS

Tots & Teddy Bears Nursery Schools are synonymous with excellence in preschool education--we know a lot about you! Because
we're interested in the same thing as you, we want you to get to
know more about us.

Stetson's Educational Amusements is an internationally respected
developer and marketer of educational toys. Our staff of educa-
tors and instructional designers develops toys especially helpful
to preschoolers, ages 2 to 5. You'll find our pegboards, musical
instruments, and, yes, even our computers, in every state domes-
tically and in 41 countries internationally.

We must be doing something right, as you are! In order that you
might join forces with us in the important area of early education,
I've enclosed our new catalog of preschool products. Won't you
call us, toll free, at (800) 555-4447, to help your preschoolers
learn that thinking is fun? Each day's delay could mean a more
difficult job for you and your staff without Stetson's Educational
Amusements to help you.

Amy D'Angelo

AMY D'ANGELO - ADVERTISING AND PRODUCTION DIRECTOR

cnj
Enclosure

PS: For a limited time only, we are offering first-time customers, <u>absolutely free</u>, a bonus of two 6' x 8' wall hangings on
learning numbers and the alphabet the visual (easy) way! Offer
free until May 1.

Fig. 6-7 In the simplified letter style, a subject line replaces the salutation.

Envelopes for mailing letters will carry the company's name and address, usually in the upper left corner, but sometimes on the back flap. The company's logo may also appear on the envelope. The receiver's name, title, and address are usually typed in block format.

Typical Business Letters

Most business activities fall into a few broad categories. Your letters will mirror these categories. There will, of course, always be special or unique letters that you and your supervisor prepare, but the majority of the letters will fall into one of these categories:

■ Request and inquiry letters

■ Response letters

■ Goodwill letters

- Refusal letters
- Claim letters and adjustment letters
- Credit and collection letters
- Sales letters

Here are some samples of each of these categories to give you an idea of how they are written, their content, and their format.

Request and Inquiry Letters These, along with response letters, make up the bulk of most business correspondence. Businesses generate a constant flow of letters seeking information, requesting goods or materials, asking for favors or reservations, and so on. These letters should be brief, to the point, and worded to encourage a fast response. See Fig. 6-5, showing the modified-block format, for an example of a letter requesting free material.

Response Letters As their name implies, these letters are written in response to a received letter, which usually has asked for information or material. Response letters should directly answer the request, and they should be prepared and sent promptly.

Organizations that receive many similar request letters usually have a form letter or boilerplate with which to respond. In a word processing or electronic office, form letters or boilerplate appear to be personalized and original by the use of the merge function discussed in Chapter 3.

A form letter would no doubt be used by the Business Network Supplies Center to reply to the customer's request shown in Fig. 6-5. In an electronic office, you could personalize the response by adding information aimed specifically at Mr. Weinstein's company, thus possibly stimulating business.

Your response letter could look like this:

Dear Mr. Weinstein:

The enclosed summer catalog includes the latest product and price listings from Business Network Supplies Center. You may find the information about our new telecommunications equipment on pages 49 to 61 especially interesting.

Your name has been placed on our mailing list as you requested. You will automatically receive all our new-product announcements as well as our seasonal catalogs. The next one will be available in September.

Thank you for writing Business Network Supplies Center. We are proud of our products and look forward to serving your company.

Cordially,

(Your name)
Product Liaison Representative

Goodwill Letters All letters should have a friendly tone and serve as goodwill builders. Some letters are written specifically to generate goodwill for a company. Such letters include announcements, invitations, and messages of sympathy, appreciation, congratulations, and praise.

Goodwill letters should be written promptly, and they should be enthusiastic, somewhat informal, and—most important—sincere. If the sincerity is forced, the letter may seem hypocritical and do more harm than good. Here is a simple goodwill-building letter:

Dear Michael:

The seminar that you organized, "Living With Automation," was the best of its kind. I want you to know how thoroughly my staff enjoyed it.

All your speakers were excellent, but my staff identified Jonah Stonington, who covered voice-activated input, as the best. He reportedly presented a very technical topic with ease and humor—not an easy task, as I'm sure you know.

Attending seminars like yours is time well spent. My staff and I look forward to the next seminar in your series on office automation.

Cordially,

Ryan Manning
Personnel Manager

Refusal Letters While you may not be able to build goodwill with a refusal letter, the objective is to avoid destroying goodwill as much as possible. The purpose of a refusal letter is to tell someone no, and few of us react well to negative news. But refusal letters become necessary when you do not have the information requested, or you are out of stock on an item, or the request is simply unreasonable.

Framing refusal letters is a real test of writing skills. You must find a way to phrase a negative response in a positive way. The refusal letter below says no in a helpful and tactful tone. It also sets a positive note by suggesting a course of action that would result in the no becoming yes.

Dear Mrs. Rios:

Thank you for your letter asking for a special discount on your quarterly copier-paper order. As a valued customer, you and your firm—Rios Hardware—know that our prices are quite competitive and that under certain circumstances we have a discount policy.

Our discount policy is explained on the back of our invoices, included with your orders. That policy allows a 10 percent discount on orders exceeding 500 sheets.

We noted in a review of your account, Mrs. Rios, that you order quarterly in amounts of about 250 sheets, which unfortunately does not qualify for the discount. May we suggest that instead of ordering for a quarter, you anticipate your paper needs for longer periods. If you combine your fall and winter or spring and summer orders, they will probably exceed the 500-sheet minimum and qualify for the discount.

We appreciate your business and hope our suggestion will help our valued customer, Rios Hardware.

Sincerely,

Samuel P. Schwartz
Marketing Agent

Claim Letters and Adjustment Letters In the business world, you will more likely be the recipient of claim letters than of adjustment letters. Despite all efforts to be precise and accurate, things can go wrong. A claim letter usually contains a complaint about something, such as slow service, faulty or wrong merchandise, invoice errors, or even discourteous service. A claim letter is an attempt to get satisfaction from a company in the form of an explanation, a compensation, or a replacement.

As the receiver of a claim letter, you promptly write an adjustment letter, in which you are trying to rectify the mistake and provide satisfaction for the person who has lodged the complaint.

If you are writing a claim letter, keep it short, direct, and specific. If you are writing an adjustment letter, be sure you are familiar with your company's policies on claims and adjustments. You must also keep customer satisfaction as your primary objective.

The following are examples of claim and adjustment letters:

Claim Letter

To Whom It May Concern:

The digital AM/FM clock-radio that I ordered from Ridgeway Electronics arrived yesterday. It was poorly packed, and the plastic shelf over the radio call numbers was smashed.

I used your mail-order toll-free number for out-of-state residents to order this product. I ordered it on January 25 and charged it to my MasterCard credit card, number 5183-0005-0992-8554. The clock-radio model number is AX 411.

I am returning the damaged product in this package and would like you to replace it with an undamaged one. If possible, please send me the replacement within the next two weeks.

Sincerely,

(Mrs.) Dorothy Marceau

Adjustment Letter

Dear Mrs. Marceau:

A new digital AM/FM clock-radio is being shipped to you today. You should receive it within two weeks.

We appreciate your detailed explanation and prompt return of the damaged product, which made it possible for us to make the replacement quickly. We are sorry for any inconvenience this has caused you. Enclosed is a copy of Ridgeway's monthly listening guide to local radio programming. We hope it increases your listening pleasure.

We look forward to serving you further.

Cordially,

Peter Levertov
Claims and Adjustments Manager

Credit and Collection Letters The clock-radio referred to in the previous letter was purchased with a credit card. Credit cards are used extensively for personal and business expenses. Perhaps you have used one. To obtain a credit card, you apply to the sponsoring store or bank using an application form. The store or bank then checks your financial record and responds favorably or unfavorably.

The credit letter telling you whether or not your application has been accepted is often a form letter or boilerplate. If you worked in a word processing or electronic office, all you would need to do to write a credit letter is call up the form letter on the computer and insert the specific information, such as the applicant's name and address.

You should use a positive, warm tone when you write credit letters either approving or rejecting an applicant. Here are samples of both:

Credit Letter (Approving)

Dear Miss Lauro:

Congratulations on joining the Halls family of credit customers. Your charge card is enclosed, and we are certain that its use will make your shopping more convenient.

As a valued credit customer, you are entitled to special treatment at Halls. Your charge card can be used to purchase all our services and merchandise. In addition, you will receive our monthly catalogs announcing sales *before they are publicly advertised*! You will be invited to our biannual fashion shows featuring the latest styles from New York, Paris, Milan, and Tokyo. And bring a friend to our exquisite dining facilities on our seventh floor—you will both be offered a complimentary dessert of your choice.

Terms for your charge card use are explained in the enclosed contract. We hope you enjoy the privileges of our special family of Halls charge-card holders, Miss Lauro. We welcome you and look forward to serving you.

Sincerely,

Danielle Watson
Credit Supervisor

Credit Letter (Rejecting)

Dear Miss Lauro:

The Halls Department Store staff always appreciates hearing from a customer. Thank you for submitting a credit application.

As is our policy, we carefully reviewed the information on your application form. Since you do, at this time, have a number of loan commitments, may we suggest that you continue to allow Halls to serve you on a cash basis.

The personnel at Halls look forward to continuing their present association with you, Miss Lauro. Should you resubmit your application for credit when you have fewer loan commitments, we will welcome the opportunity to reconsider it.

Sincerely,

Danielle Watson
Credit Supervisor

Despite careful checking, department stores and banks always encounter some credit customers who do not pay promptly. When a customer has defaulted on several payments, a collection notice is sent. Again, these notices are often form letters or boilerplate. When a person first fails to pay on time, the first notice is usually a polite reminder. If payment is not made over a period of time, the collection letters become increasingly stern. The final collection letter is a stern demand for payment, often threatening legal action. Here is an example of such a letter:

Collection Letter

Dear Miss Lauro:

This is our fourth and final reminder that your payment of $149.95 on your Halls account is overdue. If payment is not received by October 15, we will unfortunately be forced to turn your account over to a collection agency.

We realize that such a drastic step might damage your credit reputation, and we sincerely hope that it will not be necessary for us to do this. We take this action only when we believe that a customer has no intention of paying. You can prevent this action, Miss Lauro, by sending your payment of $149.95 by the above-stated date.

Sincerely,

Danielle Watson
Credit Supervisor

Sales Letters "Have confidence in *your* future—call Mutual Insurance of Tampa." "Experience what it means to relax and enjoy yourself—come to the American Riviera Hotel!" "Try us on—you'll like the way you'll stand out in Burnstein's fashionable leather shoes!"

You read words like these all the time—in newspaper ads, on billboards, and in letters. Letters whose verbal messages are like this are called *sales letters*. A **sales letter** is a written message selling a service or merchandise.

To be effective, sales letters must be aimed at specific audiences or markets. The letters try to highlight what will appeal to the particular audience. The letters also try to be eye-catching or graphically dramatic.

The electronic office makes it possible to develop eye-catching graphics in the form of tables, graphs, diagrams, and flowcharts. Also, printers in an electronic office can reproduce photographs and print in colors and various sizes.

A computer can easily make charts and graphs to visually illustrate data.

Reports A report is a lengthy and researched written message intended to communicate facts and ideas to people inside or outside the company. Because reports are in-depth, their preparation requires more time and effort than the preparation of most business letters and memos. When you compile a report, you should take the following steps:

1. State the objective.
2. Prepare an outline.
3. Carry out the research.
4. Write the report.
5. Proofread the report.

To prepare an outline, list all the sections that the report will have. Under each section list all the topics you will cover. For a very detailed outline, you could list the main point of each paragraph you will write. You use indentation to show that a paragraph or idea belongs in a broader section. Use the outline as a guide when you write the report, but be flexible and make changes as the facts and flow dictate. Figure 6-8 shows a sample outline for a business report.

Report Parts Like letters and memos, reports have specific parts. To be complete, your report should have some or all of the following features:

■ **Title page**. The first page of the report, the title page includes the report's title, receivers, author, and submission date. See Fig. 6-9 for an example of a report title page.

■ **Preface**. An introductory statement of what the report contains.

■ **Table of contents**. A list of the various sections of the report. Figure 6-10 shows a typical table of contents.

■ **List of illustrations**. A list of pictures and graphics with page numbers.

■ **Synopsis**. A brief summary of the main points and conclusions.

■ **Body of text**. The main message of the report.

■ **Appendix**. A supplementary section containing supporting documents or data.

■ **Bibliography**. A list of the books and periodicals used as sources. Each entry in the bibliography includes author's name, title of source, publisher, place of publication, and date of publication. The entries should be listed alphabetically by author's last name.

■ **Index**. An alphabetical list of significant words.

■ **Letter of transmittal**. Usually a memo accompanying the report. It explains the report and asks for reactions. The letter of transmittal resembles the interoffice memo in Fig. 6-3.

```
        REPORT OF THE OFFICE EQUIPMENT COMMITTEE


  I.   PURPOSE OF STUDY - PHOTOCOPIER NEEDED


  II.  SCOPE OF STUDY

       A.  Copying needs - by department
       B.  Equipment available


  III. PROCEDURES

       A.  How much copying do we do?
           1.  Volume
           2.  Paper sizes used
           3.  Capabilities used
           4.  How many machines?  What kinds?
           5.  Changes projected?
       B.  Machines tested
           1.  Capabilities
           2.  Performance
           3.  Costs for leasing or buying
           4.  Service contracts available
       C.  User reactions - by department


  IV.  FINDINGS


  V.   RECOMMENDATIONS AND CONCLUSIONS
```

Fig. 6-8 An outline can be an invaluable guide in helping you to prepare a report.

Report Format   The parts of the report have specific formats, just as letters do. The parts of the report usually appear in a specific order, and different formats are used to distinguish between them.

■ **Preliminary materials**. All the parts that precede the body of text. These pages are numbered consecutively with small roman numerals, except for the title page, which is not numbered.

■ **Main text**. The body of the text, the appendix, the bibliography, and the index. These pages are numbered consecutively with arabic numbers.

■ **Page beginners**. These are the first pages of major, independent sections of the report. They include the title page and the first

```
              COMPARISON AND ANALYSIS OF
                 NEW-PRODUCT REVENUE

                1984, 1985, and 1986




                     Prepared by

                   Michael Muller
                Director of Marketing

                 January 31, 1987




                     Prepared for

          General Management and Stockholders
               of Bronson Laboratories
```

Fig. 6-9 The title page of a report may sometimes include the name of the person to whom the report is being submitted.

page of the preface, the table of contents, the list of illustrations, the synopsis, the body of the text, the appendix, the bibliography, and the index. In some reports the beginners are all separate pages, just as the title page is. In others the beginning of a new section is indicated by a title for the section located about one third of the way down the page, with the body of the section starting about four spaces below that. For a very lengthy report divider pages with tabs may be used.

As you can see, written communication will fill a large part of your working day in an office. You will be a valued worker if you can use these skills effectively and adapt them to your particular work environment.

```
                    TABLE OF CONTENTS


     I.   Summary ...................................................   1


          A.  Purpose ...............................................   2
          B.  Scope .................................................   3
          C.  Objective ............................................   3


    II.   Identification of New Products,
          1984-1986 .................................................   4


   III.   Markets for New Products ..................................   6


    IV.   Market Success for New Products ...........................   8


     V.   Revenue Generated from New Products, ......................  12


    VI.   Conclusions and Recommendations ...........................  15


   Appendixes ......................................................  17

   Bibliography ....................................................  19

   Index ...........................................................  21
```

Fig. 6-10 The contents page is usually prepared last, after all the page numbers for the body of the report have been determined.

■ Summary

- ■ Writing skills in the electronic office are just as important as in the traditional office, and in some ways they are more so. Speed and the immediacy of communicating with a computer require accuracy in spelling, punctuation, and usage.

- ■ Written communication does not have the spontaneity of oral communication. But it has the advantages of giving you time to prepare a message and creating a permanent record of it. An exception to this is interactive communication via a computer, in which written words are sent and responded to immediately.

- ■ Well-written communications are a characteristic of a well-run company.

- Writing is a skill that can be acquired and improved with practice. There are general writing techniques and usage skills that you can use to improve your writing.

- Some general writing techniques are being yourself, knowing your reader, exercising empathy, being courteous, and keeping to the point. A good writer is results-oriented, organizes the message; is clear, specific, complete, and accurate; avoids jargon; and proofreads.

- The basic usage skills include knowing grammar, punctuation, and spelling. Other worthwhile usage skills include being consistent in format and style, using the active voice and the first or third person, and using the second comma where needed. Being concise, not overexplaining, and using positive expressions improve writing.

- Being a good reader is like being a good listener. Techniques to improve your reading skills include being comfortable in a noise-free environment with adequate lighting, highlighting important points in the text, learning the language of your field, and scanning the material.

- Most written communications in the office are in the form of memos, letters, or reports. Memos, the briefest and least formal of the three, are best for messages that cannot be easily communicated orally.

- Letters are most frequently used to communicate with people outside the company, and they have standard parts and accepted, traditional formats. In an electronic office, the computer can set up letter formats automatically, but you need to know which format to choose.

- Most business letters fall into these categories: request and inquiry, response, goodwill, refusal, claim and adjustment, credit and collection, and sales. Each type of letter requires its own tone.

- Some companies have standard form, or boilerplate, letters. With electronic technology, graphics such as tables, diagrams, and photographs can be easily produced and added to written communications.

- Reports are the longest form of written communication in the office. The writer must state the objective, prepare an outline, do research, write the report, and proofread. Like letters and memos, reports have specific parts and formats.

■ Review Questions

1. What are the main differences between written and oral communication?

2. List the usage skills mentioned in the text, and give examples of each.

3. What steps can a writer take to prevent miscommunication in writing?

4. Compare and contrast reading and listening skills.

5. What are the most frequently used written communications in a business office? What are their main uses?

6. Describe the four accepted letter formats.

7. What tone would you adopt in each of the following letters: a goodwill letter, a response to an inquiry, a credit refusal, a claim letter, a sales letter, and a collection letter?

8. Describe the steps you might take in preparing a written report. What parts do you want to be sure to include in the finished product?

■ Technical Vocabulary

turnaround time
interactive
jargon
thesaurus
format
logo

letterhead
inside address
salutation
postscript
sales letter

■ Discussion and Skills Development

1. To sharpen your skill in developing an outline, read an article in a newspaper or magazine. To make an outline to show the major and minor points that the writer has made, use a highlighting marker to underline the most important point in each paragraph. List these points in order, and decide which points you want to indent on the list to show related ideas.

2. Review all your mail (or that of your parents—with their permission) for a few days. Look especially at what we call "junk mail" for various examples of letters. Identify letter parts, letter formats, and kinds of letters. Answer one of the letters. How did you respond to it? Was it effective? Did it seem to meet its objectives? Write the names of the parts and the format on the letter, as well as the type of letter it is. Write a one- or two-paragraph report on your reaction.

3. Read some articles in magazines. (Look in your school library for magazines such as *Words, The Office, Management Technology, Today's Office,* and *Office Administration and Automation,* although any will do.) Look for examples of wordiness or imprecision. Decide how the wordy phrases can be reduced to one word. Edit the articles to eliminate poor writing practices. Explain your editing.

4. Wordiness—using more than one word to say something when one word will do—is something of which many writers are guilty. There are many phrases which we tend to use almost automatically and which add to the number of words without adding anything to the meaning. A common example is *due to the fact that*. It is much better to write *because* or *since*. Look at the phrases below, and think of one or two words that could replace each.

- at that/this point in time
- if you would be so kind as to
- during the time that
- destroyed by fire
- do not pay any attention to
- came into contact with

Think of other wordy phrases that you hear or read a lot. Make a list of them, and include the one or two words that can replace each one.

chapter 7
Data Creation and Input

When secretaries and other office workers take dictation or keyboard documents into a computer or perform any of a number of other similar tasks, they are inputting data. In other words, they are transferring data from the message sender's mind to a typewriter or computer so that it can be processed into information and sent out as a finished document. This, of course, is the inputting part of the IPSOD cycle.

Before data can be input, however, it must be organized using some data. Methods of preparing input vary, depending on the form of the data and the input devices available. If the media for organizing the data is dictation, and if the input device is a typewriter, then the method used might be taking and transcribing shorthand. In this case inputting involves translating data from one form into another. On the other hand, if the data consists of figures stored in a computer, and if the input device is a computer terminal, then the method used would be electronic retrieval. Inputting in this case involves extracting data.

As methods of inputting and the variety of input devices have grown, so has the range of skills needed to handle this phase of the information processing cycle.

This chapter explains different media and devices used to organize and input data to be processed. You will learn how to gather data from various sources and convert it into a form that you and other office workers can interpret and process. Then we will invite you, figuratively, to sit down in front of a computer terminal and begin to learn how to operate it.

Data Collection

If you pictured information processing in terms of building a house, the inputting step would be the equivalent of assembling the raw materials and preparing the building site before construction can begin. In information processing, your raw materials are data and your site preparation is collecting the data and inputting it into a typewriter or computer so that you can begin processing it. Of course, when you input into a typewriter, inputting and processing are going on at the same time. Inputting into a computer is a more distinct step. (See Fig. 7-1.)

You begin inputting by assembling your data, consisting of the numbers, words, and facts that will be processed into information. Data can come from a variety of sources. You collect data when you take dictation from a supervisor, when you retrieve previously processed documents from a computer disk, or when you receive the year's sales figures from the sales department.

The data you collect will come in several different forms. Some will be in the form of hard copy. Handwritten notes from a supervisor, books, typed reports, letters, and memos may all be hard-copy sources of data.

Other data will be in electronic form, that is, it will already be stored on the computer system you are using. When someone re-

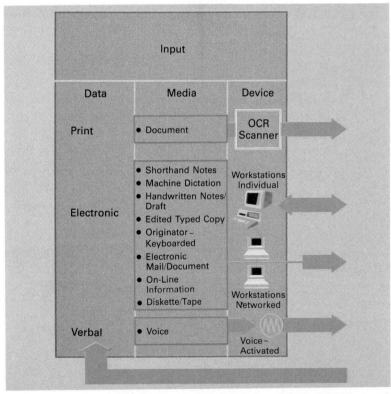

Fig. 7-1 Data that is to be input can appear in a variety of forms and in many different media.

ceives a memo by means of electronic mail or obtains data from a computer data base, he or she is collecting data that has been stored on electronic media, such as a tape or disk. The data is retrieved as soft copy.

Another form of data is spoken or verbal data. When you take down figures over the telephone or transcribe from a dictation machine, you are receiving verbal data. It is even possible to have **voice input** directly into a computer without having to use a keyboard. This technology is available today, but is still very costly.

The Role of the Office Worker

Secretaries, administrative assistants, and other office workers play a big role in the process of gathering and inputting data. We've already mentioned several ways in which office workers gather data, such as taking dictation and searching data bases. When you perform these tasks, you have to call on a number of skills. First, you have to know how to gather and organize the appropriate materials. This might mean simply pulling the right file folder, or it might mean conducting research through the use of an on-line data base.

You also have to learn to schedule your time. You need to arrange the order in which you perform each job so that you do high-priority tasks first and less important tasks later. For efficient inputting, you need a good command of basic language skills. You might be expected to reword or recast rough drafts or to fill in blanks when your supervisor doesn't have the necessary data handy. Moreover, for transcribing shorthand, good language skills are essential. You should, therefore, keep frequently used reference materials handy.

You will also need a good working knowledge of basic office procedures. It may be part of your job, for example, to plan and schedule time for office workers who share word processing or microcomputer equipment. To do that, you would need to know when the system is available, which office workers are working on high-priority jobs, and how long each job is expected to take.

Input Media

Office workers use a variety of media for inputting data. They take and transcribe shorthand, they feed hard copy into optical character scanners, they keyboard handwritten drafts into computers, they retrieve documents from computer disks. You will need to know how to work with all of these media and to recognize when one form of input is more efficient than another. If you work for more than one person, for example, it may be more efficient for each supervisor to use a dictation machine or to keyboard rough drafts than to give you shorthand dictation. You might be able to increase an office's productivity by suggesting how input can be handled most efficiently in different situations. The next few pages explain the basic types of input media you might use in an electronic office.

Face-to-face dictation is an excellent method of input because it allows for interaction between the dictator and the secretary.

Dictation   When a person dictates the contents of a document, he or she reads or says it out loud so that someone else can record it. Many executives outline the contents of their correspondence or make notes before dictating directly to a secretary or into a dictation machine.

Since most people can talk much faster than they can write in longhand or type on a keyboard, dictation is a highly efficient means of originating and organizing data for a document. The media used most commonly for dictation in the office are shorthand notes or machine dictation. A device called a shorthand machine is also sometimes used.

Shorthand   A few years ago people were predicting that dictation machines and word processors would eliminate the need for shorthand in the electronic office. On the contrary, shorthand remains such a highly valued skill that it can add thousands of dollars a year to an office worker's salary.

Shorthand remains in demand for several reasons. Some executives prefer to dictate to a secretary because they can better organize their thoughts and speak faster than they can handwrite the data. Some executives may feel uncomfortable talking out loud to a machine. Others have difficulty operating dictation machines or find it difficult to articulate their thoughts in this manner. And there are many executives who are simply accustomed to giving dictation directly to another person and don't want to change their working methods.

Dictation has a number of advantages. It offers office workers an opportunity for human contact, which they may welcome as they spend more and more time working with electronic devices. Many supervisors find that face-to-face dictation helps them organize and verbalize their ideas. And if they change their minds about something they have dictated, it is easy to go back and make corrections.

Another important reason why shorthand is still valued is that it can help preserve confidentiality in offices where executives and office workers deal with sensitive information. Until it is processed into a letter or report, the information exists only in the minds of the executive and assistant, and in hard-to-read shorthand symbols. It is not on a dictation tape, which anyone might hear, or in a draft form, which anyone might read.

Shorthand is also an invaluable tool to the office worker who must carry out a wide variety of administrative support duties. He or she may use shorthand to make notes while doing research, to take down telephone messages accurately and quickly, to take the minutes of meetings, and so on. For all of these reasons, shorthand remains an essential skill, even in the most advanced electronic office.

Taking Dictation

When you work in an office where you are expected to take dictation, you need to observe some basic rules. Preparing yourself ahead of time means that you will always be ready when your boss wants to dictate a letter or memo.

- **Supplies**. Always keep a plentiful supply of pads and pens or pencils handy, and mark off the used area of your notebook with a rubber band.

- **Special Tools**. Have a red pencil handy to note down instructions, and carry a folder and paper clips to hold and mark any papers you may have to take away with you. Some secretaries use **editor's clips**, which are brightly colored, triangular plastic clips used for color-coding related notebook pages and documents. Rush items should be marked with a paper clip or by a turned-down corner of a notebook page.

- **Separating Items**. The first notebook page you use should be dated at the bottom of the page and marked "a.m." or "p.m." so that you can locate a specific segment of the notes later on. You should also leave a space between each item of dictation so that you can add instructions in red about how to mail the item or how many copies to make and so on.

- **Changes**. You can insert small changes as you go along or add a long change at the bottom of the item and indicate where to insert it. If your supervisor tends to make frequent changes, leave one column on the notebook page free for them.

- **Spellings**. Spell out names and technical terms in longhand. You should also copy names and addresses from incoming documents to avoid misspellings and mistakes.

- **End marks**. Mark the end of each item with some distinctive symbol so that you can tell at a glance where each item begins and ends.

- **Numbering**. One way to organize your shorthand notes is to number each letter or memo requiring an answer and then number each corresponding item of dictation.

- **Questions**. If a question occurs to you while you are taking dictation, mark a large "X" in your notebook so that you can find it easily when the dictation is finished.

- **Complete Records**. If you are asked to take dictation when a notebook is not available, date the paper you take the notes on and staple it in your notebook so that you'll have a complete record of all your dictation.

- **Printed Forms**. If the dictation is material to be inserted on a printed form, number each item in your notes to correspond to each item on the form. If possible, obtain a copy of the form and attach it to your notebook.

Transcribing Shorthand Dictation

Taking shorthand dictation is only half the job. Transcribing it is the other half. Here are some procedures for transcribing shorthand notes:

- Assemble all your materials and information before you begin so you won't have to interrupt your work to look for things.

- Establish the priority or importance of each item you must transcribe, and begin with top-priority items that must be processed immediately.

- Check the instructions for each item before you begin to transcribe, and always make at least one copy of each item you transcribe.

- Check spellings, addresses, technical terms, and any other important details before you begin.

- Transcribe directly from your notes. Check each segment of your notes for grammatical errors, incomplete sentences, and any changes and additions as you work along.

Transcribing shorthand notes using a word processor enables the secretary to edit the work while it is being keyboarded and then again when it is proofread.

- Avoid making paragraphs too long or too short. Do not make a paragraph more than eight or ten lines long.

- Before you remove the document from a typewriter or print it out on a word processor or computer, check it over for errors.

- Cancel each shorthand item in your notebook with a diagonal line after you transcribe it. Keep a rubber band around the last page you've transcribed so you'll know where to begin again.

- Always check your notebook at the end of each day to make sure that you have transcribed all your notes. If any work remains undone, do it the next day after you have transcribed that day's priority items.

Machine Dictation

Office workers in many companies transcribe machine dictation as well as their own shorthand notes. With dictation machines, supervisors can dictate when no one is available to take notes. For example, managers can dictate while away from the office on a business trip or after working hours at their own convenience. This method of originating data provides a great deal of flexibility for the manager. The machines record the dictation on tape, just as a home tape recorder records music or other sounds. Office workers use similar machines, or sometimes the same machines, to play back the recordings and transcribe the dictation. Several types of machine dictation/transcription equipment are used in the electronic office.

Desk-Top Dictation Machines Desk-top machines record dictation on minicassettes or somewhat larger standard cassettes much like those used for music. Desk-top machines are used primarily by executives who dictate frequently while working in their offices. Some desk-top units can record dictation but cannot play it back for transcription. Others can be used for transcribing but not for recording. **Combination units** can be used for both purposes.

Some desk-top machines have automatic controls that can be used for indexing the dictation, scanning to find a particular spot on the tape, and other operations.

Portable Dictation Machines Small, lightweight dictation machines that run on batteries can be used in automobiles and in other places where there are no electrical outlets. These machines record dictation on minicassettes or on smaller microcassettes. Portable machines are ideal for executives who want to dictate at home or on business trips, but they lack some of the advanced features that are available on desk-top units.

Centralized Dictation Systems Organizations in which hundreds of employees originate documents may have a centralized dictation system. In such a system, originators call a central recording device to dictate.

In some centralized systems, dictation is recorded on endless loops. An **endless loop** is a long tape, joined at the ends, that stays inside the recording device and stores the dictation for hundreds of documents. As the device records the newest dictation, it erases the oldest input automatically. Many operators can transcribe different documents from an endless loop simultaneously.

In other systems, input from many originators is recorded on multiple-cassette machines. The machines also display information about how much dictation has been recorded on each cassette, whether each cassette is still receiving dictation or can be transcribed, and so on. Unlike endless loops, cassettes can be removed from the machines and distributed, so transcribers don't need to work together in one central location.

In any centralized dictation system, a supervisor assigns dictation to operators. The supervisor may use a computer terminal to keep track of the work load, turnaround times, priorities, the status of each document, and so on.

Transcribing Machine Dictation

To transcribe machine dictation without disturbing others in the office, you need a transcription machine or combination unit with earphones. Here are some procedures for transcribing machine dictation.

■ Transcription machines have hand or foot controls that enable you to stop, start, or play back dictation. If you are using hand controls, place the control unit near your keyboard so that you

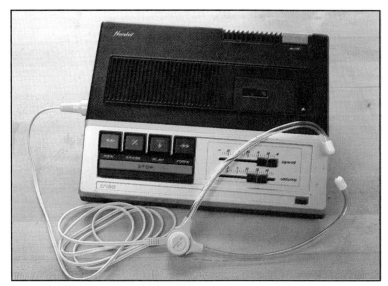

A portable dictation machine (left) is especially useful for executives who travel on extended trips. The executive may mail the cassette to his secretary so that it can be transcribed without delay. Because they are so versatile, transcription machines (right) have good sound quality and may have many optional features, such as adjustable speeds.

won't waste time or effort moving between the keyboard and the controls.

- Follow the procedures outlined in your machine's operating manual on how to insert the recorded medium. Also consult the manual for other information about operating your particular machine. Each type of transcription machine has its own procedures.

- If your supervisor uses indicator slips, place the slip for the tape you are transcribing in the space provided for it on the front of the machine. An **indicator slip**, also called an index slip, is a specially marked piece of paper on which the originator notes where each dictated document ends and any special instructions for processing it.

- If your transcription machine features electronic scanning, use this feature to scan for any special processing instructions the originator may have included.

- From the originator's instructions, determine the priority of each dictated document. Transcribe the highest-priority items first.

- Determine whether you are transcribing a finished document or a draft. If the dictation is straightforward and the originator customarily makes few changes, prepare a finished document, but if the dictation is complicated or the originator usually likes to make several changes, prepare a draft. Mark the draft with the date and the word *draft*.

■ Try to estimate how long each item is so that you can plan the margins, line lengths, and spacing.

■ Coordinate your keyboarding with your listening. If you don't hear part of the dictation, or if you don't remember it, stop keyboarding and use the playback control to listen to it again. As you develop your listening skills, your memory span will increase, and you will be able to type longer phrases without pausing.

■ Listen to complete sentences or clauses so that you can understand the context in which soundalike words are used. Examples of words that sound alike but are used in different contexts are *there* and *their*, *billed* and *build*, and *air* and *heir*.

■ Sometimes the originator indicates punctuation, but if not, listen to pauses in the dictation so that you can determine where to insert punctuation marks. The voice should indicate when you have come to the end of a sentence or a clause, whether to end a sentence with a period or a question mark, and so on.

■ Ask another office worker to listen to any part of a recording that you cannot hear distinctly. If that doesn't resolve the problem, keyboard the dictation as it sounds to you, or substitute a word that you think will be appropriate. If you do this, however, always check with the originator when you submit the hard copy to see if the word you used is correct.

■ Just as with shorthand transcription, you should always review each page for errors before you remove it from the typewriter or print it out.

Shorthand Machines

Conventional shorthand notes and tape recordings are the media most often used for dictation, but some situations call for shorthand machines. A **shorthand machine** is a portable device with keys that are pressed in combinations to produce several letters of each word. Shorthand machine operators, who have special training in using these devices, can record up to 250 words a minute, which is more than twice as fast as most people can take shorthand notes by hand.

Shorthand machines are especially useful in situations where many people are talking. They are used to record what people say during trials, public hearings, and some special business meetings, when participants require official records of the proceedings. If you make arrangements for such a meeting, you might obtain the services of a shorthand machine operator from a court reporting service, which you could find in your telephone directory.

Computer-Aided Transcription

Traditional shorthand machines quietly print the notations on paper, and the operators later transcribe them on a typewriter or word processor. On newer models, however, pressing the keys produces electrical impulses that the machine records on cassette tapes. The operator then inserts the cassette into a special computer component, which converts the impulses into words and displays them on a screen. Using the computer keyboard, the operator edits and formats the transcript and then prints out hard copies. This use of shorthand machines linked with computer technology to produce edited transcripts is called **computer-aided transcription**.

Drafts

The input data you work with will not always consist of shorthand notes or tape recordings, of course. Sometimes you may prepare documents from drafts that have been typed, written in longhand, keyboarded, or printed out from a computer, shorthand machine, or computer-aided transcription machine. A **draft** is a preliminary rough copy on which you can write corrections and editing changes to guide you in preparing a final, finished document. Drafts may be in the form of hard copy or soft copy.

Longhand   In today's offices about 50 percent of all documents are originated in longhand, while shorthand dictation and machine dictation account for about 25 percent each. Many people find that they can better express themselves by writing in longhand rather than by dictating or keyboarding. In addition, handwritten drafts offer the advantages of convenience and privacy. Executives can compose memos on airplanes and in other public places without disturbing others and without being overheard as they might be if they used dictation machines.

The biggest disadvantage of longhand, of course, is that it is not always legible to others. The reader may need to keep checking the accuracy of anything he or she cannot read clearly, causing the loss of valuable time. It is expected that as more executives become accustomed to using keyboards, the use of longhand will become less prevalent in the electronic office. Figure 7-2 shows a longhand draft that has been edited and is ready for inputting.

Keyboarded or Printed Drafts   Some of the drafts you work with may be keyboarded or printed instead of written in longhand. Supervisors sometimes keyboard rough drafts themselves or provide hard copies of old documents that they have edited for new purposes.

TO: Editorial Assistants
FROM: Lee Jacobs
DATE: April 2, 1986
RE: Free-lance data base of Personnel

I have compiled a list of the information we will use to establish the free-lance data base of free-lancers we use.

Each meaningful piece of information on the list is called a field. (In this case, name, address, street, city/zip, phone, etc.) The field name can be no longer (more) than 12 characters long, and the information in the field can only be 25 characters long.

The data base will allow you to sort free-lancers for specific jobs. For example, you could ask it to list only those free-lancers that were (who are) writers in consumer affairs. The data base would then printout only the names of people that (who) matched this description.

The printout would have the following information:

SKILLS (whether the person is a writer, editor, fact checker, artist, etc...)
SUBJECTS

NAME
ADDRESS
PHONE #
RÉSUMÉ # ON FILE (includes whether the person is a writer, editor, fact checker, artist, etc.)
J. CODE # (OF PREVIOUS JOBS) (lowercase)
COMMITMENTS (ANY COMMITMENTS THE PERSON ALREADY HAS) (lowercase)

(check spelling) I think this is the only (main) information you will need. This can be changed. If you would like different information on your printout, I can show you how to define what goes on the printout.

We will have a meeting on Friday (Monday), April 4 (7), 1986, at 10 A.M., in the conference room, to go over the procedures for (gathering and) entering the information we have on free-lancers.

Fig. 7-2 Handwritten documents remain the most popular way to originate data in the business office. This sample of a handwritten draft has been edited to indicate changes and corrections.

Keyboarded or printed drafts may contain editing marks that have been made in pen or pencil. They may also include handwritten additions or inserts. You may sometimes have to work with messy drafts that have been cut into sections, reorganized, and taped or pasted back together. Whether a draft is handwritten copy or printed or keyboarded copy that has been heavily edited, the amount of time it takes to transcribe it depends on how legible it is. If copy is difficult to read, it might save time in the end to do another draft, especially if the document is long.

To process information from edited typewritten drafts, you will need to be familiar with editing and proofreading symbols. Some of the commonly used symbols are shown in Fig. 7-3.

Originator-Keyboarded Input Some executives keyboard their input directly into a computer. For example, an executive on an extended business trip may take along a portable computer and use it to keyboard input for documents. The executive may then transfer this input to the office computer by using a modem and telephone or by sending a disk that can be processed on the office computer system. If you have to work with input keyboarded by a supervisor, you will usually be asked to make formatting and editing changes.

Here is an example of how an executive and her administrative assistant might use a computer system to input data. Julia Harris is a busy advertising executive who travels quite frequently. Her job requires her to be out of the office often, and it is necessary for her

This executive travels with a portable computer. She keyboards material and sends the disk to her secretary.

PROOFREADERS' MARK	DRAFT	FINAL COPY
ss [Single-space	ss [I have heard he is leaving.	I have heard he is leaving.
ds [Double-space	ds [When will you have a decision?	When will you have a decision?
+1ℓ#→ Insert 1 line space	Percent of Change +1ℓ# ——16.25	Percent of Change 16.25
−1ℓ#→ Delete (remove) 1 line space	Northeastern −1ℓ#→ regional sales	Northeastern regional sales
⌒ Delete space	to͜gether	together
# Insert space	It͜may͜be	It may not be
⌒ Move as shown	it is (not) true	it is true
⌒ Transpose	belie͜vable	believable
	(is it) so	it is so
◯ Spell out	②years ago	two years ago
	16 Elm (St.)	16 Elm Street
∧ Insert a word	How much ∧ it?	How much is it?
⌒ OR — Delete a word	it may not be true	it may be true
∧ OR ⋏ Insert a letter	temper∧ture	temperature
⌒ OR ⌄ Delete a letter and close up	commit͡ment to buy	commitment to buy
⌒ Add on to a word	a real⌒ good day	a really good day
⌒ OR / Change a letter	this super/edes	this supersedes
⌒ OR — Change a word	and if you won't	but if you can't
···· Stet (don't delete)	I was ~~very~~ glad	I was very glad
/ Lowercase a letter (make it a small letter)	Ƒederal Ǥovernment	federal government
≡ Capitalize	Janet L. greyston	Janet L. Greyston
∨ Raise above the line	in her new book∨	in her new book*
∧ Drop below the line	H2S0∧4	H₂S0₄
⊙ Insert a period	Mr⊙ Henry Grenada	Mr. Henry Grenada

Fig. 7-3 Secretaries should become proficient at using proofreaders' marks to edit handwritten and typed drafts before entering the drafts into their computers.

PROOFREADERS' MARK	DRAFT	FINAL COPY
Insert a comma	a large, old house	a large, old house
Insert an apostrophe	my children's car	my children's car
Insert quotation marks	he wants a "loan"	he wants a "loan"
Insert a hyphen	a first-rate job	a first-rate job
	ask the co-owner	ask the co-owner
OR Insert a dash or change a hyphen to a dash	Success—at last! Here it is—cash!	Success––at last! Here it is––cash!
Insert underscore	an issue of <u>Time</u>	an issue of <u>Time</u>
Delete underscore	a very long day	a very long day
( ) Insert parentheses	left today (May 3)	left today (May 3)
Start a new paragraph	If that is so	If that is so
Indent 2 spaces	Net investment in tangible assets	Net investment in tangible assets
Move to the right	$38,367,000	$38,367,000
Move to the left	Anyone can win!	Anyone can win!
Align horizontally	Bob Muller TO:	TO: Bob Muller
Align vertically	Jon Peters Ellen March	Jon Peters Ellen March

to send reports of her latest meetings with key accounts to her administrative assistant, Cathy Barnes. Ms. Barnes generates daily memos to Edward Moore, president of the company, updating him on the sensitive issues concerning each key account, contract changes, and newly formulated ad campaigns.

Ms. Harris travels with a portable computer so that she can input information almost as soon as any development takes place. Since her computer has a modem built in, she can simply plug it into a telephone and call Ms. Barnes's computer system. She doesn't have time to put the information into memo format. She expects Ms. Barnes to make the proper editing and formatting changes and send the completed memo to Mr. Moore using the office's electronic mail system. Figure 7-4 shows how one of Julia Harris's unformatted documents might appear on Cathy Barnes's screen. In Fig., 7-5, you can see how Ms. Barnes prepared the memo for Edward Moore and how it would appear on his screen after Ms. Barnes had sent it over the electronic mail system.

```
L //// t //// t //// t //// t //// t //// t //// t //// t //// R
 ◄
Cathy, please put this information in memo format to Mr. Moore. Be sure to

send copies to everyone on the Anderson account team. Also attach a copy of

my last memo on the Anderson account. ◄


 ◄
After my meeting with John Anderson President of Anderson Industries this

morning it seems more apparent than ever that they will remain one of our

most lucrative accounts. The following sales figures were presented for this

year and represent a marked increase in sales for Anderson over last years

sales. Q1 - $100,000 vs. 80,000, Q2 - $140,000 vs. 90,000, Q3 - $180,000, vs.

120,000 and Q4, $210,000 vs. 140,000. John largely attributes this to our

successful ad campaigns. As a result a contract was signed today to

launch two new campaigns for Anderson effective immediately. Upon my return

to the office tomorrow it is critical that the account team meets to

review the new products to be addressed through this campaign. Ed please

see that everyone can be present, and send my congratulations to each and

every one of them on a job well done!◄


Julia Harris◄
```

Fig. 7-4 Here is how one of Julia Harris's messages might appear on Cathy Barnes's computer screen.

```
L //// t //// t //// t //// t //// t //// t //// t //// t //// R
          Ed Moore◄
          cc: Anderson Account Team◄
FROM:     Julia Harris◄
DATE:     September 22, 1985◄
SUBJECT:  New Anderson Ad Campaign◄
 ◄
After my meeting this morning with John Anderson, President of Anderson
Industries, it seems more apparent than ever that this account will
remain one of our most lucrative.◄

 ◄
The following sales figures were presented for this year and represent a
marked increase over last year's figures for Anderson.◄

 ◄
 First Quarter   Second Quarter   Third Quarter   Fourth Quarter      Year◄
                                                                 _____
                                                                   Total◄
                                                                 _____
1984    1985     1984    1985     1984    1985     1984    1985     1984    1985◄
80,000  100,000  90,000  140,000  120,000 180,000  140,000 210,000  430,000 630,000◄
 ◄
John largely attributes this increase in sales to our successful ad
campaigns. As a result, a new contract was signed today to launch two new
product campaigns for Anderson effective immediately.◄

 ◄
Upon my return to the office tomorrow, it is critical that the account team
meet to review the new products to be addressed through this campaign. Ed,
please see that everyone can be present, and send my congratulations to each
and every one of them on a job well done!

JH:cb
```

Fig. 7-5 Here is how Julia Harris's finished memo appears. Miss Barnes has reformatted the memo to give it an attractive appearance and make it easy to read.

Boilerplate Another kind of soft copy you might work with is **boilerplate,** or electronic copies of frequently used paragraphs. To produce documents containing these paragraphs, you retrieve the boilerplate from your computer's storage unit and combine it with new data. For example, to process a contract you might keyboard a command to retrieve some standard paragraphs that go into all of your employer's contracts. You don't have to keyboard these paragraphs, which might make up the bulk of the contract, but you would keyboard new data that relates to the specific intent of the contract.

The procedures for using boilerplate are different for each information processing system. Generally, though, they involve locating index numbers for the boilerplate paragraphs you want to use and then using keyboard codes to retrieve those paragraphs from your electronic storage unit.

Stored Documents Documents already processed by you or by someone else in your office may serve as input for new information. For example, instead of writing a memo from scratch, you might retrieve a similar one from your electronic files and modify it for a new purpose. Or you might reply to a customer inquiry by substituting a new address and salutation on a stored letter you have already sent to many other people.

Once you have the soft copy of the original document on your screen, you can revise it to create the new document. If you want to save an electronic copy of the original document as well as the new one, you must give the new one a different name.

Data Bases Information is also stored in data bases. As you learned in Chapter 3, a data base is a collection of information that can be obtained through the use of a computer. For example, a small business might maintain a list of its customers, or a store might maintain its inventory on a computer disk or magnetic tape.

Each company has its own procedures for inputting data into and obtaining information from its internal data bases. These procedures depend on the kind of electronic equipment the company uses, the nature of the data, and the company's policies regarding data security. In some instances it may be possible to obtain information from an internal data base just by keyboarding a few computer commands. In others you may need special clearance from a data manager before you can gain access to the data.

Data Banks In addition to maintaining their own data bases, many companies subscribe to external data banks that offer a variety of information to meet different business needs. When these data banks can be accessed externally, they are called **online information services**; they are owned and operated by companies that offer information to outsiders for a fee. If you work for a company that deals heavily in stocks and bonds, for example, your company might subscribe to the Dow Jones or Media General informa-

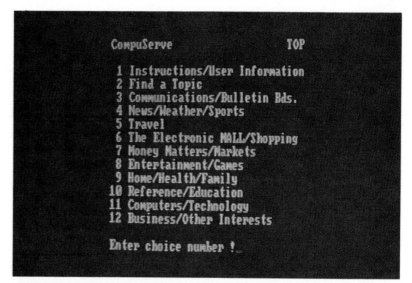

Fig. 7-6 External data bases provide many different types of information for businesses that subscribe to their services.

tion services, which provide up-to-the-minute prices for stocks and bonds. If your company's executives travel a great deal, the company may subscribe to the *Official Airline Guide*, a computerized schedule of airline flights between major cities. To obtain information from an external data bank, you use a modem to connect your computer to the data bank's computer. You then call up the information you want on your computer screen and print it out on your printer. (See Fig. 7-6.)

Data Forms Another kind of stored information found in most business offices is the preprinted form, such as an employment application or a purchase order. Forms can be hard copy, to be completed in longhand or with a typewriter, or soft copy, to be displayed on a computer screen and filled in by keyboarding the information.

You may sometimes use data from one form to process another. For example, you may use data from an invoice to prepare a customer's bill. Some computer systems can fill in parts of a form for you automatically. Suppose you are responsible for taking telephone orders for an office supply company. When a customer calls, you call up an order form on your computer screen and keyboard the customer's name and address and the quantity, description, and price of each item being ordered in the spaces provided. Once you have entered all the prices and handling costs, you can instruct the computer to add up the items and provide a total.

Electronic Mail Messages Data for input can come from an electronic mail or message system. Many organizations now have electronic message systems for internal communication among employees. In most such systems, an employee can send a message to one co-worker, to a group of workers, or to everyone whose terminal is linked to the system. Receiving an electronic message usually involves keyboarding a command so that the computer will display it on your screen.

To see how you might use an electronic message as input, suppose you have been asked to prepare a report detailing the personnel needs of each of five departments in your company. You can ask each department head to send you an electronic message about his or her personnel needs. Once the messages are sent to your terminal, you can incorporate part or all of each message into your report just by entering a few commands. This will save you the trouble of having to obtain a hard copy of each message and then having to keyboard the parts of the messages you want to use.

Input Preparation Procedures

As you have seen, there are a variety of different methods for obtaining and organizing data for processing. Now that you have learned about the different kinds of data and input media, it is time to learn about the different kinds of input devices you are likely to be using in today's business offices. In the traditional office, your input device would be a typewriter; in the fully automated office, you would input into a computer. There are several different kinds of computer attachments or devices—such as the keyboard and optical character reader—that are used to transfer data from people or paper into a computer.

Assume that you have several letters and memos to transcribe on your computer. The first order of business is to prioritize your work so that you are transcribing the most urgent documents first and the least urgent documents later. There are still several things you have to do before you can begin to work on your computer.

Microcomputers and Portable Computers

When you input on microcomputers and portable computer systems, you will need to load the appropriate operating system and software, which will be on disks. You load a disk into the computer's memory by turning the computer on and placing the disk in the disk drive. Now you must give the computer certain commands, which vary from one system to another and from one software package to another. The company you work for is certain to provide some initial training in how to perform these operations on its computer system. Or you can look up these procedures in the manual or documentation for the computer system or software program you are using.

A more detailed discussion of operating systems, software, and disks is provided in the next two chapters. However, it is important to understand that when you are working with disks, you will be responsible for their maintenance and care. Valuable information will be stored on them, and misplacing or damaging a disk can be extremely costly. Disk maintenance and filing procedures are discussed in greater detail in later chapters.

Once you have loaded the operating system and appropriate software, in this case a word processing program, be sure that the disk you will be storing your information on has enough space available to accommodate the job. If not, you will need to prepare a new disk.

Every manufacturer designs its word processing hardware and software differently. For this reason you will need to prepare every disk to store documents keyboarded with the software designed for your equipment. You cannot just take a brand new disk out of its envelope and immediately use it to store a document. The preparation procedure is called **formatting**, or **initializing**, the disk. Formatting a disk is different from formatting a document. To format a disk, you insert it in the disk drive of the computer and keyboard the formatting commands. Your equipment manual or your company's operating guide will tell you what to do.

Arrange your workstation so that it is comfortable. Adjust the screen and keyboard, and place your input media such as shorthand notes or rough drafts to the right or left of your keyboard, whichever is more comfortable for you. You are now ready to begin inputting your data.

Minicomputers

Preparing to input data on a terminal connected to a minicomputer requires fewer steps than for a microcomputer or portable computer. Since the operating system and software are housed in a central storage unit, which is usually maintained by technical personnel, you probably won't need to be concerned with this. (See Fig. 7-7.)

All you will need to do is sign onto the minicomputer system. Since many terminals may be connected to a single, central minicomputer system, there may be a security system to protect private files. If so, users will be given their own "key" to the system. The key usually consists of one or two names or codes (sometimes called a *password*) that you will type into the system so that the computer will recognize you as a valid user and allow you to access the information you want. (See Fig. 7-8.)

Input Devices

The method you use for inputting data will be determined by the input device or devices available to you. Several different input devices are used in the electronic office. You will certainly need to become familiar with the keyboard, and you may need to use other input devices as well.

Keyboards and Templates

The most frequently used input device is the keyboard. Most keyboards are similar; there is not much difference between a keyboard attached to a terminal that is linked to a centralized mainframe or minicomputer and a keyboard that is part of a standalone microcomputer or a dedicated word processor.

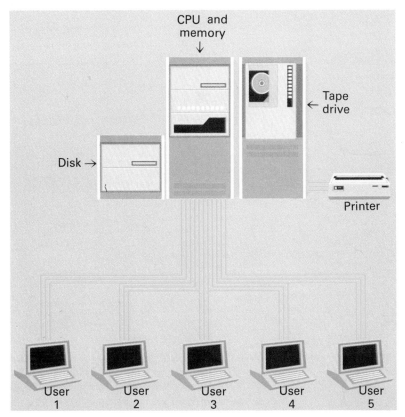

Fig. 7-7 A typical office minicomputer system allows operators at several terminals to use the computer simultaneously. Users don't have to load program and storage disks, but they usually have to enter passwords to gain access to the computer.

Fig. 7-8 On this system, the user's name is Smith. The password should be entered on the next line where the cursor is positioned.

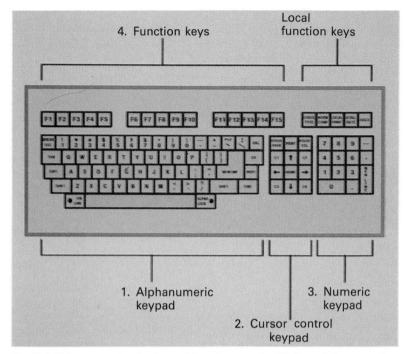

Fig. 7-9 This computer keyboard has four parts: (1) the alphanumeric keypad which is very similar to a typewriter keyboard; (2) the cursor control keypad which enables the operator to move the cursor around on the screen; (3) the numeric keypad which functions like the number keys on a calculator; and (4) the function keys which enable the operator to perform various tasks such as calling up, storing, and printing copy, formatting pages, and performing mathematical calculations.

The main portion of the keyboard, which is sometimes referred to as the **alphanumeric keypad,** closely duplicates a standard typewriter keyboard. You will use it in much the same way you use a typewriter keyboard with some minor exceptions. Depending on the type of equipment, some keys may have different uses than those used for typing. There may also be some special keys you are not familiar with. For example, instead of depressing the "SHIFT" key to lock for all uppercase letters, you might use a key such as the "CAPS LOCK" shown in Fig. 7-10.

In addition to the alphanumeric keypad, most electronic keyboards have a **cursor control keypad.** You will remember, from Chapter 2, that the cursor is the bright light or flashing symbol that marks your position on the screen. You use a cursor control key— up (↑), down (↓), right (→), left (←)—to move the cursor in the direction of the arrow that is pressed. (See Fig. 7-10.) For example, to correct the error shown on the screen in Fig. 7-11 ("tomorrow" is misspelled), you would have to press the down arrow (↓) key once

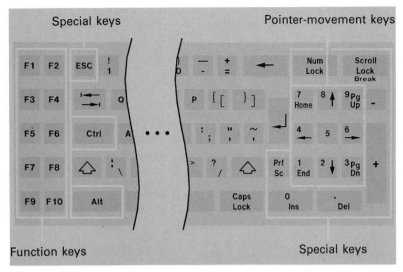

Fig. 7-10 The cursor control keys allow computer operators to move the cursor to any point on the screen.

to get to the proper line and the right arrow (→) key five times to place the cursor on the incorrect letter—*u*—to correct it to *o* by typing over it.

Perhaps the most significant difference between a typewriter keyboard and an electronic keyboard is the panel of **function keys**, which control various functions of the electronic system. The number of function keys varies from system to system; most have between 10 and 15. Each function key represents a command that the computer system can perform. A plastic or cardboard plate, called a

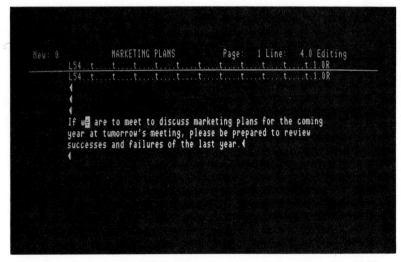

Fig. 7-11 To correct the error shown here, move the cursor key to the location of the error and type the correction over it.

Fig. 7-12 The templates shown here are for two different word processing programs. You can see from the templates that the function keys operate differently from one program to the other.

template, fits over the function keys as shown in Fig. 7-12. This template serves as a key to the functions available to you with the program you are using. It is important for you to remember that each function key performs different functions with different software programs. For example, if you were using a word processing program, function key "F10" in Fig. 7-12 (bottom) might perform an indent function. If you were working on a spreadsheet program, "F10" might do a recalculate function, and if you were working with a graphics program, "F10" might perform a graph function. The template for each program would tell you what function "F10" performs for that program.

In addition to the alphanumeric keypad, the cursor control keypad, and the function keys, many electronic keyboards have a numeric keypad as illustrated in Fig. 7-9. **Numeric keypads** have keys for each of the 10 arabic digits and are usually set up very much like calculator keypads. You can also use these keys to input numbers in place of the numeric keys located on the alphanumeric keypad.

Other keys that you might find on various computer keyboards include "CTRL," "ALT," "CMD," "ON LINE," "INS," and "DEL." Your computer manual will tell you how to use keys such as these.

Most systems have some **programmable keys**, or keys that can be customized according to the needs of the user. Following the procedures for your particular system, you could program one of these keys to underline, set margins, or define paragraphs that you want to move or delete. A programmed key enables you to use a single keystroke for a processing command that would otherwise require several keystrokes.

Although different manufacturers produce equipment with variations among the keyboards, it is not very difficult to transfer the skills you learn using one type of equipment to another. Rather than feeling intimidated when you have to learn to operate a new type of equipment, your past experience should make you feel more confident.

Optical Character Readers

An **optical character reader (OCR)** scans typed or printed pages and converts the text into electronic signals the computer can understand. As an OCR scans a page, the typed or printed contents are

In many cases, OCRs eliminate the need for rekeyboarding.

Facsimile machines can send documents electronically over long distances.

transferred to a computer storage device such as a magnetic tape or a disk. An OCR eliminates the need for keyboarding data that has already been typed or printed. Most OCRs can convert a wide range of typefaces into electronic signals. Some very specialized OCRs can even read handwritten numbers and letters, but you are unlikely to encounter these OCRs in the office. You would have to use the keyboard to add handwritten text and handwritten notes and editing marks to the soft copy just as you would use the keyboard for editing and formatting the text you have entered with an OCR.

The use of OCRs is becoming more common. For example, many grocery stores use them at the checkout counter to read and record the price of the item being purchased. The device can not only record the purchase price of the item, but can also simultaneously update the inventory record.

Digital Facsimile Machines

Some modern facsimile machines can be linked to computers so that they function as long-distance OCRs. A standard facsimile machine scans a document page and transmits signals to a receiving facsimile machine, which produces a duplicate. With newer digital units, the sending machine can transmit the signals to a computer instead of to another facsimile machine. The receiving computer displays the signals as soft copy, which can be stored on a disk or printed.

Other Input Devices

Some computer systems are equipped with special devices that enable you to enter processing commands and other input without using a keyboard. None of these devices eliminates the need for office workers to keyboard text, however. Employees without keyboarding skills can use these devices to manipulate text that someone has already entered, but they cannot create text copy with most of them. Some of the devices you might encounter are described below.

This hand-operated mouse allows the operator to move the cursor to any point on the screen. Mice are useful input devices for computer operators who are not comfortable with keyboarding.

Mouse   A microcomputer terminal may have an attachment called a **mouse**, which is a small hand-operated device that allows you to move the cursor and input processing commands without using the keyboard. As you move the mouse around on a desk top or on a special tablet, the cursor moves in a corresponding direction on the screen. Computer systems that use mice also use menus. A **menu** is a list of functions displayed on the screen. You can select a function by moving the mouse until the cursor stops at the particular menu item and then pushing a button on the mouse. For example, if you wanted to file a document that is on your screen onto a disk, you would move the mouse until the cursor arrived at the menu item "save." When you push the button on the mouse, the function is performed. These devices are used primarily by people who lack keyboarding skills, but they can also save time for secretaries and other office workers when they are working with statistical tables or other materials that require them to move the cursor frequently from place to place.

Touch Screen   Some computer systems have a **touch screen** capability that allows you to enter commands by touching the screen. Such a system displays a menu, or list of functions, such as word processing, accounting, and graphics design. When you point at the option you want and touch the screen, the terminal may display another menu that lists various tasks included in that function. If you have chosen accounting from the first menu, for example, the second menu might include the tasks of entering accounts receiva-

Graphics tablet

Light pen

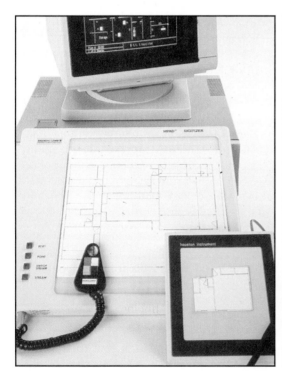

Digital scanner

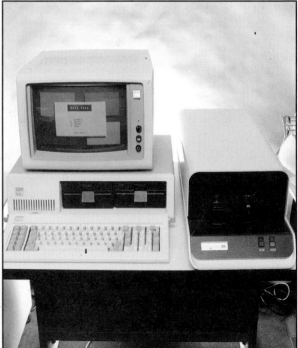

Digital camera

ble data, entering accounts payable data, and so on. When you touch the screen again, the computer might "open" a file for you or ask if you want to use an existing file. The touch screen, like the mouse, is most helpful to those who are uncomfortable with keyboards.

Voice Recognition   Some computers can recognize a few simple words and phrases of human speech as input, but scientists have not yet been able to develop a computer that can understand all the complexities of speech well enough to take dictation and convert it into soft copy. If computer scientists do succeed in developing such a computer system, it will free office workers from a great deal of dictation taking and transcribing. Then they will only need to use the keyboard to edit and format the soft copy. Voice-recognition technology is a promising area not only for office workers but for certain physically handicapped people as well.

Graphics Tablet   A **graphics tablet** is a board that you can use to create images on the screen. You use a finger, a special pen, or a mouse to draw the image on the board. The image then appears in the same position on the computer screen. Graphics tablets require special software to convert your hand movements into digital signals and then to convert the signals into pictures.

Light Pen   You can also create images on a screen with a **light pen**, which is connected to the computer terminal by a flexible wire. As you move the pen against the screen, the movements appear as light on the screen. You can use the light pen to trace drawings or maps on the screen and to create your own pictures.

Digital Scanner   Similar to an OCR, a **digital scanner** can scan charts, maps, blueprints, and pictures and convert them into digital data so that they can be reproduced on the computer screen. The digital scanner, or digitizer, is most often used in businesses such as architectural and engineering firms where employees frequently work with complex technical drawings.

Digital Camera   Some new computer systems can accept input from special cameras, called **digital cameras**, that are wired to the computer and convert photographic images into computer signals. This new technology offers increased information processing productivity for designers, engineers, and others who work with project models or who need photographs to illustrate reports and other documents.

Office workers can use digital-camera technology not only to produce photographs on documents but also to create slides and other graphic materials that can be used in meetings and presentations. The use of the digital camera is an example of how computers can be integrated with other kinds of equipment to produce more detailed information and process it more efficiently.

GUIDELINES FOR KEYBOARDING

Whether you are transcribing shorthand notes, machine dictation, or hard copy such as a rough draft, the following guidelines will help you to do the job more comfortably and more efficiently.

- **Posture.** Correct posture will help prevent the back strain and fatigue that can result from working at a keyboard and terminal for several hours.
- **Your Chair.** People who do a lot of keyboarding generally use adjustable chairs like those used by typists in traditional offices. Adjust your chair to suit your height and the position of your keyboard (unless the keyboard itself is movable). Your chair is properly adjusted and your sitting posture is correct if your feet reach the floor and rest there without pushing up your knees, if your spine is straight, and if your hips are placed firmly against the back of the chair. You should not have to move your upper arms away from your sides in order for your hands to reach your keyboard.
- **Your Computer Terminal.** Placing your keyboard and terminal correctly can also help you to avoid poor posture and the fatigue and tension that result from it.

   You may work with a keyboard and terminal that are housed in a single unit. If so, you may not be able to adjust either the tilt of the screen or·the placement of the keyboard in relation to it, but you can place the entire terminal at a height that allows you to reach the keyboard comfortably and look at the screen without slumping in your chair or straining your neck. The screen should be below your eye level so that you look slightly downward at it.

   Some offices use computer terminals with screens and keyboards that are separate from each other. If you work with one of these terminals, you can place the keyboard wherever it would be most comfortable. The screen may be mounted on an adjustable platform so that you can tilt it to a comfortable angle.

- **Computer Tables.** Your keyboard and terminal (and perhaps other system components) may all be on a special-purpose table. On many computer tables, terminals and keyboards sit on separate surfaces, and you can adjust the heights of these surfaces individually. You may also be able to adjust the tilt of the keyboard surface.
- **Using a Copyholder.** A **copyholder** is a device that holds hard copy at an angle that enables you to read it comfortably while you are keyboarding. You can place a copyholder so that you don't have to move your head back and forth constantly to shift your eyes between the screen and the hard copy. This also helps to prevent fatigue and back strain.

■ **Lighting.** Proper lighting contributes to your comfort and your productivity when you are keyboarding. In the electronic office, you need lighting that enables you to read both your screen and your hard copy without eyestrain.

Your notes or hard copy should be illuminated by an overhead light or a desk lamp, but the lamp should be placed so that it does not cause glare or reflections on your screen. If your room is lighted by windows, place your screen so that the windows are behind it. This way, the screen won't reflect light from them.

Adjusting the brightness and contrast on your screen can also help prevent eyestrain. Turn up the brightness as much as you can without hurting your eyes; then adjust the contrast so that the bright soft copy appears against a dark background.

■ Summary

■ The first step in the IPSOD process is inputting, the gathering and preparing of data for processing. You gather data from many sources, and you collect it in three different formats— print, electronic, and verbal.

■ It is an important part of an office worker's job to gather and prepare data for processing. Office workers need to be knowledgeable in language arts, researching techniques, and office procedures.

■ As an office worker, you need to be familiar with many different kinds of input media. The most common, and one of the most highly valued, is shorthand dictation.

■ Taking and transcribing shorthand requires that you follow several basic rules so that your materials are quickly at hand, so that you can organize them efficiently, and so that you can perform your work with a minimum of delays and errors.

■ Dictation machines are convenient because they don't require you to be present when your supervisor wants to dictate. Some dictation machines are portable or desk-top units, while others are large centralized units. Shorthand machines and computer-aided transcription machines convert shorthand symbols into printed words or soft copy.

■ Drafts are preliminary or working copies of documents from which you produce finished documents. Drafts can be hard copy, such as longhand, keyboarded, or printed documents, or soft copy—originator-keyboarded input, boilerplate, stored documents, and electronic messages.

- If you use a microcomputer to input copy, you have to load the appropriate software and prepare a storage disk to accept soft copy. With a minicomputer, you have to enter a password before you can use the system.

- The most common way to input on a computer is through use of a keyboard. You can also use an optical character reader to read typed or printed words or codes, or you can use a digital facsimile machine to reproduce a page of text on a computer screen.

- Other input devices include mice, touch screens, voice-recognition systems, graphics tablets, light pens, digital scanners, and digital cameras.

■ Review Questions

1. Describe the three different formats in which data may be presented, and give examples of each one.

2. Describe the office worker's role in gathering data, and list some of the skills an office worker might need to perform that function.

3. Cite at least three reasons why many executives use face-to-face dictation rather than machine dictation.

4. What details do you check when you review your shorthand notes before transcribing them?

5. Compare and contrast desk-top dictation machines with portable units and centralized dictation systems.

6. What steps would you take if you could not understand some of the words on a dictation cassette?

7. What method do executives use most frequently to create input for documents they originate? Why is this method more popular than others?

8. In general, how might you use your computer terminal to obtain input data from a data bank?

9. How does a computer keyboard differ from a typewriter keyboard?

10. Do the mouse and other input devices eliminate the need for keyboarding? Explain your answer.

■ Technical Vocabulary

voice input
editor's clip
combination unit
endless loop
indicator slip
shorthand machine

computer-aided transcription
draft
boilerplate
online information services
format
initialize

alphanumeric keypad
cursor control keypad
function keys
template
numeric keypad
programmable key
optical character reader (OCR)
mouse

menu
touch screen
graphics tablet
light pen
digital scanner
digital camera
copyholder

■ Discussion and Skills Development

1. Using a word processor or typewriter, transcribe the longhand draft shown in Fig. 7-2.

2. You are Edward Ringle's administrative assistant, and your job includes processing documents for him. Mr. Ringle usually dictates these documents to you in person, although he sometimes prepares longhand drafts instead. In both his dictation and his drafts, Mr. Ringle frequently makes grammatical errors and uses words incorrectly. In his longhand drafts, he also makes punctuation mistakes. However, Mr. Ringle thinks of himself as a good writer, and he doesn't like it when you change his dictation. In fact, just yesterday he bawled you out for rewriting a paragraph in an attempt to clarify it. This morning he has given you a draft of a letter in which he uses the word *infer* where he really means *imply*. Moreover, you think the letter would be easier to understand if the second and third paragraphs were transposed. What will you do?

3. You are Margaret Wilson's personal secretary. Ms. Wilson is away on a business trip and sends an important memo from her portable computer to your computer terminal. While you are editing the memo for transmittal to the company president, you accidentally erase it from the computer's memory. What should you do?

chapter 8
Software and Information Processing

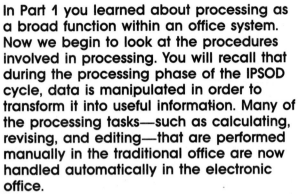

In Part 1 you learned about processing as a broad function within an office system. Now we begin to look at the procedures involved in processing. You will recall that during the processing phase of the IPSOD cycle, data is manipulated in order to transform it into useful information. Many of the processing tasks—such as calculating, revising, and editing—that are performed manually in the traditional office are now handled automatically in the electronic office.

The significance of this electronic capability goes far beyond the savings in time and effort that are achieved. Advances in computer technology, combined with the development of a vast range of applications software, have greatly expanded the tasks and procedures that make up the processing function. With the right software, people can explore a wide range of possibilities, analyze alternatives, and explore different approaches before they make significant decisions.

In this chapter we examine the interaction of computer hardware and software. You will learn more about how a computer works and what determines its capabilities.

We also take a close look at the different kinds of applications software that are most commonly used in the business office. These programs range from word processing to spreadsheets and data base management to graphics and communications.

Choosing the right software for a particular job is no easy task: thousands of software programs are available, and new ones are being released every week. You need to be a well-informed consumer if you want to locate the program that will best suit your needs. This chapter explains some important factors that you need to consider when buying any software; it gives you guidelines for choosing the right programs for your business needs.

Information Processing

The first business computers were used almost exclusively for data processing. Eventually, computerized word processing equipment became available, but data processing and word processing have continued to be handled as separate functions within most organizations. With today's technology, however, data processing and word processing functions can be performed using the same equipment. As a result, some businesses are able to integrate many tasks and functions performed by their processing departments and equipment. As organizations move toward integrating, they must deal with issues such as cost, compatibility of equipment, training required, and security. So before we look at how data processing and word processing can be integrated, we will look at each function separately.

Data Processing

Some data processing tasks must be handled by computer specialists because of the technical expertise required. Computer specialists include **systems analysts**, who determine how computer data processing can be applied to specific problems; **programmers**, who design, test, and maintain computer programs—the sets of instructions that enable computers to carry out specific applications; and **data base administrators**, who define, update, and control access to data bases.

Other data processing responsibilities are handled by computer operators and data entry clerks, jobs that require less technical

This type of large centralized data processing department is common in most big companies. Today, many functions performed by these departments can be decentralized.

training. In a large company, the data processing personnel usually work in a centralized data processing department. Some companies are too small for this kind of setup and have their data processing done outside of the company.

If an organization has a **centralized data processing system**, employees must request information from the data processing specialists who work on the centralized computer system—usually a large mainframe or minicomputer system. The specialists process reports for various departments within the organization, and they also handle special requests. For information that is not distributed routinely, there usually is a waiting period of anywhere from one week to a few weeks. You may have to wait longer if a new computer program has to be written.

Advances in computer technology make it possible today to bring some of the processing applications and the distribution of data to individual workstations. These systems are called **decentralized data processing systems**. A business can link computers throughout the organization to those in the data processing department, or it can move functions that were once handled by a centralized data processing department into the departments that carry out those functions. These changes can lead to greater efficiency and productivity. For example, if the data processing department keeps sales figures for all the territories a company covers, a sales manager may have to wait for a weekly report or request information from the data processing department. But if the computer in the sales department is linked to the main computer in the data processing department, the manager has access to the figures and can call them up instantaneously.

There are problems with decentralization. For one thing, changing an existing system is costly. Managers have to examine the needs of various departments and then decide if the cost of decentralization will eventually outweigh the benefits. Another major issue is security. Centralized data processing enables a business to maintain tight control over data. It reduces the chance that unauthorized personnel will tamper with data or see confidential information. As more companies turn to decentralized systems, security becomes a major issue.

Word Processing

Like data processing, word processing is often handled by specialists. Some organizations have word processing centers staffed by individuals who are highly skilled at operating the equipment. Input is sent to the center from various departments in rough draft form or through recorded dictation. In many centers production is a key factor, and the output is measured in keystrokes a minute and time spent on document preparation. The manager of a center can keep close track of the department's productivity.

While many large companies handle their word processing in this fashion because of the large number of documents that must be processed, some companies have found that it is not always ideal. The production orientation, with its emphasis on speed, can have a negative effect on employees. It can cause fatigue, eyestrain, and stress. In addition, productivity may suffer when documents are processed by workers who don't work closely with the originators and may not be able to understand their handwriting or dictation. Then, too, work can accumulate, and the backlog can create delays in distribution.

One way companies have decentralized word processing is by breaking up their centers into smaller satellites that serve particular parts of the organization. A **satellite** is a small unit of information processing equipment. The satellite may process the documents of one or more departments.

The most prevalent trend, however, is toward keeping the word processing function at the individual workstation. Word processing responsibilities are integrated into administrative support functions. Some companies purchase dedicated word processing equipment or microcomputers for each individual, while others decide to have several administrative assistants share equipment.

Word processing at the individual workstation has several advantages. One is that managers can have more control over the order in which the work is done. Another is that the administrative support staff can use their computers for many other applications. They might, for example, be able to use decision support software programs, such as electronic spreadsheets, database management programs, and graphics programs.

Integrated Information Processing

The role of the office worker has changed dramatically as more and more offices have linked their business operations in integrated information processing systems. Integrated information processing encompasses all kinds of computers as well as other electronic equipment, and it includes data processing, word processing, and other applications.

To understand how integrated systems work, think about how a letter is processed in an office with word processing equipment only. You take shorthand notes as your boss dictates the letter. From your notes you transcribe a draft of the letter, which you must then proofread. While you are doing that, your boss tells you that she just received a new printout with updated prices from the data processing department, and she asks you to change the figures in the letter. She also asks you to use the new figures to make a chart of price increases to go into a report she is preparing. In addition, she asks you to request the price history of the products listed in the chart. Then she wants you to send the chart to the art department to be typeset. You revise the letter, proofread it, and print it out. Then you use the data from the inside address to generate a mailing label, and you mail the letter. You also distribute copies of the letter to others in your company via interoffice mail. For the report, you request the

In an electronic office, up-to-date information is immediately available to everyone who needs it, saving time and unnecessary work in the input and processing stages of the information flow.

price history from the data processing department and set to work on the chart that you will send to the art department.

If you look at the separate tasks that have to be performed, you can see how an integrated system would increase your productivity.

■ If your boss could call up sales information on her computer while she dictates a letter, she would have the latest figures in front of her as she dictates to you.

■ If your computer were connected to the central data processing computer, you could request data by using your keyboard.

■ If you had graphics software and knew how to use it, you could have the chart drawn and typeset in a short time, without the art department's help.

■ You also could have distributed the letter through an electronic mail system.

The hardware components of the integrated system used in this example are input devices, a central processing unit (CPU), output and communications devices. Let's examine each of these further.

The input device—in this case, your keyboard—allows direct person-to-machine communication. If the keyboard is **on-line**, or connected directly to the computer system, your input goes directly into the CPU of the main computer. The CPU has three main parts:

■ The primary storage section (or memory), where input is held until it is ready to be processed.

■ The arithmetic-logic section, where the processing of the input takes place.

- The control section, which directs the operation of the system by selecting, interpreting, and executing the program instructions.

Let's look more closely at the example above. If you input a command to use the graphics program for composing the chart, the control section of the CPU will interpret the input and send graphics instructions to your terminal rather than word processing instructions or some other program in the computer's memory. When you are done processing the chart, you will insert it into the letter. Your letter appears as soft-copy output on the monitor. By inputting another command you save the document on a magnetic media. It can then be sent to the receiver via electronic mail. In this example you process, store, output, and communicate in one operation. Or you can also perform these applications on a microcomputer that is not connected to a larger computer. The only difference is that you would need to use program instructions stored on a software disk (rather than in the CPU). And if you wanted to use word processing and graphics at the same time, you would use a special integrated software program that contains both of these applications on the same disk. You will learn more about these programs later.

Software and Processing

The hardware components that make up a computer system get their instructions, step-by-step, from software. Software programs are written in special languages that perform different functions. Computer programmers need to know these languages to write software programs. They use basically two types of languages: low-level and high-level. (See Fig. 8-1.) **Low-level languages**, an example of which is assembly language, direct the computer through each step that it has to take in order to perform a particular operation. **High-level languages** use symbols that represent a series of steps.

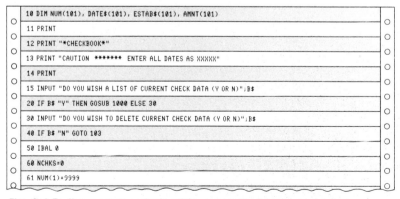

```
10 DIM NUM(101), DATE$(101), ESTAB$(101), AMNT(101)
11 PRINT
12 PRINT "*CHECKBOOK*"
13 PRINT "CAUTION ******* ENTER ALL DATES AS XXXXX"
14 PRINT
15 INPUT "DO YOU WISH A LIST OF CURRENT CHECK DATA (Y OR N)";B$
20 IF B$ "Y" THEN GOSUB 1000 ELSE 30
30 INPUT "DO YOU WISH TO DELETE CURRENT CHECK DATA (Y OR N)";B$
40 IF B$ "N" GOTO 103
50 IBAL 0
60 NCHKS=0
61 NUM(1)=9999
```

Fig. 8-1 To the person untrained in computer language and programming, this printout contains a meaningless collection of strange symbols and odd characters. To the computer, however, these symbols are recognized as commands to perform specific tasks and functions.

They save the programmer from having to input each individual step. Most high-level languages use symbols that are similar to words with which people are familiar. Among the most common high-level languages are BASIC, Cobol, Fortran, and Pascal.

Today there is a new level of computer language called **user-level**. You need little formal training to write programs in user-level languages because they allow you to use everyday terms rather than computer codes. Examples of user-level languages are PDS-ADEPT and dBase III.

Programmers use these languages for writing many different programs. But there are basically two kinds of programs: systems programs and applications programs. Let's take a close look at how these programs are used.

Systems Programs

Systems programs have two tasks: to operate the computer equipment and to translate programs into machine-readable instructions. Systems software does most of its work behind the scenes. With some computers, especially large ones, office workers may not even be aware of the systems software. But they do need to know about the system in order to select applications software for it. The programs for operating the computer are called an operating system. An **operating system** is a set of programs that controls the running of other programs. It performs such jobs as assigning places in memory, handling interruptions, and controlling input and output.

Computers with different operating systems are said to be incompatible if they cannot run the same applications software. In that case they will not be able to exchange data either, unless special translator programs are used. Several kinds of operating systems are used in microcomputers today. Let's look at some of the most popular ones.

CP/M One of the two most commonly used operating systems for microcomputers is CP/M, which stands for "control program/microprocessor." CP/M was developed by a company called Digital Research. Many computers run only CP/M systems software, but some that were built to run CP/M can be modified to run other operating systems as well. Likewise, some microcomputers with other operating systems can be modified to run CP/M.

MS-DOS and PC-DOS MS-DOS, which stands for "microsoft disk operating system," differs only slightly from PC-DOS, the operating system for the IBM personal computer (PC). MS-DOS is a product of a company called Microsoft Inc. Computers that can run MS-DOS are said to be **IBM PC-compatible**. This means that they can run the same applications software as IBM personal computers; depending on the extent of their compatibility, they may be able to use data disks created on an IBM PC.

Unix Used in microcomputers as well as in minicomputers and mainframes, Unix was developed by Bell Laboratories. Unix is regarded by some office automation experts as the operating system that provides the easiest way to integrate various brands of electronic equipment into networks that allow them to communicate. As these networks become increasingly important to the business world, these experts say, Unix or similar systems software may become standard in the office.

Proprietary Systems A mainframe or a minicomputer sometimes uses a **proprietary operating system**, which is a system designed for only one model or perhaps for other computers produced by the same company. Many microcomputer brands also use proprietary systems software. Unless they can also run one or more of the popular operating systems, computers with proprietary software are generally incompatible with other kinds of computers.

Utilities **Utilities** are programs used to speed up frequently used data-maintenance chores such as making backup copies of disks or coding data for security. Utilities can help you use your computer more efficiently. Like other software, a utility program can run only with a particular operating system. Also, some utilities run only with a particular combination of software and hardware.

Applications Programs

Applications programs are the software instructions that make computers execute required tasks. They transform a general-purpose computer into a system for performing specific tasks. As an office worker processing data into business documents, you may use many applications programs or only a few, depending on your job. For example, an administrative assistant in a large law firm might use word processing software for producing memos, communications software for sending the memos to branch offices, and a spreadsheet program for keeping track of expense reports. In another organization's order department, an office worker might use software for only two applications: for storing order information in the company's data base and retrieving it, and for sending and receiving electronic interoffice messages. Let's look at some of the applications software you might use in today's office.

Word Processing No other programs have helped automate the modern office more quickly than word processing programs. This is the application used most often by office workers. Word processing software is used for inputting, formatting, editing, and printing documents such as memos, letters, reports, and contracts. It is particularly useful for repetitive documents such as form letters. Perhaps you have heard of WordStar, Display Write III, PFS Write, and Multiplan. These are the names of four of the many word processing programs. Although these programs vary in speed, power, and advanced features, all of them perform similar basic word processing operations.

A modern word processing system is a very flexible tool. Depending on the type of word processor you use and the software available

The keyboard of a dedicated word processor displays the actual commands right on the keys. This makes it somewhat easier to use than a microcomputer with word processing capabilities because you do not need to memorize all the different commands for editing functions.

to you, you will be able to perform a number of different functions. If you use a **dedicated word processor**, you will be using a machine that is designed solely for word processing. Basically, it is a computer that only runs one program. Dedicated word processors cannot be used for programming, and they usually do not need additional software. Most of these machines offer a wide range of functions, including alphabetizing lists, checking spelling, and setting up formats automatically. And since dedicated word processors are not used for any purpose other than word processing, they usually have many word processing commands printed right on the keyboard.

Dedicated word processors do have limitations, however. They cannot be used for graphics, math calculations, spreadsheets, and other computer applications. Most computers that do have these applications, on the other hand, can also be used for word processing by loading an appropriate word processing program into the system.

While a word processor will make your job easier, you must still make editing decisions and proofread your work. And you must learn the instructions or commands for the programs you use. All the hardware and software in the world won't make a word processor do what you want it to do unless *you* instruct it properly.

Programs have two ways to tell a word processor what to do: menu selection and command. With a **menu-driven program**, the computer presents the operations available on a multiple choice basis. Each word processing program is different, but the main menu may include such choices as *Edit, Save, Print*, and so on.

PFS:WRITE MAIN MENU
----

1 TYPE/EDIT   4 GET/SAVE/REMOVE

2 DEFINE PAGE   5 CLEAR

3 PRINT   6 EXIT

SELECTION NUMBER 1_

(C) 1983 Software Publishing Corporation

F1-Help   F10-Continue

This menu presents you with choices of what function you want the computer to perform next. You make your selection by typing the one number that represents your choice and then pressing the RETURN key.

Each of these options may have a submenu of its own with further selections for the function you have chosen. The main advantage of a menu-driven program is its accuracy and ease of use. You are less likely to make mistakes when you can choose commands provided on a screen instead of having to rely on your memory of what the commands are. The main drawback of these programs is that you have to retrace some steps when going from menu to menu.

With a **command-driven program**, you must give the computer the appropriate commands to carry out the functions in any order you choose. You will need a manual to help you learn the commands for your particular program. Once you are familiar with the program, you will know, for example, that in order to delete a word, you must press the "ESCAPE" key and the letter *D*. But without the manual or a list of the commands, you will not know exactly what instructions to give. Figure 8-2 shows a list of function commands for a typical word processing program. Most word processing programs actually use a combination of menu selection and commands: a menu for the most basic functions and commands for the finer operations of manipulating data and text.

Different word processing programs offer different capabilities, but most enable you to perform a fairly standard array of text-editing functions. The most commonly used functions are usually the sim-

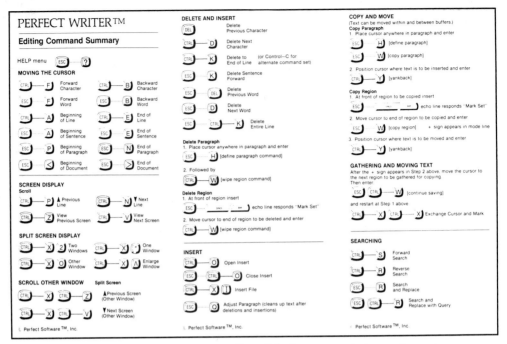

Fig. 8-2 Most software packages come with a list of commands to use for specific tasks that you want the computer to perform. If you use the program a lot, you will probably memorize the ones that you use most frequently. For those that you don't use that often, you will need to consult the list.

plest to perform. You would delete characters or words, for example, by moving the cursor to where you want to cut text and then pressing one or two keys. Other simple commands allow you to indicate letters or words that you want underlined, boldfaced, or capitalized. You can also give commands that take you straight to the beginning of the document or that allow you to move through it screen by screen. More complicated functions include copy and move operations in which whole sections of text are "lifted" and moved to another section of the document or to another document altogether. If you have ever cut and pasted a document by hand, you will appreciate the benefits of automatic text rearrangement.

Most word processing programs also allow you to search forward or backward in the document. This can be useful if you must change a word or phrase that is used consistently throughout a document. For example, suppose that you work for a record company and that you have typed a long report on your company's sales. In your report you have referred to long-playing albums as *records*. Your supervisor informs you that the company prefers the word *albums*. Instead of reading through the document and finding each place where you wrote *record* and then changing it to *album*, you could command the computer to search for the word *record* automatically. The computer will scan the document and stop at each place where the word *record* appears so that you can replace it. Depending on the program you have, you might even use a search and replace command, which would enable you to command the computer to automatically replace each *record* with *album*. The danger here is that you might have used the word *record* in another way too, as in "Our records show that 25 percent of our customers are under the age of 15." In this case you would not want the word changed to *album*. You would let the computer show you each place where the word *record* is used, and then you would decide whether or not to replace it. Most word processors can perform other more complicated tasks as well. We will examine some of these tasks in more detail in the next chapter.

Electronic Spreadsheets   Many office workers work with **spreadsheets**. In a traditional office, a spreadsheet is a large piece of ruled accounting paper on which figures are entered in columns and rows. In an electronic office, the figures appear in columns on the computer screen instead. Spreadsheet software is popular with managers and other office workers who need to produce budgets, profit plans, sales forecasts, and so on. It allows them to calculate, recalculate, and present the results in a useful format.

This kind of applications software is often called *decision-support* software because it provides people with the information they need in order to make business decisions. To get an idea of how electronic spreadsheets help in decision making, imagine yourself as the manager of a large inventory control department. If you wanted to find out how much you could afford to raise each staff member's salary, you could use a spreadsheet. The sheet would show each person's name and present salary. It would also show the total amount of money currently being spent for all employees. With an electronic spreadsheet, you could have the computer recalculate each person's salary if it were raised 5 percent, 7 percent, 10 percent, or whatever percentage you choose. In this way, you could see how large an increase the company could afford. If the spreadsheet were not electronic, you would have to make the calculations by hand—a tedious and error-prone task.

Spreadsheets are typically set up on the screen in columns and rows, which actually form a series of cells. They are usually too large to be displayed in their entirety on the screen, so most programs include a scrolling function that enables the user to move copy about in order to view different portions of the spreadsheet. The cursor on the screen becomes a cell pointer that enables the user to go to any cell in which an entry or change is needed.

Before electronic spreadsheets became available, managers and their support staffs had to develop spreadsheets by hand, using pencils, rulers, and calculators. If you wanted to change the number in any one cell, you had to erase, recalculate, and write new numbers in all the cells that were affected by that change. Since any one

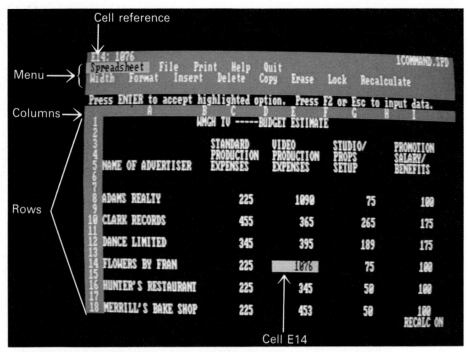

The grid of a spreadsheet contains individual cells where the information is input. The computer will automatically recalculate all variations you wish to explore.

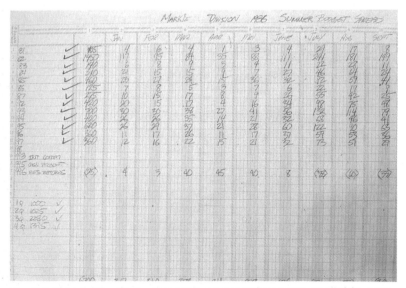

Fig. 8-3 Before electronic spreadsheet programs were available, people had to use—and still use—handwritten spreadsheets. These work well if you are good at math and can concentrate well enough to juggle all of the variables. To be done well, however, the work requires a high level of concentration.

change usually affects dozens of cells, developing spreadsheets by hand is time-consuming. In fact, one key reason why managers first bought personal computers was so that they could use VisiCalc, the first electronic spreadsheet, which was introduced in 1979.

By automating a tedious task that was once done by hand, spreadsheet software saves office workers many hours of painstaking work. This adds to office productivity by giving them more time for other work. Spreadsheet programs dramatically amplify what can be done by hand. They are fast and accurate, and they can handle complexity and detail. When you use them, you can analyze "what if" situations, allocate funds, compare alternatives, and track performance.

Data Base Management **Data base management** applications are used for entering, organizing, storing, and retrieving data in formats and orders specified by the user (for example, alphabetically or chronologically). The data can be retrieved by names, accounts, dates, and a variety of other identifying criteria. The simplest way to understand the concept of data base management is to visualize a large general filing department. The department collects all the company's sales figures, correspondence, accounts, personnel documents, and so on, over the years. These are stored in file cabinets. The file cabinets have drawers holding folders of letters, documents, periodicals, illustrations, and notes about where other documentation can be found. There are many directories to help users find the information they need.

Now imagine that all those files are stored within one computer system. In effect, data base management software duplicates the work of the filing department: it stores the information and helps users find the information they need. The big difference is in the space needed to store the information and in the speed with which information may be found. Another major advantage is that the software enables the data to be retrieved in several different ways.

For instance, suppose that you are an office worker in a medical office that uses a data base. The physicians in the practice have learned of a new treatment for hypertension in people 35 or younger. They want you to write to all the patients who might benefit from it and suggest that they make appointments to discuss the treatment with their doctors. After you have keyboarded the necessary commands, the computer system can automatically sort through the thousands of patient records stored in the data base and display or print the names and addresses of those patients under 35 who were diagnosed as having hypertension. It would take you several days of tedious work to compile this information from typewritten or handwritten records. Once you have the list, you can use your list-processing program to merge the names with a letter informing patients of the new treatment.

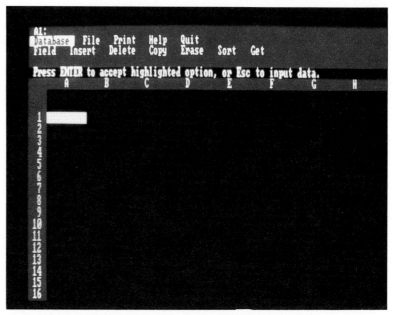

A1:

Database File Print Help Quit
Field Insert Delete Copy Erase Sort Get

Press ENTER to accept highlighted option, or Esc to input data.

A   B   C   D   E   F   G   H

1
2
3
4
5
6
7
8
9
10
11
12
13
14
15
16

Fig. 8-4 Some data bases look very much like a spreadsheet, with rows and columns to fill in with the information.

Data bases will be displayed on your screen differently depending on the software package you are using. Some may be divided into rows and columns similar to those on a spreadsheet, as in Fig. 8-4. Others might simply be arranged in a list format, as in Fig. 8-5.

It is important to know that the same basic principles apply to all data bases. A data base is made up of numerous **records**. For example, a data base in a medical practice would include a record for each patient. Each record is made up of several bits of important information called **fields**. In this case the fields might include name, address, telephone number, date of birth, physician's name, date of most recent visit, symptoms, diagnosis, treatment, and so on. In data bases arranged in columns and rows similar to those on a spreadsheet, one row of fields makes up a record. In data bases arranged with fields listed vertically, there is some sort of symbol that designates the end of one record and the beginning of the next.

Accounting If you work in a small office, your applications software may include either a general accounting program or one or more specialized accounting programs such as accounts receivable, accounts payable, payroll, inventory, and invoicing programs. In large organizations, accounting applications are used by specialists in departments such as payroll and accounts receivable.

Like spreadsheet programs, accounting software can save you work by having the computer recalculate old figures automatically as you enter new data. For example, if you enter data in the general

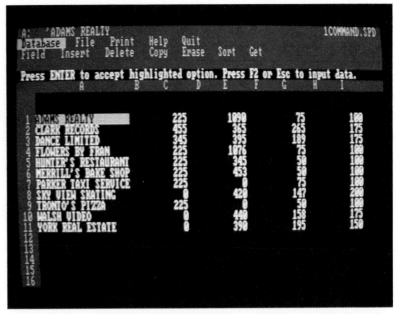

Fig. 8-5 Some data bases are compiled in a list format, with the information listed usually in some type of order (numeric, chronologic, alphabetic, or categoric). Here column A has been alphabetized.

ledger file about a $250 payment that customer Stephen Warner has sent in, the computer will automatically send this information to other files. When this information is sent to the accounts receivable file, the computer will reduce the outstanding total on Mr. Warner's bill by $250. That is, if the previous total was $800, the computer will automatically calculate that Mr. Warner now owes $550. All of this is done in one step. Without the computer you would have to make photocopies of the check, write in the numbers by hand, calculate the new amount on your calculator, file away the papers on Mr. Warner's account, and send memos about the account to other departments via interoffice mail. Chapter 17 will discuss accounting tasks in detail, along with the programs that office workers use in performing them.

Graphics Computers generate vast quantities of data, but if that data is going to be useful, it has to be converted into formats that people can understand. One way of translating lists of figures or other data into usable information is to convert them into charts or graphs using **computer graphics applications**. Charts can be prepared by hand, of course, but a software program that has a graphics capability will do the job faster and more accurately.

Charts and graphs can be used in a variety of business situations. They are useful for showing sales patterns, as a basis for slide presentations, for illustrations in reports, and for a variety of other situa-

The constantly improving quality of computer graphics is keeping pace with the demand for it in the office.

tions in which a graphic illustration aids understanding. Wouldn't you prefer to see a breakdown of a company's budget expressed as a pie chart instead of having to read and remember rows of figures? Pie charts, along with bar graphs, line graphs, and flowcharts, are just some of the forms of graphic illustration for which software is available.

Computers do not automatically create good graphics. You will need some training in chart design. As interest in business graphics grows, a wider variety of software packages is becoming available. The first computer graphics programs and hardware were slow, expensive, and difficult to use, and the results were of poor quality. The new technology is more sophisticated. It allows you to try different formats, sizes, and colors so that you can find the best way of presenting your information.

Communications **Communications applications** enable you to communicate with other office workers in your company or outside of your company and to obtain data from information retrieval services or public data bases. Communications software handles incoming and outgoing information. A communications program can tell the computer to do such things as save incoming messages, dial a phone number for you, redial if the number is busy, or log you on or off a communications network.

If you are working at a terminal that is connected to a centralized computer, chances are you won't need to be concerned with communications software. The technical staff supporting the computer will be responsible for this. They will be able to explain the communications capabilities of the computer system and tell you what commands you will need in order to transmit information from your terminal to somebody else's.

If, on the other hand, you will be transmitting data from a microcomputer, you will need communications software, a modem, and telephone lines to carry the transmission to the receiving party. The receiving party will need to have a similar setup that is compatible with yours. Once compatibility has been established, transmitting data may be as simple as dialing the phone number of the receiving computer, perhaps placing the telephone handset into an acoustic coupler, and issuing a few commands. Communications software programs vary, so you will need to refer to the documentation to find out how yours works.

Integrated Applications

In recent years software producers have been concentrating on the development of **integrated applications**, which consist of programs for several applications that are designed to work together. The purpose of integration is to bring the major business computing applications together so that data can be manipulated and converted into different formats easily. A typical integrated software product includes spreadsheet, database management, graphics, and word processing programs in a single package. Many products also include communications. With this kind of package, you can quickly switch from one application to another when the need arises. You can also move data from one application to another.

Earlier in this chapter you read about integrated computer systems. When computer systems are integrated, central data can be shared by terminals, messages can be exchanged, and the terminals can share equipment such as a printer. In this case the equipment is integrated, or linked together. In the case of integrated software packages, different applications software programs are linked together. For example, you can write and display the text of a sales report using the word processing program in the integrated package; then you can manipulate and analyze the same sales data by using the package's spreadsheet program; then you can show the results in a table; and finally, you can use your graphics program to produce charts from this data, which you can then transmit electronically.

All the programs in an integrated software package use similar menus and commands, enabling you to switch from one application to another without having to remember an entirely different set of procedures for operations such as deleting and inserting data. Well-known integrated microcomputer-based software packages include Lotus 1-2-3, Symphony, Framework, and Multiplan.

The first integrated software packages were created for stand-alone microcomputers. Increasingly, software companies are designing integrated programs for minicomputer systems and systems in which a number of microcomputer terminals share programs and data with each other and perhaps with bigger computers and other equipment. But integrated software does not have to run on integrated computer systems.

With many integrated software packages you can display data for several applications at once in different **windows**, or sections, of your screen. This enables you to switch among applications without changing screen displays. For instance, while writing a report with a word processing program, you could display part of a spreadsheet in another window and refer to the spreadsheet for data to include in your report. In a third window, you might create graphics that you will use to illustrate your report. Look at Fig. 8-6 to see what multiple windows look like.

There are some disadvantages to working with an integrated package. The programs are committed to a certain set of applications (some may not fit your particular needs), and the files produced may not be compatible with other software or systems. Also, an integrated package takes up a lot of computer memory.

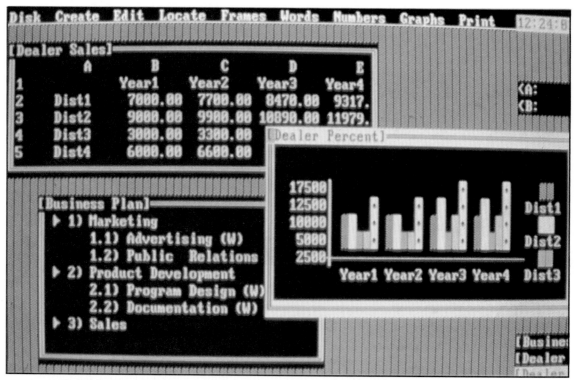

Fig. 8-6 With integrated software, you can display information for several different applications at once. Shown here are windows for word processing, spreadsheet, and graphics.

LEARNING TO USE SOFTWARE

Your first task with any new program is to learn how to use it. Learning to use a new spreadsheet or some other application is easier, of course, if you understand the underlying concepts and have already worked with similar programs. And using any program for the first time is easier if you are already comfortable with computer technology in general. Nonetheless, each program is unique, and everyone is a beginner when it comes to new software. But help is usually available from several sources:

■ **Documentation. Documentation** consists of instruction manuals and other learning materials. Some software instruction manuals are clear and thorough; others are written in highly technical language and are organized so poorly that they aren't much help to new users. In this case you will have to find other resources.

■ **Books.** Books on how to use most of the popular microcomputer programs are available in many bookstores, computer stores, and libraries. These books are often easier to follow than the official instruction manuals and may explain how to solve common problems that the official manuals do not describe.

■ **Reference materials.** In addition to instruction manuals for new users, software producers usually supply reference materials. These materials may include small cards, which you can consult quickly when you forget command codes, as well as thick volumes that include more details and technical information about the software.

■ **Tutorials.** Some software producers provide disk tutorials instead of, or in addition to, instruction manuals. **Disk tutorials** are lessons that are recorded on a disk and displayed on the computer screen. These lessons take you step-by-step, at your own pace, through each procedure. Tutorials on how to use the most popular microcomputer programs have also been produced by publishers not connected with the software producers. These tutorials, which can cost nearly as much as the programs themselves, are sold in many computer stores.

■ **Classes.** You can also learn how to use popular microcomputer programs by attending classes run by colleges, computer dealers, or businesses that specialize in teaching people to use computers and programs. These classes may be intensive one- or two-day seminars, or they may meet for shorter weekly sessions. Computer-software training classes are usually the fastest way to learn how to use a program effectively. They may cost more than the software itself, but they are usually worth the time and

money spent to learn to use the program well. Many companies offer such training free for staff members who will be using the software regularly. The companies that sell computer systems to businesses sometimes conduct classes to teach office workers how to use their systems. It's wise to take advantage of these classes if they are available.

■ **Electronic manuals and help facilities.** If the program you are using has an on-line reference manual, you can look up information without thumbing through pages of text. You select a topic from an electronic index, and the information you requested will be brought to the screen. Many programs also include a help command to find out what to do next. These electronic help facilities are slightly different from electronic manuals in that they provide you with help as you are working. With a program that has an electronic help facility, you press

the "HELP" key and get information immediately on a particular function and how to use it.

■ **Vendor support.** Some software-producing companies (**vendors**) provide a telephone information service at no extra charge. This is a way for you to talk with someone very knowledgeable about the program. Other software vendors offer newsletters that carry information about bugs, or errors, and advice on using the programs more effectively.

■ **Dealer support.** Most of the sales staff at computer stores have been trained and are familiar with the different packages they sell. They can offer help in choosing and working with software.

■ **User groups.** These are groups of people who meet to discuss a certain computer or application. They can provide help for new users and share what they've learned.

Evaluating and Selecting Software

Central minicomputers or mainframes in large offices generally run software that was written specially for them. Mainframe software for a single application can cost $100,000 or more. Because the software is so expensive and can affect a company's overall operations, decisions about purchasing software for big computers are generally made by computer specialists.

Today, however, many offices also have microcomputers that can use software not kept in the central computer. These microcomputers may be standalone units, or they may share software, storage, and other resources with a small group of other microcomputers through a network. They may also be microcomputers that are connected to a large computer system but that are also equipped with disk drives so they can run other programs besides those in the central computer. In these systems you may be responsible for helping to select software that you and your coworkers will use.

For any business function you can handle with a microcomputer, there are scores of competing software products on the market. Let's discuss how you can evaluate these products and decide which one is best for your office.

■ Compatibility

The first thing you need to determine before buying any software program is whether it will run with your computer. An application program must be compatible with your computer's operating system as well as with its hardware. As you know, most applications programs will run only on specific operating systems, such as MS-DOS. If you are buying software, be prepared to tell the dealer what operating system your computer uses. You should find this information in the computer's documentation. You can also consult the computer's documentation or your employer's computer specialists for information about your computer's hardware. Its compatibility with software may depend on the following characteristics.

Memory Computers differ in memory size and some software programs require more memory than others. A software program is loaded into the computer's memory, where it is held while processing takes place. If a software program requires more memory than the computer has, the program will not run on that computer unless a special board with additional chips is added to expand the memory. Before you select a program, be sure your computer has enough memory to run it.

A computer's memory is determined by its circuitry and is measured in kilobytes (usually abbreviated to *K*). A **kilobyte** represents roughly 1000 alphabetic or numeric characters. So a computer that can retain about 64,000 characters in its CPU at one time is said to have 64K of random-access memory, or 64K RAM. Just a few years ago, the most popular office microcomputer came with 64K as standard equipment. Since then, computer makers have developed models with greater memory capacities. Those being installed in offices today are likely to have memories of 128K, 256K, or more. As computers with greater memories have become available, software producers have created increasingly powerful programs with greater memory requirements.

Color Display Some programs run only on systems that can display color graphics. For color graphics your system needs a graphics board and a color adapter, as well as a color display monitor.

Printer A printer that produces letter-quality correspondence may not be able to produce high-quality graphics, and vice versa. Be sure your printer can make hard copies of the software's output.

Disk Drives Some microcomputers have two or more disk drives, but others have only one. If yours has only one, be careful not to buy software that requires two drives or more. Also, the floppy diskette on which the software is stored must have the diameter and capacity that your disk drive uses.

■ Comparing Products

The applications programs that are compatible with your system may vary quite a bit in what they can do and how fast they can do it. They may also have a wide range of prices. Sometimes inexpensive software is better for your needs than expensive software, but quite often it is not. If you choose software for your office, you will need to compare the following basic points.

Documentation The software should come with an instruction manual and other reference materials that are written in plain English, not computer jargon. Even if you and your coworkers have worked with computers before, look for step-by-step instructions that a future coworker with no computer experience could understand. Check to see if the reference manual is organized so that you can find the information you want without difficulty. An index, a glossary of terms, a quick reference guide, illustrations, and examples are helpful.

Ease of Use No matter how powerful the program or how good its documentation, it should also be easy to use. Its power will be wasted if you have to spend a lot of time paging through manuals to find out what to do next. Software vendors often describe their applications programs as **user-friendly**, or easy to use, even for people with no computer experience. In fact, some so-called user-friendly programs are much "friendlier" than others. So you should test programs to judge for yourself how easy they are to use before you buy them. Let's look at some features you might check.

■ **Menus**. When a program displays menus, it reminds you of the operations it can perform. Some menus are poorly organized and visually confusing, so when you test software, be sure you can understand the menus. Some programs display menus for most operations, while others rely on the user to memorize commands. Menus are extremely helpful to new users, but once you are familiar with the software, frequent menu displays can slow you down. Ideally, a program should allow users to indicate the level of help they need so that the program displays menus only when necessary.

■ **Commands**. Some software requires users to keyboard special codes for operations like saving or deleting data, searching for words, and moving the cursor from one section of a document to another. These codes may be very simple, or they may require combinations of keystrokes that can be difficult to learn and execute. The commands should be logical and easy to remember. The fewer keystrokes, the better.

■ **Help Screens**. Help screens are a good feature, but you should be able to learn how to use a well-designed program rapidly without continuously needing help. The commands for displaying help screens should be easy to remember, and the displays themselves should be easy to read.

Safeguards Everyone makes mistakes, and the best software is designed with that in mind. For instance, suppose you keyboard a

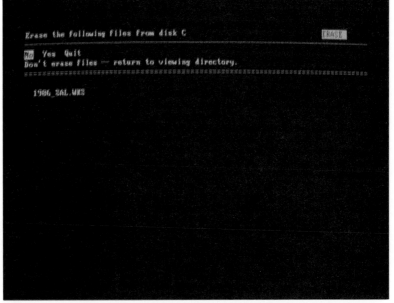

Most good software has built-in safeguards to keep you from accidentally or hastily erasing information. (Remember that once you have deleted it, it is gone for good unless you have a backup copy of the same document.) In this case, you are being given the option of reconsidering your decision to delete an entire document. If you press "Y," the document will be erased. If you press "N," the document will not be erased and you can continue processing it as needed.

command that would cause the computer to erase data from a storage disk. The program might remind you that the data will be deleted and ask you to verify the command before the computer will execute it. This makes you think twice and keeps you from erasing data you meant to store.

Buyer's Rights   When you buy software, you are actually buying the right to use it, with certain restrictions. Be sure you understand these restrictions. (See Fig. 8-7.) Here are some questions to ask:

■ Can you make backup copies?

■ If not, can you purchase backup copies cheaply?

■ Can you copy the software onto a hard disk?

Service   In addition to testing software for user-friendliness, look for information about the producer's customer service policies. If after you buy a program, you have unexpected difficulties in using it, can you turn to the company that produced it? Most software vendors have emergency numbers you can call for help. Other service considerations include whether the dealer will replace the soft-

1-2-3 from **Lotus** is the world's most popular software for business and professional use. It combines three essential analytical functions in one, fully integrated program: spreadsheet, graphics, and database. What's more, 1-2-3 is easy enough for the first time user yet provides the depth and power for the expert. 1-2-3 is an invaluable tool for business planning, analysis and decision-making.

Spreadsheet

1-2-3's spreadsheet function allows you to analyze information in a variety of ways and even perform "what if" scenarios. You can establish budgets, project cash flow, forecast sales, run sensitivity analyses. And more.

Graphics

With 1-2-3 you can graph up to six variables from information on the spreadsheet. "What if" changes can be visualized through instant graphic presentation. It's easy to change or update information on the spreadsheet and display a revised graph with a single keystroke.

Database

1-2-3's database function is an electronic filing cabinet that puts information at your fingertips. Extract individual pieces or groups of information for immediate spreadsheet analysis.

Learning is as easy as 1-2-3

You can learn to use the basics of 1-2-3 in just a few hours. A special disk, "A View of 1-2-3," gives a visual orientation to 1-2-3's spreadsheet, graphics, and database, and describes how these functions work together. The 1-2-3 Tutorial manual guides you keystroke by keystroke through the learning process. Should you forget a command or get confused about what to do next while using 1-2-3, more than 200 help screens can be accessed.

1-2-3 provides everything you need

This 1-2-3 package includes program disks, complete documentation, and function-key templates.

System Requirements:

Hardware	DOS
IBM* PC, XT,* Portable, 3270 PC	2.0, 2.1, 3.0, 3.1
IBM 3270/G, 3270/GX	2.0, 2.1
IBM PCjr*	2.1
IBM AT*	3.0, 3.1
COMPAQ* Portable, PLUS,* DESKPRO*	2.02 or 2.11
AT&T* PC 6300	2.11

Note: IBM 3270 versions supported in stand alone PC mode.
  IBM PCjr requires IBM Utility program.
Minimum system configuration is a single 5.25" double-sided, double-density disk drive and 256K bytes of memory.

Ask your dealer for a list of other personal computers and peripherals certified by Lotus as suitable for use with this product.

Fig. 8-7 Many software companies do not permit copying of their software, and other restrictions may apply as well. It is important to find out what restrictions apply to which software programs before you purchase them.

ware if it doesn't work correctly or if you damage it before copying it. Some vendors issue improved versions of their products periodically. Find out if you will be able to trade in your software for the improved versions for free or at a nominal cost.

Reputation　You can learn a great deal about what to expect from a software product by paying attention to people who have used it already. Several computer magazines, including *Byte*, publish reviews of software, and so do some big-city newspapers. These reviews can give you valuable information about the product you are considering. Also, people who have day-to-day experience with a software application may have opinions about the program that best fits the needs of your office.

Managing Your Software

Once you have received your new software program, there are a few basic procedures which should be followed for managing the software.

- Once you have opened the software package, examine its contents immediately to make sure that all the components are present. Most software packages provide the user with a checklist that lists all the components of the program.

- Inside the package you will find a **license agreement**. Read the license carefully. As the purchaser you are agreeing to certain terms for use of the program, upon opening the package. It is important for you to understand these terms.

- Most software packages contain a registration care that should be filled in and returned to the manufacturer. Registration of your purchase entitles you to receive notification of updates, upgrades, or new versions of the software. It will also entitle you to receive any corrected or new versions of the product if bugs or errors are discovered in the program or if your disk is damaged.

- By law when you purchase a software program you are entitled to a backup copy of the software. In some cases the manufacturer automatically supplies the backup in the original package. In other cases you will be required to send in your registration card to receive your backup copy or to follow instructions provided in the documentation to duplicate your own backup copy.

- Once you have reviewed the contents of the software package it is a good idea to establish a file for the pertinent information relating to the program. The file should contain a copy of the license agreement and the registration card, as well as the purchase order and manufacturer's invoice. Many manufacturers provide a service telephone number or hot line that you can call in the event of any problems with the software. This should also be kept in your file.

Software programs are powerful tools that can enable you to perform a broad range of tasks. Maintenance and recordkeeping procedures will enable you to avoid and overcome problems, and ensure that you are getting the most out of your software package.

▪ Summary

- With today's technology you can perform data processing and word processing with the same equipment. These functions can be handled by centralized departments or at individual workstations.

- The hardware components of an integrated computer system are input devices, the central processing unit, and output and communications devices.

- Software programs are written in special languages. Three types of languages that computer programmers use are low-level, high-level, and user-level languages.

- Systems programs operate the computer equipment and translate programs into machine-readable instructions. An operating system is a set of systems programs that controls the overall operation of the computer. Some operating systems used by microcomputers are CP/M, MS-DOS, Unix, and proprietary systems.

- Some of the most commonly used applications programs include word processing programs, spreadsheet programs, database management programs, and accounting software.

- The applications software most often used by office workers is that designed for word processing.

- Some word processing programs are menu-driven, and some are command-driven. Most word processing programs today use a combination of menus and commands.

- Word processing programs offer a wide variety of functions that differ from program to program. Most offer similar basic editing functions, such as deleting, underlining, and moving text.

- Spreadsheet applications enable workers to manipulate columns of figures and analyze "what if" situations. These kinds of programs are often called decision-support software.

- Data base management applications work on principles similar to those of a central filing office. Its purpose is to store and organize data so that it may be retrieved in a number of different ways.

- Graphics applications are used for creating visual representations of columns of figures and other data.

- In recent years programmers have been developing integrated software, which consists of programs for several applications—such as word processing, spreadsheet, database management, communications, and graphics—that are designed to work together and to share data.

- When evaluating software, you need to consider its compatibility with your computer in terms of its memory requirement, the type of monitor required, its printer needs, and its disk drive requirement.

- When comparing similar software programs, check the documentation carefully, test the programs for ease of use, examine the programs' safeguards, and ask about customer service policies.

- After purchasing software you should carefully read the license agreement and return the registration card. You should also maintain a file containing all information pertaining to the software package.

■ Review Questions

1. What advantages does a dedicated word processor have over a microcomputer with word processing software?

2. How is a menu-driven program different from a command-driven program?

3. Describe the main purpose of a spreadsheet. List the advantages that an electronic spreadsheet has over a manual one

4. What advantages does a data-base management program have over traditional storage and retrieval systems?

5. List some business situations for which graphs and charts would be useful tools.

6. What is integrated software? What advantages does integrated software have over individual software programs?

7. Why is a computer's memory capacity important in selecting software? How can the type of printer you have affect your selection of software?

8. What sources are available for help in learning to use software?

9. What are some important things to look for when shopping for software?

■ Technical Vocabulary

systems analyst
programmer
data base administrator
centralized data processing
decentralized data processing
satellite

on-line
low-level language
high-level language
user-level language
operating system
IBM PC-compatible

proprietary operating system	computer graphics
utilities	communications applications
applications programs	integrated applications
dedicated word processor	window
menu-driven program	documentation
command-driven program	disk tutorial
spreadsheet	vendor
data base management	kilobyte
record	user-friendly
field	license agreement

■ Discussion and Skills Development

1. Go to a store that sells word processing software, or talk to someone who uses word processing software frequently. What program does the person recommend most highly? Why? In class compare your information with what your classmates found out. Did everyone recommend the same software? How do you account for the differences, if there are any?

2. Think of something you could use a spreadsheet for in your daily living. It could be to help you figure out how much more you can spend on groceries and still have money to go to the movies, or anything that is appropriate to your situation. Prepare the spreadsheet. If you need to, get help from a book that explains spreadsheeting or from a person who has prepared spreadsheets before.

3. Suppose that you are in the market for a home computer and that you will be using it primarily for word processing. Your next-door neighbor and best friend, Bob, has a Kaypro that uses a CP/M operating system. You saw an ad for an IBM PC at a tremendous discount and would really like to buy it. The IBM uses PC-DOS for its operating system. You had hoped to be able to share software with Bob. Is it wise to buy the IBM? Why or why not?

4. Your employer has entrusted you with the job of buying word processing software for you and your coworkers to use. You have some background, but not much, in using a word processor. What steps would you take to find out what the best software would be for your purposes? Whom could you talk to? What things would you have to take into consideration? On what factors would you ultimately base your decision?

chapter 9
Information
Processing
Procedures

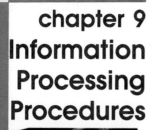

Electronic technology makes office work easier in many ways. You spend less time on routine tasks such as correcting and retyping documents or delivering messages. And tasks that once took great time and effort can now be done at the push of a few buttons. Yet that same technology also makes office life more complicated than it used to be. For one thing, you have to learn how to use the new equipment. For another, you have to be prepared to relearn when you switch jobs or acquire new equipment.

Many offices are at some stage of transition—moving from traditional equipment to word processing equipment or from semiautomated to fully electronic procedures. Even those offices which are already fully automated continue to change as new equipment renders the model of two or three years ago obsolete.

Change, then, has become a fact of office life. The secretary of a few decades ago who was able to learn office skills and then consider himself or herself trained for life has also become obsolete. Office workers today must be prepared for a lifetime of learning.

In this chapter you'll learn the basics of modern information processing. Every computer system is different, of course, and new types of equipment are being launched every week. But certain characteristics are common to most computers, and those are the ones that we focus on in this chapter.

Then we'll explore the basic procedures used in information processing. You'll learn the step-by-step procedures that you need to take when you sit down at a computer to process information. Once you've acquired the basic skills, you'll be able to transfer them to new technology as it becomes available. Each new development in the field of office technology will enable you to add to your store of knowledge.

Information Processing Equipment

When you start your office job, it is likely that you will use one of three main types of processing equipment: an electronic typewriter, a dedicated word processor, or a microcomputer that is a stand-alone, or a terminal connected to a larger system. As you learned in Chapter 2, electronic typewriters are simple word processors that can perform many of the functions which larger word processors can do, but in a more limited capacity. If you have an electronic typewriter, it will probably be "yours." That is, it will be permanently installed at your workstation, and you will probably be the only person to use it. This may also be true if you have a dedicated word processor or a microcomputer. However, these types of equipment are often shared among several employees.

Microcomputers are replacing dedicated word processing equipment in many offices today because they can perform more functions. Another reason for the change to microcomputers is that if you want to link all the workstations in your company together to form a network, the equipment must be compatible. In general, it is easier to link microcomputers with other microcomputers than to link microcomputers with dedicated word processors.

Equipment Characteristics

The processing equipment you work with might be a standalone unit or part of a network. Once you understand how to operate one type of equipment, it is generally easy to transfer that knowledge to another type. So if you understand the similarities and differences among various types of equipment, you can easily learn to use other types of equipment. Some features that vary from model to model are described below.

Keyboard The keyboard allows you to enter data into the computer. It is made up of keys labeled with numbers, letters, symbols, and words. Each type of electronic processing equipment has a keyboard as the main input device. But as you know, there are other input devices that can be used with computers, such as a mouse or a light pen. The keyboard you use will be either attached to the main unit or detached. Most electronic typewriters and dedicated word processors have attached keyboards. Many models of computers have detached keyboards that you can place in whatever position is most comfortable for you.

Most keyboards have the standard typewriter keyboard, with the QWERTY arrangement of letters. A few manufacturers provide a Dvorak keyboard, on which the most frequently used letters of the alphabet are on the home row. Some experts maintain that the Dvorak letter arrangement makes it easier to learn touch typing and to build typing speed. For these reasons they believe that the Dvorak keyboard will become more popular in time.

Most electronic keyboards have function/control keys located to the left and right of the alphanumeric keys. Some machines also have a ten-key numeric pad, usually located on the right, as well as the standard numeric/symbolic keys located on the top row. The

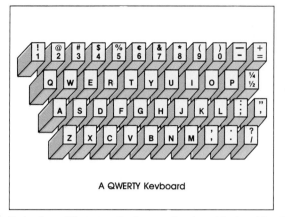

A QWERTY Keyboard

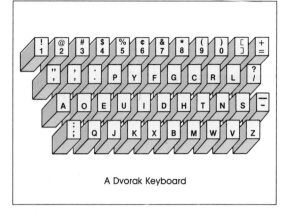

A Dvorak Keyboard

Note the difference between the two kinds of keyboards. Dvorak keyboards have the most frequently used keys in the home row.

function/control keys on a dedicated word processor have the words for some functions printed right on them. These keys are always used for the functions marked. When you use a microcomputer, you will have to learn the different uses of the function/control keys for the various software programs that you use. The templates that come with the software will help you learn the command codes for individual programs.

Memory As you learned in the last chapter, a computer's memory copies and stores the operating system and program information so that it can be used when needed. The size of a computer's memory determines the number and complexity of functions that the computer can perform. You should know the amount of memory your computer has so you can determine if it can run the applications programs you wish to use. Electronic typewriters, sometimes called *memory typewriters,* have far less memory than dedicated word processors or computers and they don't use applications programs. Most electronic typewriters have between 8 and 16 kilobytes of memory (a kilobyte, you will remember, is the unit of measure used to calculate the storage capacity of a computer). The average personal computer holds up to 364 kilobytes. The memory capacity of a mainframe or minicomputer is greater than this and is usually measured by megabytes (1,000,000 bytes or characters equals one megabyte).

If you work with an integrated system of small and large computers, you will follow a procedure that lets you know how much space is left in memory for you to store documents. When you have too many documents stored in the system, you will be told to delete files or to save them on an external storage medium—usually a floppy diskette. If you work on a microcomputer, you can determine the amount of space left on a disk by viewing the directory in most cases.

Display monitors on electronic typewriters are sometimes called "thin windows."

Display Monitors The display is what appears on the screen when you use a program or enter data into the computer. One major difference between electronic typewriters and other electronic processing devices is the size and capabilities of the display component. Many electronic typewriters have a small display area located directly above the typing keyboard instead of a large screen. Depending on its size, the display area will show either a few words or a few lines of type. On the other hand, a typical display monitor on a word processor or microcomputer is a screen that displays 80 characters on each line and 24 lines, which is considered a half-page display. Some monitors can display an entire page as well. There are color display monitors that can present graphics and text in color. The **resolution** of the display, which means the sharpness of the letters or picture, is generally determined by the number of tiny dots that the computer uses to form characters and shapes.

Examples of disk drives.

Disk Drives Disks record and store information and instructions entered into a computer, and they recall that data after they have been put into the disk drive. The disk drive is a device that is either built into the computer terminal or contained in a small, separate, boxlike plastic case. This drive contains a small electromagnetic head that is capable of reading, writing, or erasing information on the disk. Microcomputers and word processors utilize disk drives. Most electronic typewriters do not use these devices but, instead, use a built-in disk for storage which the user can't remove. A disk drive is used when you want to store data that has been input on the system. Otherwise, you access the software that is in the system.

When you want to use an applications program that is not in the system, or if you are using standalone equipment, you will need to use a disk that contains the program. Most equipment has one or two disk drives. A second disk drive can be added to any system that has only one. Since most software programs require the use of two disks, the advantage of having two disk drives is that you don't have to swap disks while you are working.

If you need to work with large amounts of data, you may have a hard-disk drive for storage. This kind of drive is almost ten times as fast as a floppy diskette drive and stores about ten times as much information on its disk. However, even if you have a hard-disk drive, you will also need at least one floppy diskette drive for loading applications programs.

INFORMATION PROCESSING SUPPLIES

When you work with electronic equipment, you use many different types of supplies. Some of these supplies have always been used in the office; others are entirely new. You may be asked to order these supplies for yourself or for your entire department. You should become familiar with the types of supplies you will be using.

Disks. A disk is used for storing data magnetically. A **floppy diskette** is a round, flat, double-sided sheet of pliable plastic that is magnetically treated and coated in a protective vinyl jacket. Floppy diskettes come in three basic sizes: the standard diameter for a microcomputer is 5¼ inches; many word processing systems take 8-inch disks; others use a micro-sized disk that is 3½ inches in diameter. Disks are usually packaged in boxes of ten. A **hard disk** is a high-volume storage device made of rigid plastic, aluminum, or ceramic and magnetically treated. It is often sealed directly inside the computer's cabinet. Hard disks can also be used in disk packs in larger computers. Here are some technical terms you will need to know when you work with disks:

■ **Double-sided**. Both sides of the disk can be used.

■ **Double-density**. The disk can store twice the amount of data that can be stored on a single-density disk.

■ **Write-protect notch**. A **write-protect notch** is an indentation on the outside edge of a floppy diskette housing. As long as the indentation is uncovered, you can add new data to the disk or erase or replace data already on the disk. Once you cover the notch, you can only retrieve and use the data or programs that are on the disk; you cannot erase them or replace them or add new information. The main purpose of the write-protect notch is to prevent you from accidentally writing over or erasing data that is important.

■ **Hub ring**. This is placed in the ring of a disk to protect the disk from damage while it is in the disk drive.

Magnetic Tape. Magnetic tape is often used for backup storage. This kind of tape is similar to the tape used to record music. It comes in reels, cartridges, and cassettes. Large reels of tape are usually used in large computer systems; smaller cassettes of tape are used by some microcomputers. In some cases magnetic tape can be used to copy data for use by other computers instead of using phone lines and modems.

Static Guard. Static is caused by electromagnetic currents in the air. Static buildup on carpets and furniture can automatically erase data from a disk. To avoid this, you might need to have antistatic desk pads, chair mats, or carpet mats. Special cleaning supplies, such as antistatic sprays and cleaning cloths, may have to be used.

Paper. Your company will provide preprinted forms, memo pads, and letterheads. For other needs you will want to have continuous-form paper that feeds automatically through the printer. There are also continuous forms for card files, mailing labels, and file labels.

Workstation Aids and Organizers. Additional supplies needed for working with software are disk labels, special marker pens that will not scratch the surface of the disks, and disk storage devices, which are discussed in more detail in Chapter 10. Additional supplies for the hardware you work with include covers for the disk drives and keyboard to protect them from dust and dirt, as well as a stand to turn and tilt the keyboard or monitor so that it is easier to use. Some offices also use filters that are placed over the monitors to reduce glare from overhead lighting.

Printer Cartridge. Just as a typewriter requires a ribbon to produce output, most printers require an ink cartridge or ribbon for printing. Although a large volume of printing can be accomplished from one cartridge, replacements will be required. Be sure to identify the type of refill needed for your printer and to have stock on hand.

Information Processing Procedures

In the electronic office, as in any other type of office system, most of your processing time will be spent on the preparation of documents. Although you may use integrated applications frequently, in most cases these applications will be used in conjunction with the processing of memos, letters, and reports, as discussed in Chapter 6. For example, spreadsheets and graphics may be used to create information for reports.

Although the specific design of the keyboard, software, and other equipment you use may differ, you will still follow certain basic procedures in order to turn data into processed information. This section will examine these procedures in detail.

Getting Ready

Applications software is built into some dedicated word processors. It begins working automatically when you turn on the machine. Other dedicated word processors use disks to store an entire application or to store certain procedures, such as storage of documents. If you are using a microcomputer, you will always need a disk with an applications program on it. This disk is called the **program disk**. You begin to use any program disk by inserting the disk into the disk drive and turning the computer on. The manual that accompanies the disk will give you the specific instructions to follow. For example, it will explain the procedure you will follow for using application software on a computer with one disk drive, as well as the alternative procedure for a machine with two disk drives.

DOS In order to operate an application program such as a spreadsheet, or word processing program, you must first load DOS (the disk operating system). Starting or loading DOS means that a set of commands contained on the DOS disk are read by the computer and stored in its temporary memory. These commands are called **internal commands**. They allow the program to run immediately and perform such functions as listing an index of the files on your disk, removing or erasing unwanted files, renaming current files, or copying individual files.

The rest of the commands on the DOS disk are referred to as **external commands**. External commands are not automatically read into the temporary memory of the computer when you load your DOS disk. You need to enter specific file names (listed on the DOS directory) to use these external commands. These commands perform functions such as copying the contents of an entire disk, comparing the content stored on one disk to the content stored on another disk, and preparing a disk to receive information.

Creating the Document

To create a document you will first need to load the applications disk containing the word processing program onto your system. Depending on the software you are using, you will either enter commands or make a menu selection to begin creating a document. If you are working on an integrated system, you will probably select a word processing function from the system menu. If you want to edit a stored document, you enter the file name of the document you wish

This menu gives you choices for opening a file for a new document.

to work on. Some word processing systems automatically assign a file name to each document in numeric order as it is created. Other systems allow you to give the document whatever name you wish with certain constraints on the length of characters and character types that can be used. Depending on what software you are using, you name the document either when you create it or when it is completely keyboarded and you are ready to save it.

Formatting the Document

The next step is to choose the page layout. This is called formatting the document, which is different from formatting a disk. In Chapter 6 you learned some standard formats for letters, memos, and reports. You must find out which formats your company uses. If there are no preferred formats, consult a style guide, such as *The Gregg Reference Manual* (McGraw-Hill). Here are the main settings you use when you format a document:

- **Margins, tabs, and paragraph indents**. Set the margins and tabs for the document as on a typewriter. You can also select the spacing for starting new paragraphs. Some programs include options such as aligning or justifying the text on either the left or the right margin, justifying the text (aligning it on both margins simultaneously), or centering lines.

- **Line spacing**. Select the spacing for the document: single spacing, double spacing, or a different amount of space between lines.

- **Page length**. Defines the number of lines on each page.

- **Page numbering**. Pages can be numbered automatically by many word processing programs. The numbers can be placed at the top or bottom of each page, and can be printed at the center or at the right or left side of the page. If you delete a page in the middle of a document while you are working on it, the computer will change the numbers of the remaining pages so that they are again in sequence.

- **Headers and footers**. In addition to the page numbers at the top or bottom of every page, insert other information, such as the author's name or the title of the document. If the information is placed at the top of the page it is called a **header**; at the bottom it is referred to as a **footer**.

Inputting and Editing the Document

After you set up the format, you are ready to keyboard the document. Most word processing programs include very similar input and edit functions. The functions listed are those most commonly provided. Depending on the software you are working with, you may not have all of these, or you may have more. Also, the function names may be different in some word processing programs.

- **Center**. Automatically centers text between the right and left margins.

- **Copy**. Designates a block of text, such as a paragraph, that needs to be duplicated in another place or several places within the document.

- **Delete**. Designate a block of text to be removed from the document. This type of delete function will require fewer keystrokes in removing large portions of text than the two delete functions listed below.

- **Delete character**. Removes one character at a time from the document.

- **Delete word**. Removes one word at a time from the document.

- **Global replace**. Replaces every occurrence of a selected word or phrase in a document with new text. For example, if the words *United States of America* appear in many places in a document and you decided to change them in each place to the abbreviation *U.S.A.*, you would use the global replace function.

- **Help**. Provides an electronic manual of the functions that can be used and details on how to use them.

- **Indent**. Automatically sets up a temporary left margin for typing indented text.

- **Insert**. Allows more text to be inserted in the middle of existing text without altering any of the text that was originally there.

- **Insert space**. Inserts just one space in the middle of existing text.

- **Merge**. Inserts another document that has been previously stored or filed into the current document being edited.

- **Move**. Designates a block of text to be moved from its original location to another place in the document.

- **Save**. Stores or files a portion of the current document being edited as a separate document in itself.

- **Search**. Locates a specific text sequence that you wish to get to quickly when you use this function.

- **Top or bottom of file**. Speeds editing operations considerably by enabling you to move the cursor quickly to the beginning or end of the document.

To further understand how these word processing functions might be used, refer to Fig. 9-1, which illustrates some of the functions listed above.

Word Processing **Features** — Center

change each occurrence to "functions."

Indent ¶

The features provided by a word processor can make editing changes much quicker and easier to do than they are with just a typewriter.

When editing changes are really needed in a document, you won't have to retype it in most cases. You will just have to bring the document to your screen from where it is stored or filed. Using the features of your word processor you can then edit the soft copy. After this is completed, you can get an updated hard copy of the document by printing it. It's that easy!

As you can see, using a word processor can be a real time-saver! As you can see, using a word processor can be a real time-saver.

In addition to this, once you become familiar with one word processing system, *and its functions* it is easy to learn how to use another. Oftentimes it's just a matter of finding your way around a new keyboard.

TR.

L //// t //// t //// t //// t //// t //// t //// t //// t //// R
◄
◄   Word Processing Functions
◄
→ The functions provided by a word processor can make editing changes much quicker
   and easier to do than they are with a typewriter.◄
◄
When editing changes are needed in a document, you won't have to retype it in most cases.
You will just have to bring the document to your screen from where it is stored or
filed. Using the functions of your word processor you can then edit the soft copy.
After this is completed, you can get an updated hard copy of the document by printing
it. It's that easy!◄
◄
In addition to this, once you become familiar with one word processing system and
its functions, it is easy to learn how to use another. Oftentimes it's just a matter
of finding your way around a new keyboard.◄
◄
As you can see, using a word processor can be a real time-saver!

Fig. 9-1 The figure on the top shows hard copy of the document that has been marked for editing corrections. On the bottom, note how the changes were made. For example, the word "features" was changed to "functions" with the global replace function. Check the list of word processing functions on page 215. Can you identify how the other changes were made?

Proofreading the Document

After you have finished keyboarding the document, you will need to proofread it for errors in keyboarding, spelling, grammar, and syntax. Check also for the kinds of errors that occur only with word processing equipment. You will quickly become familiar with these. For example, when you use a typewriter, you can easily tell the difference between one page and another. With a word processor, you will learn to check the status line to see how many lines there are on a page. If your system uses a screen symbol to show page breaks, you will also want to make sure that there is a page break at the bottom of every page. If there are too many lines on a page, or if you forget to put in a page break, the printer may print right down to the bottom of the page.

You should proofread a document on the screen before you print it, but you will still need to proofread the hard copy as well.

Spelling Checkers   Many word processing packages have electronic dictionaries, or **spelling checkers**. Some of these electronic dictionaries compare the words in the document being processed with those in the dictionary. When a word doesn't match one that is in the dictionary, the word in question will be highlighted so that the user can correct it if necessary. Since the electronic dictionary cannot possibly contain all words, it will sometimes highlight correctly spelled words, such as proper names. But you can usually add frequently used proper names and industry-specific terms to the dictionary so that they are not continually highlighted. Spelling checkers also help you find typing errors. For example, if a space is missing between two words, the dictionary will consider the error as one misspelled word rather than as two words with a missing space. You can also use some electronic dictionaries to "look up" words you are not sure of as you are inputting the document. This reduces the number of corrections needed later. Refer to Fig. 9-2 to see how a spelling checker works on a typical document.

A spelling checker cannot tell the difference between singular and plural forms of words or words with different verb endings unless they are included in the dictionary. For instance, both *phenomenon* and *phenomena* must be on the dictionary's list for them to be checked. But even if both of these words are on the list, the spelling checker cannot tell if you have used the words correctly. You must still proofread your document to check word usage. With most programs you will also have to check that you have hyphenated words correctly, although there are programs that will check word breaks for you too.

Grammar Checkers   Some packages include a grammar checker. A **grammar checker** helps you avoid common grammatical errors, such as split infinitives and the use of plural nouns with singular verbs. You will still have to check your work to make sure that you have not made other grammatical errors, such as run-on sentences, incomplete sentences, and misplaced modifiers.

```
L54..t....t....t....t....t....t....t....t....t....t.1.0R

January 17, 1986◄

◄

Mr. Jeromy Dunlap◄
1505 Elm Lane◄
New York, NY  20000◄

◄
Dear Mr. Dunlap:◄

◄
It has come to our attention that youraccount balance is
now thirty days overdue.◄

◄
We must ask that you remit your payment to us as soon as
possible.  If you have already done so, please excuse
any inconvenence this may have caused.◄

◄
Thank you.◄

◄
Sincerely,◄

◄
```

```
There are 5  words not in the dictionary. Do you wish to change them? (Y/N)█
L54..t....t....t....t....t....t....t....t....t....t.1.0R

◄

◄
January 17, 1986◄

◄
Mr. Jeromy Dunlap◄
1505 Elm Lane◄
New York, NY  20000◄

◄
Dear Mr. Dunlap:◄

◄
It has come to our attention that youraccount balance is
now thirty days overdue.◄

◄
We must ask that you remit your payment to us as soon as
possible.  If you have already done so, please excuse
any inconvenence this may have caused.◄

◄
Thank you.◄

◄
Sincerely,◄
```

Fig. 9-2 A spelling checker highlights words that are not entered in its dictionary. In this example, the first three words highlighted are proper names and don't need to be corrected. However, if they are words that you will use frequently, you should add them to the dictionary. The fifth word highlighted, "your account," is simply a typing error of two words without the separating space between them. To correct the error, you insert the space. The last word highlighted, "inconvenence," is misspelled. It can be looked up in the electronic dictionary and corrected in the document. Then the document will look as it appears on the right.

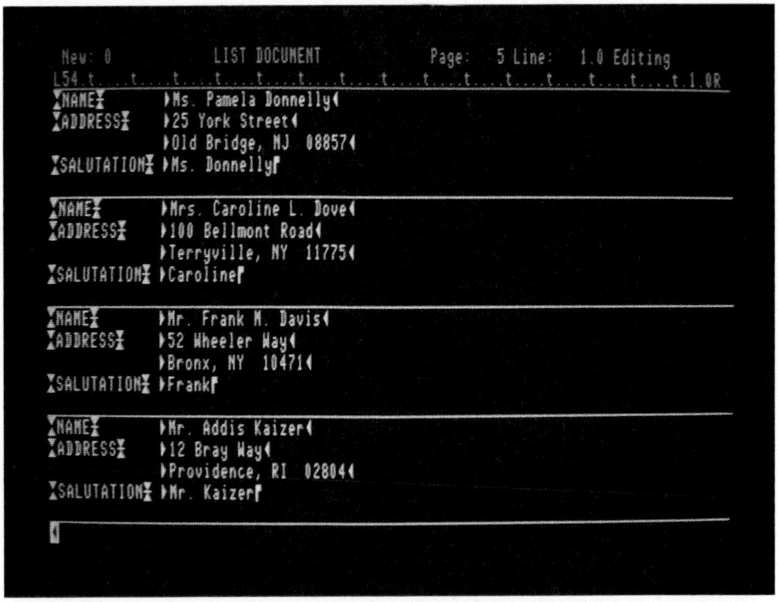

Fig. 9-3a Example of list processing—list document.

List Processing

List processing allows you to send a form letter or document to hundreds of people by automatically merging it with a mailing list that contains all the names, addresses, and salutations for the letters, and perhaps other information as well. This merging process results in a personalized letter or document for each recipient. It is more efficient than making photocopies of a form letter and filling

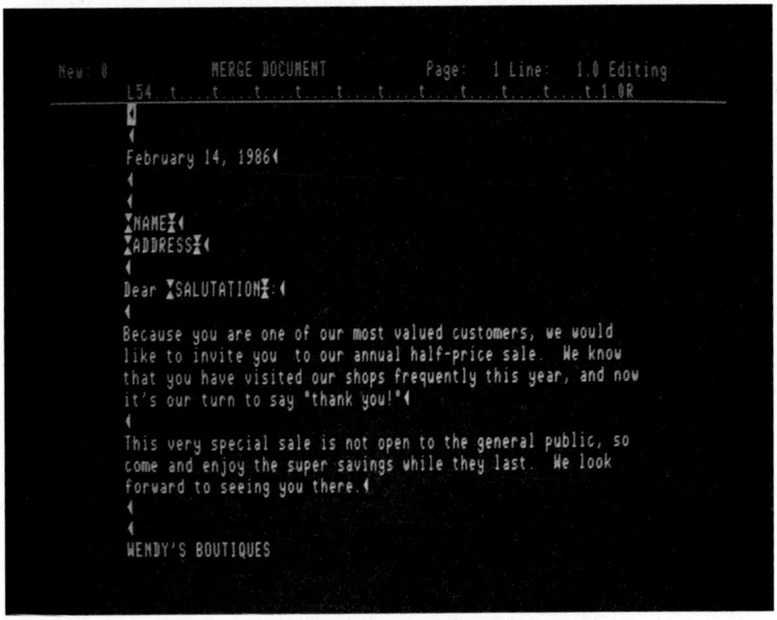

Fig. 9-3b Example of list processing—merge document.

Fig. 9-3c Example of list processing—the completed letters.

in the blanks at a typewriter. The end result is also more pleasing to the eye. With list processing software, every letter in a mass mailing will look as though it has been individually typed.

When you use such a program, you first have to input the letter or document into your word processor. You provide the appropriate commands for each bit of information (such as name, address, and salutation) that will be merged from the mailing list. After completing the letter, you input the mailing list, sometimes called the *list document,* and give the commands for the parts that will be inserted. Refer to Fig. 9-3 for examples.

Working with Floppy Diskettes

Software that is not recorded on central storage units of a minicomputer or mainframe, on hard disks, or on magnetic tape is generally recorded on floppy diskettes (Fig. 9-4). In most cases, floppy diskettes are used to record data on standalone microcomputers or word processors. You should be aware, though, that many microcomputers can be linked to minicomputer or mainframe systems where they are able to use software stored there in addition to software stored on disks that you can insert into the disk drive. When using software locally on a disk, the microcomputer usually goes off-line from the larger computer system. When you are done using the disk, you can go on-line again. If you are working with software stored on disks, changing software involves inserting the new program disk into the disk drive and keyboarding a command to reset the computer. You would use another disk to record the information you process.

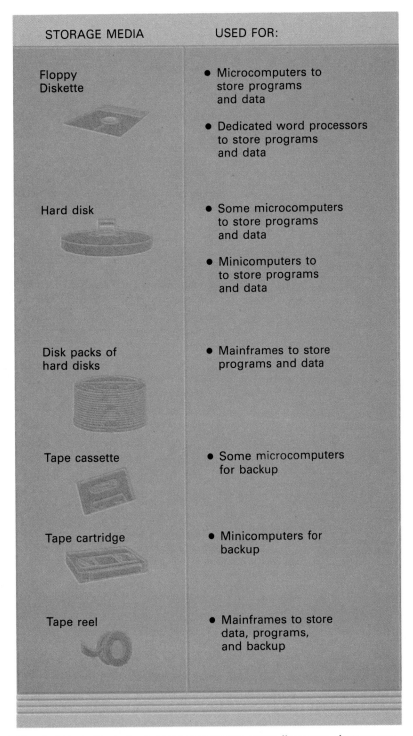

STORAGE MEDIA	USED FOR:
Floppy Diskette	• Microcomputers to store programs and data • Dedicated word processors to store programs and data
Hard disk	• Some microcomputers to store programs and data • Minicomputers to to store programs and data
Disk packs of hard disks	• Mainframes to store programs and data
Tape cassette	• Some microcomputers for backup
Tape cartridge	• Minicomputers for backup
Tape reel	• Mainframes to store data, programs, and backup

Fig. 9-4 Each kind of equipment may use more than one storage medium. Backup is often done on a medium other than the one used for information processing.

If you are using a microcomputer with two disk drives, you can use applications software and data disks at the same time without shifting them in and out of the drives as you work. If your computer utilizes a hard disk, you can copy each program from a floppy diskette to the hard disk (which stays in the storage unit at all times) so that you don't have to use the floppy diskette software again. Your computer will display a directory of the programs stored on the hard disk. You would probably use floppy diskettes for storing your data, however, and for using application programs not loaded onto the hard disk.

If you work with floppy diskettes, you need to learn how to use, store, and protect them. They are delicate and are very easily damaged. Carelessness can also lead to the accidental loss of important data.

Preventing Damage and Loss

The two most prevalent problems with maintenance of disks are physical damage and theft. As you have read, computers store data and information by recording magnetic signals on disks. They also store software instructions in this way. If you damage a disk, you can't use the data or programs that are stored on it. Guidelines for protecting disks from damage are given in the box entitled "Care and Handling of Floppy Diskettes" on page 224.

Most businesses carefully protect their central storage media from theft by restricting access to computer rooms. In small microcomputer systems, hard disks cannot be removed easily, so they are as safe as the other hardware. But some office workers may tend to be quite careless about where they keep floppy diskettes that contain critically important or confidential information. It's usually advisable to keep floppy diskettes containing such information in locked drawers.

System Failures

You can lose data if there is a power failure in the computer system. As you know, a computer stores input in a temporary memory until you instruct it to store it on a disk. If the computer breaks down as you are working, or if there is a power failure, you may lose the data you entered since the last time you entered a "save" command unless the computer system you are working on automatically and periodically "saves" data for you.

Sometimes computer failures generate electrical signals that damage disks too, and so even the data you have stored may be lost. The best way to guard against this is to make backup copies of data disks and keep them as up to date as possible. You can also use a surge protector, which looks like a heavy-duty extension cord. A surge protector eliminates power surges, spikes, and line noise so that they don't damage equipment or affect data stored in the system.

Making Backup Disks

Technical specialists are responsible for making the backup copies and performing other maintenance operations for minicomputer and mainframe systems. Office workers using microcomputers, however, are responsible for protecting the programs and data they store on disks. You will need to make backup copies of software and data recorded on both hard disks and floppy diskettes. The steps involved in making backup copies will depend on the computer and the software you are using. In general, you will keyboard a "copy" command and insert the disk you wish to duplicate and a blank disk into the disk drives of your computer.

Security

Software is valuable. An organization may pay hundreds of thousands of dollars for an elaborate set of programs for a mainframe computer, and microcomputer software on floppy diskettes is expensive too. Data you process with the software is valuable as well. It may be difficult to duplicate, requiring many hours of work repeating what you have already done if the software is lost. Since electronic offices need to prevent unauthorized people from gaining access to confidential information or from changing or erasing data, they establish procedures that you will need to learn. Here are some of the procedures office workers use to control access to data:

- **Identification codes**. In a large organization, employees usually have to **log on**, or keyboard their individual identification codes, before they can use a terminal linked to a central computer. This is also true in some small networks. An **identification code** may tell the computer what data the employee is—and is not—authorized to use. The system may keep records of each employee's work which the employer can check.

- **Passwords**. In addition to an identification code, you may have to keyboard a **password** to identify yourself to the central computer. This provides more protection against improper use of data files. Some offices change their passwords regularly. A password generally provides you with a key to your own files on the system, and an identification code identifies you as a valid user on the computer system.

- **Encryption**. To guard highly confidential data, businesses may use a process called **encryption**, which is the use of a code to scramble data so that it looks like gibberish. A computer system will unscramble encrypted data only for users who keyboard the required password. Computer programming specialists are responsible for encrypting sensitive data that is kept in central computers. An office worker at a separate workstation can encrypt the data stored on floppy diskettes or a hard disk with a special utility program.

CARE AND HANDLING OF FLOPPY DISKETTES

Here are some procedures you can use to guard the disks against damage and accidental loss of data.

- If your software is stored on a floppy diskette, cover the write-protect notch with a sticker before you use the disk or even make a copy of it. A box of blank floppy diskettes usually includes a package of write-protect stickers. Computer supply dealers also sell them. Apply write-protect stickers to new software disks and to any disks containing data that should not be changed.
- Handle a floppy diskette only near the label at the top of its rigid protective cover. Never remove a disk from its protective cover, and never touch the parts of the disk that are exposed through openings in the cover.
- Do not fold, crease, or bend a floppy diskette.
- Do not use pens, pencils, or erasers on the surface of the protective cover of a floppy diskette. Instead, write on an adhesive-backed identification label before you apply it to the disk cover. Remove any old labels, if possible, instead of adding new labels on top.
- Keep disks out of direct sunlight and away from radiators, lamps, and other heat sources.
- Store disks at room temperature.
- When they are not in the disk drive, keep floppy diskettes in their protective paper jackets.
- Store floppy diskettes, in their paper jackets, so that they are standing on their edges, not in stacks, in specially designed containers. These are available from computer supply dealers.
- Keep magnets away from floppy diskettes and hard disks, because magnetism can erase data. Keep metal paper clips away from disks too, because many office workers use magnetic paper-clip containers that magnetize the clips themselves. And a ringing telephone can create a magnetic field, so don't leave your disks near telephones or set a telephone on top of a disk drive.
- Follow the procedures for handling disks outlined in your computer's instruction manual, and be careful when you insert floppy diskettes into disk drives.
- Keep floppy diskettes away from water and other liquids. If they should get wet for some reason, dry them with a lint-free cloth.

■ Summary

- The three major types of processing equipment you are likely to find at workstations in an office are electronic typewriters, dedicated word processors, and microcomputers which may be standalones or terminals connected to a networked system.

- Information processing equipment includes a keyboard, memory, display monitor, and disk drive. Supplies for processing include floppy diskettes, hard disks, magnetic tapes, a static guard, and continuous-form paper.

- The main settings you can choose when you format a document are margins, tabs, paragraph indents, line spacing, page length, page numbering, headers, and footers.

- Input and edit features usually found in a word processing program are center, copy, delete, search, replace, help, indent, insert, move, read, and save.

- Some word processing software includes a spelling checker or a grammar checker that helps when you proofread a document.

- List processing merges a form letter with a list of names and addresses.

- Because floppy diskettes are valuable, you need to learn procedures for protecting them against damage, loss, and system failures. You will need to make backup copies of the disks as well.

■ Review Questions

1. Give two reasons why microcomputers are replacing dedicated word processors in today's office.

2. What are the differences between the QWERTY and Dvorak keyboards? How do these differences affect information processing?

3. How does the size of a computer's memory affect information processing?

4. In what ways can list processing make office work easier?

5. What are some techniques for the care and handling of floppy diskettes?

6. Describe the different kinds of magnetic storage media. When would you use each one?

7. How does a computer help you format a document?

8. Why should you still proofread a document, even though you have software with spelling checking and grammar checking functions?

9. What kinds of problems can cause data stored on disks to be erased?

■ Technical Vocabulary

resolution
floppy diskette
hard disk
double-sided
double-density
program disk
header
footer
spelling checker
grammar checker

write-protect notch
hub ring
program disk
internal commands
external commands
log on
identification code
password
encryption

■ Discussion and Skills Development

1. Choose one component of information processing equipment that you will research: keyboards, memory, display monitors, or disk drives. Then find two computer magazines, such as *Byte* and *PC*, at the library or newsstand. Look through the articles, pictures, and ads for the equipment you have chosen. Take notes about the different types of that equipment available today and the range of options offered. Make a summary chart of the similarities and differences you find.

2. Visit an office supply store. Identify the different types of workstation aids the store carries for working with computers. Find at least three products besides those mentioned in this chapter, and be prepared to describe their uses to the class.

3. Write a memo to the class that tells what aspect of the electronic office you would like to study next and why. Type the memo, and then proofread it. Then input the memo using a word processor or microcomputer, proofread it on the screen, print it out, and proofread it again. Explain to the class what differences and similarities you found in the proofreading tasks.

4. Imagine that you want to buy ten new floppy diskettes for your IBM PC. Call or visit several different computer supply stores, or department stores, and find out what choices are available to you. Make a list of the different disks you could use and the prices. Ask the salespeople to explain why some disks are more expensive than others. Share your findings with the class.

chapter 10
Storage and Information Management

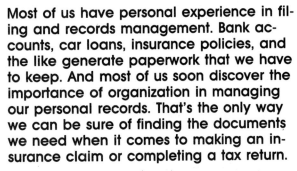

Most of us have personal experience in filing and records management. Bank accounts, car loans, insurance policies, and the like generate paperwork that we have to keep. And most of us soon discover the importance of organization in managing our personal records. That's the only way we can be sure of finding the documents we need when it comes to making an insurance claim or completing a tax return.

The same is true of managing important information in the business world. Good organization is essential. Without it, any filing system—whether it consists of traditional file cabinets or stacks of computer disks—is useless. People have to be able to retrieve the information stored in the system. And unlike your personal file system consisting of maybe 10 or 20 files (not too many to search through should you misplace something), an office system might consist of literally millions of records.

Businesses retain records for a number of important reasons. They need some documents as legal records of business transactions. Some financial records must be kept by law for a stipulated number of years. And many documents are kept so that people can refer back to them when necessary.

Information management involves the storage, protection, retrieval, use, and disposal of records. The records may be in the form of paper documents, computer disks or tapes, or various types of miniaturized film called microforms.

This chapter examines the equipment and procedures used to set up and maintain information management systems. You will see where procedures for handling manual filing and electronic filing systems overlap and where they differ. Finally, you will gain an overview of the field of information management that covers handling records on a broad scale.

Filing Systems and Procedures

Almost all office workers spend some of their time filing. Even if their filing duties are limited to organizing their own files, they need to develop and follow a simple system. Those who are responsible for filing and retrieving records generated by supervisors and co-workers may need to become familiar with some sophisticated electronic systems.

The first step in easy retrieval is to use a storage method that fits the kind of record being filed. Different methods work best with different kinds of records, so you should know different filing rules and procedures. First, let's look at some of the methods that workers use to store their own records and materials.

■ **In/Out Boxes**. Many forms, letters, and memos are most efficiently handled by an in/out box. Such a device usually consists of two or three stacked metal or plastic trays labeled "in," "out," and perhaps "hold." The purpose of the in/out box is to organize papers coming in to you for processing and going out from you for further action. The "hold" tray is for papers that do not demand immediate attention or that you cannot act upon immediately. For these papers you must devise a system that will remind you to attend to them at the appropriate time. You will learn how to do this later.

■ **Desk-Drawer Files**. For your own personal records—items that no one else will need—a desk-drawer file is probably the answer. A desk-drawer file is the perfect place to keep blank forms, carbon paper, requests for information, copies of your time sheets, com-

This office worker keeps his often-used files close at hand.

pany policy handbooks, and the like. The filing system for this drawer should be set up in whatever way makes the most sense for you, since you will be the only one using it.

- **Log Books**. Log books are kept for recording recurring events, such as long-distance phone calls, express mailings, messenger trips, and petty-cash outlays. The log shows the date, time, and description of each event, as well as the personnel involved in the transaction. It also usually contains a place for comments regarding the transaction in case it varied in some way from the usual procedure.

- **Correspondence Book**. Sometimes called a **chronological file**, this is a loose-leaf binder in which you place a copy of each piece of outgoing correspondence, always in chronological order. This will give you a record of all correspondence pertaining to any given transaction and makes it easy to retrieve. It also provides you with an easy way to check on what happened in response to specific actions, should this ever become necessary.

Filing System Design

The procedures listed above form a system for filing records at your workstation. The idea of a system can be applied to all the business records of a department or organization. The filing system consists of procedures and rules for filing (storing), retrieving, and updating the information in your files. How can you decide the best way to store any given record? Since no two offices are exactly the same and no two people have exactly the same needs for their files, there are no hard-and-fast rules for setting up a filing system. There are some guidelines, however—factors to consider that will help you figure out what is best for you and your coworkers. Follow the steps in Fig. 10-1 as you read the description of what takes place at each phase.

Define the Filing Needs This first step requires you to examine the records and the needs of the people who will be using them. You must identify the kinds of materials that will be filed and then decide if they are a homogeneous group of records. That is, do they relate to each other in some way so that it makes sense to group them all together? If they do, you only need one filing system. If there are many different types of records, you may have to consider making several different filing systems.

Next, look at how you can organize the files. Can they be organized alphabetically? geographically? numerically? Would it make more sense to organize them by subject and have a different file for each subject? You will learn more about these and other specific filing systems in the next section.

Finally, who will be using the files? Some files contain confidential material that should not be available to most people. Will clerical

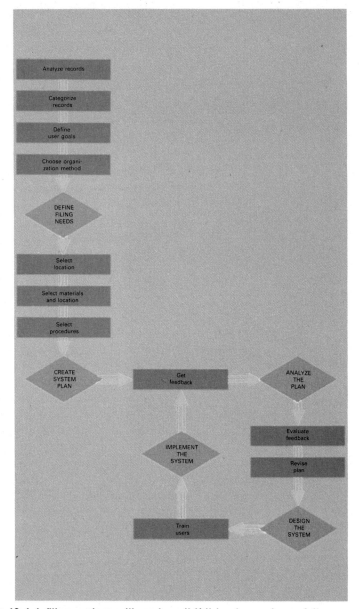

Fig 10-1 A filing system will work well if it is planned carefully.

personnel or managerial personnel use the files? Depending on the answer, you may organize the files differently. A sales manager might find files that are organized according to geographic region to be most helpful. An inventory clerk, on the other hand, might find it more useful to have files organized alphabetically by product name. If both people will be using the same files, you may need to either cross-reference the material or have two separate files.

Plan the Filing System   Once you have defined the goals of the filing system, you can begin to plan. You will want to look into exactly where the files ought to be placed, which will depend on who uses them most often. Another thing to consider is the procedure for borrowing, or **charging out**, the files. Choose the procedures that you think will work best, and then write a proposal. As you consider various options, you will solve problems before they happen.

Analyze the Plan   Take your written proposal to the people who will be using the files, and get feedback from them regarding your system. Because they will actually be using the files, they may have suggestions that will help make their job easier.

Design the Filing System   Evaluate all the suggestions you were given in the previous step, and try to work as many of them into your plan as possible. Remember, you are designing this system for people to use, so the other users must be satisfied with your plan.

Implement the Filing System   When you have all the details of the plan worked out, put your system to work. It is helpful to all those concerned, including you, to have an orientation meeting on how the files are set up, what the procedures are for charging out files, how the files are updated, and so on. Be sure that everyone understands the procedures.

Evaluate the Filing System   After the system has been in use for a while, ask the people who have been using it if the system works well for them. You can use their comments to improve the system.

Filing Rules and Procedures

Records are stored in a variety of ways. They may be papers in file cabinets, data on disks, reductions on microfiche, and so on. Even though the physical forms for storing data differ, the basic rules for organizing stored data are the same. Each record is filed under a **caption**, which is a name or some other type of reference that denotes the contents of the file. **Indexing** is the selection of the caption under which a record will be stored. Whether you or your co-workers can find records when you need them depends on how carefully they are indexed and on whether they are filed under the correct captions. Records should always be filed under captions by which they are most likely to be requested. Let's look at some of the indexing methods you will use in organizing records for fast and easy retrieval.

Alphabetic Files   Most files are organized alphabetically. This is true whether the captions are names of people, geographic names, or names of forms. There are standard rules for alphabetizing correctly. Following these rules helps everyone who uses files to find records quickly and efficiently.

RULES FOR ALPHABETIC FILING

These rules are adapted from *The Gregg Reference Manual*, sixth edition, list of 25 rules for filing.

- **Alphabetic order.** Alphabetize names by comparing the first units of the names letter by letter. Consider second units only when the first units are identical. Consider third units only if the first and second units are identical, and so on.
- **Nothing comes before something.** A name consisting of a single letter comes before a name consisting of a word that begins with the same letter (that is, *H* comes before *Hancock*). Similarly, a name consisting of one word comes before a name that consists of the same word plus one or more other words (that is, *Harley* comes before *Harley House*).
- **Last name first.** Treat each part of the name of an individual as a separate unit, and consider the units in this order: last name, first name or initial, middle name or initial.
- **Prefixes.** Consider a prefix (such as *Mc* in *McDonald*) as part of the name, not as a separate unit. Ignore variations in spacing, punctuation, or capitalization. Alphabetize the prefix *St.* as though it were spelled out—*Saint*.
- **Hyphenated individual names.** Consider the hyphenated part of a name as one unit. In other words, ignore the hyphen.
- **Titles.** Ignore a title used with the last name plus one or more other parts of the whole name, but consider a title as the first unit if it is used with only one part of an individual's name. Consider the title *Mrs.* as a unit if a woman uses her husband's first name and you do not know her first name. Treat *Mrs.* as it is spelled.
- **Seniority terms and other designations following the name.** Ignore a seniority term (such as *Sr.*, *Jr.*, *II*, or *2d*), a professional or academic degree (such as *CPA*, *M.D.*, or *Ph.D.*), or any other designation following a name.
- **Abbreviated names and nicknames.** Consider any abbreviated part of a name (such as *Wm.* for *William*) as if it were written in full. (For the purpose of this rule, initials standing for a first or middle name are not considered abbreviations.) Consider a name such as *Al* or *Kate* as the full name only if it is the person's true name or if the true name is unknown.
- **First word first.** Treat each word in the name of an organization as a separate unit, and consider the units in the same order as they are written. When the name of an organization includes the last name of an individual plus one or more other parts of that person's full name, transpose only the parts of the personal name (that is, *Frank Balcom Construction Company* would be filed under *Balcom, Frank, Construction Company*).
- **Articles, conjunctions, and prepositions.** Ignore an article, a conjunction, or a preposition in the name of an organization unless it is a distinctive part of the name.
- **Abbreviations.** Treat an abbreviation in an organization's name as if it were spelled out. When a company name contains a person's initials plus a surname, do not treat those initials as abbreviations—that is, do not spell out the full name.

- **Single letters**. Treat single letters that are not abbreviations as separate units, whether separated by spaces or not. Consider single letters that are hyphenated as one unit.
- **Hyphenated organization names**. Consider the hyphenated parts of an organization's name as one unit.
- **One or two words**. Consider as one unit the part of an organization's name that may be written as one word, as two words, or with a hyphen (that is, in *Supreme Soft Ware Company*, *Soft Ware* would be treated as one word). Consider a compound compass point (for example, *Southeastern*) as one unit, even when the term is spaced or hyphenated.
- **Possessives and contractions**. Ignore the apostrophe and consider all letters in a possessive or a contraction.
- **Numbers**. Consider a number in the name of an organization as though it were written in words, and treat it as one unit. Express the number in as few words as possible.
- **Parts of geographic names**. Consider each part of a geographic name as a separate unit. However, treat hyphenated parts of a geographic name as one unit.
- **Addresses**. When two names are identical, alphabetize them according to their addresses.
- **Banks and other financial institutions**. Consider each part of the name of a bank or some other financial institution in the same order as it is written.
- **Hotels and motels**. Consider each part of the name of a hotel or motel in the same order as it is written. If the word *Hotel* or *Motel* appears at the beginning of the name, consider the distinctive parts of the name first.
- **Hospitals and religious institutions**. Consider each part of the name of a hospital or a religious institution in the same order as it is written. However, transpose the elements of a personal name that appear in the name of the institution.
- **Educational institutions**. Consider each part of the name of a school or library in the same order as it is written. If a word like *University* or *College* appears at the beginning of the name, consider the distinctive parts of the name first. Transpose the elements of a personal name that appear in the name of the institution.
- **Federal government names**. For any organization that is part of the federal government, consider *United States Government* as the first three units. Then consider the name of the department, and finally the name of the bureau, division, commission, board, or other subdivision.
- **State and local government names**. For any organization (except an educational institution) that is part of a state, county, city, or town government, first consider the distinctive name, followed by the word *state*, *county*, *city*, or *town* or by some other appropriate classification. Then consider the name of the department, bureau, or other subdivision.
- **Foreign government names**. For an organization that pertains to a foreign government, first consider the distinctive name of the country, followed by the word *Dominion*, *Republic*, or *Kingdom* or by some other appropriate classification. Then consider the name of the department, bureau, or other subdivision.

Subject Files When the subjects of documents are more important to your office than the names on them, file the documents alphabetically by subject. A file labeled "Proposals" would be filed between records labeled "Organizations" and "Questionnaires."

Like name files, subject files can be subdivided into categories to allow for more efficient storage and retrieval. For example, if your records include dozens of files relating to insurance policies of different kinds, your main subject file would be labeled "Insurance." Subcategories would be "Hospitalization," "Malpractice," "Fire," "Theft," and so on. The subjects you choose as captions or key words in filing will depend on your office's business and the kinds of records it keeps. The more familiar you are with your employer's records and the way they are used, the easier it will be for you to set up subject files that allow for the most efficient storage and retrieval.

While subject filing is generally regarded as an efficient method, trying to locate records in a subject file can be frustrating and time-consuming. This is because people often use different words to identify the subjects. For example, you might file a document under "Automobiles," and someone else might look for it under "Motor Vehicles," "Cars," or "Transportation." The solution to this problem is to use cross-references, which are explained later in this chapter. Another method is to maintain an alphabetic listing of all the subjects that are included in the system. This allows for a quick review of all the listings, if necessary, prior to locating the materials in the files.

Numeric Files Sometimes records can be retrieved more easily if they are filed by number rather than by name or subject. For example, a bank has thousands of customers, and some may have savings accounts as well as checking accounts, retirement accounts, mortgages, and personal loans. Rather than mix up the records on all of a customer's accounts under the customer's name, a bank files them according to account numbers.

Unlike records that are filed alphabetically according to name or subject, numeric files generally require office workers to also keep separate indexes that list the files alphabetically by name or subject and indicate their corresponding numbers. Thus if you worked in a bank and were handling a transaction for a customer who had forgotten his or her savings account number, you would look in the index under the customer's name to find that number so you could retrieve the file for the account.

Numeric filing offers several advantages that make it the most productive method in many situations. It is very useful when the files themselves are numbers, as in the example of bank accounts. Beyond this, however, there are other advantages. One is that you can add unlimited numbers of new records and files without running out of captions. Another advantage of numeric filing is that you can use it to conceal the names and subjects of confidential records. Still another advantage is that with numeric filing you never have to make decisions about what captions to use or how to label folders.

Offices use two systems of numeric filing. One is the **consecutive numeric system**, which uses consecutive numbers: 1, 2, 3, and so on. In a consecutive numeric system, a record labeled "97334" would go between those labeled "97333" and "97335." In a **terminal-digit system**, numbers are assigned for the purpose of classifying records into groups, and the last number in a caption indicates where to start looking for a record. For example, in the caption 97334, "97" might refer to a drawer number, "33" might refer to a folder number, and "4" might refer to the sequential position of the record within the folder. To make terminal-digit index numbers easier to read, offices may use hyphens, spaces, or periods to separate the components. In the terminal-digit system just described, 97334 might be written as 97-33-4.

Geographic Files Geographic filing is useful when the records apply to particular geographic locations. For example, a large company might want to break down its operations by country, by region, by state, or even by town. Branch offices, real estate firms, government agencies, and public utilities frequently use geographic filing systems.

When organizing a geographic file, you should first break down the categories into the largest or most important geographic divisions that are relevant to your company's operations. Use these as the primary guides. Divide these major geographic regions into subdivisions, and then alphabetize the files within each subdivision. Figure 10-2 illustrates how a geographic file drawer might look. The

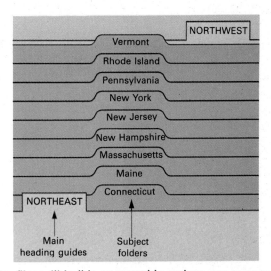

Fig. 10-2 The files within this geographic system are arranged alphabetically.

drawer is divided into sections of the United States: Northeast, Southeast, Northwest, Southwest. The part shown in detail, the Northeast, is divided into subdivisions: the states of Connecticut, Maine, Massachusetts, New Hampshire, and so on. Note that the states are listed in alphabetic order within the section. Within each state, the files are broken down into towns and cities. The companies within those folders are alphabetized according to the rules for alphabetic filing.

Tickler Files A common name for a follow-up file is **tickler file**. The most common tickler file is an accordion file that is designed to hold items for a one-month period. You will find this type of file most useful when it is used to remind you of some action that is to take place in the future, or as a follow-up file.

The captions are usually the days of the month—1 to 31. Within such a file, arranged by day of the month, are forms or other papers that need to be attended to on particular days. Each day, time is set aside to review the tickler file. If there is something in the file that must be done that day, the task is attended to. If the task indicated in the file has been postponed to another day, the paper is moved to the appropriate day, where it will again be reviewed and attended to.

Another common tickler file is a box holding 3 × 5 index cards with the names of the months as file captions on the tabs. With this type of system the office worker types reminders of future actions on the file cards and reviews them at the designated time.

For an example of how a tickler file is used, let's look at the following situation. Say you are a secretary in a real estate office. On the morning of the tenth, you look in the tickler file and find a form that tells you that the Petersons will be closing the deal on the sale of their house on the eleventh, so you must type up the necessary forms today and have them ready. However, when you go to the Peterson file to get the information you need, you find that the closing has been delayed until the twentieth. You return the Peterson folder to its file and then move the reminder to a new slot in the tickler file. You should put it in the slot for the nineteenth—a day ahead of the closing date—to remind yourself again to prepare the appropriate documents. That way, on the twentieth everything will be prepared and organized. Note that in a tickler file, you must pay attention to what day of the week any given day of the month falls on. If something is filed in the slot for a weekend day or a holiday, that task will not be attended to. File all such papers in the slot for the business day *ahead* of the nonbusiness day.

Forms Files Most businesses use different kinds of forms. These should be organized in a logical, neat manner. Depending on the types of forms, it may make sense to organize them alphabetically, numerically, chronologically, or geographically. For example, it might be adequate to file them by name, such as "Applications," "Contracts," "Expense Vouchers," "Requisitions," and so on. If the forms are referred to by number, you could use a numeric system. The rule here is to use whatever system works best for you and the other workers in the office.

Filing Procedures

Each company has its own rules and guidelines for filing, but there are some general guidelines that apply to just about every situation. First of all, remember that not all records need to be filed. Some may be disposed of after you look at them or use them, and some may have to be redistributed. Find out exactly what should be kept and what should not before you jam your files with useless records. Second, it is always a good idea to establish procedures for filing or to follow those already made. Set aside a time each day or every few days for filing. Keep papers to be filed in a designated place—a basket marked "To Be Filed" or an "Out" box will do.

There are essentially five steps in filing, and they are generally done in this order: inspect, index, code, sort, and store. Let's look more closely at what's involved in each of these steps.

Inspect   Review each record to make sure that it is something you must file. If it needs attention before filing, attend to it. If it does not need filing and you are sure it can be disposed of (check guidelines for which records are disposable and which are not), throw it out. If your inspection tells you that it must be filed, move to the next step.

Index   You have just learned about the different ways of filing records. In the indexing step of filing, you must determine under which caption within your files the particular record should be filed. Indexing is really a mental process, requiring you to make a decision. If the record is incoming or outgoing correspondence and your files are organized by names, you might file it under the name of the corresponding person or organization. If your files are organized by subject, you might file the letter under the subject it pertains to. If your files are geographic, you might file the letter under the geographic location that it pertains to. If you have a cross-referencing system, you might file one copy under the name of the person and one copy under the subject. Cross-referencing is explained below.

Code   Once you have determined the caption of the record to be filed, you must assign a code before filing it. One way to do this for a document on paper is to underline or highlight the name under which the paper will be filed. Just as indexing is a mental process, coding is the physical process of highlighting and underlining. The underlining or highlighting serves as a permanent reminder to anyone using the file in the future to refile the record under that name. Another method is to write the caption in the upper right corner of the paper. This is necessary when the caption name or subject does not appear anywhere on the page and therefore cannot be underlined or highlighted.

Cross-referencing, as mentioned above, is useful in filing systems. A **cross-reference** notifies people looking for a record in a particular file that it is filed elsewhere. One way to provide a cross-reference is to make an extra copy of the record and then file the copies in the referenced files, noting in the upper right corner of the paper that it is cross-referenced material. Another way is to use a cross-reference sheet and file this instead of an actual copy. The sheet contains the name of the individual and/or organization found on the original record, the date it was filed, a brief description of the subject of the record, and the place(s) in which that record can be found. If you have ever used a library card catalog, you have probably seen a cross-reference card, which refers you to other places where the book you want is listed.

Sort   Once you have properly coded the records to be filed, you are ready to sort them. Arrange them in the order in which they will be placed in the file. If your file is alphabetic, you will put them in alphabetic order. If your file is numeric, you will put them in numeric order, and so on.

Store   Finally, you are ready to store the records. When placing them in the file folders within the drawer, be careful to check and double-check that you are filing them correctly. Once they are misfiled, it will be very difficult to retrieve them. A little extra time spent at this stage will save you work later.

HOW TO PREVENT MISFILING

Every time a record is misfiled, it takes time for office workers to find it. Sometimes the record is lost completely. The following guidelines can help you manage records efficiently and prevent these costly mistakes.

- **Use simple headings**. If the headings on tabs and file-folder labels are too complex, they may confuse people and cause them to file records in the wrong places.
- **Type the headings in capital letters**. This will make them easier to read. Never write them by hand.
- **Use enough guide tabs, but not too many**. A full file drawer should contain no fewer than five tabs to guide people

to the sections they want. However, more than 15 guide tabs can clutter the drawer and confuse people.
- **Don't overcrowd file drawers**. A full file drawer should have 3 or 4 inches of extra space so that people can flip through folders easily to locate the ones they need.
- **Don't overcrowd folders**. If a folder is too full, the papers in it may obscure the tab, and so people won't be able to find the folder easily.
- **Code papers clearly**. Before filing a document, write its file heading in the upper right corner, or underline it in color where it appears in the text.

Manual Filing Supplies and Equipment

The types of filing supplies and equipment vary some from office to office, but not much. There are a few products that are recognized as doing any job best, and these are found in most offices. Let's look at some of these products and how they are used.

Supplies **Filing supplies** are used to organize the many papers and records stored in offices and are fairly standard from office to office.

- **File-Drawer Guides**. File-drawer guides are used for separating a file drawer into sections to make it easier to locate records. They are usually made out of thin but rigid cardboard, and each guide has a tab on it that extends above the top when the guide is placed in a drawer. Some of these guides have hooks that allow them to hang from the sides of the drawer like pockets. The purpose of the extending tabs is to separate groups of records. File-drawer guides are described according to the width of the tab. The positions on the tab are referred to as first cut, second cut, third cut, and so on. A one-fifth cut means that the tab takes up one-fifth of the horizontal width of the guide; a one-fifth-cut guide can have five tab positions. When the positions of tabs are staggered, each tab is readily visible, as shown in Fig. 10-3.

- **File-Guide Captions**. File-guide captions go on the tabs of the file-drawer guides. A caption indicates what lies between the guide you are looking at and the one directly behind it. If a guide caption says "A," then all records beginning with the letter *A* will be found behind that guide. A caption that reads "Ban—Baz" tells you that only names falling alphabetically between these groups of letters will be found behind this guide.

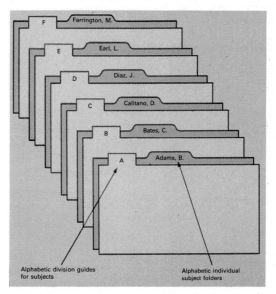

Fig. 10-3 File guides separate groups of files for easy retrieval.

■ **File Folders**. File folders are used for organizing papers in file drawers and cabinets, and they are also used for keeping papers neat, clean, and together when they are carried from one place to another. You might, for example, carry a freshly typed letter from your desk to your supervisor's desk in a folder. But the main use of file folders is to keep papers arranged in order in file drawers. Like file-drawer guides, folders have tabs on them for identifying captions. Many people like to stagger the positions of the file-folder tabs as they would the positions of the file-guide tabs, but others like to have the tabs of all file folders in a category in the same position. This can be an aid in categorizing files and can help you locate a given folder more quickly.

■ **File-Folder Labels**. Many labels are already gummed and come attached to a special paper backing that allows you to peel them off when you are ready to use them. The headings should be typed on the labels while they are still attached to the backing. Then they can be peeled off and placed on the folders. There are labels available that can be used with word processors. Labels are also available in many sizes, shapes, and colors. Depending on your filing system, you might want to use a color code, or you might simply use white labels.

Equipment **Filing equipment** refers to the actual structures in which files are stored. There is probably more variation in equipment from office to office than in supplies. But here, too, there is much similarity. While manufacturers offer many different models at different prices and in different colors, most pieces of equipment still have basic features in common. Let's look at some of the more common kinds of manual filing equipment.

Vertical files fit into many offices.

■ **Vertical Files**. Until recently, the most common kind of file was the vertical file. Vertical files come in two-, three-, four-, and five-drawer models. The drawers are stacked one on top of the other and frequently have locks. They are designed to accommodate either 8½- by 11-inch (letter-size) files or 8½- by 14-inch (legal-size) files. The cabinets are usually made of metal and provide sturdy, often fireproof, protection of files. And the documents are placed in the vertical cabinet with the heading or top of the document located at the left.

■ **Lateral Files**. A lateral file is similar to a vertical file except that the longest side opens, and the files are stored as if they were on a bookshelf. Lateral files are most often found in two-drawer models that have the added advantage of providing a countertop for reviewing files removed from the cabinet or for displaying books and other materials. Like vertical files, lateral files are designed to accommodate letter- or legal-size files.

- **Open-Shelf Files**. Open-shelf files are not enclosed the way vertical and lateral files are. They consist of metal frames arranged to suit the size and space needs of the user. Their main advantages over enclosed cabinets are that they take up less space and you can change them easily. They are also useful for files that are constantly in use. You may have seen open-shelf files in a doctor's office, where each patient's folder is pulled when he or she goes in to see the doctor. This arrangement eliminates the need to open and close drawers each time a record must be pulled or refiled.

- **Rotary Files**. A rotary file consists of a large, round shelf with a hole in the middle through which the supporting post passes. The shelf can be moved in a circular fashion to locate files. Because of the round shape, rotary files are very useful for filing loose-leaf binders, which have a wedge shape and fit on the shelf like pieces of a pie. Rotary files also make sense when workers are seated around the files.

- **Tub Files**. The main advantage of a tub file, which is usually a small container that opens at the top, is that it can be moved from one location to another. When files must be used by people in many different locations, a tub file may be the answer to carrying individual folders back and forth, for these actions risk loss and create traffic problems within the office.

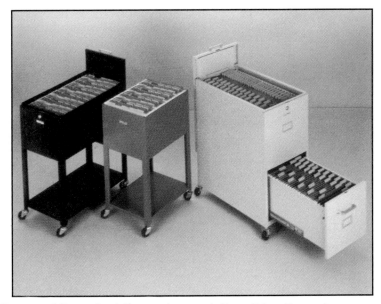

These mobile vertical files work especially well in offices where several people require access to the same files.

■ **Card Files**. Card files come in an assortment of styles and sizes, depending on how the cards are used. All the above-mentioned types of filing equipment are available in scaled-down versions for use as card files.

Electronic Storage and Retrieval

As you know, some records appear on electronic media rather than on paper. (See Fig. 10-4). When filing electronic media, you follow the rules for filing paper documents, but the procedures and equipment are different. You will still follow the five steps of filing mentioned in the previous section: inspect, index, code, sort, and store. But you will be able to use your computer to speed up these functions.

The computer performs the indexing, cross-referencing, and retrieval functions. Also, you can store data on or retrieve data from the electronic media instantly during any other phase of the IPSOD cycle. This capacity for instant storage/retrieval is at the heart of the information processing cycle in the electronic office.

Memory, Storage, and Retrieval

You already know that a computer has a memory. Actually, computers have two kinds of memories: ROM and RAM. **ROM** stands for **read-only memory**. This means that what is stored on the ROM chip is only for the computer to use; the data stored on a ROM chip is not meant to be manipulated by the user. For this reason ROM is also referred to as permanent storage. The information in ROM tells the computer what to do in any given situation. When you turn a computer on, messages appear on the screen before you even touch a key. These messages are made possible by the information stored in ROM.

RAM stands for **random-access memory**. The data that you input and manipulate on the computer is stored in RAM. You can retrieve this data at will, change it, and restore it whenever you want. RAM is also called temporary storage because the data must be stored before the computer is turned off. The amount of data you will be able to store on a computer will be determined by how much

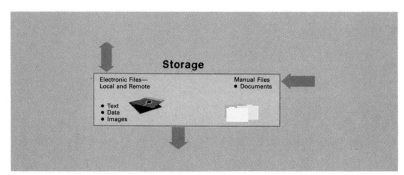

Fig. 10-4 Files can be stored manually and electronically. Those stored electronically can be retrieved instantly.

RAM (measured in kilobytes) the computer has. Today few personal computers are equipped with less than 128K of RAM, and many now have 512K or more.

▪ Electronic Storage Systems

The specific equipment you will use depends largely on what is available to you and on your company's needs. At your own workstation, you will probably use a manual filing system for your own papers, but you may also use at least one type of electronic storage system. There are two basic types of electronic storage systems: decentralized and centralized.

In many offices, particularly if microcomputers make up the primary computer system, a **decentralized storage system** is used. This means that each worker stores his or her own files on floppy diskettes or tapes. These files must be stored on disks or tapes because the size of the computer's memory is limited. Users still often share files by making multiple copies of data files or borrowing disks as needed.

If the workstations in a system are part of a local network and are capable of communicating with each other, a different type of storage system is possible. Users can call up files stored in any part of the network, including the central computer. This is known as a **centralized storage system**. In a system like this, a user might use a modem to contact someone at the workstation where the files

In a centralized file system, this worker does not have to leave the workstation to retrieve files located in another part of the office. The computer helps retrieve the file.

are stored. That person would insert the requested file into his or her computer and transmit the information to the user via a modem. In another system, you enter your request into the computer, and the computer finds where the file is stored, calls up the file, and sends the information to you. This is only possible when the file is permanently stored in the computer and does not have to be retrieved from a separately filed disk. These storage systems may be completely centralized or a combination of centralized and decentralized.

In decentralized systems, you decide which disk should store your information, and you must maintain an index of what files are on the disks. In centralized systems, this is done electronically. In other words, because the specific storage place for your information is handled by the central computer and the technical staff, you do not need to know which disk or tape it is stored on. Instead, the computer does the indexing and helps you retrieve documents. Many centralized filing systems today allow you to file your documents just as you do in your manual filing system. If you are working with one of these systems, you can do your electronic filing by creating electronic groupings, using key terms. The terms you use have only slightly different meanings from those used to describe a manual filing system:

- **Cabinet**. You call your collection of records a cabinet. Electronic cabinets can store data for private use only or for the entire department to share. If a user creates a personal cabinet, only he or she can have access to information stored there. Generally, a password is used when signing onto the system.

- **Drawer**. Within each cabinet the user can create sections, or drawers. In most cases these can be named to duplicate your manual filing system.

- **Folder**. Within each drawer users can create smaller sections, or folders, as they would in a manual system. As with the drawers, the user can generally name the folders in any way desired.

Not all centralized systems work precisely this way, but they all ease the burden of indexing your files by automatically doing much of this task for you in one way or another. To more clearly illustrate how these systems can assist you, let's look at how the type of system described above would work.

Figure 10-5 shows how this type of electronic filing system is set up. Jennifer, Tracy, and Mark work in the Corporate Training Department. They all need to be able to edit and update training manuals. Jennifer is also the department manager and works closely with Phil, director of corporate training. Jennifer and Phil need to work together on some upcoming programs that should be kept confidential. Jennifer also maintains a personal file, which nobody, including Phil, has access to. Figure 10-6 shows what the filing system might look like. As you can see, there is great flexibility and security in filing documents with a centralized filing system. There is so much flexibility because *any* type of document can be filed electronically, including word processing documents, spreadsheets, data bases, and graphics.

Storage space is not as limited in a centralized system as it is when only disks are used. But it is a good filing habit to be aware of what space is left. Another thing to consider when using a centralized system is that in many cases files are shared. This means that you must be careful when you delete files. You will need to follow a procedure for reviewing files regularly to suggest which ones to discard. Consult the other users to find out if they will need the files you intend to delete. You may wish to transfer the files to backup tapes.

Electronic Storage Media

Computers store data by recording electrical impulses on magnetic disks or tapes. The disks and tapes come in several sizes and storage capacities. For example, with a standalone workstation or a small

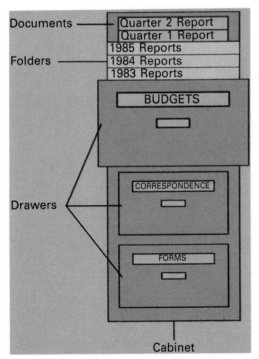

Fig. 10-5 Some electronic filing systems are set up in much the same way as traditional files. The advantage is that the computer can search for documents and help in finding documents that have been misfiled. Also, security is easier because passwords can be used to limit access to personal files.

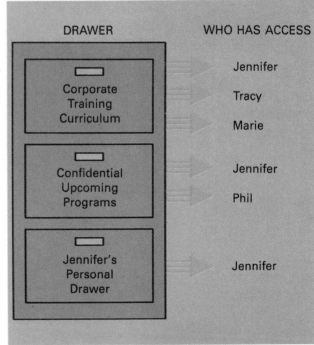

Fig. 10-6 This illustrates how access to the drawers is limited for security in a centralized storage system.

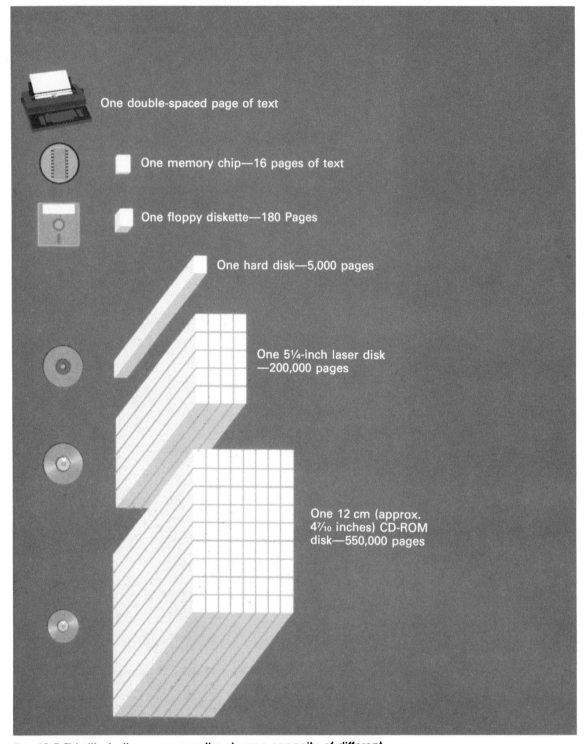

One double-spaced page of text

One memory chip—16 pages of text

One floppy diskette—180 Pages

One hard disk—5,000 pages

One 5¼-inch laser disk —200,000 pages

One 12 cm (approx. 4⁷⁄₁₀ inches) CD-ROM disk—550,000 pages

Fig. 10-7 This illustration compares the storage capacity of different types of disks.

computer network, you may use floppy diskettes for all data and program storage needs. Office workers in these decentralized systems are responsible for managing their own disks. On the other hand, most of the integrated office systems that run on central computers provide a centralized system for storing documents. The media used for this storage can be magnetic tapes, hard disks, or disk packs (stacks of hard disks that work together).

If you work at a terminal linked to a mainframe or minicomputer with central storage, you may also use floppy diskettes to store records that only you or your immediate coworkers will use. And you may also use larger hard disks to store information shared throughout the network. In other words, some terminals in a centralized computer system can use decentralized filing systems as well as centralized files. In this case the storage media will determine the filing systems you can use. Let's look at the most common forms of electronic storage media.

Floppy Diskettes Even though a floppy diskette is smaller than a sheet of letter-size paper, it can contain much more information. (See Fig. 10-7 for a comparison of the storage capacity of different types of disks.) Floppy diskettes come in 8-, 5¼-, and 3½-inch sizes. The method of storing data on a diskette is essentially the same regardless of the size of the disk. When a disk has been formatted in the disk drive of your computer, it is ready to record information that is written on it. Information is written on floppy diskettes along concentric circles called **tracks**. These concentric circles are very much like the narrow grooves or tracks on a record. The read/write head of the disk drive moves back and forth from one track to another. This is how the disk drive head finds certain data to read or a place to write information on the diskette.

The tracks on the diskette are divided into **sectors** (see Fig. 10-8). The space on the diskette is measured in **bytes**. One byte holds one character. The number of tracks, sectors, and bytes on a diskette will vary depending on the type of diskette and disk drive you are working with. When the storage space of a floppy diskette becomes full, you can delete some of the files to create new space, or you can store the full disk and format a new disk for your next task.

Many data files may be stored on one floppy diskette. One way to keep track of which files are on which disks is to label each disk with its own identifying number or code. A separate index can then list all the file names and the numbers or codes of the disks on which they may be found. Then you can file the disks alphabetically or numerically, according to how you have indexed them. For example, you might want to have one disk for memos, another for reports, and others for items arranged alphabetically by subject (the disks would be labeled "A–D," "E–H," "I–L," and so on). The choice should be based on the way you usually file hard copy documents. For each disk a subindex, or list, of files stored on that disk

Floppy diskettes.

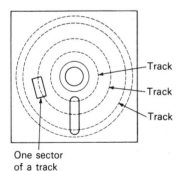

Track

Track

Track

One sector
of a track

Fig. 10-8 Information is written on the tracks of a floppy diskette. When information is retrieved, the disk drive head finds the sector on which the information has been stored.

Magnetic tape has a very large storage capacity, but is rarely used with microcomputers.

A hard disk is usually housed in the disk drive.

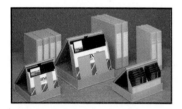

Desk-top storage for floppy diskettes.

Desk-top storage for floppy diskettes. This can be locked for security reasons.

can be housed in the disk envelope with the disk for quick reference. If you wanted to retrieve a memo you had named "JWVAC," you would look up that name in the index to find what disk it is stored on. Then you would find and load the disk and keyboard a command for the soft copy of "JWVAC" to appear on your screen.

Office-supply dealers sell several kinds of specially designed storage units for floppy diskettes. These include plastic and wooden desk-top boxes, rotary files, and ring binders with vinyl pages that have pockets. The dealers also sell panels and racks that you can use to adapt your existing file cabinets for storing floppy diskettes safely and conveniently. The storage equipment you will use will depend on your office design and preference as well as on cost.

Hard Disks   Your computer may have one or two floppy diskette drives, or it may have a hard disk drive. Hard disks are permanently encased in the disk drive. Hard disks have much more storage space than floppy diskettes, but because hard disks can't be removed from the computer, you need to be aware of the space left for storage. A hard disk will hold about 10 million bytes, which equals 4000–5000 pages of copy. When the hard disk becomes full, you must transfer some files to a floppy diskette or delete them if they are no longer useful. Generally, you transfer the records you retrieve least often, since they will no longer be readily available on the disk in your disk drive.

Magnetic Tape   **Magnetic tape** is the most popular storage medium used in large-volume data processing operations because of its large storage capacity and relatively low cost. Magnetic tape can store about 6000 characters per inch, which means that 100 million characters can be stored on a single reel of tape. Most microcomputers use magnetic disks instead of tape, although some systems do use tape cassettes for storage or have cassette disk drives that allow the use of tapes for backup storage. Most mainframe computer systems still use magnetic tape as the major storage or backup storage medium.

Optical Disks   The **optical disk**, also known as the **laser disk**, has a greater storage capacity than does a hard disk. One 5¼-inch laser disk can hold up to 200,000 pages of copy. A laser disk is nonmagnetic and is far more durable than magnetic media. These types of disks are created through laser recording, which uses laser light beams to burn tiny holes into the metal of the disk. Sounds and images are then recorded in these tiny holes which can be read by the machine that plays back the recording. You may have heard of videodisks, a type of laser recording that is widely used for commercially developed products, such as movies and other types of audiovisual presentations that require sound and motion. These types of disks are known as read-only disks, that is, they cannot be written on. There are also erasable laser disks, which can be used for recording and reading data.

Optical disks can store data, graphics, or sound.

A new type of optical disk coming into widespread use is **compact disk–read-only memory** or **CD-ROM**. CD-ROM is a durable, nonmagnetic storage medium which has the capability of storing vast quantities of data, graphics, or sound. Compact disks were originally developed for audio use. Today many record stores are selling compact disk recordings as a replacement for records and tapes because of the high quality of sound which can be stored on this durable medium.

In business compact disks are being used for data processing and data base applications because of their desirable features, such as high-capacity storage, speed, cost effectiveness, durability, and flexibility. For example, one CD-ROM disk can store 40 file cabinets full of documents or 270,000 pages of a book with over 2000 characters printed on each page (equaling approximately 550,000 typed pages). The CD-ROM disk is an ideal medium for most data storage and retrieval because programs and data can be easily stored or retrieved from a single disk. In the future many businesses will have CD-ROM disk players or disk drives attached to personal computers, enabling workers to access vast quantities of information at the workstation.

SOME HELPFUL HINTS FOR ELECTRONIC FILING

When your files are stored on disks, they may be hard to organize. Here are some steps to make retrieval easier.

- **Be sure to label each disk.** Complete the label using a felt-tip pen before placing it on the disk.
- **Print a current index of documents on the disk each time you add a new document to it.** You can either fold this and place it in the jacket with the disk or put all disk indexes in a three-ring binder for easy reference.
- **Store disks in an easily accessible, safe place.**
- **If you fill up a disk and need to format another one with the same label, use "-1," "-2," "-3," and so on,** for example, "Memos-1," "Memos-2," and "Memos-3." You should also mark each with the date it was formatted and first used.
- **If you want to ensure that your disks**

Write-Protect Notch

will not be erased by another office worker, you can place a write-protect tab in the protect position. When the tab covers the notch, you can't store documents on the disk. If there is a particularly important disk you wish to protect, cover the notch when you are finished with the disk and uncover the notch when you need to store on it again.

Micrographics

We've seen how computers help reduce document storage space, costs, and retrieval time compared with manual filing systems. But not all records can be computerized. For example, birth certificates, fingerprints, canceled checks, and credit card receipts contain prints or signatures that are very difficult to convert into accurate soft copy. These documents need to be retained, but banks, insurance companies, government agencies, and others encounter so many of these documents that their storage space fills quickly, and retrieval methods are very clumsy. How do companies keep all the records they need to satisfy the laws and to conduct business?

One solution to the problem of overcrowded files is to reduce the size of the records. This is done by storing small images of the records on film. You have probably seen newspapers on film in libraries. The process of reproducing newspapers and other documents on film is known as **micrographics**. The rolls or sheets of film that have images which are exact duplicates of the original records are called **microforms**. The images are many times smaller than the originals—so small, in fact, that you cannot read them without the aid of a special machine called a **microform reader**. A library could not possibly store thousands of copies of newspapers, but it can store thousands of microforms. Storage, however, is only one reason for using micrographics. Let's examine some of the other reasons.

Uses of Microforms

It is much quicker to find a document on a microform reader than to sift through stacks of papers. In addition, many microform readers can print as well as read, so you can read and print the information all in one operation. Reading information through a machine also means that originals of important documents will not be subjected to the damage that results from frequent handling of paper documents. If the microform is damaged, a new copy can be made from the original. Because micrographically reproduced material is so small, many documents can be reproduced on a single microform. This often means that all the information related to one topic can be contained on a single microform, making it less likely that one piece of information will become separated and perhaps lost. These are distinct advantages over the use of paper, which is frequently misplaced, lost, damaged, or destroyed.

Micrographics also has some advantages over the process of computerizing records. For one thing, the images are exact duplicates of the original documents. Some computer records are not the documents themselves but rekeyed information. Errors can be introduced in the rekeying. And since micrographics produces an exact duplicate in miniature, graphic data such as pictures and drawings can be stored as well. This is not always possible with computer records. In general, the conversion of documents into microforms is easier than conversion to computerized files. Micrographics is a photographic process; pictures are taken with special equipment to produce the tiny images, and then the film is processed. With computerized files, someone must keyboard all the information.

Types of Microforms

The term *microform* refers to a variety of micrographic media. These media make is possible to record miniature images of documents on film negatives. They all have advantages and disadvantages, as well as specific uses for which they are best suited. Here is a list of the types of microforms used by businesses.

■ **Microfilm Rolls**. The oldest micrographic medium is the **microfilm roll**, which is a continuous roll of film that can hold the images of hundreds of pages of documents. Businesses have been using microfilm since the 1920s. Microfilm rolls come in two sizes. The smaller size, 16 mm, is used for photographing pages that are 8½ by 11 inches or smaller. These include letters, invoices, and so on. The larger size, 35 mm, is used for photographing blueprints, newspapers, and other large documents. All microfilm rolls, regardless of size, are stored on reels or in cassettes or cartridges. These holders, in turn, are generally kept in specially designed file cabinets or desk-top files. Microfilm is especially useful when many pages of information relating to the same topic or document must be kept together. With microfilm all the information can be stored on one roll of film, eliminating the possibility of losing part of a file.

The miniature images on this roll of microfilm will be a readable size when they are projected through a microfilm reader.

- **Microfilm Jackets**. A **microfilm jacket** consists of two sheets of clear plastic that are sealed together to form horizontal slots for holding strips of microfilm. Microfilm jackets come in several sizes, but the most common is 6 by 4 inches. The top of each jacket has a strip of tape on which you can write labeling information. Microfilm jackets can be stored in ring binders, folders, or file drawers. Because they hold only short strips of film instead of the entire roll, microfilm jackets are most useful when many different documents that should be separated are reproduced on one roll of film.

- **Aperture Cards**. An **aperture card** is a card with a rectangular hole that holds usually only one image. You can write on the cards to label them. Aperture cards are a convenient medium for storing one-page documents and drawings. Because of this, they are most commonly used for storing engineers' drawings.

- **Microfiche**. A **microfiche** is a sheet of film, usually 4 by 6 inches, that can hold the images of several hundred letter-size pages. These images are smaller than the images on microfilm. This medium takes its name from the French word *fiche*, which means index card. A microfiche takes up less space than a microfilm roll bearing the same number of document images. Because they are flat, microfiche sheets are easier to file and mail than microfilm rolls. A sheet of microfiche is also easier to use than microfilm because you can find what you are looking for more easily. The images recorded on a microfiche are arranged in rows and columns. The columns are numbered across the top of the microfiche, and the rows are labeled with letters along one side. Using the numbers and letters as guides, you can locate the image of a specific document the way you would locate a town on a map.

This piece of microfiche contains many pages of material. Enlarged, they are a normal size that can be read easily.

Another advantage of a microfiche is that it can be updated by adding pages. This is not possible with microfilm except by splicing the roll of film, a risky and time-consuming process. A microfiche sheet can also be edited by photographically blacking out portions of the sheet.

- **Ultrafiche**. The smallest micrographic images are stored on an **ultrafiche**, which resembles a microfiche, but a single sheet can hold the images of 4000 letter-size pages. An ultrafiche is a very expensive micrographics medium because it can be processed only in photographic laboratories. Nonetheless, it offers a practical way of storing catalogs, directories, encyclopedias, and other documents that may have thousands of pages.

Advantages and Disadvantages

The main advantage of using microforms is that they take up very little storage space. If microform readers are available and documents will not be edited much, microforms provide a good way to store large amounts of information. Another advantage is that documents can be retrieved quickly.

One disadvantage of microforms is that a special machine is needed to read them. Other disadvantages are that the paper copies you can make from them are of poor quality, and microforms can't be easily updated and edited. It is true that new documents can be added to a microfiche, but they can only be inserted in blank spaces. Old documents must be blacked out and new ones inserted elsewhere. The blackened-out spaces are not reusable. As mentioned before, microfilm can only be updated by splicing into the film. Splicing creates weak areas in the film, and too much splicing can make the roll of film unusable.

Retrieving and Reading Microforms

Because records stored on microforms are too small for the naked eye to read, retrieval of records from microforms involves three steps. The first is to use an index to find out where on the microform a given document is located. Then you must find the microform. Finally, you use special projection equipment to locate the document on the microform itself.

How you find documents on microforms depends on the kinds of microforms you are using and how they have been indexed. Let's look at some equipment and procedures that you may find.

Microfilm Readers A microfilm reader is a device that enlarges the images on microfilm rolls and projects them onto a screen so that you can read them. Some microfilm readers can also print paper copies of the images. A microfilm reader may have a crank that you turn to advance the film, or it might use a computer to find documents automatically. The computerized models have keyboards that you use to enter the index numbers or names of the documents you want.

Microfiche Readers Like a microfilm reader, a microfiche reader enlarges the images on the microform and projects them onto a screen. It may also be capable of copying these images on paper. To find a document on a microfiche, you need to look in an index to find its location on the grid. A microfiche reader is equipped with a pointer and a lens. As you move the pointer, the microfiche is moved around under the lens. When the pointer reaches the correct location, the document you want will appear on the screen.

Aperture-Card Readers An aperture-card reader works in much the same way as a microfiche reader, but it has a bigger screen to accommodate the large maps and drawings that are usually stored on aperture cards.

Computer-Assisted Retrieval Computers can be linked with micrographics equipment to retrieve information from microforms automatically. This application of computer technology is called **computer-assisted retrieval (CAR)**. To understand how CAR works, imagine that you have been asked to locate some information about copper mining, and you go to a library that has CAR equipment. In either an index that resembles a telephone directory or an electronic index, you find an entry on the subject of copper mining. Included with the entry is the alphanumeric index code LDMSL6586,R-3. Working at a computer network terminal in the library, you keyboard the index code. Within a few seconds, the first page of the system's material on copper mining appears on the screen. You use the keyboard to advance the text, just as you would to advance soft copy that you had processed or retrieved by other means.

CAR is an important retrieval method for employers who frequently need information from files that would be either too bulky or too costly for them to keep in their own offices. These employers include not only library systems but also law firms, hospitals and physicians' offices, and insurance agencies.

With a microcomputer and a modem, you can use CAR to obtain records not only from your employers' files but also from libraries and data banks. There are many data banks that provide access to information in many specialties. For example, by calling up LEXIS, a legal secretary could quickly locate an opinion issued by a court in another state. LEXIS is an on-line library of legal information. Other useful data banks are computerized news services and bibliographic retrieval services.

Information Management

You already know that businesses run on information. They input it, process it, store it, output it, and distribute it, in all its many forms. With so much information and so many records, businesses would find themselves drowning in paper, microforms, and computer disks if they did not have a way of managing their records. To run efficiently, businesses must establish logical and usable systems for storing and retrieving information. This need has given rise to the field of **records management**, or what many people are now calling information management. **Information management** is the function of organizing and controlling all aspects of business records, from their creation, protection, and use to their storage and ultimate disposal. Most businesses manage their own records. But some large corporations turn to outside companies that specialize in setting up information management systems for other organizations. Whether your company manages its own records or uses specialists, one of your most important information management tasks is deciding which records to keep.

Records Retention

All of us have had the experience of not wanting to throw something away because we might need it later. After we threw the item away, we realized that we really needed it. Similarly, sometimes the things we keep end up being of no use.

Today, good records management procedures are critical, particularly when both electronic and manual or paper files are being managed. Office workers must determine which files should be saved in electronic form and which should be stored as hard copy documents. In many cases, the same document is stored in several forms unnecessarily. Documents that should be maintained in electronic form include only items such as monthly reports or other documents that may be used frequently or used to generate other documents. Hard copies should include items such as reports or correspondence with attachments or documents which will never

Warehouse storage is useful for boxes of inactive records that must be kept until they are no longer useful. There should be a review period for these records so that they can be destroyed when they are no longer needed.

be used to generate future documents. To make these decisions, it is necessary to understand the importance and future use of all documents. Studies have found that more than half of the documents on file in offices are not needed. To avoid adding to the mountains of unnecessary paper, film, and disks that waste space, you need to make careful decisions about which records to store, which to discard, and which to transfer to **archives**, which are off-site storage locations for inactive files.

Since making the wrong decision about records retention can be very costly, most businesses have strict guidelines regarding what records must be kept and what records can be disposed of. Such decisions should never be left to the subjective judgment of individual workers. If you work in an office, make sure you know your company's policies regarding records retention and disposal. While each company has different requirements that will affect specific records, there are some general guidelines you can follow.

Legal Records   Many records must be kept by law. Employers today often need to prove to the government that they have not violated equal-opportunity laws in their employment practices, that they meet federally mandated quotas in the employment of different groups of people, and that they do not practice any form of discrimination in their policies. They may also need to show that they have acted in accordance with environmental guidelines established by the government. All records dealing with such issues must be retained in case they are needed. Any correspondence containing information that could be useful in a lawsuit should also be kept.

Vital Records   Some records are so important that they should be kept permanently, even if it is not required by law. Records in this category include the corporate charter; the deed, mortgage, or bill of sale for the company's place of business; minutes of all meetings of the company's directors or stockholders; stocks and bonds; trademark registrations and patents or other proprietary records; and tax records. These records are so important that they should be kept in a fireproof, theftproof vault or safe, and copies are often retained in another protected location. Most office workers will not come in contact with these documents, and if they do, they will probably know enough not to destroy them.

Important Records   Many records are extremely important to the operation of a business, but they are not vital. Generally, these should be retained for six or seven years. Important records include accounts receivable and accounts payable ledgers, invoices, canceled checks, inventory records, purchase orders, payroll records, and employee time sheets and expense vouchers. These records may be needed if there is a question regarding financial transactions. Most companies have a policy that allows these kinds of records to be destroyed after being held for approximately seven years.

Useful Records Useful records are usually retained for one to three years, depending on the company. These include general correspondence, bank reconciliations, employment applications, stenographers' notes, expired insurance policies, and petty-cash vouchers. Many office workers know not to throw away a vital record, such as the company charter, or an important record, such as a canceled check, but the category of useful records is often unclear. What one company considers a useful record, another may consider garbage. It is always best to check with your employer before throwing away any record.

Other Records Common sense can help you figure out when to discard some records. These include papers that only you use, such as reminders of meetings, notes to yourself regarding tasks to be done (discard only if the tasks are done!), out-of-date announcements and pamphlets, duplicates of filed material (make sure the originals are filed before discarding the duplicates), rough drafts of documents that are now finished (and filed), and so on. Experience will tell you which records in this category you can dispose of safely. But if you have any doubt, check first.

Active Versus Inactive Records

Active records are those that must be kept in the office. They are used regularly, or at least often enough to justify the amount of space they take up. Active records include recent correspondence, proposals, accounts receivable and payable files, purchase orders and invoices, and any records that relate to ongoing projects. Active files should be located conveniently for the person or people using them.

Active files do not necessarily remain active indefinitely. When a file is no longer used regularly, it becomes an **inactive record**. Files should be reviewed periodically to select those that should be moved to inactive storage or discarded. A good information management system includes a schedule for the review of active records and guidelines for what records should be destroyed after how long and what records should be moved to inactive storage.

Inactive records may be housed on- or off-site. The decision about where to store inactive records depends on how many records there are and what kinds of facilities are available. A company that has only a few boxes of inactive records will be best off finding room for them in a protected, out-of-the-way place somewhere on-site. On the other hand, a company that has many inactive records to store should consider an off-site location such as a warehouse. As with active records, inactive records should also be reviewed and eventually discarded. A records retention schedule will indicate how long records should be stored.

Centralized Versus Decentralized Systems

Active records, whether electronic or traditional, can be filed in a centralized or decentralized system, as discussed earlier in this chapter. In a manual centralized system, there is usually an area or room designated as the records center. With the exception of personal files, the records center houses all records that people within the company use. Depending on how large the company is and how many records the company has, the records center may operate on a self-serve basis or have trained personnel who are in charge of maintaining the files. The main advantage of a records center is that all the files you might want are located in one place. If you want a file, you go to the records center and ask for the file or find it yourself, depending on the procedure.

A decentralized system has files stored in different places, either near the people who use them most often or where they fit best in the office. The advantage of this type of system is that the people who are most likely to use a given file are located near it. The disadvantage is that it is not always easy for people in other areas or departments of the office to locate the files.

Establishing an Information Management System

If you are put in charge of setting up an information management system, there are some basic steps that you should follow. If the task involves many hundreds or thousands of records, you may want to consider going outside for professional help. Setting up a major in-

In a large organization, records are often stored in a records center. Depending on how the system is set up, trained personnel help workers get the files, or workers get the files themselves.

formation management system is a time-consuming task requiring specialized knowledge, and you must make sure that you have enough time and training to do the job well.

The first step in setting up an information management system is to survey the records in question and make an inventory. Go through all the files, baskets, boxes, shelves, and other places where the records you will include in your system are currently stored. Talk to the people in the office, and find out where they keep their files. Have respect for people's personal files. Most likely these will not be included in your system. It is up to workers to establish their own management systems for their personal files.

Once you have located and surveyed the records, you are ready to categorize them. Use the information found in other parts of this chapter to help you come up with useful ways of categorizing and organizing files. When you have the files organized into the categories that make the most sense, you are ready to draw up a retention and disposition schedule. You must be very careful at this stage and be sure that you know the laws and guidelines for records retention. Consult with your boss and seek legal advice if necessary. Once you are confident that you know the rules for retention, you can draw up your schedule. Establish a period for review and transfer. This may be a matter of months or a year or more, whatever makes the most sense for your office. When this period has passed, the files that were inactive are moved to transfer files. Then they are evaluated to see if they should be disposed of or stored in archives. The files that were active become inactive and are moved to drawers or boxes for inactive files. Now you have room for your new active files. This cycle is repeated whenever the review period comes around. Current papers are kept in the active files, less recent papers are available in the inactive files, and outdated papers are disposed of if they are not needed or held in archival storage if they are important.

■ Summary

■ Information management is the function of organizing and controlling all aspects of business records, from their creation, protection, and use to their storage and ultimate disposal.

■ Records must be organized so that people can retrieve them quickly and easily when they need to refer to them, and there should be a planned schedule of review for all stored records to determine when they can be disposed of permanently.

■ There are many systems and devices for organizing files. To set up a filing system, take the following steps: define the needs, plan the system, analyze the plan, design the system, implement the system, and evaluate the system.

■ Files can be organized in a number of ways. The most common are alphabetic, subject, numeric, geographic, and follow-up.

- The steps for filing are inspect, index, code, sort, and store. A fixed time every day or every few days should be set aside for filing. Special care must be taken to avoid misfiling.

- There are standard filing supplies and equipment. The most frequently used supplies are file folders, file-drawer guides, and labels. Filing equipment comes in many shapes and sizes, the most common being the standard vertical file. Other popular units are the credenza-style lateral file and open shelves.

- A computer's ability to store and retrieve information depends on its memory. Computers have two kinds of storage: ROM, or permanent storage, and RAM, or temporary storage.

- Decentralized electronic files are controlled by the people who use them and are located near the people who use them. Centralized electronic files can be accessed via computers from workstations within the network.

- Electronic files are categorized and labeled in much the same way as traditional files. Electronic files must be reviewed periodically to see how much storage space is left and what files can be deleted. Special procedures for deleting files must be followed.

- Microforms are photographically reproduced records in miniature. A special machine is needed for reading them. Microforms include microfilm, microfiche, aperture cards, and ultrafiche.

- Computers can help retrieve micrographic materials through CAR.

- Records can be classified as active or inactive. Active files are current and are used often. Inactive records are less recent and may be held in archival storage or reviewed for destruction.

- Records can be organized in a centralized system, in which all records in an office are stored in a records center. In a decentralized system, records are stored near the people who use them most or wherever space is available.

- To establish an information management system, you must first find and take inventory of the records to be included in the system. The next step is to categorize the records. When this is done, you can draw up a retention and disposition schedule.

■ Review Questions

1. Why is it important to define the filing needs before beginning to design a filing system?

2. List and give an example for 5 of the 25 rules for alphabetic filing given in the text.

3. In what way(s) do geographic files differ from subject files? In what way(s) are they the same?

4. What are the five steps to follow in proper filing procedures? Give a reason why it is important to do each one correctly.

5. What are five ways to avoid common misfiling problems?

6. What is the difference between RAM and ROM?

7. In what ways are centralized electronic files different from decentralized electronic files? What are the advantages and disadvantages of each system?

8. Why are microforms often used for inactive or archival storage of important files?

9. What kinds of records are usually classified as vital? important? useful?

10. What are some considerations that must be attended to in drawing up a retention and disposition schedule?

■ Technical Vocabulary

chronological file
charging out
caption
indexing
consecutive numeric system
terminal-digit system
tickler file
cross-reference
filing supplies
filing equipment
ROM (read-only memory)
RAM (random-access memory)
decentralized storage system
centralized storage system
tracks
sectors
bytes
magnetic tape
optical disk

laser disk
CD-ROM (compact disk–
     read-only memory)
micrographics
microform
microform reader
microfilm roll
microfilm jacket
aperture card
microfiche
ultrafiche
computer-assisted retrieval (CAR)
records management
information management
archive
active records
inactive records

■ Discussion and Skills Development

1. Gerald Hansen is one of four secretaries on a team that shares a filing system. He is the newest member of the team. Frequently the folders he wants to retrieve from the files are missing. All of the team's members except one, Betty Washington, spend a few minutes each day filing. Ms. Washington seems always to be behind in her work, and the file tray on her desk is always overflowing. To the surprise of no one, the missing folders usually turn up in Ms. Washington's tray or on

her desk, but only after a time-consuming search. Mr. Hansen has begun to resent the amount of time he spends looking for the folders Ms. Washington has failed to return to the files, especially since his own workload has begun to increase. What should he do?

2. Visit or contact an information management company. Ask if the company will give you a copy of its brochure explaining the kind of work it does. (Most companies have printed copies of such materials for distribution.) If you can get brochures from several companies, compare and contrast their approaches to information management.

3. Joan Milo works at Hanes Publishing Company. Joan and her coworkers do most of their writing and editing on microcomputers. Although the company usually has several projects going at the same time, there are some software programs that all the staff members need at different times during the course of these projects. One is a program that automatically tests the reading level of passages from the text that is being developed for the books. There are several copies of this program in the office, and they are supposed to be filed in one place with the other programs that staff members share. But every time Joan goes to get a copy of the program, all the copies are out of the file. She spends time hunting down a copy of the disk, and finally, after half an hour, she is back to work at her own machine. She puts the disk in her computer and discovers that someone has altered the program to suit his or her specific needs in testing reading levels. What can be done about the problem of making this program available to all who need it? What can be done about the problem of "personalizing" software that others in the office use?

4. Everyone has files and records—at work, at school, or in the home for personal use. Choose one of these types of records that you use, and create a filing system for the records using the procedures in this chapter.

5. Go to the library. Make a list of all the different kinds of filing systems you can find there. Include card-catalog files, micrographics files, magazine files, and so on.

chapter 11
Output and Reprographics

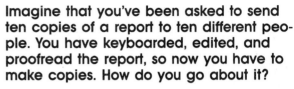

Imagine that you've been asked to send ten copies of a report to ten different people. You have keyboarded, edited, and proofread the report, so now you have to make copies. How do you go about it?

Depending on the kind of office you work in, you may have one or several ways of making your copies. Making copies is part of the output stage of the IPSOD cycle. Output involves transforming letters, reports, and other documents into a form that can be distributed to other people. The most common form of output is paper. No matter how automated your office becomes, you can expect to continue working with large quantities of paper because paper remains the most common and convenient form for people to transmit information to one another.

In Chapter 1 we mentioned a study that showed that American business offices produce 76 million letters a day. But letters represent only the smallest part of the daily deluge. Businesses also generate 600 million computer printouts and 234 million photocopies a day.

This chapter explores the output phase of the information processing cycle. You'll see how reprographics work is distributed and performed in large and small offices, and you'll learn about various capabilities of modern printers and photocopiers. You'll also be introduced to different kinds of electronic copier/printers, and you'll learn how phototypesetting fits into the modern reprographics scene.

It's a scene that has been totally transformed in the past 20 years or so. It's likely that the vast majority of people training to be secretaries today will never encounter a piece of carbon paper. Yet just a generation ago, carbon paper provided one of the few ways of making a replica of an original document.

Reprographics Equipment and Procedures

The primary function of workers in today's office is to generate useful information. Although this has always been the case in business offices, the use of computers has had a major impact on the form in which the information can be presented. For many years typewritten documents, such as letters, memos, and reports have been the primary form of output for processed information. Today output can be generated in print form or transmitted electronically to be received on the computer screen as soft copy. Other options are available as well: computer graphics or charts can be viewed on high-resolution color CRTs and then printed in color using a piece of equipment called a *plotter*; reports can be printed using a wide variety of typefaces or fonts without being sent to an outside compositor or typesetter. Today some computer systems can even generate voice output.

The selection of the form of output required is now a major part of the decision-making role of office workers. It is important to understand the different types of output devices used in the electronic office and the forms of output that each can generate. This chapter covers hard copy output. Sending and receiving soft copy output is discussed in Chapter 12.

Many people think only of copying machines when they hear the word *reprographics* but the term includes a wide and growing array of electronic equipment. One electronics company, for example, recently marketed an easel that executives can use to draw charts and diagrams during business meetings. When a drawing is completed, the speaker can push a button and produce paper copies of it to give to each listener. *Reprographics*, then, can refer to any piece of mechanical or electronic machinery that produces multiple copies of an original.

Since computers have made it possible to produce hard copies from soft copy, reprographics now encompasses not only copying machines but also electronic typesetters and computer printers. When these devices are connected to a computer system they are said to be on-line and are referred to as **output devices**. Computer users can keyboard commands to instruct the printer or photocopier to produce copies of the letters or reports they've just processed.

With microcomputers, printers are usually connected to only one computer terminal, but with minicomputers and mainframe computers, one or more printers can be on-line with an entire network of terminals and CPUs. The electronic link between a computer terminal and an output device can be permanent (by means of electronic cables), or it can be a temporary connection established with telephone lines and modems. Over the next several pages, we will discuss several kinds of computer printers, photocopiers, and typesetters, as well as some procedures for using them.

Printers

The reprographics device you are most likely to use in the electronic office is a computer printer that produces hard copies from the soft copy stored in the computer's storage devices. A printer may also have a small, temporary electronic memory of its own called a **buffer memory** that enables it to store and print bits of a document. In the case of microcomputers the printer's memory is usually very small, from 1K to 2K—not enough to store a letter—but additional buffer memory can be added to enable a computer to store and print out one document while you are keyboarding another. With printers connected to a mainframe or minicomputer this is not a problem since there is ample memory available.

Printers differ from one another in their speed and the quality of their output. **Letter-quality printers** produce pages that look as if they were typed on a high-quality electric typewriter, but they are generally expensive and slow. Other kinds of printers, sometimes called **draft-quality printers**, are more economical and faster, but their output may be faint and difficult to read. A typical letter-quality printer may produce only 12 to 55 characters a second, while a draft-quality printer can print up to 400 characters a second. In recent years computer manufacturers have greatly improved draft-quality printers and have developed faster printers for producing letter-quality print. Another difference among printers is that some cannot produce graphics such as charts and diagrams. If you work on an information processing system that includes different kinds of printers, you will have to choose the printer that is most appropriate for the work you are doing. For example, you might print a letter on one printer, a 50-page report on another, and an engineering drawing on still another kind of printer called a plotter. Let us look at the kinds of printers you might encounter.

Impact Printers

An **impact printer** prints by striking metal or plastic letter shapes, or type, against inked ribbon over paper, as a typewriter does. This means that an impact printer can produce carbon copies along with the originals.

Character Printers   A **character printer** is an impact printer that prints one character at a time. The output of character printers is usually letter-quality. Other kinds of printers produce an entire line or even an entire page in one stroke, but the output with some of these other printers is not as presentable as that of a character printer.

Daisy Wheel Printers   A **daisy wheel printer** is a kind of letter-quality character printer with a round, flat type element. If you think of this type element as a daisy, its "petals" are bars with type characters on their ends. A daisy wheel spins very rapidly, and when the correct character is in position over the ribbon and paper, a tiny hammer strikes it.

Daisy wheels are available in many type sizes and styles and are interchangeable, like the type elements on element typewriters. This means that you can change the daisy wheels to produce hard

ITC AVANT GARDE 10   ABCDEFGHIJKLMNOPQRSTUVWXYZ
abcdefghijklmnopqrstuvwxyz
0123456789

ABCDEFGHIJKLMNOPQRSTUVWXYZ abcdefghijklmnopqrstuvwxyz 0123456789

ITC SOUVENIR 10   ABCDEFGHIJKLMNOPQRSTUVWXYZ
abcdefghijklmnopqrstuvwxyz
0123456789

ABCDEFGHIJKLMNOPQRSTUVWXYZ abcdefghijklmnopqrstuvwxyz 0123456789

Super Focus 10   ABCDEFGHIJKLMNOPQRSTUVWXYZ
abcdefghijklmnopqrstuvwxyz
0123456789
ABCDEFGHIJKLMNOPQRSTUVWXYZ

ABCDEFGHIJKLMNOPQRSTUVWXYZ abcdefghijklmnopqrstuvwxyz 0123456789

Prestige Pica 10   ABCDEFGHIJKLMNOPQRSTUVWXYZ
abcdefghijklmnopqrstuvwxyz
0123456789

ABCDEFGHIJKLMNOPQRSTUVWXYZ abcdefghijklmnopqrstuvwxyz 0123456789

The daisy wheel consists of a rotating wheel and a set of spokes or "petals," each containing one character. Daisy wheels are interchangeable and offer a wide variety of type fonts.

copies in many different type styles, or fonts. One printer manufacturer offers more than 100 daisy wheels in different fonts and for several foreign languages and technical symbols. A secretary might choose a font such as orator for speeches and transparencies, italic or script for announcements, and elite for regular correspondence. Secretaries in law firms, medical offices, and engineering and architectural offices may also use daisy wheels containing special symbols commonly used in those professions.

On many printers you can change not only the typeface but also the pitch of the letters, just as you can on electric typewriters. **Pitch** refers to the number of characters to the inch in a single line of type. Printers usually offer a minimum of two standard pitches—10 characters to the inch and 12 characters to the inch—and many offer several more. The capability to change pitch is important because it allows you to set up a wide variety of formats. You might use a pitch of 15 to format a spreadsheet on wide paper or a pitch of 8 to space out the words in a speech. Daisy wheels are often manufactured in both standard pitches, so if you are shopping for an elite-type daisy wheel, for example, you may have a choice of purchasing it in elite-10 or elite-12 type.

A **thimble printer** is similar to a daisy wheel printer, except that the typebars are bent so that the type element is shaped like a thimble. Like the daisy wheel, the thimble spins constantly as it travels back and forth across the page.

Dot Matrix Printers   Another kind of impact printer is the **dot matrix printer**, which does not use cast metal or plastic type but instead forms characters by projecting tiny metal bristles or pins in patterns. If you look closely at the output of a dot matrix printer, you will see that each letter or number is actually a collection of dots formed by the impact of the bristles against the ribbon and paper. In dot matrix printing, the closer the dots are to each other, the better the quality of the print. In the past dot matrix printers produced fuzzy, draft-quality print, but they have been greatly improved in recent years. Generally, dot matrix printers are available in three levels of quality—high, medium, and low. The high-quality printer approaches or equals letter-quality printing.

Unlike daisy wheel and thimble printers, dot matrix printers can produce graphics. This is because they can project their metal bristles to form any pattern, not just numbers and letters. Some dot matrix printers can print graphics in several colors.

Dot matrix printers are also much faster than daisy wheel or thimble printers. A daisy wheel printer can produce between 12 and 55 characters a second, while a dot matrix printer can produce 50 to 400 characters a second. The fastest dot matrix printers are **line printers**, which print an entire line at a time. A line printer can produce 300 to 2000 lines a minute.

Dot matrix printers usually cost less than thimble or daisy wheel printers. Many offices use letter-quality printers only for documents that will go to clients. They use faster, less expensive dot matrix printers for internal correspondence and drafts of documents that will be edited and reprinted.

Dot matrix printers can produce output of varying quality. Generally, they are not considered to be letter-quality printers; rather, they are thought of as producing "draft-quality" output. "Letter-quality" generally describes fully formed print characters. (Figure 11-1 shows a comparison of draft-quality and letter-quality output.) Dot matrix output can range from very poor to near letter-quality. The difference lies in the number of dots used to form each character. The more concentrated the dots, the higher the quality of the output generated. Additional features of some of the newer dot matrix printers include the ability to print characters in several type sizes and fonts. Typical type sizes include condensed print, standard print, and enlarged print. Common typefaces include pica, elite, italic, and gothic.

Plotters   Another kind of impact printer you may encounter is the **plotter**. A plotter is a device that converts computer output into drawings on paper or on display-type terminals. The most common kind of plotter consists of a movable arm that holds a pen or set of pens of different colored inks. The arm travels back and forth over paper fastened to a flat surface or a drum to produce a high-resolution drawing.

```
        Mr. William Chang
        Personnel Director
        The New Jersey Sentinel
        315 Terrace Avenue
        Hackensack, NJ 07004

        Dear Mr. Chang:

            Your advertisement for a well-rounded student with organi-
        zational skills for a summer word processing job was posted in
        the guidance center of Carlton Business School, where I am a
        student.  I believe I am the student for whom you are looking.
        Let me explain why.
```

```
        Mr. William Chang
        Personnel Director
        The New Jersey Sentinel
        315 Terrace Avenue
        Hackensack, NJ 07004

        Dear Mr. Chang:

            Your advertisement for a well-rounded student with organi-
        zational skills for a summer word processing job was posted in
        the guidance center of Carlton Business School, where I am a
        student.  I believe I am the student for whom you are looking.
        Let me explain why.
```

Fig. 11-1 These documents were produced on the same printer. Draft quality may be used for copy that is to be proofread, edited, and revised. Letter quality is used for output that is being printed to be mailed.

Some plotters are a combination of printers and plotters. These printer-plotters allow users to label and add comments to charts, graphs, and drawings. Plotters are used to produce engineering drawings, maps, blueprints, schematics of machine parts, and so on. In business offices they are used for statistical analyses, financial and sales projections, and meeting presentations. They produce better graphics than most of the other kinds of printers, but they are expensive and are most useful in offices that frequently produce complex drawings and graphs.

Nonimpact Printers

Nonimpact printers produce hard copy without striking type elements against ribbons and paper. They are more expensive than daisy wheel, thimble, or dot matrix printers, and most require special paper. They also lack the ability to produce carbon copies that impact printers have. However, nonimpact printers can produce either text or graphics very fast, and their output generally is of extremely high quality. What is more, nonimpact printers are much quieter than impact printers.

Plotters are graphics printers that can reproduce complex drawings and diagrams.

Ink-Jet Printers An **ink-jet printer** is a nonimpact printer that sprays ink right onto the paper. Like the characters produced by a dot matrix printer, the characters made by the ink-jet printer are registered as patterns of dots. Ink-jet printers can produce almost letter-quality print because the dots are very close together. They are very quiet and fast, printing between 150 and 270 characters per second. They can also produce characters in many fonts, pitches, and sizes.

Laser Printers Another kind of nonimpact printer is the laser printer, which uses a narrow beam of light to form images on paper. These images are brought out, or developed, by using a toner. Laser printers are more expensive than most of the other kinds of printers, but they produce the highest-quality print at the fastest speed—up to 21,000 lines a minute. They can reproduce forms and letterheads, and they can print in different colors and different type fonts on a single page. Laser printers can even produce signatures that are virtually indistinguishable from handwritten signatures.

Laser printers have been most useful to organizations that produce high volumes of personalized mail for political campaigns, mail-order selling, and the like. Until recently they were too expensive to be practical for most office systems. However, they are rapidly becoming cheaper and more compact. Offices of all sizes are beginning to use laser printers, and some office automation experts predict that they will soon be used more often than any other type of printer for producing letter-quality documents.

Laser printers are fast and versatile. They can produce high-quality printed material that looks like professional printing.

CONDENSED PRINT — NORMAL CHARACTERS
CONDENSED PRINT — EMPHASIZED CHARACTERS

STANDARD PRINT — NORMAL CHARACTERS
STANDARD PRINT — EMPHASIZED CHARACTERS

ENLARGED PRINT — NORMAL CHARACTERS
ENLARGED PRINT — EMPHASIZED CHARACTERS

These are Roman regular, *Roman italic, and* **Roman bold.**
Many people prefer the Sans Serif regular or *Sans Serif italic,*
but the most proper and high-minded among us prefer Script or even
Old English

Today's printers produce a broad range of options for producing printed documents. Since many offices have a variety of printers, it is increasingly important to first understand the usage of the information being produced. Then the best printing device and combination of print characters can be selected.

Most printers, whether they are impact or nonimpact printers, are **bidirectional**, that is, able to print from right to left as well as from left to right. If a printer is not bidirectional, it prints from left to right only, returning to the beginning of each line before it starts to print. A bidirectional model prints one line from right to left and the next line from left to right so that it doesn't waste time or motion. The fastest bidirectional printers can produce about 3600 characters a second, or about 720 words a minute. Slow models produce about 120 words a minute, which is faster than most typists.

Printer Accessories

There are some optional devices that increase the efficiency of printers and automatically perform nonprinting tasks that office workers would otherwise perform manually. Let's look at some of these accessories.

Tractors   A **tractor** is a device with moving sprockets that guides continuous-form paper through a printer. **Continuous-form paper** is what we commonly think of as computer printout paper, or fan-fold paper. Each sheet of paper is attached at the end to the next sheet, and each has ½-inch-wide borders with evenly spaced holes that catch on the tractor's sprockets. This hole-and-sprocket mechanism keeps the paper straight and carries it evenly through the

Most printers have tractors which guide continuous-form paper through the printer. Each sheet of continuous-form paper can be separated from the next, and the perforated edges can be removed to make the paper look like a sheet of ordinary office stationery.

printer. The sheets can be separated from each other, and with most continuous-form paper, the perforated edges can be removed so that each sheet can be made to look like a standard sheet of letter paper. Some printers stop printing and give off a sound signal when the tractor feeder runs out of paper or if the paper jams.

Continuous-form paper comes in various sizes and widths, and it can be blank or preprinted with just about any kind of form imaginable. The most common continuous form is the company paycheck. As the computer processes the week's payroll, it automatically fills in the name of an employee, the amounts of his or her gross and net pay, and the deductions for taxes and payroll savings on each paycheck form. Some tax consulting companies have the federal income tax form printed on continuous-form paper so that clients' tax returns can be processed by computer and output on the standard government form. Many companies print bills, receipts, and invoices on continuous-form paper. Using continuous-form paper is a tremendous time-saver because it eliminates the need for an office worker to feed separate forms into the printer one at a time.

Bursters   A **burster** is a device that automatically separates continuous-form paper sheets from each other and from their borders. A burster may be equipped with a device that stacks the sheets in order as it separates them. Without a burster, an office worker must separate continuous-form paper sheets and remove their borders by hand.

Sheet Feeders   If you are printing on letterhead or other special paper that is not available in continuous form, you may want to use a **sheet feeder**, which feeds individual sheets into the printer automatically from stacks. Otherwise, you must insert and remove the sheets one at a time by hand.

Most sheet feeders hold between 100 and 200 sheets at once in a bin. The sheet feeder also uses a sound signal to alert its operator if it runs out of paper or if paper jams. Some sheet feeders have two bins so that you can print documents using two kinds of paper, such as letters consisting of one letterhead and one or more plain pages. Sheet feeders also have receiver trays to accept the printed pages that emerge from the printer.

Envelope Feeders   **Envelope feeders** work like sheet feeders, eliminating the need for an office worker to insert each envelope into the printer individually.

Computer Output Microform

Computer output microfilm (COM) is among the many kinds of output you can produce in the electronic office. With COM, you don't have to print a document on paper in order to transmit it. One reason for using microforms is that it is easier and less expensive to

This sheet feeder can accommodate more than one kind of paper. Hence, a two-page letter could be printed without changing paper bins. One bin could hold letterhead; the other, plain bond.

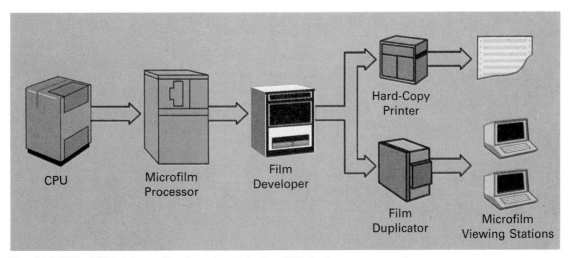

CPU

Microfilm Processor

Film Developer

Hard-Copy Printer

Film Duplicator

Microfilm Viewing Stations

Fig. 11-2 With COM, information is entered in the CPU, is then processed as microfilm, and is then developed. The film can then be printed as hard copy or duplicated for viewing.

distribute or mail many pages or documents on microforms than on paper. According to one vendor, COM equipment transferred 280 billion pages of information directly from computer memories to microforms in 1983.

Figure 11-2 shows how COM works. Output information is entered into the computer and then processed by the microfilm processing unit. The film is then developed and sent to a hard-copy printer to produce a printed document or to a film duplicator to be viewed at a microfilm viewing station.

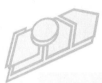

DECISION MAKING

Since more options for producing output exist in the electronic office, it is important to choose the most appropriate output device and the best form for the type of document wanted. When choosing the best possible method of producing a hard-copy document, it is important to consider the following:

1. What is the purpose of the document?

2. Who will read or use the information?

3. How will the document be used?

4. Does the document require any special features, such as graphics, color, a special type size or typeface?

5. How many copies of the document are needed?

Once you have answered these questions, you can make a better decision as to the appropriate printing device and features for a particular job.

Reprographics Systems

Before photocopiers and computers came into wide use in the 1960s and 1970s, the typewriter was the output device for originals and copies. Copies were made by sandwiching carbon paper between sheets of typing paper and then typing over all the layers. Another way to make copies was to type the document onto a stencil or spirit master. These were used on duplicating or mimeograph machines to produce copies of the original.

Making copies in those days was often messy or time-consuming or both. The carbon paper ink and duplicating fluids often stained hands and clothes, the copies had to be separated and stacked, and corrections had to be made on each copy as well as on the original. It was also clear, with duplicated and carbon copies, which was the original and which were the copies. The copies looked and sometimes felt different from the original because they had to be made on special paper or printed with special ink.

In the electronic office, computer printers and photocopiers make the process of producing copies as clean and easy as pushing a button. And electronic technology has blurred the distinction between originals and copies. For example, if you keep printing out the same letter again and again on a computer printer, you are producing not an original and several copies but **multiple originals**. Each is identical with the others, but none is a copy of any of the others because each was generated independently.

The reproduction of documents has become such a large, important, and costly part of office automation that **reprographics systems** have evolved. These are ways of organizing reproduction work so that it can be carried out as efficiently and economically as possible. Depending on the size of a company, its specific needs, and the level of technology it uses, these systems can be either centralized or decentralized. As we discuss these two kinds of systems, you will see that many offices use systems that do not fall neatly into either category but contain elements of both.

Reprographics Centers

Large offices that make heavy use of reprographics may have **centralized reprographics systems**. In other words, they have **reprographics centers**, sometimes called **copy centers**, where specialists use different kinds of equipment to produce hard copies.

Companies that reproduce large quantities of documents usually have a copy center like this one where trained specialists operate the photocopying equipment.

While other office workers may use copiers near their workstations for small copying jobs, they generally rely on the copy centers when they need large numbers of copies or copies of long documents.

A copy center may serve an entire organization, including its branch offices in other buildings, and it may reproduce millions of document pages each year. To handle this volume of work, copy centers generally use equipment that can make copies very quickly and can automatically perform functions such as **collating**, placing pages in the correct order, and binding them together.

Centralized reprographics systems help companies operate more productively in several ways. A centralized system allows office workers to spend time on other duties instead of spending long hours making copies. It also allows management to centralize control of maintenance of the equipment.

Requesting Copies When you work for a company that has a copy center, you usually have to fill out a standard form to be sent to the copy center with your copying job. On this form you should specify the priority of each copying task, how many copies you want, the kind of paper on which they should be made, whether the copies should be stapled or bound, and so on.

Checking Output When your work is returned from a copy center, you should always check it before you distribute the copies to others. Reprographics specialists make mistakes now and then, and automatic copying equipment sometimes malfunctions without warning. Checking the copies carefully can help you avoid sending out copies that are incomplete or unreadable.

You should make a checklist of things to look for. Are there any missing pages? Are all the copies legible? Are they in correct order and right side up? Has the original been reduced or enlarged to the specified size? If the number of copies you have ordered is too large to check each one, pick two or three copies at random and check them thoroughly. You should also make sure the copy center returned your original intact before you distribute the copies.

Decentralized Reprographics Systems

Instead of having copy centers, many employers use **decentralized reprographics systems**, in which all copying machines are located in work areas where employees use them to make their own copies. In a small organization, the volume of reprographics work may not be large enough to keep a copy center busy, so a decentralized reprographics system is more suitable. Large offices use both kinds of systems: a centralized system for big jobs and a decentralized system of relatively small and simple copiers scattered around the office for small jobs. The use of these **convenience copiers**, as they are sometimes called, keeps the copy center from becoming overloaded with small jobs that office workers can complete faster and more efficiently on their own.

In a decentralized reprographics system, employees are usually responsible for keeping the photocopiers supplied with paper and toner.

Access Control The drawback of decentralized reprographics systems is that employers have less control over the operation of copy machines. Some organizations equip their copiers with mechanical or electronic locks, and they distribute keys only to certain employees who are authorized to make copies. Some employers may also keep logs in which office workers are required to note all the copies they make.

Equipment Maintenance In a decentralized reprographics system, maintaining the photocopiers may be the responsibility of the regular office staff rather than specialists. Photocopier maintenance may be assigned to one member of a support staff. In other companies, the entire staff may share this responsibility.

Mechanical Failures A broken copier can slow down an office operation tremendously. Office workers in charge of maintaining copiers should know where to call for a repair technician if their copiers break down. Most offices have repair service contracts with the companies from which they lease or purchase photocopiers.

Supplies While the office workers who are responsible for maintenance in a decentralized reprographics system are not expected to repair photocopiers, they do need to keep the machines filled with paper and **toner**, which is the powder or fluid that develops photographic images on blank paper. Each copier has its own operating instructions, which specify how to add more supplies.

Paper Jams The operating instructions also specify what to do if a piece of paper jams the copying machine. With some models, paper jams occur frequently, but office workers familiar with the operating procedures can generally clear them up easily.

Photocopiers

Although a printer can reproduce the same original any number of times, it is usually more efficient to use a photocopier if you need more than a few copies. If you work in an office where several office workers have to share one printer, you can't afford to tie it up for the length of time it usually takes to produce several copies of a document. Most printers only produce one character or one line of type at a time, while photocopiers can deliver nearly letter-quality copies at a much faster rate because they produce an entire page at a time. Assume, for example, that you need to produce ten copies of a 50-page report. Unless it is essential to distribute multiple originals, it would be more efficient to print the original on your computer printer and then make the copies on the photocopier.

When offices first began using photocopiers in the 1960s, office workers had to feed originals into them one page at a time. They were slower than today's models, and they usually produced copies that looked and felt quite different from the originals. Today's copiers vary widely in their production methods and in their capabilities and features. Some copiers can analyze and enhance print quality, and they can inform you when the paper jams or the ink runs low. Some can put the pages of a multipage document in the correct order and can even staple and bind each copy of the document. Sophisticated copiers, which make copies extremely quickly and have many of these automated features, are usually found in centralized copy centers that handle huge volumes of work. The machines in decentralized reprographics systems are generally smaller and may be somewhat slower and have fewer automated functions.

SPECIAL PHOTOCOPIER FEATURES

Copiers differ markedly in the kinds of special features and capabilities they can offer to save money and produce copies suited to the needs of most business offices. Here are some of those features:

■ **Reduction and Enlargement.** A copier in today's office may also be able to print images that are either smaller or larger than the originals. An office worker might use this feature to enlarge a graphic to make it more attractive and easier to read, or to shrink an oversize computer printout or ledger page so that a standard-sized copy can be placed in a file folder.

- **Color**. Some copiers can print not only on colored paper but also with toners of different colors. Some of these machines can also make high-quality color copies from photographic slides or color transparencies.
- **Automatic Document Feed**. Another feature found on many copiers today is **automatic document feed**, or the ability to feed one sheet at a time automatically from a stack of originals placed in a feeder tray. Without this feature, office workers must feed in pages one at a time.
- **Collating**. **Collating** can be a time-consuming, tedious task when done by hand, but many of today's copiers collate automatically by stacking sets of pages into separate bins.
- **Stapling**. A copier may also be able to staple the collated documents automatically, which saves yet another step for the office worker.
- **Duplex Copying**. Some copiers are capable of **duplex copying**, or copying on both sides of a sheet of paper automatically. This saves money for employers by cutting down on paper use, postage costs, and filing space.

Types of Photocopiers

Coated-Paper Copiers   **Coated-paper copiers** make copies by projecting images of the originals onto special chemically coated paper. Before the copies emerge from the machine, they pass automatically through a toner that develops these photographic images. Coated copying paper does not look or feel like standard business paper, but copies made on coated paper are inexpensive. Some offices use coated-paper copies for internal distribution but make plain-paper copies of documents that will be distributed to outsiders.

Plain-Paper Copiers   A **plain-paper copier** uses a process in which an image of the original is projected onto a drum or belt inside the machine. Powdered toner adheres to this image, and the machine uses heat and pressure to transfer the toner permanently onto ordinary business paper. (See Fig. 11-3.) Plain-paper copiers can make copies on colored papers, letterheads, business forms, and other special papers, in addition to standard white bond paper. When copies are made on high-quality plain-paper machines, it is sometimes difficult to distinguish them from the originals.

Roll-Fed Copiers   Copiers differ not only in their photographic processes but also in the ways blank paper is fed into them. A **roll-fed copier** makes copies on paper that is cut from a roll as it is fed into the machine. Roll-fed copying machines can make copies of as many as 40 different sizes. They are especially useful in offices that copy many special business forms or other odd-size documents.

Sheet-Fed Copiers   A **sheet-fed copier** automatically takes cut sheets of paper from a tray inside the machine. Sheet-fed copiers

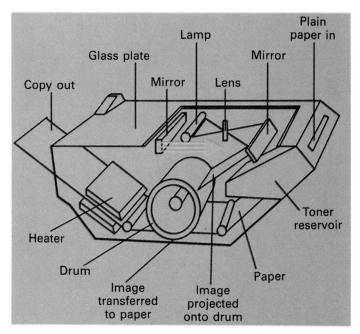

Fig. 11-3 Plain-paper copiers work by projecting the image of the original onto a drum. Powdered toner adheres to the image on the drum; then the toner is transferred to the paper by means of heat and pressure. The finished copy can be almost identical to the original.

generally use letter-size or legal-size paper. Some machines can make copies of several other sizes as well.

Electronic Copier/Printers

So far, we have talked about photocopiers that require hard-copy originals and are not linked to electronic networks. Today's office may also include an electronic copier/printer, which can make copies at high speeds directly from the soft copy that appears on a computer screen. An electronic copier/printer is generally used on-line, which means that office workers can send soft copy and printing instructions to it from keyboards that are connected to the same computer. The computer and its terminals may be located in the same office as the copier/printer, or they may be separated by vast distances.

Electronic copier/printers represent a combination of the technologies found in computer printers, photocopiers, and facsimile machines. Like printers, they can be instructed to produce hard copies from soft copy; like photocopiers, they can reproduce entire pages at 120 pages a minute; and like facsimile machines, they can transmit exact duplicates of pages over long distances. Because they are very expensive, electronic copier/printers are used almost exclusively in reprographics systems that produce 20,000 copies or more a month.

Intelligent Copier/ Printers

Some of the most sophisticated electronic copying machines are **intelligent copier/printers**, which have their own small internal processors. With the appropriate software, these copiers can combine and process several different kinds of input in the same document automatically. For example, they can combine words and graphics on the same page, they can input and combine hard and soft copy, and they can send copy to and receive copy from other intelligent copier/printers.

Dumb Copier/ Printers

Electronic copier/printers without their own internal processors are called **dumb copier/printers**. These machines lack many of the features and capabilities of intelligent copier/printers. For example, they can follow your keyboarded instructions as to how many copies to print and what type style and format to use, but they cannot accept commands for more complex processing operations such as merging form letters with mailing lists.

Composition Systems

Another reprographics device is the phototypesetter. A **phototypesetter** uses photographic technology to set text into special styles and column widths. Typesetting is used for printing books, magazines, annual reports, and other widely distributed documents that must look polished rather than for making copies of everyday documents, such as letters and memos.

At one time typesetting was done by casting type in lead—either by laboriously inserting each letter into a row by hand or by molding lead into lines of type on a linotype machine. Columns of lead were arranged on page forms that were fitted into printing presses. Today the most common method of setting type is phototypesetting.

Phototypesetters, which are usually operated by specialists, resemble word processors and computer terminals because they have keyboards, storage units, internal processors, and, generally, display monitors. An office worker whose terminal is on-line with a phototypesetter can send soft copy to the phototypesetter electronically in seconds, regardless of whether the typesetter is in the same building or hundreds of miles away. The soft copy would include some special instruction codes to tell the phototypesetter's processing unit what sizes and fonts of type to use for the body and headings of the text, how wide to set each column of type, and so on. The specialist who operates the phototypesetter may then keyboard some additional, more technical instructions. For example, the specialist would keyboard codes indicating how much space should appear between columns of text and where space on the page should be left blank for illustrations.

If there is no electronic communications link between the phototypesetter and the office worker's computer, the office worker may be able to output the text to a disk that can be read by the typesetter as long as the operating systems of the computer and the typesetting equipment are compatible. If the two systems are not compatible, the office worker must produce a hard copy of the text and the typesetting instructions. The hard copy is then delivered to a specialist, who must keyboard it into the typesetter.

Phototypesetters also have photographic units that contain light sources, master images of all the type sizes and fonts the phototypesetter can produce, and light-sensitive paper onto which these images are projected. The phototypesetter stores the previously input text and instructions on a magnetic tape or disk that is then fed into its photographic unit. In this unit the type images are developed like a photographic print. This unit can create photographic images at a speed of 1000 lines a minute.

When the paper with type developed on it—or galley proof, as it is called—emerges from the typesetter, it is generally cut into strips and pasted onto paper boards in position for the printed pages. These boards are then sent to some kind of printing press, where the final output is produced. This manual paste-up process is called **page composition**. Some phototypesetters create photographic images of entire pages, which eliminates the need for manual page composition. These special phototypesetters are called **photocompositors**.

Companies that generate large volumes of printing, such as newspaper and magazine publishers or stores that frequently publish catalogs, often have their own phototypesetters. Other companies use the services of commercial phototypesetters. In either case the phototypesetting devices may be on-line with the employer's central processing unit and its computer or word processor terminals. As you have seen, the electronic link between an office worker's terminal and a phototypesetter may be permanent, or it may rely on a temporary telephone connection by means of a modem.

Typesetters, like copiers and computer printers, have made life much easier for today's office workers. Office reprographics has come a long way from the days of carbon paper and hand-cranked mimeograph machines when reproduction was expensive and time-consuming. In those days an executive might have circulated only one copy of a memo for everyone to read and initial, or several people might have had to share one copy of a report. Electronic technology has transformed the way in which office workers reproduce documents. Today every employee can get a copy of the latest memo, meeting agenda, or sales report. In fact, technology has contributed greatly to the paperwork explosion confronting many modern American business offices because it has become so easy to churn out copy after copy of even the longest and most complicated documents. Just as computers have made it possible to process so much more information than ever before, modern reprographics has made it possible to share that information quickly and easily with many more people than ever before.

HOT OFF THE PRESS

After printers or photocopiers produce the pages of a document, the pages must be assembled into the finished document. The collating and binding operations are all part of the reprographics process. If you have to collate by hand, you arrange the copies of each page in stacks and then take one copy from each stack in the correct order until each document is assembled. Your office may also have a manual, mechanical, or automatic collating device to help you.

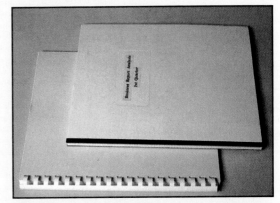

Flat-comb binding (right) and spiral-comb binding (left) are two methods of binding sets of documents after they have been printed.

- A **manual collator** has from 4 to 100 bins to hold each page. A manually operated feeder arm pushes up the top copy in each bin so that an office worker can gather it quickly and easily.
- A **mechanical collator** works the same way, but its feeder arms are motorized.
- An **automatic collator** gathers the top copies in the bins and deposits the completed sets in receiving trays.

The most common way to bind sets of documents is to staple them. Other kinds of binding usually require special equipment:

- In **spiral-comb binding**, a curled plastic comb is inserted through a line of rec-

tangular holes punched along the side of each page of the document.

- In **flat-comb binding**, half of a two-part rigid plastic comb is inserted through the holes along the side of the document and heat-sealed to the other half.
- When **adhesive binding** is required, pellets of glue are inserted into the binding device and melted, or a strip of fabric is glued to the edge of a document and then sealed to each page with heat and pressure.

Summary

- Even though business offices are being automated, office workers can expect to produce large quantities of paper copies. Since not all offices are fully automated, paper remains the most common form for transmitting business information.

- The most common on-line output device is the computer printer. Impact printers include slow, letter-quality daisy wheel and thimble printers and fast, lower-quality dot matrix printers and plotters. Nonimpact printers, such as ink-jet and laser printers, are faster and quieter than impact printers.

- Printer accessories such as tractors, sheet feeders, and bursters help office workers perform time-consuming nonprinting tasks.

- Large companies may have centralized reprographics systems where specialists perform all of the company's copying tasks. Smaller companies may have decentralized reprographics systems, in which copying machines are scattered throughout the company. Most companies have a combination of the two kinds of systems.

- Office workers often have to know how to request a copying job from a centralized system and how to operate and maintain the copiers they use in a decentralized system.

- *Reprographics* refers to the production of multiple copies. To make hard copies from soft copy, a printer or photocopier must be connected to a computer system.

- Photocopiers are more efficient than printers for producing large numbers of copies. Coated-paper copiers require special paper, while plain-paper copiers use ordinary business paper.

- Some copiers can print in different colors, reduce and enlarge originals, and collate and staple copies automatically.

- Electronic copier/printers can produce copies from soft copy stored in computers. Intelligent copier/printers can combine hard and soft copy and communicate with other intelligent copier/printers.

- Typesetters are used to produce books, manuals, magazines, catalogs, and reports. Computers can send soft copy and instructions directly to typesetters.

■ Review Questions

1. Define *reprographics,* and explain how it fits into the IPSOD cycle.

2. Explain why most large companies have centralized and decentralized reprographics systems.

3. Explain the steps you would take to make sure copies returned to you from a copy center are in acceptable form.

4. Define *on-line.* Explain the function of an on-line output device.

5. Compare daisy wheel and dot matrix printers. What are the advantages and disadvantages of each?

6. How do impact and nonimpact printers work?

7. Discuss the drawbacks and advantages of nonimpact printers.

8. Compare coated-paper and plain-paper photocopiers.

9. Cite a task that could be performed by an intelligent copier/printer but not by a dumb copier/printer.

10. How do phototypesetters work? When would you use one?

■ Technical Vocabulary

output devices
buffer memory
letter-quality printer
draft-quality printer
impact printer
character printer
daisy wheel printer
pitch
thimble printer
dot matrix printer
line printer
plotter
nonimpact printer
ink-jet printer
bidirectional
tractor
continuous-form paper
burster
sheet feeder
envelope feeder
multiple originals
reprographics system
centralized reprographic system
reprographics center

copy center
collating
decentralized reprographics
    system
convenience copiers
toner
automatic document feed
duplex copying
coated-paper copier
plain-paper copier
roll-fed copier
sheet-fed copier
intelligent copier/printer
dumb copier/printer
phototypesetter
page composition
photocompositor
manual collator
mechanical collator
automatic collator
spiral-comb binding
flat-comb binding
adhesive binding

■ Discussion and Skills Development

1. Jeremy Richards is an administrative assistant in a big office that has a copy center as well as convenience copiers. The last several times he has sent documents to the copy center to be reproduced, he has found mistakes in the finished work. In one instance some pages were in the wrong order. In another recent case one page was missing altogether from each copy and some pages were missing the bottom lines of text. Mr. Richards has begun to feel that the copy center is unreliable. Discuss what you would do if you were in his position.

2. Assume that you have been asked to purchase a computer printer for a small business office. The printer will be used for both word processing and graphics, and it must produce almost letter-quality print. Research computer magazines for articles on printers, or go to a computer store that carries several different kinds of printers, and pick out one that you think would be best suited for your office. Compare these features:

print quality, speed, buffer size, pitches, fonts, ink colors, types of paper feeds, and graphics capabilities. Did you choose an impact or a nonimpact printer? What were the differences in prices? Prepare a short report explaining your choice.

3. Check your local Yellow Pages for the name of a nearby commercial copy center. Arrange for your class to visit the center as a whole or in small groups. Bring a list of questions with you about what you would like to see and how the equipment is used. Ask the staff at the center to demonstrate how they use the different machines. Ask to see special features such as automatic collating, reduction and enlargement, binding, duplex copying, and color reproduction. To summarize what you have learned, make a chart of the kinds of jobs that can be done on the different machines.

chapter 12
Distribution/
Communication

There is no point in processing information unless it is going to be sent somewhere. That would be like cooking a meal but then not serving it. The distribution/communication phase is an important step in the IPSOD cycle. Without it, all the other steps would be useless.

This chapter explores the many different ways people can distribute information in the office. Traditionally, the most common way office workers distributed information was by placing a hard copy of it in an envelope and mailing it. In the electronic office, a vast number of computer-based methods of sending information have developed. We've already mentioned a few of these, such as electronic mail and facsimile machines.

Electronic communication allows all the offices of a company to interconnect, or integrate, their information processing systems so that they can communicate with each other and with other companies. This enables businesses to send and receive information instantaneously instead of having to wait hours or days for telegrams or mail delivery. Using electronic communication equipment, for example, a teller at a bank branch can instantly record a transaction on the main office computer, and a multinational corporation can send a contract from Zurich to New York in a matter of minutes.

Of course, even if you work in a fully electronic office, you will still have to know about manual methods of distributing information, since you will sometimes be communicating with people who work in traditional offices. And no matter what type of office you work in, you will have a number of distribution methods to choose from. This chapter explains the choices you will be offered and looks into the advantages and disadvantages of each type of distribution/communication system.

Manual Distribution Methods

When you pick up the day's mail after your letter carrier has dropped it in your mailbox, or when you walk across the hall to deliver a copy of a letter to someone in another office, you are using a manual distribution system. Manual distribution, or traditional mail, refers to any system in which people, rather than electronic machines, carry messages from one place to another. It includes not only the U.S. Postal Service but also private couriers and delivery services, such as Emery and Federal Express. It also includes office messengers, mail rooms, and interoffice mail systems.

The electronic communication methods we have already discussed are usually the most efficient and cost-effective ways to deliver messages between fully automated offices that can link up with each other electronically. However, even the fully automated offices still need manual delivery services to communicate with other businesses or offices that are not automated and that cannot, therefore, communicate electronically. Sometimes an automated office may need to use a manual delivery system because its electronic equipment does not have the capability to transmit certain kinds of graphics or text, or because the receiving equipment doesn't have the capability to receive the transmission. In addition, traditional methods are still needed to deliver periodicals and parcels.

U.S. Postal Service

The U.S. Postal Service faces growing competition from private courier and delivery services, but it remains the most widely used system for conveying mail between companies. One reason for this is that in most cases the U.S. Postal Service still offers the least expensive means of manual distribution despite rising postage costs. It also usually offers the most convenient means, and it is by far the most familiar delivery service.

High-speed mechanical equipment, which can sort ZIP-Coded mail much faster than manual sorters, greatly speeds the delivery of first-class mail.

CLASSES AND SERVICES OF MAIL

The cost and speed of U.S. Postal Service delivery depend on the class of mail sent. Here is what you should know about the classes of mail and the special services available.

■ **First-Class Mail**. You generally use first-class mail to send letters, personal notes, and payments. Any item can be sent by first-class mail if it weighs less than 70 pounds and if its combined length and circumference do not exceed 108 inches. First-class mail usually reaches its destination in less than a week. The U.S. Postal Service ships first-class mail by the fastest means available. First-class postage assures that letters will not be opened for postal inspection, so they are private. First-class mailings that are not letter-size should be clearly marked "First Class."

■ **Priority Mail**. Priority mail is designed for sending small packages. Fees are set by zone as well as by weight, but they are usually lower than those charged by private couriers. Priority mail can be used for items weighing up to 70 pounds and measuring no more than 108 inches in length and circumference combined. The minimum weight for priority mail is 13 ounces. All priority mail should be clearly marked on all sides.

■ **Second-Class Mail**. You may use second-class mail, which is less expensive than first-class, for mailing copies of newspapers and magazines. Publishers of periodicals are the biggest users of second-class mail.

■ **Third-Class Mail**. For bulk mailings, especially of advertisements, you might use third-class mail. Third-class mail can include printed materials and parcels that weigh less than a pound.

■ **Fourth-Class Mail**. For packages that weigh a pound or more, you might use fourth-class mail, which is also known as parcel post. A fourth-class parcel can weigh up to 70 pounds and can measure up to 108 inches in combined length and circumference. For books, records, materials for blind people, catalogs, and some other parcels, the Postal Service offers reduced rates.

■ **Express Mail**. Express Mail is the Postal Service's fastest manual delivery system, and you can use it for any urgent letter or package weighing up to 70 pounds. The Postal Service guarantees that an item sent by Express Mail from a designated post office before 5 p.m. will reach its destination by 3 p.m. the next day (unless the destination is in a rural area classified as a two-day delivery zone). Express Mail is more expensive than other Postal Service services, but it is often less costly than similar services from private couriers. To send letters or parcels by Express Mail, you use special envelopes or address stickers that you can obtain from post offices.

■ **Special Delivery**. Special delivery, which you can obtain for any class of mail, assures that your letter or parcel will be delivered as soon as it reaches the post office nearest its destination. Otherwise, it would go out with the next regular mail delivery, which might not be until the next weekday morning. Special-delivery mail should be labeled with stickers that are available from the post office.

■ **Special Handling**. Special handling speeds up the sorting and transportation of third- or fourth-class mail but does not provide special delivery. The fee for special handling depends on the weight of the item. Packages for this service should be clearly marked with the words "Special Handling." For especially urgent mail, you can specify both special handling and special delivery.

■ **Certified Mail**. The Postal Service will provide a record that certified mail has been delivered to the addressee. Your employer may need such a record for documents such as contracts. For an , extra fee, the Postal Service offers restricted delivery, which means the mail will be delivered directly to an individual rather than to anyone at the delivery address. Only first-class mail can be certified.

■ **Registered Mail**. Valuable first-class mail or priority mail can be registered or insured. Registered mail is used for items such as stock certificates, cash, and precious metals. To register mail, you must declare its full value. For an additional fee, you can obtain restricted delivery of registered mail.

■ **Insured Mail**. Because registration is available only for first-class and priority mail, post offices offer insurance for mail of other classes that is sent to U.S. destinations. Insurance fees are based on the declared value of the item, and you can insure a package for up to $200.

■ **COD Mail**. You send an item COD, which stands for "Collect on Delivery," if the addressee has bought the item from you but has not yet paid for it. The mail carrier collects the amount you specify (up to $200) and returns it to you in the form of a postal money order.

■ Courier and Messenger Services

Couriers and messengers generally guarantee that they will manually deliver documents and packages overnight. They can often make deliveries over short distances quickly. Couriers and messengers usually make pickups and offer other services that are not available from the U.S. Postal Service. In addition, they frequently offer faster delivery, and their rates are usually comparable to Postal Service rates, or even lower.

Some courier services operate only in the United States or within a smaller geographic area, while others make pickups and deliveries internationally. Most large courier services will pick up envelopes or packages from your office, but with others you drop off your materials at their offices. Courier services may also require that you use specially marked envelopes. If your employer uses couriers frequently, it may have a contract with one of the courier services. There are special procedures, such as getting authorizations or setting special pickup times, for using each service.

Some private couriers have recently begun to offer facsimile transmissions that they deliver within a few hours. One of these couriers is Federal Express, which offers the facsimile transmission service called Zap Mail.

Messenger services may operate only within a city and its suburbs. Many offices in large cities have contracts with messenger services that they call on when they need to rush documents or parcels to other offices nearby. Messenger service within a city generally costs less than Express Mail and is much faster. Many large and medium-sized offices employ their own messengers to make pickups and deliveries at nearby offices or other locations. For example, a typesetting company might employ a messenger whose job is to deliver documents to and pick up documents from publishing houses and design studios.

Mail Rooms and Interoffice Mail

All large offices, including those with electronic mail systems, have mail rooms. These mail rooms are staffed by employees who sort and deliver **interoffice mail**, which includes all mail exchanged between people who work in the same location or at the company's nearby branches. An example of interoffice mail is a memo from a supervisor to managers in other departments.

In a large office, each floor usually has a location for depositing interoffice mail as well as letters and parcels that will be mailed through the U.S. Postal Service. This mail drop may have separate bins for interoffice and outgoing mail. Mail-room employees generally make several pickups from these locations during each workday, and office workers should be aware of pickup and delivery schedules.

Some companies use an interoffice mail system called **mail-mobile**. This system uses a mailcart that automatically follows a magnetic track on the floor. It is programmed to stop at various points and ring a bell to remind office workers to pick up and deposit mail. The layout of the track can easily be altered if the floor plan is changed.

In addition to collecting, sorting, and distributing interoffice mail, mail-room employees sort outgoing mail and may be responsible for delivering it to post offices. Incoming mail is generally delivered to the mail room, where the mail-room staff sorts it for delivery to individual offices and employees along with interoffice mail.

Outgoing Mail Procedures

If you work in a large office where outgoing mail is processed by mail-room employees, you can still expect to be responsible for wrapping packages and for stuffing, addressing, stamping, and presorting envelopes. You should keep a ZIP Code directory among your reference materials to make sure outgoing envelopes bear the proper ZIP Codes. Your post office can tell you how to purchase a ZIP Code directory from the Government Printing Office. If your office is too small to have a mail room, you may be responsible for the processing operations described below.

Sorting Outgoing mail should be sorted according to destination and service class. When processing many outgoing envelopes, you can save money for your employer by sorting them according to ZIP Codes, because the Postal Service offers discounts on sorted mail. Some employers have OCR devices that scan ZIP Codes and sort envelopes automatically. (These devices are different from the OCRs used as input devices, which you read about in Chapter 6, but

Postage meters make it easy for office workers to stamp outgoing mail with the correct amount of postage. The meter registers the amount of postage for each item and subtracts this amount from the total amount of postage remaining in the meter.

they employ some of the same technology.) If you don't have an automatic sorter, you can sort mail manually.

Weighing Unless you are certain of how much postage it requires, you must weigh outgoing mail on a postal scale. A postal scale, which may be mechanical or electronic, shows the weight of an item in ounces and pounds. The postage is determined by both the weight and the class of mail.

Stamping Once you determine the amount of the postage, you affix a stamp to each envelope or parcel. Depending on the quantity of mail you handle, you may do this by hand with ordinary stamps, or you may use a postage meter.

Using a Postage Meter A mail room that routinely processes large quantities of mail generally uses a **postage meter**, which prints postage fees on gummed strips of paper that are used as stamps. A company purchases a postage meter from an office-equipment company, but the meter must be licensed by the Postal Service, which also supplies a meter record book. Before using a new meter, you take it to a post office and purchase a specific amount of postage. A postal worker records the amount of the purchase on the meter's dials. At the end of each workday, you record in your meter record book the amount of postage you have used that day and the amount that remains on the dials. When the amount remaining on the meter runs low, you go to the post office again to buy more postage and have the dials reset. With newer, more sophisticated postage meters, postage can also be purchased electronically.

Electronic Communication Methods

One early way to distribute information over long distances was by mail, though not in the way that we think of the mail service today. From the Middle Ages, when commerce began to flourish, until the nineteenth century, camels, horses, sailing ships, and stagecoaches carried the mail between the cities and ports of Europe and America. It often took weeks or months to send mail from one place to another by stagecoach or ship, and even today with trains, trucks, and airplanes to speed mail on its way, it can take several days for a letter to reach its destination.

In the 1830s Samuel Morse perfected the first practical electronic communications system: the telegraph. The telegraph was a great boon to business and government because it was the first communications system to provide nearly instantaneous transmission of messages across hundreds or thousands of miles. In the early twentieth century, other electronic advances, such as the development of the telephone and telex, continued to improve business communications. Then, in the 1960s and 1970s, the electronic revolution brought a new array of machines that could send hard or soft copies at astonishing speeds. Today electronic offices can choose from electronic mail systems, computer-to-computer communications, time-sharing systems, facsimile transmission, and computer-based mail services. And, of course, electronic offices also have the option of sending mail by traditional manual delivery systems such as the U.S. Postal Service and private couriers (see Fig. 12-1).

If you work in an electronic office, the method you choose to distribute a document will depend on several factors. What kind of a document is it? Where is it going? Who will receive it, and how urgently is it needed? If it is a big, bulky report consisting of several hundred pages, it may be best to send it by regular mail, but if it consists of only a few pages of text or graphics, you could send it by facsimile transmission. If a document is going to be delivered to a rural area or a foreign country, some delivery methods may not be available. In addition, the recipient may not have electronic equipment available to receive a document sent by computer or facsimile machine. If a branch office must have a copy of a contract for a meeting in an hour, you should send it by the fastest available

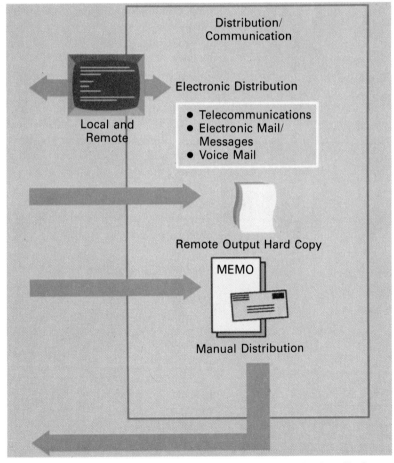

Fig. 12-1 The distribution/communication of data can be handled manually, by traditional means, or electronically.

means. But if you are mailing copies of the company's annual report in preparation for a stockholders' meeting next month, regular mail service will do.

Electronic Mail Systems

The use of computers and other electronic equipment to send and receive documents instantaneously is known as electronic mail. Companies can use electronic mail among their own departments and to send messages to other companies or to distant branch offices and plants. You may recall that when a company's terminals, computers, and peripheral equipment are all connected, they make up a network. To use electronic mail internally, a company has to have a network of cables and devices interconnecting its computers so that they can all communicate with one another. This system is called a **local area network** (LAN). LANs are interconnected systems that communicate over an internal, private network and are located within several hundred yards or several miles of each other.

Local area networks offer many advantages. They allow a company to place its terminals, printers, and other hardware where they can be used most conveniently and still have them linked together. A company can also save a lot of money by purchasing the hardware to set up a LAN that permits it to integrate older, incompatible equipment with newer equipment instead of having to replace the older equipment.

LANs are usually laid out, or configured, in three basic ways. The way in which a LAN is configured is called its topology. A linear bus connection means that each piece of hardware is connected in a line so that additional equipment can be added on at the end. A ring connection means that the devices are strung together in a closed loop or circle, and a star connection means that each device is connected by a single, separate link to a central computer. Each configuration has advantages and disadvantages. The configuration your office uses will depend on its size and communications needs.

A company generally uses its internal electronic mail system to send one message to an individual employee, to send the same message to several employees at once, and to gather comments and ideas from various employees at the employees' convenience. When you send a message by means of an electronic mail system, you keyboard the message at your terminal. Then you keyboard a series of special commands that tells the computer where to send the message.

Electronic mail permits computers to send, store, and receive messages. The messages you send go to the recipient's **electronic mailbox**. To receive electronic mail, you would keyboard in special commands that instruct your electronic mailbox to display a list of your messages. This list will indicate who sent each message, what time it arrived, its subject, and whether or not it is urgent. Some electronic mail systems require that a user identification code be

```
SCAN         for a summary of your mail
READ         to READ messages or LISTS
PRINT        to display messages nonstop
CREATE       to write an MCI Letter
CREATE LIST  to make a distribution list
DOWJONES     to Dow Jones News/Retrieval
ACCOUNT      to adjust terminal display
HELP         for assistance

Command (or MENU or EXIT): create

TO:      Elisabeth Allison
TO:      117-5798 Elisabeth K. Allison                    Belmont, MA

CC:      William Buckley
CC:      121-0059 William F. Buckley, Jr.   The National Re New York, NY

Subject: Speaking Invitation

Text: (Enter text or transmit file. Type / on a line by itself to end.)

Please confirm speaking engagement at National Association of
[Command: ^]
```

An electronic mailbox lets you send, receive, store, and copy messages on your computer terminal.

entered prior to displaying messages. A recipient's identification code is usually known only to the recipient (and perhaps one or two others who work closely with the individual). This allows electronic mail to be kept private. You can leave messages in your electronic mailbox until you are ready to read them (see Fig. 12-2). You can also print them, make additional soft copies, add notes, and forward them instantly to other people in the network. You can transfer soft copies of messages from your mailbox to be electronically filed with other files on disks, tapes, or other electronic media. If you have no further use for a message, you can erase it from the computer's memory.

Computer-to-Computer Communications

We've been discussing short-range electronic information distribution using electronic mail and LANs. *Computer-to-computer communications* is a general term that includes electronic mail and LANs, but we are using it here to refer to two basic types of computer exchanges: communicating with large central computers and communicating with individual workstations.

Computer-to-computer communications grew out of **data communications**, the exchange of data between computers. The first business computers were big mainframes housed in central locations. Data had to be manually delivered to the computer center and manually distributed to users after processing. With the advent of minicomputers and computer networks, companies could process data both at their centralized data processing centers and at remote

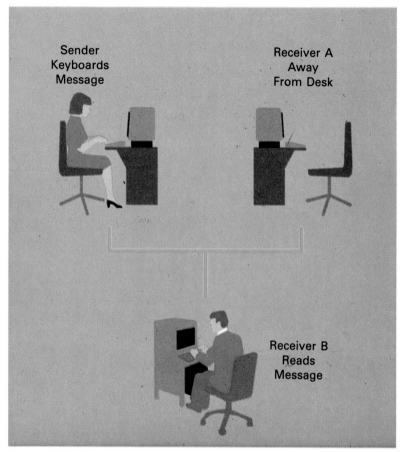

Fig. 12-2 Electronic messages can be sent at any time and received immediately or at the recipient's convenience.

sites such as warehouses, manufacturing plants, and branch offices. In addition, the central and remote computers could exchange data between themselves over cables or telephone lines.

This teleprocessing, as it is sometimes called, offered tremendous advantages. Salesclerks in distant stores could check central warehouse inventories, or a day's banking transactions could be collected and held in a branch computer until the central computer was ready to process it.

Data can be transmitted in different ways and over many different kinds of media. Two computers sitting side by side can use simple copper wires; a larger number of computers would require a LAN. Remote transmission may be via telephone lines, microwave, or even satellite.

One problem with some computer communications is that it is possible for formatting instructions to be lost during transmission, and part of the document may be garbled. Sentences may be received as strings of meaningless letters and symbols, every comma may become a quotation mark, and so on. An office worker at the receiving end may have to spend some time restoring the soft copy to its original form, and this may require some discussion with the sender over the telephone.

To avoid garbled messages, computer manufacturers have devised rules or procedures called **protocols** that allow different models of computers to communicate with one another. These rules, incorporated into various kinds of hardware and software, can identify and correct errors, control the speed and sequence of events during a transmission, establish and terminate transmissions, and edit and format transmitted documents. One set of protocols, for example, prescribes exactly how a person may ask a computer terminal to call up a data base; another dictates the commands a person can keyboard on a word processor to edit text.

Sometimes a message is garbled because the sending computer transmits a control code that the receiving computer can't interpret. Computers usually use one of two **control codes**, or kinds of binary language to represent each letter, number, and symbol—the American Standard Code for Information Interchange (ASCII) and the Extended Binary Coded Decimal Interchange Code (EBCDIC). Computer operators can correct the problem of incompatible codes by using a **protocol converter**, a device that translates the transmission code of one computer into the transmission code of the other.

When computers in distant locations send messages to each other, the messages usually travel over ordinary telephone lines. Telephone lines generally carry analog signals. These are continuous but variable electrical waves. Computers, on the other hand, produce digital signals, which are discrete electronic units transmitted in very quick succession like rapid-fire Morse code. Computers cannot send or receive analog signals, and most telephone lines cannot carry digital signals. Therefore, in order for two computers to communicate over long distances, a signal converter must convert the transmitted signals from digital to analog and back to digital as they are carried from computer to computer.

Modems One device that performs these conversions is the modem, which you first read about in Chapter 2. The term *modem* was made up from parts of the words *mo*dulate and *dem*odulate. Modems are devices that can be attached to a computer either internally or externally. Some computers can be purchased already equipped with modems, or modems can be purchased separately and added to the computer.

The speed at which a modem transmits data is known as its **baud rate**. A modem with a baud rate of 300 can transmit roughly 30 characters a second. Most modems used in offices with microcom-

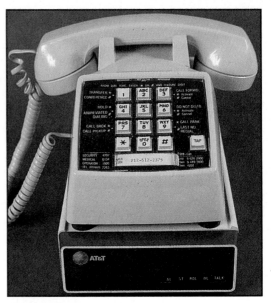

Modems are available in several forms. Some are circuit boards that fit inside microcomputers. Others are separate units that are linked directly to telephones and terminals.

puters are either 300 or 1200 baud, although there are modems that can transmit data much faster. Some modems can operate at several baud rates, and if you are using such a device, you may have to select the baud rate yourself, either by flipping a switch or by keying a command. The baud rate you select must match that used by the receiving modem.

Many public data banks offer users a choice of receiving data at either 1200 or 300 baud. A modem at 1200 baud lets you receive data faster. This saves money in two ways. The data bank fees, which are based on the length of time you are connected to the computer, would be lower. And the telephone charge, which is also based on the amount of time your modem is connected to the computer, would also be lower.

Acoustic Couplers A less costly device for translating digital signals into analog and vice versa is the **acoustic coupler**, which has two openings that accommodate the earpiece and mouthpiece of a telephone handset. Like a modem, it modulates and demodulates signals, and it can send data at 300 or 1200 baud. The trouble with using an acoustical coupler is that the phone may pick up loud noises that can garble the data.

Acoustic couplers are used mostly for linking telephones with facsimile machines or computers. In fact, many facsimile machines have acoustic couplers built in. The main difference between modems and acoustic couplers is that most modems are plugged directly into the telephone line, using the same kinds of plugs that

Acoustic couplers let you transmit copy using a telephone handset held in a cushioned cradle.

connect the parts of modular telephone systems. Acoustic couplers use a cushioned cradle to hold the handset. Sales representatives and other employees who travel a lot often use acoustic couplers to feed information to their company computers because they can use couplers with any telephone.

Communications Software In Chapter 8 you learned that in addition to modems, communicating computers need communications software. These are programs that can perform several communications functions. A communications program connects one terminal to the other, transfers files from one terminal to another, repeatedly dials busy telephone numbers, and takes the user through the proper log-on sequence when he or she calls an external data base. It can also store information about the computers with which you communicate most frequently, such as their telephone numbers, passwords, and baud rates, so that you do not have to rekeyboard the information each time you call. Different communications programs have different capabilities. Some "combination" communications programs are written to be used with specific brands of modems. The Hayes Smartcom II program, for example, is intended to be used with the Hayes Smartmodem.

A communications program can allow you to access specific external data bases, such as Compuserve, Dow-Jones, and The Source. Your company may subscribe to these data bases to access a wide variety of information, such as stock market reports, airline schedules, and research services. Certain specific communications programs also allow you to create mailing lists and access computer-based mail services such as Telex and EasyLink. We will discuss these services later in this chapter.

Transmission Media   While most long-distance communication between computers involves sending signals over telephone wires, some offices also transmit information over microwaves and by satellite. When you use electronic communications equipment in an office, you probably will not even know which transmission medium you are using, but you should know something about them.

Microwaves travel invisibly in straight lines through the air, carrying data and voices between dish-shaped antennas. Because microwaves cannot bend or pass through obstacles such as buildings, the antennas must be placed at high altitudes—on top of buildings or hills. Microwave transmission is used by companies to link facilities that are scattered over a limited area. It might be used by a bank in a city, for example, to communicate with its suburban branches. The Federal Communications Commission regulates microwave channels and assigns them to users.

Communications **satellites** orbit about 22,000 miles above the earth. They are equipped with transmission devices known as **transponders**, which receive signals beamed to them by an earth station. They amplify the signals and relay them back down to another earth station. Satellites permit communication between companies that are separated by very long distances or are located on different continents. Poor weather and electrical interference occasionally affect satellite communications, but despite this drawback, satellites are very useful for transmitting not only data signals but voice and video signals as well (see Fig. 12-3).

Time-sharing Systems

Time-sharing is the use of a central computer by many companies that are linked with it through a network of telephone lines and, perhaps, microwave and satellite transmissions. Traditional offices and word processing offices often use time-shared computers for big data processing jobs such as payrolls and billing. Electronic offices use time-shared services, too, when their own computers are not powerful enough to meet all their business needs. Figure 12-4 illustrates how a time-sharing system works.

If your office subscribes to a time-sharing service, you can use the central computer at the same time as many other users. An example of a time-sharing service is an airline's reservations system. Reservations clerks in many distant cities can use their terminals to make reservations at the same time that the central computer makes and transmits immediate changes in the availability of flights and seats. Another example of a time-sharing service is a company that leases its system exclusively to one kind of organization—for example, hospitals. In this case all the hospitals can use the computer to

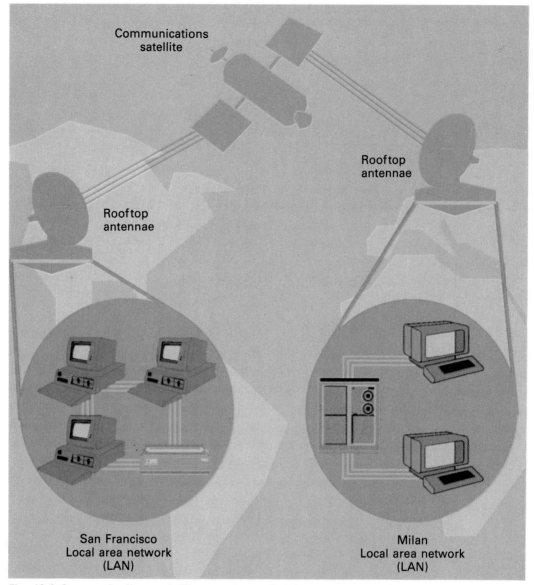

Fig. 12-3 Communications satellites can transmit data over very great distances.

perform tasks specific to hospitals, such as patient billing, diagnostics functions, and recordkeeping.

You can use a time-sharing service to send electronic messages to coworkers down the hall as well as to people in distant branch offices. In addition, you can use it to send electronic mail to other people and organizations that subscribe to the same service. Your messages can reach their destinations within seconds, just as they

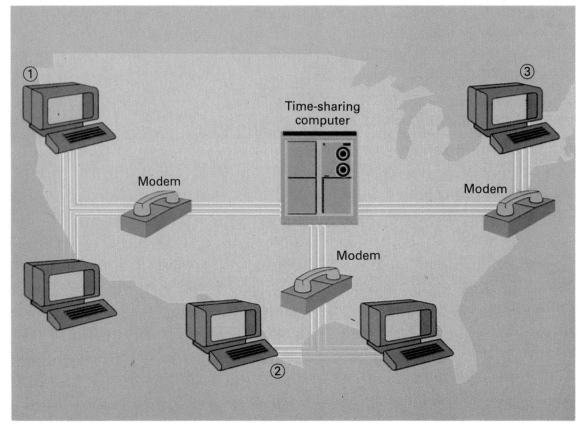

Fig. 12-4 Time-sharing systems allow several companies to lease time on one central processing unit which can perform big data processing jobs or deliver electronic mail.

can in internal electronic mail systems. The procedures for sending messages through a subscription service are different for each system.

Electronic offices sometimes subscribe to a time-sharing service because electronic mail might overburden their own computers and interfere with other business functions. They may also use a subscription service to save money. A subscription service may have local telephone access numbers in hundreds of cities, so using such a service to communicate with branch offices may be more economical than exchanging messages through the employer's computer with long-distance telephone connections. One well-known electronic mail subscription service is Telemail. It uses the Telenet time-sharing network, which has local phone numbers in 300 U.S. cities and 45 other countries. Another popular subscription service, OnTyme, uses the Tymnet network, which has local numbers in 400 U.S. cities and 40 other countries.

Facsimile Machines

Facsimile machines use telephone lines to transmit exact duplicates of entire pages of text and graphics over long distances. Like communication by telegraph, facsimile transmission is another form of electronic communication that began in the nineteenth century. The first facsimile machine was invented by a Scottish clockmaker in 1842. This machine used an electric wire to translate a document into an electrical signal. In 1907 a German inventor introduced photoelectric scanning, which used reflected light to translate light and dark areas on a page into electrical signals. By the 1920s RCA, AT&T, and Western Union had all developed commercial picture transmission systems, which were used mainly by newspapers to send and receive news photos and copy. Facsimile transmission did not become practical in most business offices until the late 1960s, when Xerox brought out a line of telecopiers that could access public telephone lines.

Today's facsimile machines operate by using a photocell or laser beam to scan a printed page and convert the image into analog signals, which are then sent to a receiving facsimile machine. The receiving machine reverses the conversion process and prints the image on blank paper, using much the same methods as coated-paper and plain-paper copiers or laser printers. The newest and most sophisticated machines can convert images into digital signals and then send the signals to a computer rather than to another facsimile machine. The computer can then produce hard or soft copies of the pages and store them on magnetic tape or disks.

Facsimile machines are regularly used for contracts, drawings, charts, and photographs.

You will probably have to operate a facsimile machine if you work for a company that needs to send a large number of documents from one office to another on a regular basis. Facsimile machines allow offices to send exact duplicates of complicated drawings and statistical charts, but some of them produce only low-quality copies that many companies would not want to distribute to outsiders. Some of the kinds of offices that would use facsimile machines are public relations firms that forward press releases and photographs, sales offices that process high volumes of orders, and engineering firms that routinely transmit drawings and designs.

Facsimile machines are relatively slow compared with other kinds of electronic communications devices. Analog equipment can take several minutes to transmit a page of text, as opposed to seconds for electronic mail or computer-to-computer transmissions. The major cost for most facsimile systems is the expense of using the telephone lines—up to $2 a page. With a high-speed digital facsimile system, it may cost as little as 93 cents a page to use the telephone lines, but the monthly rental cost of this equipment can be very high and would not be justified except in offices that transmit a high volume of documents.

One cheaper alternative to using telephone lines is to subscribe to a facsimile service that lets you send documents over a private network of lines at reduced or flat rates. FAXPAK, MCI International, RCA Q-FAX, and Federal Express's Zap Mail are some of the facsimile services that provide both nationwide and international facsimile transmission. Rates vary from 15 cents to 40 cents a minute for domestic transmissions and from $6 to $12 a page for overseas transmissions.

Computer-Based Mail Services

In addition to the electronic mail systems we've just described, you may use mail services that combine electronic technology and manual delivery systems. Several of these computer-based mail services are available from the U.S. Postal Service, Western Union, and other sources. These services offer two main advantages over traditional mail. One is that they can quickly and efficiently handle large mailings. When you use a computer-based mail service, you and your coworkers don't have to prepare a hard copy of each letter, stuff it into an envelope, and stamp it. Computers, folding machines, or postal service workers will perform these chores for you. The other advantage is distribution speed. In many cases a letter that normally would take a week to reach its destination through traditional mail delivery can arrive in hours, minutes, or even seconds through a computer-based mail service.

Telex and TWX

Two of the oldest electronic systems for distributing messages over long distances are Telex and TWX, both now operated by Western Union. TWX began as a competitor of Telex, but Western Union

Teletypewriters are communicating typewriters that can send and receive printed messages.

purchased it and merged the two systems. Originally, these systems transmitted information between terminals called **teletypewriters**, which are keyboard devices with printers that can send and receive messages over telephone lines. Today Telex and TWX use computer, satellite, and microwave technology for faster communication, higher-quality hard copies, and lower costs. Most of the time-shared electronic mail subscription services are integrated with Telex, TWX, or both to allow for communication with nonsubscribers. You are most likely to use Telex or TWX if you work for an organization that has branch offices in distant cities or that communicates frequently with offices overseas.

Many offices now use computer terminals to send and receive electronic mail through TWX and Telex, but some still use teletypewriters, especially for communicating with branch offices. Teletypewriters are generally slower and noisier than computer terminals and printers. They receive messages by printing low-quality hard copies, so the messages have a crude appearance. However, teletypewriters are less expensive than computer terminals, and many organizations find them quite adequate for internal communications.

Most teletypewriters have keyboards and can be used for sending documents as well as receiving them, but some have no keyboards and are used only for receiving. TWX teletypewriters print faster than Telex terminals and have keyboards that are arranged somewhat differently, but the two systems are very similar.

Telex and TWX have a store-and-forward feature that allows you to send a message to a teletypewriter even if it is busy. The system's storage unit holds the message until the receiving unit is free. Since teletypewriters print messages automatically and operators don't have to be present when the messages arrive, they are very useful to organizations that communicate with distant offices in different time zones.

EasyLink

At one time only a Telex machine could communicate with another Telex machine, only a facsimile machine could communicate with another facsimile machine, and only a computer could communicate with another computer. But, as we have seen, electronic technology makes it possible for different kinds of equipment to communicate with each other. For example, computers can send messages to Telex machines, and facsimile machines can send messages to computers. This enables fully automated companies to communicate electronically with companies that have achieved only a certain level of automation. EasyLink is a Western Union network service that allows you to use your office computer terminal to send telegrams, Mailgrams, or Telex messages to people who do not have computers. An office worker in Houston, for example, could use a computer terminal and modem to access EasyLink and send messages that might be received on a Telex machine located in Kenya or hand-delivered to an office in Singapore. EasyLink can be cheaper than traditional telegram or Mailgram distribution because you type the message yourself. Your company would have to pay an access fee, however, so EasyLink may not be worthwhile unless your office regularly sends a large number of messages.

Mailgrams

The **Mailgram**, which was developed jointly by the U.S. Postal Service and Western Union, is a combination of a telegram and a letter. To send a Mailgram, you can either telephone or hand-deliver a message to a Western Union office, or you can send a message directly to Western Union by computer or Telex machine. A Western Union operator then transmits the message electronically to a post office near its destination. At the post office, another operator prints out a copy of the message and inserts it into a distinctive blue and white envelope. The message is delivered the business day after it is received by a regular U.S. Postal Service letter carrier.

Mailgrams have several advantages and disadvantages. They are delivered much faster than regular mail, and they can be sent to

```
┌─────────────────────────────────────────────────────────────────────┐
│  ┌─────────────────────────────────┐                                  │
│  │ ELLEN HORAN, CLAIMS AND ADJUST  │ Western Mailgram®   🦅           │
│  │ 211 CLERMONT AVE                │ Union               U.S.MAIL     │
│  │ BROOKLYN NY 11205 25AM          │                                  │
│  └─────────────────────────────────┘                                  │
│                                                                        │
│   4-0196735084 03/25/86 ICS IPMMTZZ CSP NYAD                          │
│   7182309536 MGMB TDMT BROOKLYN NY 89 03-25 0118P EST                 │
│                                                                        │
│                                                                        │
│  ▶    ROSE MARIE ROSSI                                                 │
│       THE GREGG DIVISION                                               │
│       MCGRAW HILL BOOK COMPANY                                         │
│       1221 6 AVE                                                       │
│       NEW YORK NY 10020                                               │
│                                                                        │
│                                                                        │
│                                                                        │
│       DEAR MS ROSSI:                                                   │
│                                                                        │
│           A NEW DIGITAL AM/FM CLOCK RADIO IS BEING SHIPPED TO YOU.     │
│       YOU SHOULD RECEIVE IT WITHIN TWO WEEKS.                          │
│                                                                        │
│       WE APPRECIATE YOUR DETAILED EXPLANATION AND PROMPT RETURN OF THE │
│       DAMAGED PRODUCT, WHICH MADE IT POSSIBLE FOR US TO MAKE THE       │
│       REPLACEMENT QUICKLY. WE ARE SORRY FOR ANY INCONVENIENCE THIS HAS │
│       CAUSED YOU. WE LOOK FORWARD TO SERVING YOU FURTHER.              │
│                                                                        │
│       CORDIALLY,                                                       │
│         ELLEN HORAN, CLAIMS AND ADJUSTMENT MANAGER                     │
│         HENEOCH INC                                                    │
│                                                                        │
│       13:17 EST                                                        │
│                                                                        │
│       MGMCOMP                                                          │
│                                                                        │
└─────────────────────────────────────────────────────────────────────┘
```

Mailgrams are faster than regular mail delivery, but they lack the impressive appearance of business stationery.

people who have no computers or other electronic communication devices. This makes them useful for sending urgent messages to places that cannot be linked electronically to the equipment in your office. The disadvantages of Mailgrams are that they can be sent only to destinations in the United States, and they lack the impressive appearance of messages printed on high-quality business stationery. You are more likely to send Mailgrams to branch offices or company sales representatives than to customers or clients.

INTELPOST

INTELPOST is another example of how electronic and traditional mail can be combined. INTELPOST stands for International Electronic Postal Service. It is not really a computer-based mail delivery system because it uses facsimile machines rather than computers. It is a U.S. Postal Service system that transmits documents over microwave and satellite channels between cities in the United States, Canada, England, Germany, Japan, Brazil, and many other countries that have INTELPOST systems. Many brokerage houses and banks use INTELPOST to carry out international financial transactions.

If you work for a bank in Washington, D.C., and want to send a credit-guarantee letter to a bank in London, you can take the letter to a Washington post office that offers INTELPOST (see Fig. 12-5). A facsimile machine there would convert the letter into electronic signals that would travel by way of microwaves to a satellite earth station in Toronto, Canada. The earth station would beam the signals to an orbiting satellite that in turn would send them overseas. A facsimile machine at the London post office would receive the signals and reconvert them to produce a hard copy of the original document. The addressee could pick up the document at a London post office, or it could be sent out by special delivery or with the next day's regular mail.

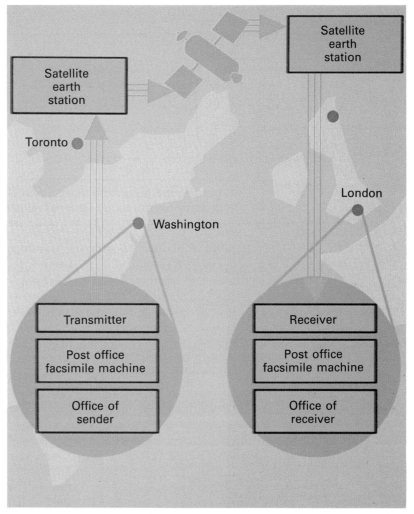

Fig. 12-5 Using INTELPOST, your documents are sent to a satellite orbiting the earth and are sent back down to a receiving device

Handling Incoming Mail

Most office workers process incoming mail every day. If you work in an electronic office, you will probably handle both traditional and electronic mail. This will include the letters and parcels that are hand-delivered by mail-room employees or postal workers as well as the soft copy you receive in your electronic mailbox (or perhaps your supervisor's electronic mailbox). In the next few pages we will look at the procedures for handling each kind of mail.

Receiving Traditional Mail

If your company has a mail room, the people who work there will separate and sort your mail. They may also use a machine to open all envelopes that are not marked "Personal" or "Confidential." If your company doesn't have a mail room, one of your duties may be to sort the incoming mail.

Sorting You should first sort the mail according to addressee, and then according to priority. Personal and confidential mail gets top priority, followed by telegrams, Mailgrams, special deliveries, and registered or certified mail. Next comes first-class mail, then inter-office mail, then parcels. The lowest priority goes to second- and third-class mail, which normally consists of magazines, advertisements, and catalogs.

Opening Mail Open traditional mail according to priority: first telegrams and other special mail, then first-class letters, and so on. Don't open confidential or personal mail addressed to others. If you mistakenly open such a letter, return it to its envelope without reading it, and mark the envelope with the words "opened by mistake" and your initials.

Letters that are not confidential should be opened with a letter opener to ensure that the envelope and its contents will not be damaged. Mail rooms are generally equipped with electric letter openers, but unless you handle huge quantities of mail, you will probably use a manual opener instead. If you cut a letter by accident while opening the envelope, tape it together immediately.

Checking the Contents Remove letters from the opened envelopes, and attach any enclosures to the letters with paper clips. (Remember to use plastic clips if you keep magnetic storage media such as disks at your workstation. You must avoid the risk of demagnetizing them.) If a letter indicates that enclosures were sent but you do not find them in the envelope, attach a note that says the enclosures are missing, or mark on the letter that the enclosures are missing, and initial it. If appropriate, you can call the correspondent and request the enclosures. If a letter does not include the sender's full name and address, clip it together with its envelope, or note the information on a separate piece of paper and attach it to the letter.

Date- and Time-Stamping After the mail is sorted and opened, each piece of correspondence must be marked near its top edge with the date you received it. Most offices have a rubber stamp for this purpose, but it can also be done by hand with a pen or pencil. Many employers want both the date and the time stamped on each piece of mail. This provides a record of when the mail was received, which helps in planning response time and serves as proof of receipt in the event of a dispute. Your employer may also want you to keep a log in which you note the date and time each letter arrives. Some offices keep logs as an added precaution in case there is disagreement over when documents reach them.

Reading and Annotating Mail   Your next step is to read each piece of correspondence. If a letter refers to another document, you should retrieve that document and attach it to the letter. In some cases you may be able to call attention to important passages in a letter by underlining or highlighting them, making notes in the margins, or making notations on a separate sheet of paper (see Fig. 12-6). A temporary way to annotate a letter is to use self-sticking notes. They come in a variety of sizes and colors and are neat and easy to use. You simply make your notation on a self-sticking note and then stick it to the margin of the letter next to the passage you want to call attention to. The notes can be peeled off and discarded when you and your supervisor are through with them. If a letter will be photocopied and the copies will be forwarded to others, notations can be made on the letter with a nonreproducing pencil or pen. Notations made with this kind of pencil or pen are invisible on photocopies of the document. How you annotate your supervisor's mail will depend on his or her preferences and on the nature of the correspondence.

The mail you process will include professional journals and other magazines as well as correspondence, and you can annotate them in much the same way that you annotate letters. However, instead of reading them from cover to cover, you check their tables of contents for items that might be of particular interest to your boss. When you find such an article, you might scan it and highlight the key points. Then attach a note to the magazine's cover to call your boss's attention to it. Some managers prefer that their support staffs prepare written summaries of important articles to save reading time.

Presenting Mail   Try to anticipate what materials your supervisor might need in order to respond to the mail, and attach them to the incoming correspondence. For example, if you have written a margin note on a letter saying "See Invoice 233807-B," give your supervisor a copy of the invoice.

Most executives keep in boxes on their desks for depositing incoming mail. Others prefer to have it presented in a folder, with personal and confidential correspondence on top followed by the rest of the mail in order of priority. In any case, confidential mail should never be left on a desk for inspection by passersby. It should

Westport University

School of Business Administration
1500 Western Way
Westport, California 91432
(213) 555-6200

January 31, 1987

Mr. William Santos
Rockford Publications
1600 South Avenue
Minneapolis, MN 55302

Articles sent 12/5
Deadline for review
was 1/15
P.S.

Dear Bill:

Attached is my review of the two articles you sent me last month, "Managerial Effectiveness in the Eighties" and "Success is More than Luck." I found them to be interesting and well written. My notations are brief, but I think they will help your writers in sharpening the focus for your audience.

My fee for these two reviews is $500.00. *Check request attached for your signature.*

Please let me know if you have any questions. I enjoy doing *P.S.* this kind of work and hope you will call on me again.

Sincerely,

Paul

Paul L. Watson
Professor, Business Administration

PW/ps
Enclosures

Fig. 12-6 Here is an example of an annotated incoming letter. Marking key passages helps supervisors process their mail quickly and efficiently.

always be placed in a folder. If there is a lot of mail, divide it into categories, and place each category in a separate folder.

Routing Mail If you want to bring a letter or journal to the attention of other people in the office, you can circulate it by stapling to it a **routing slip**, which is a piece of paper with a column of names (see Fig. 12-7). When you drop the item in the interoffice mail, the mail room routes it to the first person on the list. That person then reads the item, checks off his or her name, and returns the item to the interoffice mail so that it will be delivered to the next person on

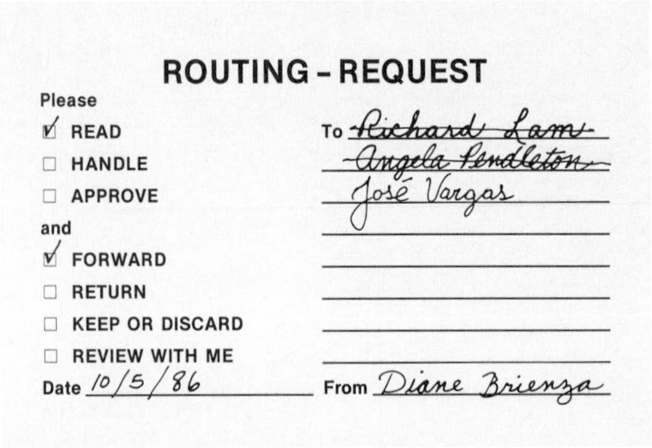

ROUTING – REQUEST

Please

☑ READ

☐ HANDLE

☐ APPROVE

and

☑ FORWARD

☐ RETURN

☐ KEEP OR DISCARD

☐ REVIEW WITH ME

Date _10/5/86_

To _Richard Lam_
Angela Pendleton
José Vargas

From _Diane Brienza_

Fig. 12-7 Routing slips enable you to circulate one document to several people within your office or company. Crossed out names indicate which coworkers have seen the document and passed it on.

the list. Circulating mail with routing slips can take several days. Therefore, it is best to use this procedure for periodicals and other items that cannot be duplicated. When you are in a hurry for people to read an item, it's faster to photocopy it and address the copies individually.

Responding to Mail Prompt responses to letters are necessary for good relations between correspondents, so reply as soon as possible to inquiries and requests that are addressed to you or to your office in general. This includes forwarding payment checks or invoices to appropriate departments and forwarding any letters that have been addressed to your office by mistake. If your supervisor is away from the office for more than a day or two, you may also be expected to read your principal's mail thoroughly and respond to it with appropriate actions.

When you are sure you have the information and the authority to do so, answer any requests or inquiries that arrive in your supervisor's absence. Otherwise, you can simply acknowledge many letters with notes explaining that your supervisor is away and stating when you expect him or her to return. Keep copies of all the responses and acknowledgments you write, and pass these copies on to your manager along with the incoming letters when he or she returns.

Receiving Electronic Mail

Procedures for receiving electronic mail are very similar to those for receiving traditional mail. However, an electronic mail system can do automatically many of the things, such as date-stamping and time-stamping, that you would do manually with traditional mail. In addition, an electronic mail system can automatically prioritize items so that the most urgent messages always appear first on the screen.

In an electronic office, each user on the electronic system has an electronic mailbox, or in box. This is a private receptacle for mes-

```
Urgent Message(s)!        Mar 21,86 12:11 PM Document:
                          INBOX for Janet Kimball

Msg    Postmark          Cert    Sender      New      Subject
 1 Fri Mar 21,86 10:45 AM  Y   Pam Brown     Y    URGENT: Budget
 2 Fri Mar 21,86 10:43 AM      Pam Brown     Y    MEETING:  Mar 31, 86
 3 Thu Mar 20,86  4:00 PM      Sally Jones   Y    Lunch
 4 Thu Mar 20,86  3:18 PM  Y   Jack Small    Y    Sales Figures
 5 Thu Mar 20,86  3:17 PM      Mary Klein         Phone message from Tim
 6 Thu Mar 20,86  2:41 PM      Tom Jackson        Vacation




Pick one: (1. View, 2. File, 3. Reply, 4. Forward, 5. Delete,
           6. Reformat or Print menu, 7. Print Message, 8. Remail) █
Message number(s):
```

Fig. 12-8 An electronic mail in box lists all the messages that have been received, placing the urgent ones first.

sages to which only the "owner" has access. However, most electronic mail systems allow users to give other people access to their in boxes. Your supervisor would probably give you access to his or her mailbox.

Viewing Electronic Mail Imagine that you've been away from your office for a couple of hours. During that time several of your colleagues used the electronic mail system to leave messages for you. When you return to your office, your computer will list for you all the messages that came in, indicating the time each was received, the sender, the classification (such as "urgent" or "classified"), and the subject. Figure 12-8 shows the kind of information that might appear on an individual's screen. In this case Janet Kimball can see at a glance who has contacted her. Notice that the computer has automatically placed the urgent message at the top of the list, even though it was received later than some of the other messages.

Once you have read the list, you can use the view option to read the messages, in any order you choose. You do this by indicating the number or numbers of messages you wish to view. Some systems allow you to select only one message at a time; others allow you to choose several through number entries (such as 1–5, 9, 10) or through commands (such as ALL for all messages or NEW for only new messages). In the example shown in Fig. 12-8, Janet Kimball selected the message marked "Urgent" first and then some of the more important messages by keying in the view option and then the message numbers.

```
Msgs: New:  3              Mar 21,86 12:34 PM Document:
                              MESSAGE DISPLAY

   TO    Janet Kimball

   From:  Pam Brown
   Postmark:  Mar 21,86   10:45 AM
   Status:   Certified  Urgent
   Subject: Budget
------------------------------------------------------------------
Message:
        Mr. Johnston asked me to obtain a copy of last year's budget for a
        meeting he's attending in 45 minutes.  Can you please get a copy to
        me as soon as possible?

        Thank you.



------------------------------------------------------------------
Pick one: (1. View content, 2. File, 3. Reply, 4. Forward,
           5. Delete, 6. Next message, 7. Print, 8. Remail)
```

Fig. 12-9 Once you select the view option, the complete messages will appear on your screen. You then decide which of the other options is appropriate for each message. The forward option was chosen here.

Once you've read your electronic messages, you'll need to act on them. Depending on the type of message you receive, you might want to forward it to someone else, file it, send a response, or delete it from your in box.

Forwarding Electronic Mail Most electronic mail systems have a forwarding feature that allows you to send a message that you have received to somebody else, with your comments attached. We'll continue to use Janet Kimball's in box, as shown in Fig. 12-8, to illustrate how electronic mail is processed. The urgent message listed as number 1 on her in box is shown in Fig. 12-9. When Janet reads the message, she knows that she does not have the information that Pam Brown has asked for. But she knows that Sally Jones has a copy of the budget. So instead of sending a message back to Pam telling her that Sally is the one to ask for the documents, Janet can simply forward Pam's message to Sally. Janet therefore selects option 4, the forward option. She indicates the person to whom she wishes to forward the message and can then keyboard any comments or instructions she might want to give the person receiving the message. Figure 12-10 shows what Janet's screen will display when she is forwarding the message. Figure 12-11 shows what will appear, seconds later, on Sally's screen. As you can see, the system automatically attached Janet's comments to Pam's original message.

Filing Electronic Mail Any time you receive information in your in box that you might need to refer to again in the future, you

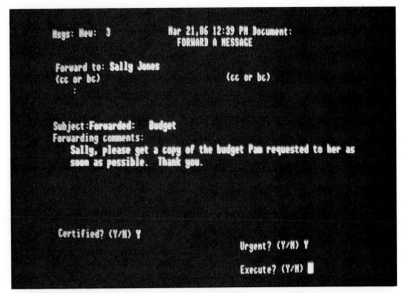

Fig. 12-10 Electronic mail makes it easy for you to forward messages to other people, after you have added your comments.

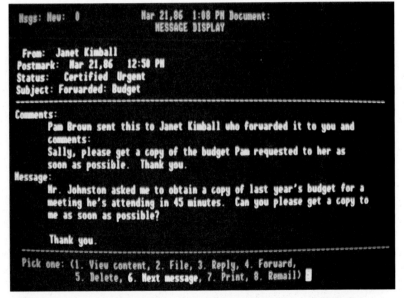

Fig. 12-11 The receiver of this message can see immediately the steps it has been through before it reached her.

should file it. To file information, you use the file option (listed as number 2 in Fig. 12-8). Once you select the file option, you will have to indicate where within the electronic filing system the information should be placed. You will also have to give the information a document name so that you will be able to access it in the future.

```
Msgs: New: 2              Mar 21,86  1:00 PM Document:
                          REPLY TO A MESSAGE

To: Pam Brown
(cc or bc)                              (cc or bc)
 :
Subject: Reply to MEETING: Mar 31, 86
Original message text:
        A one-hour secretarial meeting has been scheduled for March 31 at
        noon.  Please let me know if you can attend.



Reply Text:
        I will be attending the secretarial meeting.




Certified? (Y/N) N
File this reply? (Y/N) N       Urgent? (Y/N) N        Execute? (Y/N) ▊
```

Fig. 12-12 Electronic mail enables you to send immediate responses to your messages.

Replying to Electronic Mail   When you receive any type of mail, traditional or electronic, you often need to respond. With traditional mail, you respond by mailing back your answer, which may take several days, or by using the telephone or some form of express mail. With electronic mail, you can respond immediately.

Most electronic mail systems include a reply function. This automatically sends your response to the person who sent you the message. Suppose that Janet Kimball has viewed message 2 on her in box. She learns that Pam Brown has scheduled a one-hour secretaries meeting for March 31 at noon. Janet wants to let Pam know that she will attend, so she selects the reply option. Figure 12-12 shows what might appear on Pam's screen. Notice that the original message is included on the screen for easy reference. Electronic mail systems vary, and not all of them include this capability.

Deleting Messages   As you process electronic mail and take the appropriate action, such as replying to a message or filing important information, you should clean out your in box. Just as you wouldn't keep the mail you processed yesterday in the in box on your desk, you shouldn't do so in your electronic in box either. After each mailbox item is processed, it should be deleted. Then you should go on to process the next item. Deleting processed messages is the final step in electronic mail processing.

■ Summary

■ Computer-based mail services such as Telex, EasyLink, Mailgrams, and INTELPOST let office workers use a combination of electronic and manual delivery systems to transmit messages.

- Traditional, manual delivery systems include the U.S. Postal Service, private courier and messenger services, and company mail rooms and interoffice distribution systems.

- To handle outgoing mail, it is necessary to address, sort, weigh, and stamp it. Company mail rooms handle many of these chores for office workers.

- Workers in automated offices can choose from among a wide range of electronic equipment to transmit messages, or they can use traditional, manual methods such as the Postal Service system or courier services.

- Electronic mail utilizes computers to send and receive messages. Electronic mail can be sent to people within a company by means of computers linked together in a local area network.

- Computer-to-computer communications refers to the transmitting of messages between computers using telephone lines, microwaves, or satellites. Modems and communications software make computer-to-computer communication possible.

- Other kinds of electronic communication include time-sharing, or subscribing to large external computers, and facsimile transmission, or the sending of duplicates of entire pages of text or graphics.

- To handle incoming traditional mail, you must sort and open it, check it for missing enclosures, read and annotate it, and present it to your supervisor.

- To handle incoming electronic mail, you view what is in the electronic in box and then process each item by using the appropriate functions of your system, such as forwarding messages, replying electronically, and filing or deleting processed messages.

■ Review Questions

1. What advantages do private courier services offer over the U.S. Postal Service?

2. What is the most widely used means of distributing mail to outsiders? Why?

3. Why do office workers or mail-room employees weigh outgoing mail?

4. How would you go about choosing a method for distributing a document in an electronic office? What factors would enter into your decision?

5. Describe an electronic mailbox, and discuss how it is used.

6. What is the difference between a modem and an acoustic coupler? Describe how each works.

7. What is the purpose of communications software? Describe some of the functions it performs.

8. Name and describe two computer-based mail services that combine electronic technology with manual delivery.

9. How do you send a message from your computer terminal to a coworker in the same electronic mail system?

10. Describe the major differences and similarities in procedures for handling incoming traditional mail and incoming electronic mail.

■ Technical Vocabulary

interoffice mail
mailmobile
postage meter
local area network
electronic mailbox
data communications
protocol
control code
protocol converter

baud rate
acoustic coupler
microwave
satellite
transponder
time-sharing
teletypewriter
Mailgram
routing slip

■ Discussion and Skills Development

1. Suppose that you work in an office in Dallas. What class of U.S. mail or what special service offered by the U.S. Postal Service would get each of the following items to its destination on time and without unnecessary expense?

   a. A letter requesting information about a convention that is being held in two months.
   b. One routine invoice.
   c. Eight thousand routine invoices mailed at once to destinations around the country.
   d. A manuscript that has to reach an office in New York before that office closes tomorrow.
   e. A stock certificate.
   f. A sales contract.
   g. A personal note to a business acquaintance in another organization.
   h. A box containing a new supply of product brochures for a sales representative in Wisconsin.
   i. Five thousand copies of your employer's latest merchandise catalog.
   j. An item costing $175 for a customer in Maine who has not yet paid for it.

2. Carol Zeitz is a receptionist in a small office. One of her duties is to process all incoming mail. After opening a letter addressed to a supervisor one day, she was embarrassed to discover that its contents were personal, although its envelope was not marked "Personal" or "Confidential." Today a letter with the same return address has arrived for the same supervisor. Again, it is not marked to indicate that it is personal. How should Ms. Zeitz handle the letter?

3. Christopher Weiss, a senior partner in a large law firm, handles several sensitive legal accounts and normally exchanges many confidential messages with lawyers in the firm's branch offices by means of electronic mail. One day Mr. Weiss's secretary, George Barnes, accidentally discovered that an unauthorized employee had obtained Mr. Weiss's identity code and that she routinely read Mr. Weiss's electronic mail. Mr. Barnes didn't want the employee to get in trouble or be fired, but he wanted to put a stop to her nosiness. How could he handle the situation?

chapter 13
Telephone Technology and Techniques

"Mr. Watson, come here; I want you!" This, as we all know, was the extent of the first telephone conversation. It took place in 1876 when Alexander Graham Bell spilled acid on his trousers and called for help to his assistant through his newly invented speech transmission device. Nothing could have delivered that first telephone message more immediately than that first telephone. Now, more than 100 years after its invention, the telephone continues to be the most common and most important communications device in the world because using it is one of the fastest and easiest ways to transmit messages over long distances.

In Chapter 12 you learned how telecommunications technology enables office workers to use machines, such as computers and facsimile machines, to communicate with one another. In this chapter you will see how technology also enables people to communicate with each other directly over the telephone. You will learn about such advanced technological inventions as voice mail, which enables you to send and receive messages at any time, and teleconferencing, which enables people separated by great distances to confer over speakers or television circuits as if they all were in the same room.

Chapter 13 will introduce you to different kinds of telephone systems, such as key systems and private branch exchanges, and it will discuss the many new features that telephone technology can offer. For example, you will learn about mobile phones and about answering machines that help people keep in close touch with their offices and homes. You will learn the basic telephone techniques that office workers need to know to handle business telephone calls. You will also gain a more thorough understanding of how teleconferencing systems work and how you go about arranging teleconferences.

Telephone Companies Today

Some experts estimate that as much as 90 percent of all business is conducted over the telephone. It's easy to see why this is so. It's a great deal faster and easier for an executive or a secretary to place a call than to go through all the steps required to dictate, type, and mail a letter. Moreover, telephoning allows business people to build and maintain interpersonal relations with people at other companies or branch offices.

Telephones are such familiar parts of our lives that we generally don't give them much thought. Until a few years ago, we didn't need to give much thought to purchasing telephone service either. Nearly everyone—businesses and individual consumers alike—rented telephones and telephone service from one of the many local Bell telephone companies that made up the American Telephone and Telegraph Corporation (AT&T). Bell was known universally as "the telephone company." If you wanted to call Australia, "the telephone company" put the call through and added the charge to your monthly bill. If something went wrong with your telephone, "the telephone company" sent someone to fix it. All that changed in 1984 as a result of a court order aimed at encouraging competition in the telephone industry. AT&T was obliged to give up its monopoly of the industry and divest itself of its local companies. The local phone companies became independent of AT&T, and consumers were allowed to buy their own phone equipment. Although AT&T continues to offer telephones and long-distance service, it now has many competitors. Because of the changes brought about by the divestiture, businesses and consumers now obtain telephone equipment and services from a number of sources. They also use different companies for local service and long-distance service. The benefits of AT&T's divestiture include many new telephone products and lower prices for some services. On the other hand, many people find it difficult to choose among the services and equipment available.

Many businesses now obtain long-distance service from companies other than AT&T. Companies such as MCI, SBS, Sprint, and Allnet are among AT&T's best-known competitors, but there are many others. Businesses can determine which of these companies can provide the best service at the lowest cost. They can compare such factors as long-distance rates, the quality of transmission, and the range of services offered.

In addition to purchasing services from AT&T or other long-distance carriers, businesses purchase local service from the phone companies that serve their immediate area. The local phone company owns and maintains the service lines to which the telephone equipment is connected, but the local company may not own or repair the equipment itself.

In most cases long-distance calls must travel over local phone company lines between the caller's office and the long-distance company's switching station. This means that each long-distance call has a local phone bill charge as well as the long-distance carrier

Telephones have changed dramatically over the years from those modeled after early styles, to the midcentury rotary dial phone, and finally, to the modern telephone with a pushbutton keypad that can be used to input data into computers.

fee. However, many large organizations have direct-access connections with long-distance carriers that allow them to bypass their local telephone companies.

Telephone Equipment Today

Telephone equipment is changing along with telephone service. Although nearly everyone still speaks of "dialing" calls, the rotary-dial phone has given way to pushbutton phones with 12 buttons: 10 numbered keys plus keys labeled * and #, which are used for dialing special codes that provide additional services. You can make calls much faster with pushbutton phones than you can with rotary-dial phones. And pushbutton phones can serve as input devices for computers.

While some businesses continue to rent telephone equipment from AT&T, more and more are purchasing their own telephone systems. In either case, there are several methods you can use for directing the flow of incoming and outgoing calls, or switching calls as it is called. Two basic types of telephone switching equipment are available today: key systems and private branch exchange systems.

Key Systems

In a **key system** the phones have several keys, or buttons, that represent different phone lines. When the phone rings, one of the buttons lights up. To answer the call, you press the lighted button and pick up the phone. Key system phones also have hold buttons. If you are talking on one line and another line rings, you press the hold button to put the first call on hold before answering the incoming call. If you answer a call for someone else, you can put the caller on hold while using an intercom or a separate telephone line to alert the person being called. A key system has the advantage of letting office workers use any phone in the system to answer calls.

Key system telephones are most useful in small offices that don't require elaborate switchboards and complicated features.

Key system telephones come with a variety of features. One telephone system has an electronic memory that stores frequently called numbers. If you had to call a branch office several times a day, for example, you could assign a single digit to the branch's telephone number. Then you would only have to press the button for that one digit instead of having to dial the entire telephone number each time.

Another kind of key system offers distinctive ringing sounds so that you can tell if the caller is telephoning from outside the office, from another office line, or over an intercom line. By pushing a button, you can also use the telephone as a microphone to summon coworkers over wall-mounted loudspeakers. Key telephone systems can be set up so that if one line is busy, a call coming in on that line will automatically be switched to another line. And they can be programmed to provide background music to entertain callers on hold.

In an organization too small to need a switchboard, a key system may be the only means of directing telephone traffic. In a larger office, key systems may be linked with other switching equipment.

Private Branch Exchanges

A **private branch exchange**, or PBX, consists of the equipment needed to switch calls among the telephone extensions in an office. A switchboard operator controls the central switching station of a PBX, but many offices today have **private automated branch exchanges**, or PABXs, with some automated switching operations.

Digital PABXs can carry the digital signals from computers as well as the analog signals from human voices. A digital PABX can link computers and other electronic equipment into a network, in addition to directing telephone traffic. However, most PABXs are still analog.

Both digital and analog PABXs offer several features not found on the manual switchboards. With one feature, **direct outward dialing**, you can make outside calls by dialing an access number first. In a manual PBX you have to call the switchboard operator to ask for an outside line. Some PABX systems also have centrex systems. A **centrex system** can work in two ways. If you know the extension number of the person you are calling, you can call that office directly, without speaking to the switchboard operator. On the other hand, if you don't know the extension number, or if you are calling for information and don't have a specific person you want to speak with, you call the company's number. Then the switchboard operator will transfer your call to the right extension. On systems without centrex, all calls go through the general number and the operator.

Computerized Telephones

Some companies have computerized phones that offer a variety of special features. The features your phone has will depend on how big your company is and how much business is handled over the telephone. Your phone could have computerized features such as call waiting, speed dialing, and call forwarding, which are explained below. Some computerized phone systems are relatively simple to use; others are more elaborate and may be difficult to use at first, because their automated features require you to learn special dialing codes. For example, instead of simply pressing a hold button if a call you have answered is for a coworker in another office, you may have to key in a code, such as "#4," and then key in another code and the coworker's extension number to transfer the call. However, most users find computerized phones convenient once they have mastered their features. Computerized telephone systems can offer more than 300 features, but most companies use about 40 of them. Here are a few of the most commonly used features:

Call Waiting   If you are using your telephone line when another call comes in, a special tone will inform you that you have a call waiting. You can then either finish the call with your first caller or place that caller on hold while you answer the second call. Businesses ask for call waiting more often than for any other feature of computerized telephone systems. This feature, which is popular on home telephones as well, prevents people from missing important calls.

Speed Dialing   One convenient feature of a computerized phone is an electronic memory that allows you to store the phone numbers you use most often. Once you have done this, you can call any of those numbers by keying in a one- or two-digit code rather than the entire number. Most computerized phones also have a code for redialing the last number you called. This feature is especially handy when you are trying to reach someone whose number is busy.

Call Forwarding   Another convenient feature, call forwarding, allows you to key in a code that automatically forwards all your incoming calls to another number. If you are going to be working in a conference room down the hall or a branch office across town, this feature enables you to receive your calls without imposing on your coworkers.

Conference Calls   Suppose that you are talking with a regional manager in another city, and you want to have two other department heads participate in the conversation. One way to do this is with a **conference call**, which is a telephone call involving three or more people (see Fig. 13-1). If your computerized phone has a conference call feature, you can set up a four-way call in just a few seconds. You ask the regional manager to hold while you ask the two department heads to pick up their phones. Then all four of you can finish the conversation.

Automatic Callback   This feature lets you call back somebody whose line is busy as soon as the line becomes free. To do this, you

Fig. 13-1 Conference calling, a popular feature of computerized telephone systems, allows office workers to confer with each other without having to meet face-to-face.

hang up, dial a command code, and redial the busy number. When the line becomes free, the telephone system first calls you. When you pick up your phone, it dials the number you are trying to reach. This feature is particularly useful when you need to reach a very busy office, such as an airline reservation office.

Automatic Route Selection As you learned earlier, businesses may use several long-distance services to save money on toll calls. Many computerized phone systems automatically place long-distance calls through the most economical service. Office workers, as a rule, are not even aware that this is taking place.

Call Timing Some companies, especially professional offices such as law firms and accounting firms, bill each client for the time spent handling the client's business. Since they may handle a lot of business on the phone, they need to keep track of these telephone calls. Many professional offices are installing computerized telephone systems with call-timing features in an effort to keep track of phone calls. Some of these systems can also automatically provide the total time spent on phone calls to each client since the last billing.

Call Restriction   Some computerized phone systems require users to key in authorization codes before placing calls. This enables organizations to keep track of the calls people make, and it discourages workers from making personal long-distance calls from the office.

■ Voice/Data Networks

In the past most telephone systems only had the capability to transmit voice or analog signals. Today digital computer-based communications systems are being created that will support the simultaneous transmission of both voice and data. This means that your telephone system cannot only be used for voice conversations, but it can also be connected directly to your computer, enabling you to send and receive data. No modem is required to send or receive data within this type of system. Local telephone wires can be used rather than special cabling.

Today several voice/data telecommunications systems are available. One of the better-known systems is the PBX. Although the PBX system was once only a voice-based system, today it can be used by businesses to support teleconferencing, voice messaging, and data communications. This allows office workers to send and receive electronic mail and messages or to access central processing systems and data bases by simply dialing a telephone number. Many experts believe that computer controlled digital telecommunications systems are rapidly becoming the hub of future office communications.

■ Other Equipment and Accessories

Many businesses today use telephone-related equipment and accessories that add to the functions their phones can perform. Some of the devices that you may encounter are mobile phones, paging devices, and answering machines.

Mobile Telephones   Recent advances in electronic communications technology have made cordless portable telephones inexpensive and relatively reliable. As a result, more and more business people, especially sales representatives and others who spend a lot of time on the road, have installed telephones in their cars. Some telecommunications experts predict that soon many people will carry portable telephones in their briefcases. Already, one type of mobile phone is available on Amtrak's Metroliner trains, and another kind of mobile phone is available aboard airplanes.

Paging Devices   Another way that businesses stay in touch with people who are traveling is with pocket-sized **paging devices**, sometimes known as "beepers." A paging device emits a high-pitched sound that makes the person carrying it aware that someone is trying to reach him or her. There are several types of paging devices. Some have tiny screens that display messages, such as telephone numbers where calls can be returned. Others just beep, and the sound is a signal to call the office.

Beepers can be used to transmit messages or to alert people to call their offices no matter where they are or what they are doing.

Voice Mail

Answering Machines If you work in a very small office, your employer may have a machine that answers calls automatically and records messages when nobody is in the office. Your job may include recording the message the machine will play for callers when it answers. People are often annoyed when they reach answering machines instead of people. A cheerful but professional-sounding message delivered in a friendly tone of voice can help overcome this problem. The message should ask the caller to leave a name and telephone number, a brief message about the nature of the call, and the time the call was made. It should assure the caller that someone will call back as soon as possible.

The procedures for recording an answering message depend on the machine you are using, as do the procedures for playing back messages left by callers. With some answering machines, it is possible for the owner to play back the messages by calling the machine from another phone. This feature requires using a beeper or dialing a special telephone number that instructs the machine to play back the messages.

A much more sophisticated automatic answering system is called *voice mail*, or voice messaging. More and more medium-sized and large companies are using voice mail to communicate with traveling executives and with people at offices in other time zones.

Voice mail is something like electronic mail, except that to send a message, you use your phone instead of your computer terminal, and the message is stored in the form of recorded words instead of soft copy. The person receiving the message gains access to his or her voice mailbox and gives it instructions by punching in certain prearranged codes on the pushbutton telephone keypad. Assume, for example, that you are a secretary in an office that uses a voice mail system. You are going to be away from your desk for several hours, so you key in a code on your telephone that sends all your incoming calls to a voice mailbox controlled by a computer to which the phone is linked. While you are away, the computer will answer your phone automatically, instruct callers on how to leave a message, and record messages of any length. Messages can be left on the system by outside callers as well as by coworkers from within your own company.

When you return to your desk, you can check for messages on your voice mailbox by dialing your authorization code on the phone. You can also use the telephone keypad to instruct the voice mailbox to play your voice mail messages or store them for replay later, to erase the messages, or to forward them to others. When you retrieve a message, you can reply to it immediately, and the system will automatically route your answer back to the sender. You can also add something to a message you have received and send the entire package to one or more other people who are also on the voice mail network.

As with electronic mail, no one can listen to messages in your voice mailbox without using your identification code. Also, like electronic mail, a voice mail system can be an internal, closed system, or it can be an external subscription service similar to a computer time-sharing service.

For employers who can afford a voice mail system, its major advantage is that it can put an end to "telephone tag," the time-wasting and frustrating phenomenon of two people who are often away from their desks trying repeatedly to return each other's calls. It is also a convenient way for workers who must be away from the office to communicate with coworkers or subordinates.

Telephone Techniques

When callers telephone your office, they can't see you. They can only judge you and the office or business you represent by the professionalism and courtesy you convey through your voice. This is why it is important to develop the oral communication skills we discussed in Chapter 5.

It is also important for you to be familiar with your employer's telephone system so that you don't accidentally cut people off or transfer them to the wrong office. Before you begin using any telephone system, learn the procedures for transferring calls, putting calls on hold, and other operations. Then practice these operations with your coworkers until you can perform them without error.

Answering Calls

In any office you should show courtesy and efficiency by answering calls promptly, on the first or second ring. Answering quickly with a pleasant and businesslike tone of voice makes callers feel welcome. It also inspires confidence in you and your employer. And you should always have message forms or a pad and pencil handy to take down messages and record the gist of telephone conversations. Here are some guidelines you might follow when answering calls.

Identifying the Office Answer the phone by identifying the office the caller has reached. The way you answer will depend on the preferences of your supervisor. Many executives prefer that you answer with their names first and then your own, as in "Dr. Bradley's office; Mr. Quinn speaking." Others prefer that you answer with the name of your department.

Screening Callers You may be required to screen calls for a supervisor who does not want to answer every call he or she receives. You will quickly learn which callers should always be put through right away, which you should take a message from, and which you should handle yourself or direct to another office. If you have to screen callers, it may sometimes require all your tact to identify callers without giving them the impression that you are stalling them. You might say, "Ms. Reynolds is away from her desk at the moment. May I take a message or ask her to call you back?"

A client's first contact with a business office is often by telephone, so it is important for office workers to develop good telephone techniques and oral communications skills.

Monitoring Calls on Hold   Sometimes you will have to put a caller on hold. You might have to check with a supervisor before putting a call through, or you might have to answer another call. Callers who are kept on hold too long may feel annoyed. So if you leave a caller on hold for more than a few seconds—while waiting for a supervisor to finish another call, for instance—keep the caller informed about the delay. If you need to put a caller on hold while you search for information, offer instead to call back when you find it. Then be sure to note the name and number.

Forwarding Calls   If your supervisor is not available to answer a call, or if someone else can be more helpful to the caller, you might forward the call. This can irritate callers, however, especially those who have already described their requests to several people in your organization.

One way to avoid this irritation is by explaining why another person can be more helpful. You might say, "Ms. Reeves handles inquiries about delivery dates. May I transfer your call to her office?" It's also a good idea to ask if the caller would rather be called back than transferred. If so, get the caller's name and telephone number, try to determine the nature of the caller's request, and tell the caller the name and extension number of the person who will call back. This will save time for both of them, and it will help to ensure that the caller gets a satisfactory response.

If you must forward the call, state the name and number of the person to whom you are forwarding it. The caller can use this information if the call is cut off accidentally or if the number to which you forward it is busy or goes unanswered.

Taking Messages   Offer to take a message from a caller when your supervisor is not available to speak with the caller. Keep a notepad near your phone for taking messages. Write down the caller's name and telephone number (including the area code) as well as any additional information the caller wishes to leave. Take time to verify the information. Your boss may be embarrassed—and annoyed with you—if he or she returns a call using incorrect information. Finally, put your name or initials on each message so that the recipients know whom to ask if they need more information. Many offices use standard message forms that can be purchased in any office-supply store. These forms remind you to take all the necessary information. Figure 13-2 shows a form with space for the time; the date; the caller's name, company, and phone number; the type of response desired; a short message; and your name.

Handling Problem Calls   Some callers can be difficult to deal with or even unpleasant. For example, a caller may refuse to give a name, saying only that the call is personal. If you refuse to put through such a call, you run the risk of offending someone who is important to your company or your supervisor. In general, it's best

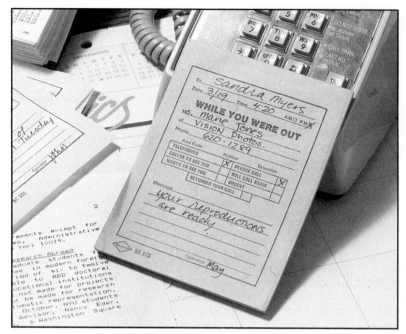

Fig. 13-2 These forms remind you of what information you should ask for when taking messages.

to put a difficult caller on hold and check with your supervisor before putting the call through. Always be as courteous and tactful as possible with problem callers. There is no set formula for dealing with unpleasant calls, but with time and practice you will become skillful at handling them.

Placing Calls

Making outgoing business calls requires oral communication skills that are similar to the ones you use for answering calls. In addition, you need to know how to place local and long-distance calls using the public telephone system. We will deal with how to place calls first and then with the oral communication skills you need to practice in order to make the best impression on the people you are calling.

Checking the Number Be sure of the number before you dial. Consult your phone list, a telephone directory, or a phone company information operator. Phone companies usually charge for directory assistance, so if you must use this service, add the number you request to your telephone list so that you won't have to ask for it again.

Checking Time Zones If you make long-distance or overseas calls, you need to be aware of time zones. Most telephone directories

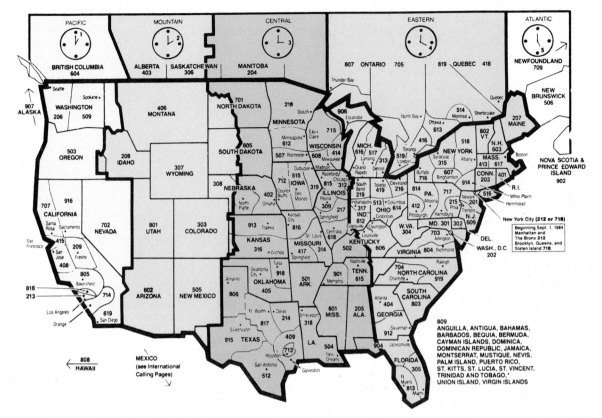

Fig. 13-3 It is important to check time zones when making long-distance calls. This map shows the standard time zones for the United States and Canada.

include a map showing the four time zones in the United States, as well as lists of overseas cities and their time zones (see Fig. 13-3). If you check the time zone, you won't waste time trying to reach an office before or after business hours. If you are calling someone's home, check the time zone to avoid disturbing people in their sleep.

Planning Your Phone Calls   Before you make a call, outline what you want to say on paper; then check off the items as you cover them in your telephone conversation. That way, you won't forget something important.

Knowing Your Options   When you make long-distance telephone calls through AT&T, there are several different ways you can call (see the box entitled "AT&T Long-Distance Services"). Some options are cheaper than others, so check with the company before placing your call.

PLACING LONG-DISTANCE CALLS

When making long-distance calls, you should choose the service that will complete your call most efficiently and economically.

■ **Person to Person**. If you wish to speak only to one person who may not be there to answer your call, place a person-to-person call by dialing "0" as the first digit of your call. When an operator comes onto the line, tell him or her that you want to place a person-to-person call, and identify the person you are trying to reach. The rates for these calls are higher, but the charges don't begin until you reach the person you want to speak to.

■ **Collect**. When you call collect, the person or office you are calling agrees to pay for your call. Again, you dial "0" as the first digit. You tell the operator that you are calling collect, and you identify yourself. The operator then checks that the person you are calling will accept your call.

■ **Direct Dialing**. Use direct dialing if you are willing to talk with anyone who answers. Calls that you place without help from a phone company operator are cheaper than calls that require an operator's assistance, but charges begin as soon as the phone is answered. You can direct-dial calls to any place within the United States and to many foreign countries as well.

When placing long-distance calls, be brief and clear when you state your business.

"Operator, I'd like to place a person-to-person call to Ms. Marilyn Thomas, please."

"Operator, I'd like to place a collect call to Ms. Marilyn Thomas, please. My name is Mary Smith, calling from Southwest Travel Services."

"Hello, this is Mary Smith from Southwest Travel Services. I'd like to speak with Marilyn Thomas, please."

Communications Skills

Here are some communications skills you should practice when placing outgoing calls:

Identifying Yourself Identify yourself, or the executive for whom you are placing the call, to the person who answers (unless you reach the switchboard of a large office). You might say "Dr. Bradley is returning Mr. Jackson's call" if you are placing the call for a supervisor. When calling on your own behalf, you might say, "This is Rebecca Lasker from Centercomp Inc. Could I please speak with Mr. Jackson?" If a switchboard operator answers your call to a big organization, simply state the name or extension number of the person you are calling.

Avoiding Sexism Many people make assumptions about the roles of men and women in the business world. Indeed, many people assume that executives are always men and secretaries are always women. These assumptions are increasingly incorrect. If your call is answered by a woman, do not assume that she is a secretary and ask to speak to her boss. Instead, ask for the person who handles what you are calling about. Address all office workers, not just managers, with respect and courtesy regardless of whether they are male or female. It is important to remember that terms such as *young lady* and *girl* or *boy* may seem offensive and condescending when you use them to refer to adults, even if you think of these terms as neutral or complimentary.

Stating Your Business When your call is put through to the person you wish to speak to, identify yourself again, if necessary, and state your business politely in as few words as possible. Depending on how well you know the person you are calling, you might say, "Good morning. This is Rebecca Lasker from Centercomp Inc. I'm calling about a delivery we are expecting from your company tomorrow" or "Hello, Abdul. This is Rebecca. I'm calling to confirm our delivery tomorrow." When you call people you know, of course, you may exchange pleasantries before you get down to business. The idea, though, is to get to the point and deliver your message without wasting anybody's time.

Leaving Messages If the person you are trying to reach is not available, you may want to leave a message. The message may contain all the information you wanted to convey in the call, or it may be a request for that person to call you back. What type of message you leave will depend, in part, on who answers the call. If you wish to leave a lengthy or very important message, try to determine whether or not this would be appropriate. You might ask, "Do you work for Mr. Jones?" or "Are you in Mr. Jones's department?" If the answer is no, it would probably be best for you to simply request that Mr. Jones call you back.

If you are attempting to call someone at home or in a small office, your call may be received by an answering machine instead of by a person. Answering machines allow only a limited time for you to record a message. It's best to avoid trying to leave a long or complicated message. Simply state your name as well as your employer's name and telephone number, the date and time of the call, and the reason for the call. Enunciate as clearly as possible, because the recording quality on some machines is poor.

When you call someone who works in an electronic office, you may reach a computerized voice-mail recorder. Because a voice-mail message can be as long as you wish and the recipient will hear your words instead of another person's interpretation, you may leave a more complex message than you would otherwise. This may eliminate the need for the person to return your call. For example, if you are calling to provide detailed information, you can convey it in the voice-mail message. The recipient can replay the message as often as necessary and can even forward it to others who need the information.

Teleconferences

One use of telecommunications that is gaining acceptance among electronic offices is the teleconference. In a teleconference, people in widely separated locations can use a variety of electronic communications technologies to conduct a meeting.

Increasingly, employers are using teleconferences to cut the costs of business travel. Executives and other employees often travel long distances to attend meetings that last only a few hours. For each out-of-town participant in even a brief meeting, a company may have to pay for one or two nights in a hotel, several restaurant meals, and an airplane ticket. Moreover, the participants are taken away from their regular duties for a day or more. Even executives who take portable computers and dictation machines on business trips are less productive away from their files and their support staffs.

In a teleconference, managers and other employees can participate in decision-making processes that might otherwise exclude them. For example, a manager might not be willing to send a supervisor to a meeting that would keep her or him away from the office for two days, but the same manager might not object to the supervisor's spending three hours taking part in a teleconference down the hall.

A teleconference can be as simple as a three-way telephone call, or it may involve the use of more sophisticated technologies for the exchange of visual, printed, and spoken information. Let's look at the different types of teleconferences and how they might be used.

Audio Teleconferences

An audio teleconference is basically a conference call. However, audio teleconferences involving large numbers of people are generally conducted with speakerphones rather than with ordinary desk telephones. A **speakerphone** is a telephone device that amplifies a call for an entire room rather than for one person, and it can transmit voice messages from a roomful of people as well. An audio teleconference can be an economical and effective means of distributing information to large numbers of people and receiving instant feedback from them.

For example, suppose that the Zeppelin Automobile Corp. in Detroit runs into financial problems and has to trim its budget immediately. Through an audio teleconference, Zeppelin's president explains the financial situation to executives at the company's plants and offices throughout the country. Then the president orders that several cost-cutting measures be put into effect immediately. Finally, the president asks for questions and suggestions from the participants. Some of these questions and suggestions could result in more ways of cutting costs. As you can see, the teleconference enables Zeppelin's president to receive instant feedback and to consider revisions for the cost-cutting plan.

Video Teleconferences

When people talk about teleconferences, however, they are usually referring not to conference calls but to **video teleconferences,** in which participants can see and hear each other over closed-circuit television. You may have seen this technology on TV news shows where, for example, a senator in Washington, D.C., might debate with a professor in Boston. In video teleconferences, participants can demonstrate procedures, display new products, and exchange other kinds of information—visual as well as verbal. Using facsimile transmissions or computer communications, they can also exchange hard copies of documents.

A video teleconference may involve two-way video and two-way audio communication, or it may involve two-way audio but only one-way video. In a teleconference with one-way video, one video teleconference room has a television camera, but the video teleconference rooms in the other locations have only video screens. The people in the room with the camera cannot see the other participants, but the other participants can see them.

A few very large companies have installed teleconference rooms in their headquarters and branch offices. These rooms are equipped with television cameras, large video screens, and microphones, and they may be equipped with other electronic devices, such as facsimile machines, computer terminals, and printers.

Several companies have begun renting video teleconference facilities to organizations that are too small to afford or need their own video teleconference rooms but that still want to hold teleconferences now and then. For example, some of the major hotel chains have equipped several of their hotels with teleconference facilities that corporations can rent for meetings and that trade associations and similar groups can use for televised conferences and conventions.

Arranging a Teleconference

Even the simplest video teleconference involves complicated equipment that has to be operated correctly. If your company has its own conference room with technicians and built-in equipment, your duties may be to make the same kinds of arrangements that you would make for face-to-face meetings, such as fixing a time and assembling the documents the participants will need. On the other

Video teleconferences allow groups of people to meet without having to go through the time and expense of traveling to distant points.

hand, if you have to arrange a teleconference in rented facilities, your duties will be more extensive.

If you have to rent a room at a hotel or conference center, make the reservation as far in advance as possible, because rooms suitable for teleconferences are usually in demand. The room you select should be large enough to accommodate the participants and the equipment. If you have to set up the equipment or assist in arranging it, you should be aware that color television requires more lighting than black-and-white TV and that the lights should be arranged so they don't reflect from the conference table or other objects. You may have to experiment with lighting for some time before you can arrive at an arrangement that creates a pleasant setting. Television lights give off a great deal of heat, so you may want to turn down the room heat or increase the air-conditioning before the conference.

You should check with the hotel to make certain that there will be enough telephone lines to handle your microphones and other transmitting equipment. If there are not enough telephone lines, you may have to lease lines from your local telephone company for the duration of the conference. Microphones should be placed in front of each seat or between every two seats. Some teleconferences use microphones that can be clipped to clothing or placed around a person's neck. If loudspeakers are not already installed in the room, you may have to place some on the walls so that the participants can hear the speakers at the other ends of the teleconference.

The television screen has to be set up so that all the participants in the room can see it. The seats should be arranged so that the participants can see both the screen and each other. The best seating arrangement has the participants seated along the outer curve of a crescent-shaped table, with the inner curve of the crescent facing the screen.

If the camera setup is relatively simple, with only one preset video camera, it may be up to you to load and monitor the camera. You may even have to switch it from speaker to speaker during the course of the conference. If you do have to monitor or operate the camera, you will need special instructions prior to the conference. When several cameras are being used at your end of the teleconference, they probably will be set up and operated by a trained technician, but you will need to discuss any special requirements. For example, you may need to have a camera with a zoom lens stationed so that it can focus on a chalkboard or on a slide projection screen.

A number of devices are available to transmit graphics during a teleconference, such as light pens and graphics tablets (which transmit images to television screens) and electronic blackboards (which transmit images written or drawn on them over telephone lines). If your company uses any of these devices, you will probably need to learn how to operate them. The simplest ways to transmit graphics at a teleconference are to send the materials beforehand; to have a television camera focus on the slide projection, chalkboard, or flip chart; and to use a facsimile machine or computer.

Arranging the scene and the equipment is important, but don't forget to consider the participants when you are arranging a teleconference. If a featured speaker has no experience with teleconferences or television appearances, you might offer to arrange a practice session. That way, the speaker can become familiar with the microphone system and can learn where to stand or sit and where to look when different cameras are being used.

Telecommuting

Telecommunications technology enables many employees to work from their homes using computers and modems to communicate with their offices. This phenomenon is known as **telecommuting**. Telecommuters are often more productive workers because they tend to work more hours, and they experience fewer distractions at home than workers in offices. They also don't have to expend energy traveling to and from work. Businesses find that they can save on office and parking facilities, and they can recruit workers from among the handicapped and from distant geographic areas.

Telecommuting also presents some problems. At-home workers are isolated from any social contact with coworkers. Some telecommuters don't have the self-discipline to work without supervision, but even superior workers may be overlooked for promotions and advancement because they have less contact with their supervisors. As more and more businesses turn to telecommuting to keep down business costs and increase productivity, employers and workers

More and more people are becoming telecommuters. Telecommuting involves working at a home-based computer which is linked to the company computer. Telecommuters enjoy flexible hours and freedom from the distractions of an office, but they may also miss the interactions with coworkers.

will have to deal with these issues as well as with other important issues such as union representation and insurance coverage for employees who work at home.

■ Summary

- Businesses and consumers used to rent telephones and services through subsidiaries of AT&T, but since 1984 many other companies have been providing telephone systems and long-distance services as well.

- Businesses can purchase key systems with buttons or private branch exchanges with manually operated or automatic switchboards to route company calls.

- Computerized telephones provide many specialized services, such as speed dialing, call forwarding, conference calling, and call-timing.

- Other telephone equipment and accessories include mobile telephones, beeper devices, and answering machines.

- Voice mail is a sophisticated message system that allows users to leave, receive, answer, and reroute recorded messages at any time.

- Office workers need to be courteous and efficient when screening and forwarding calls, placing callers on hold, and taking messages.

- When office workers place calls, they need to be sure of the number, check time zones, plan their calls, and use the most efficient and economical means of placing long-distance calls.

- Office workers making business calls should identify themselves clearly, avoid sexism, state their business promptly, and leave clear messages.

- Teleconferences allow people in widely separated locations to hold a business meeting without having to travel.

- Audio teleconferences involve the use of speakerphones so that groups of people at each end of a conference can hear the entire conversation.

- Video teleconferences let participants see and hear each other over closed-circuit television.

- To arrange a teleconference, you must make sure that the facilities and equipment are adequate and are arranged properly and that the participants are well prepared.

- Telecommuting means using computers and telephone equipment to work at home instead of at the office.

■ Review Questions

1. Explain how you would answer and hold a call on a key system.

2. What are two features found in PABX systems that are not available in manual PBX systems?

3. Name and describe four features a business can purchase with a computerized telephone system.

4. Explain how a voice mail system works.

5. Describe how you might handle a problem caller.

6. Why would you check time zones before making a long-distance telephone call?

7. What are the three long-distance services available for placing calls through AT&T?

8. What is the difference between a conference call and an audio teleconference?

9. Explain the difference between a one-way video teleconference and a two-way video teleconference.

10. Describe at least four things you would have to do to arrange a teleconference.

■ Technical Vocabulary

key system
private branch exchange
private automated branch exchange
direct outward dialing
centrex system

conference call
paging device
speakerphone
video teleconference
telecommuting

■ Discussion and Skills Development

1. Assume that both you and the people you need to call work from 9 a.m. to 5 p.m. During what hours could you place calls from your office to offices in the following places? Check the phone book and other library references for time zone information.

   ■ New York
   ■ Dallas
   ■ San Francisco
   ■ Mexico City
   ■ Anchorage
   ■ Rome
   ■ Minneapolis
   ■ Singapore
   ■ Harrisburg
   ■ Melbourne
   ■ Salt Lake City

2. Rose Sanchez is a secretary to sales manager James McFarlain, and it is part of her regular duties to place and take telephone calls for him. How should she handle the following situations?

   ■ Mr. McFarlain is attending a sales meeting at a branch office, and he receives an urgent long-distance telephone call from his boss, who is calling from an airport pay phone while waiting between planes.
   ■ While she is attempting to transfer a call to Mr. McFarlain, Mrs. Sanchez accidentally hangs up on an important caller.
   ■ Mr. McFarlain asks Mrs. Sanchez to try to discover which employees in his department have been making personal long-distance calls on the office telephone system.

3. Imagine that you work for a large corporation that is experimenting with telecommuting. You have been asked to participate. In the experiment you work at home processing letters using a desk-top computer provided by the company. You work at home four days a week. One day a week you go to the office to pick up materials and discuss the experiment with your supervisor.

   What aspects of telecommuting do you think you would enjoy? What aspects would you dislike? Do you think you would start postponing the start of your workday, or would you stop working earlier than you would if you worked in an office? Do you think you are self-disciplined enough to telecommute? Would you ask to be taken out of the experiment, or would you want to continue telecommuting after the experiment is over? Do you think you would be candid in discussing your telecommuting experience with your supervisor? Make a list of the work habits and types of jobs you think would be most suitable for telecommuting.

part 3
Administrative Support Functions

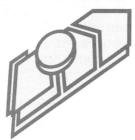

"More interesting," "More versatile," "More challenging," "More productive."

These phrases describe the role of office workers in the electronic office. Computers take over the routine tasks, freeing workers to perform jobs that require more thought and planning. While providing more exciting job possibilities, the change puts a premium on being well organized and having efficient work habits.

To provide administrative support effectively, you must first be able to manage your time, plan your tasks, and maintain an orderly workstation. Part 3 shows you how to accomplish this.

Of the many administrative support services you will provide, two of the most important are organizing meetings and arranging business trips. Part 3 covers the steps involved in setting up meetings of whatever size and the support services you can render during and after a meeting.

To arrange business trips, you must deal with travel agents, hotel reservation clerks, and automobile rental clerks. You will learn how to organize a well-planned business trip whether your boss is going overseas or just on a one-day journey to a nearby city.

In your job, you may be called on to do tasks related to accounting, banking, and legal matters. As computers become ever more sophisticated and integrated, you may even be asked to perform tasks previously handled in separate departments, such as the accounting department. The final chapter in this part gives you a working knowledge of the procedures and documents you could encounter.

chapter 14
Time Management and Work Organization

In your personal life, your time is your own, and you can spend it as you wish. If you'd sooner spend three hours watching a ball game than cleaning your room and doing your laundry, that's fine. You're the only person who has to live with the consequences. But in the business world, things are different. Your time is not your own; your employer is paying you for it. And other people are affected by your decisions and actions.

Employees often represent an employer's most valuable—and most costly—resource. One of the main reasons employers automate their offices, in fact, is to make better use of their human resources. Instead of doing tasks that can be done faster and better by machines, people who work in electronic offices can spend their time on tasks that require judgment, human relations skills, and other attributes that machines don't have.

Because time is money in business, office workers are expected to use their time carefully and economically. They need to schedule their assignments and plan their work days so that they produce the most work possible in the time available to them.

Efficiency in the workplace can be divided into three main areas: organization of time, organization of assignments, and organization of the workstation. Guidelines for improving your performance in all three areas are included in this chapter. You'll learn about the equipment that can help you plan your time and your supervisor's time. You'll also learn about some tried-and-true techniques that can help you organize schedules and meet deadlines. The final part of the chapter focuses on the workstation itself. It shows you how to organize the space around you so that the materials you need for your job are located logically for the greatest efficiency.

Office workers need many time-management skills to do their jobs well. These skills include planning, scheduling, and organizing.

Time Management

There's more to working efficiently than knowing how to do each task. You also need to know when to perform each task, how to choose which job to do first, how long each project will take, and so on. This is called **time management**. Time management in the office involves planning your work, scheduling your work, and avoiding wasted time.

Time management begins with **planning**. When you plan your work, you outline the steps for carrying out all the aspects of a project. If you plan the whole project before you begin working on it, you will be able to foresee problems and handle changes without getting bogged down. You will also need to develop a **schedule**, which indicates when each stage of the project will be completed and in which sequence the stages will be performed. Schedules are the most widely used time-management tools in business.

Electronic Time-Management Systems

Most integrated electronic offices have **electronic time-management systems.** These may include electronic calendars and reminder facilities. With systems such as these, many of the time-management tasks that are traditionally done manually, such as scheduling meetings and maintaining things-to-do lists, can be done electronically. The main advantage of these systems over manual methods is that they are much more efficient and provide for considerable time savings.

There are many electronic time-management systems available today. You may find yourself using an independent, or standalone,

```
Msgs: New:  0              Feb 07,86  2:38 AM  Document: MARKETING PLANS
         CALENDAR for Terry Smith              Date: Mon Feb 10,86
    Ev        Time          Type         Location        Rem Rec     Subject
    1    9:00 AM-10:30 AM  Meeting   Conference Rm. 1              Staff Meeting
    2   10:30 AM-11:30 AM  Meeting   John's Office                Budget
    3    2:00 PM- 4:00 PM  Appoint   Starbright Offices           New Ad Campaign




         Pick one: (1. Different date, 2. Change display, 3. View or Change, 4. Insert,
                    5. Delete, 6. Confirm or Decline, 7. Print, 8. Scheduling) 1
         Pick one: (1. Next, 2. Previous, 3. Specific) █
```

Fig. 14-1a The option of viewing calendars in different ways provides the flexibility needed to get the global picture with a month or week at a glance, and the details needed on each event with a day at a glance. A calendar for one day is shown here.

system running on a microcomputer. A more popular alternative is a system that is just one part of a larger integrated electronic office system.

Just as you might be expected to maintain your principal's calendar manually in a traditional office, you may also be expected to do so electronically in an electronic office. Since the calendar contains personal information, you will probably have to use a password to access the principal's electronic calendar. The key difference between using an electronic calendar and using manual methods is that the electronic system is much easier to maintain.

Electronic calendars allow you to display information in different ways. You may be able to choose to view a day at a time, a week at a time, or a month at a time. Figures 14-1a, 14-1b, and 14-1c illustrate what your screen may look like with each of these options.

Now that you have seen how an electronic calendar might look, let's examine the ways electronic time-management systems help office workers schedule events.

Electronic Calendar/Scheduler

Although each system will differ in features, all electronic calendar and scheduler systems make it easy to organize items and manage office resources. In using such a system, you will be able to electronically record calendar events, reserve office resources, and update and modify calendar events. Some systems even have reminder facilities that allow the user to automatically be reminded of upcoming events.

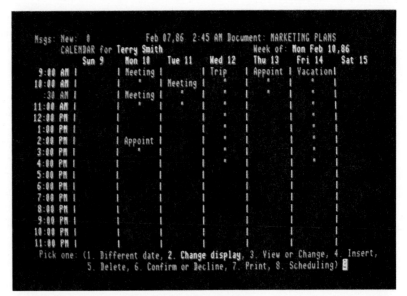

```
Msgs: New:  0              Feb 07,86  2:45 AM Document: MARKETING PLANS
       CALENDAR for Terry Smith                    Week of: Mon Feb 10,86
            Sun 9      Mon 10    Tue 11    Wed 12    Thu 13    Fri 14    Sat 15
    9:00 AM |         | Meeting |         | Trip    | Appoint | Vacation|
   10:00 AM |         |    "     | Meeting |    "    |    "    |    "    |
     :30 AM |         | Meeting |    "     |    "    |         |    "    |
   11:00 AM |         |    "     |    "     |    "    |         |    "    |
   12:00 PM |         |         |         |    "    |         |    "    |
    1:00 PM |         |         |         |    "    |         |    "    |
    2:00 PM |         | Appoint |         |    "    |         |    "    |
    3:00 PM |         |    "     |         |    "    |         |    "    |
    4:00 PM |         |         |         |    "    |         |    "    |
    5:00 PM |         |         |         |         |         |    "    |
    6:00 PM |         |         |         |         |         |    "    |
    7:00 PM |         |         |         |         |         |    "    |
    8:00 PM |         |         |         |         |         |    "    |
    9:00 PM |         |         |         |         |         |    "    |
   10:00 PM |         |         |         |         |         |    "    |
   11:00 PM |         |         |         |         |         |    "    |
    Pick one: (1. Different date, 2. Change display, 3. View or Change, 4. Insert,
              5. Delete, 6. Confirm or Decline, 7. Print, 8. Scheduling) █
```

Fig. 14-1b This is a calendar for one week.

```
Msgs: New:  0              Feb 07,86  2:48 AM Document: MARKETING PLANS
       CALENDAR for Terry Smith
     Sun       Mon       Tue       Wed       Thu       Fri       Sat
                                  Apr 1986
   -------------------------------------------------------------------
             |1        |2        |3        |4        |5        |
             |         |         |         |         |         |
   -------------------------------------------------------------------
   |6        |7        |8        |9        |10       |11       |12       |
   |         |         |         |         |         |         |         |
   -------------------------------------------------------------------
   |13       |14       |15       |16       |17       |18       |19       |
   |         |         |         |         |         |         |         |
   -------------------------------------------------------------------
   |20       |21       |22       |23       |24       |25       |26       |
   |         |         |         |         |         |         |         |
   -------------------------------------------------------------------
   |27       |28       |29       |30       |
   |         |         |         |         |
    Pick one: (1. Different date, 2. Change display, 3. View or Change, 4. Insert,
              5. Delete, 6. Confirm or Decline, 7. Print, 8. Scheduling) █

   There are 18 more lines in this display.
```

Fig. 14-1c This is a calendar for one month.

For example, suppose that you had to schedule a meeting for ten principals. Using manual methods, you might expect to spend a good part of your workday just determining a day and time when all can attend. You may then need to schedule a meeting room and other resources such as audiovisual equipment. Obviously, this can be very time-consuming. To compound this further, it would not be uncommon to find that the time you have established as a good one for all the participants is unavailable for the conference room needed. In this case you might find yourself starting the scheduling process all over again—repeating telephone calls, playing telephone tag, and so on. Using an electronic scheduler, you could expect to spend only a few minutes completing the task.

To schedule a meeting for several busy principals, you indicate to the system the meeting's participants and the date, time, and length of the meeting. The system automatically surveys the electronic calendar of each individual, whether there are 2 or 20. If a participant or resource is not available for the stated date and time, you will be notified. You can then decide whether to go ahead and schedule the meeting or, if those unavailable are crucial to the meeting, request that the system determine the earliest possible date and time when all the participants and resources are available. The main advantage is that this procedure can take place within moments rather than hours.

To illustrate this, let's assume that Patty Curran, administrative assistant to Jack Thompson, president of Thompson and Kelly Advertising, needs to schedule a meeting of the seven top executives of the firm. These include Jack Thompson, three vice presidents, two assistant vice presidents, and the controller. Mr. Thompson would like the meeting to be held in the executive conference room on Tuesday, February 18, from 2 to 5 p.m. He will need a slide projector and an overhead projector.

In using the electronic scheduler on her system, Patty might find that her screen looks like the one shown in Fig. 14-2a. Keep in mind that different systems may provide slightly different displays.

After completing her screen with the above information, Patty asks the system to execute her request. At this point the system is checking the calendar of each individual and resource indicated for availability at the stated date and time. If all were available, the system would indicate so, and Patty could continue the scheduling process. However, as shown in Fig. 14-2b, conflicts exist.

Patty sees that three of the seven individuals needed for the meeting are unavailable. She is given the option of scheduling the meeting at the stated date and time, but she declines. In this particular case Patty knows that the presence of all seven individuals is required. If, however, she was scheduling a meeting for 20 individuals and only three could not attend, she might decide to go ahead and schedule the meeting anyway if the unavailable individuals were not critical to the meeting. Conflicts should be evaluated on a case-by-case basis. Personal judgment will need to be used in making each decision.

In this case Patty wants to be sure that all seven can attend. Thus she requests that the system determine the earliest possible date and time after the date and time already indicated when all seven are available for the three-hour meeting.

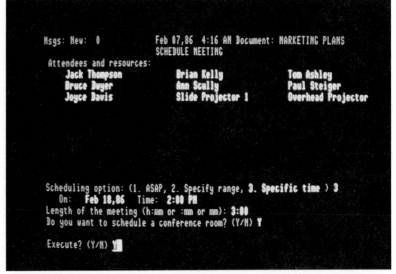

Fig. 14-2*a* This screen shows all the people and the kinds of equipment that should be at the meeting.

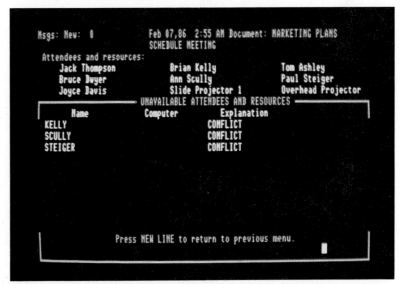

Fig. 14-2*b* This indicates that three of the people who should attend the meeting have something else scheduled at that time.

Her screen will look very similar to the one shown in Fig. 14-2*a*. The only exception is that she now chooses the ASAP scheduling option. After she does this, the system indicates the next available time slice of three hours when all the individuals and resources are available. This is illustrated in Fig. 14-2*c*.

Now that the system has determined that February 19 at 1 p.m. is suitable for all the attendees and resources, Patty can continue the

```
Msgs: New: 0               Feb 07,86  3:15 AM Document: MARKETING PLANS
                                SCHEDULE MEETING
    Attendees and resources:
       Jack Thompson             Brian Kelly             Tom Ashley
       Bruce Dwyer               Ann Scully              Paul Steiger
       Joyce Davis               Slide Projector 1       Overhead Projector




    Scheduling option: (1. ASAP, 2. Specify range, 3. Specific time ) 1
    After:   Feb 18,86   Time: 2:00 PM
    Length of the meeting (h:mm or :mm or mm): 3:00
    Do you want to schedule a conference room? (Y/N) Y

    Execute? (Y/N) Y



    Scheduled for Wed  Feb 19,86  at  1:00 PM in Exec. Conf. Rm.     OK? (Y/N) ▉
```

Fig. 14-2c Since the meeting couldn't be held on February 18 at 2 p.m., the computer found the first available block of three hours when all the participants could attend.

```
Msgs: New: 0               Feb 07,86  3:18 AM Document: MARKETING PLANS
                                SCHEDULE MEETING
    Attendees and resources:
       Jack Thompson             Brian Kelly             Tom Ashley
       Bruce Dwyer               Ann Scully              Paul Steiger
       Joyce Davis               Slide Projector 1       Overhead Projector


   ┌─────────────────── SCHEDULING SUPPLEMENT ───────────────────┐
   │ Subject: Starbright Contract                                 │
   │ Description:                                                  │
   │   We will need to develop a strategic plan for winning the   │
   │   Starbright Toothpolish contract over the Hamilton Ad Agency.│
   │   Bring all account information to the meeting as well as new │
   │   ad campaign developments.                                  │
   │                                                              │
   │ Do you want mail confirmations from attendees? (Y/N) Y       │
   │ Is this a recurring meeting? (Y/N) N                         │
   │ Do you want to be reminded of this meeting? (Y/N) ▉          │
   └──────────────────────────────────────────────────────────────┘
```

Fig. 14-2d A detailed description of the meeting is provided for the information of the attendees.

scheduling process. Keep in mind that everything illustrated from the beginning of this scheduling session takes only a couple of minutes to complete, as opposed to numerous hours if traditional methods are used.

After she completes the scheduling session, Patty might be given the option of providing a detailed description of the purpose of the meeting. This will serve as a reference for the attendees, and it can be accessed when each person views his or her own calendar entry for the meeting. Figure 14-2d shows what the description screen might look like.

Once the scheduling supplement is completed, the scheduler automatically reserves the resources requested and inserts the meeting event in each attendee's calendar. If the system used is an integrated electronic office system, the scheduler may even send a notification message to each attendee's in box. This is the case in the example given. Since Patty requested confirmation from the attendees, as shown in Fig. 14-2d, she will get a message in her in box from each attendee as to whether he or she will attend the meeting. The meeting event in each attendee's calendar is a tentative notation until it is confirmed or declined. If an individual must decline the meeting because of previous commitments not yet in his or her electronic calendar, Patty may then again reschedule the meeting. It is important to remember, however, that whenever this happens, it takes only moments. There is no need for telephone tag and follow-up.

Modifying Calendar Events Electronic calendaring and scheduling systems make it easy not only to schedule events but to modify and update those events as well. All information pertaining to each event is electronically stored in the calendar, and so it is easy to make changes.

Very often you will need to change the time of appointments, adjust meeting dates, or reschedule events to reflect the changing needs of your office. Electronic systems let you do this quickly and easily with a change entry option. If rescheduling of several individuals is needed, use of the electronic scheduler will complete this for you as described in the previous section.

Electronic Reminders and "Things-to-do" Facilities

Some more advanced features that may be a part of an electronic time-management system are reminders and "things-to-do" facilities. These are additional tools that can help office workers perform the time-management tasks that they face on a day-to-day basis.

Reminder facilities can be used effectively to remind you or your principal of upcoming meetings, commitments, or projects. A reminder indicator will automatically be displayed on your screen on the date and at the exact time that you set it for. You can think of this type of facility as an electronic alarm clock. Obviously, this type of facility is much more sophisticated than a standard alarm clock, since you can attach detailed information on what you'll need to be reminded of, and you can set it for a specific day as well as time. This can replace the manual tickler file when all that is needed is limited information on a specific date and at a specific time.

Either during the scheduling process or after completing the scheduling of the meeting on the Starbright Toothpolish contract,

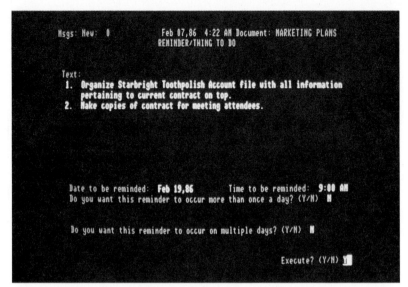

Fig. 14-3*a* This is a reminder for Mr. Thompson. It describes what he should do to prepare for the meeting.

```
Msgs: New: 0              Feb 07,86 4:24 AM Document: MARKETING PLANS
                              REMINDER/THING TO DO

Text:
    Tell Mr. Thompson that meeting is to begin in 15 minutes and give him
    account file and contract copies.




Date to be reminded:  Feb 19,86       Time to be reminded:  12:45 PM
Do you want this reminder to occur more than once a day? (Y/N)  N

Do you want this reminder to occur on multiple days? (Y/N)  N

                                                Execute? (Y/N)  Y
```

Fig. 14-3*b* This is to remind Patty that she should remind Mr. Thompson about the meeting 15 minutes before it starts.

Patty may choose to set a reminder for herself for things she needs to prepare for Mr. Thompson prior to the meeting. She may also want to set a reminder to prompt him about the meeting 15 minutes before it begins so that he can prepare himself for it. Once the reminder facility is accessed, Patty's screen might look like the ones in Fig. 14-3 for the two reminders that she wishes to set regarding this meeting.

As you can see from these examples, many reminder facilities allow you to set reminders that will occur more than once in a day. You just decide how often you wish a reminder to occur if this option is chosen (for example, every two hours). You can also set reminders so that they occur over several days. Once these reminders are set, it is possible to view all the reminders set for a specific date. Just as calendar entries are easy to modify, so are reminders. Dates and times are easily changed, and reminders can be deleted entirely if necessary.

In addition to reminding you about specific events, commitments, and so on, some more advanced time-management systems may provide you with a **"things-to-do" facility.** A "things-to-do" list can be maintained electronically on the system for items that you don't need to be reminded about at a specific time. Items on your "things-to-do" list can usually be prioritized in some way, and items can be added, deleted, changed, or reprioritized quickly and easily at any time. The "things-to-do" list is stored electronically and can be referred to at any time.

Also, any good time-management system will allow you to print out your "things-to-do" list as well as your calendar.

Manual Time-Management Systems

There are many obvious advantages of electronic calendaring systems over manual methods. However, there may still be the need to continue the use of manual calendars, even though an electronic system has been put in place. One reason for this is that there will always be cases where access to the electronic system is not possible.

For example, a principal who spends much of his or her time out of the office will find it necessary to carry a pocket calendar for scheduling appointments with clients and others. This is obviously easier to do than calling the office to check for free time on the appropriate electronic calendar every time there is a need to schedule an event. Although this may be the case, if an electronic system is in place in the office, the principals should be urged to provide you with their manual calendars on a daily basis so that the electronic calendars can be updated accordingly. In this way, other individuals in the office needing to schedule time with your principals can be assured that their electronic calendars are effectively maintained, and meetings can be scheduled as requested.

Of course, manual systems will be used in cases where an office has not yet implemented a fully electronic system. Many times office automation takes place in a phased manner. If this is the case, not all office workers will be provided with access to the system at the same time. A small department may be a pilot location for testing the new system. Then other departments may be added in a piecemeal fashion. Thus it may not be possible to use the electronic calendaring facility effectively during the implementation process, because not all the office personnel are part of the system.

Keeping Desk Calendars

The best manual tool you have for keeping track of your schedule is a desk calendar. In the office you can use daily, weekly, or long-term calendars to record appointments, deadlines for projects, and so on.

You should write calendar entries neatly with a pencil so that you can change them easily. If your notes are clear and if your calendar is kept in a convenient place, your supervisor and coworkers can get any information they need about your schedule when you are away from the office. Don't make personal or confidential notes on this calendar. It is for business.

To keep your own and your boss's calendars up to date, you may need to meet regularly with your boss to discuss additions and changes in your schedules. The kind of calendar you keep will depend on your schedule and your responsibilities. You may find that a combination of the types listed below will work best for you.

■ **Daily Calendar**. You may have a daily calendar on your desk. This kind of calendar has one blank or ruled page, or pair of pages, for each day of the year. The ruled pages may divide the workday into segments of an hour or less, which can help you schedule appointments and tasks. If someone asks for an appointment, a quick look will tell you when you are free.

These are the different desk calendars you can use. Make sure your notes include all the information about the appointment you are scheduling: person's name, phone number, time and place of the meeting, and subject.

- **Weekly Calendar**. Some calendars display a week's schedule at once. On these calendars, too, days may be divided into segments, and there may be blank areas for general entries. Many weekly calendars are notebook-size, with pages large enough to allow room for detailed entries. The advantage of a weekly calendar is that it allows you to see what you have planned for an entire week in one glance. So if your boss asks when you can prepare a budget for your department, which will take three or four days, you can simply refer to your weekly calendar.

- **Monthly Calendar**. You would use a monthly calendar to schedule events such as vacations or long-term projects that occupy big blocks of time. These calendars, which must be large enough for a month's worth of entries, generally hang on the wall. Office workers sometimes use color coding with wall calendars. For example, you might use blue lines to indicate when you will be out of the office and red lines for your boss's vacations and business trips. These color codes will give you information about your long-term schedule quickly.

- **Yearly Calendar**. A yearly calendar is a master calendar which includes events which always occur at set times during the year. Holidays, the preparation of annual budgets and reports, employee evaluations, and conferences are just some of the things that might be listed on a yearly calendar. A yearly calendar is especially helpful to new staff members.

Tickler Files

Another kind of daily reminder system is the tickler file, which stores reminders and other notes until you need them. One type of tickler file uses index cards and divider guides in two colors. The divider guides in one color are labeled with the months, and one is labeled "Future Years." The divider guides in the other color are numbered 1 through 31, for the days of the month. The divider guide for the current month is at the front of the numbered guide cards, and the other months are behind them.

To use this kind of tickler file, you write notes on index cards and file them behind the appropriate dates. For example, if it's June 3 and you need to remind yourself to call a client on, say, June 20, you place a note in the file behind the guide card labeled "20." If you want to remember to make a follow-up call in October, you put a note farther back in the file, behind the card labeled "October." To remind yourself that you should begin to prepare for a conference in March next year, you file a note behind the "Future Years" card. Some tickler files are designed to hold originals or file copies of documents that need follow-up at a later date. These are larger so that they can hold letter- or legal-size documents.

Of course, tickler files are only useful if you remember to check them every day.

Maintaining Daily Schedules

Whether you use electronic or manual methods, your calendar and tickler file remind you of what needs to be done each day. To work most efficiently, you will also need to create a schedule for the next day's work before you leave the office each evening. Or you could schedule your work for the day when you arrive at your office in the morning. In either case, you can use these suggestions to develop your schedule:

- **Make lists**. If you list all the tasks that need to be done, you can then estimate how much time each task will take. This helps you see how much work you can do in one day. List all pending tasks, not just those you must do that day. But you don't need to list daily routine chores, such as opening mail or sharpening pencils. Delete each task from your list as you finish it, and add any new assignments to your list. Any tasks you don't finish that day go on the next day's list. Keep your list in sight during the day to remind yourself of what needs to be done next and how you can best spend your time.

- **Set priorities**. Most of the time you won't finish all the tasks on your list in a single workday. If you rank each item on your list by its **priority**, or its level of urgency and importance, you will be able to spend your time on the most important tasks. To do this, you can divide the items on your list into these three categories: *A* for tasks you should do immediately, *B* for tasks you should do that day, and *C* for tasks that can be done whenever you have time. For example, arranging to have an important out-of-town visitor picked up at the airport tomorrow morning would get an *A* rating. Tasks you could postpone for a short time, such as transcribing shorthand notes for routine correspondence, would be ranked *B*. Priority ratings of *C* would go to tasks such as rearranging the books on your shelves, ordering supplies (unless you are running low on them), and putting new labels on file-folder tabs.

- **Be flexible**. You might have to change your plans during the day. Suppose that an unexpected visitor shows up or that your boss has a sudden "rush" project. You can cope with unexpected events if your schedule for the day is flexible. One way you can allow for flexibility is to rank your priority list by assigning numbers after the letters: *A-1, A-2, B-1, B-2, C-1, C-2,* and so on. Then you can choose easily among tasks that have the same urgency. Sometimes, however, you can't be flexible with your schedule. For instance, your boss may need you to finish a special project in one day. In this case you could ask your coworkers if you could rely on them for help with some tasks.

- **Make use of slack time**. It's a good idea to keep a list of things you'd like to do in the office when you have extra time. This could include tasks such as consolidating files, rearranging reference materials, and updating procedures manuals. Tasks like these are

Adjust your priorities and work schedule according to your supervisor's needs.

good for two reasons: they give you something interesting to do in slow times, and when they are done, your regular tasks are easier. Be sure to check with your boss before starting one of these jobs.

■ **Consult your supervisor**. Your supervisor may want to develop daily schedules with you, or he or she may prefer to check the schedules you make. In either case, you should consult your supervisor when you have schedule questions or conflicts. If you work for more than one person, it may be difficult to coordinate plans. Each person may want his or her work done first. In general, you should do the work of the highest-ranking person first unless another person's work is more urgent. You might ask your supervisors to assign a priority to each task routinely.

MAKING APPOINTMENTS

Most office workers schedule appointments with people outside the office for both themselves and their supervisors. The following guidelines will help you perform this time-management task efficiently and courteously.

■ When you request an appointment, identify yourself (and the person for whom you are scheduling the appointment). Identify your employer, as well, if you are speaking to someone who is unfamiliar with you and your company.

■ State the reason for the appointment.

■ Indicate how much time you think the appointment will take.

■ Have your schedule (or your supervisor's) in front of you so that you can suggest a time or respond to a suggestion from someone else without delay. If the time slot requested is not available, suggest an alternate time.

■ When you must clear an appointment with your supervisor, confirm it as soon as possible.

■ Write down (or keyboard) the details of any appointment you make: date, time, location, purpose, and the other person's name and title. Note any additional information that you need to pre-pare for the appointment, such as files you should review.

■ Confirm the details with the other person to make sure you have communicated clearly.

■ Ask the other person to get in touch with you if the appointment must be changed.

■ Leave some time between appointments in case some of them last longer than expected.

Avoiding Time-Wasters

If you have trouble sticking to your plans and schedules, you may have to change them. Perhaps you underestimated the time a certain task would take, or you were uncertain about its priority. You can work at solving these problems using the skills outlined in this chapter, but there is another aspect of time management that you ought to consider. You need to become aware of the time-wasters in your office procedures and work habits. And you need to learn to control and reduce time-wasting factors.

Telephone Calls   Answering the telephone will probably be part of your job. But there will be times when telephone calls will get in the way of your other work. At such times you can ask the caller if you may return the call. You could say, "May I call you back with that information this afternoon? I have a project due in one hour." Be sure to get the caller's name and phone number and the reason for the call. And do remember to return the call at the time you specified.

Electronic message systems can also help eliminate many of the disruptive telephone calls you receive. Messages can be stored in your computer terminal until you are ready, or your boss is ready, to attend to them. You can set aside a block of time each day for responding to interoffice communications.

Interruptions by Coworkers   Interruptions by supervisors and other coworkers waste time in the same way that telephone calls do. That is, when you are in the middle of a task and someone interrupts with a question or comment, you must stop what you are doing and answer. One way to reduce the number of interruptions is by exchanging some information in writing with your coworkers. Unless you urgently need the answer to a question, you can write a note and wait for the note to be answered either in person or in writing. Or if your office has an electronic message system, you can send it to your coworker's electronic mailbox rather than interrupt while he or she is handling other priorities. Another way is to arrange in advance to talk with your supervisor or coworkers at specific times. You can save your questions for these times.

Socializing Chatting with coworkers also steals time from your work. This problem is especially troublesome in landscaped offices. Because these offices have fewer doors and walls that serve as barriers between people, their layouts encourage conversation. Some socializing is acceptable and even desirable because it helps employees understand each other and work together better, but work must take first priority. You will probably find it necessary now and then to say to a coworker, "Please excuse me. I've got to get back to my work."

Unnecessary Work Your routine may include tasks that are unnecessary. One example of unnecessary work is filing papers that should be discarded. Another example is routinely filling in forms with details that your company already has in its data base. Analyze the tasks you perform as well as the different elements of those tasks. When you suspect that a task or some part of it has no point, consult your supervisor to see if it can be dropped from your routine.

Organizing Individual Tasks

Just as following a daily schedule can help you use your time more effectively, working according to a plan can help you perform individual tasks more efficiently. If you plan the steps you will take to complete each task, you will save yourself time and effort and avoid making mistakes.

Scheduling Big Projects

Your job functions will probably include both small tasks that can be finished quickly and bigger projects that will take some time. Big projects may sometimes seem overwhelming and difficult to plan, but you can make them manageable. There are several ways that this can be done.

Break Big Jobs into Segments Divide a big project into segments, and think of it as several small tasks. For example, suppose that you work for an employment agency. Your supervisor wants you to write a report that will help her to do more business next year. The report must include a detailed account of the people the agency placed this year, the jobs they were placed in, and how each match was made. Because this is a large agency and you have other tasks to do as well, the report will take you several months to prepare. You will have to break this job into small segments. For example, first you can make the list of the people who were placed by the agency. Then you can put the list in a format that will allow you to fill in the additional information, such as the name of the company an applicant was placed in and the position the person filled. You can then go about finding and filling in this information. Finally,

The keys to planning time wisely are predicting how long a task will take and using short-term goals along the way.

you can organize the report. When it is done, you will type it, proofread it, make a copy, and give the original to your boss. Each of these tasks is a segment that you can handle one step at a time.

Set Short-term Goals   You can set **short-term goals** for the individual segments of the task. Your success in reaching short-term goals on time will help you to determine how likely you are to reach your long-range goal. If you take more or less time than you had planned to reach a short-term goal, you will have to revise your plans. For the assignment to write the report for the employment agency, you might set short-term goals of finishing the first task in two weeks and the second task in another week. If you do not finish the first task at the end of two weeks, you will know that you need to devote more time to that task each day if you are to reach the next goal on schedule.

If you don't reach the first goal on schedule, figure out why. Then you can adjust your plan so that you can finish the work on time. You may find that you should give higher priority to this project and perhaps devote three hours each week to it rather than two. You may even decide that you are unlikely to finish the job, perhaps because you have more work than you can handle over the next few months. In this case you must decide whether to ask for help with the report or with your other work or for more time to finish the report. Without a plan you would have no way to determine how close you were to completing the report or whether you would need help to get the job done.

Establishing Deadlines

Other people may have established **deadlines**, a specified date on which a task must be completed, for many of the tasks you perform in the office. For tasks that don't have deadlines already, you should set your own. Deadlines can push you to finish tasks that you might put off indefinitely. Also, deadlines help you plan and schedule work. For example, if you know that a letter must be written by next Friday, you can plan time for it more easily than if you didn't know when it should be finished. When all your projects have deadlines, you can arrange your schedule so that you finish each one on time.

If you have a big project, you may need to set **interim deadlines**, dates for completing parts of the project, as well as a final deadline for others in your office. Interim deadlines can help you finish the parts of the project that involve other people. In other words, they function like the short-term goals you set for yourself, but they also apply to other people.

If you and your supervisor faced a November 16 deadline for submitting your division's proposed budget for the next year, you would note the final deadline on your long-term schedule. You would also schedule interim deadlines. For instance, you might set an August 30 deadline for reviewing this year's costs and your supervisor's plans for the division. You might also schedule an interim deadline for budget requests from managers who report to your supervisor. You would enter these deadlines on your long-term and daily schedules too.

Analyzing Daily Tasks

Each morning you should spend some time analyzing the tasks on your daily schedule. Make lists of the information, supplies, and other materials that you will need to perform each task. Then think about where you will do the work, how long you expect it to take, and what steps are involved.

If a task is complex, write down the steps in the order that you will carry them out. Then look at what you have written to see if you can simplify the task by combining some of the steps, performing them in a different order, or delegating some of them. For example, if you are arranging a business trip for an executive, perhaps you can delegate some tasks, such as reserving airplane seats and hotel rooms, to a travel agent. Here are some tips for analyzing and completing daily tasks.

■ **Study your instructions**. Unless you are thoroughly familiar with the job you are about to do, ask for instructions. Write these down, and study them until you understand exactly what you are supposed to do and how you are to do it. Ask questions about anything you don't understand, but avoid interrupting your co-workers more often than necessary. If this is a task that may be repeated in the future, keep the instructions for future use.

■ **Group your tasks**. Your plan for the day may include several tasks that involve similar steps or the same location. You can save time and effort by grouping these tasks and doing them all at once. For example, suppose that several tasks on your list involve looking up phone numbers and making calls. If you look up all the numbers and make the calls at the same time, you will spend less time and effort reaching for your telephone directory, address file, and telephone.

■ **Gather your materials**. Before you begin any task, gather all the materials you will need, and arrange them in the order that you will use them. You will concentrate better and you will finish each task faster if you don't have to stop in the middle of it to search for supplies, information, or equipment.

Managing Your Workstation

Efficiency begins with a well-organized workstation. You'll be able to carry out all your tasks more effectively if your workplace is properly arranged. Keep supplies, reference books, and other materials you use in your work where you can find them quickly. An orderly workstation not only makes your work easier but also gives others a favorable impression of you.

When your workstation is organized, you can find everything you need quickly.

Organizing Your Desk

Your desk may be the most important tool you have for organizing the materials you use in your work. You will probably be the only person who uses your desk, which means that you can arrange it however you like. Here are some guidelines you can follow to arrange your desk.

Your Desk-Top   You should keep your desk-top orderly and uncluttered. Don't allow mail, coffee cups, papers, and other items to pile up. Ideally, the only items on your desk should be the ones you are using at the moment, such as the papers you are working with, and the ones you use often during the day, such as a desk-top calendar and a telephone. Place these items where you can reach them easily.

You will probably want to keep some papers on your desk, of course. But if they are spread over the desk-top, you won't have room for writing or other tasks, and the papers could be misplaced or damaged. Desk-top organizers can help you sort the papers on your desk and arrange them so that you can find them quickly. There are two basic types of organizers for papers: vertical organizers and trays. Both types take up no more desk surface than a piece of stationery, but they can hold many papers or files. In a vertical organizer, files stand upright between dividers so that you can read their tabs and add documents to them easily. In organizer trays, files or papers are stacked on top of one another. The trays themselves may also be stacked. If you work for more than one executive, assign a different colored in/out box to each person.

Most workers have a telephone at their workstation. If you keep your phone on your desk-top, place it to the left of the writing surface (unless you are left-handed). That way, you will be able to talk on the phone and write at the same time. You may also want to keep small items that you use constantly on your desk-top, such as tape, pens and pencils, and a pad of telephone message slips. Keep supplies for taking messages next to your phone. Use an upright container for pens and pencils, and store them with their points up so that you can see what color they are and whether they are sharp. Keep paper clips in a container too. If you use magnetic tapes or disks at your workstation, don't use a magnetic paper-clip container, and beware of metal clips that might have become magnetized in another office.

Most office workers keep a few reference materials on their desk-tops. These materials might include an address file, a dictionary, a reference manual, and other sources of information that they refer to often. If you work in an electronic office, you might have some of these materials filed on disks, which you would keep in a disk file box. Keep your reference materials away from your writing surface but within arm's reach, and use bookends to stand them upright so that you can read the titles easily and remove the one you want without displacing the others.

Your Desk Drawers Organize your drawer space so that you won't have to search for the items you need. You will work more efficiently if your desk drawers are neat and if you arrange their contents so that the items you use most frequently are closest to hand.

If your desk has a shallow center drawer, you can use it to store many small items such as scissors, rubber bands, a spare ribbon for a printer or typewriter, stamps, and rulers. Containers of liquid, such as glue or correction fluid, should be stored upright so they don't leak.

Use the top side drawer of your desk for shorthand notebooks, frequently used forms, and other paper supplies. With a vertical divider, you can create a section where envelopes stand on edge, which makes them easier to remove. If you keep several kinds of paper in this drawer, you may want to use a diagonal divider with separate sections for letterheads, second sheets, and so on. The top side drawer is also a good place for storing a tickler file, a stapler, a coffee cup, and other frequently used items that are too large for the center drawer.

You may want to keep a few current or pending files in your bottom drawer. If you do, review these files, and transfer them to file cabinets when you don't need to see them very often. This way, you won't use up valuable space in your desk with rarely needed files. You can use a divider panel to keep file folders upright, or you can obtain a rack for the drawer and use hanging files. Either way, store the files loosely so that you can locate the files you need quickly.

Your Computer Terminal If you work in an electronic office, your workstation will probably include a computer terminal. Ideally, if you have your own printer, it will be kept on a specially designed table. However, if your terminal is attached to a large centralized system, many users may share several printers. These will probably be placed in convenient central locations. The terminal and keyboard (and perhaps a unit housing the computer and disk drives if you have a microcomputer) will be kept on another table. However, they might be placed on your desk-top instead. If the terminal is on your desk, place it off to one side at an angle so that you still have a clear surface for writing by hand and performing other tasks.

Whether your terminal sits on your desk or on a special table, arrange it so that you can work comfortably and so that the equipment will operate smoothly. Make sure that all cables and wires are out of the way so that they can't trip anyone or make your workstation messy.

Shelves Your workstation may include shelves that you can use for storing reference materials that shouldn't stay on your desk, such as an employee manual, telephone directories, a thesaurus, and an almanac. You might want to store other items on shelves too. For example, most file boxes for floppy diskettes fit neatly on shelves so it is convenient to store them on a shelf near your disk drive. Remember, though, to store disks with expensive software or confidential data securely in locked boxes or drawers, not in open boxes on shelves. Also remember to store all disks on their edges and in protective envelopes; never store them on top of the computer, because

If you organize your supply area properly, you'll be able to see at a glance when certain items are running low.

they may become demagnetized. A shelf may be a safe, out-of-the-way place to keep a plant, a photograph, or some other item you bring in to personalize your workstation. Arrange the materials you store on your shelves so that the items you use most often are the easiest to reach.

Supply Cabinets

Your workstation may also include cabinets and closets for storing items that are too large to fit in your desk. In a cabinet you may store oversize envelopes as well as large quantities of supplies such as pencils, notepads, floppy diskettes, typewriter ribbons, stationery, and file folders. Use locked cabinets for storing software disks and confidential-data disks.

Ordering Supplies You should check your supplies regularly and order new stocks of any items that are running low. This way, you won't run out of them. In a large office, you will probably place orders for supplies through your employer's central supply room. In a small office, you may order them yourself from a stationery store.

When you get new supplies, they may be wrapped in plain paper. Label each package clearly with a marking pen so that you can see what the package contains without opening it. When you receive a new quantity of an item, place it behind or under what remains of your old supply so that the old supply is used first. These steps, like others involved in organizing your workstation, your schedule, and your assignments, will help you to do your job with the least possible waste of time, effort, and materials.

■ Summary

- Doing your job well requires skill in organizing your time, your assignments, and your work materials.

- Careful planning is essential to managing your time well. It can help you finish assignments on time with a minimum of mistakes and frustrations. You will probably use a daily desktop calendar for scheduling, and you may also use weekly, monthly, or yearly calendars.

- You would use a tickler file to keep reminder notes on events or responsibilities you must deal with in the future.

- Note your plans as far in advance as possible to help avoid conflicts. Schedule tasks that you perform regularly, as well as events, far in advance.

- To develop a daily schedule, list the tasks that need to be done, estimate how long each one will take, and then rank each task by priority. Try to develop a schedule that is flexible enough to allow for unexpected events.

- Consult your supervisor when you have schedule questions or conflicts. If you have slack time, use it for low-priority tasks.

Avoid time-wasters, such as phone calls, interruptions, socializing, and unnecessary work.

- A big project will be more manageable if you break it into segments and view each segment as a short-term goal on your way to the long-term goal of finishing the project. Your progress in reaching the goals on schedule can help you determine whether you can finish the project on time.

- If you set deadlines for tasks, you can manage your time better. For a long-term project, set interim deadlines in addition to a final deadline.

- Analyze the tasks on your daily schedule to see which ones you can simplify or delegate. Study your instructions before you begin each task. If tasks involve similar steps, save effort by grouping them together.

- Your work will go more smoothly if you keep your desk-top free from clutter. Organize the materials that must stay on your desk. Keep supplies, reference books, and other materials where you can find them quickly.

- Well-organized desk drawers are important to orderly work. Shelves and supply cabinets should also be kept well organized.

■ Review Questions

1. How is a schedule related to a plan?

2. What is the most widely used scheduling tool in the office?

3. When would you use both a daily calendar and a weekly calendar?

4. Describe how you would use a tickler file to keep track of a reminder that you want to see on May 15 of next year.

5. What is the first step in developing a schedule for each day?

6. Summarize the steps you should take when scheduling appointments for yourself or your supervisor.

7. What two techniques can you use for cutting down on interruptions while you are working?

8. If you don't reach a short-term goal on schedule, why is it important to determine the reason?

9. What are some steps you can take that will help you get your daily tasks completed more efficiently?

10. Why is it important to keep your workstation clean and well organized?

■ Technical Vocabulary

time management
planning
schedule
electronic time-management system
electronic calendar
reminder facility

things-to-do facility
priority
short-term goal
deadline
interim deadline

■ Discussion and Skills Development

1. Georgia Miller is an administrative assistant to Robert Drenning, who is the manager of a busy department. Although Ms. Miller likes Mr. Drenning, she sometimes finds it frustrating to work for him because he is disorganized. For example, he habitually makes appointments without telling her, so she often discovers that she has scheduled conflicting appointments for him, which she then has to cancel. He frequently misplaces files, and when he takes work home in the evening, he sometimes forgets to bring all the materials back to the office the next day. His office is messy too, with papers, coffee cups, and personal items cluttering his desk and his coat slung over a chair. Should Ms. Miller try to help Mr. Drenning get organized? If so, how can she do this without offending him?

2. Robert Fleming has recently been promoted to a job where he will be responsible for keeping track of the progress of the many projects in his department. Along with charting progress, he will have to see to it that deadlines are met; he will have to know when these deadlines are approaching and check that each project is on schedule. What time-management and scheduling tools can help Robert do his job efficiently?

3. Go to a stationery or office-supply store. Look at the various desk and supply organizers that are available. Make a list (that includes descriptions) of items that you think would be most useful in organizing your workstation. Compare your list with your classmates' lists, and be prepared to justify or explain your choices.

4. Think of all the appointments, dates, errands, and tasks you juggle in your daily routine. What time-management method(s) and tool(s) could help you organize and plan your schedule? Try using some of the methods and tools discussed in the chapter, and see if they help you run your life more efficiently.

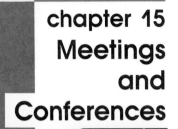

chapter 15
Meetings and Conferences

According to *Newsweek* magazine, business executives spend about 50 percent of their work time in meetings. In fact, they devote more of their time to meetings than to any other single business activity. With so much executive time, and therefore, so much corporate money, going into meetings, it is important that the time be well spent.

Meetings come in many shapes and sizes; they range from two people talking informally in an office to 2000 or more people gathering in a hotel for a conference. If such widely differing events have one thing in common, it is that their success and usefulness largely depend on the planning that went into them.

Arranging meetings might be one of your most important responsibilities. Certainly, it will be one of the more challenging parts of your job. Organizing people, equipment, transportation, caterers, and speakers so that they all get together in the right place on the right day can take many hours of careful planning.

Each meeting that you arrange will present you with a different set of tasks. Usually, though, the success of any meeting depends on four key elements: information, planning, preparation, and follow-up. In this chapter you'll learn how you will use communication skills to obtain and convey the information you need to arrange a successful meeting. The chapter also discusses the kind of planning you need to do in order to ensure that meetings run smoothly. You will learn how to avoid those last-minute aggravations that can cause people to lose both time and patience.

Preparation for a meeting involves such tasks as informing those who will attend, reserving rooms, arranging meals, and generally making sure that all the needed seating, tables, and equipment will be in place and operational on the day of the meeting. This chapter helps you make sure that you will overlook nothing in this important phase.

Finally, it explains follow-up procedures. You'll see how careful follow-up can prevent problems in the future and make it easier for you to arrange subsequent meetings.

Types of Meetings

Companies function best when their employees hold meetings frequently. A carefully planned, orderly meeting is often the best way for a group and its individual members to exchange information, solve problems, make plans, and accomplish their business goals.

Meetings range from informal talks to highly structured events involving panel discussions, exhibits, votes, and other activities. They can last for a few minutes or for several days, and they can involve two or three participants or several hundred. Meetings can be held in offices, conference rooms, auditoriums, restaurants, and conference centers. When people talk about **informal meetings**, they are usually referring to discussions of everyday business activities that take place in an office or conference room.

Informal Meetings

Most meetings held in the office are informal. They generally do not involve complicated arrangements or scheduling. The three basic types of in-office meetings are staff meetings, committee meetings, and supplier/client meetings.

Staff Meetings   Perhaps the most common in-office meeting is the staff meeting. You may arrange informal staff meetings frequently, and you will probably participate in them from time to time. A staff meeting is generally held in a supervisor's office or in a conference room. It is attended by employees who report to that supervisor. The purpose of a staff meeting is to discuss and solve problems, make decisions, review progress, plan projects, or distribute assignments. Some supervisors meet with their staffs monthly, weekly, or even daily; others call staff meetings only when they need to deal with special problems or unusual circumstances.

Committee Meetings   Another kind of informal in-office meeting is the committee meeting. Office workers often serve on committees that are formed to investigate problems or complete special projects. These committees hold meetings to exchange information and plan action. For example, you could serve on a committee assigned to investigate word processing software and suggest which type would be best for your office.

Supplier/Client Meetings   An executive may also hold informal supplier/client meetings, either in the office or at a restaurant. A meeting between a law firm administrator and representatives of a company that supplies telephone equipment for the firm would be an example of a meeting in which the executive acts as a client. In the same firm, attorneys might meet frequently with their clients to discuss work the firm is doing for them.

Formal Meetings

Formal meetings may be held inside the office or at another location. These meetings involve more preparation than informal meetings. Sometimes a special setting has to be rented to accommodate the meeting. Formal meetings of groups like professional associa-

A staff meeting provides an opportunity for face-to-face discussion among people working together. Because the participants can understand different points of view, a staff meeting often produces workable solutions and plans.

tions or corporate boards of directors usually follow the procedures set forth in *Robert's Rules of Order*, which is a guide that organizations use to conduct meetings in which they make decisions and set policies. The rules set forth in this book are known as **parliamentary procedure**. Formal meetings can follow other procedures too. The basic types of formal meetings are conventions, conferences, and official meetings.

LEADING AND PARTICIPATING IN MEETINGS

You can learn how to conduct and participate in formal meetings by studying *Robert's Rules of Order*. In addition, keep these guidelines in mind whenever you lead or participate in a meeting, whether it is formal or informal:

■ Every meeting should have a clearly defined purpose.
■ A meeting should start promptly and be adjourned as soon as the group finishes its business.
■ Only one topic at a time should be discussed, and each discussion should be finished before discussion of the next topic begins.
■ Discussions should focus on issues that are of concern to the group as a whole, not on personalities or subjects unrelated to business.
■ Participants should speak one at a time, and only when the leader of the meeting has called on them. The statements they make should be brief and to the point.

For some gatherings, you may have to reserve meeting rooms at a nearby hotel or convention center. These arrangements may include catering services for meals or light refreshments, as well as overnight accommodations for participants from out of town.

Conventions and Conferences   A **convention** is one kind of formal meeting at which members of a large professional group elect officers, establish policies, conduct other business, and exchange information of interest to the profession. A **conference**, on the other hand, is a meeting at which the primary objective is to exchange information rather than to make group decisions. The main difference between conventions and large-scale conferences is that conferences usually don't involve voting, committee meetings, and other official business, since the participants are not members of an association.

Conventions and conferences are usually held in hotels or in special convention centers, often in major cities or at resorts. The sites for these large-scale meetings often have exhibit halls where vendors display products and services they hope to sell to participants. The displays provide a convenient way for participants to learn about new products in their profession. In smaller meeting rooms at a convention site, individual speakers present research papers or deliver talks on topics of interest to the profession. These smaller meetings may also feature panel discussions, films, slide presentations, and question-and-answer periods. Conventions and conferences help participants find out about technological, legal, political, and marketing developments in their field. For example, at the annual Office Automation Conference, office automation managers can attend panel discussions about new telecommunications technology and other current subjects, and they can view exhibits by information processing equipment vendors.

In addition to official business sessions, speeches, and panel discussions, conventions and conferences often involve social events, such as luncheons, cocktail parties, and dinners. The social events provide an opportunity for members of a profession to get to know each other and exchange useful business information.

Official Meetings Some companies have official meetings from time to time that are open to their stockholders or, if they are nonprofit organizations, their members. The elected officials of these groups also hold smaller official meetings more frequently. These meetings are formal, and discussion and decision making are generally carried out according to parliamentary procedure. The kinds of decisions that are made, however, vary according to the organization's purposes and bylaws. Official meetings may be held for special purposes, or they may be conducted annually, monthly, or on some other regular schedule.

Planning and Scheduling Meetings

The first thing to consider when you arrange a meeting is when it will take place. If the meeting is for a small group, you generally find a time when everyone can attend. But for larger conferences, stockholder meetings, or other gatherings that involve hundreds or thousands of participants, you generally arrange a time that is convenient for the people who will lead them.

Gathering Information

Before plans can be made for any meeting, it is important to gather as many facts as possible about the meeting. These facts include such details as the purpose of the meeting, the number of participants, and desired location. Obtaining as much information as possible will make your planning more efficient.

As soon as you begin to arrange a meeting, you should establish a file folder for any information that will help you plan the meeting, prepare for it, or conduct it. For example, you could include the correspondence between your boss and a client on the matter they will be discussing. You may also include information that your boss wants to give to the client.

When you make notes about conference room reservations, equipment, and supplies that will be needed during the meeting, include them in the folder as well. Check whether you will be asked to prepare slides or overhead transparencies to support a presentation.

Prepare a separate file folder for the day of the meeting that contains all the information your boss will need to conduct the meeting. Arrange these materials in the order of presentation.

Reserving Meeting Places and Equipment

The next thing to consider is where the meeting is to take place. Some formal meetings or informal gatherings are too large to take place in an office. In this case you will need to reserve conference rooms or other meeting places, either on the company's premises or

You will prepare two file folders for a meeting. The first you will use for filing information on the arrangements as they are made. The second you will give to the meeting's leader to help conduct the meeting.

at a hotel or conference center. The meeting place should be large enough to accommodate the group comfortably, but not so large that the group occupies only a small corner. A small group may feel uncomfortable in a room that is too large, and the members may have trouble hearing each other.

If you are making arrangements for a meeting with a hotel or conference center, you may be able to obtain a conference planning guide from the facility. The guide will provide you with basic information, such as sample floor plans, dining and catering information, descriptions of rooms, price lists and a variety of special information. This material can be very useful, especially if you are not able to visit the facility in advance.

Check that the room is appropriate for the equipment needed. For instance, if the meeting will include a technical presentation, make sure that the room you reserve can accommodate a projection screen or whatever equipment has been requested and that there are enough electrical outlets. You should also make sure that the room can be made dark enough for the screen to be seen easily.

Your file notes on room reservations and other arrangements should include the following items:

■ Descriptions of the rooms, services, and equipment you have ordered.

■ The dates when you plan to use the facilities.

■ The length of time you will be using the facilities.

■ Fees and payment methods.

■ The names of the people you made the arrangements with.

■ A copy of the letter you sent confirming the reservations.

This information will be helpful if you need to make changes in the arrangements as plans for a meeting progress. And written confirmation helps prevent misunderstandings.

You may also have to reserve equipment for an individual presentation. To reserve a slide projector or other equipment that your company owns, you would follow company procedures. If your company does not have the equipment you need, you may be able to rent it from a dealer listed in the Yellow Pages. And if the meeting is in a hotel or a similar location, you may be able to rent a meeting room that is already equipped for audiovisual presentations.

Notifying Participants

You will need to notify each participant of the meeting's time, location, and subject. How you go about telling participants and how far in advance of the meeting you do it will depend on the meeting's size and purpose. There are three basic ways of notifying participants of meetings.

Telephone Calls For small, informal meetings, you can notify participants by telephone. These meetings are usually scheduled only a few days before they occur, so make the calls as soon as you find out about the meeting. When time allows, meetings arranged by telephone should be followed up with a written confirmation.

Written Notices Because larger meetings involve many people, written notices are more efficient than telephone calls. You can compose a notice, process it, and distribute copies to two dozen participants in much less time than it would take to telephone all the participants. Written notices also reduce the chances of miscommunication.

Electronic Calendar If your company has an electronic calendar system you may be able to set aside coworkers' time for your meetings automatically. After you keyboard information about a meeting, the computer will check the participants' schedules and will either add the meeting to their calendars or let you know which participants already have plans for the proposed meeting time.

Composing a Meeting Notice

A meeting notice is supposed to do two things: give notice of a meeting and serve as a reminder. It should state the date, time, place, and purpose of the meeting. Figure 15-1 shows an example of a meeting notice displayed on an electronic mail system. If partici-

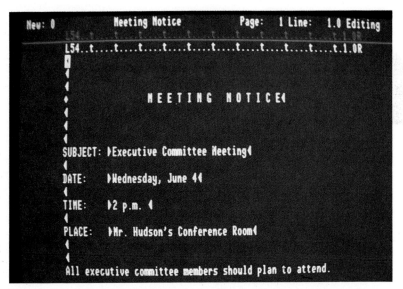

Fig. 15-1 For regularly scheduled meetings you can create a soft-copy notice form that includes standard information and blanks where you can keyboard date, time, place, and other information about each meeting. This form will save you time composing new notices each time the group meets.

pants are invited to present items for discussion at the meeting, the notice should request that they notify you of their presentation topics so you can add them to the meeting agenda. You should keep a copy for your own files and note the responses you receive from participants.

When you're preparing to send out a meeting notice, you should be aware of any group bylaws that might affect the content or timing of the notice. Some groups, for example, have a bylaw that specifies how far in advance of a meeting notices must be distributed. If you're arranging a meeting at which attendance is voluntary, you might also want to ask people to let you know if they intend to come. Then you'll be able to let caterers and other people involved in the event know the size of the group they can expect.

Following up on Notices You will need to follow up on meeting notices. Some people will respond; others will not get around to it, and you will have to telephone them. You should keep track of all responses in your file. One way to do this is illustrated in Fig. 15-2. Divide a sheet of paper into four columns: one column for the group members' names, one column for their department or other relevant information, one column with the heading "Yes," and one column with the heading "No." Make a check mark in the appropriate column next to each member's name as soon as you hear from that person.

For small, informal groups, you might follow up your meeting notices by calling the participants a few hours before the meeting and asking if they plan to attend. Explain tactfully that you are making a last-minute check on attendance. Your calls will serve as reminders for the participants, and the information you gather about who will be absent or late will help ensure that the meeting begins on time.

EXECUTIVE COMMITTEE MEETING: Attendance for June 4, 1987			
Name	Department	Yes	No
Leslie Amato	Marketing	✓	
George Johnson	Finance	✓	
Randolph Miller	Production		✓ (vacation)
Fay Peterson	Creative Services	✓	
Judith Smith	Product Development	✓	
Albert Sutton	Administration	✓	

Fig. 15-2 In order to make the practical arrangements for a meeting, you will need to know how many people will be coming. Here is one way of keeping track of responses to meeting notices.

```
                    ON-LINE INFORMATION SERVICES

                      Executive Committee Meeting

                           June 4, 1987


                              AGENDA

        1.  Review of marketing plans for ART INFO ON-LINE (Leslie Amato).

        2.  Review of second-quarter expenditures (George Johnson).

        3.  Production status report (Randolph Miller).

        4.  Review of third-quarter creative services budget (Fay Peterson).

        5.  New business.
```

Fig. 15-3 An agenda acts as a guide for a group's discussion.

Developing an Agenda

Meetings are generally better organized and more productive if they follow an agenda. An **agenda**, which may also be called the order of business or the calendar, is an outline of what will take place at a meeting. (See Fig. 15-3.) Agendas are almost always used for formal meetings and .are sometimes used in informal meetings as well. They help to guide the discussion and keep participants on track. Sometimes an agenda may include a schedule indicating how much time should be taken up for each order of business listed.

Using a word processor to prepare the agenda can be helpful since last minute changes often occur. Another advantage is that once the final agenda has been prepared, various output devices can be utilized to produce a document that looks like it was typeset. Often graphics can be used to provide a more "finished" look.

It may be part of your job to develop an agenda for any meeting that you organize. To do this, you will need to obtain a list of the items that will be discussed at the meeting. For an official meeting, you will also need to review the minutes of the group's last meeting to see if there was any unfinished business that was to be carried over. Finally, you will need to check for agenda items in the meeting file folder you have been keeping.

PARLIAMENTARY PROCEDURE

The usual order of business for a group following parliamentary procedure is something like this:

- The presiding officer calls the meeting to order by stating, "The meeting will now come to order."
- The secretary calls the roll (or notes silently who is present).
- The secretary announces whether the attendance constitutes a **quorum**, or the number required by the group before a vote can take place.
- The secretary reads the minutes of the last meeting and asks whether members would like to offer any additions or corrections.
- The group votes on whether to approve the minutes of the last meeting. If something is incorrect or has been left out of

the minutes, the group may vote to amend them. If there are no additions or corrections, the secretary states that the minutes stand approved as read.
- The officers read their reports to the group and give copies of them to the secretary. These are followed by reports from standing committees and then reports from special committees, copies of which are given to the secretary.
- Items of unfinished business remaining from the last meeting are discussed.
- Items of new business are discussed.
- Any new committee appointments are made.
- The group nominates and elects people for any group offices that are open.
- The next meeting date is established.
- The meeting is adjourned.

If the meeting group has bylaws, you should review them to see if they set forth a specific order for discussing business. If the bylaws don't specify the order of business, or if the meeting group does not have bylaws, check minutes and agendas from previous meetings to see if the group's agenda usually follows a set order. Otherwise, set up an agenda according to the steps in the box on parliamentary procedure.

Preparing for the Meeting

On the day of the meeting, check to see that the room in which the meeting will be held is clean and tidy. You also need to make sure that it has everything you need. Check the following items:

- **Atmosphere**. The room should be a pleasant temperature, with sufficient light and ventilation.

You can establish the tone of the meeting with your arrangements.

- **Furnishings**. Make sure that there are enough tables and chairs and that they are set up so that the participants can see each other and projection screens, if used.

- **Equipment**. If you have requested special equipment, such as a tape recorder, a slide projector, or a computer, you should check to see that the equipment is in place and works properly.

- **Supplies**. Be sure that you have provided paper, pencils, markers, and any special materials the participants need. If the meeting has many participants who do not know each other, you may provide name tags as well. If smoking is permitted, you should supply ashtrays.

- **Other meeting materials**. You might also supply materials that relate to the meeting, such as a list of the names and affiliations of the people attending, copies of the last meeting's minutes, or the agenda for this meeting.

- **Refreshments**. Often participants are offered coffee, tea, and simple refreshments such as doughnuts. If tea and coffee are not available in your office, perhaps you can obtain them from the company cafeteria or have them catered.

Support Duties During Meetings

Your boss will probably expect you to perform a number of duties while a meeting is in progress. The first of these may be to greet participants as they arrive. Make sure they know where to leave coats and which room to go to. Unless somebody is hired to prepare a transcript of the meeting, you will probably be asked to take notes. Efficient note-taking requires some advance planning.

Taking Notes

Before the meeting begins, take time to study the agenda, review the previous meeting's minutes, and look over the other materials in your meeting folder to acquaint yourself with the items that are likely to be discussed. The more you know about what is going on, the easier it will be to take notes.

Sit next to the person who will lead the meeting so that you can hear everything that is going on. If you miss something a speaker has said, ask the speaker to repeat it, or give the leader of the meeting a prearranged signal that will prompt him or her to ask for a repetition. If you miss a speaker's name, make a note to determine his or her identity after the meeting.

Note the names of group members who are present, of those who are absent, and of those who arrive late or leave the room during the meeting. This information may be important for the voting records of the group, especially if the group votes on a controversial issue.

Your notes should cover everything of consequence that occurs, but they don't need to cover everything that is said. If you are not sure if a statement is important enough to be included, take notes on it and decide later. If the meeting is being tape-recorded, your notes should include any data that are not on the tape, such as the names and titles of speakers and the times when the meeting started and ended.

Obtaining Transcripts Stockholders' meetings and some other official meetings often require **transcripts**, which are word-for-word records of everything that was said during the meeting. Transcripts are generally prepared by specialists who use shorthand machines to record speeches and who then transcribe the shorthand. Transcripts generally have to be approved and signed by the group's presiding officer.

Using a Tape Recorder Your duties may include operating a tape recorder during a meeting. If possible, you should set up two tape recorders before the meeting; then you won't have to interrupt the meeting or lose information while you change tapes. All you have to do is remember to activate the second recorder when the tape on the first is about to run out. Keep tapes of meetings until the transcripts, minutes, or summaries have been signed by the group's secretary or approved by your supervisor.

Special Meeting Considerations

So far this chapter has focused primarily on meetings in which the participants gather in an office or in a conference room. However, some of the meetings you help to organize may take place under different circumstances. To arrange these meetings, you will need to make additional plans and preparations.

Small Mealtime Meetings

Some meetings involve meals in restaurants, hotel dining rooms, or executive dining rooms. Most meetings like these take place at lunchtime or in the evening, but breakfast meetings are becoming popular. A small mealtime meeting usually involves two or three executives who discuss a project among themselves or with outside clients or suppliers.

Reserving Tables   When you schedule a small mealtime meeting, you need to make a table reservation. If you are asked to select a restaurant, choose one that offers privacy and where the food, service, and atmosphere are highly recommended by business people. If the restaurant is especially popular, you may need to call days or weeks in advance. Otherwise, you can call just an hour or two ahead of time to reserve a table. State your supervisor's name, the number of people who will be at the table, and the time they will arrive. When you note the time of the reservation, include the name, address, and phone number of the restaurant as well as the name in which you made the reservation.

Other Considerations   If you would like any special treatment, such as getting a table next to a window or a small, private dining room, request it when you make the reservation. If the group includes vegetarians or other people with special diets, mention this to the restaurant staff in advance. Ask about the restaurant's policy on smoking; if it segregates smokers from nonsmokers, specify the area in which you want your table. Also, find out which credit cards the restaurant accepts.

Large Mealtime Meetings

For larger meetings, you must make more elaborate arrangements. For example, you may have to select a menu and organize place cards, flowers, and other decorations. The meeting may include a

Luncheon and dinner meetings can provide an excellent atmosphere for top executive sessions, director's meetings, and award presentations.

predinner cocktail hour and after-dinner entertainment, which you might also have to arrange.

Most hotels and restaurants with large dining rooms have employees who are trained in arranging mealtime meetings. They can help you plan the meal, choose the decor, arrange the seating, and deal with many of the other details. Usually they will offer you a number of options, depending on your budget. You would probably discuss the options with your supervisor.

USING SPREADSHEETS TO PLAN MEETINGS

You can use an electronic spreadsheet or integrated software to help organize the many separate details of a large-scale meeting. For instance, on a spreadsheet you can label the rows to represent individual expense items, such as the cost of an airline ticket for a speaker and the fee you must pay for a dinner-dance orchestra. The columns represent expense categories, such as entertainment and transportation. When you enter an expense item on the grid, the computer can automatically recalculate the other figures on the grid that are affected. For example, after you enter the cost of an airline ticket, the computer can recalculate the total expenditure for travel, the total expendi-

ture for the conference, and the amount remaining in your budget for travel and for the entire conference. This can help you determine easily whether you are likely to stay within your budget for expense categories and for the whole event or whether you need to adjust your plans.

You might also consider how the computer software you normally use can eliminate duplication of work when you organize a meeting. You can use word processing, list merging, data base management, graphics, and communications programs to process and distribute the many notices and letters you will handle and record.

Conventions and Conferences

If your supervisor attends a convention or conference, your responsibilities will probably include filling out registration forms, making travel and hotel reservations, and preparing a cash advance. At some point, though, you may be asked to help plan a convention or conference. Since no convention or conference is ever like any other, there is no set formula for organizing one. When you plan one of these events, you perform many separate tasks. Because the job of arranging a convention is so complex, you need to be very well organized.

Most large-scale meetings include a number of smaller meetings. There may be exhibit rooms in which vendors display equipment or information on their services. There may also be various speeches or panel discussions in rooms adjacent to the main meeting place.

The people who attend conventions and conferences generally divide their time between visiting the main exhibit rooms, or listening to the main speakers, and attending some of the smaller discussion groups and specialized meetings. They might also attend mealtime meetings and cocktail parties.

In a way, then, planning a convention or conference is like planning several smaller meetings and coordinating them so that they fit together. But several additional considerations are involved:

Site Selection   Selecting a site for a convention or conference is much more complex than choosing a location for an ordinary business meeting. Conventions or conferences are generally held in resorts or large cities. The meeting sessions and accommodations may all be at a single location, or participants may stay at several hotels near a convention center that houses the meeting rooms and vendors' exhibits.

Speakers   You may be involved in booking speakers or members of discussion panels. You can do this by writing letters or making phone calls that explain the nature of the meeting, the topics for discussion, and how long the talks should be. You should also ask each speaker for biographical data to include in publicity for the conference. Also, ask if the speaker will require any particular type of meeting room or equipment for the discussion. Follow up your phone calls with letters confirming the arrangements you have made.

Registration   There are several ways to register for a conference. Written notification of conference dates generally includes forms the recipients can use to register for the meetings by mail. You may

Once the convention has begun, the administrative assistant should move away from the registration area, circulate to troubleshoot any problems, direct speakers to rooms, and answer hotel staff members' questions.

be responsible for distributing or receiving these forms. And you will need to set up a registration desk at the entrance to the convention center for participants who didn't register by mail. The people who staff the desk are responsible for collecting registration fees and distributing name tags and packets of information about the conference.

Reporting the Conference   Academic and professional organizations sometimes publish the proceedings of important conferences so that members and outsiders can obtain them. These publications are written and edited by specially trained reporters, and they may contain copies of research papers that speakers presented at the conference. You may be asked to help prepare such materials for publication. You will need to obtain copies of speeches and papers presented at the conference, as well as the speakers' permission to publish them, and you may be expected to locate reporters.

Tape Recordings   Some companies specialize in tape-recording the meeting sessions at conferences and producing tape cassettes that they sell to members of the group. This service can be helpful to participants who cannot attend all the sessions that interest them, perhaps because two or more sessions of interest are scheduled for the same time. You may be responsible for arranging this service.

CONVENTION BUREAUS

Most cities and resorts that are suitable for large-scale meetings have convention bureaus. Your first step in selecting a site is to write or call the convention bureaus or resort staffs at the places you are considering. Ask for this information:

- The names, addresses, and phone numbers of hotels and descriptions of their facilities.
- Transportation between the hotels and the airport and between the hotels and the convention center.
- Weather conditions at the time of year the convention is scheduled for.
- Sightseeing and other recreational opportunities.
- The sizes of the meeting rooms.
- Catering arrangements.
- The location of the hotels with regard to the convention center and the downtown area.
- The overall quality of the hotels.
- The number of hotel rooms available at the time you want.

Teleconferences and Computer Conferences

As you have read, large-scale meetings are sometimes conducted as teleconferences or computer conferences rather than as gatherings at single convention centers. This enables participants to sit in on meeting sessions without traveling great distances or staying out of the office for several days.

A computer conference is a variation of electronic mail. It can include graphic and verbal messages. For instance, a participant could use a light pen to draw a picture of a proposed package design to display to the other participants.

Teleconferences are also used for small meetings. Growing numbers of organizations with several distant offices are installing teleconference rooms so that employees at different locations can hold staff meetings together, without traveling. If your company has several offices, you may be responsible for scheduling a teleconference. You would have to reserve the teleconference room and equipment, using the same skills you use to reserve other kinds of meeting places. You might also be asked to sit in at one of the teleconference sites to take notes, to operate equipment, and to provide other kinds of support, just as you would if the participants were all gathered in one place. If the meeting is an audio teleconference, your duties could include scheduling and placing calls and connecting all the participants through an operator or a computerized phone system. Also, you may be asked to listen to the conference and take notes.

Another way that people can hold meetings without leaving their offices is through a computer conference, in which participants use linked computers to send each other messages. All the participants may be at their terminals at the same time for a computer conference, or the messages can be stored in the computer and read at a participant's convenience. Your role in a computer conference might include keyboarding messages and retrieving stored messages, or scheduling the conference and organizing materials.

Teleconferences and computer conferences should be planned in advance so that you can distribute background materials to the participants ahead of time. And you can sometimes send documents electronically while a meeting is going on.

Follow-Up on Meetings

After a meeting you generally perform some follow-up tasks. Some of these tasks relate to the meeting itself; others may result from decisions that were made during the meeting.

One very important follow-up duty is to prepare a report about what took place at the meeting. The report may be in the form of a summary for the participants of an informal meeting, or it may be an official record of the meeting called the **minutes**. The minutes are kept in an organization's permanent files. When you transcribe your notes into a report, you should emphasize the actions the group took rather than what each member said.

Processing the Minutes

Most groups keep minutes of their meetings, although in many offices this is not done for informal meetings, such as staff meetings. However, keeping minutes of meetings is always advisable. Even though the minutes may not be disseminated, a record of the proceedings can be kept on file, in case they are needed. If confidential items are discussed, the person conducting the meeting can request that they be left out of the minutes. For informal meetings the principle may have the secretary take minutes or may request that it be done by a member of the group. Figure 15-4 is an example of the minutes of an informal meeting.

Corporations are required by law to keep minutes of stockholders' and directors' meetings. If you serve as the secretary of an ongoing group, one of your official duties will be to record its minutes.

You should begin the minutes by stating the name of the group, the date, place, and purpose of the meeting, its starting time, the name and title of the person who led the meeting, the names of those in attendance, and whether a quorum was present. You should also indicate whether the meeting was held according to a

```
                      ON-LINE INFORMATION SERVICES
                    Meeting of the Executive Committee
                               June 4, 1987

ATTENDANCE

     The monthly executive committee meeting was held in the office of
J. R. Hudson, Vice President and General Manager, at 2 p.m. on
June 4, 1987.  Mr. Hudson presided.  Those present were Leslie Amato,
George Johnson, Fay Peterson, and Albert Sutton.  Randolph Miller
was absent.

AGENDA ITEMS COVERED

     1.  Leslie Amato presented the marketing plans for the new product,
ART INFO ON-LINE.  It was decided to move the launch date from
June 1 to September 1, due to delays in getting the program up and
running.  The rest of the plan was approved.

     2.  George Johnson reviewed second-quarter expenditures.
All departments were within or under budget for the quarter to date.

     3.  Randolph Miller presented the production status report.
ART INFO is the only major project not on schedule.  It was agreed
to reschedule it as stated in item 1 above.

     4.  Fay Peterson reviewed the creative services budget for third
quarter.  It was estimated that an additional $30,000 would be needed
to cover promotional plans for the launch of ART INFO.  It was decided
that Fay would meet separately with Leslie Amato and George Johnson
to develop a strategy for implementing the original plan without going
over budget.  Mr. Hudson asked Fay to present a report and
recommendation by June 15.

DISCUSSION

     Judith Smith presented a proposal for a new product that would
supply information to businesses on convention sites in the United
States and throughout the world.  Members of the committee were asked
to review the proposal and prepare a response for next month's
meeting.

     Mr. Hudson requested that each department prepare a report on the
status and utilization of microcomputers by all personnel within the
department.

ADJOURNMENT

     The meeting was adjourned at 3:25 p.m.
```

Fig. 15-4 Here is an example of the format used for the minutes of a business meeting. Most business organizations do not use the terms "old and new business," but many private organizations use these terms. You should check to find out the specific terminology used in the organization you work for.

regular schedule or if it was called for a special purpose. Next you should establish that the presiding officer called the meeting and notified members in accordance with the bylaws. The minutes should summarize the group's discussion of each topic rather than quote speakers verbatim. For formal meetings you must include the exact wording of each **motion**, or proposal, that was introduced as well as the names of the people who introduced and seconded it and how the group voted (or why it did not vote) on it. You should also give the details of any action the group took. Acknowledge the efforts of individual members, and mention any correspondence the group received from former members.

Use a professional tone in writing the minutes, and be careful not to write them in a way that reflects your opinions. The purpose of the minutes is to provide an unbiased record of what occurred, so phrases such as *heated discussion* and *thorough and accurate report* are inappropriate.

Devote a separate paragraph of the minutes to each item discussed or acted on at the meeting. Rather than record what happened in chronological order, you can group related discussions or actions together if this makes the minutes easier to follow. You should transcribe your notes while the meeting is still fresh in your mind. Here are some guidelines to help you prepare the meeting report:

■ Capitalize and center the heading that indicates the group's title or purpose, and include subject headings to help readers find information in the minutes.

■ Use either single spacing or double spacing for the final copy. (Double spacing makes the report easier to read.)

■ Leave generous margins, and indent five to ten spaces at the beginning of every paragraph.

■ Number the pages at the bottom, and if the minutes are likely to be used for reference at future meetings, include line numbers in the margin (this will make it easier for the group to follow the discussion involving the minutes).

■ Capitalize business titles and words that refer to the meeting group or the organization that employs its members, such as *Committee, Company,* and *Corporation.*

■ Print out or type the hard copy of the report on plain white paper.

You may be asked to distribute copies of the minutes before you read them aloud at the next meeting. The minutes of the last meeting are usually approved without comment, but occasionally someone may point out an error or omission. If this happens, use a pen to write in the correction and strike out the incorrect portion. A copy of each meeting's minutes, signed by the secretary, should be filed with the group's permanent records. The bylaws may also require that the minutes be signed by the president.

Tying Up the Loose Ends

After the meeting or conference is over and you have processed the minutes, there will still be some miscellaneous tasks that will need your attention.

Paying Bills   Within a short time after a meeting or conference, you will have to process and pay the bills for meeting rooms, audio-visual equipment, transcripts, meals, and any other facilities or services that were rented or purchased for the meeting. It is a good idea to check these bills against the confirmation letters in your meeting folder.

Processing Correspondence   During a meeting, participants may make decisions or raise questions that require correspondence. Your follow-up work may include writing and processing letters that provide information requested during the meeting.

Processing Resolutions   During an official meeting, a group may adopt a **resolution**, which is a formal expression of opinion or intention that it wishes to convey to another group or person. Resolutions are often written before the meeting by the participants who propose them, but sometimes a group will ask its secretary to compose one. The group's secretary—or a support worker on that person's office staff—is also responsible for processing the resolution, having it signed by the group's officers, distributing it, and incorporating it into the meeting minutes.

Evaluating the Meeting   An evaluation is another important task when you follow up on a meeting. Review the meeting file, and consider the ways in which the meeting was a success and how it might have been better. Think about any problems that arose and what you might do to prevent or solve them at future meetings. Also, keep notes on any people or businesses that helped to make the meeting a success. These might include speakers, hotels, restaurants, interpreters, and any other person or organization whose services you might wish to obtain again in the future. When you follow up each meeting with an evaluation, you give yourself information you can use to organize successful meetings in the future.

■ Summary

- The success of any meeting depends on information, planning, preparation, and follow-up.

- Meetings range from informal to highly structured formal events. Informal meetings, which generally occur in the office, involve discussions of everyday business. Formal meetings include those that follow parliamentary procedure and large conferences where participants exchange information.

- Staff meetings, committee meetings, and supplier/client meetings are usually informal. Conventions and conferences are formal, as are official gatherings of ongoing groups.

- Scheduling an informal meeting can be as simple as making a phone call and a calendar notation of the time when all the participants can attend. To schedule a large-scale meeting, you must reserve meeting rooms and other facilities months in advance.

- For each meeting you arrange, keep a file folder that includes copies of confirmation letters and any information that can help you prepare for it. Prepare a separate folder for the day of the meeting that contains all the materials needed for conducting the meeting.

- Notify participants through phone calls or written notices of the date, time, and place of the meeting and its topic or the fact that it is a regularly scheduled meeting.

- On the day of the meeting, check the room where it will take place. See that it is clean, orderly, and comfortable. Also, check any equipment and supplies that will be needed.

- Some meetings require special arrangements. For example, if a group is meeting over a meal, you may need to make a restaurant reservation. For a conference or convention, months of planning will be necessary.

- Meetings generally require follow-up work by office employees. This work may include processing the minutes of the meeting, writing summaries, paying bills, processing correspondence resulting from the meeting, and evaluating the meeting.

■ Review Questions

1. What four elements are essential to the success of any meeting?

2. Where would you look for information on parliamentary procedure?

3. What is the difference between a conference and a convention?

4. What information should you include in a letter confirming the rental of a meeting room?

5. What information should you include in a meeting notice?

6. What is the first item on a standard agenda for an ongoing group?

7. Describe the most efficient way of tape-recording a lengthy meeting.

8. Do all the participants in a computer conference need to be at their terminals at the same time? Explain your answer.

9. Distinguish between meeting minutes and meeting summaries.

10. How can evaluating a meeting when it is over help you plan future meetings?

■ Technical Vocabulary

informal meetings
formal meetings
parliamentary procedure
convention
conference
agenda

quorum
transcript
minutes
motion
resolution

■ Discussion and Skills Development

1. Using the information below, compose a meeting notice to inform members about the next meeting.

   The New Jersey Truck Dealers Association, which has its headquarters at 32 River Road, Stockton, N.J. 08559, meets on the first Thursday of each month at 3 p.m. to hear a speaker or panel discussion. This is followed by a question-and-answer session, cocktails, and dinner. The location varies from month to month. Each meeting features a speaker or panel discussion. To make final arrangements for each month's meeting, you need to know a few days in advance how many of the group's members will attend. Your office phone number is 609-555-1017.

2. You have reserved a conference room down the hall from your office for a large staff meeting at 3 p.m. Another group is scheduled to meet there this morning. After lunch you go to the conference room to prepare it for your meeting and discover that it is a mess. The room smells of cigarette smoke and greasy food. The conference table is littered with coffee cups. Your meeting is set to begin in an hour. What options do you have?

3. Choose one of the major convention cities in the United States (for example, Atlanta, Chicago, San Francisco, or New York), and use reference materials from your school or public library to find out all you can about the facilities it has to offer. Prepare a report for your class in which you describe the convention facilities, hotel accommodations, and restaurant and entertainment facilities.

4. Go to a nearby hotel that handles conferences, and observe the facilities that the hotel has to offer. Make a list of the

equipment and services that the hotel provides in order to attract conference customers.

5. Imagine that you have been asked to arrange a meeting at a local hotel for 30 business people. They will be coming in from out of town and staying for two days and two nights. Make a list of all the arrangements you will need to take care of.

chapter 16
Arranging Business Trips

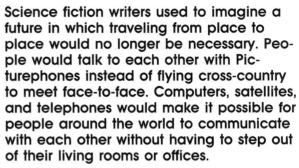

Science fiction writers used to imagine a future in which traveling from place to place would no longer be necessary. People would talk to each other with Picturephones instead of flying cross-country to meet face-to-face. Computers, satellites, and telephones would make it possible for people around the world to communicate with each other without having to step out of their living rooms or offices.

This technology exists now, and some electronic marvels, such as conference calling and electronic messages, have become familiar tools in the modern office. But business people still travel as much as they ever did. Company professionals still go to conventions. Real estate dealers still travel to inspect factories and offices in far-flung corners of the world. Sales representatives and managers attend regional sales meetings. And company executives take contracts and plans to clients in far-away cities.

It will probably be an important part of your job to help get business people to their destinations. You will be expected to make arrangements for your supervisors' hotel rooms, rental cars, and meals and to get them back home again—all with a minimum of fuss. You will have to prepare lists of travel arrangements and business appointments, and you will have to make sure your supervisors have the proper business documents to take with them.

Finally, it will be up to you to keep the office running smoothly while your supervisors are away and to help them evaluate their trips once they return. To do all these things, you will need to use information-gathering, communications, and decision-making skills. In this chapter you'll learn about the many details that you'll need to take into account when planning a business trip. And you'll learn to use computers and other electronic equipment to make your trip planning more efficient.

The first step in planning any trip is to start a file folder. As you gather the information you need, place it in the file folder. If you're arranging a trip for some of your company's executives, you'll need to ask them many questions before you can make the arrangements for them. Here are some of the things you need to know:

- At what time of the day do they want to leave and return?
- How many days will they be gone?
- Will they travel by plane, train, or car?
- If they are flying, do they prefer smoking or nonsmoking sections? aisle or window seats?

- Does anyone require a special meal (for example, vegetarian) on the plane?
- Does anyone prefer one airline over another?
- Should you reserve a rental car for them at their destination?
- Do they prefer a particular hotel?
- How many rooms will be needed?
- Should you make restaurant reservations for them?
- What documents will they need to take with them?
- Do they need any special equipment, such as a tape recorder or slide projector?

Making Travel Arrangements

When you are making travel arrangements, you have several options to pursue for making the actual reservations. For example, you may use a travel agency, work with your company's travel department, use your computer to access an electronic on-line reservation service, or contact the airlines, hotels, and car rental agencies yourself. What you do usually depends on the size of your company and the kinds of arrangements you are asked to make. Some companies are too small to have their own travel department, while other companies maintain a contract with a travel agency. Even if your company routinely uses a travel agency, you might prefer to arrange simple trips yourself. On the other hand, you would need the services of a specialized travel agency to arrange for a complicated trip like a company trade mission to China.

Travel Agencies

Travel agents can make airline, railroad, rental car, and hotel/motel reservations for you easily. They use computerized data bases to find the lowest fares and most convenient flight schedules. They also use printed guides and schedules to determine hotel room rates and facilities. Travel agents are paid commissions by the airlines and hotels they book. They usually do not charge a client.

Selecting a Travel Agent   Your company may require you to use a particular agency, or you may have to pick one yourself. If you choose the agency, be sure to pick an agency that specializes in

Most travel agents have computer terminals that enable them to check schedules and make reservations directly with airlines, car rental agencies, and hotels. Your travel itinerary can be printed out automatically once all of the arrangements have been confirmed.

business travel. These agencies usually deliver tickets and other documents to your office at no extra charge.

Working With the Agent Call the travel agent as soon as you're prepared to make flight and hotel reservations. By making reservations as far in advance as possible, you can save your company money and make certain that your travelers get the flights and hotels they want.

Have your trip file folder in front of you, and be prepared to pass on the information you have gathered. For example, if you're arranging for two company executives to go from Los Angeles to Detroit, you might provide the travel agent with the following information:

■ They plan to fly to Detroit on March 3 and return on March 5. They do not plan to make any other stops, and they will spend two nights in Detroit.

■ They have no preference for any particular airline, but they want to fly nonstop to Detroit in the morning and return to Los Angeles on an evening flight.

- They both want to fly first-class, and they both prefer aisle seats, but one wants to be in a nonsmoking section.

- They want a rental car to be waiting for them at the airport in Detroit, preferably a large four-door sedan.

- They require separate rooms in a downtown hotel for the nights of March 3 and 4. They prefer double, rather than single, rooms.

- If your company will pay for the airline tickets, car rental, and hotel rooms by credit card, you need to give the agent the credit card number and expiration date. The travel agent could also bill the company directly.

Some companies may require their employees to fly in coach class or to use certain airlines or hotel chains which offer special corporate rates or discounts. If your company has any such policies, you should inform the travel agent. Once the agency makes the arrangements, it will mail or deliver the tickets and an **itinerary**, which is a document that lists departure and arrival times, flight numbers, hotel addresses and telephone numbers, and other details of the trip. Examine the tickets and the itinerary carefully to make sure that the arrangements they describe are the ones you requested and that the information they contain is complete and correct.

Corporate Travel Departments

Some large companies have their own travel departments for booking business trips. They function just like travel agencies and may even receive the same commissions from hotels and airlines. If your company has a travel department, you will provide it with the same information that you would give to a travel agency. The travel department will then give you a choice of flights and hotels so that you or the traveler can pick the most convenient schedule. The travel department will also provide tickets and a travel itinerary.

Arranging Trips Yourself

If you work for a small company, or if you have to arrange a trip at the last minute, you may have to make all the arrangements with airlines, hotels, and car rental agencies on your own. The next few pages will explain the procedures you will follow when making travel arrangements on your own.

Transportation

If you have to arrange transportation for company executives, the first question to ask is how they will travel. Will they take a train or plane to their destination? Will they take cabs or limousines to and from the airport or train station? Will they require rental cars? Most people fly when they have to go 300 miles or more because flying is the fastest way to get there. Large airlines can take travelers to any major city in the United States. **Commuter airlines** can carry them from major airports to smaller airports or between major airports that are not far apart.

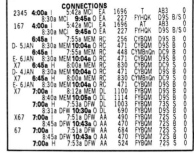

Fig. 16-1 Official airline guides are published monthly for international travel and every two weeks for domestic travel. These publications help you determine connections available and the time needed for traveling from one city to another.

Airlines If your company frequently makes airline reservations, it may subscribe to the *Official Airline Guide*. This directory, published every two weeks, lists airline routes and schedules between major American cities. Figure 16-1 provides a sample listing from the *Official Airline Guide* showing flights from Houston, Texas, to Chicago, Illinois.

The first line of the table tells you that Houston is on central standard time and that the official airport code for Houston is HOU. The second line provides one-letter abbreviations for airports; for example, *1-IAH* means that *I* stands for the International Airport in Houston. Reading from left to right across the next line of the table, you learn the following:

- Column 1 indicates flight frequency. Each number represents one of the seven days of the week. *2345* means the flight is every Tuesday, Wednesday, Thursday, and Friday; *X67* means every day except Saturday and Sunday.

- Column 2 shows the time the flight departs. The plane leaves at 4:18 a.m.

- Column 3 is the one-letter abbreviation for the airport from which the flight is leaving.

- Columns 4 and 5 indicate the time the flight will arrive and the airport at which it will land. In this case, the first flight lands at 6:30 a.m. at O'Hare Airport.

- Column 6 indicates the name of the airline. The letters *EA, AA, WN,* and *UA* stand for Eastern Airlines, American Airlines, Southwest Airlines, and United Airlines.

- The numbers in column 7 are the flight numbers.

- The letters in column 8 are codes for the classes (*T* is coach economy discounted, *A* is first class discounted, *F* is first class, *Y* is coach economy, and so on).

- Column 9 shows the kinds of planes used on the flight: *AB3* means the plane is an airbus industrie, *72S* means the plane is a

727, and so on. The letters *B*, *L*, *S*, and *D* in the next column mean that breakfast, lunch, a snack, or dinner will be served on the flight.

■ The 0, 2, or 3 in column 11 means either that the flight is nonstop or that it will make two or three stops.

If nonstop flights are not available, you should consult the part of the table labeled "Connections." This shows where and when connecting flights can be caught. For example, the first entry shows that a traveler can take an Eastern Airlines flight from Houston at 4 a.m. and arrive in Kansas City, Missouri, at 5:42 a.m. He or she would then leave Kansas City at 8:30 a.m. and arrive in Chicago at 9:45 a.m.

The *Official Airline Guide* used to list fares between cities, but airlines today have become very competitive and offer too many different kinds of fare plans. Many companies subscribe to an electronic version of the *Official Airline Guide*, which allows a computer operator to call up flight information and airfares on a computer screen. Companies can also subscribe to an electronic data base, such as Duns Net or Computravel, that provides detailed information about flight schedules and airfares.

Selecting an Airline

Most big cities are served by several major airlines. You should choose the airline that has the most convenient schedules and the best fares. If you were arranging a trip by plane from Houston to Chicago, for example, you would start by choosing three or four possible flight times, after consulting the *Official Airline Guide*, an electronic data base, or individual airlines.

```
FROM-NEW YORK,NY:NEWARK,NJ,USA
# TO-SAN FRANCISCO:OAKLAND,CA,USA
1* 1000A  EWR  110P  SFO PE   5 747 F 0
2  1040A  LGA  300P  SFO RC 343 72S L 1
3* 1100A  JFK  148P  SFO UA  25 767 L 0
4* 1200N  JFK  248P  SFO AA  17 767 L 0
5* 1225P  LGA  535P  SFO AA 491 D10 L 1
6  1228P  EWR  617P  SFO EA 201 757 L 2
  * THOMAS COOK TICKETING ONLY
ENTER +,-,CX,X#,F#,RS,B#(#=LINE NUMBER)
  #  <

          DIRECT FLIGHTS     TUE-01 APR
FROM-NEW YORK,NY:NEWARK,NJ,USA
# TO-SAN FRANCISCO:OAKLAND,CA,USA
1*  200P  EWR  510P  SFO PE  21 747 F 0
2   335P  LGA  850P  SFO DL  99 L10 S 1
3*  355P  EWR  840P  SFO TW 171 L10 S 1
4   400P  EWR  910P  SFO WO  79 D10 D 1
5*  415P  JFK  720P  SFO PA  85 747 D 0
6*  530P  JFK  835P  SFO AA  19 767 D 0
  * THOMAS COOK TICKETING ONLY
USE +,-,0,CX,X#,F#,RS,B#(#=LINE NUMBER)
  0  <
  Receiving B:OAG  (ALT-R or PgDn to Terminate)
```

One benefit of the electronic guide is that up-to-date information on alternative flights and fares is available automatically. You have more choices and can make better decisions with this information.

When you use a frequent flier bonus, you may be given a coupon or number by the travel agent. Or the bonus mileage may be credited when you check in at the airport.

It is part of your job to obtain the lowest fares available for the required flights. Fares vary according to how far in advance reservations are made, how many days passengers intend to spend at their destinations, and which days of the week or hours of the day they intend to fly.

In order to attract repeat business, some airlines offer "frequent-flier bonuses" to business customers. One airline, for example, offers free round-trip tickets between any two of the North American airports it serves to travelers who book at least 15 trips with that airline. If your employer is enrolled in an airline's frequent-flier program, you will want to book flights on that airline as often as possible to earn credits toward free flights.

■ Making Reservations

Airlines have either toll-free numbers or local telephone numbers you can call to make reservations. Again, you will be passing on much of the information you collected when you interviewed your employer about his or her trip. The reservations clerk will need to know the traveler's destination and the desired dates and times of day for traveling. The clerk may then offer you a choice of flights that more or less fit your requirements.

When you make reservations, try to choose a nonstop flight or one that does not require a change of planes. Most business travelers do not want to waste time with stopovers or risk missing a connecting flight. Travelers who are flying long distances or overseas may want to arrive a day or so in advance of their appointments so that they have time to recover from **jet lag**, the fatigue and confusion that result from flying across several time zones.

The reservations clerk will need to know whether the traveler intends to travel first-class or coach. First-class travel is more costly but provides extra comforts and conveniences. Some companies may require all their employees to fly coach, while others expect high-level employees to travel first-class so that they can arrive at their destinations rested and ready to work.

Many travelers prefer to fly on airlines that allow seat selection when reservations are confirmed, because this saves them time at the airport. If the airline you have chosen permits advance seat assignments, the reservations clerk will ask whether the traveler wants to sit in a smoking or nonsmoking section and whether he or she prefers an aisle or window seat. If your boss requires a special kosher, vegetarian, or salt-free meal, this is the time to inform the airline clerk.

Finally, the airline clerk will want to know how your company will pay for the tickets and whether the airline should send them to your office or hold them for the traveler to pick up at the time of the flight. You will need to make careful notes about the flight numbers, the dates and times of arrival and departure, the seat numbers, and other details. Repeat this information to the clerk to make sure you have noted it correctly. Find out whether the airline can confirm the arrangements immediately or whether you must call again to confirm them later. It is usually necessary to confirm overseas flights three days before departure.

Last-Minute Changes   You might have to cancel or postpone a trip at the last minute or make some other changes in the reservations. If so, telephone the airline as soon as possible. Some airlines may charge your company a higher fare or a penalty fee for changing the reservations. If you book your supervisor on a flight that will require additional payment if the reservation is changed, be sure that he or she is aware of this before you confirm the reservation. If your employer decides during the trip to change the return reservation, you can usually do that with a call to your local airline office. Major airlines keep reservation information in a central data base that is accessible to all their reservations clerks. You can obtain a refund or credit card adjustment on unused tickets by submitting them to the airline or your travel agent.

Special Commercial Flights   When suitable airline flights aren't available, companies may charter planes or helicopters to take employees to their destinations. Some companies also use air taxis, which are small planes and helicopters that carry a few passengers at a time on frequent flights between nearby cities. These services are generally more expensive than regular airline flights, but sometimes they are the only way to get from one place to another in a hurry.

Railroads Business people traveling from one nearby city to another may find it more convenient to take a train than to fly. In many cities business offices and train stations are centrally located, while the airports are located miles away. So taking a train is a more convenient way to travel. For example, you can fly from New York to Washington, D.C., in about an hour, but it may take an hour or more to get from an office in midtown Manhattan to an airport and another hour to get from a Washington airport to a downtown office. A three-hour Metroliner train ride between the business districts of the two cities may be easier and more relaxing. It may also be cheaper because on heavily traveled routes, train fares are usually less expensive than airfares.

You can reserve seats and sleeping accommodations in advance on many trains, but some travel agents will not book train trips within the United States, so you may have to make the arrangements yourself. To find out about train service between cities, you would call Amtrak or look under *Railroads* in your local Yellow Pages. Your company may also subscribe to the *Official Railway Guide*, a directory similar to the *Official Airline Guide*, which includes the schedules of all railroads in the United States and Canada.

Traveling by Car In some cases the best way for a business person to get from one place to another is by car. Some firms provide company cars or pay employees so many cents a mile to use their own cars. Others rent

Train travel lets an executive work while traveling.

The administrative assistant should be aware of any available discounts and make certain they are used when reserving cars.

cars from rental agencies. Car rental agencies usually charge either a flat daily, weekly, or monthly fee or a flat fee plus an additional amount for each mile driven. They also charge for insurance, and they may charge a drop-off fee when a driver picks up a car at one place and leaves it at another.

Most airports and cities offer a wide choice of rental agencies. Your company may have a long-term contract with an agency that provides discounts for frequent use, or your supervisor may belong to an automobile club that provides car rental discounts at specific agencies. If you have to choose an agency yourself, you need to compare the fees and services of several firms. Some companies encourage their employees to avoid big agencies and deal with smaller companies that offer lower rates.

Renting a Car   When you telephone the car rental company, give the reservations clerk your supervisor's name, and specify when and where he or she will pick up the car. If the car will be picked up at an airport, give the clerk the traveler's flight number so the rental agent can hold the car if the flight is late. Describe the kind of car your boss prefers, including the model and size. Big cars with extra features cost more than smaller, standard models but may be worth the extra cost. If your supervisor has to spend much time driving, a big, comfortable car will be less tiring. It can also make a good first impression on an important business client.

Ask the reservations clerk what the fees will be and whether there will be any additional charges for dropping the car off at another agency office. You will need to tell the clerk whether to charge the fees to a personal or company credit card or bill the company directly.

Planning a Car Trip   People who drive to their destinations must know what routes to follow, what signs to look for, where to stop for the night, and so on. If your boss asks you to prepare driving instructions, you will need a road map. You should always get directions from the clients your supervisor will be meeting, but you also need to gather other information.

You can use the map to locate the final destination and any stops along the way. Then you can determine the best road and the shortest, most direct routes to take. You can give written directions, or you can highlight the routes with a transparent marker so that the traveler can easily consult the map during the trip.

Other Trip-Planning Help   People who frequently drive long distances often find it helpful to pay a small annual fee to join an automobile club such as the American Automobile Association (AAA). These clubs can help you plan a car trip by providing you with maps marked to show the recommended routes. Usually the maps show the locations of restaurants and motels along the way. Automobile clubs also provide emergency road services, such as free towing for their members.

If you work for a company whose employees travel by car a great deal, your employer can purchase computer software that will help you plan an automobile trip. To use such a program, you enter the trip's starting point, the destination, and any stops along the way. The program then chooses the fastest, most direct route. If you were mapping a trip for a regional sales representative, you could use this program to work out a route that included calls on customers in several different cities.

Personal Cars Business professionals often use company cars or their own cars for business trips within a state or region. If they use company cars, the company may provide them with a gasoline credit card, or they may pay for gas themselves and then submit expense accounts for reimbursement. When people drive their own cars, the company usually pays them so much a mile to cover wear and tear, insurance, and the like. The company also customarily pays all tolls and parking fees. You should be prepared to keep records and expense accounts for supervisors who use their own cars or company cars extensively for business trips.

Taxis and Public Transit Some travelers find it cheaper and easier to get around a strange city by using taxis or public transit rather than by driving. If your boss plans to get around without a car in an unfamiliar city, you should learn as much as you can about these alternate methods of travel. You may be called upon to provide a list of taxicab company telephone numbers in San Francisco, a map of the Philadelphia subway system, or bus schedules for Seattle. You can obtain this information by talking to your travel agent, by looking at tourist guidebooks for the city your supervisor intends to visit, and by questioning hotel clerks.

Limousine Services Airport limousine services carry passengers between the airport and various downtown terminals or hotels. Limousine rates are usually lower than taxi fares. Most cities also have private limousine services that provide cars and drivers for local trips. These services require reservations, which you can make by telephone a day or two in advance. Some companies based in big cities have long-term contracts with limousine services that entitle them to discounts. If your employer does not use a service regularly, you may have to choose a limousine service. As with car rental companies, you will need to compare the rates and services of different companies. Limousine services may charge an hourly fee or a flat fee for drives they make often, such as trips to the airport.

International Travel

More and more people are making business trips to other countries as companies seek to open new markets and purchase raw materials abroad. Some corporations, such as IBM and Exxon, are called **multinational companies** because they have corporate headquarters, manufacturing plants, and other properties in several different

Travel in foreign countries can sometimes be especially difficult. The secretary can eliminate many potential problems by researching and planning the trip carefully.

countries. In addition, some lawyers, accountants, and consultants provide professional services for multinational companies, so they have foreign offices. You may be asked to arrange international as well as domestic trips. When you plan an international trip, you follow the same steps as for planning a domestic trip, but you have to do more research, planning, and preparation.

Research and Planning

When you plan a trip to a foreign country, you need information about its customs and cultures. For example, if you did not know that July 14, Bastille Day, is a national holiday in France, you might try to schedule business meetings on a day when all French business offices are closed. Information about social customs can help the traveler avoid offending people in other countries. It would be highly offensive, for example, for your supervisor to offer a bottle of wine to a Moslem business associate in Saudi Arabia, where Islamic law prohibits the use of alcohol.

The U.S. State Department publishes a series of pamphlets entitled *Background Notes on the Countries of the World.* There is a pamphlet for every country in the world, and each pamphlet describes the geography, history, social customs, economy, and trading patterns of the country it covers. Check your local library and bookstores for other reference works and guidebooks about the country your supervisor will be visiting.

Travel Documents

People traveling outside their own countries may be required to carry documents such as birth certificates, passports, visas, and papers that identify them and their employers and state the pur-

This is a page from a valid passport. When a traveler enters or leaves a foreign country, an official stamps the page with the date.

poses of their trips. They should carry these documents at all times and be ready to produce them upon request.

Passports   To visit most countries, the traveler needs a **passport**, which is an official identification document issued by the U.S. State Department. Passports identify travelers and prove that they are U.S. citizens. A traveler applying for a passport for the first time must appear in person at the passport office with an application, photographs, and some proof of citizenship, such as a birth certificate. It sometimes takes several weeks to obtain a passport, so travelers should apply as soon as they know they are going abroad.

Visas and Other Documents   **Visas** are permits granted by governments to allow foreigners to enter their countries. Most Western countries do not require American travelers to obtain visas, but Eastern European and Asian countries usually do. To find out whether a country requires a visa, you can ask your travel agent or contact the country's nearest consulate. The consulate can also tell you whether your traveler needs to obtain a special permit to work in the country.

Currency   A traveler visiting another country will need some money in that country's currency, even if it's only to buy a cup of coffee during an airport stopover. You can purchase a packet of currency worth about $10 in American money for each country the traveler will be visiting from a currency exchange office, your travel agent, or a large bank. Generally, however, travelers can exchange American money and traveler's checks for foreign currency at currency exchange offices in banks, hotels, and airports in the countries they visit. It is a good idea to find out what the current rate of exchange is between foreign currency and American dollars to help your employer calculate tips and other expenditures abroad.

Vaccinations   Travelers are often required to be vaccinated against diseases that are prevalent in the countries they plan to visit. Travel agents and consular offices can tell you which vaccinations are required. Travelers can obtain vaccination records from the physicians who vaccinate them. They must also obtain International Certificates of Vaccination and submit them to their local or state health departments. These certificates can be obtained from a travel agent, a passport office, or the traveler's doctor.

▮ Local Transportation

It can be a trying experience for travelers to find their way from airports to hotels or meeting places in a foreign country, especially if they don't know the language. In addition to gathering information about local transportation, as you would for any domestic business trip, you can help your supervisor cope with this situation by making some transportation arrangements in advance.

Trains Many foreign countries, particularly in Europe, have excellent train service, with passenger trains running frequently to all big cities and most smaller cities and towns. European railroads usually offer different classes of service. A first-class ticket costs more but ensures the traveler a comfortable seat in an uncrowded compartment. First-class tickets usually require reservations. You may be able to make reservations through your travel agent. If not, the traveler can make reservations through a travel agent overseas.

Car Rentals Most major American car rental agencies have toll-free numbers that you can call to make reservations for overseas rentals. Car rental rates in foreign countries can differ substantially from American rates, so be sure to ask the reservations clerk about rates in advance. You should also ask whether your supervisor will need an international driver's license. Many countries accept U.S. driver's licenses, but if an international license is required, it can be obtained from the American Automobile Association (AAA).

Booking Hotel Rooms

Now that you've arranged to get your boss to Houston, or Cincinnati, or London, you have to reserve a hotel or motel room where he or she can stay during the trip. If the traveler has no personal preferences and your company does not require you to use a specific hotel chain, you will have to choose the hotel yourself.

Costs and Location

Cost and location are the two most important factors for you to consider in selecting a hotel for your supervisor. Suppose, for example, that you have arranged for your two company executives to fly to Detroit. If they were planning to drive from the airport to a suburban office for a one-day business meeting, it probably would be more convenient for them to stay at a hotel near the airport. But, in fact, they are going to have a series of meetings over two days with clients at a downtown office. In that case it's more convenient to reserve rooms at a downtown hotel close to the meeting place.

Hotel Guides If you make hotel reservations frequently, your company should subscribe to a directory such as the *Official Hotel and Resort Guide*, the *Hotel and Motel Redbook*, or Leahy's *Hotel-Motel Guide*. These directories give the names, addresses, telephone numbers, room rates, and services of hotels in most cities.

The hotel directories usually indicate what services a hotel offers, such as room service, garage service, laundry and valet services, secretarial services, and transportation to and from airports. Most large hotels and motels have toll-free 800-numbers that you can call to make reservations. If no 800-number is listed for a hotel in your hotel directory, you can call (800) 555-1212 to find out if the hotel has one.

When you make a room reservation, you will need to tell the hotel clerk when your supervisor will be arriving and departing. You should also tell the clerk whether you want to reserve a single or double room or a suite. To hold a room for a traveler who will arrive late in the day you will need to make a **guaranteed reservation.** This means that the hotel will hold the room as long as is necessary. You may have to provide a credit card number and agree to pay for the room whether or not the traveler shows up. If the hotel provides transportation from the airport, you should ask for information on how the service operates. If there is time, ask the hotel to send you a written confirmation specifying the date of the reservation, the length of stay, and other details.

Preparing for the Trip

Once you've made all the transportation and hotel arrangements, you still have a number of tasks to perform to help your employer prepare for the trip. A day or two before departure, you will have to confirm all flight and room reservations unless they were confirmed earlier. You will also have to confirm arrangements for getting the traveler to and from the airport. In some cases you may have to make some last-minute changes in the airline or room reservations. Always make such changes as soon as possible, and always ask how a change will affect the cost. If your boss wants you to make restaurant reservations or arrange for theater or concert tickets, it's a good idea to hold off on these arrangements until just before departure, when all the other details have been worked out.

Preparing an Itinerary

Your travel agent or travel department has already provided you with an itinerary showing all the flight and hotel arrangements that have been made. Now you will use that information and all the other data that has been accumulating in your trip folder to prepare a more detailed itinerary. This itinerary includes not only travel and hotel information but also all business appointments, speaking engagements, entertainment events, and other activities planned for the trip.

Organizing the Itinerary Prepare an outline of the itinerary using all the reservation confirmations, calendar notations, letters, and appointment notes you've collected as you've planned the trip. The outline should list all activities in chronological order. It should be organized in a clear, logical format with separate heads for each day or for each scheduled activity. Figure 16-2 shows an example of a complete itinerary.

When you are preparing an itinerary, try to include as much information as possible to show where the traveler should be at all times. Be sure to list the names of companies and individuals the traveler will visit as well as their addresses and telephone numbers. If your supervisor is delayed, he or she can then call ahead without having to look up the numbers.

```
                    Itinerary for Gina M. LoCicero
                         January 19-20, 1987

        SUNDAY, JANUARY 19

           6:30 p.m.    Pick-up by All-Boro Limousines at
                        2 Charles St., New York, N.Y., for ride to
                        LaGuardia Airport (New York).

           7:40 p.m.    Leave LaGuardia on TWA flight 538, direct
                        to Columbus, Ohio.

           9:05 p.m.    Arrive at Port Columbus, Columbus,
                        Ohio.

                        Confirmed reservation for rental of
                        Lincoln Town Car from Hertz at Hertz
                        counter, Port Columbus.

                        Guaranteed reservation at Marriott Motor
                        Lodge, 3293 W. Broad St., Columbus,
                        614-829-8130.  (Travel instructions from
                        airport attached.)

        MONDAY, JANUARY 20

           9:00 a.m.    Appointment with Daniel Georgiton,
                        Universal Data, 4300 Sullivant Ave.,
                        614-274-1212, to discuss contract.  (Travel
                        instructions from hotel attached.
                        Correspondence relating to contract also
                        attached.)

           4:15 p.m.    Leave Port Columbus on TWA flight 508,
                        direct to LaGuardia (New York).

           6:30 p.m.    Arrive at LaGuardia.
```

Fig. 16-2 If you prepare an itinerary on a word processor, you can update it and change details as the plans become final.

Appointment Schedules Some managers prefer to have their business appointments listed separately from travel and hotel arrangements. You can easily prepare a separate schedule containing the same information that you would have included in a complete itinerary. Figure 16-3 shows an example of an appointment schedule.

Making Copies Make several copies of the itinerary. Your supervisor should keep a copy handy in a jacket pocket, briefcase, or purse. You should keep a copy so that you will know where to reach him or her, and key coworkers and members of the traveler's family may also receive copies.

```
                              APPOINTMENTS

    Thursday, January 3      Miami, Florida

            10 a.m.          James Fletcher, Sea King Industries,
                             332 Oceanside Drive, 305-555-0200, to
                             discuss plant addition.  (Background
                             attached.)

             7 p.m.          Michael Weinstein of Beach Motels, for
                             dinner at Neptune's, 2413 Collins
                             Avenue, 305-555-1881.  Table for two
                             reserved in your name.

    Friday, January 4        Key West, Florida

             1 p.m.          Martin Halden, of The Conch, 110 Palm
                             Boulevard, 305-555-4311, for lunch and
                             discussion of new restaurant construc-
                             tion.  (Background attached.)
```

Fig. 16-3 There is no set format for an appointment schedule. You should select a style that is easy to read and consistent.

Travel Funds

Another part of your job is to see that your boss has cash, traveler's checks, and credit cards to cover expenses that arise during the trip. Some expenses may be billed directly to the company or to company credit cards, but travelers still have to pay for such things as meals, cab rides, parking, and tips.

Credit Cards Some companies give their employees credit cards to use for most of their trip expenses. Other companies expect their employees to use their personal credit cards and then submit receipts for reimbursement. Using credit cards makes it easier for companies and their employees to keep track of travel expenses.

Your supervisor is responsible for carrying the credit cards, but you may be asked to keep all credit card numbers on file so that you can notify the credit card companies if the cards are lost or stolen.

Cash Advances When travelers must pay for tips, cab fares, highway tolls, and other such expenses in cash, many employers issue cash advances for business trips. To obtain a cash advance, you probably will have to fill out a request form and submit it to the company cashier. Most such forms require certain authorized signatures, an explanation of the request, employee identification numbers, and other details. Keep copies of cash advance requests for your expense records.

Traveler's Checks It is usually a good idea for the traveler to carry only a small amount of cash and to carry the bulk of his or her travel funds in the form of **traveler's checks**. Traveler's checks can be spent almost as easily as cash in stores and restaurants, but they are insured against theft or loss. The checks are available from banks and American Express offices. Some banks issue their own checks, while others sell checks issued by companies such as Visa or American Express. They come in denominations of $10, $20, $50, and $100. The person who will use the checks must pick them up and sign each one in the presence of a teller or bank officer. Traveler's checks come with a receipt that is a record of the check's serial numbers. Keep one copy of this receipt in your files and give the other one to the traveler so that if the checks are lost, he or she can be reimbursed. (Remind the traveler that the receipt should be kept separately from the checks.)

Organizing the Traveler

Shortly before your supervisor leaves for a business trip, you should organize all the information, documents, and materials he or she will need to take on the trip. Your boss can use your checklist to organize the materials in his or her briefcase. The briefcase should contain all the files and documents your supervisor will need to read or distribute at meetings while he or she is away. Include any background information available on the companies and individuals your supervisor will visit as well as any correspondence relating to the trip.

On your checklist be sure to include any guidebooks, maps, and directories that will help the traveler find public transportation, entertainment, and restaurants at his or her destination. Also include any equipment and supplies the traveler may need during the trip.

Managing the Office While Your Boss Is Away

Most supervisors delegate major business decisions to other managers before they leave on a trip. But they also expect you to be responsible for handling day-to-day decisions and for seeing that the office runs smoothly while they're away.

Handling Letters and Telephone Calls Your responsibilities will probably include replying to calls and mail that your employer

TRAVELER'S CHECKLIST

Keep a checklist like the one below, and use it each time you need to prepare materials for your supervisor to take on a business trip.

- Tickets
- Itinerary
- Appointment record

- Hotel confirmations
- Rental car arrangements
- Travel funds and traveler's checks
- Equipment and supplies
- Address book
- Files, documents, slides
- Miscellaneous items (maps, city guides, and so on)

would ordinarily answer. If mail cannot wait for your supervisor to return, you can handle it in one of three ways:

1. Forward it to the appropriate person.
2. Refer it to another supervisor who can handle it.
3. Answer it yourself.

For example, a letter to your supervisor regarding a real estate transaction probably could be handled by your company's real estate manager or by another supervisor. On the other hand, you could easily handle a letter requesting an appointment with your employer yourself. Handle telephone calls the same way that you handle the mail. Help the callers yourself when you can, or refer them to someone else who can help. If the callers must speak to your supervisor, take messages and tell them when you expect your boss to return. Keep the originals and copies of letters you receive while your employer is away. Place all letters, telephone messages, and documents that your supervisor must handle personally when he or she returns in a file folder labeled "Important." Place copies of all materials that you have already handled or directed to someone else in a file folder labeled "Information Only." Always arrange the materials in order of importance. If your employer will be away for a long time, he or she may want you to forward copies of any materials that require immediate attention.

Handling Projects and Problems Your supervisor may have specific tasks or assignments for you to handle while he or she is away. If you are not busy, you can undertake projects for which you don't normally have time, such as updating the office files.

Communicating With Your Boss Some supervisors place daily telephone calls to the office when they are away. Others expect their employees to call them at scheduled times or when there are problems to be discussed. You should ask your supervisor how often

You can expect to be in frequent contact with your boss by phone when he or she is away on a business trip.

he or she intends to telephone the office. Keep notes on matters you need to discuss, and have your notes handy when your supervisor calls.

Keeping a Log   Many office workers keep daily logs of all office activities while their supervisors are away. In these logs they record all visitors, incoming letters, and telephone calls as well as their own projects and activities. These logs help them keep track of all information regarding what transpired during the boss's absence.

Following Up on the Trip   When your supervisor returns from a trip, you need to perform some follow-up tasks. One task is to return to your files all the materials that your boss took along on the trip. You also need to help your supervisor prepare an expense account and to return any unspent funds to the cashier's office.

Another follow-up task is to handle correspondence arising from the trip. This may include notes to thank hosts or letters confirming sales orders, contracts, or other such business deals. You should also talk to your supervisor about the trip itself. Discuss any problems the traveler encountered with airlines, accommodations, and other aspects of the trip. Then try to determine how your planning and preparations contributed to the trip and what you should do differently the next time you plan a similar trip.

Expense Accounts

Executives who travel generally have to submit expense accounts when they return. **Expense accounts** are forms that business people fill out in order to be reimbursed for using their own money to meet business expenses or to account for any cash advances they

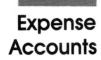

have received from their employers. It may be part of your job to fill out an expense account for your boss.

Employers generally require monthly expense accounts, which may be known as **travel and entertainment (T&E) reports**, but some require the reports immediately after business trips. Expense account formats differ from one employer to another, but Fig. 16-4 depicts two sides of a typical T&E form. All business expenses are listed on one side, and entertainment and miscellaneous expenses are explained on the other.

Expense Records

Because of federal tax regulations, employees must submit receipts for reimbursable expenditures over the amount of $25. Some employers may require receipts for other expenditures as well. One reason for the popularity of credit cards among business people is that cardholders automatically get receipts when they use them. In most places, though, people can get receipts for cash payments. In addition to obtaining receipts, most travelers keep logs of expenses for which they don't have receipts. Since employers generally reimburse a set amount per mile for business use of personal cars, drivers may also use these logs to keep track of their mileage. You will need to obtain your supervisor's receipts and log in order to prepare the expense account.

Reporting Expenses

Before you begin filling out an expense form, sort the receipts and logged expenses by day, and determine the nature of each expense so that you will know where to insert the information about it on the form. Note that the form includes separate columns for different kinds of transportation and living expenses.

When you fill out a T&E form such as the one in Fig. 16-4, you should follow these procedures:

■ Next to the preprinted date, write the departure point and destination of each trip.

■ Enter the expenses for each day in the appropriate columns following the preprinted date. On the reverse side of the form, provide details of entertainment and miscellaneous expenses.

■ Total the auto mileage column. Then multiply the total miles for the month by the employer's per-mile reimbursement rate to calculate the total auto expense for the month.

■ Total the other expense columns, and enter each monthly total at the bottom of the column.

■ Total the rows, and enter the totals at the far right, in the "Daily Totals" column.

■ Total the "Daily Totals" column, and record the "Grand Total" at the bottom of it.

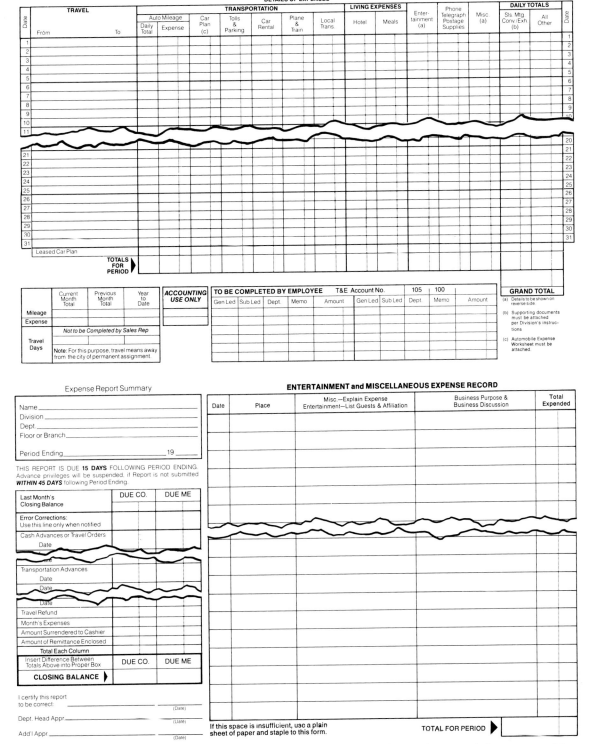

Fig. 16-4 To fill out a T&E form, you must have receipts and information on how each item was paid.

- Check the grand total by adding the monthly totals that appear at the bottoms of the other columns. You should get the same grand total that you got by adding the daily totals.

Reconciling Expense Accounts

On the side of the T&E form on which entertainment and miscellaneous expenses are explained, there is also a section labeled "Expense Report Summary." This section is used to reconcile the amount of money that the employer owes the traveler or vice versa. To reconcile a T&E account, follow these steps:

- Enter your name, division, department, and floor or branch.

- Enter the ending date for the T&E report.

- Enter any amount that is still owed to you or the company from the previous month's summary.

- If you are aware of any errors in previous expense summaries, enter those here.

- In the "Due Company" column, enter the dates and the amounts of any cash or transportation advances your supervisor has received during the reporting period.

- In the "Due Me" column, enter the total expenses or refunds for the month, using the grand total you recorded on the other side of the form.

- Total the "Due Company" and "Due Me" columns.

- Subtract the smaller total from the larger one, and enter the closing balance.

Expense Account Software

With the right software, you can use a computer to prepare expense. accounts and store them electronically. For example, with a spreadsheet program, you could store input about expense items on a data disk as you obtain it from your supervisor throughout the month. At the end of the month, you would retrieve the data, which the computer can sort and total automatically by category and by date. The computer can do even more of the work for you. You can use the software to create and store a soft copy of a T&E form, complete with your supervisor's name, department, and account number. After sorting and calculating the expenses for you, the computer would transfer them to the appropriate rows and columns on the electronic form. You could then print a hard copy of the filled-in form to be signed by your supervisor and submitted to your employer's accounting department.

You can also use the computer to keep running totals of expenses for a longer period, such as a budget year. Then, with a few keystrokes, you can find out how much remains in your department's budget for a particular category, such as travel.

■ Summary

- Questions that you need to ask when you plan a trip include: When will the travelers be going? How long will they be gone? Where are they going? What methods of transportation will they use? What kinds of hotel reservations will they need? What documents, equipment, or information will they need?

- Travel agents or travel departments of large companies can make arrangements for you. Or you can make reservations yourself. You can use airline, railroad, and hotel directories to assist you in making the reservations.

- Schedules and connections are two main points to consider when you make airline reservations. Others include which airline to use, seat assignments, frequent-flier bonuses, and special food requirements. The main points to consider for train reservations are schedules and the types of train service.

- Car rental companies will ask about dates and times, the place where the traveler will return the car, and the size, model, and special features of the car. You will have to compare rates and mileage fees and ask about insurance and discounts. Make sure that your boss knows the best route to take.

- People traveling to other countries need passports, visas, and other documents. When you plan an international trip, you follow the same steps as for planning a domestic trip, but you do more research, planning, and preparation.

- Cost and location are the two most important factors for you to consider when you select a hotel for your supervisor. Hotel directories usually indicate the services a hotel offers.

- You should use all the trip information you have gathered to prepare a detailed itinerary for your boss. The itinerary should include travel and hotel arrangements, business appointments, and all the other activities planned for the trip.

- While your supervisor is away, you will handle correspondence, telephone calls, projects, and problems. You should deal with these according to their priority, and you should take notes about what to do.

- Preparing a trip expense report is the first step in following up. Also, you might ask for feedback on specific arrangements and outline for your boss what went on in the office during the trip.

- Most people have to submit an expense account after a business trip. You should gather and save all receipts and logged expenses before filling out a T&E form.

■ Review Questions

1. If your supervisor is planning a business trip, what information do you need to gather before you can begin making travel arrangements?

2. What services do travel agencies and corporate travel departments usually provide?

3. If you had to rent a car for your supervisor, what information would you have to give the agency so that it could select and reserve a car for you?

4. If your supervisor intends to drive to a client's offices, how would you go about planning his or her car trip?

5. Name the documents your supervisor might need to carry on an international trip, and explain how to go about getting them.

6. What information would you need to give to a hotel reservations clerk to reserve a room for your supervisor?

7. What information would you include in an itinerary? Where would you get the information?

8. Describe how software can be used to prepare an expense account.

9. What information would you include on a traveler's checklist?

■ Technical Vocabulary

itinerary
commuter airline
jet lag
multinational company
passport

visa
guaranteed reservation
traveler's check
expense account
travel and entertainment report (T&E)

■ Discussion and Skills Development

1. Explain how you would handle each of the following situations that occur while your supervisor is away on business.

- An interoffice memo arrives; it asks your supervisor to provide some urgently needed technical information.
- You receive notice of a meeting that your boss should attend, but that is scheduled to take place while he or she is away.
- You receive a phone call from a client whom your supervisor will visit at the end of his or her trip. The client wants to change the time of the meeting.

- An unscheduled visitor comes to the office to talk to your supervisor.
- While opening your boss's mail, you come across a notice from the personnel department announcing the promotion of a staff member in your department.

2. Using the information below, prepare an itinerary for Ms. McGuire.

   Ms. McGuire is leaving from the Los Angeles airport at 6 p.m., Wednesday, on American Airlines flight 79, and she will land in Seattle two hours and ten minutes later. Roger Stern of CCL Industries will meet her at the arrival gate at the airport and take her to dinner with several CCL executives. Ms. McGuire has a guaranteed reservation at the Seattle Hyatt Regency, 4335 Pines Parkway, (206) 555-7500. She will spend the entire next day in meetings with various executives at CCL, including Mr. Stern. The address of CCL is 331 Pacific Avenue, Seattle, and its phone number is (206) 555-6000. She has a reservation for that evening on American Airlines flight 112, which leaves Seattle at 8 p.m. and arrives in Los Angeles at 9:50 p.m.

3. Your boss, sales representative Darrell Nelson, will be flying from Portland, Oregon, to Atlanta, Georgia, to meet with a prospective client. Mr. Nelson will get there just in time for the meeting, because obligations in the office and at home prevent him from flying there the day before. Mr. Nelson has never been to this client's office before, and the client will not be picking him up from the airport. Mr. Nelson also told you that he thinks the meeting will last until late in the evening. What steps can you take to ensure that your boss's arrival goes as smoothly as possible?

4. Suppose that your supervisor and three other executives from your company have planned an international business trip that will take them to Rome, Athens, Senegal, and Melbourne. Choose one of these cities, do some research, and write a short outline to give to your boss. Consider the kinds of information that will be needed and where you might obtain the information. Show your outline to the class, and discuss how you developed it.

chapter 17
Financial and Legal Functions

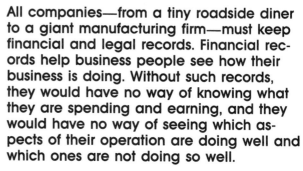

All companies—from a tiny roadside diner to a giant manufacturing firm—must keep financial and legal records. Financial records help business people see how their business is doing. Without such records, they would have no way of knowing what they are spending and earning, and they would have no way of seeing which aspects of their operation are doing well and which ones are not doing so well.

Most companies also need to use legal documents from time to time—for example, when they rent new premises or sign a credit agreement.

As an office worker, you can expect to perform some financial and legal functions. These functions might include sending and receiving bills, paying for materials and supplies, banking the receipts, keeping accounting records, paying employees, budgeting expenditures, and so on. Secretaries and administrative assistants perform many of these functions, but the extent of their involvement depends on the size and nature of the business that employs them. For example, if you were an administrative assistant in a small company, you might be responsible for processing the entire company payroll each week. In a large corporation, you would not be responsible for the payroll, but your supervisor might require you to maintain electronic payroll records of the employees in your department and provide that information for the payroll department.

This chapter will introduce you to many of the financial and legal functions you can expect to encounter in an administrative support role. You will learn about accounting and banking procedures, credit transactions, payrolls, and budgeting. You will also learn about the different kinds of legal documents commonly used in business, such as contracts and real estate documents, and you will learn how to prepare these documents.

General Accounting

No matter how big or small a company is, its managers need to have certain financial information to make decisions about the company and to evaluate its performance. They have to know how much money the business has, how many goods or services it has sold over the course of a month or a quarter, how much money the business owes to its suppliers, and so on.

Accounting is a means of gathering financial data and processing it into information that managers can use to analyze their financial situations and make decisions. In a large company, accounting may be done by a special department. A small business may pay an outside accounting firm to do its accounting, but office workers perform many day-to-day accounting tasks. If you were an administrative assistant at a small company, for example, you might be asked to keep the **accounts receivable** records, which list money owed to the company by customers, and the **accounts payable** records, which show money owed by the company to suppliers and creditors.

Types of Business Entities

The accounting process is essentially the same for any business, but there are some specific differences in the ways that financial information is processed for different types of businesses. The three major types of business entities are the sole proprietorship, the partnership, and the corporation.

Sole Proprietorship   Many small businesses are **sole proprietorships**; that is, they are owned by one person. The owner is legally responsible for the business's debts, and the owner's personal income is combined with the income of the business for tax accounting purposes. For business accounting purposes, however, only the company's financial transactions are computed to allow the owner to obtain a true measure of the company's performance.

Partnership   A **partnership** is a business owned by two or more people. Many doctors, lawyers, and architects form business partnerships. When a partnership is formed, the partners enter into a contract that spells out each partner's contributions, duties, and share of the profits. Each partner shares the responsibility for the firm's debts and taxes, but again, only the firm's financial transactions are subject to the accounting process.

Corporation   A **corporation** is a business that is privately owned by a specific group of individuals or publicly owned by hundreds or thousands of people who have purchased stock in it. Each share of stock is a unit of ownership and represents one vote on major decisions about operating the company.

One major difference between a corporation and the two other kinds of business entities is that corporations generally last longer. A sole proprietorship may last only as long as the life of its owner. And a partnership may last only as long as the life spans of its partners. But a corporation can go on indefinitely, even though its ownership can change daily as shares of stock are bought and sold on stock exchanges. The owners, or **stockholders**, of a corporation are not personally responsible for its debts and taxes, and they can lose only the amount of money they invested in their shares. Sole proprietors and partners can be held responsible for all of their business's debts. For accounting purposes, the corporation's financial transactions are also accounted for separately from the owners' transactions.

Accounting and IPSOD

Accounting is a form of data processing, so accounting procedures generally follow the IPSOD cycle. First, the unprocessed data that is required to produce accounting information is organized and input into manual or electronic journals and ledgers. When accountants input data, the first thing they do is gather all the necessary **source documents** that serve as records of business transactions. Source documents consist of purchase orders, bills, checkbook stubs, invoices, credit agreements, and so on. Accountants also gather any other financial records that have been kept during the accounting period, such as accounts receivable records, accounts payable records, payroll records, tax records, facilities and equipment inventories, and credit records. These records are some of the kinds of data that reflect the company's financial condition.

Next the data is processed or reorganized to produce useful information. For example, by totaling all of its individual weekly payroll expenditures, a company can determine how much it spends on employees' salaries and benefits in a month or a year. Similarly, when a company breaks down its yearly sales figures by month, it can determine when it makes the most or fewest sales each year, and it can then plan its advertising and sales campaigns accordingly.

In accounting, processing the data involves transferring it from the source documents to journals and ledgers where items can be grouped in a logical order and manipulated mathematically. We will discuss ledgers in more detail later in this chapter.

Once the data is processed and stored, it can be output in the form of financial statements. Usually the financial statements consist of an income statement, which shows the business's net income or loss for the accounting period, and a **balance sheet**, which shows the company's total assets and liabilities (debts). (See Fig. 17-1 for an example of a balance sheet.) This document is called a balance sheet because the total of a company's assets always equals the total of its liabilities and owner's equity. **Owner's equity** is the owner's financial interest in the company.

Just as with any other kind of data processing output, accounting records can be stored on paper or on computer storage media, and they can be printed out, reproduced, and distributed.

```
                              JULIA'S BOUTIQUE
                               Balance Sheet
                             December 31, 19XX
                           (in thousands of dollars)


                                   ASSETS

        Current Assets
           Cash                                    $100
           Accounts Receivable                      175
           Inventory                                250
           Prepaid Expenses                          25
                Total Current Assets                         $  550

        Fixed Assets
           Land                                    $150
           Building                                 300
           Furniture                                100
              Total Fixed Assets                               550
              Total Assets                                   $1,100

                      LIABILITIES AND OWNER'S EQUITY

        Current Liabilities
           Accounts Payable                        $160
           Taxes Payable                             25
           Other Accrued Expenses                    75
              Total Current Liabilities                      $  260

        Long-Term Liabilities
           Notes Payable                                       350
              Total Liabilities                              $  610

        Owner's Equity
           Julia Bond, Capital                     $400
           Net Income                                90
              Total Owner's Equity                             490
                 Total Liabilities and Owner's Equity       $1,100
```

Fig. 17-1 Accounting produces financial records, such as this balance sheet, that help companies analyze their financial situation.

Accounting information is distributed to managers and business owners, who make decisions such as whether to build a new plant, drop a line of products, or hire or lay off employees. It is distributed to stockholders so that they can evaluate the financial health of their company; to banks, which decide whether to approve a loan to a company; to the Internal Revenue Service, which determines taxes; and to investors, who decide whether to buy shares in a company.

Accounting Procedures

One accounting task that you may be asked to perform is to maintain a journal. Accountants use several different kinds of journals, but you would most likely keep a general journal. A **general jour-**

ACCOUNTING TERMS

These are some of the terms you will need to become familiar with if you work with financial information:

- **Account.** A grouping or classification of similar transactions, such as accounts payable or payroll.
- **Account balance.** The difference between the total debits and the total credits in an account.
- **Accounting period.** The period of time covered by the analysis of a company's financial records, usually quarterly (every three months) or annually (once a year).
- **Assets.** Money and other items of value owned by the company.
- **Balance sheet.** A financial statement that sums up a business's assets, liabilities, and owner's equity. On a balance sheet, the total of the assets always equals the total of the liabilities plus the owner's financial interest in the business.
- **Credit.** An amount that is entered on the right side of an account.
- **Debit.** An amount that is entered on the left side of an account.
- **Journal.** A record in which each business transaction is listed in chronological order.
- **Journalizing.** Maintaining the journal or making entries in the journal.
- **Ledger.** A record of each business transaction organized according to account.
- **Liability.** A debt or obligation owed by a company to its creditors.
- **Owner's equity.** The owner's financial interest in the business.
- **Posting.** The process of transferring data from a journal to a ledger.

nal is a list in chronological order of each business transaction that a firm is involved in (Fig. 17-2, top). Each entry in the journal shows the date, the names of the accounts that must be debited and credited to record the transaction, a brief description of the transaction, and the amount of the transaction. The description would identify the nature of the transaction—a cash sale, a purchase of goods on credit, the payment of employee salaries, and so on.

An **account** is a grouping of similar transactions. Accounts can be assets (showing items of value owed by the business) such as cash, equipment, and accounts receivable, or they can be liabilities (showing debts owed by the business) such as accounts payable and loans payable. Accounts can also represent owner's equity, revenue, and expense items.

You may also be asked to keep a **general ledger**, which is a record of all the business transactions, grouped according to account (Fig. 17-2, bottom). Each account is recorded on a separate page of the ledger. You would use the journal as a guide to list each item in its appropriate account. Transferring items from the journal or a source document to the ledger is known as **posting**. Usually each item is posted in the ledger as a debit in one account and as a credit in another. For example, if you have a journal entry showing that a customer made a $3000 payment to your company, you would list it as a debit on the ledger page designated "Cash" and as a credit on the ledger page designated "Accounts Receivable." In other words, since the payment has been received, it is no longer part of the money that the company is owed. Instead, it is added to the actual cash the company has on hand. The general ledger is, in effect, a master file of every business transaction, classified by account. It is a useful tool that accountants and business owners use to analyze a company's performance and financial health.

Another accounting procedure that you may be asked to perform involves adding and subtracting transactions. For example, you might be asked to total each day's receipts or keep a running total of the balance in each account. You can use computers and calculators to perform many of these functions, but you should also be able to perform basic arithmetic operations yourself. The accuracy of computer or calculator output depends on the accuracy of your input. If you enter a decimal point in the wrong place or key in a number incorrectly, you will get an incorrect answer. You should always check the calculator tape or computer entries against your source documents. Another way to guard against errors is to round off your input figures and estimate what the output should be. If the output is very different from your estimate, redo the calculation.

GENERAL JOURNAL — Page 2

DATE	ACCOUNT TITLE AND EXPLANATION	POST. REF.	DEBIT	CREDIT
19— May 30	Cash	101	3000 00	
	Accounts Receivable	102		3000 00

GENERAL LEDGER

Cash — Account No. 101

DATE	EXPLANATION	POST. REF.	DEBIT	CREDIT	BALANCE DEBIT	BALANCE CREDIT
19— May 30		J2	3000 00		3000 00	

GENERAL LEDGER

Accounts Receivable — Account No. 102

DATE	EXPLANATION	POST. REF.	DEBIT	CREDIT	BALANCE DEBIT	BALANCE CREDIT
19— May 30		J2		3000 00		3000 00

Fig. 17-2 Journal entries (top) are made chronologically as each transaction occurs. Ledger entries (bottom) are listed according to categories called accounts.

Some electronic calculators simply add, subtract, multiply, and divide figures. Others can perform many other functions as well. The following review of standard and optional features may help you select a calculator that meets your needs.

- **Keypad.** An electronic calculator has a key for each digit, a decimal key, and keys for functions such as adding, subtracting, and clearing the calculator's memory. Select one which has the function keys you need and which you can use comfortably.
- **Floating decimal point.** On a calculator with this feature, a decimal point appears automatically whenever you use the calculator. (It's still up to you to see that the decimal point appears in the right place.) This feature is especially useful if you are calculating sums of money.
- **Memory.** Like a computer, many electronic calculators have an internal memory. This memory allows you to clear a figure you have entered without erasing all the other figures you have input. It also lets you shift from one function, such as addition, to another, such as division, without having to rekey your input.
- **Display.** Calculators are available with several types of displays, such as light-emitting diode (LED) and liquid crystal. Be sure the numbers are easy for you to read.
- **Printer.** Some calculators print their output on a paper tape instead of display-

A good quality calculator can help you perform many financial tasks.

ing it electronically. Others can do both. Sometimes you may want to attach printed output to reconciliation sheets and other documents. But at other times, printed output would just be thrown out. So a calculator that allows you to choose the type of output is very useful.
- **Programmability.** Some calculators can be programmed, like computers, to perform specific applications. You can choose a calculator that you can program yourself, or you can buy a preprogrammed model. Some programmable calculators can store programs on magnetic media and retrieve them later. This feature is most useful to accountants and other people who repeatedly apply the same complex mathematical formulas to different sets of numbers.

Accounting Software

There are well over 200 accounting software programs on the market. Many of these are full-scale accounting systems that were originally designed to run on large computer systems. These products have now been modified to run on personal computers. There are

```
                          Copy Machines                          848486
                          GENERAL LEDGER                          Page 1
                            84-84-86

  Entry  Date  Description              Document  Jl   Debits   Credits   Balance

  (8828.      )                         PETTY CASH
         818184  BALANCE FORWARD                                          -1888.88
    98   122785  dep                    881       A    1888.88

         TOTAL PETTY CASH                              1888.88    8.88      $8.88


  (8188.      )                         Petty Cash
         818184  BALANCE FORWARD                                          188.88
    38   818284  petty cash replenish   89173     D     75.88
    69   812584  Legal Pads             v275      D              13.75
    81   122685  supplies               ck 188    C    188.88



              Press 'RETURN' to Continue    'S' to Stop: _
```

Computer software, like this ledger program, makes it easy for small businesses to do their own accounting.

also many smaller-scale programs that were created for use with popular microcomputer software applications, such as Lotus 1-2-3.

The design of these products parallels traditional accounting subsystems: general ledger, accounts receivable, accounts payable, and payroll. Some also provide additional functions, such as job costing, inventory, and sales order entry. While the smaller-scale programs are easier to implement and run, most accounting software systems require some technical expertise so that they can be tailored to the individual needs of a particular business. However, your job may require you to prepare data for entry into the system or even may require that you enter data directly. For example, you may be asked to reword the hours worked by each employee in your department on a computer input form. In some cases your manager may ask you to retrieve data from the accounting system to prepare a report. Or, perhaps you may be asked to obtain monthly sales or inventory figures.

If you work for a company that requires the selection and use of accounting software, you will probably have to consult an accountant or some other outside expert. One source of printed help is *The Guide to Accounting Software for Microcomputers*. This guide contains detailed analyses of the popular accounting software products.

Banking

If you deal with accounts, you might also have some banking responsibilities. All businesses deal with banks; your level of involvement in your employer's banking will depend upon the size and nature of the company you work for. Remember that banking tasks carry a high level of responsibility because they involve money and confidential information. Some of the banking tasks you might be asked to undertake include making deposits and payments, reconciling account balances, dealing with dishonored checks, and transferring funds.

Making Deposits If you work in an office that receives payments from customers, you may be responsible for depositing them in your company's checking account. You will need to sign signature cards that the bank will keep on file so that the tellers can compare your signature with the one that appears on the checks and forms. The bank will also need written authorization from your employer to honor your signature.

Deposit Slips To make a deposit, you need to fill out a deposit slip. First you fill in the date and the amount of currency and coins you are depositing. (Traveler's checks and money orders are considered currency.) Then you fill in the amount of each check on a separate line. If you have more checks than the deposit slip can accommodate, you can attach an adding machine tape listing the amount of each check and write only the total on the deposit slip. (See Fig. 17-3 for an example of a deposit slip.)

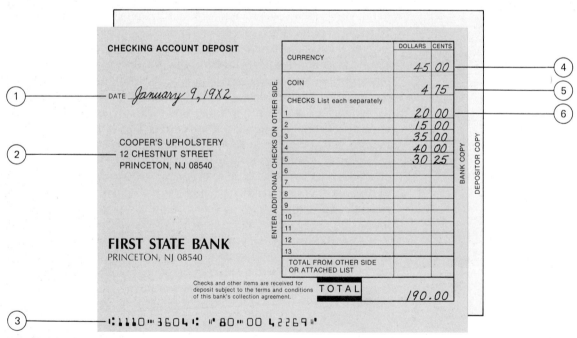

Fig. 17-3 When making out a deposit slip, you must fill in the date (1), the account name and number if they are not preprinted on the slip (2 and 3), the amount of currency (4), and coins (5), and the amount of each check (6).

Depositing Currency and Coins If you frequently deposit currency and coins as well as checks for your company, you need to obtain a supply of coin rolls and bill wrappers from the bank. Before you wrap the coins and bills, mark the wrappers with your employer's name and account number so that the bank can notify you if the wrappers contain too much money or too little. Some banks do not accept large amounts of currency or coins if they are not already wrapped. Others charge businesses a fee for separating and counting loose bills and coins.

Depositing Checks Before you deposit any checks, you should examine them to see that they are written correctly. Make sure that the date, the amount, and the signature are correct. Otherwise, the bank may return the check uncashed and charge your company a handling fee.

Endorsements Each check you deposit must be endorsed, or signed on the back, by the **payee**—the person or organization to whom the check is written. The endorsement is a legal procedure that transfers ownership of the check from the payee to the bank so that the bank can collect payment from the **drawer**, or the person on whose account the check is drawn. If it is one of your duties to endorse checks for your employer, there are several different types of endorsements you can use (see Fig. 17-4).

A check with a **blank endorsement**, consisting only of the payee's signature, can be cashed by anyone. Don't put a blank endorsement on a check until you are about to deposit it, and never send checks with blank endorsements through the mail. A **restrictive endorsement** sets conditions such as "for deposit only" to a specific account. A **special endorsement** or **full endorsement** is used to transfer ownership of a check from one payee to a second. In this case the first payee signs his or her name and then writes "pay to the order of" and adds the second payee's name. A **corrected endorsement** is used to reconcile signatures if the payee's name on the front of the check does not match the name on the payee's checking account. To correct an endorsement, the payee first endorses the check with the name that appears on the front of the

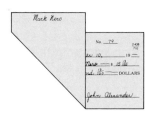

Blank Endorsement

Restrictive Endorsement

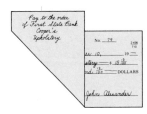

Full Endorsement

Fig. 17-4 The check at the left shows a blank endorsement, the check at the center shows a restrictive endorsement, and the check at the right shows a full endorsement.

check; then the payee signs it again, using the name that appears on his or her account.

Automatic Teller Machines Automatic tellers are machines that let you deposit and withdraw funds by using a special access card and identification code. An ATM is similar to a computer terminal. A special keypad enables you to instruct the machine about the types of transactions you require and the amounts, and a display screen tells you how to proceed with a transaction. ATMs permit you to make deposits and withdrawals after banking hours, and they can save you long waits on bank lines during the day. You should, however, take a few precautions when using an ATM.

Use an ATM for depositing only checks with restrictive or special endorsements that assign them to the bank. Never use one for depositing cash or other items that can be used by unauthorized people. The ATM will give you a receipt, but it cannot give you a copy of your deposit slip so that you can prove you deposited a specific check. Notify the bank immediately of any discrepancies between its records of your ATM transactions and your employer's records, such as a deposit you made that is not listed on your employer's monthly bank statement. Also notify the bank immediately if your company's ATM access card is lost or stolen. If an unauthorized person uses the lost or stolen card, your employer's liability is limited to $50 if the loss is reported promptly, but it could be much greater if the loss is not reported.

Night Depositories If your company must deposit large amounts of currency after business hours, you can use a night depository. This is a slot on the outside wall of a bank through which customers can drop their deposits after banking hours. Businesses that collect money after banking hours often use night depositories as a safety precaution. That way, they don't have to keep money on the premises overnight. Banks provide deposit bags with locks on them for customers who frequently use night depositories. Bags containing deposits are dropped through the night depository slot and opened the next day.

Banking by Mail Mailed deposits, like those made in ATMs, should include only checks with restrictive or special endorsements. Never send currency through the mail unless you use registered mail. Most banks provide special envelopes and deposit slips for banking by mail. The bank will send you a validated copy of your deposit slip as well as a new deposit slip and envelope by return mail.

Making Payments

Businesses generally use checks rather than cash to make payments. In large companies, these checks are handled by the accounting or payroll department. If you work in a small office, though, it may be your responsibility to prepare checks and main-

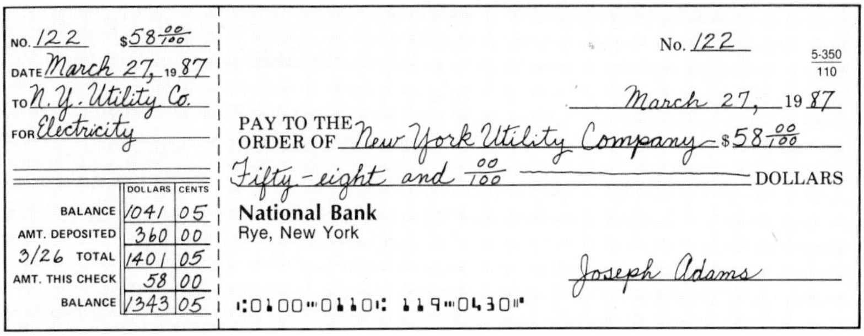

NO. _122_ $58 $\frac{00}{100}$
DATE _March 27,_ 19 _87_
TO _N.Y. Utility Co._
FOR _Electricity_

	DOLLARS	CENTS
BALANCE	1041	05
AMT. DEPOSITED	360	00
3/26 TOTAL	1401	05
AMT. THIS CHECK	58	00
BALANCE	1343	05

No. _122_

5-350 / 110

March 27, 19 _87_

PAY TO THE ORDER OF _New York Utility Company_ $58 $\frac{00}{100}$

Fifty-eight and $\frac{00}{100}$ _____ DOLLARS

National Bank
Rye, New York

Joseph Adams

⑆0100⑆0110⑆ 119⑈0430⑈

Fig. 17-5 Here is how a properly written check and check stub should appear. Always make out the check stub first so you don't forget what the check was for.

tain records of them. You may also be responsible for ordering new checks when your supply is low.

Banks issue books of checks with **stubs** or **check registers** in which you record the number, date, and amount of each check as well as the payee's name and the reason for payment. Some registers are electronic. If you use an electronic register, you input this information into the computer. You also subtract the amount of a check from the checking account's **balance**, or the funds contained in the account, and write in the new balance. If a deposit has been made, you enter the date and the amount, and then you add that amount to the account balance. This information will be helpful for accounting and tax preparation, and it will help you keep track of how much money is in the account.

The signature on a check authorizes a bank to remove money from one account and give it to someone else. The check indicates how much is to be transferred and to whom the money should be paid. This information can be printed out by a computer or written by hand (see Fig. 17-5). These guidelines can help you issue checks properly with either method:

■ Date each check and stub.

■ Number checks and stubs consecutively if they don't already have numbers printed on them.

■ Give the payee's full name, and make sure that it is correctly spelled and legible. Omit courtesy titles, such as *Ms.* and *Mr.*

■ Begin the amount close to the dollar sign on the check, and use bold, clear figures. If you are writing, write the figures close together so that no one can insert new figures between the ones you have written.

■ On the next line write the amount of the check in words. Begin at the left end of that line, and capitalize the first letter only. Express cents as fractions of 100; that is, *38 cents* would be *38/100*. Use hyphens, periods, or a line to fill any blank space on the line.

- Indicate the purpose of the check in a corner of the check. Some checks include a "memo" line for this purpose.

- If you make a mistake on a check, write the word *void* in large letters on the check and on its stub. Don't try to correct a mistake on a check by erasing or crossing out what you have written. Save any checks that you void, and file them in numerical order with those that are cashed by the bank and returned to you.

Other Types of Checks   Most payments processed by office workers are in the form of checks drawn against company checking accounts, but companies sometimes use other kinds of checks as well.

- **Certified check**. A certified check is drawn against a company checking account and certified by a bank teller. The teller immediately subtracts the amount of the check from the account. People use certified checks when the payee requires a guarantee that the check will be honored. They are most often used in transactions involving large sums of money, such as a real estate sale.

- **Cashier's check**. Banks issue cashier's checks for the amount of the check plus a small fee. Like certified checks, cashier's checks are guaranteed by the bank and are most commonly used in transactions that involve large sums of money. Cashier's checks are also called official checks, teller's checks, or treasurer's checks.

- **Bank draft**. A bank draft is similar to a cashier's check except that it is drawn against one bank's account in another bank. Bank drafts are used to transfer large sums of money quickly between banks in distant cities.

- **Money order**. Money orders are similar to cashier's checks, but they are usually issued for $250 or less. People who don't have checking accounts may buy money orders from a bank or post office and send them through the mail to pay for goods or services.

- **Stop-payment requests**. If a check that your company has issued is lost or stolen, or if it was written for the wrong amount, you may be able to stop payment on it. To request a stop-payment order, call the stop-payment desk at your company's bank and give the checking account number, the name of the account holder, the amount, the date, the number of the check, the payee's name, and the reason you want to stop payment. If the bank has not cleared the check yet, a bank employee will process a stop-payment request. You must follow up your oral request either by sending the bank a confirmation letter or by filling out and returning a form that the bank supplies. Most banks charge a fee for issuing a stop-payment order.

Reconciling an Account Balance

Each month banks send their customers statements of all activities involving their accounts, including deposits, withdrawals, checks that have cleared, interest paid to the accounts, and fees charged against them. With these statements, banks generally return the last month's **canceled checks**, or checks that have been cleared against the account. If you keep your employer's checkbook, your duties may include reconciling the balance, which involves comparing the balance reported on the bank statement with the balance recorded on the check stubs or in the check register and accounting for any difference between them (see Fig. 17-6).

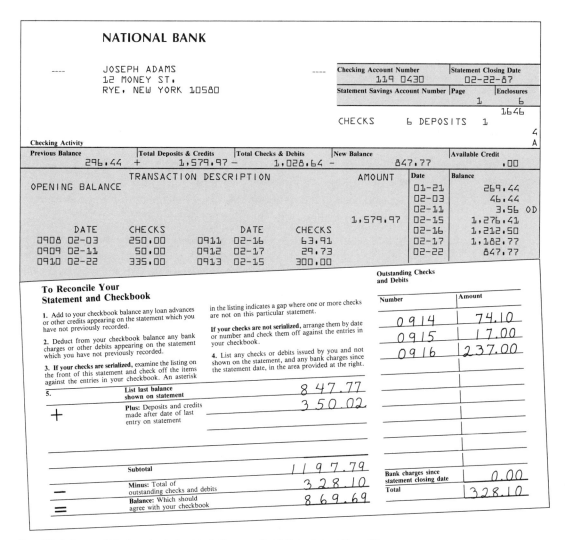

NATIONAL BANK

JOSEPH ADAMS
12 MONEY ST.
RYE, NEW YORK 10580

Checking Account Number	Statement Closing Date
119 0430	02-22-87

Statement Savings Account Number	Page	Enclosures
	1	6

CHECKS   6 DEPOSITS   1

1646

4
A

Checking Activity

Previous Balance	Total Deposits & Credits	Total Checks & Debits	New Balance	Available Credit
296.44 +	1,579.97 −	1,028.64 −	847.77	.00

TRANSACTION DESCRIPTION	AMOUNT	Date	Balance
OPENING BALANCE		01-21	269.44
		02-03	46.44
		02-11	3.56 OD
	1,579.97	02-15	1,276.41
		02-16	1,212.50
		02-17	1,182.77
		02-22	847.77

DATE	CHECKS	DATE	CHECKS
0908 02-03	250.00	0911 02-16	63.91
0909 02-11	50.00	0912 02-17	29.73
0910 02-22	335.00	0913 02-15	300.00

To Reconcile Your Statement and Checkbook

1. Add to your checkbook balance any loan advances or other credits appearing on the statement which you have not previously recorded.

2. Deduct from your checkbook balance any bank charges or other debits appearing on the statement which you have not previously recorded.

3. If your checks are serialized, examine the listing on the front of this statement and check off the items against the entries in your checkbook. An asterisk

in the listing indicates a gap where one or more checks are not on this particular statement.

If your checks are not serialized, arrange them by date or number and check them off against the entries in your checkbook.

4. List any checks or debits issued by you and not shown on the statement, and any bank charges since the statement date, in the area provided at the right.

Outstanding Checks and Debits

Number	Amount
0914	74.10
0915	17.00
0916	237.00

5.

List last balance shown on statement   847.77

+ Plus: Deposits and credits made after date of last entry on statement   350.02

Subtotal   1197.79

− Minus: Total of outstanding checks and debits   328.10

= Balance: Which should agree with your checkbook   869.69

Bank charges since statement closing date	0.00
Total	328.10

Fig. 17-6 A monthly bank statement shows all of the deposits, withdrawals, and service charges that have been made in each account during the month. Many banks also provide a convenient form on the back of the statement to reconcile the balance.

If you have an electronic banking system, you can use the computer to reconcile the balance. Even if you don't bank electronically, you might be able to use your computer terminal to reconcile the balance by using a special program. The procedure for reconciling the balance, manually or electronically, is as follows:

- Arrange the canceled checks according to the check numbers.

- Compare the amounts of the checks with the amounts listed for them on the bank statement.

- Compare the checks with the checkbook stubs, and place a check mark on the stubs to indicate that the checks have cleared. On the reconciliation form, list the numbers and the amounts of any checks still outstanding, and add their amounts.

- Compare the deposit amounts shown on the check stubs or in the check register with those listed on the statement. List any deposits not reported on the statement, and add the amounts.

- Add the total of unlisted deposits to the balance shown on the bank statement, and subtract the total of outstanding checks. The resulting figure is called the adjusted bank balance.

- Examine the statement for service charges or interest payments. Subtract the service charges from the balance recorded in your checkbook, and add the interest payments.

- The resulting figure should equal the adjusted bank balance. If it does, record the service charge and interest payment amounts in the checkbook, and write in the new balance.

If your new checkbook balance and the adjusted bank balance don't agree, you will need to determine the reason for the difference. First, look for mistakes in the calculations on the reconciliation form. If the calculations are correct, go through the check stubs to verify that each check is listed either among the cleared checks (on the bank's statement) or among the outstanding checks (on your reconciliation form). Then check the bank's list to be sure that you have a stub for each of the checks on the list and that the amounts agree. Also, make sure that no deposits have been omitted from the lists. Each deposit recorded in your checkbook should be listed either on the bank statement or on your reconciliation form. Then see that each deposit listed on the bank statement is also recorded in your checkbook.

If you still haven't found the error, look at your checkbook to be sure that the balance you brought forward to each new page is correct. Then, if you find no errors in the forwarded balances, you should verify your calculations in the checkbook. When you find a check stub with an error on it, circle the error and write on the stub: "True figure is $_____. Correction is on stub #_____." Make the appropriate adjustment on the stub where the current balance appears. Enter the amount of the error on the reconciliation form, showing where the error occurred and the number of the stub where you corrected it. When you have reconciled the balance, write on the last stub covered by the bank statement: "Agrees with bank statement" and the date of the statement.

Reconciliation Follow-Up After you reconcile the balance each month, you should file the bank statement, reconciliation sheet, and canceled checks. File all statements and reconciliation sheets in chronological order. Either fold the checks inside the statements on which they are listed, or file them numerically in a separate place. Canceled checks have legal importance as proof of payment. Your company's policies will determine how long you should keep bank statements and canceled checks.

You should also trace what happened to any outstanding checks that have still not cleared when the next month's bank statement arrives. If a check hasn't cleared, the payee may not have received it, or it may have been lost. Call or write to the payee to find out. If the check has been lost, request a stop-payment order and issue a replacement check.

Finally, if you are also responsible for maintaining the general journal, which we discussed earlier in this chapter, you should make the same corrections in the journal as you have made in the checkbook, if necessary. For example, if you have made a miscalculation on a check stub, the chances are that you also listed the same incorrect figure when you made the journal entry regarding that transaction.

Handling Dishonored Checks

Sometimes you may deposit a check that the bank cannot collect on, either because the check was altered, misdated, or made out incorrectly or because there were not sufficient funds in the drawer's account to cover the check. When a check can't be paid, it is called a **dishonored check**. The bank will return the check to the depositor and subtract the amount of the check from the depositor's account. Some banks will also charge the depositor a fee for handling the check. If the bank dishonors a check made out to your company, you will have to notify the drawer. The drawer may then deposit additional funds in his or her account and either issue a new check or instruct you to redeposit the dishonored check.

Electronic Funds Transfer

As more and more businesses have turned to office automation, businesses and banks have developed the means to transfer funds electronically from one account to another. You may be responsible for recording these transactions. The automatic teller machine is one electronic means of transferring funds. Other forms of electronic funds transfer (EFT) include direct deposit, telephone transfers, and computer transfers (see Fig. 17-7).

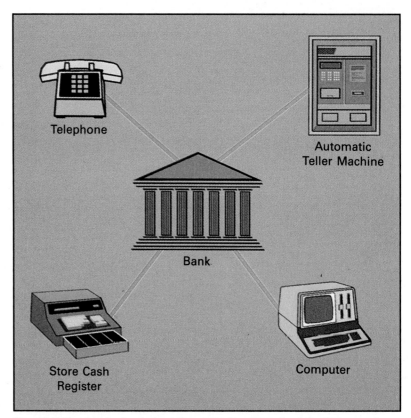

Fig. 17-7 Electronic funds transfers can be done by telephone, automatic teller machines, computer, and by point-of-sale transactions.

Direct Deposit   Some businesses use direct deposit transfers to deposit paychecks directly into their employees' accounts. A company may also pay recurring bills, such as rental fees or charges for utilities, by direct deposit. In such cases the company authorizes the bank to take the required amount out of its account and transfer it to the creditor's account. Both of these types of direct deposit save the company and the bank time and paperwork.

Telephone Transfers   Customers of investment funds and stock brokerages routinely use telephone transfers to switch their investments from one fund or stock to another. Certain bills can also be paid in this way.

Computer Transfers   If you use a computer terminal and modem to bank electronically, you can also keyboard instructions to transfer funds from the company account to pay bills.

Point-of-Sale Transfers   **Point-of-sale transfers** means that customers use bank identification cards instead of credit cards or checks to pay for goods and services. The store clerk inserts the card into the store's computer and links up with the bank's computer, which immediately transfers the amount of the sale from the customer's account to the store's account. Point-of-sale transfers are listed on the monthly bank statements of both the customer and the store.

Credit Transactions

Companies often have to borrow money, or obtain credit, in order to purchase expensive goods or raw materials or to pay bills while they wait for payments from customers. They can obtain that credit from banks, finance companies, retail stores, and credit card companies.

In a small company, you may be responsible for processing credit documents and handling the company's credit card accounts. Big companies usually have credit departments that investigate loan applications from customers, develop credit terms, process applications for credit cards, and so on. Even in a company with a credit department, you may still be responsible for receiving and forwarding your supervisor's credit card statements and receipts, so you should have a general understanding of credit transactions.

Credit Agreements

Before a business extends credit to a customer, it usually checks the customer's credit rating to ensure that the customer will be able to pay the debt. Once the loan application is approved, the borrower and the lender must agree on the credit terms and repayment schedules. Credit terms establish how much the borrower is seeking, how much interest the lender will charge, and what penalties the borrower will incur if the credit terms are violated. The interest rate is a percentage of the loan, and it represents the charge that the lender is making for lending money. The federal Truth-in-Lending Act is a law that requires businesses to spell out all of these credit terms to the borrower.

Repayment schedules specify how the borrower will repay the loan. One common business arrangement is for a company to ship merchandise or raw materials to a customer with the understanding that the customer will pay for the goods in full within 30 days. Another common arrangement is for the borrower to repay the loan in **installments**—that is, in portions that are paid at regular intervals. For example, many stores, finance companies, and credit card companies collect payments from customers in monthly installments. The borrower, in most cases, has to pay a **finance charge**, an amount based on a specific percentage of the unpaid balance, with each installment payment.

Using Credit Cards

One form of credit is the credit card. Your supervisor may have a company credit card that he or she can use to charge meals, hotel rooms, office supplies, and other legitimate business expenses. Credit card companies, such as American Express and Visa, issue cards to businesses. When an employee uses a company credit card, at a restaurant, for example, the credit card company pays the restaurant and then bills the employee's company for payments and interest charges. When companies don't provide credit cards, employees may use their personal credit cards for both personal and business expenses. The credit card company bills the employee who is then reimbursed by the company for the business expenses.

If your supervisor uses a credit card for business, it may be part of your job to maintain credit card records. For example, you may have to keep receipts, check credit statements, and fill out expense vouchers. You may also have to keep a record of credit card numbers in case they are lost or stolen.

Just as banks provide bank statements each month, credit card companies provide credit card statements that show when and where each purchase was made during the billing period, the total amount of outstanding charges, and the amount of interest owing on the account. If you are responsible for maintaining credit card records for your supervisor, you will need to keep copies of all the receipts of expenditures to compare with the monthly statement. If your supervisor cannot account for an expenditure on the statement and you do not have a receipt for it, you may have to contact the credit card company to determine whether an error in billing was made.

Budgeting

So far, we have discussed the various financial procedures that are part of the day-to-day operations of a business office, such as keeping a journal, banking, and handling credit transactions. You may also be asked to help with a financial procedure that usually occurs once a year: preparing the budget.

A **budget** is a company's financial plan of operations for a given period of time, commonly a year. Usually the company has an overall budget that dictates the expected income and expenditures for each division and department. Each division and department of the company has its own separate budget that governs only its operations. A department manager's budget (see, for example, Fig. 17-8) will describe the department's expected expenditures for salaries, supplies, furniture, and so on.

A budget sets the company's financial goals, keeping its expenditures in line with its revenues in order to achieve an acceptable level of profit. Company executives and department managers are responsible for making sure that expenditures do not exceed the budgeted amount or for making cuts, if necessary, to achieve the company's financial goals. For example, if the company you work for decides that it has to cut its salary expenditures by 10 percent in the coming year, that reduction will be reflected in the budget section marked "Salaries." Then each department manager must work to achieve the reduction, perhaps by leaving vacant positions un-

| DEPARTMENT BUDGET | | | | |
| JANUARY–MARCH 19_ | | | | |
EXPENSE	JAN.	FEB.	MARCH	TOTAL
SALARIES	6,300	6,300	6,300	18,900
EMPLOYEE FRINGE BENEFITS	1,660	1,660	1,660	4,980
TRAVEL & ENTERTAINMENT	600	600	600	1,800
PHOTOCOPYING CHARGES	100	100	100	300
LEGAL FEES	0	0	500	500
TELEPHONE & TELEGRAPH	125	125	125	375
MAILING EXPENSES	100	100	100	300
STATIONERY & SUPPLIES	300	50	50	400
MAGAZINES & BOOKS	100	100	100	300
FURNITURE & EQUIPMENT	200	600	200	1,000
MAINTENANCE & REPAIR	50	50	50	150

Fig. 17-8 Budgets help managers see at a glance how much money will be received or spent in each area during the budget year.

filled, or by withholding merit raises and bonuses, or by laying off workers. If the company cannot achieve a 10 percent salary reduction, its executives will have to revise that goal or look for some other area to cut.

Preparing a Budget

When company managers prepare a budget, they include all the available information about both income and expenses under separate headings, such as "Raw Materials," "Revenues," and "Labor Costs." Under each heading they list all the line items for that heading. A **line item** is a category of expenditure or income (similar to an account) that is given a separate line in a budget so that anyone can tell at a glance how much will be received or spent in that area during the budget year. Examples of line items are salaries, fringe benefits, supplies, equipment, office space, and postage.

Budgets are very flexible. You can prepare a budget for any aspect of a business, but the two most common types of budgets are the operating budget and the capital expense budget. The **operating budget** spells out the expected income and costs of the day-to-day operations of a company. It is broken down into a revenue or sales budget showing income and an expense budget showing expenditures for such items as salaries, supplies, and raw materials. The **capital expense budget** shows long-range expenditures for such items as new facilities, equipment replacement, land purchases, and mortgages. Another type of budget is a **project budget**. A film studio might use this kind of budget to plan the expenses for production and promotion of each film project. If you work in an office that operates according to project budgets, you might be asked to log expenses, process invoices, and monitor expenses for each project.

Many companies now use electronic spreadsheet software for developing their budgets so that they can plan more thoroughly and in less time than with paper and pencil methods. Electronic spreadsheets are also useful for preparing budgets because they enable planners to see how a change in one calculation affects all the related calculations. For example, assume that a budget planner anticipates that the company will spend more for fuel oil in January and February of next year than it spent in the same months of this year. When the January and February fuel oil figures are changed on the spreadsheet, the computer automatically adjusts the fuel oil total for the entire year, and the planner can tell at once how much to budget for fuel oil for the year.

Graphics, data base, and word processing software can also help you perform many budgeting chores, such as developing charts to show how much of the budget is devoted to each income or expense category; keeping a running tally of expense data that you can store, retrieve, and sort in various ways; and preparing reports to explain how your department is meeting its budgetary goals.

Whatever type of budget your company uses, you are most likely to participate in the budgeting process at the department level. At budget time your department manager may ask you to gather information and documentation about various departmental line items such as office supplies or equipment maintenance costs. If you regularly pay the bills or order office supplies, you may be able to suggest ways to reduce these expenses.

Monitoring the Budget

Department managers are usually required to keep track of their expenditures on a monthly or quarterly basis so they can judge how well they are adhering to the annual budget. For example, if a department has exceeded its overtime budget each month for three months, the manager may have to ban overtime for the rest of the year to avoid exceeding the annual budget for overtime.

Managers often have limits on the amounts they can spend for each line item during a budget period. Your department manager probably would have to obtain approval if he or she wanted to exceed the limits, especially on expensive items such as furniture and equipment. You, in turn, may be required to obtain your supervisor's approval if you need to make a large expenditure. In any event, you may be asked to monitor specific line-item expenditures such as those for supplies, travel, telephone service, or magazine subscriptions throughout the budget year so that your department can keep within the limits.

No. _28_   Amount $ _12.30_

PETTY CASH VOUCHER

Paid to _Fleet Equipment Co._

For _Index cards_

Charge to _Office Supplies_

Approved by   Received by

Susan Berman   _Mark Schaeffer_

Fig. 17-9 Office workers who are entrusted with the petty cash fund use vouchers such as this one to keep track of expenditures.

Petty Cash

Most offices keep **petty cash** which is a small cash fund used to pay for small day-to-day expenses that can't conveniently be paid for by check or credit card. If you are responsible for maintaining the petty cash fund, you should keep cash on hand to cover about two weeks' worth of expenses. It is not a good business procedure to keep large amounts of cash in the office, and you should be sure to lock up even small amounts of petty cash each night in a cash box stored in an office vault or safe. Figure 17-9 shows how to fill in a petty cash voucher.

Recording Withdrawals

You will need to keep a record of each withdrawal from the petty cash fund. The best way to do this is to use a petty cash voucher: a preprinted form with blanks for the date, amount, and purpose of the withdrawal, the name of the payee, and the signature of the person who is making the withdrawal. You may also be required to keep a petty cash register in which you record each petty cash transaction.

Replenishing the Fund

A petty cash fund should have a fixed amount of money. The total of the cash in the fund and the withdrawals noted on vouchers should equal the fixed amount. When the fund runs low on cash, replenish it to the full fixed amount. How you go about this will depend on your employer's policy.

Payroll

One other financial area where you may have certain responsibilities is that of processing and distributing the payroll. A large company will probably have its own payroll department, and you may be responsible only for providing the department with weekly time cards and for distributing paychecks to the employees in your department. In other companies you may be responsible for using a computer system to process the payroll, and in some small businesses, you may even have to process the payroll by hand. We will discuss each of these situations in more detail later in this section.

Payroll Deductions

Every pay period your employer should provide you and each of your coworkers with a pay statement detailing your **gross pay** (the amount of pay before any deductions are made), the amount of and reason for each deduction, and the **net pay** (the amount remaining after the deductions have been made). Usually a pay statement is in the form of a stub or voucher attached to your paycheck (see Fig. 17-10), which you can detach and keep for your personal records.

Your employer is required to withhold a percentage of your gross pay as advance payment on your annual federal income taxes. In some states, employers may be required to withhold state and local income taxes as well. The Internal Revenue Service (the federal government taxing agency) provides employers with tables for calculating the amount to be withheld for federal income taxes. The amounts vary according to marital status and the number of exemptions individuals can claim. The method of computing the amount of the withholding for state and local taxes varies from place to place. Employers are required to forward these tax payments to each government agency periodically.

Your employer is also required to withhold federal social security tax and, in some states, state unemployment insurance tax. You

EARNINGS	HOURS	CURRENT	YEAR TO DATE	DEDUCTIONS	CURRENT	YEAR TO DATE
REGULAR PAY	70 00	692 30	2 076 90	FICA	55 38	166 14
TOTAL PAY	70 00	692 30	2 076 90	FEDERAL	96 92	290 76
				STATE	34 62	103 86
				CITY	2 77	8 31
				NET PAY	502 61	1 507 83

SOCIAL SECURITY NUMBER	DEPT.	CO.
306-26-0210	WP20	01

PERIOD ENDING	FED. EX.	STATE EX.
03/31/-	02	02

Fig. 17-10 This corporate pay statement shows gross pay, net pay, and deductions. FICA stands for Federal Insurance Contributions Act, and that deduction is the social security payment.

may authorize your employer to withhold voluntary contributions to pension plans, contributions to charities such as the United Way, contributions to payroll savings plans, and monthly union dues.

Payroll Records

In order for the payroll staff to process each week's payroll, it has to maintain certain permanent information on each employee, such as the employee's name, salary or hourly wage, and social security number. Your duties may include forwarding changes in this data to the payroll department when new employees are hired, when employees resign or retire, or when they receive raises, promotions, or transfers. The payroll staff can then call up the payroll records, stored on computer storage media or in manual files, and update them with the new data. In large companies this updating has to be done every pay period.

When employees are paid by the hour, they usually either punch in and out on a time clock or fill out time cards to indicate how many hours they worked during the pay period. Most hourly employees are covered by the federal Fair Labor Standards Act, which sets a minimum wage and requires employers to pay one-and-a-half times the regular wage for overtime, or time worked beyond 40 hours a week.

To figure an hourly employee's gross pay, the payroll department computer multiplies the hourly wage by the number of hours worked. It then computes overtime pay separately and adds it to the regular wages.

Processing the Payroll

Businesses usually designate one day each week or every two weeks as payday. On that day each employee receives a check or cash for the amount of his or her net pay for the last pay period and a pay statement detailing all the deductions that have been made. If your company has its own payroll department, the payroll department computer will perform all the processing, and your only duty may be to distribute paychecks to your coworkers.

If, however, it is one of your duties to process your company's payroll by computer yourself, you need to keyboard in the hours of work for each hourly employee and add any changes in the payroll records since the last pay period. The payroll accounting software you use will have the formulas for computing income tax, social security deductions, and so on. It will calculate wages, deductions, and net pay, store all this information for tax and accounting purposes, and print each check and stub automatically.

If you work in a very small office where you are required to process the payroll by hand, you will need to keep a **payroll register**, which lists each employee by name, his or her number of exemptions, regular and overtime pay for the pay period, and each deduction in separate columns. To compute deductions, you will have to use withholding tables provided by the Internal Revenue Service, the Social Security Administration, and the state and local taxing authorities. Once you have computed each employee's gross pay, deductions, and net pay, you must total each column to determine your employer's total costs and the amount of taxes to be sent to each taxing agency. Then you must fill out and distribute checks and pay statements for each employee.

You may recall that some businesses use direct deposit transfers to transfer each employee's pay from the company's bank account to the employee's account. In this case the employees still receive pay statements showing their gross and net pay and deductions so that they can maintain their personal records. Whatever your role may be in processing or distributing the payroll, keep in mind that salary information is private and not to be shared with anyone.

Legal Functions

Businesses, like individuals, are governed by hundreds of federal, state, and local laws that determine their legal rights and responsibilities. Many of the laws involve important issues of civil rights, environmental protection, and malpractice. To comply with these laws, businesses often need to input, process, store, output, and distribute various kinds of legal documents. You may be involved in these tasks. If your company purchases a factory, for example, you might file a copy of the deed and mortgage with the county recorder in the county where the factory is located.

Businesses also use many legal documents, such as sales and credit agreements and contracts, to carry out routine financial transactions. These documents spell out the terms of a transaction and protect the company if the terms are violated. In addition, businesses occasionally sue or are sued to resolve a debt or disagreement or for any number of other reasons. Such litigation always involves the preparation of a number of legal documents.

If you are a member of a support staff, your main responsibility in most legal matters will be to prepare legal documents. The extent of your involvement will depend on the nature and size of the company you work for. You may work for a large corporation that has its own legal department to prepare documents and represent the company in legal matters. Nevertheless, even in a large organization, you may routinely prepare certain legal documents, such as contracts and credit agreements, that are commonly used by your department.

In a small organization, you may also be responsible for preparing other kinds of routine legal documents, such as leases and employment contracts. Of course, if you are employed in a law office, the bulk of your work will be processing a wide variety of complex legal documents, and you may decide to seek additional training to become a legal secretary, a paralegal, or a lawyer.

Legal Documents

Your job responsibilities may include inputting legal documents, processing legal documents, or having these documents notarized.

There are several types of commonly used legal documents that you may be asked to prepare.

Contracts and Agreements **Contracts** and **agreements** are the most common kinds of legal documents used in the business world. Contracts and agreements are legally enforceable understandings or arrangements between two or more parties. They are used most often to state a company's intention to buy or sell specific goods or services and to set the terms of the sale. A contract or agreement can be a sales slip, a memo, a letter, or even an oral promise made by one person to another.

When a contract is a formal written agreement, the person who prepares it should include the names of the parties to the agreement, the date and place of the agreement, the purpose of the contract, the responsibilities of each party, a description of the goods or services to be sold, the amount of payment expected, the duration of the agreement, and the signatures of all parties to the agreement.

Affidavits **Affidavits** can be required in many business situations. Affidavits are sworn, written statements of fact. When a person makes an affidavit, he or she swears under oath, before a judge or some other public officer, that the facts contained in the affidavit are true. For example, people sometimes have to make affidavits to prove their citizenship or to prove that there are no financial or legal judgments pending against them.

Power of Attorney A **power of attorney** is a legal authorization for one person to act as an agent for another. The power of attorney may apply to all of a person's business, financial, and legal matters or only to certain specific matters. For example, a corporate executive might give a lawyer in another state the power of attorney to carry out all the transactions necessary for the corporation to purchase a building in that state.

Real Estate Documents When a company purchases a piece of land or a building, it usually has to process several legal documents. The buyer and seller have to draw up a contract of sale that details the sales price, the down payment, and other terms of the sale and that describes the property being purchased. The buyer will also have to enter into a mortgage agreement, which is an agreement between the buyer and a financial institution describing how the property will be paid for. The buyer will receive a copy of the title, which affirms ownership of the property, and will file copies of the title and mortgage with the county recorder. Another kind of real estate document is a lease, which is an agreement between the owner of a building and the lessee. The lease gives the lessee the right to occupy the building for a specific period of time in exchange for a stated rental fee. Figure 17-11 shows an example of a preprinted real estate document with blank spaces for the variable information.

Williams & Dunn

COUNSELLORS AT LAW

316 South Street

Jacksonville, Florida 32210

(904) 555-7500

JOHN K. WILLIAMS
WILLIAM N. DUNN
MEMBERS OF FLORIDA BAR

, 198-

RE:

File No.

Dear

Please be advised that the closing in the above-captioned matter has been set for on , 198-, at the office of . You must meet me there at that time.

You must vacate your home by this date, and it should be broom clean so the purchasers are able to move in at their convenience after the closing. The purchasers may inspect the property prior to the closing.

A few days in advance you should notify your utility companies, i.e. telephone, water, gas and electric, etc., of the sale, and they will prepare final bills for you and send them to your new address. If you have oil, you should have the tank read and get the written report to me as soon as possible. You will be paid for the oil in the tank at the closing.

Please supply me with the following marital information which is required by the mortgage institution: the date of your marriage, maiden name, and if this is the first marriage for both of you. If this is not, please send us a copy of the divorce decree.

Please advise me if there are any additions or alterations made to your house since the date of the contract.

Please bring a check covering my fee in the amount of $, made payable to Williams & Dunn, Esqs. If you have any questions, please do not hesitate to contact me.

Very truly yours,

WILLIAMS & DUNN, ESQS.

BY:
JOHN K. WILLIAMS

JKW:baw

Fig. 17-11 Stored legal documents are a convenient way to produce legal documents when the same legal language can be used again and again.

Litigation Documents Lawsuits usually involve the preparation and filing of several different kinds of legal documents. These documents are often complex and usually require the preparation of one or more drafts. You are not likely to be responsible for preparing litigation documents unless you are employed in a corporate legal department or by a law firm.

Some of the more common litigation documents include complaints and answers—that is, the actual filing of a lawsuit by the complainer, or plaintiff, and the written response to the lawsuit by the opposing side, or the defendant. Either side may also make a number of motions to the court, which ask that the suit be dismissed, or that other parties be added, or that the judge make an immediate judgment, and so on. In addition, both sides are likely to file notices stating the time and place of a trial or pretrial conference, announcing the withdrawal of an attorney, and the like. The judge may issue a **court order**, which is a formal instruction to one side or the other to either do or stop doing a specific action. Finally, a witness may receive a **subpoena**, which is an order to appear at a trial or hearing in order to testify. Sometimes the subpoena also orders the witness to bring certain documents or records to the hearing.

Processing Legal Documents

Most companies have their own legal forms; however, many legal documents can be purchased from stationery stores as printed legal forms. Each contains the same standard legal language, because the legal provisions of the transaction don't vary; only the specific details differ from one transaction to another. Examples of printed legal forms include mortgages, deeds, real estate sales contracts, office leases, and various litigation forms, such as notices and subpoenas.

Legal documents that deal with the same kind of transaction are often very similar to each other; large parts of the text may be almost identical from document to document. Because these documents are legal, binding agreements, they must contain no errors, and all copies of the documents must be originals (photocopies usually are not acceptable as legal documents). For all these reasons, it makes sound sense to process legal documents on a word processor rather than on a typewriter.

When you process a printed legal form, sometimes called a **law blank**, you must first obtain the information to be filled in from your supervisor or from source documents. Then you should study the form to make certain that you have all the information you need to fill in every space. Legal forms can be stored as soft copy and corrected or changed without retyping the entire document each time.

When you process legal documents, whether on a word processor or on a typewriter, you must observe several basic formatting rules. Traditionally, legal-size paper is used, that is, 8½ by 13 or 14 inches, but sometimes letter-size paper (8½ by 11 inches) may be used. Here are some other rules you should observe when processing legal documents.

■ Use a pica typeface if you can regulate type fonts on your word processor or typewriter. Never use italic or script.

■ Always double-space legal documents. If you are using paper with preprinted margins, leave one or two spaces blank on each side within the margins. If you are using blank paper, leave a 1½-inch margin on the left and at least a ½-inch margin on the right. Use a 2-inch margin at the top of each page and a 1-inch margin at the bottom.

- Indent each paragraph ten spaces, and number each paragraph with a roman numeral and a period followed by two blank spaces.

- Set off quoted material by indenting the material five to ten spaces from the left margin. This material can be single-spaced.

- Page numbers should be centered at the bottom of each page. Each draft should also be numbered, dated, and labeled "First Draft," "Second Draft," and so on.

- Single-digit dates and the year are written out (for example, the third day of August, nineteen hundred and eighty-five); double-digit dates can be written in numbers (the 23d day of September, 1985).

- Numbers are usually written in both figures and words—for example, "Ten thousand dollars ($10,000)," or "Twenty (20) acres of land."

- Insert signature lines for all the parties to a legal document at the end of the document. Never place signature lines by themselves on a separate sheet of paper. Always include two or more lines of text on the same page. You may type either the name of each signer under the line or the designation of each signer, such as "Buyer," "Seller," "Lessor," or "Lessee." If the parties are companies, you can also include the names and titles of the persons who are representing the companies, such as "President," "Vice President," or "Sales Representative."

Photocopies of legal documents are usually not acceptable. Each copy must be an original duplicate, so you must determine the number of copies you require. In some cases you can make carbon copies, but in others you have to execute each copy individually. You may not erase errors or use correction fluid or correction tape to correct or block out portions of a legal document, but you can use Xs to cross out portions of printed legal forms on a typewriter. You can also type hyphens or draw lines through words and sentences to strike them out so long as the deleted words remain legible. With a word processor, this would not be necessary.

If the typewritten material you are adding is short and the space allotted for it is long, draw a Z in ink to fill up the unused space. You can also use a Z to cross out paragraphs or blocks of preprinted legal language that do not apply to the transaction you are recording. If the space is short and the material you are adding is long, you can type it on a separate sheet of paper called a **rider**. Cut off any unused portion of the paper, and paste the rider onto the appropriate space on the form. Then fold the rider to fit neatly into the form.

Notary Publics

Legal documents usually become valid when they are signed. A **notary public** is a person commissioned by a state government to verify signatures on documents for legal purposes. A notary witnesses the signing of documents and attests to the authenticity of the signatures. The notary then **notarizes** the documents by stamping and signing them. Property titles, assignments of mortgages, wills, deeds, partnership agreements, and affidavits are some of the kinds of documents that usually must be notarized.

Many companies find it convenient to have one or more office workers commissioned as notary publics so that employees don't have to travel to a notary's office every time a signature needs to be notarized. If your employer asks you to apply for a notarial commission, you can obtain an application at most stationery stores. You or your employer may have to pay a fee, and you may have to take a test. The state office that commissions notaries will inform you of the requirements. If no one in your office is a notary, keep the names and addresses of a few nearby notary publics on hand.

■ Summary

- ■ Accounting is a means of recording financial data and processing it into information that managers can use to evaluate a company's performance.

- ■ There are three types of business entities—sole proprietorships, partnerships, and corporations.

- ■ Accounting is a form of information processing; it follows the IPSOD cycle.

- ■ Secretaries and administrative assistants may be required to keep journals and ledgers to record business transactions.

- ■ Banking chores include depositing checks and currency and using automatic tellers, night depositories, or bank-by-mail services.

- ■ If an office worker is required to pay the company's bills, he or she must know how to write checks and how to reconcile a checking account balance.

- ■ Electronic funds transfer means the transfer of funds from one bank account to another by means of the telephone, computers, direct deposit, or point-of-sale transfer.

- ■ When companies borrow or lend money, they make credit agreements that describe the interest rates and repayment schedules of their loans.

- ■ A budget helps a company set financial goals and acts as a standard of measurement so that the company can determine if it is meeting its goals.

- ■ Administrative support personnel are often required to help prepare and monitor departmental budgets.

- Petty cash funds pay for small expenditures that cannot conveniently be paid for by check or credit card.

- Payrolls can be processed by computer or by hand. A payroll check usually includes a statement of the employee's gross pay, deductions, and net pay.

- Office workers who process payrolls by hand must know how to compute taxes and other deductions.

- Businesses deal with many legal documents such as contracts, affidavits, real estate documents, and litigation documents.

- Secretaries must follow several specific rules for processing legal documents and for filling out printed legal forms.

■ Review Questions

1. What are the three kinds of business entities, and how do they differ?

2. Explain the difference between a journal and a ledger.

3. Describe two methods you can use to avoid making errors when using a calculator.

4. Describe how to fill out a deposit slip for various items of currency and checks.

5. Name and describe three different kinds of check endorsements.

6. Explain how to reconcile a checking account balance.

7. Define *certified check, cashier's check,* and *bank draft,* and explain how they differ from one another.

8. Explain how a point-of-sale transfer works.

9. Describe five different kinds of payroll deductions.

10. Name and define four types of legal documents.

■ Technical Vocabulary

accounts receivable	general ledger
accounts payable	posting
sole proprietorship	payee
partnership	drawer
corporation	blank endorsement
stockholder	restrictive endorsement
source documents	special endorsement
balance sheet	full endorsement
owner's equity	corrected endorsement
general journal	stub
account	check register

balance
canceled check
dishonored check
point-of-sale transfer
installment
finance charge
budget
line item
operating budget
capital expense budget
project budget
petty cash
gross pay

net pay
payroll register
contract
agreement
affidavit
power of attorney
court order
subpoena
law blank
rider
notary public
notarize

■ Discussion and Skills Development

1. Suppose that you are responsible for a petty cash fund. In the cash box there is $11.84 in bills and coins. You have vouchers for withdrawals of the following amounts: 83¢, $1.98, $3.50, $20, $4.75, $6, and $1.10. What is the total amount of the petty cash fund? Remember that the cash and vouchers add up to the total amount of money in the fund.

2. What is the total amount of the cash deposit that includes the following bills and coins?

   - 57 pennies
   - Four $10 bills
   - One $20 bill
   - 37 quarters
   - 18 dimes
   - Four nickels
   - Twelve $5 bills
   - One $50 bill

3. Roberta Jensen, the only secretary in a small real estate company, pays the company's bills and reconciles the monthly bank statement. One month she discovers that the company check register shows a balance of $698, while the bank statement indicates that the balance should be $935. Mrs. Jensen has checked and rechecked all the checks, stubs, outstanding checks and deposits, and service charges, but she cannot find the error. What should she do?

4. Go to a stationery store and make a list of all the different types of legal forms that are available. Then, using this book and other reference sources, find out what each document is used for. Write a brief description of each type of form, and explain its applications.

part 4
Management and Career Development

You will not step right into a supervisor's job, but knowing what a supervisor does and, in particular, how your job relates to that position will make you a more satisfied and valuable worker. Not the least important reason for knowing what supervisors do is wanting to be promoted to a supervisory position.

Another reason for knowing about managerial duties is that the new technology is changing the nature of the work in the business office. Functions that were once purely managerial are now being handled by administrative support workers. The more familiar you are with managerial duties, the readier you will be to help perform them.

Part 4 will help you understand how a company operates and particularly how the work you do relates to the job and goals of your supervisor and managers.

Knowing how and why a company goes about automating its business office will give you the ability to use your talents more effectively. Part 4 examines the benefits companies derive from automation and looks at the complex issues involved.

Identifying careers in the electronic office, knowing what you need to acquire a job, and recognizing what you need to advance and succeed are covered in the final chapter of Part 4.

chapter 18
Managing Human Resources

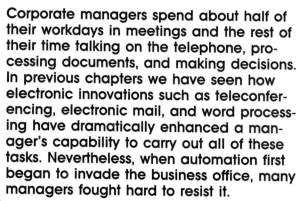

Corporate managers spend about half of their workdays in meetings and the rest of their time talking on the telephone, processing documents, and making decisions. In previous chapters we have seen how electronic innovations such as teleconferencing, electronic mail, and word processing have dramatically enhanced a manager's capability to carry out all of these tasks. Nevertheless, when automation first began to invade the business office, many managers fought hard to resist it.

Many of these were executives who could see the benefits of automating their companies' assembly lines but couldn't see any use for a terminal on their own desks. Now that attitude is changing rapidly as managers see the benefits of office technology and as new workers, many of whom have learned to work with computers, join the work force.

Secretarial work and other types of office work in the electronic office can lead to management careers. It is possible that you may become a manager someday, or at least you may find yourself performing many of the same functions as a supervisor or manager. To succeed as a manager, you will need to be well versed in all the basic office skills, and you will need a good working knowledge of computers and other electronic equipment now used in modern business offices.

You will also need to learn other essential management skills such as how to make decisions and how to supervise employees. Chapter 18 gives you an overview of these skills. It shows you how managers plan, carry out, and evaluate a business operation. You will also see how executives use different kinds of leadership styles to run their operations and how supervisors train, motivate, and evaluate their employees.

The Functions of Managers and Supervisors

The difference between managers and supervisors is that managers decide what has to be done, and supervisors determine how to do it. In a small company, one person may do both jobs, but in a large company, these functions are distributed among several levels of personnel.

A large company like General Motors, for example, is headed by a board of directors, which makes the major decisions such as whether to build a new plant or produce a new product. The president of the company is the chief operating officer. He or she is answerable to the board and responsible for all the day-to-day decision making and operations of the company. Large companies typically are divided into several departments, such as payroll, production, data processing, and sales. A manager heads each department, and within a department, several supervisors are in charge of different groups of personnel. In a production department, for instance, each work shift has its own supervisor and assistant supervisor, who oversee the workers on that shift. Figure 18-1 shows the organizational chart of a computer hardware manufacturing company.

Long- and Short-Term Planning

Managers and supervisors are responsible for planning, implementing, and evaluating the operations of a business. They are concerned with both long-term and short-term planning. **Long-term planning** refers to projects that take a year or more to implement, while **short-term planning** refers to proposals that can be carried out within a few weeks or months.

Assume, for example, that a soft-drink company decides to introduce a new kind of beverage that it hopes will capture 10 percent of the total soft-drink market within two years. First, the company must set the long- and short-range goals and objectives that it needs to accomplish before it can produce the new soft drink. Its long-range goals will be to develop the new flavor and to construct a new plant to produce and bottle the drink. These goals are likely to take a year or more to complete.

To begin the project, the company must find a site for the new plant and must obtain financing from the banks. These are short-term goals. They can be accomplished quickly, and they represent separate, small steps that need to be carried out to accomplish the long-term goal of producing the new drink. Planning can also include mid-range goals. In this case mid-range goals might be to hire a construction company to build the plant and to engage an advertising agency to begin planning a sales campaign.

To make long-term plans, managers need to gather and analyze a variety of information. Before it decides to produce a new drink, the soft-drink company will probably want to know the size of the market, what its competitors are planning to do over the next two years, whether it can obtain the financial resources it needs to carry out the project, whether it can hire or train enough skilled workers to produce the new soft drink, and so on. Computers have dramatically

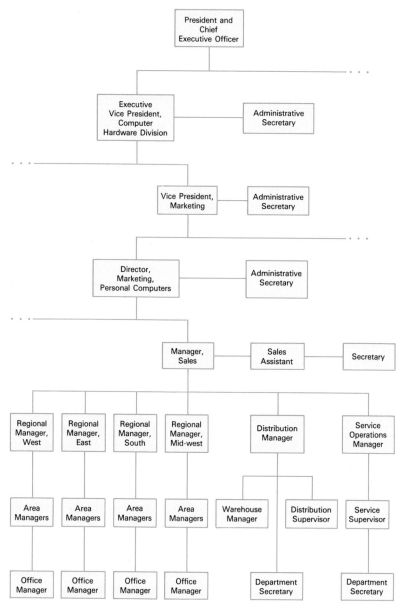

Fig. 18-1 A company's organizational chart shows how its management is organized and spells out its chain of command.

enhanced the process of analyzing information because they enable managers to organize data quickly and efficiently in several useful formats.

Managers also need similar kinds of data to carry out short-term planning. The soft-drink company's financial officer may want to know, for example, whether the company might save money by waiting a month to borrow the money for the new plant, or the manager of the research department may consult the department's work schedules to determine whether a particular team of chemists can be reassigned to begin working on the new formula. Management often delegates such short-term planning to supervisors and their staffs.

Today, more and more managers are using computers to carry out the planning function. The computer gives the manager direct access to information that would take hours to acquire (or even longer) in a traditional office environment. In addition to having access to internal files, many managers use modems to access external data bases which provide up-to-date information about events in the market, competition, and many other topics.

Implementing the Plan

Implementing a plan involves carrying out the company's long- and short-term objectives. Several steps and tasks are involved.

Organizing Organizing is determining how the company can best use its employees, plants, materials, information, and money to carry out its plans. If you were the manager of a department that was assigned the task of producing a new product, you would have to assign supervisors to the job of hiring and training new employees, and you would probably also promote some existing employees to supervisory positions and reassign others so that they could begin work on the new project. In business management, **organization** usually refers to the way in which a business divides responsibilities among its departments and divisions. It also refers to how the business assigns various tasks and functions to employees and to the way it structures its chain of authority or command. This structure is usually spelled out in the company's organization chart.

Controlling Companies establish standards to control the costs and production of each product or service they offer. If you were a manager, it would be a major part of your job to control the costs for such things as supplies and employee overtime within your department. You would also be responsible for making sure that your employees produce the expected number and quality of goods they have been asked to deliver. Production control is most common in assembly-line operations, but computers are now making it possible to monitor the quantity and quality of production in the business office as well. In Internal Revenue Service branch offices, for example, computers are used to monitor how many income tax returns each worker processes in an hour.

Directing In order to succeed with any project, a company needs to provide direction or leadership. In other words, it needs to assign managers who are authorized to make the decisions that ensure that a project runs smoothly. Managers must make decisions that will affect their companies' profits. A manager may have to decide

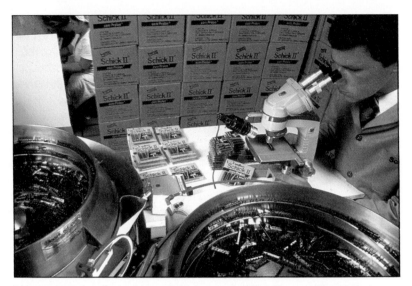

Managers are often responsible for controlling the quality of their company's products. Here a lab technician tests a sample of one of his company's products to make sure it meets the company's and the government's minimum standards.

whether to cease production of a product line, whether to close a plant, or whether to acquire another company. Leadership and decision making will be discussed in detail later in this chapter.

Evaluating the Operation

Evaluating means reviewing the plans and their implementation to determine whether they have been successful. In the case of the soft-drink company, an evaluation of the new drink project might seek answers to questions such as these: Was plant construction completed on schedule? Did the plant start production and make its first shipments according to the plans? Did consumers like the new soft drink? Did it capture 10 percent of the market? Should the advertising campaign be changed?

Competent managers informally evaluate their projects continually as well as at the end. Ultimately, the evaluation process provides a way of comparing the actual results with the original long-term goals. If a project did not return enough profits, if it cost too much, or if it took too long to complete, the managers can reconsider their plans and goals and make new decisions about the project.

The processes of planning, implementing, and evaluating are repeated over and over again, often in overlapping sequences, as managers and supervisors fulfill their responsibilities. They may revise a plan midway in its implementation to meet new goals or circumstances. They may also formulate new plans and make new decisions to put their plans into action. In fact, making decisions is probably the most important function a manager performs.

Decision Making

At the beginning of this chapter you read that managers spend most of their time attending meetings, talking on the telephone, processing documents, and making decisions. In essence, what managers are doing when they hold meetings, talk on the telephone, and read documents is gathering and analyzing information. They then use that information to make the decisions they are required to make to keep their businesses running smoothly and profitably.

Managers could not perform their jobs without making dozens of decisions every day, but they are not the only decision makers in the business office. Virtually everyone who works in an office has to make any number of decisions over the course of any given workday. Some decisions are complicated and difficult to make, while others are trivial and easy, but all decision making involves the same basic steps, depicted in Fig. 18-2:

Basic Steps in
Decision Making

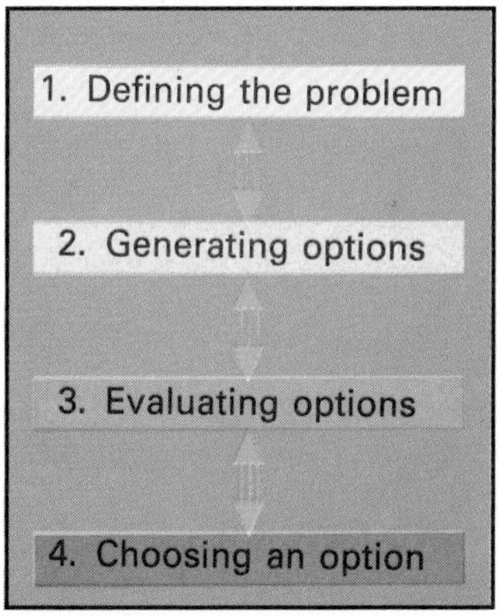

1. Defining the problem

2. Generating options

3. Evaluating options

4. Choosing an option

Fig. 18-2

1. **Defining the problem**. First, you need to determine what must be done. We've called this defining the problem, but the word *problem* doesn't necessarily mean something negative. It can mean an opportunity, a choice, or a project. Your "problem" may be to decide whether to accept a promotion that requires that you transfer to a company branch office.
2. **Generating options**. Next, you must think of the possible solutions to the problem or the methods for arriving at the solution. You might want to discuss some of the possibilities with one or more of your colleagues.
3. **Evaluating options**. Once you've thought of several solutions, you need to consider the possible outcomes of each one and weigh the advantages and disadvantages of each.
4. **Choosing an option**. Finally, you must select the option that you are going to try. You should be aware that you may change your mind at any stage by redefining the problem and generating new options.

Of course, each of us makes hundreds of decisions every day. The vast majority of these decisions are so routine and trivial that we are not even aware that we are going through the decision-making process. For instance, when you decide what to wear to work, what to have for lunch, or what assignments to work on for the day, you define the problem and evaluate and choose options in each case, even though you are not conscious of each distinct step.

In an active, growing organization, managers and supervisors are constantly making decisions. Here are some examples of the kinds of decisions they need to consider:

- **New products and services**. Should we make the new automobile part out of plastic or metal? Which would be safer, more durable, or less costly?

- **Improved procedures**. Should we set up a toll-free, 24-hour hot line to take customer orders and complaints?

TRADITIONAL OFFICE ENVIRONMENT	ELECTRONIC OFFICE ENVIRONMENT

Executive
(decision making)

Middle Management
(analyzing/presenting)

Supervisors
(analyzing/presenting)

Office Workers
(gathering/processing)

Executive
(decision making)

Middle Management
(analyzing/presenting)

Supervisors
(analyzing/presenting)

Office Workers
(gathering/processing)
(decision making)
(analyzing/presenting)

Fig. 18-3 In the electronic office, relationships between office workers and those higher on the hierarchical pyramid change primarily in that some decision making and analyzing can now be done by office workers using electronic equipment.

- **Changes in policies**. Should we adopt staggered work hours for our employees?

- **Changes in equipment**. Should we replace all of our electric typewriters with electronic typewriters?

- **Sources of materials**. Should we buy our supplies from a discount supplier who is cheaper but farther away?

- **Methods of control**. Should we computerize our accounting procedures?

Effective decision making is a skill that you can develop just as you develop the clerical and interpersonal skills you need to work in a business office. Figure 18-3 shows the changes taking place in decision-making responsibilities from a traditional to an electronic office environment. And just as you can learn to use tools such as the computer and telephone, you can learn to use certain tools that can help you make decisions. Two of the most useful tools in decision making are brainstorming and modeling.

Brainstorming   The most efficient managers communicate with their staffs constantly to gather new ideas and learn about problems that interfere with productivity. This process is called **brainstorming**. When a manager brainstorms, he or she discusses a problem with an employee or with a group of employees who are affected by the problem and who will benefit from the solution. For example, a manager might pose the question, "Should we have staggered work hours?" When one member of the group proposes an option, others may think of the advantages and disadvantages of the option, or they may offer alternative ideas. Employees may know of obstacles of which the manager is unaware, or they may offer ideas that are cheaper and easier to implement than any solutions that the manager has proposed.

The manager's role in a brainstorming session is to make sure that the brainstorming is done in a positive atmosphere so that no proposals are ridiculed or dismissed out of hand. The manager must also evaluate each idea carefully to arrive at the best solution.

Sometimes the best solution to a problem generates a different set of problems. For example, when an office staff is placed on staggered hours, the office can be kept open longer, employees can select the hours they want to work to some extent, and rush commuting is reduced. New problems may include not having a full staff during certain hours, increased expenses for lights and heat, and the inability to give everyone his or her first choice of working hours.

Modeling

Part of the decision-making process may include modeling or testing. **Modeling** involves setting up a formula or model that can be used to forecast the possible outcome of a decision. For example, the soft-drink company might set up a mathematical model that could predict whether producing a new drink would be a profitable undertaking when projected costs and sales figures are factored in.

Mathematical models can be very useful in making decisions about manufacturing, retailing, financial planning, or any other kind of business for which statistics—objective, quantitative data— are available. Electronic technology has proved to be particularly valuable in modeling because computers can process a large quantity of data over and over again. New software is continually being produced to help managers make decisions in many different kinds of business situations. These programs allow managers to pose "what if" scenarios in order to determine the outcomes of various options. Spreadsheets are one kind of software that can be used this way.

Although modeling is very useful in making decisions about products, sales, and profits, it is less useful for predicting how people will act or react. Instead, businesses use various testing and surveying techniques to gauge the impact of a product on potential customers or users. For example, before going ahead with full-scale production, our hypothetical soft-drink company might test-market its new drink in one geographic area, or it might employ a market research company to conduct taste tests or shopper interviews in different parts of the country.

Whether managers use brainstorming, modeling, or testing to

gather data and ideas, as a general rule, the more information they have about a problem, the better able they are to make useful decisions. Once a manager makes a decision, it usually falls to supervisors to decide how to carry it out.

The Role of Supervisors

The primary responsibility of supervisors is to implement, or carry out, management's plans. Supervisors usually work directly with the materials and employees of the company, and their main functions are hiring, training, assigning, motivating, and evaluating the people who work under them.

Hiring

Hiring includes recruiting, interviewing, and making job offers. In small companies, supervisors may do all of these things themselves. In large companies, a human resources department (the modern term for a personnel department) is responsible for performing many of these tasks.

What commonly happens when an opening occurs in a large company is that the supervisor informs the human resources department and provides a job description, which defines the duties and the qualifications needed to fill the opening. The human resources department then advertises the opening in newspapers, posts announcements within the company, or contacts job placement companies.

The human resources department may do the preliminary screening and interviewing of applicants. Then the supervisor interviews applicants, selects the finalists, and makes the job offer. Once the new employee begins work, he or she will probably undergo some kind of training program to learn how to operate equipment or follow procedures used by the company.

Training

Employees on the job as well as new employees need training from time to time. Employees usually need to be trained when new equipment is installed or when new production procedures or techniques are adopted. Sometimes companies also retrain workers so that they can perform new tasks when their old jobs become obsolete. Usually, supervisors have the responsibility for training and retraining employees. **Initial training** refers to the training of new employees, and **in-service training** refers to the retraining of existing employees.

Initial Training New employees need to know everything from where to hang their coats to how to run the computer terminal. They also need to know about such things as company work rules and vacation and sick leave policies. Orientation sessions are designed to fill these needs.

Some orientation programs, designed for large groups of incoming employees, use films, lectures, and employee handbooks to do the job. But an orientation can also be an informal session in which

Supervisors are responsible for training new employees and retraining existing employees.

a supervisor or another employee shows the new worker around and answers his or her questions. In some cases a supervisor may simply stay with new employees to teach them how to perform their jobs until they feel comfortable on their own. Supervisors sometimes delegate this role to another employee, but most responsible supervisors prefer to work closely with new employees while they are learning a new job.

In-Service Training   Supervisors are also usually responsible for training or retraining on-the-job employees when they need to learn about new equipment or work methods. In-service training can be conducted for large groups, using films, training manuals, and lectures, or it can be one-on-one, with the supervisor working with the employee until he or she masters the new skill.

Training Techniques   Assume that you are a supervisor responsible for training a group of employees to operate a new piece of equipment. No matter whether you are teaching one employee or a hundred, you should follow a structured training program that covers these four basic steps:

1. **Prepare the employees**. You should put the trainees at their ease. Explain the purposes and advantages of the new equipment or task. Let them know that you will be available to help them for as long as it takes them to learn how to use the new equipment. Start with what they know, and try to interest them in the new equipment or job.
2. **Present the task**. If you are training workers to operate new equipment, provide them with a training manual or written set of instructions. If you are training employees to perform a new job, provide a written job description. Explain the equipment or job, giving clear, complete instructions at a speed the trainees

can absorb. Then demonstrate the job, emphasizing the major points.

3. **Provide practice**. Have the trainees walk through the job until they feel comfortable with it. Be patient and encouraging. Provide feedback for each employee, and reexplain any steps that seem unclear.

4. **Put workers on their own**. Let the trainees do the job themselves. Be available to help, and provide written sources of help if necessary. Check on the trainees with decreasing frequency.

Always invite questions at every step. This way, you can tell whether you are providing clear, comprehensible instructions.

Job Descriptions

Job descriptions are a key element in training, assigning, and evaluating employees. They spell out what employees are expected to do, what knowledge and skills they are expected to possess, and what criteria will be used to evaluate them. Supervisors are usually responsible for writing job descriptions or for helping the human resources department prepare them.

Often employees help refine or revise their own job descriptions, usually as part of their annual evaluations. For example, photocopying may be listed as a task in a job description, but employees may no longer be responsible for photocopying because the company has established a copy center. In addition, it frequently happens that employees are assigned responsibilities over the course of the year that were not included in their job descriptions. These responsibilities should be added to the job descriptions when they are revised.

Written job descriptions are typically divided into three categories:

- **The description itself**. This includes a summary of the overall functions of the position and a detailed list of the specific tasks and responsibilities the employee is expected to perform.

- **Knowledge and skill requirements**. The job description spells out the minimum education or training requirements for the job.

- **Accountability**. This part of the job description tells employees who their supervisors are and whom they are expected to supervise. It may also describe any equipment, expenditures, or areas of operations the employee is expected to oversee.

Earlier in this book, you learned that a function is an operation or series of tasks performed by a person as part of his or her job and that a task is a piece of work or step in carrying out a function. In a job description, a function is frequently called a **position function**. For example, a job description for an administrative assistant might read as follows:

Position functions: Provide support services for general manager of division; maintain and prepare records; schedule appointments, meetings; screen calls and visitors; retrieve, synthesize necessary information.

The job description then specifies the tasks required for carrying out the position function. A sample list might include the following:

- Update appointment calendar daily; review with manager.
- Make all travel arrangements as required.
- Answer telephones; greet visitors.
- Retrieve information as necessary from electronic or manual files.
- Take dictation; type reports, letters, and memos.
- Compile retrieved data into monthly reports.
- Set up electronic meetings (telephone conferences or video conferences).
- Receive, review, and prioritize both electronic and traditional mail.
- Make computer printouts of electronic information as needed.

DELEGATING— A FINE ART

In many situations the work to be performed by employees is clearly identified. For example, the operators in a word processing center process documents, and the supervisor makes assignments and oversees the work flow. Often, though, the division of labor is not so clear. A supervisor is given authority over a group of employees and is responsible for achieving a particular goal—producing the weekly payroll, for example—but it is not spelled out how the supervisor is to go about meeting that goal. The most skillful supervisors perform only the most complex and critical tasks themselves, and they **delegate**, or assign, routine and time-consuming tasks to members of their staffs.

Generally, the more duties and responsibilities supervisors have, the more likely they are to delegate individual tasks to others. This frees the supervisors to con-

centrate on management functions— planning, implementing, and evaluating— and it gives their employees the kinds of additional experience they need to develop into more productive and self-reliant workers.

Some inexperienced supervisors find it difficult to delegate. They are afraid to depend on other people, and they believe it is easier to just go ahead and do a job than to explain it to someone else. These supervisors end up trying to do everything themselves and quickly become bogged down. Other supervisors err in the other direction and try to assign all the work to subordinates. The art of delegating lies in the supervisor's ability to strike a balance between the two extremes—to identify and do the important jobs and to leave the routine work to others.

Assigning Work

One skill that supervisors need to develop is the ability to match their employees' training and capabilities to the work that needs to be done. Supervisors also need to be aware of their employees' preferences in work assignments. One employee may have a talent for research and writing, while another may prefer to work with numbers. A good supervisor tries to make assignments in accordance with such preferences whenever possible. Of course, there are times when it is not possible to match an employee's preference to a task at hand, and it is up to the supervisor to make assignments based on the best interests of the company.

Motivating Employees

Since supervisors work most closely with the work force, it is an important part of their jobs to **motivate** employees. Employees who are motivated perform their jobs as enthusiastically and energetically as possible. They try to solve problems, they show initiative, and they have a positive attitude about their work and their company. They are the kinds of workers who are willing to put in the extra effort or time that is sometimes required to get a job done.

How does a supervisor motivate an employee? No one knows all the elements that contribute to developing a well-motivated worker, but later in this chapter you will read about some theories about motivation and see how they relate to developing an effective leadership style.

If you become a supervisor, you can help motivate employees by treating them fairly and equally when making assignments and work schedules, by making them feel that they are important members of your team, and by listening to their complaints and suggestions. You should make requests rather than demands, and you should issue clear, comprehensible instructions. You should also make sure that you recognize your employees' efforts and accomplishments, and you should let them know frequently how well they are performing their jobs.

Evaluating Performance

Supervisors are normally responsible for evaluating employees, and they do this in one of two ways. They can evaluate workers informally, on a day-to-day basis, simply by saying "Good job on that report" or "There are some problems with this. Can you straighten it out?" This kind of evaluation should occur constantly.

The other kind of evaluation is the formal performance review, which occurs annually in most companies. The supervisor and staff member will sit down to discuss the employee's progress during the past year and to plan for the coming year. The annual review usually includes a written report or evaluation form (see Fig. 18-4) that rates the employee on such traits as work habits, dependability, appearance, accuracy, decision-making ability, efficiency, and so on.

Supervisors often use an employee's job description as the basis for evaluating his or her work. For example, a secretary's job description might require a number of clerical duties. The perform-

Office Employee Performance Evaluation

Soc. Security No.	Employee Name	Division	Department	Wk. Location	Date of Hire
Position Title	Grade Level	How Long Under Your Supervision?	Postpone This Appraisal Until (Date)		

Performance Analysis

In the appraisal, focus on the key aspects of job performance. Check only those factors that are applicable to the employee's job. Space is provided for you to add any other job-related factors you think are important. Be sure to complete this section as fully as possible; it will help you determine the employee's overall performance rating.

JOB RESULTS
- Thoroughness of work
- Accuracy-lack of mistakes
- Quantity-output of meaningful work
- Coverage of total job responsibility

JOB KNOWLEDGE
- Understanding work procedures, methods and techniques
- Learning and adapting to new methods and techniques
- Understanding equipment

DEPENDABILITY
- Adherence to instructions and directions
- Consistency and reliability of work habits
- Efficiency under pressure
- Supervision required
- Ability to get things done

RELATIONSHIPS
- Cooperation with other in group
- Respect and consideration for others
- Acceptance of constructive criticism
- Impressions created outside department

INITIATIVE
- Efforts to improve own qualifications
- Efforts to improve the way work is done
- Coping with problems as they arise
- Willingness to assume responsibility

OTHER JOB RELATED FACTORS
-
-
-
-

ATTENDANCE

	IN A 6-MONTH PERIOD	IN A 12-MONTH PERIOD
Poor	☐ Absent 4-5 Days	☐ Absent 7-8 Days
Excessive	☐ Absent 6 or More Days	☐ Absent 9 or More Days

PUNCTUALITY

Poor	☐ Late 7-8 Times	☐ Late 11-12 Times
Excessive	☐ Late 9 or More Times	☐ Late 13 or More Times

Performance Comments

What aspects of the employee's duties are handled in an exceptional or commendable manner?

What aspects of the employee's duties are not handled as well as should be expected?

Performance Rating

Considering all the employee's performance factors, please check the statement that most nearly fits this employee's overall performance on the current job in the last twelve months:

1 ☐ Exceptional — Superior performance. Consistently exceeds job standards.
2 ☐ Commendable — High standard of performance. Consistently meets, and occasionally exceeds, job standards.
3 ☐ Good — Performance normally expected of qualified employee.
4 ☐ Needs improvement — Performance not up to desired standard; should show improvement.
5 ☐ Unacceptable — Poor performance. Cannot be retained on job without immediate improvement.

Development Plans

The employee's career objectives and your department's staff needs will dictate the development plan. The plan should help to improve the employee's skills, increase job knowledge, or provide a means of correcting problems. Use the following code list to identify the appropriate training programs.

State your plans and objectives for improving the employee's performance (consider increased responsibility, coaching, on-the-job training, etc.)

If formal training programs will help the employee, please code (using the course list in the instructions) those programs that the employee needs.

1 _____ 2 _____ 3 _____ 4 _____ 5 _____ Write in other _____

A. Business Writing & Editing	I. Business Math	Q. Receptionist Training
B. Copy Editing & Proofreading	J. Business Correspondence	R. Supervisory Training
C. Make-up & Production	K. Business English	S. Accounting
D. Graphics, Art & Design	L. Shorthand Refresher	T. Word Processing
E. Advertising & Marketing	M. Shorthand I	U. Computer Technology
F. Promotion	N. Typing Refresher	V. Language Arts
G. Research & Statistics	O. Typing I	W. Other (specify).
H. Office Practices Seminar	P. Telephone Techniques	

Employee's Comments

Employee's Signature
(Your signature indicates only that you have read this appraisal.)

Appraised By _____ Date _____

Appraisal Approved By _____ Date _____

FORM 09-873.00 (Rev. 7/85)

Fig. 18-4 Evaluation forms are corporate "report cards" that tell employees how well they are performing their jobs and how well they are developing as reliable, self-motivated workers.

465

ance evaluation will determine whether the secretary has been adequately performing those duties.

In some companies, supervisors supplement the job description with a written statement of objectives as a basis for evaluating employees. The **statement of objectives** is a description of the goals or objectives that the employee is expected to accomplish during a set period of time, usually a year. A statement of objectives for a secretary might require him or her to reduce typing errors by 75 percent by the end of the evaluation period.

A formal performance review can be a positive and motivating experience for employees. It provides an opportunity for a supervisor and an employee to discuss the company's goals and the employee's goals. In addition, they can try to resolve any work problems the employee may be experiencing. All too often, however, employees come to dread the performance review because they are surprised by negative comments about their work. Supervisors who practice constant informal criticism throughout the year can eliminate this element of unpleasant surprise.

One of the greatest weaknesses of supervisors and managers is their tendency to avoid formal performance reviews with their employees. However, the review process should be viewed in a positive light. When supervisors conduct performance reviews, their basic goals should be to identify and reinforce each employee's strengths and to identify the employee's shortcomings. In addition, the review should include programs and plans for the coming year that will help the employee grow and correct his or her weaknesses.

In many companies, supervisors and managers conduct formal annual or more frequent performance reviews with workers, during which progress toward goals is assessed and plans for the next period discussed and agreed upon.

A good performance review requires experience and skill, but inexperienced supervisors can get help from a broad range of literature on the subject. Some companies also provide formal training programs for their supervisory staffs on employee evaluation and other aspects of supervision.

Handling Stress

Despite all of its positive contributions, the electronic office has created some special problems for both managers and employees. One such problem is **stress**, the body's response to change and stimulation. High levels of unrelieved stress can cause physical and emotional problems for workers.

Job-related stress in the electronic office occurs when employees perceive themselves as being controlled by their machines rather than the other way around. Workers may also experience stress when they are required to learn to operate complicated new machines or when they are required to meet unreasonable production quotas. There have been cases reported in the news media of overworked employees who shredded, threw out, or hid thousands of unprocessed documents in order to relieve the pressure of their work load. Workers who experience stress in the automated office generally feel uncomfortable or threatened if there are changes in their routine, and they react by underutilizing the new equipment or by sticking to old ways of doing things. One way you can overcome the problem is to involve employees in the process of making changeovers. Provide training in the use of new equipment, be patient and responsive to problems, and ask the employees for their opinions and evaluations of the new equipment or procedures.

If you become a supervisor, you must take stress into consideration when you motivate and evaluate your staff. It is important to let employees know whether or not you are satisfied with their work. Being "left in the dark" about their performance will create more stress for employees than will an open discussion of any negative aspects of their work. Providing constructive criticism will allow them to improve their performance and will relieve stress on both sides.

Leadership Styles

Managers and supervisors develop different leadership styles, or ways of carrying out their functions and dealing with their employees. Each manager's style is a blend of his or her experience, training, and personality. Some managers like to be friendly and outgoing; others prefer to maintain a distance between themselves and their employees. Some are intuitive and creative; others are methodical and plodding. Managers develop their own leadership styles as they move up through the ranks by imitating those above them and by trying out different ways of doing things until they find the methods that best suit their own temperaments and circumstances.

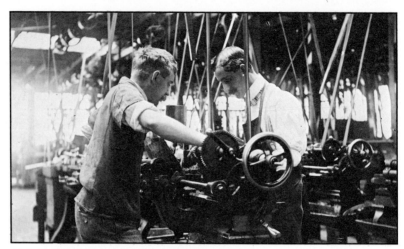
At the start of the Industrial Revolution, workers were considered extensions of the machines they operated.

A manager's leadership style can have a great impact on how well he or she motivates employees. Social scientists have been studying management theory and human behavior in the workplace for decades, and they have developed several different theories about how managers motivate their employees.

Workers and Machines

For a long time after the start of the Industrial Revolution, factory owners looked upon their workers as extensions of the machines they operated. They were just one component of an array of tools and materials the manufacturer could use to produce a product, and they were as interchangeable as the machinery. If a worker couldn't perform well, he or she was replaced by another worker who could do a better job. Workers' rights were nonexistent, and most factory owners had little regard for their employees' needs or desires.

At the beginning of the twentieth century, an engineer named Frederick Taylor became the first person to study the effect that workers could have on production. But Taylor's efficiency studies overlooked human factors and focused only on quantitative data such as how much material a worker could move most efficiently in an hour.

The Hawthorne Effect

The effect of good human relations on production was discovered almost accidentally in a famous experiment at the Hawthorne, New Jersey, plant of the Western Electric Company. While experimenters were studying the effects of improved working conditions, such as better lighting, on worker productivity, they had frequent contact with the workers and paid them a good deal of attention.

One startling result of the study was the discovery that the increased attention alone resulted in higher productivity—regardless of any other factors in the study. When working conditions were improved (good lighting, music, frequent breaks), the workers' performance improved. But when all those improved conditions were removed, the workers still continued to better their performance. The workers had been made to feel special, and the attention that was paid to them was as important as or more important than any specific working conditions.

Theory X and Theory Y

Douglas McGregor, in his 1968 work *The Human Side of Enterprise*, described what he called **Theory X** and **Theory Y**. Theory X assumes that most people dislike work and will avoid it if possible. They will work only if forced to or only to provide themselves with life's essentials. In addition, Theory X supposes that most people prefer to avoid responsibility and creativity in the workplace. Theory Y assumes just the opposite: that most people find work fulfilling and enjoyable and that given the chance, they will be creative, self-directed, and responsible workers.

According to McGregor, managers who subscribe to Theory X have an authoritarian style. They do not communicate with their employees or seek their opinions, and they are likely to assume that as long as their employees are paid, they will work satisfactorily. Theory Y managers are much more democratic. They communicate frequently with employees, solicit their opinions, and give them more control over their work lives.

Recent studies have shown that in some respects both theories are valid and useful, depending on the specific workplace where they are applied. The assembly-line worker who performs the same limited tasks day in and day out may dislike his or her work intensely and may only be working to earn a living. On the other hand, an administrative assistant who performs many different, challenging tasks every day may find work very rewarding and satisfying. Usually, most jobs involve elements of both theories. In any case, social scientists believe that involving workers in making work-related decisions helps motivate them to perform better. Letting workers take an active, positive part in running their workplace is known as **participatory management**.

Maslow's Hierarchy of Needs

Abraham Maslow developed a theory that everyone has certain physical and psychological needs that are fulfilled by work. He theorized that these needs can be divided into levels and that as each level of needs is met, the worker is motivated to satisfy the next level (see Fig. 18-5). At the lowest level of Maslow's scale is the need to obtain food, clothing, and shelter. That is followed by the need to feel safe, the need to feel a sense of belonging, the need for recognition and self-esteem, and finally, the need for self-actualization, that is, the need to achieve one's highest potential. Fulfilling all of these needs, Maslow believed, results in job satisfaction.

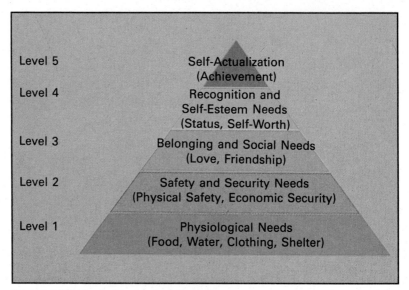

Level 5   Self-Actualization
           (Achievement)
Level 4   Recognition and
           Self-Esteem Needs
           (Status, Self-Worth)
Level 3   Belonging and Social Needs
           (Love, Friendship)
Level 2   Safety and Security Needs
           (Physical Safety, Economic Security)
Level 1   Physiological Needs
           (Food, Water, Clothing, Shelter)

Fig. 18-5 Maslow's hierarchy of needs.

Herzberg's Motivation Hygiene Theory

Frederich Herzberg used Maslow's needs hierarchy as the foundation for developing the theory that the presence or absence of certain elements in a job can affect motivation. He identified these elements, which he called **hygienes**, as pay, advancement potential, status, work conditions, and interpersonal relationships. He theorized that these elements prevent employee dissatisfaction if they are present but that they do not, in themselves, motivate. Herzberg believed that other elements such as recognition, achievement, and responsibility are the real motivators but that they can be outweighed by the effects of missing hygienes.

Management by Objectives

Management by objectives (MBO) is a participatory management style that responds to the theories of McGregor, Maslow, and Herzberg and that seems to succeed very well in actual practice. MBO brings managers and employees together periodically to set specific goals or objectives. After deciding what the goals should be, managers and workers decide how to go about achieving those goals, set deadlines, and agree on the standards to be met. They put their plans into writing and then meet from time to time to review objectives and evaluate progress. In effect, this is nothing more than involving employees in the management functions of planning, implementing, and evaluating that were discussed in the first part of this chapter. For management by objectives to succeed, managers and employees have to develop realistic goals. They have to agree on how the goals will be met, and when the deadline has passed, they must evaluate the actual outcome against their expectations.

MANAGEMENT BY OBJECTIVES

This simplified statement of goals shows the essential ingredients of objectives that a worker and a manager would establish. Goals for increasing skills are combined with tasks and standards needed to get the job done. In parentheses after each statement is a suggestion of how achievement will be evaluated. The goals are also weighted to show that some are more important than others.

Goal Statements	Weight
1. To increase typing speed to 70 wam. (Year-end test)	10%
2. To keep electronic and paper files up to date with no more than a day's lag. (Files)	30%
3. To maintain current telephone log. (Log)	10%
4. To return dictated letters for review or signature within four hours. (Files/log)	30%
5. To learn use of computer graphics generation capabilities by midyear. (Generation of graphics)	20%

Management by Walking Around

MBWA, a takeoff on the acronym MBO, stands for **management by walking around**. The book *In Search of Excellence* (Peters and Waterman, Harper and Row, New York, 1982), which is a study of companies geared for success in the eighties, devotes quite a bit of time to this leadership style. The authors say that MBWA contributes substantially to the success of some of America's best companies.

Managers who use MBWA are highly visible leaders. They spend little time in their offices, preferring to be out in the production areas or on the road visiting their company's plants, salesrooms, and offices. They communicate constantly with employees, and they see and hear for themselves how things are going instead of relying on information processed by other managers within the organization.

The benefits are obvious. No matter how good communication may be in a business, direct observation is a very reliable way to gather information. The charge "you never see the boss around here" is never heard with MBWA; the boss gets seen, and the boss sees. More and more, a leader's personal interest and enthusiasm are being recognized as important ingredients in a company's success; MBWA is a powerful demonstration of that interest.

In Search of Excellence also describes other successful management techniques and leadership styles used in many American companies.

A Style for You

As you develop your own leadership style, it is important for you to understand the different management theories and to be able to use them to devise ways of motivating your employees. Your leadership style should be a good "fit" between your personality, the composition of your staff, and the kind of business you are involved in. For example, the supervisor in charge of a word processing center in which each worker expects to be given every assignment would need a different leadership style from that of the manager of a sales department in which each employee is expected to be an aggressive self-starter.

You need to know your own strengths and weaknesses. You might be the kind of manager who relies on past experience and intuition when making a decision. You may rely on your business sense or on your personal likes and dislikes. Or you may like to gather a lot of information and make objective, intellectual analyses of each problem before making a decision. Most managers have a mixture of all of these attributes, but some elements are much

Managers who practice "management by walking around" learn about their employees' problems first-hand and show their employees that they are interested in them.

stronger than others. If you can integrate all of these attributes, you will have a great advantage over managers who must always be compensating for their weaknesses.

Makeup of a Successful Manager

As you become more experienced in your role as a secretary, office worker, or administrative assistant, you will have an opportunity to develop many work habits and skills that will help you become a good supervisor or manager. For example, when you perform administrative support tasks such as accounting and budgeting, you are already participating to some degree in the management functions of planning and evaluating. In addition, if you are required to train or oversee other employees, you are already learning the major function of supervisors.

Leadership style, as we have said, is a highly individual trait, but there are also some common characteristics that help identify people who are likely to become successful managers.

Basic Job Skills If you want to become a manager, you need to develop good basic skills. These include technical skills such as typing, shorthand, and the ability to operate computers and other electronic equipment. They also include such personal traits as punctuality, dependability, good personal appearance, ethical behavior, loyalty, good organizational skills, and a solid knowledge of and interest in the company you work for.

Good Self-Image In addition to basic job skills, you need to have self-confidence and a good perception of yourself. Do you have a good feeling about yourself? Do you approach new challenges with enthusiasm and an eagerness to learn rather than with fear and anxiety? Potential executives say yes to these questions.

Good Communication Skills Managers often have to speak before large groups of people. They serve on boards and committees where they try to persuade others to adopt certain courses of action. They write letters and reports, and they deal constantly with subordinates. All of these activities require good communication skills. This means learning to write concisely and to the point, learning to plan speeches and telephone conversations, and learning to communicate effectively with employees who may come from many different social, economic, and educational backgrounds. As you learned in Chapters 5 and 6, secretaries and other office workers also need to develop these skills.

Ability to See the Big Picture You need to be able to see how each job contributes to the company's overall goals. Some employees are concerned only about their own jobs or their own departments. They may feel that they are in competition with other employees or offices within the company, and they fail to realize that all employees are, or should be, working toward the same goals. The employee who has a broad perspective and who promotes the inter-

Managers must have good communications skills since they are often required to speak before large groups of people.

ests of the company as a whole stands a better chance of being offered a management position.

The introduction of office automation offers an illustration of how the ability to see the big picture can contribute to a company's efficiency and productivity. Some companies have electronic equipment that is not fully utilized because the managers who planned for it failed to take an overall view. One office may have one kind of computer equipment, and another office may have another, incompatible system. In one office, word processors may be used only to improve the typing speed of secretaries, while other offices remain unautomated, and employees must carry out time-consuming tasks by hand.

In companies where management took a look at the big picture, the managers planned for computer systems that would enhance the entire company's operations. Terminals, printers, and copiers can communicate with one another, and secretaries can use their word processors not only to type but also to send electronic mail and to search data bases. And each office can use the computer system for its own needs: to process purchase orders, take inventory, perform accounting and budgeting tasks, and so on. This kind of overall planning can save a company enormous amounts of time and money.

Initiative and Self-Motivation The ability to start and complete assignments on your own and the willingness to look for new undertakings are probably the most important characteristics you can possess if you are interested in being promoted to a management-level job. These traits demonstrate that you are capable of making decisions and that you are comfortable with responsibility.

As you gain experience on the job, you will acquire many of the skills that managers need. Your self-confidence, for instance, will grow as you learn your job and become comfortable in it. You will develop good judgment, which will enable you to exercise your abilities at the right time and in an appropriate manner. Initiative may be perceived as aggression or ambition in some circumstances, and it will be up to you to recognize when and how to assert yourself. This in itself is another qualification for management responsibility. Once you have measured yourself against these characteristics and decided that you have the desire and ability to become a manager, you need to do some career planning. Chapter 20 will explore careers in the electronic office and show you how you can plan for your own future.

■ Summary

- Managers decide what has to be done, and supervisors decide how to do it.

- The three main functions of managers are to plan, to implement, and to evaluate company operations.

- Implementing consists of organizing the company to carry out the operations, controlling the costs and quality of the product, and directing or leading the company and employees.

- A major task of managers is to make decisions. The basic steps in decision making are defining the problem, generating and evaluating options, and choosing an option.

- Two useful tools to use in decision making are brainstorming and modeling.

- The main functions of supervisors are to hire, train, assign, motivate, and evaluate employees.

- To train employees to do a new job, the supervisor should tell them about the job, demonstrate it to them, let them practice it, and then let them do it on their own.

- Job descriptions explain the functions and tasks of a job, list the minimum qualifications and training for the job, and tell employees who their supervisors are.

- Supervisors need to delegate work to others and to match their employees' abilities and preferences to jobs.

- Supervisors should evaluate employees informally all the time and should hold formal performance evaluations once a year.

- Supervisors must consider job-related stress when motivating and evaluating employees.

- Leadership style is the manner in which managers carry out their functions.

- Most theories about motivation assume that workers need to be involved in controlling their workplace and that they need to satisfy certain needs such as the need for recognition, achievement, and self-esteem.

- Management by objectives involves employees in planning and carrying out corporate goals.

- The characteristics of a successful manager include basic job skills, a good self-image, good communication skills, the ability to see the big picture, and initiative and self-motivation.

■ Review Questions

1. List and explain the major functions of managers.

2. Describe the three tasks involved in implementing a corporate plan or operation.

3. Describe the steps involved in decision making.

4. Explain brainstorming and modeling.

5. List and explain the major functions of supervisors.

6. Describe the four basic steps in training employees.

7. How do supervisors use job descriptions and statements of objectives to evaluate employees?

8. What is the Hawthorne effect, and what does it indicate?

9. Describe the main characteristics of management by objectives.

10. What characteristics identify employees who would make good managers?

■ Technical Vocabulary

long-term planning
short-term planning
organization
evaluating
brainstorming
modeling
initial training
in-service training
job description
position function
delegate

motivate
statement of objectives
stress
Theory X and Theory Y
participatory management
hygienes
management by objectives
  (MBO)
management by walking
  around (MBWA)

■ Discussion and Skills Development

1. Imagine that you have just been promoted to the position of office manager. One of your first tasks is to replace yourself in your old position of secretary. Using the job description on

page 462–463, define the qualifications the job requires and the questions you should ask to find out if a candidate has them. Then write down ten interview questions to ask candidates for the job. Try to include questions about technical skills and about work habits.

2. Think about a job you have had—paying or nonpaying—and about the person who supervised you. How would you characterize your supervisor's leadership or management style? Write down your thoughts in two columns, with the strengths in one column and the weaknesses in the other. If you had been in your supervisor's position, what would you have done differently?

3. Find two or three people in your circle of family or friends who have been promoted recently to more responsible jobs in their companies. Ask them what steps they took to move into their new positions and what kinds of problems they encountered when they assumed the new responsibilities. Ask them to tell you how they overcame some of the problems and to explain what they might do differently the next time.

4. With a small group of students in your class, set up a decision-making exercise. As a group, select a "problem" to work on: for example, planning an event or choosing a new word processor for classroom use. Follow the decision-making steps outlined in this chapter, and record each step on a chalkboard. Brainstorm for solutions, evaluate them, and eventually choose one. Make note of the kinds of information your group felt it needed to make a choice. If you could, how would you obtain and analyze that information? Decide and agree on how you would evaluate your choice. Did anyone in the group emerge as a leader? When you have completed the exercise, write down at least three things you learned about decision making by doing this.

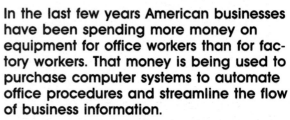

chapter 19
Managing Automated Office Systems

In the last few years American businesses have been spending more money on equipment for office workers than for factory workers. That money is being used to purchase computer systems to automate office procedures and streamline the flow of business information.

In recent years the cost of purchasing computer systems has been declining, and computers have become easier to understand and use. Nevertheless, the costs are still high enough and computers are still complex enough that successful companies make it a point to carefully study their automation needs before investing in a computer system. The studies are expected to answer these questions: How much will the system cost? What benefits will it provide? How will the staff react to it? The company that rushes into buying a computer system before it answers these questions risks wasting a substantial investment and costing itself countless hours of lost time.

As someone entering the business world, you may one day be involved in helping to plan and create an electronic office. To do that, you will need to be aware of the issues and decisions that go into automating an office. You will also need to see how automation changes job functions and responsibilities.

Modern business computer systems no longer require such highly technical employees as computer programmers and systems analysts. The need in the future will be for people who understand office functions and procedures. This will create new opportunities for office workers to move up the career ladder into positions where they will be managing electronic offices. Chapter 19 will show you how automation changes and enhances office functions, and it will describe just how companies carry out the planning process to create an electronic office.

The Benefits of Automation

The goal of office automation is to increase productivity, either by saving time and money or by enabling businesses to produce more goods or services. In the factory, automation has usually been used to perform a particular task faster than it could be done by hand or to reduce the number of workers needed to perform the task. In the office, too, automation means faster work or fewer people. But it also means doing tasks in new ways. This can result in a reorganization of the office and changes in employees' job functions.

Both kinds of changes are important. If a typist can type twice as fast using a word processor, then that person will be able to produce twice as much work for the company in the same amount of time. The company saves money because it needs only one employee instead of two to perform the same work, and it saves time because letters, orders, and reports can be processed at twice the previous rate.

Changes in job functions can also lead to increased productivity. You have seen throughout this book how automation has changed the functions of secretaries and other office workers by freeing them from repetitious, mundane tasks and by giving them the opportunity to assume management responsibilities. Because these employees can perform more complicated functions, they are much more valuable to the company. Automation has also freed supervisors and managers from having to perform many routine tasks, and it has speeded up the flow of information processing so that managers can gather information and make decisions more efficiently.

It doesn't automatically follow that the company that automates will reduce the number of its employees. Automation may eliminate some jobs, and the employees in those jobs may be retrained, laid off, or offered early retirement incentives. What often happens is that because the company's employees can produce more work, the company expands production. Automation makes it possible for the company to reach more customers. It sells more goods or services and generates more income. It may even have to hire more people to help meet the increasing demands for its products.

Automation also enables companies to provide better services for customers. It can greatly increase the speed at which information flows within a company and outside to customers, suppliers, and others with whom the company must interact. This results both in more service and in better-quality service to customers.

People in various departments within an organization can have immediate access to the data and information they need to perform their jobs (see Fig. 19-1). Information can be shared and feedback given almost immediately. Many functions that are redundant from one department or branch office to another can be streamlined, increasing efficiency and productivity. Through automation companies also have access to outside sources of information, such as data banks and information services. All of these factors work together to improve the productivity of the organization.

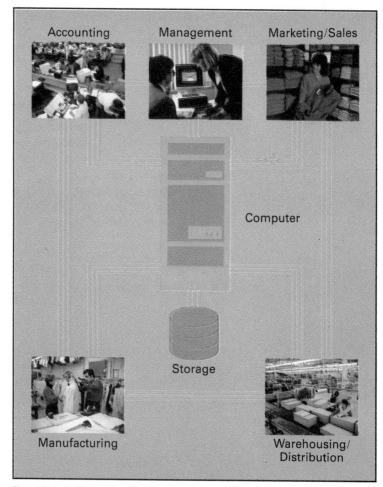

Fig. 19-1 Automation enables a clerk to send a purchase order to many different offices simultaneously.

THE
BOTTOM LINE

When a company increases productivity through automation, one of the outcomes should be an improvement in the "bottom line." Managers have to determine how the cost-benefit ratio will affect the bottom line. This is simply common business jargon for "How much is it going to cost?" and "How much profit will it generate?" **Bottom line** means the net profit—the amount of profit remaining after the company has deducted all of its expenses. The term *bottom line* refers to the very last figure—literally the bottom line—on a company's annual financial statement, which always shows the company's net profit for the year.

A **cost-benefit ratio** is a comparison of the costs of carrying out a plan or operation with the profit or benefit the company can expect to receive. It is a kind of mathematical model that helps management decide whether or not to go ahead with a given proposal. If the ratio is low—that is, if the company can expect a large return for its investment—the project will probably be approved. If the ratio is high—that is, if the profits or benefits are only slightly greater than, equal to, or less than the costs—management will probably decide to shelve the project.

A cost-benefit ratio is a useful tool in making decisions. One problem with it, however, is that it does not include certain intangible benefits. A proposal might, for example, offer improved employee morale or improved client relations, but it is often difficult or impossible to estimate these benefits in monetary terms.

Planning an Automated Office

As you read earlier, people who are planning to automate an office try to answer four basic questions:

1. How much will it cost, not only for installation but also for maintenance and training?

2. What benefits will be derived in time and money saved or in improved services offered customers?

3. How will the staff react?

4. What current systems and procedures will change?

The first two questions are often stated as a combined question: What's the cost-benefit ratio? In planning for office automation, however, it is often better to consider costs and benefits separately. The reason is that it is often difficult to express the potential benefits of automation in specific monetary terms. This is particularly true when a planner is considering new ways of doing things.

To demonstrate the cost-benefit ratio resulting from increasing a typist's speed by 50 percent is relatively easy. It is less easy to specify the cost-benefit ratio resulting from making it possible for a secretary or administrative assistant to access a data base or develop a sales graph. Yet in the long run, the company's benefits will probably be greater as a result of the latter changes.

How Changing Technology Affects Planning

Before looking at steps involved in planning office automation, let's first consider how changes in technology have affected the process of planning and implementing a system.

As you have read, automation first entered the business office in the form of huge, expensive mainframe computers that were used for data processing tasks such as handling payrolls, inventories, and billing. Not only were they expensive in themselves, but they also required special technicians to program them and run them. Secretaries, administrative assistants, accountants, and other office workers could not use these computers. They merely provided the necessary data, which was then processed by the newly hired special systems technicians. A host of new jobs appeared in the business world, mostly with the words *systems*, *programmer*, and *analyst* in their job descriptions.

The financial investment in equipment and staff for these early systems was extremely high, and businesses thought long and carefully before making it. They conducted months-long studies. They hired special consultants to help them decide about equipment or to custom-design a system.

The situation today is dramatically different because of the advent of minicomputers and, in particular, microcomputers. Not only are the newer computers inexpensive and powerful, but they can also be used by anyone with a little training. The software programs for today's computers are also less expensive and more powerful. And today's micros can process voice, text, and image as well as data.

Today's computer systems can also perform several different functions at once instead of just one function at a time. Terms such as *multitasking* and *parallel processing* have been coined to describe these multiple capabilities. **Multitasking** means that a computer system that is being operated by several users at separate terminals can move back and forth from one user's tasks to another's so quickly that the users are not even aware of it. **Parallel processing** refers to the ability of a computer to run two or more programs, such as data processing and word processing, simultaneously. Offices in which there are computers that are capable of doing several tasks simultaneously and in which all pieces of hardware are interconnected are said to be **integrated**.

All of these high-tech advances are providing office workers with more power at a lower cost. A company does not need to make a large initial investment when it decides to automate its offices. It does not need to have software programs specifically designed for it; it can buy them off the shelf. And if one program doesn't work out, the company can get another one. It will not have wasted much money.

This means that in many cases companies no longer need to hire outside consultants when they decide to automate, nor do they need to conduct long-term studies. Secretaries and other office workers can evaluate and recommend software. Who knows better what is needed to perform the tasks? Nor is it necessary for companies to hire squads of systems analysts, programmers, or other specialists, because office workers can operate the sophisticated computers of today with minimal training.

In many fully integrated electronic offices, the technical specialists are being phased out as office workers acquire the necessary skills to run the systems. This change accelerates automation because companies realize that they no longer need to augment their traditional staffs with a host of expensive technicians who could wipe out most, if not all, of the supposed savings from automation.

Major Challenges Today

Planners of office automation do face particular challenges today. One has to do with timing and the other with the compatibility of different computer systems within a company.

Timing Deciding when to automate can be a worrisome problem for a company. Computer systems and software programs are constantly being improved and upgraded, so it is always tempting to delay automation. Of course, by waiting, the company is losing all the potential benefits of automation while a competitor is moving ahead and realizing them.

Incompatible Systems As you learned earlier, different computer systems are often **incompatible**—that is, they cannot communicate with one another. Computer hardware and software have become so inexpensive that middle managers sometimes go out and get their own systems. When this happens, a company can end up owning several different, incompatible systems within the same building. The computer industry is working on ways of overcoming problems of incompatibility.

Automating the Business Office

Although computer systems have become much cheaper and much easier to program and operate, companies still face a relatively costly and complicated process when they decide to make a changeover from a traditional office to an electronic one. It's true that many companies don't have to hire technical consultants to help them automate, but when they assign their own employees to the task of devising an office automation system, the employees have to become at least moderately knowledgeable about computers. Otherwise, they may be overwhelmed by incomprehensible technical jargon and by the great quantity and variety of equipment and software that are available in today's electronic marketplace.

Companies must give careful thought to automating or to replacing an outdated computer system with a new one. They need to choose a system that can carry out all the functions expected of it and that is powerful enough (has enough memory) to meet all of the company's processing needs. If a company chooses the wrong system for its needs, it may be stuck with that system for years to come, or it may lose a sizable investment in time and money and have to automate all over again.

One way in which companies go about automating is by conducting a **system study**. This is a study that focuses on the company's overall system of procedures and functions rather than on individual tasks, although the results will affect the tasks. The study is intended to result in the creation of a complete office automation system capable of performing various functions such as word processing, data processing, graphics production, and interoffice communication. There are seven main steps in the typical system study, beginning with a preliminary survey.

Many office workers have acquired the skills necessary to automate office systems without the help of technical specialists.

Preliminary Survey

The first step is to identify the need or problem. The people best able to define the need are usually those who will be using the system. Everybody who will be affected by the system should, therefore, be involved, directly or indirectly, in the preliminary survey. Also, people who are involved in the planning will be more committed to implementing the plan.

A large company considering ways to automate its offices would need to involve employees from every department. A payroll clerk could suggest ways to automate payroll production. A salesclerk could specify exactly what information he or she needs to include on an order form. Employees in the bookkeeping department would know best what features they would require in a spreadsheet program. This process would continue until the needs of every department and every group of employees had been examined and identified.

Office Automation Study

Once needs have been determined and some broad goals established, the next step is to examine the existing system. What is being done, and who is doing it? Why is it being done? This study tracks data such as sales orders or employee records as they go from department to department to see exactly how records are processed and who handles them.

The study is conducted by an office automation committee or team, which is usually made up of a small, representative number of managers and employees. The team should include an administrator whose job it is to handle the paperwork and conduct cost-benefit analyses. The administrator is usually a manager who can make decisions about such things as expenditures and budget allocations.

Another essential member of the team is the **office automation (OA) specialist**. This person knows about computer systems. He or she is responsible for ensuring compatibility between old and new systems and for explaining the various features of a computer system, such as electronic mail, to the users. The OA specialist also writes the specifications for the new system, works with vendors of computer systems, and oversees the installation of the new system.

The third essential member of the team is the trainer. This person is the users' representative on the committee. It's the trainer's job to generate enthusiasm among the workers for the new system, to explain the system to the users, to arrange for training, and to be available to help the users when they have problems operating the new system.

System Design

Once the office automation study is completed, the team must determine how a computer system can be designed to perform the tasks and functions identified in the system analysis. It must determine, for example, which employees need word processors, which need data processing equipment, which need communications hardware, and which need letter-quality or graphics printers.

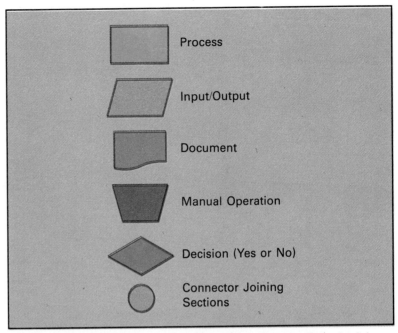

Fig. 19-2 These standard symbols are used in flowcharts to depict how information or work flows through a system.

Remember that an automated system not only performs functions faster but also performs functions in different ways. It is up to the automation team to determine, step by step, exactly how the new system will perform each function and how it will change the way that function is being performed now. Often the results of the analysis are presented graphically in a **flowchart**. A flowchart uses standard symbols to present various steps to illustrate in graphic form the flow of information or work in a system (see Fig. 19-2).

Consider, for example, the function of preparing and distributing in-house memos. In the traditional office, the process follows the path shown in Fig. 19-3 (top). A manager dictates a memo to a secretary, who transcribes the shorthand notes and types up a copy of the memo. The manager proofreads and approves the memo, and the secretary then makes the required number of copies on a copying machine. Finally, the secretary files a copy of the memo and hand-delivers or mails a copy to each recipient.

In the automated office, the process may take different paths, as shown in Fig. 19-3 (bottom). Managers may dictate memos, or they may use desk-top computer terminals to originate copy. They may either edit, proofread, and file memos themselves or have this done by their secretary. The manager or the secretary can then send the memos instantly by electronic mail to all the recipients. This requires that all recipients have their own terminals, electronic mailboxes, and access codes. They would need to be trained to use the terminals and the electronic mail program. If recipients are located

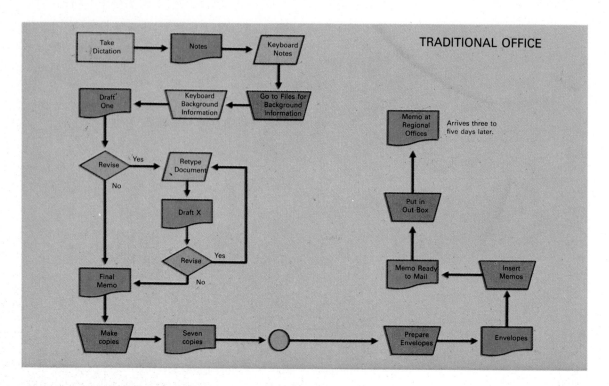

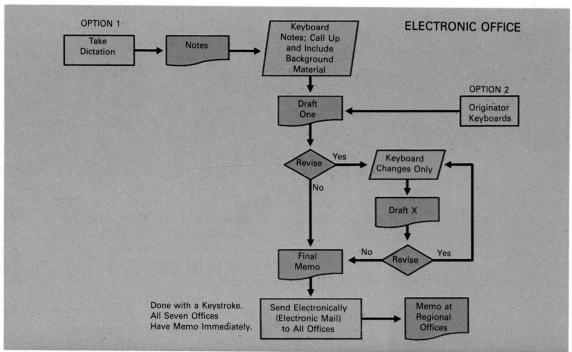

Fig. 19-3 These flowcharts illustrate how automation can alter the tasks and procedures involved in performing a function (in this case, preparing a memo for seven regional offices).

in distant offices, the computer system will have to include telephone modems and communications software.

Notice that in this example the secretary's functions of transcribing, typing, copying, and delivering memos have been transferred to the manager and the computer system. As a result, both the manager's functions and the secretary's functions and responsibilities have been changed.

In order to plan an automated system for each function, the automation team must answer a great many technical questions. These include the following:

- What is the physical geography of the company? Is it contained entirely on one floor of one building, is it spread out over several floors, or is it housed in different buildings?

- What specific equipment is needed at each workstation, in each office, and on each floor, and how can the pieces of equipment be wired or connected to each other?

- How will existing files be transferred to the new media? Some files may need to be transferred by hand from paper to disks; others may be transferred by computer from magnetic tape to disks.

- Which machines will communicate with other machines? How can the old and new systems be made compatible? What communications equipment is required?

- How can the computer's files be protected? Should each workstation have access to every file in the system, or should access be limited to certain users? For example, should access to payroll records be limited only to personnel in the payroll department? What kind of access should each user have? The team may decide that one user may only read a computer file while another may be able to both read it and change it.

- How will the new system change job functions and responsibilities? The clerk whose job has included taking telephone purchase orders and passing them on to other departments for processing by hand may now be required not only to take the orders but also to process them from beginning to end on a computer terminal.

Programming/ Applications Design

Designing the hardware for a new computer system is only part of the automation team's job. Another major part is designing the software, or programs, to be used in the system. Large corporations that still use mainframe computers to carry out applications such as payroll and inventory control probably would have their programmers write programs that would allow minicomputers and microcomputers to gain access to these operations. But as software vendors continue to develop and market more and more "off-the-shelf" software, companies have less need to employ their own programmers.

The automation team's technical expert can work with the users to help them find the right software and can tailor it to meet the specific needs of their business applications. This may mean selecting spreadsheet and data processing programs for the accounting department, choosing graphics programs for the engineering department, buying typesetting software for the copying center, and deciding on the right word processing, communications, electronic mail, and data base management programs for the general use of the entire company.

Implementation

Once the system has been designed, the automation team must oversee its implementation. It must purchase the equipment, supervise its installation, and train employees to use it. First the team prepares **bid specifications**, a list of requirements describing the kind of equipment the company needs and what the company expects the equipment to be able to do. Then it receives and evaluates bids from the vendors who are hoping to sell their computer system to the company. The team selects the vendor whose bid comes closest in price and features to what it is looking for. Then the team enters into contract negotiations with the vendor. The contract negotiations determine the actual costs, set the requirements for training and maintenance, establish the installation timetable, and so on. The automation team needs to work very closely with the vendor as implementation proceeds. Together they draw up diagrams of each workstation and installation site, detailing requirements for wiring,

The office automation team must plan carefully to implement a new system as smoothly as possible.

telephone connections, cabling, and the like. They formulate a training plan so that users will be ready to operate the new system as soon as it is installed, and they develop a delivery schedule so that the pieces of equipment can be delivered in stages as each site is prepared and each group of employees completes its training.

Training is an important part of implementation because an automated system is of little value if the employees won't use it or if they underuse it. The users must fully accept the system and quickly become comfortable using it. Commonly, the vendor trains the company's supervisors to use the new system, and they, in turn, train their employees, using the training techniques described in Chapter 18. The vendor and the software supplier usually provide documentation, consisting of handbooks and manuals, that explains how to use the system and its software.

Maintenance

Nothing is more costly to a company than an automated system that is frequently "down," or not working, particularly when the company or any of its departments cannot function without the system. If an airline's computers are not functioning and it cannot make reservations, customers go to other airlines. If a daily newspaper cannot produce an edition because its computer system is out of commission, it loses thousands of dollars in advertising revenue and newsstand sales. Other kinds of businesses experience similar losses of revenue and customer goodwill when their computer systems aren't working for any length of time. Proper maintenance is, therefore, critically important to ensure that breakdowns occur infrequently and that when they do occur, repairs are made as quickly as possible.

When a company purchases a new computer system, it usually asks for a service contract which is an argreement that the vendor will provide major maintenance service and replacement parts. The vendor might also be required to solve software problems. Large companies may also employ in-house computer service and repair specialists, and smaller companies sometimes designate one or two employees, such as production supervisors, to receive some technical training in computer maintenance from the vendor so that they can solve minor problems quickly. When the vendor and the automation team draw up a maintenance plan, they must take into consideration the need to service and repair equipment in distant branch offices as well as in the main office.

Maintenance also includes special "housekeeping" chores such as periodically purging the computer's memory banks to keep them from becoming overloaded, developing security codes, and even such simple things as making sure all the terminals are turned off at the end of each day. More and more office workers today are undertaking the responsibility for these basic tasks. In large offices one person may be designated and trained to perform the housekeeping function.

Review and Modification

Nothing has changed more rapidly within the last few years than the computer industry. What computers couldn't do five years ago they are doing today, and nobody can predict what they'll be able to do five years from now. Some companies that automated early on in the electronic revolution have already replaced their computer systems two or three times, and their first system would seem rather primitive if it were compared with their current equipment.

It will be up to the automation team or to the automation specialist to keep track of changes and advances in computer hardware and programming and to recommend improvements for the system when new, more efficient components are developed.

In addition, the automation needs of the company may change from time to time as conditions change. The company may need new machines to help produce a new product, or it may hire more employees and need more workstations. Then the automation team will be responsible for designing the new elements of the system and ensuring that they are compatible with the existing equipment.

Managing Automated Office Systems

People used to regard the business office as a place where a series of separate tasks was carried out: dictating, taking dictation, typing, filing, mailing, telephoning, and so on. But office automation has changed the way people look at and describe what occurs in the business office. As we have emphasized throughout this book, the electronic office is now seen as a place where information is processed, and each task is part of IPSOD, an integrated system to carry out that function.

The way in which people use automation in the business office has also changed. At first, only specially trained personnel operated the large mainframe computers in the data processing department, and they needed technically trained managers to oversee their operations. In the mid-1960s, automated office systems came to be referred to as **management information systems (MIS)**. The phrase was intended to stress the idea that managing information was the function of these "keepers of the data."

The development of management information systems created the need for trained personnel to help design and operate them. Colleges and universities began to offer undergraduate and graduate degrees in MIS. These technically trained managers represented a new element in the business office.

Today the movement away from large centralized automation and toward user-friendly computer systems and purchased software is changing the way information systems are managed. Now computers have become a familiar tool in the electronic office, and virtually everyone works with them to some extent. Businesses no longer need large numbers of technically trained managers. Instead, they need people who can understand office functions and procedures and can adapt automated equipment to perform them.

The development of mini- and microcomputers and off-the-shelf software will reduce the need for this kind of large, centralized data processing department in many businesses.

Operating and managing the electronic office still requires some specialized training, but in many job categories, this training can be acquired on the job or with minimal additional schooling. A secretary, for example, can become a word processing trainer, a word processing specialist, or a supervisor. These jobs require only a little additional training in the same technical skills the secretary already uses to operate his or her word processing equipment. This change is opening up many new career paths for traditional office workers. Careers in the electronic office is the topic of the next chapter.

■ Summary

■ The goal of office automation is to increase productivity by saving time and money or by expanding business to generate more income.

■ To plan the automation of an office, you must determine how much it will cost, what benefits it will provide, and how the staff will react to it.

■ Those planning to automate an office or update an automated system need to be concerned about time and about the compatibility and integration of old and new systems.

■ Before a company can automate, it must appoint a team of managers and workers to perform a system study.

■ A preliminary survey identifies the company's needs and problems.

- The office automation study examines how each office currently carries out its functions.

- The office automation team must design the hardware to perform the functions it has identified in the office automation study.

- The automation team also selects the software that each office will need to operate the new system.

- Implementation involves purchasing the system, arranging for the training of employees, and overseeing the installation of the system.

- A good maintenance plan keeps breakdowns to a minimum and ensures speedy repairs.

- The automation team makes recommendations about changing the system when new components are produced or when the company's automation needs change.

- In the future, people will need less knowledge about automation and more knowledge of office procedures and functions to manage the electronic office.

■ Review Questions

1. How does a company benefit from office automation?

2. Define the terms *bottom line* and *cost-benefit ratio*.

3. What three questions does a business have to answer when considering automation?

4. How do the issues of timing and compatibility affect automation planning?

5. List and explain the seven steps required to automate an office.

6. Why is a good maintenance program an important part of an office automation plan?

7. Explain the role of the vendor in the implementation of office automation.

8. Discuss the factors an automation team must consider when designing the hardware for an automation system.

9. What is a flowchart and how is it used?

10. How has technology changed the requirements for managing an electronic office?

■ Technical Vocabulary

bottom line
cost-benefit ratio
multitasking

parallel processing
integrated
incompatible

system study
office automation (OA) specialist
flowchart

bid specifications
management information
systems (MIS)

Discussion and Skills Development

1. You have to write a letter to the human resources manager of a company asking for an employment interview. Write down each logical step involved in this assignment. (First you decide what you are going to say, then you get paper, then you put the paper in your typewriter, and so on.) Prepare a flowchart, using the flowchart illustration in this chapter. Your flowchart should show what each task is and how it is related to the other tasks. Assign each task to the appropriate symbol on the illustration.

2. Joyce Kanter is a trainer/clerical worker on an office automation team that is planning to computerize the insurance office where she works. One day the president of the company's clerical union came to her and told her that the union members were very upset at the thought of having to learn to operate computers and were discussing plans to stage a strike when the new system is installed. What steps can Miss Kanter take to reassure the office workers and involve them in planning for the new system? Review the training procedures outlined in Chapter 18, and explain how Miss Kanter can apply those procedures to this situation.

3. All through this text you have learned about input, processing, storage, output, and distribution—or IPSOD. To prepare a system study, the whole IPSOD process would be repeated over and over. Go back to the section of the chapter that describes the steps in a system study. Analyze each step of the study to determine when each of the parts of the IPSOD process would be used. Write these down using either words or, if you prefer, symbols. You may find that all parts of the study require the IPSOD steps but that the degree to which each is used may vary. What does this tell you about work organization and decision making? Write down your observations. If you were a secretary or an administrative assistant in a setting where this process was occurring, how would it affect your job?

4. Together with your teacher, locate a systems analyst and/or a programmer, and invite the person to come and speak to your class. Ask this person to discuss the training for and the work of systems analysts and programmers and to explain how that work has been affected by the rapidly changing technology of recent years. Ask the person to compare the work when he or she first started working with the work now. Can the person predict what future changes might occur?

chapter 20
Your Career: Growing and Advancing

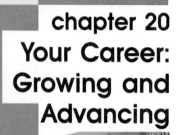

Secretarial work was once a limited career. A good secretary could progress up the career ladder from pool typist to private or executive secretary, or even administrative assistant, but that was about as far up as he or she could go. This is not true anymore. Technology not only has changed the way in which office workers perform their jobs but also has vastly increased the opportunities for new jobs and for career advancement.

Today you can enter the business world at an entry-level job such as secretary, data entry clerk, or word processing operator and move up through the ranks to a specialist, supervisory, or management position. Or once you have gained skills in one company, you can move on to another company that offers better advancement opportunities. If you specialize in one particular area of technology such as systems analysis or telecommunications, you can join a company that provides these services for businesses, or you can even go into business for yourself.

What you make of your career largely depends on what you put into it. Don't let the electronic office scare you. You won't walk into your first job knowing all there is to know about the technology, procedures, and skills we've discussed in this book. Little by little, you will learn these skills, and you can speed up the process by planning your career carefully and by continuing to educate yourself throughout your working life.

This chapter is designed to help you plan your own career. We will discuss some of the career paths open to you, and we will take you step by step through the procedures you need to follow to acquire your first job and any subsequent jobs. We will also tell you how to assess your progress as you continue to grow and change in your own chosen career.

Setting Career Goals

Careers can be constructed in a variety of ways. Some people's careers are characterized by careful planning and preparation, while other's have been shaped by unexpected opportunities and luck. A person's lifetime work history can be called a **career path**. In this text career path means a progression of jobs or positions that build upon one another as a person develops skills, knowledge, and experience.

A career path may take the form of a career ladder. A **career ladder** involves a logical succession from the initial entry-level position through promotions to various supervisory and managerial levels within a company's organizational structure. When a person wants to take advantage of an opportunity that is not a promotion, he or she might decide to make a **lateral move**. This involves taking a different job at the same level of responsibility and pay as the old one, or at a similar level, in the hope that the new job will provide opportunities for progress along a career path.

Some people's career paths are marked by **career moves**—changes from one department or field to another, sometimes related and sometimes not. For example, someone who has worked for a while in information management might make a career move to marketing. To make a career move, it might be necessary to take a lower-level position in order to get a start in the new area.

The path your own career takes will almost certainly involve a combination of careful planning and sheer chance. There's no way for you to know exactly what the future holds for you, but the planning you do will prepare you to take whatever opportunities come your way. When you think you are ready for a promotion, you can do many things to stand out in a crowd of competitors. You can learn as much as possible about the equipment you operate, you can take courses—for example, in management, accounting, or business administration—and you can develop the interpersonal and managerial skills discussed in earlier chapters. Then when an opportunity is available, you'll be ready to step forward and be recognized.

Developing a Personal Profile

Before you can plan a career, you need to take time to assess your background, personality, and life goals. In other words, you need to develop a **personal profile**. You then have to assess the job opportunities and the companies offering them to see how closely you can match your personal profile to the employment requirements. The better the fit, the better your chances of success.

You are more likely to find the right fit if you have a realistic understanding of your abilities and personality. Here are some questions to ask yourself:

- What skills have I learned in my schooling, from previous jobs, and from my hobbies and social activities? (Some examples might include typing or word processing, speaking a foreign language, working with people, writing, doing math, organizing events, and using a computer.)

- What kinds of activities satisfy me, and what kinds of work situations do I seem to like best? (For example, do you like working with people or with things? alone or with a group? Do you like to take responsibility for others, or do you prefer to make an individual contribution? Do you like working with words or with numbers, or do you enjoy a combination of both?)

- What do I hope to accomplish in the short run or in the long run in my life, and what values do I have that might affect the career I choose? (For example, at this time you may be looking for an entry-level position, but what will you want to be doing five or ten years from now? What things hold the highest value for you? Money? Security? Authority? These priorities in your value system will make a difference in the path your career takes.)

Many of your answers to these questions will change as you grow older and your experiences and circumstances change. You may want to start out in a small business office where you can experience a wide range of office duties, or you may want to work in a large company where you can specialize in a specific area such as information processing in an advertising agency or medical center. If you are single, you may welcome frequent company transfers so that you can live in different places. If you are married and have a family, you may want to stay in one place.

The type of environment you work in will depend a great deal on the type of company, organization, or institution you work for.

Office Job Opportunities

Every company, whether it manufactures goods or provides services, has a business office. You may find yourself working for a doctor, a lawyer, an insurance company, a construction contractor, a lumber company, a government agency, a jewelry wholesaler, a school, a bank—any one of thousands of different kinds of businesses and public agencies. The chances are very good that you will be able to match your personal abilities and goals to a company whose product or service interests you.

The U.S. Department of Labor predicts that the number of secretarial and clerical jobs in the United States will increase by at least 25 percent in the next decade. The nation will need an estimated 5 million more clerical workers of all kinds, 600,000 more secretaries, and 150,000 more clerical supervisors by 1995, according to Department of Labor projections.

The only clerical jobs for which employment is expected to decline are those of data entry clerks and stenographers, but many of the people who would have taken these jobs will become word processing operators and secretaries instead. Even if secretarial work and other office work did not increase over the next ten years, there are already so many jobs in these areas that thousands of new employees would be needed each year just to fill vacancies and replace retirees.

Careers in Today's Office

What career paths are available in office automation, and what kinds of job skills are needed for them? The major categories are described in the pages that follow. Be aware that although they are discussed separately, in the electronic office you can cross over from one career path or ladder to another (see Fig. 20-1). Within each category, jobs are listed in order of progression, from entry-level positions to those at the management level. To succeed in each area, you must be well organized, flexible, and attentive to detail, and you must have good verbal skills.

Administrative Support—Traditional Office

In the traditional office, administrative support workers are mainly secretaries and clerks, who perform all routine secretarial tasks and functions. They range from entry-level secretaries who do routine information processing to administrative assistants who work closely with top managers and oversee the work of other secretaries and assistants.

Standard administrative support positions in the traditional office include:

■ **Secretary**. This is the basic job classification, which is known by several other titles: Associate Administrative Secretary, Secretary Assistant, Level I Secretary, and so on. In large organizations several levels exist in this classification with the title indicating the level. Higher levels represent more experience and ability. At all levels tasks include traditional secretarial duties, such as tak-

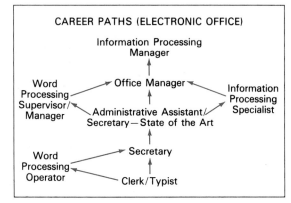

Fig. 20-1 The electronic office has opened up new career paths for office workers.

ing and transcribing dictation, processing correspondence, answering telephones, greeting visitors, opening mail, and filing. Usually works for more than one principal or in a pool. A Secretary Assistant might report to an Administrative Assistant.

■ **Administrative Assistant/Secretary.** Few purely secretarial functions, such as typing and filing. Reports to only one principal, a top officer in the organization. In addition to regular support services, such as maintaining schedules and arranging meetings, helps with research. Oversees others. Secretary assistants may report to this person.

■ **Administrative Support Supervisor**. Also called office manager. In large organizations where there is a typing or secretarial pool, this person assigns work. May be a top-level or senior secretary with additional supervisory responsibilities.

Administrative Support—Electronic Office

The administrative support positions of the traditional office occur in the electronic office, but there are significant differences and new positions, as this text has indicated. The differences involve handling higher-level responsibilities dealing with both the technology and with decision making.

In the electronic office, the line separating administrative support services and managerial functions shifts, even blurs. Functions, heretofore purely managerial, become part of administrative support services. Manager and support personnel work more closely together.

There is a twofold reason for this change. First, with routine tasks being automated, administrative support people have time to devote to more creative tasks. Second, the entry of sophisticated equipment into the office increases the value of those operating it. Managers do not have the time to learn to operate the equipment. They rely on administrative support personnel, and the more tasks the electronic equipment performs, the greater the reliance. This translates into greater opportunity for those working in electronic offices.

Two new positions found in the electronic office illustrate these changes and the opportunities they offer: In many offices these jobs will still carry the title of *secretary* or *administrative assistant.* However, in many cases the job title will change to reflect the change in responsibilities.

■ **Administrative Assistant/Secretary—State of the Art**. This position with corresponding levels, replaces the various levels of secretaries up to the level of administrative assistant in the traditional office. This person has the state-of-the-art skills needed for using electronic equipment in a workstation-specific environment. In a sense, the traditional secretary's duties have evolved into information processing functions. This position demands increased skills in creating, retrieving, synthesizing, and making available information and requires knowledge of word and data processing, electronic mail, and electronic records management. (See Fig. 20-6 on pages 518–519 for a complete job description.)

■ **Information Processing Specialist**. This person is responsible for operating the integrated information system and providing site support to system users and administrators. Emphasis is on coordinating the system to improve communication and information access through the use of software applications. Responsibilities also include training and administering standards.

■ **Information Processing Manager**. This person is responsible for providing support to those departments involved in the planning, installation, training/use/operation, and maintenance of integrated information processing systems. Primary emphasis is on assistance and support services associated with equipment and software selection, physical installation and arrangement of office workstations, and the development of information schemas and systems. Responsibilities also include training and administering standards to ensure success of the automated office concept.

Word Processing

The processing of documents on a computer will continue to be an important secretarial function in an electronic office, but in many large companies, word processing has become an entirely separate job category with many entry-level jobs and levels of advancement. In these companies, the word processing center has replaced the typing pool, and word processing operators have replaced typists. Word processing jobs include:

■ **Word Processing Trainee**. Has little or no prior experience. Needs to know how to type, and must have a knowledge of grammar, spelling, formatting, and other basic secretarial skills. Trainees transcribe dictation and process rough drafts and other documents. When they gain sufficient experience, they become word processing operators.

- **Word Processing Specialist**. Has 18 months to two years of experience as a word processing operator. Is skilled at producing, revising, and formatting lengthy, complicated reports such as legal documents and medical reports and is also skilled at preparing statistical tables. Can proofread and edit documents and retrieve documents from electronic files.

- **Word Processing Supervisor**. Oversees the day-to-day operations of a word processing center, trains and assigns operators, determines the priorities for producing work, and sets quality standards. May make budget recommendations, purchase equipment and supplies, and monitor production procedures.

Data Processing

Increasingly, office managers are coming to perceive all aspects of office automation—data processing, word processing, and telecommunications—as information processing. Data processing is no longer seen as a separate function, and it is losing its identity as a separate job classification. In Chapter 19 you learned that the business office has less need for the specialists usually listed in this category, such as computer operators, programmers, and systems analysts. Nevertheless, there will still be many jobs for these specialists within the broad field of information processing. Large companies will continue to need data processing personnel in their inventory control or payroll departments, and smaller companies may hire data processing specialists as consultants from time to time to solve temporary hardware or software problems. Jobs are also available for highly trained people in companies that research, manufacture, and sell equipment and software that businesses need.

In the average business office, most of the jobs in this category are at the entry level, and people seeking promotions would have to acquire additional skills, such as the ability to use a computer language, or move to another career path. The person who wants to advance in data processing needs an aptitude for technical work and a broad knowledge of all types of office automation equipment. Some jobs in data processing include:

- **Data Entry Clerk**. Also called a keyboard/input operator. An entry-level position requiring little technical knowledge or experience operating a computer terminal. The data entry clerk must have good typing skills and be able to enter data and figures quickly and accurately. In many companies this position requires employees to work different shifts.

- **Programmer**. Must know one or more computer languages, and must be able to design, write, and test programs so that they fit a company's specific needs. Needs to be logical, organized, and patient.

- **Systems Analyst**. Works with managers and supervisors to determine their needs, then designs a group of programs to carry out the required functions. Also designs hardware, trains employees to operate the system, and oversees programmers.

Telecommunications

Career opportunities in telecommunications are expected to increase as more and more companies integrate their electronic equipment and as the demand for instant communication between offices and between companies continues to grow. People are needed to oversee the sending and receiving of electronic mail, to operate telex machines, to arrange teleconferences, and to set up and maintain telecommunications networks. The person who goes into this field needs to be a decision maker and problem solver and also needs to be technically oriented. A person could move from any other office career path to telecommunications jobs such as these:

■ **Technician**. Helps set up and maintain electronic equipment; provides technical support for teleconferences.

■ **Electronic Mail Supervisor**. Supervises the operation of a company's electronic mail system, including facsimile machines, telexes, teletypewriters, electronic copiers, and computers. Coordinates telecommunications with word processing and data processing activities.

Businesses are increasingly using electronic capabilities to hold long-distance meetings. With the use of audiovisual equipment, personnel in offices scattered about the country can "meet" electronically, thus saving thousands of dollars in travel costs as well as time. Setting up such meetings is a new skill that secretaries can acquire.

- **Telecommunications Manager**. Manages the planning, installation, and day-to-day operation of the telecommunications system and oversees supervisors and technicians.

Records/Information Management

Secretaries, file clerks, and data processing personnel used to keep business records as part of their daily routine, but some electronic offices now maintain separate records centers in which most recordkeeping functions are coordinated. The management of records and information involves archiving, filing, handling micrographics, and destroying records. Archiving is the preservation of records for scholarly and historical purposes. Filing is, of course, the process of sorting and storing records. Micrographics involves transforming paper records to microfilm or microfiche for more compact and safer storage. Records/information management personnel also periodically destroy outdated records and records that are no longer needed.

Records/information management personnel are usually in charge of both paper and computerized records. Their jobs generally include data base management, that is, maintaining, updating, and managing a company's computerized data bases. Some of the jobs in records/information management include:

- **File Clerk**. This is a clerical position and involves filing office records in whatever systems are currently used by a company. At a higher level, a file clerk may be involved in disposing of records according to already established retention schedules and legal requirements. Some higher-level file clerks are also involved in the creation of microforms.

- **Classification Clerk**. This is also a clerical position and is sometimes referred to as *coding file clerk*. A classification clerk classifies materials by their subject matter and assigns them numbers or symbols according to already established coding systems. A classification clerk may revise a currently used coding system if he or she thinks it can be improved.

- **Files Supervisor**. This clerical job is also referred to as *records-section supervisor*. A files supervisor is responsible for overseeing the workers who maintain a central records file. With specialized knowledge of common filing errors, this person helps retrieve lost or missing files. A files supervisor also oversees the periodic disposal of obsolete files, in accordance with company guidelines and legal requirements.

- **Records Manager**. This is a managerial job that usually requires four years of college and a degree. A records manager is involved in all phases of information management and has the ultimate responsibility for seeing to it that files are organized efficiently and that they are reviewed for transfer and/or destruction periodically. Many records managers are certified by ARMA, the

Association of Records Managers and Administrators. Certification is based on specific training and a demonstration of competency in the field of records management.

- **Micrographics Technician**. Operates equipment to reduce records to microfilm and microfiche under the direction of a supervisor.

- **Archivist**. This position is more likely to exist in government offices, libraries, and educational institutions than in business organizations. Archivists determine which records should be preserved, arrange the records, and take precautions to protect the records from environmental damage.

If you want further information on these or other careers in information management, consult a current edition of the *Occupational Outlook Handbook*.

Job Hunting

You have set some career and personal goals and have given thought to the kind of business that interests you. Now it is time to find a job. Here are the four steps you will need to follow to find a job:

- Locate a prospective employer.

- Prepare and send a résumé and cover letter, or fill out an application.

- Obtain an interview.

- Follow up on the interview.

At the end of this four-step process, either you or the employer will decide if this is the right job for you. If it is not, then you begin the process again.

Locating Prospective Employers

There are many places where you can look for prospective employers, starting right at your school. Some of them are described below.

School Placement Services Many schools offer placement services, and employers may even come to your school to meet prospective applicants and to describe the kinds of jobs they have to offer. Find out where your school's placement office is, and visit it regularly. Usually, the placement office maintains a bulletin board on which job announcements and visits by company recruiters are posted. Your school placement office will not find you a job, but it can help you write a résumé, line up references, and research potential employers. Many placement offices will keep copies of students' résumés and reference letters on file and send them to prospective employers at the students' request.

Employment Agencies An employment agency is in the business of bringing job hunters and companies in search of personnel to-

School placement offices can help you prepare a résumé and locate prospective employers.

gether. It attempts to match a job hunter's education, work experience, and employment preferences to the needs of the companies that come to it for referrals. Employment agencies that place office workers are almost always fee-paid agencies; that is, they charge the prospective employer, not the job hunter, a percentage of the employee's salary for the first year. That fee does not come out of the employee's salary.

One way to enter the job market is to sign up with a temporary employment agency that supplies clerical workers and word processing operators to businesses for short periods of time. If you work for a temporary service, you gain valuable on-the-job experience, you learn how to operate different kinds of computer systems, and you get to see how different business offices function.

If you go to an agency that does both permanent and temporary placements, it can put you into a temporary job while it lines up employment interviews for you. Sometimes you can also find a permanent job with a company that has employed you in a temporary position and likes your performance.

Newspapers The help-wanted ads in newspapers are a very good source of employment opportunities. Get into the habit of reading the classified advertisements for job listings. Large city newspapers often have extensive listings grouped together in categories such as *business*, *education*, and *secretarial*. Employers often purchase display advertisements describing their company and the career opportunities and benefits they offer. Reading these ads helps you gain an impression of companies for which you might like to work.

Friends and Contacts Often people find jobs because they hear of job openings from friends or acquaintances. The advantage of word of mouth is that your source may be able to answer many of your questions about the job and will be able to describe frankly the company and your prospective coworkers. The friend might also know someone at the company and might be able to put in a good word for you. Another advantage of word of mouth is that you might hear of a job opening before it is advertised.

Blind Letters and Calls You might find a job by sending your résumé with a cover letter to a company for which you want to work. Try to follow up the letter with a visit to the personnel office. This could be a good way to introduce yourself to a prospective employer, who may think of you if a job opening occurs. Once in a while, but rarely, a company may be looking for new talent and may create a job opportunity if the right individual comes along. Showing this kind of initiative in seeking a job could generate a positive interest in you.

Preparing a Résumé

A **résumé** is a brief summary of your educational and employment history. Employers use résumés to screen job applicants so that they don't waste valuable time interviewing job hunters who don't possess the education, training, or experience they need for a specific job. For example, a manager who needs to hire a computer programmer can quickly sort through a pile of résumés and pick out the applicants who list training or experience in programming. The manager may then arrange interviews with several of those applicants. Using résumés to screen job seekers not only saves the manager's time but also saves you the time and expense of interviewing for jobs for which you are not qualified.

Résumés usually contain the following information (see the example in Fig. 20-2):

- **Your name, address, and telephone number**.

- **Your employment history**. You can list this either in reverse chronological order or in descending order of importance. If you choose reverse chronological order, you list the last job you held first, the second-to-last job next, and so on. If you choose to list your jobs in order of importance, you list the job in which you exercised the most authority, earned the highest salary, or held the most responsibility first and then the next most important job and so on. Your employment history should tell you which presentation is likely to make the best impression on a prospective employer.

    Always list the starting and ending dates for each job along with the name of the company, address, and telephone number; the position you held; and a brief explanation of your responsibilities if they are not self-evident from the job title.

```
                              David A. Diaz
                              1632 Hillside Ave.
                              Rockford, IL 61109
                              (815) 555-2805

POSITION SOUGHT

    Administrative Assistant


WORK EXPERIENCE

    Secretary/Assistant Office Manager.  Vanguard Insurance Company, 4500 Michigan
    Avenue, Chicago, IL 60653.  September 1985 to present.  Supervisor:  Mrs. Anna
    Robinson.  Telephone:  (312) 555-9530, Extension 419.

    Kitchen aid.  McCarthy's Catering, 93 West Mill Road, Rockford, IL 61104.
    September 1983 to June 1985.  Supervisor:  Mr. Maurice Doher.  Telephone:
    (815) 555-4987, Extension 2167.


EDUCATION

    Will be graduated with a B average from East Chicago Community College in June
    1987.

    Participated in the Office Education Training Program.
    Specialized in business courses and attained:

    1.  Typewriting speed, 60 wam; shorthand speed, 120 wam.
    2.  An understanding and operating knowledge of transcribing machines, the IBM
        Personal Computer, and all components of the Wang Alliance System.
    3.  A working knowledge of electronic calculators.
    4.  An understanding of human relations in dealing with coworkers, superiors,
        and subordinates.


OTHER EXPERIENCE AND ACTIVITIES

    Member of Chicago Chapter of Illinois Office Education Association.
    Chairperson of Future Business Leaders of America Fund-Raising Drive to raise
      $2000 for club activities.
    Member of Illinois chapter of Phi Beta Lambda.


REFERENCES

    Mr. Richard Loo, Office Manager, Vanguard Insurance Company, 4500 Michigan
    Avenue, Chicago, IL 60653, (312) 555-9530.

    Ms. Jennifer Best, Dean, East Chicago Community College, 4398 West 22 Street,
    Chicago, IL 60616, (312) 555-9208.
```

Fig. 20-2 A résumé is a brief summary of your educational and employment history.

■ **Your educational background**. Start with the highest level of school attended. Give the date of graduation from each school, the names of the schools, your majors, and the degrees or diplomas earned.

   If you attended a college, vocational school, or graduate school but did not graduate, state that you attended the school and give the dates. You can also list the courses you took if they seem relevant to the job you are seeking. It is customary to list your employment record before your educational background on a résumé, but if you have only just completed school and have no employment experience in your career area, you should list your educational record first.

- **Your accomplishments**. Give the names of any professional or school organizations you belong to and any offices you hold or have held. Also list any honors you have received for professional, academic, or athletic achievements. Carrying out the duties of a club officer, graduating in the top 10 percent of your class, or being named secretary of the year demonstrates your determination to excel and your ability to shoulder responsibility.

- **Your hobbies, interests, activities, or special abilities**. Can you speak Spanish? Were you the editor of your college paper? Can you operate a video camera? These abilities may give you an advantage over your competition for the job you are seeking.

- **References**. It is up to you to decide whether you want to list references on your résumé. Some people list the names and addresses of three or more personal references; others state that references are available upon request. References may be former employers or supervisors if you have previous work experience, or they may be teachers, guidance counselors, and advisers if you have just completed your schooling.

  You should always check with the people you intend to list as references beforehand to make sure that they are willing to be listed and that they will recommend you without reservation to a prospective employer. If you have the slightest doubt about whether a person will give you a good report, do not list that person as a reference. You may also obtain letters of recommendation from your references. Keep copies of these in a folder, and take them with you to job interviews, but do not include them with your résumé.

Presentation   Your résumé should be clearly written and well organized. Avoid vague, flowery phrases, and make sure your spelling, grammar, and punctuation are impeccable. If possible, keep your résumé to one page. Some employers only scan résumés and won't take the time to read a long résumé.

You may prepare your résumé on a typewriter or word processor, or you may have it printed. If you type it, you can tailor each résumé to a particular employer and the job opportunity you are seeking, but you will have to type out a new résumé each time you apply for a job. With a word processor, you can store a boilerplate résumé and tailor a copy to each employer without having to rekeyboard the entire résumé. If you use a word processor, be sure to print your copies on a letter-quality printer. If you plan to apply to a large number of companies, you can have your résumé printed. A printed résumé can look very attractive and professional, but you cannot alter it to fit each employment opportunity. Whichever way you produce your résumé, avoid ornate typefaces or overdramatic layouts that make the résumé difficult to read.

Applying for a Position

Once you have located a prospective employer and prepared a résumé, your next task is to apply for a position. Usually, the first step is to prepare a cover letter to accompany your résumé. The cover letter or application letter tells the prospective employer which job you are applying for, highlights your qualifications for the job, and includes any relevant information that is not already incorporated in your résumé. The cover letter is, in effect, your chance to make a short sales pitch for yourself. It should lead the employer's attention to the résumé by making direct reference to it. See the example in Fig. 20-3.

If you are replying to a help-wanted ad, mention the advertisement in your cover letter, and state when and where it appeared.

1632 Hillside Ave.
Rockford, IL 61109
April 29, 1987

Ms. Anne Jacobs
General Manager
World-Wide Tours
7800 Olive Drive
Downers Grove, IL 60515

Dear Ms. Jacobs:

Will you please consider me an applicant for the administrative assistant position that you advertised in the April 27 *Evening Star.* My enclosed resume will support my belief that I am qualified to handle the job.

I will be graduated from East Chicago Community College on June 16, 1987, and will be ready for full-time employment anytime after that date. While in college, I maintained a perfect attendance record and a B average. During my senior year, I have been able to acquire on-the-job experience as an assistant office manager/secretary for the Vanguard Insurance Company. Here my duties include taking dictation, transcribing, handling routine correspondence, and managing the administrative records for the office. In this position, I have discovered an aptitude and liking for administrative work, and I hope to pursue this interest in business.

As you will note from my resume, I have participated actively in professional organizations. Probably the most challenging activity was chairing a successful campaign to raise $2000 for the Future Business Leaders of America club. Professional involvements, teamwork, and responsibility have become more significant to me because of such activities.

Mr. Richard Loo, office manager for Vanguard Insurance Company, and the other person listed in my resume have given me permission to use their names as references. You may call them or write to them for further information concerning my character and work abilities.

Will you please allow me a personal interview? If you wish, you may call me at (815) 555-2805 after 4:30 p.m.

Sincerely yours,

David A. Diaz

David A. Diaz

Enclosure

Fig. 20-3 A good cover letter should make the employer want to look at your résumé.

Then explain in one brief paragraph why you feel your education and employment background qualify you for the job. The entire letter should be no more than three or four paragraphs long. The major purpose of the letter is to get the applicant an interview.

If the ad asks you to state your salary requirements, find out what the general salary range is for the job. Your placement office or employment agency, published career guidebooks, and professional associations should be able to help you find the appropriate salary range. Use that range as a guide to arrive at a range or figure that would be reasonable on the basis of your current salary and your qualifications and experience. If you ask for too much, your application may be rejected before you even get an interview.

The cover letter is also the place to provide information such as temporary addresses or telephone numbers and to ask for an interview. If you must travel to a distant city for an interview, you may want to arrange several interviews in that city over a one- or two-day period. In your cover letter, you can tell the company when you expect to be in the area and ask if it would be possible to schedule you for an interview then.

Some companies ask job seekers to fill out an application form as well as submit a résumé. If you are asked to fill out an application form, read it through first, and then fill it out carefully. Companies often use application forms to judge job seekers' handwriting or typewriting skill and their ability to follow directions. In this case neatness does count.

Job applicants are often asked to take one or more skills or aptitude tests. The company may ask you to type a sample letter on an electronic typewriter or word processor to determine your typing speed. If you are not familiar with the equipment, the tester should allow you a warm-up period. You may also be asked to take a shorthand test or to proofread a document so that the company can test your knowledge of spelling, grammar, and punctuation. Some companies also test applicants on their arithmetic skills.

The employment application may ask you personal questions about such things as age, race, and marital status. You are not required by law to answer such questions. You are also not legally required to take any psychological or lie detector tests the company may request. You will have to decide for yourself what to do in these situations. You can simply leave an objectionable question unanswered on the application form, and if you wish to avoid a test, try to decline as gracefully as possible. You should be aware, however, that your refusal to answer a question or take a test is likely to reduce your chances of obtaining the job.

The Employment Interview

Some companies like to have their human resources departments conduct preliminary interviews and then follow up with an interview by the supervisor for whom the job seeker would work. When you fill out an application or when you attend an interview, you should be shown a job description. (See Fig. 20-4 for page 1 of a job description. The complete description appears on pages 518–519.) As you learned in Chapter 18, a job description describes the tasks and functions of a job, the qualifications required, and the accountability or reporting relationships. As you read through the job description, write down any questions that occur to you so that you can get answers to them during the employment interview. The job description is your best measure of how closely your background and career goals match the job to be done.

Preparing for the Interview The first thing you should do to prepare for a job interview is research the company. You can find out about a company from newspaper and magazine articles, busi-

---

POSITION DESCRIPTION

Job Title ___Administrative Assistant/Secretary--State of the Art___ Date _____

Name _____

Department _____ Location _____

Manager: Name _____ Approved _____

1. **MAJOR FUNCTION:**

Responsible for using the integrated information system to process and prepare office documents. Primary emphasis is on using the interactive capabilities of the system to improve the coordination and efficiency of document preparation, storage, and retrieval. The integrated information system may be resident on a local or remote network, or disk-based at each secretarial station. This position reports to management and in some cases to the information processing specialist as well.

2. **SPECIFIC DUTIES:**

	% Time
1. Establishes station-specific procedures for information processing functions, including: document formats, electronic file management, document distribution and controls, and use and operation of equipment.	5%
Defines forms and document formatting.	
Develops electronic filing procedures.	
Develops and defines procedures for information/records management, determining how information will be archived and stored.	
Defines document distribution methods and controls.	
Develops procedures for use and operation of equipment.	
2. Utilizes new and/or advanced interactive capabilities of the integrated information system to improve the efficiency of office functions.	5%
Maintains a working knowledge of software capabilities.	
Uses new features of software and integrated software as appropriate.	
3. Maintains the equipment inventory system and prepares reports based on data base analyses.	5%
Uses data base system to build inventory files.	

Fig. 20-4 Seeing a job description helps you match your skills to the requirements of the job.

ness directories, and your local chamber of commerce. Your public library should have back copies of newspapers and magazines like *The Wall Street Journal*, *Business Week*, and *Fortune*. In the library's reference section you can find several directories such as *Standard and Poor's Register of Corporations*, *America's Corporate Families*, and the *Thomas Register of American Manufacturers*.

These books contain information about the products and services the company provides, its annual revenues, the number of employees, its divisions and subsidiaries, the names of its corporate officers, and the stock exchanges that list the company's stock if it is a publicly owned corporation. All of this information will help you form a mental picture of the company so that you can ask intelligent and informed questions at your job interview. Similar directories are also available on law firms and doctors.

Next you should write down all the questions that you have about the job, about salary and fringe benefits, and about company policies. The interviewer will probably answer many of these questions during the course of the interview. Then you can ask any questions that have been left unanswered at the end.

Once you have learned as much as you can about the company and determined which questions you plan to ask at the interview, you should also spend some time trying to anticipate the questions the interviewer is likely to ask you and preparing suitable answers.

Having the Interview   The employment interview is usually the first time you will be seen by a company representative. First impressions are important, so dress appropriately, be well-groomed, and be on time.

Grooming for the Interview   Image is important and rightly so. When going for a job interview, consider your image. This is not to say that image should replace substance as the measure of a person. It is to say that image—the way we present ourselves—is an effective way to communicate. When dressing for an interview, consider what you wish to communicate about yourself.

What you wear should be natural for you *in the situation*. Wearing jeans may be naturally you—but not in a job interview situation. You know from television commercials that companies spend millions of dollars creating an image, one that will engender trust and confidence. Your prospective employer will be looking for someone with these qualities as well as someone who indicates a serious interest in the job by his or her appearance.

In a good interview, the interviewer will give you an overall explanation of the requirements of the job and of the company's policies and benefits. He or she will ask you questions about yourself and will give you an opportunity to ask questions about the job and the company. It's normal to be nervous, but try to act naturally. Expect some in-depth questions about your education and previous work experience, listen attentively, and answer the questions fully and honestly. Give concrete examples whenever you can.

A good interviewer tells you about the job and the company, asks questions about you, and gives you a chance to ask questions as well.

Here are some questions the interviewer may ask you:

- Why did you choose to become a secretary?

- What future professional or educational plans do you have?

- What characteristics or traits do you have that you think will make you a good secretary?

- What skills did you learn in previous positions or in your summer and after-school jobs?

- What experience do you have with computers?

- Where do you hope to be in your profession ten years from now?

- Why did you leave your last position?

- What do you think are your strengths and weaknesses?

- What do you think your references will say about you?

- Why should this company hire you?

Interview questions such as these are intended to both ascertain your skills and abilities and explore your personality to determine whether you will fit in with the company team and with the manager's leadership style. Interviewers may ask you to cite specific examples of projects you have worked on or to discuss how you would handle different types of work situations.

One particularly tough question is the question of salary. Usually, the interviewer will tell you what the company expects to pay for the position, but sometimes an interviewer will ask you what salary you want or expect. If you expect to be asked about salary, you can prepare for the question beforehand by following the same steps we discussed in the section on cover letters. You can also simply tell the interviewer that you would be willing to accept the prevailing salary for the position.

When it is your turn to ask questions, keep in mind that the questions you ask also reveal something about your personality. Asking questions can make a good impression. It shows that you are interested and aware. Be sure to ask questions about the duties and responsibilities of the job as well as about salary and fringe benefits, or the interviewer may wonder about your dedication.

When the interview is over, you need to know what the next steps should be. Employers usually interview several applicants before they make a job offer, so you will probably have to wait one or two weeks before you can learn whether you have the job. The interviewer should tell you whether he or she will call or write to you and how long you can expect to wait. If you are offered a job at the interview, you can ask for a short time to think about the job offer if you wish.

Following Up the Interview As soon as you can after the interview, evaluate your own performance. Make a list of the things you feel you did right and the things you would do differently at another job interview. Even if you have to go through several job interviews before you are offered a position, you will not have wasted your time. Each interview is a learning experience. The more familiar you become with the job interview, the more relaxed and confident you will be.

INFORMATION ABOUT THE COMPANY

You should get as much information as possible before accepting a job with a company. Questions about salary, benefits, working hours, and other company policies must be worded tactfully in the interview situation. Many companies provide written brochures to answer many of these questions. However, you may also wish to discuss them with the human resources person who handles your position (rather than with the immediate supervisor). Here are some common questions that job seekers ask about company benefits and policies.

■ What will my hours of work be? Will I have regular lunch hours and breaks?

■ If I work overtime, will I be paid, or will I receive compensatory time off?

■ May I expect to have an accurate job description so that I will know exactly what is expected of me?

■ When will I be eligible for a vacation, and how much vacation time will I receive each year?

■ Will I be required to join a union or professional association as a condition of employment?

- What is the salary range for the job, and how often could I expect to receive a raise?
- What is the company's policy regarding sick days, personal leave days, and holidays?
- What fringe benefits will I receive? Is there a medical insurance, dental, eyeglass, or prescription plan?
- Is there a pension plan, and will I be able to contribute to it?
- Does the company have an employee credit union?
- What is the company's policy regarding maternity and paternity leave? Does the company provide day-care facilities for the children of employees?
- Does the company have a stock purchase or profit-sharing plan?
- Does the company pay bonuses, and how does an employee earn a bonus?
- Will the company pay tuition for employees who take job-related courses, and does it offer any in-service training or seminars?
- Does the company provide free parking for employees?

EVALUATING THE INTERVIEW

How do you evaluate your performance at a job interview? Here are some questions to ask yourself:

- Did you prepare questions and research the company beforehand?
- Did you remember to bring reference letters, work samples, and any other requested documents to the interview?
- Were you on time for the interview?
- Did you talk too much or too little?
- Did you answer the interviewer's questions honestly and completely?
- Did you dress appropriately?
- Did you display any nervous behavior such as fidgeting, giggling, or forgetting things you wanted to say?
- If you handled any questions badly, how would you answer them differently the next time they are asked?
- Were you courteous at all times?

Another follow-up task to do after the interview is to write down any details about the job that you want to remember, such as salary, hours, duties, and so on. Now that you know more about the job, you have to decide whether you want to accept it if it is offered to you. You should consider whether the position matches your background and goals. Ask yourself how the company lets you know what it expects of you, how you will be evaluated, and who will evaluate you. Also ask yourself whether the company can provide you with the career path you've chosen. Will it provide educational assistance and offer career development opportunities?

You may send the interviewer a brief thank-you note, but you should avoid calling or writing before the decision deadline to inquire about the status of your application. After the deadline it is acceptable to call or write to ask when a decision will be made. This shows that you are still interested in the job.

Making the Big Decision As you look at several job possibilities, you may find it difficult to sort them all out so as to concentrate on the most desirable. A useful tool to help you organize your priorities is a decision-making matrix. You can make one of these easily.

A matrix is a grid on which you list your job possibilities vertically on the left and the characteristics you desire in a job horizontally on the top. See Fig. 20-5. Rate the job characteristics according to how important you feel they are to you. Give the least important characteristics a "1" and the next least a "2." If you have identified seven characteristics, as shown in the illustration, the most important will have a value of "7." Opposite each option, check the appropriate box. If the job meets your salary goal, put a check there. Then add the value for the boxes checked. The total values can help you make your decision. If there is a tie, you can add other characteristics.

The Job Offer

The company may offer you the job while you still have interviews scheduled with several other companies or while you are waiting to hear about a job that you would prefer. The company making the job offer may be willing to wait a short while for you to decide. You may consider calling the other company to tell the supervisor or human resources manager that you have received an offer and need to make a decision. In that case the second company might be willing to make a job offer also, or it might not. In any event, the decision is yours. Once you have made it, stick to it.

DESIRED JOB CHARACTERISTICS

	Salary (6)	Fringe Benefits (4)	Challenge (5)	Opportunity (7)	Prestige (3)	Location (1)	Hours (2)	Totals
Job option 1			✔	✔	✔			15
Job option 2	✔	✔				✔	✔	13
Job option 3	✔		✔		✔			14

Fig. 20-5 A decision-making matrix such as this one is a simple device you can create to help you in selecting the best job option to pursue.

Even though the company does the hiring, think of yourself as "hiring" an employer and before applying for or accepting a job, do your best to determine if you will fit into the company. Ask yourself how closely the offered position fits your background and goals.

Sometimes an interviewer will tell you that you are not suited for the job you have applied for. Try not to take the rejection personally, and continue to be polite, because you never can tell when the company will have a position for which you are suited. You should not be afraid to turn down a job offer if you decide that your interests, background, and skills do not fit well or if you are not confident that you can do the job.

Advancing on the Job

Getting a job is one accomplishment; getting ahead in the job is an even more important achievement. We said at the beginning of this chapter that your career will be what you make of it. You can put in your eight hours every day and do only what's expected of you, or you can seek new challenges and opportunities to grow. To do that, you need to become as competent as you can in your present job. Study your superiors and coworkers so that you can begin to develop interpersonal and management skills. Learn all you can about the electronic equipment you operate, and take on administrative support responsibilities. If you can accomplish all of these goals, you will make yourself a valued employee, and you may even be picked to take the **fast track**. People are said to be on the fast track when they are singled out as potential management material and given rapid promotions.

Growth Potential

Many businesses have tools designed to help employees develop and grow on the job. These tools are job descriptions, which you have previously read about, and performance appraisals. Job descriptions define the job. They identify exactly what it is the employee must do. Performance appraisals are conducted by supervisors with employees. They are intended to monitor performance so an employee can eliminate weaknesses and improve strengths.

At first glance, it might seem to you that job descriptions and performance appraisals are solely management tools to make sure you do the work. While it is true they could be solely used in this way, they are also intended to protect employees and help them develop. If the tasks you are expected to do are clearly spelled out and agreed to, you are protected from whims or arbitrary actions of supervisors. This protection is increased if you are given periodic performance evaluations based on your job description.

If you do not get a periodic evaluation, ask for one. Seek an appropriate time to discuss with your supervisor the scope and responsibilities of your job and how you are responding to them. Also ask what areas need improvement and what you can do to increase your chances of being promoted.

A clear job description is necessary to ensure effective evaluation of potential. If one does not exist for your position, developing one could be a useful exercise increasing your understanding of your job and what it requires from you.

A good job description defines the overall job function and shows how it fits into the organization. Then the various functions and tasks that make up the job are identified. Often the estimated amount of time the employee is expected to spend on each task is given. The description shows the relationship of the employee's work to his or her boss.

A job description for an Administrative Assistant/Secretary—State of the Art is shown in Fig. 20-6 on pages 518–519.

Growing Professionally

To grow professionally, you need to keep up with the changes and developments in your field. Your company may be willing to pay for your membership in a professional organization or for a subscription for you to one or more professional publications. Even if you have to pay for these things yourself, you will probably find that they are worth the expense. Professional organizations and periodicals keep you informed of new equipment and procedures. They provide contacts, advice on common problems, and ideas you can use to make your job easier and more interesting.

Some professional organizations that you might be interested in joining include the Professional Secretaries International and the National Association of Executive Secretaries. There are organizations for supervisors and managers such as the Association of Information Systems Professionals, Administrative Management Society, and the National Association of Office Managers, and there are

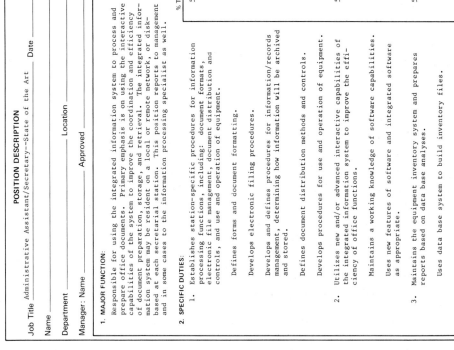

POSITION DESCRIPTION

Job Title Administrative Assistant/Secretary--State of the Art ___ Date ___
Name ___
Department ___ Location ___
Manager: Name ___ Approved ___

% Time

1. MAJOR FUNCTION:

Responsible for using the integrated information system to process and prepare office documents. Primary emphasis is on using the interactive capabilities of the system to improve the coordination and efficiency of document preparation, storage, and retrieval. The integrated information system may be resident on a local or remote network, or disk-based at each secretarial station. This position reports to management and in some cases to the information processing specialist as well.

2. SPECIFIC DUTIES:

1. Establishes station-specific procedures for information processing functions, including: document formats, electronic file management, document distribution and controls, and use and operation of equipment. 5%

   Defines forms and document formatting.

   Develops electronic filing procedures.

   Develops and defines procedures for information/records management, determining how information will be archived and stored.

   Defines document distribution methods and controls.

   Develops procedures for use and operation of equipment.

2. Utilizes new and/or advanced interactive capabilities of the integrated information system to improve the efficiency of office functions. 5%

   Maintains a working knowledge of software capabilities.

   Uses new features of software and integrated software as appropriate.

3. Maintains the equipment inventory system and prepares reports based on data base analyses. 5%

   Uses data base system to build inventory files.

   Updates data base regularly.

   Analyzes data fields using sort/search commands.

   Prepares reports based on data base analyses.

4. Processes documents for order fulfillment electronically and/or manually. 5%

   Gathers information on order requests.

   Verifies prices using data base and print sources.

   Obtains approval signatures.

   Processes order request documents.
   Formats, enters, and proofs documents.
   Edits documents electronically.
   Stores and files documents electronically.
   Distributes documents electronically and in print (as appropriate).

   Forwards order request documents to purchasing departments or directly to vendor (as appropriate).

   Follows up order requests and communicates status of order to originator of requests.

5. Processes documents for invoice billing. 5%

   Uses electronic invoicing system, including client information, project rates, billing schedules, etc., or accesses manual invoice record systems.

   Updates billing/invoice system regularly.

   Gathers and/or electronically retrieves billing and invoice information for the billing schedule.

   Generates the invoice electronically or manually.

   Stores/files monthly invoice information.

   Distributes invoice information to billing clerk or processes invoice forms (if appropriate).

   Follows up invoice sent and reissues invoice (if appropriate).

6. Processes payroll records electronically and/or manually. 5%

Updates timesheet/timecard record system.

Calculates totals on timesheet/timecard records for appropriate employees.

Stores and files records.

Distributes payroll information to accountant or processes payroll checks (if appropriate).

7. Processes business correspondence, including reports, letters, memos, etc., electronically or manually.   35%

Gathers information from electronic (data bases, spreadsheets, and word processing documents) and print sources.

Determines document format.

Processes documents.
  Formats, enters, and proofs documents.
  Edits documents electronically.
  Stores and files documents electronically.
  Distributes documents electronically and in print (as appropriate).

Revises documents as needed.

Integrates spreadsheet, data base, and graphic data (if appropriate).

Uses a variety of input devices (keyboard, mouse digitizer, voice, etc.).

Uses advanced word processing features to improve document preparation.

8. Processes financial information, e.g., departmental budgets, and maintains spreadsheet files electronically or manually.   15%

Builds budget spreadsheets using application software.

Uses spreadsheet functions to modify and recalculate data.

Submits departmental budget reports to the manager.

9. Prepares visuals for management presentations, electronically or manually.   5%

Gathers information for graphics/visuals needed.

Uses graphic/charting software packages to prepare visuals.

Integrates graphics/visuals in word processing documents.

Produces computer-generated visuals in variety of forms: overhead transparencies, slides, print, etc.

10. Coordinates office communications, including: incoming/outgoing mail, phone calls, and messages, electronically or manually.   10%

Establishes incoming/outgoing mail system (collection, distribution).

Establishes electronic/manual phone and phone message system.

Uses electronic/manual mail systems for interoffice communications.

11. Coordinates staff schedules by arranging meetings and updating calendars, using interactive capabilities of the system and takes minutes of staff meetings.   5%

Coordinates meeting schedules.

Uses scheduling and calendar planning software (if available).

Updates management calendars.

Records minutes of meetings.

Orchestrates meetings using teleconferencing/videoconferencing.

Fig. 20-6 Illustrated here is a complete job description for the position of administrative assistant/secretary—state of the art. The description under "major functions" provides an overview of the job, including the primary emphasis. Also included are reporting relationships for this position. The numbered items under "specific duties" are the job functions. Under each of the functions are the job tasks. As you can see, the tasks are more specific than the functions. At the right side of each page of the description is the percentage of time each function requires of the overall job.

To get ahead professionally, it is necessary to read about changes and advancements in your field.

also many groups for people who perform specific business functions such as data processing and accounting. You can find out more about these and other professional associations by consulting the *Encyclopedia of Associations* in the reference section of your local library.

Professional associations usually publish their own newsletters and periodicals, which you receive when you enroll as a member. You can learn a great deal about the industry you work for from reading these publications. Reading to keep up with the changes in your company's business and in your own field is essential if you hope to advance in your career. You can also keep informed by subscribing to newspapers and magazines such as *The Wall Street Journal, Secretary's World, The Office, Administrative Management,* and *Business Week.*

Some professional organizations offer certification programs, which enable you to demonstrate your competence in your profession. The largest and best known certification program is the Certified Professional Secretary certificate program, which is offered by Professional Secretaries International. PSI gives a certificate to candidates who pass a two-day examination in six business areas, including accounting, law, administration, and technology. PSI and other organizations also offer courses and seminars to their members to improve their secretarial skills. Many companies pay tuition and grant time off from work so that their employees can attend these seminars and courses.

Ongoing Education

If you cannot attend a course or seminar offered by a professional organization, you may want to seek out classes on your own. As you advance up your career ladder, you are likely to discover that professional advancement involves lifelong learning. Many successful people find that they must repeatedly return to school throughout their working lives to retrain themselves for new careers, to keep up with technological advances in their fields, or just to grow in their own careers and explore other career options.

Day or evening courses are available for adults in most four-year colleges, community colleges, vocational schools, and high schools. Many privately operated trade schools offer courses in legal and medical secretarial training, computer programming and electronics, and a wide variety of other careers.

When you begin to assume administrative support and supervisory functions, you may want to take courses in accounting, business law, business administration, telecommunications, data processing, and even psychology. You may have taken several of these courses already as part of your secretarial studies program. In that case you may just want to take the courses you missed, or you may want to take refresher courses in some subjects. This does not mean that you have to return to school on a full-time basis or run yourself

Lifelong learning has become a characteristic of our society and people of all ages are attending school for a number of reasons: to broaden their horizons, to change careers, or simply to enrich their lives with a hobby.

ragged trying to work and carry a heavy load of classwork at the same time. You can take one or two courses a year or every couple of years or proceed at any other pace that is comfortable for you. Part-time courses are usually fairly inexpensive at public schools and community colleges, and your employer may be willing to pick up some or all of the costs.

Adult education can be an enjoyable and relaxed experience because you no longer have to compete for grades. If you pay for your own courses, no one needs to know or care whether you pass or fail a course except you. And you will probably be very interested in the courses you take because you can apply what you're learning directly to your employment experience.

Reassessing Career Goals

After you've been in a position for a while, you may feel the need to reassess your career goals. It is normal for people to discover that they have new ideas about their careers after they have held a position for a while. Sometimes this happens because they learn more about themselves and their abilities on the job. Sometimes they discover a new interest. You may initiate the reassessment of your goals. You might also be helped in the process by your company. To reassess your career, it might be a good idea to ask yourself again the questions you asked when you first considered your career. Have the answers changed? If so, how? How would you reprioritize the job characteristics on your decision-making matrix?

In the course of a performance evaluation, your supervisor may be able to advise you on career directions by commenting on your strengths and weaknesses. Your supervisor may suggest a career path you could follow, advise you on what you will need to know, and even suggest courses you could take that would prepare you for your next opportunity.

Another thing you will need to consider is whether you want to continue on a traditional career path or branch out into a specialty. A traditional path might begin with a secretarial job that leads to the positions of administrative assistant, office supervisor, and manager of office services, in that order. You can stay on a path like this, or you can decide to retrain yourself for any one of a number of specialized jobs. If you decide to pursue an office technology career, you could become an information processing manager or get additional training to become an office automation specialist or trainer. You could become a legal or medical secretary, or you could become a secretary in a research laboratory, where your duties would include preparing documents containing many unusual scientific symbols and words. Sometimes secretaries become familiar enough with their companies' products to move into another career in the same business. A secretary in a plastics manufacturing company could become a salesperson, for example.

After you have been in a job where you have been operating a variety of electronic equipment, you may discover that you have a flair for working with technology. You could become a specialist in one of the technical areas we described earlier in this chapter, such as computer programming or telecommunications. Since many of these technical areas are related, it is often possible to move from one career path to another with only minimal additional training. If you specialized in word processing, for example, you could go from being a word processing supervisor to selling, installing, or repairing word processing equipment. You could even become a self-employed consultant who helps companies plan and install office automation systems.

After you reevaluate your career goals and explore the opportunities your company has to offer, you may decide that you want a career change or a change in assignments that requires new skills and knowledge. You will probably need to do some reading off the job or take some courses to prepare yourself for your new job.

Making a Change

Once you are ready for a career change, you will have to begin the job-hunting process all over again. This time it can begin with your own company. Many companies have a regular policy of recruiting and promoting from within, and they will post new job openings in the personnel office or on an employees' bulletin board. If, after a reasonable amount of time has passed, there seem to be no opportunities for advancement at your present company, you will have to look outside the company for a new position.

You will have to go through the same steps of preparing a résumé, getting interviews, and following up again, only this time you will have more experience, and you will feel more self-confident.

Once you have obtained a new job, you need to resign gracefully from your present job. Inform your supervisor of your resignation as soon as possible, and provide a written letter of resignation if it is requested. The following is an example of a letter of resignation.

Dear Mr. Brooks:

Please accept my resignation as executive secretary for the Research Department effective June 10, 19___.

Since I plan to move to Denver, Colorado, on July 1, I will need a few weeks to get things ready and packed. Prior to my leaving, I will be happy to train my replacement if you wish.

Thank you for the opportunity to work with your Research Department. This job allowed me to expand my experience and thus become a more efficient secretary. My replacement has much to look forward to!

Respectfully yours,

Common practice is to give at least two weeks' notice so that your employer can begin searching for your replacement. Make sure you are reimbursed for any benefits, such as pension contributions and unused vacation days, that are due you. Even if you have been unhappy in your present job, maintain good relations with your employer and coworkers until you leave. You may need them in the future for references or professional contacts.

Attitudes for Success

In the first part of this chapter, we talked about careers in office automation and the qualifications for those jobs. You will recall that many of the jobs require flexibility, good communication skills, and initiative. As you grow on the job past your entry-level position, you will discover that your future progress depends more and more on your attitude and human relations skills than on the basic job skills that enabled you to land a job in the first place.

Your willingness to work with a team, cooperation, and good communication skills will help you get along with your coworkers. Initiative, self-motivation, and enthusiasm will show your supervisor that you have leadership potential. Curiosity, a willingness to learn, and flexibility will enable you to acquire new skills and grow in your career.

By taking this course in electronic office procedures, you have already shown an interest in the office of the future. If you maintain an interest in new technological developments and if you are willing to accept changes and try new procedures, you will keep pace with the rapid changes to come, no matter what career you choose.

Willingness to work with a team, cooperation and good communication skills will help you keep your job and advance in it. Displaying initiative, self-motivation, and enthusiasm will mark you as a potential leader.

■ Summary

■ A career path is a person's work history. It consists of vertical moves up a career ladder or lateral moves to another department or field.

■ To choose the right career path, you must first understand your own personality, abilities, and goals.

■ The number of office jobs will continue to increase over the next ten years.

■ The major office job categories are administrative support, word processing, data processing, telecommunications, and records/information management.

■ When you go job hunting, look for a prospective employer through your school placement services, through employment agencies, in newspaper ads, through friends and contacts, and by sending blind letters and making calls.

■ Résumés usually contain your identification, your work history, your educational background, a list of your achievements and interests, personal information you wish to include, and references.

■ To apply for a job, you must send your résumé and a cover letter to the employer. You may have to fill out an application form and take various tests.

■ Always research the company and list any questions you want to ask when preparing for an interview.

- During the interview, the interviewer will tell you about the job, ask you questions about yourself, and give you a chance to ask questions as well.

- After the interview, evaluate yourself and determine what you would do differently the next time.

- To get ahead in a job, become as competent as you can, learn about the equipment you use, take on administrative support duties, and develop management skills.

- You should join professional organizations and read job-related newspapers and magazines to grow professionally.

- You should also expect to take various educational courses from time to time as you advance on the job.

- If you decide to change your career path, you will have to retrain for a new career and go job hunting all over again.

- Job advancement often depends on positive attitudes such as cooperativeness, initiative, and flexibility.

■ Review Questions

1. Compare the terms *career path* and *career ladder*.

2. What specific traits do you need to consider in preparing a personal profile?

3. Describe at least three positions in the administrative support job category.

4. Describe how a records management center handles business records.

5. What steps are involved in job hunting?

6. What information should a résumé contain?

7. What is the purpose of a job interview? What can you expect to happen during an interview?

8. What items should you consider when evaluating your performance at a job interview?

9. What part-time courses could you take to improve your knowledge of administrative support duties?

10. Describe some of the things you will have to consider in reassessing your career goals.

■ Technical Vocabulary

career path
career ladder
lateral move
career move

personal profile
résumé
fast track

■ Discussion and Skills Development

1. Prepare a basic résumé. Use the illustration on page 506 as a sample to follow, but organize it to highlight information about you. Once you have it drafted, type it, making sure that it has impeccable spelling, grammar, and punctuation. Then get together with a friend, and have that person critique your résumé. Ask him or her to develop possible interview questions based on what your résumé says. Does your résumé make it possible for you to get across the most important information about you? If it does not, rewrite your résumé.

2. For a couple of weeks in a row, read the classified advertisements for job openings. On Sunday read the display advertisements for career opportunities. Write down the positions you think you might be interested in if you were job hunting. Pick one company and one job opening, and analyze them carefully. Research the company: learn the answers to the questions posed in this chapter, and use all the local sources of information available to you. Write the information down. Then analyze the job to discover what skills and qualifications might be required in the job. Write those down. Compare your résumé with what you know about the company and the job. How good is the fit? Finally, write a cover letter, using the sample on page 508 as a guide. What can you say about yourself that would make an employer want to look at your résumé?

3. You may already have a good idea about what you think you would like to do in your future work. By inquiring among your friends, family, or professors at school, get the name of someone who has a position similar to the one you think you are interested in having. Call and make an appointment with that person, explaining that you would like to talk with her or him about the work the person does and the preparation required for it. Be sure to explain that you are not asking for a job but are only exploring career options. When you meet the person, ask what the work is like. What is most likable and least likable about it? What qualifications does the job require? What is the person's background, and what skills does the person have? What advice would he or she give someone entering the same career? Be sure to take notes. When the meeting is over, compare the answers you got to your questions with your life and career goals and the résumé you have prepared. How do all these things compare? Make a list of the qualifications you already have; write down the ones you still have to acquire.

Glossary

Account A record of financial transactions.

Account payable The amount owed to creditors for goods and services bought on credit.

Account receivable The amount to be collected from customers to whom goods and services are sold on credit.

Acoustic coupler A device for translating digital signals into analog and vice versa that has two openings to accommodate the earpiece and mouthpiece of a telephone handset.

Active records Records that must be kept in the office because they are used regularly.

Adhesive binding A binding technique in which pellets of glue are inserted into the binding device and melted or in which a strip of fabric is glued to the edge of a document and then sealed to each page with heat and pressure.

Administrative support Primary functions of an administrative assistant making travel arrangements.

Affidavit A sworn, written statement of fact.

Agenda An outline of what will take place at a meeting.

Agreement A legally enforceable understanding or arrangement between two or more parties.

Algorithm Logical, ordered, repetitive steps that carry out a task.

Alphanumeric data A mix of numbers and words or letters.

Alphanumeric keypad The main portion of an electronic keyboard, which closely resembles a standard typewriter keyboard.

Aperture card A card with a rectangular hole that holds only one microform image.

Applications programs Programmed instructions that make a computer execute a required task.

Archive An off-site storage location for inactive files.

Archiving Storing a file on a back-up medium.

Audio teleconference Relating to the use of a telephone linkage to allow people in widely separated locations to speak together at the same time.

Automatic collator A device that gathers the top copies in each bin and deposits complete sets in receiving trays.

Automatic document feed The ability to feed one sheet at a time automatically from a stack of originals placed in a feeder tray.

Balance The total funds contained in an account.

Balance sheet A financial statement that shows the company's total assets and liabilities.

Baud rate The speed at which a modem transmits data.

Bid specifications A list of requirements describing the kind of equipment a company needs and what the company expects the equipment to be able to do.

Bidirectional printer A printer that is able to print from right to left as well as from left to right.

Blank endorsement The payee's signature.

Body language Nonverbal communication that depends on behavior such as gestures, facial expressions, and posture.

Boilerplate A section of text that is repeated; often stored electronically.

Bottom line 1. The net profit; the amount of profit remaining after all expenses have been deducted. 2. The last figure on a company's annual financial statement.

Brainstorming The process in which a manager communicates with the staff to gather new ideas.

Budget A company's plan of expenditures and income for a given period of time.

Buffer memory A feature of some computer printers that has a small, temporary electronic memory, enabling it to store and print bits of a document.

Burster A device that automatically separates continuous-form paper sheets from each other and from their borders.

Business communication The exchange of information in the workplace.

Byte A group of bits (the smallest unit of information recognized by the computer) strung together to form a character (letter, number, etc.), which are used to measure the space on a diskette.

Canceled check A check that has been cleared against the account it was drawn on.

Capital expense budget A budget that shows long-range expenditures for new facilities, equipment replacement, land purchases, and mortgages.

Caption The title that appears on the guide tab of a file folder.

Career ladder A series of successive steps that mark the stages of a person's work history.

Career move A change in a person's career path; going from one department or field to another.

Career path The progression of jobs that forms a person's work history.

Cathode-ray tube (CRT) A display screen used on a word processing terminal to display information.

Centralized data processing system A computer system in which the users must request information from specialists who work on the centralized computer system.

Centralized reprographics center A type of copy center most commonly found in offices that make heavy use of reprographics where many different kinds of equipment are located and operated by specialists.

Centralized storage system A computer storage system in which individual work-stations in the system are part of a local network and are capable of communicating with each other.

Centrex system A phone switching system in which users can choose between dialing directly and using the operator's assistance.

Character printer An impact printer that prints one character at a time.

Charging out A procedure for borrowing files.

Check register A log in which you record the number, date, and amount of each check, as well as the payee's name and the reason for payment.

Chronological file A loose-leaf binder or file folder in which is placed a copy of each piece of outgoing correspondence, always in chronological order.

Coated-paper copier A copier that uses chemically coated paper and liquid toner to develop photographic images.

Collating Putting copies of the pages of a multi-page document into the correct order.

Combination unit A desk-top dictation machine that can record dictation and play it back for transcription.

Command-driven program A program that uses commands rather than menus to perform functions.

Communicate To send, or distribute, information to others.

Communications applications Relating to computer software programs that enable workers to communicate with other workers both within and outside the company and to obtain data from information retrieval services or public data bases.

Commuter airline A company that provides air transportation between a major airport and a smaller airport or between major airports that are not far apart.

Compact disk–read-only memory (CD-ROM) A new type of optical disk with the capacity to store vast quantities of data, graphics, or sound.

Compatibility The ability of one kind of computer to accept and process disks or tapes that were prepared on another type of computer.

Computer-aided transcription The use of a short-hand machine linked with a computer to produce an edited transcript.

Computer-assisted retrieval (CAR) A process of automatic microform retrieval that uses an electronic index.

Computer graphics Pictorial representations of data, such as graphs or charts, on a computer screen.

Computer language Instructions, coded to be understood by a computer, that tell a computer what to do (for example, Cobol, BASIC).

Computer-literate Having an understanding of computer technology, its terms and uses.

Computer-output microform (COM) Normal printed computer output reduced to microform by a special output device.

Computer systems Relating to computers and the different basic units that make them up.

Conference A formal meeting at which the primary objective is to exchange information.

Conference call A telephone call involving three or more people.

Consecutive numeric system A filing system that uses consecutive numbers: 1, 2, 3, and so on.

Continuous-form paper Computer printout "fan-fold" paper with sheets attached to each other and borders with evenly spaced holes that catch on the tractor's sprockets.

Contract A legally enforceable understanding or arrangement between two or more parties.

Control code A binary language that represents each letter, number, and symbol.

Convenience copier Copy machines situated close to the employees' work area so that they might easily be used for small copying jobs.

Convention A formal meeting at which members of a large professional group elect officers, establish policies, conduct business, and exchange information of interest to the profession.

Copy center A centralized group of reprographic equipment run by specialists.

Copyholder A device that holds hard copy at an angle that enables you to read it comfortably while you are keyboarding.

Corporation A business that is privately owned by a specific group of individuals or publicly owned by stockholders.

Corrected endorsement An endorsement that consists of the payee's name as it appears on the front of the check and the payee's name as it appears on the payee's account.

Cost-benefit ratio A decision-making tool used by comparing the costs of carrying out a plan or operation with the benefits the company can expect to receive.

Court order A formal instruction issued by a judge to a party in a lawsuit to do or stop doing a specific action.

Cross-reference A message that refers you to another location for the file you are searching for.

Cursor A lighted indicator on a display screen that can be moved to show where functions are to be performed.

Cursor control keypad The portion of an electronic keyboard that controls the movement (up, down, left, right) of the cursor on the computer screen.

Daisy wheel printer A letter-quality character printer with a round, flat type element.

Data An often unorganized group of facts, usually made up of words or figures, such as a list of names and addresses or a sheet of sales figures.

Data bank A data base or collection of data bases.

Data base A stored collection of data on a particular subject.

Data base administrator A computer specialist who defines, updates, and controls access to data bases.

Data base management A computer software application used for entering, organizing, storing, and retrieving data in formats and orders specified by the user.

Data communications The exchange of data between computers.

Data processing The application of a programmed sequence of operations upon numerical data.

Deadline A specified date on which a task must be completed.

Decentralized data processing system A computer system that links computers throughout an organization with those in the data processing department.

Decentralized reprographics center A copy center in which all copying machines are located in work areas where employees themselves use the machines to make their own copies of documents.

Decentralized storage system A computer storage system in which each worker stores his or her own files on floppy diskettes or tapes.

Decision-support tools See *Productivity tools*.

Decode To interpret a message.

Dedicated word processor A computer that is designed solely for word processing.

Delegate To assign tasks to members of the staff or other employees.

Digital Relating to information represented by a code made up of digits.

Digital camera A special camera wired to a computer that converts photographic images into computer signals.

Digital scanner A device that scans charts, maps, and blueprints and converts them into digital data so that they can be reproduced on a computer screen.

Direct outward dialing A feature of computerized telephone switching systems that allows users to make outside calls directly by dialing an access number first.

Dishonored check A check that the bank can't collect on either because it was altered, misdated, or made out incorrectly or because there were not sufficient funds in the drawer's account to cover it.

Disk drive A device that contains a small electromagnetic head that is capable of reading, writing, or erasing information on a disk.

Disk tutorial A lesson, recorded on a disk and displayed on a computer screen, that explains procedures and programs.

Distribute To send, or communicate, information to others.

Distributed logic system A multiterminal computer system that shares storage and peripheral equipment, while individual workstations have processing capabilities.

Documentation The instruction manuals and other documents that explain a computer system or software.

Dot matrix printer An impact printer that forms characters by projecting tiny metal bristles or pins in patterns, producing draft-quality output.

Double-density disk A disk with twice the storage capacity of a single-density disk.

Double-sided disk A disk for which both sides can be used.

Draft A preliminary rough copy of a document.

Draft-quality printer A computer printer that produces output that looks fainter and is more difficult to read than that produced by a letter-quality printer.

Drawer 1. A section in a filing cabinet or electronic filing system for storing files. 2. The person on whose account a check is drawn.

Dumb copier/printer An electronic copier/printer without an internal processor.

Dumb terminal A computer terminal that has a keyboard for inputting data and a display screen for output, but no local processing capability.

Duplex copying The ability to copy images on both sides of a sheet of paper.

Editor's clip A brightly colored, triangular plastic clip used for color-coding related notebook pages and documents.

Electromechanical Referring to all *electric* devices, such as electric typewriters and calculators, used in the office, as opposed to *electronic* devices.

Electronic calendar An office calendar that has been electronically stored and that can be called up for viewing on the computer screen.

Electronic file Documents stored electronically on tape or disks.

Electronic mail The distribution of messages through computers and telecommunications systems.

Electronic mailbox A program that permits computers to send, store, and receive messages.

Electronic network A linkage in a computer system that permits different departments located throughout the organization to utilize the resources provided by the larger system.

Electronic time-management system A system that makes use of electronic rather than traditional, manual methods for performing time-management tasks such as scheduling meetings.

Element An interchangeable type font ball used by some impact printers and typewriters.

Encode To convert a sender's message into a form through which it can be interpreted.

Encryption The use of a code to scramble data so that only people with approval to use the code can access and read the data.

Endless loop A long piece of magnetic recording tape that stays inside the recording device and stores dictation for many documents.

Envelope feeder A device that feeds individual envelopes into the printer automatically from stacks.

Ergonomics The study of how the physical work environment affects workers and job performance.

Evaluation The review of business plans and their implementation to determine whether they have been successful.

Expense account A form that businesses use to reimburse employees for using their own money to meet business expenses or to account for cash advances they receive.

External commands Commands on the disk-operating system that are *not* automatically read into the computer's temporary memory, thereby requiring the entering of specific file names to be used.

External files Data held on computer systems outside a given organization.

Facsimile machine A device that (*a*) distributes information by scanning pages and converting words or images on them into signals that travel over telephone lines and (*b*) receives information by converting the signals into words or images and reproducing them on paper.

Fast track Rapid advancement in job positions.

Feasibility study A study of office procedures, equipment, and productivity in regard to time, costs, and benefits that a company performs to determine if specific changes are desirable.

Feedback A response that indicates how the receiver has understood a message.

Field A unit of information in a record.

Filing equipment The variety of structures used in an office for the storage of files.

Filing supplies Standard supplies (such as file folders) used to organize papers and records stored in an office.

Finance charge A fee charged the borrower by the lender, which is an amount based on a specified percentage of the unpaid balance and that is paid with each installment payment.

Flat-comb binding A binding method in which half of a two-part rigid plastic comb is inserted through the holes in the side of a document and heat-sealed to the other half.

Floppy diskette A round, flat, double-sided sheet of pliable plastic that is magnetically treated and coated in a protective vinyl jacket.

Flowchart A step-by-step graphic description of a process or operation.

Footer A line of identifying information that appears at the bottom of a page of text.

Formal meeting A meeting that is held either within the office or at another location, but that requires more preparation and that usually has a more formally planned agenda than an informal meeting.

Format 1. A procedure that prepares a floppy diskette for use in an operating system. 2. The arrangement of information on a page.

Full endorsement A special endorsement that transfers ownership of a check from one payee to another by using the phrase "pay to the order of."

Function A series of acts or responsibilities involved in carrying out work.

Function key A key on a keyboard that controls a specific processing function.

Garbage in, garbage out (GIGO) An expression that means if what we input into a computer is wrong, what we get out will also be wrong.

General journal A list in chronological order of each business transaction in which money is received or spent.

General ledger A record of financial business transactions, grouped according to account.

GIGO See *Garbage in, garbage out.*

Grammar checker A feature available in some word processing packages that checks for some common grammatical errors.

Graphics tablet A device that converts the movements of a hand drawing on a board into digital signals and then converts the signals into pictures.

Gross pay The amount of pay before any deductions are made.

Guaranteed reservation A hotel reservation in which the hotel guarantees that the room will be held as long as is necessary. Payment is usually required whether or not the room is used, unless cancellation is requested.

Hard copy Computer output in a permanent, visually readable form, usually on paper.

Hard disk A high-volume storage device made of rigid plastic, aluminum, or ceramic and magnetically treated.

Hardware The physical components of a computer system.

Header A line of identifying text that appears at the top of a page.

High-level language A computer language that uses symbols to represent series of steps.

High tech Another term used for *electronic technology.*

Hub ring A device placed in the ring of a disk to protect it from damage while in the disk drive.

Hygienes Specific elements of a job—pay, advancement potential, status, work conditions, and interpersonal relationships—that can affect a worker's motivation by their absence or presence.

IBM PC-compatible Referring to a computer's capability of running MS-DOS, that is, microsoft disk operating systems.

Identification code A code needed by employees to log on to a terminal linked to the central computer.

Impact printer A type of printer that generates characters by striking metal or plastic type against an inked ribbon over paper.

Inactive records Records that may be moved to inactive storage or discarded because they are no longer used regularly.

Incompatible Unsuitable for use together.

Increased productivity Referring, in the narrow sense, to work that employees can do more of in the same period of time or that employees can do in a shorter period of time. In the broader sense, it means workers have greater flexibility in performing their tasks.

Indexing The process of selecting a caption under which a record will be stored.

Indicator slip A specially marked piece of paper on which the originator notes where each dictated document ends and instructions.

Informal meeting A meeting that takes place in an office or conference room at which discussions of everyday business activities occur.

Information Facts that have been processed or organized in some fashion so that they may be communicated to others in a useful manner.

Information management The function of organizing and controlling all aspects of business records, from their creation, protection, and use to their storage and ultimate disposal.

Information processing The transformation of data into useful information.

Information processing cycle The process through which all information in the office environment flows, that is, input, processing, storage, output, and distribution/communication.

Initial training Referring to the training of new employees.

Initialize A procedure that prepares a floppy diskette for use in an operating system.

Ink-jet printer A nonimpact printer that sprays dots of ink onto paper.

Input 1. The task of entering data into the computer. 2. The data entered into the computer.

In-service training Referring to the retraining of existing employees.

Inside address The part of a letter that consists of the name, title, and address of the receiver.

Installment A portion of a loan that is paid at regular intervals.

Integrated Relating to efficiently combined components.

Integrated applications A computer software program with several applications designed to work together.

Integrated software A package that consists of programs for several applications that are designed to work together.

Intelligent copier/printer An electronic copier/printer with an internal processor.

Intelligent workstation Individual workstations within a multiterminal computer system that have processing capabilities.

Interactive Relating to a method of exchanging information by computer in which users carry on a dialogue by inputting their comments and reading the responses.

Interim deadlines Dates on which completion of various parts of a major project are set to be completed.

Internal commands A set of commands contained on the disk-operating system that are read by the computer and stored in its temporary memory.

Internal files Data held on the computer system within a given organization.

Interoffice mail The mail exchanged between people who work at the same location or at the company's nearby branches.

IPSOD Acronym signifying the stages of processing information in the electronic office: input, process, storage, output, distribution.

Itinerary A list of travel arrangements that includes departure and arrival times, flight or train numbers, hotel addresses and telephone numbers, and other details.

Jargon Specialized technical language not normally used in everyday communication.

Jet lag The fatigue and confusion that result from flying across several time zones.

Job description The expected skills and responsibilities of an employee.

Key operator The person in an office responsible for photocopier maintenance.

Key system A type of telephone switching equipment using phones equipped with keys or buttons that light up when in use.

Kilobyte (K) A measurement of computer memory.

Knowledge worker A person who works with information.

Labor-intensive Relating to tasks that require many work hours to complete.

Laser disk Another term used for *optical disk.*

Laser printer A high-speed printer that uses a combination of electronics and photography to produce high-quality originals.

Lateral move A sideways step on a career path.

Law blank A printed legal form with blanks to be filled in with information supplied by a supervisor or from source documents.

Letterhead Stationery printed with a heading, usually including the company name and/or logo, as well as the address.

Letter-quality 1. Relating to high-quality printing, suitable for business use. 2. Relating to a kind of printer that uses a typing element to produce sharp, high-quality characters.

License agreement A license found in software packages that obligates the purchaser to certain terms for use of the software program.

Light pen A pen-shaped, light-sensing input device used to "write" or "draw" on a computer screen.

Linear In order, in a straight line.

Line item A category of expenditures or income that is given a separate line in a budget.

Line printer The fastest printer; can produce an entire line at a time.

Local area network (LAN) A system that makes it possible for a company to use electronic mail internally; requires a network of cables and devices interconnecting a company's computers so they can all communicate with one another.

Logo The identifying symbol of a company.

Log on To "sign in" with an individual identification code, which must be entered into the computer before access is authorized.

Long-term planning Referring to business projects that take a year or more to implement.

Low-level language Computer instructions that direct the computer through each step it must

take in order to perform a particular operation; assembly language.

Magnetic tape Tape coated with magnetic material used to record and store information.

Mailgram A combination of a telegram and a letter.

Mailmobile An interoffice mail system that uses a mailcart that automatically follows a magnetic track on the floor and is programmed to stop at various points for collection.

Mainframe A powerful computer with large storage capacities, capable of quickly processing vast quantities of information.

Management by objectives (MBO) A style of management whereby workers meet with managers periodically to discuss objectives.

Management by walking around (MBWA) A leadership style that stresses highly visible managers who spend a lot of time communicating directly with employees rather than in their offices or in meetings.

Management information system (MIS) An integrated system of office automation that is used in decision making; provides management with rapid access to all available data bases.

Manual collator A device with a manually operated feeder arm that pushes up the top copy in each bin so an office worker can gather it quickly and easily.

Mechanical collator A device that functions like the manual collator, but with motorized feeder arms.

Memory 1. Where information is stored in a computer; can be either permanent (ROM) or changeable (RAM). 2. The capacity of a computer to store information.

Mental filters The unique elements in a person's mind—ideas, facts, attitudes, emotions, experience, and memories—that interpret (or decode) messages in an individual way and trigger a response.

Menu A list of choices displayed on the computer screen from which the operator can select the next activity or process.

Menu-driven program A program that uses menus rather than commands to perform functions.

Merge To combine.

Microchip A tiny piece of semiconductor material (usually silicon) with photoelectronically etched circuits; used to store computer memory.

Microcomputer A small computer containing a single microchip; also called a desk-top computer or personal computer.

Microfiche Flat sheets of easy-to-use film that can hold hundreds of pages of micrographic images, arranged in rows and columns.

Microfilm jacket A clear plastic sheet, sealed to form horizontal slots, that holds short strips of microfilm.

Microfilm roll A roll of film that can hold hundreds of pages of miniaturized documents.

Microform Film containing reduced images.

Microform reader A machine used to enlarge microforms to a readable size.

Micrographics The process of reducing documents to tiny images and storing them on film.

Microwave An electromagnetic wave that travels in straight lines through the air and carries data and voices between disk-shaped antennas.

Minicomputer A medium-sized computer, less powerful than a mainframe but with more capacity than a microcomputer.

Minutes Official records of a meeting.

Miscommunication A failure in the sending and receiving of a message.

Modeling Setting up a formula that can be used to forecast the outcome of a decision.

Modem An electrical device that converts computer signals into telephone signals (and back again) for sending and receiving information over telephone lines.

Modular furniture Furniture of uniform design that allows flexibility for arrangement and can be adjusted to individual needs and tastes.

Motion A proposal for action made during a formal meeting.

Motivate To help employees perform their tasks with enthusiasm and initiative.

Mouse A hand-operated device which controls the cursor and which inputs processing commands without the use of a keyboard.

Multinational company A company with corporate headquarters, manufacturing plants, and other properties in several different countries.

Multiple originals The product that results from the repeated reproduction of a document on a computer printer, each of which is an identical original rather than a copy because each was generated independently.

Multitasking Relating to a computer system which is operated by several users and which does several tasks at the same time.

Net pay The amount of pay remaining after deductions are made.

Network Computer systems linked by communications wires, telephone lines, or paths.

Networking Tying computer systems together.

Nonimpact printer A type of printer that produces hard copy without striking type elements against a ribbon and paper.

Notarize The stamping of a signed document by a notary public.

Notary public A person commissioned by a state government to verify signatures on documents for legal purposes.

Numeric data Numbers.

Numeric keypad The portion of an electronic keyboard with keys for each of the ten arabic digits.

Office automation (OA) specialist The person responsible for overseeing the implementation of an electronic office system and for explaining the various features of a computer system to its users.

Office landscaping A flexible arrangement of office space using movable partitions (rather than fixed walls) to provide economical workstations.

On-line Directly connected to a central computer system.

Online information services Companies that, for a fee, provide access to particular types of information from their data banks to meet the needs of various business professionals.

Operating budget A statement that lists the expected income and costs of the day-to-day operations of a company.

Operating system A set of programs that controls the overall operation of the computer.

Optical character reader (OCR) A device which converts typed or printed copy into electronic signals that the computer can understand and store.

Optical disk A durable, nonmagnetic storage medium of great capacity, which uses laser beams to burn tiny holes into the metal of the disk.

Organization The way in which a business divides responsibilities among its departments and divisions, and how it assigns various tasks and functions to employees and structures its chain of authority or command.

Output 1. The finished product; hard copy. 2. Computer results.

Output device A device directly connected to a word processor or computer system that can produce hard copies of keyboarded documents.

Owner's equity The amount of the owner's financial interest in the company.

Page composition The manual process of cutting galley proofs and pasting them onto paper boards in position for printing.

Paging device A small, portable device that alerts the person carrying it when someone is trying to reach him or her; also called a beeper.

Parallel processing The ability of a computer to run two or more programs simultaneously.

Parliamentary procedure The rules that structure a formal meeting.

Participative approach A modern management technique in which employees are consulted and involved in the decision-making process.

Participatory management A technique in which employees are allowed to take an active part in running the workplace.

Partnership A business owned by two or more people.

Passport An official government identification document that grants citizens permission to travel abroad.

Password A personal code used by an individual to identify himself or herself to the central computer.

Payee The person or organization to whom the check is written.

Payroll register A record that lists each employee by name along with regular and overtime pay and all of his or her deductions.

Peripherals Equipment such as printers, modems, scanners, and terminals that can be added to the CPU.

Personal profile An outline of a person's characteristics, including personality, abilities, and goals.

Petty cash A small cash fund kept by most offices to pay for small day-to-day expenses.

Photocompositor A phototypesetter that can create photographic images of entire pages; eliminates the need for manual page composition.

Phototypesetter A reprographics device that uses photographic technology to set text into special styles and column widths.

Pitch The number of characters in an inch in a single line of type.

Plain-paper copier A copier that uses heat and pressure to transfer powdered toner permanently onto any ordinary paper.

Planning Developing an outline of steps required to complete a task.

Plotter A computer printing device that converts computer output into drawings on paper or on display-type terminals.

Point-of-sale transfer A customer's use of a bank identification card to pay for goods and services.

Position function Specific tasks that are listed in the job description.

Postage meter A machine, licensed by the U.S. Postal Service, which prints postage fees on gummed strips of paper that are used as stamps.

Posting The process of transferring data from a journal to a ledger.

Postscript A message placed after the main body of a letter, added as an afterthought or for emphasis.

Power of attorney Legal authorization for one person to act as an agent for another.

Printer The output device that allows the computer to present a paper copy of its results.

Printout Text or copy printed out on paper by a computer.

Priority A certain level of urgency or importance.

Private automated branch exchange (PABX) Telephone switching equipment with automated switching operations.

Private branch exchange (PBX) A type of telephone switching equipment that requires a switchboard operator to control the central switching station for all the telephone extensions in an office.

Procedure A series of steps followed in a regular, definite order.

Process 1. To organize data into useful information. 2. The organization and calculation of words and numbers by a computer.

Productivity tools Referring to a variety of business applications (such as data base management, spreadsheeting, or graphics) which can be done on a computer.

Program disk A disk with an applications program on it for use with a microcomputer.

Programmable key A key on a computer keyboard that can be custom-programmed by the user.

Programmer A person who designs the sets of instructions (or programs) that enable a computer to function.

Project budget Log of expenses for individual programs of a company, for example, an advertising campaign or film project.

Proprietary operating system A system designed for use by only one model or perhaps for other computers produced by the same company.

Protocol 1. A set of rules or procedures that allows different models of computers to communicate clearly with one another. 2. The exchange of predetermined signals in a specific sequence.

Protocol converter A device that translates the transmission code of one computer to the transmission code of the other.

Quorum The number of people required by the group before a vote can be taken.

Random-access memory (RAM) 1. Computer memory in which data is temporarily stored and from which it can be retrieved by the user. 2. The amount of data a computer can store, measured in kilobytes (K).

Read-only memory (ROM) Preprogrammed information that is permanently stored by the manufacturer in the computer's memory and cannot be changed by the user.

Receiver One who detects and interprets a message.

Records Pieces of important information that, collectively, make up a data base.

Records management The organization and control of business records; developing systems to store, protect, retrieve, use, and dispose of records.

Reminder facilities A feature of an electronic time-management system in which a reminder indicator (of a meeting, commitment, project, and so on) will automatically be displayed on the computer screen at the exact time and date for which it is set.

Reprographics center The area in an office where the equipment for reproducing documents is located.

Reprographics system A system (centralized or decentralized) that makes multiple copies of hard- and soft-copy originals.

Resolution 1. A formal expression of opinion or intention. 2. The sharpness of the picture on a computer screen.

Restrictive endorsement An endorsement that sets conditions such as "for deposit only" to a specific account.

Résumé A brief summary of a person's educational and employment history used by employers to screen job applicants.

Rider A separate sheet of paper attached to a legal document to add necessary space.

Roll-fed copier A copier which makes copies on paper that is cut from a continuous roll as it is fed into the machine.

Routing slip A piece of paper with a column of names that is used to circulate material to several people in an office.

Sales letter A written message whose purpose is the sale of a service or merchandise.

Salutation The word or phrase of greeting that comes before the body of a letter.

Satellite A small unit of information processing equipment.

Schedule A timetable for a project that indicates the sequence of work and sets deadlines.

Sectors The divisions of the tracks on a diskette.

Sender One who creates and transmits a message.

Sensory receiver A body part or mechanical device that receives and interprets stimuli.

Shared logic system A multiterminal system in which one CPU does all the processing for several workstations.

Shared resource system A multiterminal computer system that can share printers, modems, and other pieces of compatible equipment.

Sheet-fed copier A copier that automatically takes cut sheets of paper from a tray inside the machine.

Sheet feeder A device that feeds individual sheets of paper into the printer automatically from stacks.

Shorthand machine A portable input device with keys that are pressed in combinations to produce abbreviations of words or phrases more rapidly than by handwriting.

Short-term goal A goal to be reached.

Short-term planning Referring to business projects that can be carried out within a few weeks or months.

Signal 1. Stimulation from an individual's environment; something a person sees, hears, tastes, smells, or feels. 2. An electronic pulse used to transmit information.

Smart terminal A workstation with processing capabilities; part of a distributed logic system.

Soft copy Computer output displayed temporarily on a screen.

Software A set of instructions, or programs, directing the operation of a computer.

Sole proprietorship A business owned by one person.

Source documents Various base forms (such as purchase orders, bills, checkbook stubs, invoices, and credit agreements) used to record accounting information.

Speakerphone A telephone device that amplifies a call so that many people can hear it at once; widely used for audio teleconferences.

Special endorsement An endorsement that is used to transfer ownership of a check from one payee to a second payee.

Spelling checker An electronic dictionary used with word processing software.

Spiral-comb binding A binding method in which a curled plastic comb is inserted through a line of rectangular holes punched along the side of each page of a document.

Spreadsheet 1. Ruled accounting paper on which figures are entered in columns and rows. 2. Graphic applications software that presents figures in a grid format on the computer screen.

Standalone A microcomputer; a self-contained workstation with all the equipment and processing power it needs to operate independently.

Statement of objectives A description of the goals or objectives that an employee is expected to accomplish.

Stockholders The owners of a corporation.

Store 1. To place information onto computer disks or tapes for later use. 2. To save information permanently in a computer.

Stress The body's negative response to change and stimulation.

Subpoena An order to appear at a trial or hearing to testify.

System study A study that focuses on overall procedures and functions rather than on individual tasks.

Systems analyst A computer specialist who determines how computer data processing can be applied to specific problems.

Tact A sense of what to do or say to avoid offending or embarrassing people.

Task An assigned piece of work.

Telecommuting Using computers and telephone equipment to work at home instead of at the office.

Teleconference A conference among people at different locations electronically linked by audio and/or visual connections.

Teletypewriters Keyboard devices with printers that can send and receive messages over telephone lines.

Template A plastic or cardboard plate that fits over the panel of function keys on an electronic computer keyboard; used as a guide to the function keys of a particular program.

Terminal The workstation; consists of a keyboard and a display screen.

Terminal-digit system A filing system that uses numbers specifically assigned to classify records into groups; the last number (terminal digit) indicates where to start looking for the file.

Theory X and Theory Y Two competing claims on whether people naturally avoid work or actually are fulfilled by their jobs.

Thesaurus A book that lists words and their synonyms (different words that have nearly the same meaning).

Thimble printer A letter-quality, fast, single-element character printer that resembles a thimble.

"Things-to-do" facility A feature of an electronic time-management system in which a list of items that the user does not need to be reminded about at a specific time is stored electronically for future viewing on the computer screen as needed.

Tickler file A follow-up file, arranged by day of the month, which serves as a daily reminder of tasks that must be acted upon.

Time management Planning, organizing, and using time effectively.

Time-sharing Simultaneous access by many users to a shared central computer facility.

Toner The powder or fluid used in a photocopier to develop photographic images on blank paper.

Touch screen A screen with sensors that allow the user to select computer commands without the use of a keyboard.

Tracks Concentric circles on floppy diskettes (similar to the grooves on a record) along which information is written.

Tractor A device with moving sprockets that guides continuous-form paper through a printer.

Transcript A word-for-word record of everything said during a meeting; a written or printed copy.

Transistors Electronic devices consisting of substances that conduct electricity.

Transponders Transmission devices on communications satellites; they receive signals beamed to them from one earth station and then amplify the signals and relay them back to another earth station.

Travel and entertainment (T&E) report A form on which employees formally report, on a regular basis, all their business expenses to their employers.

Traveler's check A form of money which is used like cash and which is purchased from a bank or express company and payable only when signed by the owner; used by travelers because it is safe to carry.

Turnaround time The time from when a task is assigned to when it is expected to be completed.

Ultrafiche Flat sheets of film that hold miniaturized images which are even smaller than those on microfiche; ultrafiche can only be produced by an expensive photographic process.

User-friendly Relating to applications programs that are easy to use.

User-level language A computer language that uses everyday terms rather than computer codes and requires little formal training in writing programs.

Utilities Programs used to speed up frequently used data-maintenance chores.

Vendor A person or company that produces and sells computer software equipment.

Video display terminal (VDT) A screen used on a word processing terminal to display information.

Video teleconference (VTC) The use of closed-circuit television to allow people in widely separated locations to hold a meeting without having to travel.

Visa A permit granted by the government of a country to allow foreigners to enter the country.

Voice input Direct input of verbal data into the computer without the use of a keyboard.

Voice mail A sophisticated message system that uses a telephone linked to a voice-activated computer.

Windows Sections of a display screen that allow information from several different sources to appear on the screen simultaneously.

Word processing 1. Using a computer to create, edit, revise, format, or print out text. 2. The organizing of words by a computer.

Word wrap The feature on a word processor that automatically returns the carrier to the left margin as copy is entered; sometimes called automatic carrier return.

Workstation The area in the electronic office that incorporates all the equipment, furnishings, and accessories needed to perform one's work.

Write-protect notch A safety device on the floppy diskette jacket; with the notch covered, information cannot be written on the diskette or erased from it.

Index

Account, 422
Accounting, 419–425
  business entities, 419–420
  procedures, 422–423
  software for, 192–193, 424–425
  terminology of, 422
Accounts payable, 419
Accounts receivable, 419
Acoustic coupler, 298–299
Active record, 257
Administrative support function,
  15–16, 497–499
Affidavit, 443
Agenda, 377–378
Air quality, 92
Algorithm, 4
Alphabetizing rules, 232–233
American Standard Code for
  Information Interchange
  (ASCII), 297
Answering machine, 327
Aperture card, 252
Applications software, 212
  accounting, 192–193, 424–425
  communications, 194–195, 299–
    300
  DBMS, 191–192
  decision-support, 189–191
  grammar checker, 217
  graphics, 193–194, 200
  integrated, 195–196
  spelling checker, 217
  spreadsheet, 189–191
  utility program, 185
  word processing, 185–189
Archives, 254–258
Arithmetic-logic unit, 38, 182
ASCII (American Standard Code
  for Information Interchange),
  297
AT&T (American Telephone and
  Telegraph), 321, 331
ATM (automatic teller machine),
  428
Automatic collator, 283
Automatic document feed, 279
Automatic teller machine (ATM),
  428
Automation, office (*see* Office
  automation)

Backup, 83, 222–223
Balance sheet, 420
Banking, 425–435
  balance reconciliation, 431–433
  deposits, 426–428
  EFT, 433–435
  payments, 428–430

Baud rate, 297
Bid specification, 488
Bidirectional printing, 271
Binding, 59, 283
  flat-comb, 283
  glued, 283
  spiral-comb, 283
Blank endorsement, 427
Block format, 128
Body language, 100, 108–109
Boilerplate, 161, 219–220
  (*See also* Mail/merge)
Bottom line, 480
Brainstorming, 458–459
Budgets, 436–438
  capital expense, 437
  monitoring of, 438
  operating, 437
  preparation of, 437–438
  project, 438
Burster, 272
Business letters, 131–137
  claim, 134
  collection, 136–137
  credit, 135–136
  goodwill, 133
  refusal, 133–134
  request, 132
  response, 132
  sales, 137
Business trips, 392–416
  airlines, 395–399
  automobiles, 400–402
  expense accounts for, 412–415
  hotel booking, 405–406
  international, 402–405
  itinerary for, 395, 406–407
  railroads, 400
  travel arrangements for, 393–395
  travel funds for, 408–409

Calculator, 424
Calendar:
  electronic, 346–351, 375
  manual, 354–355
Canceled check, 431
Capital expense budget, 437
Caption, 231, 237, 239
CAR (computer-assisted retrieval),
  254
Card file, 242
Career ladder, 495
Career path, 495
Careers, 494–523
  administrative support work, 15–
    16, 497–499
  advancement, 516–521
  application procedures, 508–509

Careers (*continued*)
  continuing education, 518–519
  in data processing, 500–501
  goal setting for, 495–497
  interviewing, 110, 509–515
  job hunting techniques, 503–516
  lateral move, 495
  office job opportunities, 497
  in records management, 502–503
  résumé writing, 505–507
  in telecommunications, 501–502
  in word processing, 499–500
Cathode-ray tube (CRT), 39, 41–
  42, 89–92, 124, 199, 210
Central processing unit (CPU), 38,
  40–42, 182
Centralized data processing, 180
Centralized storage system, 243,
  244, 258
Centrex system, 323
Character printer, 265
Charging out process, 231
Check register, 429
Checks, 428–430
  canceled, 431
  dishonored, 433
  types of, 430
Chronological file, 229
Coated-paper copier, 279
Collating, 59, 279, 283
Combination unit, 152
Command-driven program, 187–
  189, 200
Communication, 99–113
  business, 99–100
  listening skills, 108
  message preparation, 102–105
  miscommunication, 100–102
  nonverbal, 100, 108–109
  oral, 105–107
  person-to-group, 111
  person-to-person, 109–110
  telephone techniques, 328–334
  written (*see* Writing)
  (*See also* Business letters;
    Letters; Reports)
Communication/distribution of
  information, 7, 12–13, 60–63,
  287–317
  computer-based mail services,
    304–308
  electronic mail, 12, 61–62, 162–
    163, 294–302, 312–316
  electronic methods, 292–294
  facsimile transmission, 303–304
  mail-room practice, 291–292,
    309–312
  manual methods, 288–292
Communications satellite, 300